Antisemitism on the Campus:
Past & Present

ANTISEMITISM IN AMERICA

Series editor
Eunice G. Pollack (University of North Texas)

ACADEMIC
STUDIES
PRESS

ANTISEMITISM ON THE CAMPUS: PAST & PRESENT

Editor
Eunice G. Pollack

Boston
2018

Library of Congress Cataloging-in-Publication Data

Antisemitism on the campus : past & present / editor, Eunice G. Pollack.
    p. cm. -- (Antisemitism in America)
 Includes bibliographical references and index.
 ISBN 978-1-934843-82-6 (hardback : alk. paper)
1. Antisemitism--United States. 2. Antisemitism--History--21st century.
3. Universities and colleges--United States--History--21st century. I.
Pollack, Eunice G.
 DS146.U6A594 2011
 305.892'4073--dc22
                        2011002604

ISBN 978-1-61811-324-5 (paperback: alk. paper)

Book design by Ivan Grave

Published by Academic Studies Press in 2011
Paperback: 2018
28 Montfern Avenue
Brighton, MA 02135, USA
press@academicstudiespress.com
www.academicstudiespress.com

Table of Contents

Preface
CONFRONTING ANTISEMITISM ON THE CAMPUS

Eunice G. Pollack

Although overt antisemitism declined in the West in the aftermath of the Holocaust, over the last half century it has reemerged, spread, and increasingly intensified. Perhaps most ominously, the world's oldest and longest hatred has reappeared in the universities, where it has acquired a high profile, a new patina, and even academic garb. There the "old-new antisemitism,"[1] though often cloaked in its latest attire, has been granted a certain legitimacy. To be sure, antisemitism is not confined to the campus. In Britain, as Robert Wistrich shows, it has become "part of mainstream discourse, continually resurfacing among the academic, political, and media elites."[2] It is on the campus, however, where the old antisemitic tropes and charges have been incorporated into new, seemingly academic paradigms. Here the hoary charges of theological and economic antisemitism have been updated, molded to fit the racial paradigm predominant on the contemporary campus. Evil Jews, become Zionists in the current lexicon, menace the world from a "white colonialist settler state," born in sin, this time conspiring to conquer, to "ethnically cleanse," to sacrifice the innocent, "people of color." Instead of dehumanizing or animalizing Jews, campus anti-Zionists demonize the Jewish state, now a secular "Synagogue of Satan." A well-placed voice of the academic movement to delegitimize Israel warns that it has "lost any moral justification for its existence,"[3] echoing Christianity's former antisemitic claims against Jews. Campus groups congeal around insistent calls for the boycott of Israel, "an essential tool of antisemites for at least a thousand years."[4] Campus activists predict that only when Zionists, in effect, convert, and relinquish the homeland will the promised millennium — the world at peace — arrive. This Manichean schema, this secular Oberammergau — or modern Western, the players all outfitted in white or black hats — is not being enacted on the big screen or Bavarian stage, but in the academic arena.

Certainly, anti-Zionism and criticism of Israel's actions need not be antisemitic, in effect or intent. In a number of academic venues, however, anti-Zionism appears to have become the new language of antisemitism, the latest form the old hatred has assumed.[5] As Benjamin Ginsberg concludes, the contention that "anti-Zionism and antisemitism are not one and the same thing...is true in principle, but not often in practice."[6]

In the first section of this study, the authors approach the modern face of antisemitism from various angles, examining its features, and consider how and why the monster has come to stalk American and British campuses in recent decades. In exploring its growth, Benjamin Ginsberg focuses on the role of university administrators, who "respond with alacrity to the slightest indication of racist, sexist or homophobic activity on their campuses," but "refuse to take action against antisemitic activists." He attributes these divergent responses to the alliance that administrators, anxious to "enhance their own power," have typically forged with left-liberal and radical activists on campus, as well as with those currently designated "minority groups." Often the consequence of the coalition is administrations' "selective enforcement" of speech codes. Willing to cancel a talk that might offend Muslim students, they protect the right of a "professional 'anti-Zionist' speaker" to lecture on campus.

Jerold Auerbach follows the well-trod path of the monster at Wellesley College over the course of the last century, and finds that even so late as the 1980s, "From admission to graduation, antisemitism infested virtually every corner of Wellesley life." The "pattern of discrimination" did not consist simply of "isolated acts of individuals," he shows, but of institutional discrimination. Like Ginsberg, Auerbach exposes an administrative double-standard at Wellesley. Even in the 1990s, when an African-American professor was teaching "scurrilous lies" about Jews, the college "declined to defend academic integrity." Although the school "promptly and properly" denounces "racism and Islamophobia...for what they are, [ ] antisemitism, blandly labeled 'prejudice' or 'intolerance,' is routinely stripped of Jewish content." Auerbach also considers why so many Jewish students and alumnae — "assimilated Jews," "Jewish universalists," "Court Jews," "self-hating Jews," "Jews of silence" — refuse to acknowledge or denounce the antisemitism that surrounds them.

Edward Alexander also examines the responses and actions of Jews, but of Jewish faculty at the University of California, Berkeley, who are often in the forefront of the "campaign to depict Israel as the center of the world's evil" or the movement that demands "the end of Zionism." Although refusing to recognize how their actions further the hatred of Jews, these "Jewish professors," Alexander concludes, are, in fact, making antisemitism "academically respectable." He shows how these otherwise careful scholars rely on convoluted arguments to deny the petitions they champion are antisemitic, how they manage to ignore masses of evidence that contradict their ideologically-driven positions, and repeatedly reverse cause and effect in their determined efforts to "assign responsibility for anti-Jewish aggression to Jewish misbehavior."

Robert Wistrich completes this section with an analysis of the situation in Great Britain, where antisemitism has become "something of a crisis" and London "a world center for Muslim antisemitism and the demonization of Jews and Israel." He uncovers deep roots of antisemitism, finding that Britain's "liberal democratic tradition has . . . been far more ambivalent toward Jews than is often assumed." It was, he points out, an "eminent member of the British establishment, the renowned historian Arnold J. Toynbee," who, in the 1950s, became the "intellectual pioneer of the idea that Zionism is a form of Nazism." This "would eventually become a mantra of the British Left," which is so prominent on the contemporary campus. Thus Wistrich shows how in Britain, as in the United States, "the thin boundary between antisemitism and anti-Zionism has increasingly been breached," and "how easily anti-Israel defamation slides into antisemitic imagery."

Section II of this volume turns the spotlight on an earlier incarnation of antisemitism on the campus, when colleges and universities severely restricted the admission and hiring of Jews. In his examination of the reasons for the founding of Brandeis University in 1948, Stephen Whitfield points to the heightened barriers that the elites erected in the 1920s to protect their educational institutions from the children of East European Jews, who were now applying in large numbers. The elites apparently feared the "tenor and tempo that Jewish students injected into campus life." Established in response to these "No Trespassing" signs, and formed as a "non-sectarian institution" under Jewish sponsorship, "Brandeis University would guarantee that at least one institution of higher learning would be bereft of antisemitism."

Much remained unsettled, however, and Whitfield traces the conflict that developed between the esteemed professor of comparative literature Ludwig Lewisohn, who sought to preserve or cultivate Jewish difference, "psychologically, morally, intellectually," and Abram Sachar, Brandeis's first president, who, Lewisohn charged, "refus[ed] to invest the university with a serious and demanding Jewish character." The larger question — of the nature and degree of Jewish identity — was becoming a critical one, as academia began to lower its barriers and Jews had to assay the cost of inclusion.

Andrew Winston also considers Jewish identity as he explores the widespread refusal of universities to hire Jewish psychologists as faculty members because of their supposed "objectionable traits." Winston exposes the lengths to which faculty went in their letters of recommendation — or rather, letters advising against placement — to determine if a candidate was a Jew or of Jewish origin and to calibrate his fitness for a faculty position as a measure of the "degree of [his] Jewishness" or "defects of his race." Although some, such as the leading sociologist E.A. Ross, considered Jews' disqualifying traits — their "inborn love of money-making" — to be racial, progressive psychologists explained the odious characteristics — their "defensive aggressiveness" — as the "psychological result of the prejudice" itself. All the letter-writers were certain, however, that they were not antisemitic, but were only scientifically assessing the suitability of the Jew. An astute observer concluded that the Jew who was allowed to continue in graduate school or was hired as a faculty member often found that he could succeed only if he became "a simulated WASP: WASP wife, WASP tastes, even WASP sports." In short, he had to become invisible as a Jew.

Henry Fetter's focus is on elite law schools, where the approach to hiring Jewish faculty somewhat resembled that of psychology departments, but where the openness to admitting and retaining Jewish students was distinct, even exceptional. Fetter notes that even when an elite university introduced a quota system to limit Jewish enrollment, often it was not evident in its law school. The result of the "relaxed admission standards," he explains, was an emphasis on "academic merit within the school itself." The elite schools were committed to a "grades-driven ethos," which derived from the conviction that law was a science in which student performance could be measured objectively. With exams graded anonymously, and faculty thereby prevented from "play[ing] favorites," with even the board of editors of Law Review chosen "automatically" on the basis of the highest scores, Jews did extremely well.

This meritocracy ended upon graduation and most large law firms remained closed to Jews, even to editors of Harvard Law Review. The chances of being hired as a faculty member in an elite law school appear to have been worse. This began to change, however, after World War II. In 1954, after undergoing scrutiny for the "disagreeable characteristics," a Jew was even appointed dean of Yale Law School. Indeed, Fetter points out that after his death the following year, the next four men to hold the office were Jews. Although no longer explicitly evaluated by a committee for the tell-tale traits, one wonders if the chosen were, for the most part, invisible Jews.

Notably, as late as 1966, the head of the Harvard Law School Placement Office concluded that there is "no question in my mind that the Jewish boy [graduating from Harvard Law] is slower to receive an offer than his twin who is not Jewish…." She explained that since firms have an "unemotional, Anglo-Saxon pattern," Jewish students would find it hard to fit in, and even if hired, "would probably still not be happy in the firm." She noted that at times she tried to combat the "old prejudices" by sending a "tall, handsome, extremely bright Jewish boy" to these firms. An editorial in the Harvard *Law Record* recognized the difficulty of proving discrimination, at least in some cases: "Of course, hiring partners, with their extensive (often Harvard) legal educations, can be expected to be more subtle in their bigotry than Alabama rednecks."[7]

Closing this section, Edward Shapiro considers an event that occurred at the end of the 1940s, when educational institutions had begun to discard their old policies of excluding Jews. He examines the fate of the offer of a sizeable grant — reported to be worth as much as $50,000,000 — by George Washington Armstrong, "one of America's most prominent antisemites during the 1930s and 1940s," to Jefferson Military College in Mississippi, alma mater of Jefferson Davis, provided the school teach "the doctrine of racial supremacy and not admit Jews [or blacks] as students." Although the school accepted the gift without reservations, within a few days, the outraged response of "Northerners and Southerners, Jews and Gentiles alike," led the trustees to reverse themselves, falsely contending that the stipulations had been unclear. The spokesperson for the school now insisted that Armstrong's antisemitism was "utterly foreign to the thinking of all the members of the board," although one wonders what they understood antisemitism to be. They would not agree to bar Jews, although the admission of "colored" students remained "unthinkable."

More recently, massive monetary gifts to schools have come not from the "Deepest South," but from Arab and Muslim lands, and the stipulations are more indirect and the expectations updated to include the teaching of the doctrine of anti-Zionism. In 1976, for example, after the University of Southern California established the King Faisal Chair in Islamic Studies, endowed by Saudi Arabia with a gift of a million dollars, the Saudi Minister of Finance and National Economy informed the school's president, "It is our understanding that… [f]uture incumbents [of the chair] shall be chosen by

the university in consultation with the Saudi Minister of Higher Education."
Even in the present century, after Georgetown University accepted money
from Turkey's Gulen movement, the head of the school's Prince Alwaleed bin
Talal Center for Muslim-Christian Understanding sponsored a conference in
honor of Fethullah Gulen, the cult's leader, "whitewashing both [his] Islamism
and his anti-Semitism."[8]

Although Jews were now present in significant numbers as students and
faculty at major universities, they were increasingly confronted with campus
movements fraught with anti-Zionism and antisemitism. Section III examines
three groups that have been in the forefront of those movements. Stephen
Norwood begins this section with a study of antisemitism in both the Old and
New American Left. After the Six Day War, he notes, "hostility toward Israel
became a central defining issue for the far left," which was now largely campus-
based. Unlike the Old Left, whose approach to Israel was inconsistent, and
which at times even supported it as "the progressive, democratic force in the
Middle East," in contrast to the authoritarian, intolerant and reactionary Arab
regimes, the New Left, he shows, was relentlessly opposed to what it considered
only a "racist and expansionist" state. Though a secular movement, its
denunciations often rang with vile theological as well as economic antisemitic
charges and epithets. Despite its own — unacknowledged — antisemitism,
the New Left always considered antisemitism a "non-issue," and flatly denied
that it was, or had ever been, significant in the Arab and Muslim worlds.
Promises to turn the Mediterranean red with Israeli blood were dismissed
as "meaningless bombast." Explaining the ceaseless Arab attacks on Israelis
simply as rational responses to oppression, the New Left denied that Jews
needed a separate state. By contrast, at one critical juncture, Norwood shows,
part of the Old Left even acknowledged the "Jews' long, historical connection
to Palestine," and the need for a Jewish state.

Still, the New Left's understanding of antisemitism derived from the
narrow approach of the Old Left, which recognized only its economic roots.
At times, Norwood explains, the Old Left maintained that antisemitic
outbreaks could even be useful in raising workers' consciousness, as they
would proceed from denunciations of Jewish exploiters to a broader attack
on capitalists. Thus in 1929, the American Communist Party supported
the Arabs' barbaric pogroms against the Jews of the Yishuv, characterizing
them only as a "revolutionary Arab uprising," the "expropriated [ ] peasants"
rising up against "British imperialism" and its "Zionist agents." Norwood
observes that this set a precedent for the New Left's "backing of, or excusing,
Palestinian terrorist attacks against Jews," and its "overlook[ing], and

sometimes encourag[ing], the overt antisemitism [in the black ghettos] and the destruction of Jewish stores," which it championed as "ghetto rebellions."

By contrast, during the period of the Popular Front against fascism, the American Communist Party "did not fully back the Arabs in their violent uprising...against Jewish immigration to Palestine" in 1936–1939. And in 1947, at the beginning of the Cold War, the Party "abandoned its [old] hard-line opposition to Zionism and...threw its support behind partitioning Palestine," the *Daily Worker*, the party organ, even stating that "Arab consent should not be required for Jewish immigration to Palestine." By 1948, however, the Soviet Union had initiated a "new antisemitic campaign" and Zionism had become only a "bourgeois nationalist doctrine." Still, in 1956, after Khrushchev's secret speech "denouncing Stalin's crimes," large numbers of Jews left the Party as they came to believe long-standing charges about Soviet antisemitism and became distressed over "Soviet hostility to Israel" during the Suez War. Even in the sixties, Norwood shows, members of the Old Left appeared to have retained "latent pro-Israeli sympathies," even as "far left youth seemed solidly in the Arab camp."

The next chapter, which I wrote, explores how and why, beginning in the 1960s, African Americans — mainly black nationalists and their acolytes — helped legitimize antisemitism on the campus. Long after the demise of the New Left in the early seventies, the nationalists' impact remained, serving, in effect, as a link, even a template, for the Arab- and Muslim-Americans who took the lead near the beginning of the new century. Malcolm X, who has been honored on a postage stamp, and whose autobiography has been required reading for incoming freshmen for decades, was an anti-Zionist and antisemite. For Malcolm X and many other nationalists in these years, antisemitism and anti-Zionism were central to their message, and were seamlessly merged. Indeed, I analyze the pervasive impact of the *Protocols of the Elders of Zion* on the thought and teachings of Malcolm X and the other nationalists whom students came to revere. Classical Christian antisemitism also pervaded their speeches and worldview. The counter-narrative of America and the world that black nationalists and their followers self-consciously forged had the ubiquitous evil Jew at its core, the gross distortions and preposterous charges quickly becoming staples of students' papers and published articles.

In the last chapter of this section, Edward Alexander continues his discussion of the "crucial role" played by academics and journalists who are Jews — or were born to Jewish parents — in "the current upsurge of antisemitism, the likes of which we have not seen since the Hitler era." He finds that these "Jewish prosecutors of Israel" have "disproportionate influence" because "they demonize Israel precisely as Jews." For many, it is, in fact, "the demonization of Israel that *makes* them Jews." Alexander observes that many of them "resemble medieval apostates who confided to their new Christian co-religionists that Jews made Passover matzohs out of Christian blood" — now elevating their status among their gentile campus colleagues. Aside from lending credibility to their compatriots' condemnations of Israel, their presence is actively used to immunize their colleagues against charges of antisemitism. Many appear to belong to the long tradition of Jewish self-hatred, Alexander observes, now appearing as "hatred of Israel." They complain of the "shame and embarrassment" Israel has caused them to endure at cocktail parties, and call "for an end to Israel" because its efforts to defend itself are "bad for [*them*]."

Earlier, as shown in section II, Jews who wanted to enter the academy learned that they had to erase any "Jewish traits," convert to Protestantism, or try to pass as "a WASP." Now, having been admitted, they may, on some level, believe that acceptance requires ridding themselves of any *Zionist* traces, or better, conversion to anti-Zionism.

Section IV turns the discussion to the student organizations that led the anti-Zionist campaigns on campus. Dave Rich focuses on the campus in Great Britain, where in 1977 the National Union of Students (NUS), in effect, banned Jewish societies. He notes that in the early 1970s, political activists on the left were engaged with the liberation struggles in South Africa and Vietnam, not the Arab-Israeli conflict. Still, they generally agreed that "Zionism was a racist ideology and that Israel was comparable to apartheid South Africa," and the Young Liberals became "the first [organization on the British left] to call for Zionists to be excluded from mainstream political structures." The end of the Vietnam War in January 1973, however, "left a campaigning vacuum," which, Rich observes, the Middle East conflict could fill. And with the Yom Kippur War in October of that year, the activists had found their new "national liberationist" cause.

Thus in April 1974, the NUS passed its "No Platform" policy, which "refuse[d] any assistance (financial or otherwise) to openly racist or fascist organizations." Even before this policy was approved, some students were trying "to restrict campus Zionist activities on the grounds that they were racist," but it was, Rich observes, the United Nations' 1975 resolution that "Zionism is a form of racism" that "lent respectability to the idea that Zionism…should be banned." Thus in 1977, student unions on many campuses passed resolutions equating Zionism and racism, which, following NUS policy, meant that Zionist activities would be banned. Since it was the Jewish societies that supported Zionism, in practice this threatened them. Incredibly, some of the activists claimed they had not realized at the time that their resolution would lead to the banning of the Jewish societies. (The ban would not extend to a Jewish chess club, after all, and Jewish anti-Zionists would be permitted to organize and speak.) And certainly their intent could not be construed as anti-Jewish, they claimed, because some of the prominent campaigners for the resolutions were Jews — anti-Zionist Jews. To be sure, later that year NUS voted to rescind the entire No Platform policy. It is notable, however, that even when one university passed a motion reinstating the Jewish society that had been expelled there, 45 percent of the Students Union voted to retain the ban. And one wonders if any Students Unions at the time considered banning antisemitic activities and Islamist speakers, or simply characterized their harangues and threats only as anti-Zionist speech.

In the following chapter, Gregg Rickman lifts the anti-Zionist cover off the actions and speeches of student organizations in South Africa, often revealing the mass of antisemitism barely hidden underneath. As in Great Britain, the left — often the far left — controls the Student Representative Council on many campuses there, but in South Africa, as one observer points out, the "government is itself a sponsor of anti-Zionism" and "it, in effect, licenses the actions of Muslim student associations that spread anti-Israel/anti-Zionist hatred and antisemitism." The Muslim Students Association (MSA) and Palestine Solidarity Committee (PSC) conduct ferocious, sustained campaigns on campus, focused single-mindedly on equating Israel with South Africa under apartheid and the national "liberation struggle" of the Palestinian Arabs with that of South Africans. Because the analogies are drawn by South Africans, the international community automatically accords them moral authority. Groups not only invert apartheid, but the Holocaust, proclaiming "Holocaust Victims threatening a new and even bigger Holocaust." They appropriate the cry "Never Again!" "applying it to Israel's supposed current actions against the Palestinians." A PSC celebrates the "two-time plane hijacker" it brings to campus, and Muslim students sponsor talks by a columnist they "pointedly describe as 'a well-known and observant Jew.'" Norman Finkelstein, son of Holocaust victims, tours South African campuses, where he charges that Jews exploit the Holocaust for monetary gain and as a "cover for Israel's ostensibly illegal acts against the Palestinians," though there is no talk of the exploitation of the "Nakba" to attract massive funding to the Palestinians or to justify the persistent violation of Israelis' human rights.

Using the definitions of antisemitism adopted by the U.S. State Department in 2008, Rickman concludes that the "criticism of Israel" or Zionism on South African campuses has often been antisemitic. Still, the students deny they can be antisemitic, because they know "it is wrong to hate 'a religion.'" Apparently they have determined not only that Jews are only a religious group, but that there is no relationship between Judaism and Zion.

Kenneth Lasson's chapter rounds out this section with an examination of what currently passes as anti-Zionism in the American academy. He exposes the myths about Israel and the Israel Defense Forces that are endlessly propounded by students and faculty in the effort to turn the Jewish state into a satanic pariah. He surveys the methods of threat and intimidation deployed by "pro-Palestinian" student organizations, which leave many of their fellow students feeling "terrified for anyone to find out" they are "Jewish and…support a Jewish state," fearing they would be physically attacked. Often the students do not even disguise their shouts or scrawls as anti-Zionist, as in "Hitler did not finish the job" or "God Hates Jews" or "Burn the Torah." Lasson also analyzes the speeches, writings and actions of anti-Israel faculty, systematically exposing the double-standards they apply, the absurdity of the analogy they draw between Israel and apartheid South Africa, the specious arguments, the wanton distortion of data, and the complete absence of context, which allows them to reverse cause and effect. When writing about Israel, ordinarily careful authors present a "conspiratorial view of history" and a former president "manufactures sins 'to hang around the necks of Jews when no sins have actually been committed.'" In short, much of the writing Lasson presents appears to be propaganda masquerading as scholarship. "An academic voice" disguises ideologically driven polemics. Often, it appears, anti-Zionism becomes the language of a born-again antisemitism.

Section V moves on to consider students' exposure to antisemitism through youth culture. Glenn Altschuler and Robert Summers examine the impact of "bad rap," exemplified by the group Public Enemy (PE), the "prophets of rage," who "dominated the political rap landscape" in the late eighties. This was a time when "black leaders with 'street cred'…exhibited enmity for Jews" and when Jesse Jackson's negative stereotyping of Jews, long familiar in some circles, was first widely reported by the mainstream media.

It was in this context that in 1989, "Professor Griff," "Minister of Information" for PE, informed a reporter that "ninety percent of the [music] business is operated by Jews," although he warned that "A lot of people are not ready for the truth." He also divulged that "Jews are wicked and we can prove this," their wickedness including their "culpability in the slave trade." His source, he later explained, was Henry Ford's *The International Jew* — renowned for featuring the antisemitic tract *The Protocols of the Elders of Zion*. It appears that this minister of information and his followers were people of the antisemitic book. Altschuler and Summers comment that Griff, Chuck D, PE's lead singer, and others may "well be regarded as Malcolm [X]'s grandchildren." This is certainly the case: as I show in the chapter on African Americans, Malcolm X was greatly influenced by, and promoted, the *Protocols*. And while Malcolm X taught that Jews dominated the black ghetto, Griff now had Jews controlling the exit out of the ghetto. Griff's charges were openly antisemitic, and before long, Chuck D attempted to reframe them, stressing that "Griff's real beef was 'with Israel and its involvement in South Africa, which hurts his people, black people.'" He never mentioned that this trade had occurred only after the other African countries had isolated Israel; nor did he complain about the Arab and European nations that provided South Africa with critical oil and military supplies.

In February 1990, Griff spoke at Columbia University, invited by the Black Students Organization (BSO). Altschuler and Summers explain that his appearance elicited protests and petitions. And Griff did not disappoint, as "he charged that AIDS had been invented by Jews and (somehow) injected into black Africans." Here again he was only updating Malcolm X, who, as I show, portrayed Jews as poisoning blacks. He was also echoing Steve Cokely, an African-American aide to the acting mayor of Chicago, who had been forced to resign a week after his antisemitic charge became public, whereupon he was welcomed as a speaker on college campuses.[9]

Columbia's BSO defended its invitation to Griff, noting that he "would speak on education." This was likely not disingenuous — he was, after all, *Professor* Griff and a minister of *information*. And he, along with the members of the Nation of Islam whom I discuss, always maintained that the students were being mis-educated, and only they could provide the knowledge they lacked. Thus students who were in the academy to understand their past and present chose to invite speakers who boasted that *The International Jew* was their major guide. A BSO spokesperson explained that "the BSO did not necessarily endorse Griff's comments on Jews: 'We're not saying, yes, he's right, or no, he's wrong.'" These students at an elite university could not challenge Griff's antisemitic claims or worldview.

In the next chapter Andre Oboler focuses on the Internet as a major source of antisemitism on the contemporary campus. Students now spend much of their time online, where they encounter masses of antisemitic material, which in the past would have been confined to restricted-access library shelves, to newsletters mailed to already converted subscribers, or, being privately published, would have remained largely unknown. On the Internet, however, as Oboler points out, even small groups can have massive outreach. Search engine algorithms assign a high rank, he explains, to well-optimized sites, which then appear on the first page of a search, where students are more likely to access them. An example is the antisemitic, but well-organized, JewWatch. com, with sections on "Zionist Occupied Governments [ZOG]," "Jewish Mind Control Mechanisms," and other "scholarly" topics. Antisemitic groups often reproduce or provide links to materials found on each other's websites, where students, repeatedly finding the same "information," may infer, Oboler notes, that this enhances its credibility. He provides the example of the increasing number of Islamist and Muslim community sites, which frequently reprint documents originally posted on neo-Nazi and Holocaust denial sites. Social and media sites, such as Facebook or YouTube, which promote the formation of networks of online friends, have become the venues for the broad dissemination of antisemitic materials and the rapid organization of "communit[ies] of hate." Oboler cites a user whose info box declares, "Jihad is our way. Dying in the way of Allah is our highest hope," and notes that this user has "4,388 friends."

Antisemitic sites often pose as "an educational tool and research archive" and explicitly assure their viewers, "This is NOT a hate site." And the culture of the Internet, monitored by few trained gatekeepers or referees, accords a rough equality to informed and uninformed comments, to the signed or anonymously posted alike. Like the rappers and speakers favored by students, who deliver their lines in the studiedly nonacademic language youth prefer, the antisemitic websites package themselves as providing "controversial," non-traditional, anti-authoritarian points of view, often highly appealing to those at the students' stage of life. Although more youth than ever before are attending colleges and universities, the academics' challenge to ensure their pursuit and recognition of accurate information and proximate truth is becoming increasingly difficult.

The last section of the book is devoted to an examination and assessment of recent efforts to combat antisemitism on the American campus — in most cases, efforts made by the authors themselves. Kenneth Marcus traces the failure of the Office for Civil Rights (OCR) of the U.S. Department of Education to respond appropriately to a complaint filed in 2004, documenting the "hostile environment for Jewish students" that had developed at the University of California, Irvine, "in violation of the prohibition on racial and national-origin discrimination contained in Title VI of the Civil Rights Act of 1964." OCR refused to act because it recognized Jews strictly as a religious group and considered the national origins claims only to determine if Israeli students had been subjected to "national origin discrimination." Notably, in 2004, when Marcus was the head of the OCR, he issued policy directives, based on recent decisions and dicta of the U.S. Supreme Court, stating that the OCR would henceforth "exercise its Title VI jurisdiction to defend members of groups, such as Jews, which exhibit both ethnic and religious characteristics." His successors, however, have ignored these guidelines. As Marcus points out, they understand the nature of neither Jewish identity nor modern antisemitism, and generally will not act to defend the rights of Jews.

Next, Rachel Fish discusses her ultimately successful effort, begun while a graduate student, to have Harvard Divinity School reverse its decision, announced in 2000, to accept a grant from the dictator of the United Arab Emirates, endowing the eponymous Sheikh Zayed al Nahyan Professorship in Islamic Religious Studies. Searching the sheikh's record, Fish learned that the Zayed Centre he had founded, which was directed by his son, promoted antisemitism, including Holocaust denial. Yet the Terms of Agreement between Harvard and Zayed privileged academic exchanges between the Centre and the school. Fish notes that the "majority of the Jewish students" privately supported her effort, but, "with a few exceptions, they were reluctant to get directly involved." The majority of faculty, "tenured and untenured," "refused to take a public stand." And the dean proved uncooperative, to say the least. It was only after Fish publicized the issues beyond the campus through the press and the Internet that Zayed was finally led to close the Centre and Harvard to freeze the funds. Still, some of the information Fish uncovered would have been readily available to Harvard at the time it accepted the tainted money, which it chose to retain for as long as it could.

Fish then relates her subsequent experiences working with Columbia University students who were distressed that some faculty in the Middle East and Asian Languages and Cultures Department (MEALAC) were using the classroom "to promote [an] anti-Israel agenda, intimidating any students who supported Israel and Zionism." Once again, it was only after she and the students made the film "Columbia Unbecoming," documenting some of their experiences, and released it to the public that the university responded by forming a committee to consider the charges. The committee was, however, comprised of faculty who were compromised by their support for divestment from Israel or their close connections to the accused, and its "findings," which protected the professors and skirted the students' concerns, were a foregone conclusion.

The issue students raised — that in some MEALAC classes "academic integrity was being subordinated to a rigid political agenda" — is a critical one, but difficult to resolve. Some campuses and classrooms have come to resemble charged courtrooms, with faculty (and students) assuming the role only of prosecutor or defendant. There are only competing narratives, argued tendentiously, positions chosen and hardened to sustain political views. Academic freedom was not intended as a cover for the teaching of false or highly distorted data and concepts and conclusions the evidence cannot reasonably support. As Middle East Studies is one of the few growth areas on campus, and the tendency of departments is to hire only those who share their perspective, it is urgent that the university uphold the academic ideal of the disinterested pursuit of proximate truth, however often it has been ignored in the past.

Evelyn Avery conveys her experiences combating the attempts of a Radical Caucus (RC) to politicize an academic organization, the Modern Language Association (MLA), and put it on record as censuring and condemning Israel and in support of scholars of "Palestinian culture," who alone are alleged to be "under attack for pursuing such work." In response, Avery and two other MLA members drew up their own resolution, which "supported all Middle Eastern scholarship and refused to censure either side." Along with their resolution, Avery and her colleagues submitted documentation showing that it was "radical Islamists [who were] propagandizing at universities" and "Israel advocates who were under assault in U.S. higher education, not Palestinian or Arab supporters," as the RC claimed. Avery's resolution was never put to a vote, as the MLA Executive Council decided that it, along with a new, even "more viciously" anti-Israel, RC resolution, was "not in the interests of" the association. The MLA did, however, vote online to adopt the RC's previous resolution, though the percentage of members who voted was minuscule, the vast majority choosing not to condemn, but also not to endorse, the biased statement or a politicized organization. Still, the hundreds who voted for the resolution teach tens of thousands of students and are training a segment of the next generation of the professoriate.

Avery also discusses her efforts to combat the politicization of her own campus, Towson University. She reveals the impact that even one newly hired Israel-bashing professor can have on the campus culture and discourse. In 2002, when, for the first time, the university conducted a search for a professor of Islamic history, the History Department chair assured Avery that it would choose "a real scholar, dedicated to fairness and balance," and after completing the process, "shared his relief" that it had hired "an impartial educator." Within only a few months, however, Avery had discovered "how wrong" his assessment was, when her new colleague organized her first anti-Israel event, and then "rejected [Avery's] recommendation" that she consider a "fair, more balanced program." The historian instructed Avery that it "was fair; there was no other side." Having completed her training at an Institute of Middle Eastern Studies, it appears that she, like many other recent graduates of such a course of study, had been taught to dismiss any other perspective out-of-hand.

Tammi Rossman-Benjamin shows that scholarly standards have been even more widely flouted on her campus, the University of California, Santa Cruz (UCSC), in service to the anti-Zionist cause. She finds that since 2001, all the campus events on the Israeli-Palestinian conflict sponsored by university departments and centers have been "biased against Israel." Though billed as "an academic event," a 2007 conference was, she concluded, only "an open exercise in political indoctrination, bent on promoting an anti-Zionist agenda and encouraging activism against the Jewish state." Speakers clamped the currently favored paradigms and tired tropes on Israel, only Israel — a racist entity from its beginnings, an imperialist and colonialist settler state that engages in ethnic cleansing and attempts genocide, "an apartheid regime," "worse than apartheid," that takes "pride in domination" to boot. The organizer characterized the conference as "an historic event" and the presentations as exemplars of academic freedom. Rossman-Benjamin, by contrast, found the papers "scholarly questionable, politically motivated," and "much of the discourse...antisemitic," according to the "working definition of the term adopted by the U.S. State Department." In addition, Rossman-Benjamin, along with a group of concerned colleagues, found that some faculty appeared to have been inserting "anti-Israel or anti-Zionist materials unrelated to the course" into their lectures, and others to have turned the classroom into a "platform for politically biased and unscholarly" indoctrination in an "anti-Israel perspective," while "encourag[ing] students to engage in anti-Israel activism."

Confronted by what they believed to be the misuse of the university, Rossman-Benjamin and her group examined California's policies on academic freedom and its limits. Although the policies were revised in 2003, they continued to require that "teaching and scholarship be assessed by reference to the professional standards that sustain the University's pursuit and achievement of knowledge." But while the older set of rules had listed what constituted abuses of academic freedom, the new policy shifted the responsibility for defining the limits to faculty and administrative bodies.

Having systematically documented how the conferences and courses had egregiously violated the limits of academic freedom, Rossman-Benjamin and her group proceeded to bring their evidence to those charged with enforcing the policies and upholding the core academic values of the University — from administrators and faculty at the highest levels of governance of the statewide University of California system to those at UCSC. Their efforts, however, were repeatedly thwarted or rebuffed. At UCSC, they submitted their materials showing the "pattern of political bias and advocacy" on campus to the Academic Senate and asked that it "investigate this problem." The report, issued by the Committee on Academic Freedom a year later, "not only ignored our primary concern," Rossman-Benjamin states, but included an investigation it had conducted of members of the group — for *their* "alleged violations of [the] academic freedom" of those whom they had accused. She could only conclude that the "investigation of our group and its inclusion in the report were intended to discredit us and stifle further inquiry into this matter." It is hard to be confident that the university will acknowledge the severity of the problem and adequately regulate itself.

In the final chapter, Alvin Rosenfeld analyzes the ideological wars being waged against Israel on a number of campuses and suggests several appropriate responses. He contends that the conflict has become acute largely on the coasts, and finds "little evidence to date of chronically persistent anti-Israel manifestations" on campuses elsewhere. At Indiana University, his own school, for example, Israel is not "habitually discredited, maligned, and demonized." He shows how it has been able to avoid the politicization that has corrupted the academic culture on coastal campuses, and offers its approach as a proactive model others might adopt "to discourage...hostility [to Israel] from arising in the first place."

In order to develop effective strategies to combat the conflict already raging on coastal campuses, however, it is necessary to understand, Rosenfeld explains, that they are "ideological battles," "unlikely to be won by mounting carefully composed counter-arguments based on verifiable facts." Those "responsible for most anti-Israel agitation on university campuses" are, he suggests, driven by "identity politics" and thus are "not open to...rational arguments in support of Zionism or Israel." "Such politics serves as a quasi-religion," he observes, providing them with "a sense of community" based on "shared affirmations...and shared denigrations."

In an era in which the traditional sources of community have eroded and a coherent personal identity has become increasingly problematic, these ideological bonds appear to satisfy powerful needs — needs which appear to have overwhelmed any commitment to reasoned inquiry. Indeed, as converts to a "quasi-religion," many seem to have assumed the role of missionary, using the conference and lectern as a pulpit, from which they spread their gospel truth about the new Satan, the Jewish state.

Rosenfeld identifies the two groups that he believes provide "much of the energy behind today's most strident anti-Zionism" — "politically active Muslims and so-called 'progressive' anti-Zionist Jews" — and indicates the intellectual sources of their rage. Many, to whom "Israel appears... anachronistic... and needs to be opposed," are inspired in part by a "range of intellectual and ideological currents — Islamism, Third-Worldism, Marxism, postmodernism," etc., each of which "may encourage a predisposition to regard Israel from an adversarial posture." Their positions are, however, inconsistent, laced with contradictions, which betrays that they are not based *only* on intellectual or ideological grounds. Thus, as postmodernists, who are "unsympathetic to the idea of nation states and nationalities," they are "biased against... a Jewish state... [but] readily support Palestinian nationalism and national identity," and rarely criticize Muslim states' enforced uniformity. As post-colonialists and anti-imperialists, they "see Israel as heavily corrupted by both," but rarely "voice dissent against the imperialist schemes of radical Islamists to create a global caliphate."

We still need to explain, however, the near hysteria and obsessiveness with which they — and especially the young adherents to the cause — defend their (contradictory) positions and the tenacity with which they cling to them, ignoring or denying the data that undermine their view. Thus, along with identity politics, we may be witnessing an impassioned form of what might be called sibling politics, played out between anti-Zionist and Zionist Jews. The anti-Zionist, unsure of acceptance in the academic family, driven to convince the gentile authority-figure that he is the good son, goes to extreme lengths to show how different he is from the evil — Zionist — Jew. (In calling for boycotts of Zionists/Israelis, he is insisting that none of the parents' treasure should be bestowed on them.) In some cases, we may also be witnessing, however, the displacement of a form of what might be called domestic separation politics onto the Middle Eastern scene. Israel's behavior that evokes the most intense negative reaction of the young campus warriors is, after all, its alleged expulsion of the Palestinians, always portrayed as innocent children, from their homes. Worse, they cry, Israel has replaced them with the favored (Jewish) son. The activists are enraged above all that the new "settlers" have taken over their home. This drama appears to have dislodged the fears and rage of those whose parents have divorced and remarried, with a new spouse and children "settling" into their home. They want to reverse the "catastrophe" — and insist on their "right of return."

ENDNOTES

1   Robert Wistrich, "A Deadly Mutation," in this volume.

2   Ibid.

3   Joel Beinin, former head of the Middle East Studies Association (MESA), quoted by Edward Alexander, "Blushing Professors," in this volume.

4   The historian Anthony Julius and the legal scholar Alan Dershowitz, quoted by Robert Wistrich, "A Deadly Mutation," in this volume.

5   Thus the title of Stephen Norwood's chapter, "Old Wine [or poison] in New Bottles," in this volume.

6   Benjamin Ginsberg, "Why University Administrators Tolerate Antisemitism," in this volume.

7   Harvard *Law Record*, December 1, 1966.

8   Seth Crospey, "Arab Money and the Universities," *Commentary*, April 1979; Michael Rubin, "Turkey, from Ally to Enemy," *Commentary*, July/August 2010, 86.

9   See, for example, "Emory University…Anti-White and Anti-Semitic Speakers Welcome," *Project 21 News*, October 8, 1996; Nat Hentoff, "Strange Speech on Campus," Washington *Post*, May 21, 1999.

I

ANTISEMITISM:
THE HYDRA-HEADED MONSTER

WHY UNIVERSITY ADMINISTRATORS TOLERATE ANTISEMITISM

Benjamin Ginsberg

As the papers in this volume indicate, a good deal of antisemitic rhetoric and more than a few instances of antisemitic vandalism and even violence have plagued American college and university campuses in recent years. In some instances, antisemitism is expressed in the form of attacks on "Zionists" but, often enough, antisemitic speakers and vandals are happy to make their hatred more explicit and point to the Jews as their targets. At the University of California, Irvine (UCI), for example, antisemitic speakers have informed their campus audiences that Jews need to be rehabilitated, that they suffer from a communal psychosis and, ominously, that the Jews' days are "numbered."[1]

Much of this antisemitic vitriol seems to originate with radical Muslim campus speakers from groups such as the Council on American-Islamic Relations (CAIR) and the Muslim Students Association (MSA). In some instances, unfortunately, Muslim faculty members — perhaps carried away during the heat of academic debate — have allowed their opposition to Israeli policy to lead to intemperate remarks to Jewish students, as has been well-documented at Columbia University and elsewhere.

It is hardly surprising that the Muslim campaign against Israel has come to involve attacks on American (as well as European and Canadian) Jews. America's Jews work vigorously to maintain the U.S. support upon which Israel is militarily and economically dependent. Thus, for Muslim activists, the American Jewish community is simply a second front in the war against Israel. If American Jewish support for Israel can be delegitimated and America's Jews cowed into silence, then Israel's isolation and vulnerability will be increased. College campuses are useful battlegrounds along this second front. The presence of a sizeable contingent of Muslim students along with their various American sympathizers provides a force ready and willing to do battle with the "Zionists." College campuses also hold millions of impressionable American students who, on any given day, can be convinced of just about anything. If a few are persuaded each year that Israel is a vicious, racist, Apartheid, Fascist state, supported by a conspiracy of Zionists, aka Jews, who manipulate the press and Congress, then this part of the war may eventually be won.

This much is obvious. What at first glance seems more surprising is that a number of college and university administrators appear unwilling to speak out against, much less actively work to combat, antisemitic activities on their campuses. At UCI, for example, where Jewish students have been subjected to a number of antisemitic attacks, campus authorities have generally remained silent. The same has been true at Columbia and a number of other schools. Typically, administrators cite the university's tradition of free and open debate as well as First Amendment concerns when they refuse to take action against antisemitic activists. Such concerns are certainly important, but it is worth noting that many college administrators who ignore the most vicious antisemitic speeches respond with alacrity to the slightest indication of racist, sexist, or homophobic activity on their campuses. In other words, they exhibit what is sometimes called "First Amendment opportunism," invoking the Constitution only when they find it useful.[2]

What explains this peculiar state of affairs, especially given the prominence of Jews in America's academic world? One factor that is often mentioned in connection with the reluctance of university administrators to take issue with antisemites on their campuses is the growing importance of Middle Eastern contributors and students to schools' finances. It is certainly the case that the governments of Saudi Arabia and the Gulf states have donated tens of millions of dollars to American universities and it is also true that tens of thousands of Middle Eastern students — fifteen thousand from Saudi Arabia alone — are important sources of tuition revenue at some schools. Nevertheless, Jewish donors and Jewish students are far more important factors in American higher education than their Muslim counterparts. Jews donate billions of dollars every year to America's schools, which also enroll nearly 400,000 Jewish students. Rather than provide an explanation, these numbers merely add to the mystery of campus antisemitism.

The actual reason that administrators are reluctant to confront antisemites has less to do with money and more with campus politics, in particular, with the peculiar relationship between university administrators and left-liberal and radical activists, a vocal force on many university campuses. Though the precise composition of this group varies from school to school, it generally includes middle-class white radicals, black activists, radical feminists, gay rights activists and others advocating major changes in American society, the American economic structure and America's place in the world. Though this coalition includes many Jews, it has long been hostile to Israel and sympathetic to Israel's (and America's) various Middle Eastern foes. In recent decades the campus Left has come to include, as members in good standing, Palestinian and other Muslim activists who have been welcomed with open arms as representatives of a third-world people with the courage to stand up to America and its Zionist surrogate. Hence, when UCI Muslim groups organized their annual anti-Israel week in 2009, the event was co-sponsored by such organizations as the Afrikan Student Union, the Workers' Student Alliance, the Radical Student Union and other campus activists.

If the Jewish members of this coalition are untroubled by their partners' (Muslim and other) antisemitic rhetoric, they must be pretending that attacks on Zionists could not possibly include them. Perhaps they thought CAIR coordinator and frequent campus speaker Affad Shaikh was referring to O.J. Simpson when he posted a sign declaring "DEATH TO ALL JUICE" on his blog. And, perhaps, they simply were not listening when former University of Colorado Professor Ward Churchill, who famously called the World Trade Center victims "little Eichmanns," downplayed the importance of the Shoah, declaring during his 2008 University of Toronto "Israel Apartheid Week" comments that the mass murder of the Jews was "not a fixed objective of the Nazis."[3] Could it be that the Nazis only wanted to kill Zionists? Rather than object to this sort of rhetoric, Jewish members of the left-liberal coalition dismiss those Jews who do express outrage as "right-wing Zionists."[4]

UNIVERSITY ADMINISTRATORS AND THE CAMPUS LEFT

On most campuses, administrators are reluctant to criticize left-liberal activists, whatever they may do or say. Indeed, on many campuses, administrators have forged what amount to tactical alliances with local activist groups. Since it was not so long ago that campus presidents responded to the legitimate grievances of minority groups and liberal activists by calling the police, it is fascinating to observe the apparent sympathy shown for these same groups by university administrators today.

At my university, for example, the administration strongly supported liberal activists' protests in response to what some termed a fraternity's racial insensitivity. The fraternity had called its 2006 All Hallow's Eve party, "Halloween In the Hood," invited guests to wear their "bling" and decorated its chapter house with a plastic skeleton in pirate garb dangling from a rope noose. The precise meaning of this display was far from clear. A noose might have a racist connotation, but skeletons and pirates would seem, at first blush, to be devoid of racial antecedents. Campus and community activists, however, chose to interpret the unfortunate skeleton as a symbolic affirmation of the idea of lynching black people. This understanding was vigorously contested by the fraternity, which boasted a multiethnic membership. The university administration, nevertheless, supported the activists' interpretation and agreed with them that investigations, punishments and policy changes would be required to prevent such events from occurring in the future.[5]

In a similar vein, during the Spring of 2008, Brandeis University administrators overrode a finding by the faculty's Committee on Faculty Rights and Responsibilities (CFRR) regarding the case of Donald Hindley, a long-time and somewhat cantankerous political science professor who had been accused of racial harassment by an anonymous student in his Latin American politics class.[6] The accuser averred that Hindley had used the term "wetback," to refer to illegal immigrants from Mexico. Hindley asserted, in response, that he had employed the term during a historical discussion as an example of the racist invective to which Mexican immigrants had been subjected. While the facts continue to be a matter of dispute, university officials seemed to have little or no interest in determining exactly what was said in Hindley's class. Instead, they quickly sided with campus activists and treated the episode as an opportunity to take a strong public stand against racism and discriminatory conduct. The university's provost assigned human resources staffers to conduct a brief investigation, sent a deanlet to monitor Hindley's classes, and threatened the professor with termination if he failed to modify his classroom conduct. CFRR and the faculty senate vehemently protested these actions as violations of due process and the university regulations, but these institutions were ignored by the president and provost, who asserted that they alone possessed legal authority and responsibility in these matters.

What accounts for the solicitude shown by university administrators for campus activists and minorities? In some instances, perhaps, administrators themselves possess deep and abiding commitments to social justice and change and support the same causes espoused by the minority and activist communities. Yale's Kingman Brewster was a leading example. Many university administrators, however, are dull bureaucratic functionaries whose main commitments involve planning the next conference or retreat. Others are opportunists, firmly focused on their own administrative careers. Rather than their own deep and abiding concern for social justice, two other factors explain the cooperative stance that administrators typically adopt toward their campuses' liberal activists and minorities.

The first of these factors is, of course, a desire to protect themselves from criticism from the often vocal and vehement campus Left.[7] Since the 1960's, the campus Left has been well-organized and active, especially at major colleges and universities. Administrators have learned, through the application of repeated electric shocks, as it were, that a failure to pacify the liberal Left can result in demonstrations, disturbances and the potential destruction of administrative careers. During the 1960s and 1970s, university presidents who sought to battle campus protests, like Columbia's Grayson Kirk, saw their careers ruined, while those who learned to work with and placate militant forces, like a subsequent Columbia president, Michael Sovern, had relatively uneventful presidencies.[8]

Administrators who come into conflict with campus radicals or, for that matter, minority groups are, at the very least, likely to be labeled "controversial," and shunned by the search firms that hold the keys to new positions and promotions in the administrative world. Corporate head hunters will never touch a "controversial" individual though of course such traits as indolence, ineptitude and out-and-out stupidity are rarely disqualifications for career advancement in the field of higher education administration. The demands of the campus Left, moreover, are seldom counterbalanced by conservative or moderate opinion. There are virtually no conservatives on leading campuses while the moderate liberal majority generally takes little or no part in university politics. Only on the issue of Israel, where campus Jews are usually well-organized and prepared to engage in political struggle, is significant opposition likely to be voiced to the views of the strident campus left.

Take, for example, the now-infamous 2006 case of the three Duke lacrosse players falsely accused of raping an African American exotic dancer. Radical activists, though constituting only a small fraction of the Duke faculty, were outspoken in their demands for summary punishment of the accused athletes even before the facts of the case were examined. The campus's more mainstream liberals were dubious about the allegations but generally remained aloof from the fray, reluctant to be seen as taking the side of privileged white students against a poor black woman. The university's president and other administrators, with the notable exception of the school's provost, shamelessly backed the outrageous claims of campus and community activists even after the case began to publicly unravel.[9]

A desire to avoid clashes with vocal and well-organized college groups is only one reason that administrators often find it expedient to maintain good relations with liberal activists and minority groups on their campuses. A second reason is that this alliance can, in several ways, help administrators to bolster their own power vis-à-vis the faculty. Because most professors are progressive in their political commitments they are, as in the Duke case, unwilling to be seen as siding with putative oppressors against the oppressed and, hence, are generally reluctant to oppose programs and proposals that are presented as efforts to foster campus equality, diversity, multiculturalism and the like. At some point during the past several decades one or more administrators, perhaps possessing a bit more political savvy than the average deanlet or deanling, became aware of the political possibilities inherent in this situation and developed a model that the others could imitate.

Put simply, university administrators will often package proposals designed mainly to enhance their own power on campus as altruistic and public-spirited efforts to promote social and political goals, such as equality and diversity, which the faculty cannot oppose. This tactic can succeed if and only if administrative proposals are endorsed by the school's political activists, as well as spokespersons for the women's groups and various racial and ethnic groups that, together, constitute a self-appointed but effective political *Vaad Ha'ir* on many campuses. For this reason, administrators view these coalitions of minorities and activists as important allies and frequently work to retain their support with symbolic and material rewards including positions for spouses, funding for scholarly initiatives, released time for research and higher salaries than are received by other professors. For example, faculty in such programs as "Gender and Sexuality Studies" usually have more perks than students. At the same time, they can usually be counted upon to support the campus administration in its various endeavors.

The political alliance between administrators, minorities and liberal activists, an alliance born in the turmoil of the 1960s, serves the interests of both parties and has become an important force at a number of colleges and universities. The most obvious and best-documented expression of this alliance is the strong support shown in recent years by so many university presidents for affirmative action and other racial preferences in both graduate and professional school admissions.[10] Other institutional expressions of this alliance include the proliferation of multicultural programs and centers; the expansion of administrative influence in faculty hiring and promotion, nominally designed to promote racial and gender diversity; the emergence of a punitive regime of speech and "civility" codes on a number of university campuses, and the development of often ideologically freighted "student life" or "residence life" curricula at many schools.

DIVERSITY

The case of the current nationwide administrative campaign for greater faculty diversity illustrates one way in which their alliance with campus activists serves administrators' interests. Most colleges and universities in the United States appear to be struggling to promote faculty diversity, that is, the hiring and retention of women and people of color as full-time professors. Usually led by the president and provost and other high-ranking officials, university administrators throughout the nation have declared diversity to rank among their institutions' very highest priorities. University of Rochester president Joel Seligman, for example, recently declared that faculty diversity was an institutional priority and a "fundamental value" of his university.[11] The school adopted a thirty-one point program to enhance the diversity of its tenured and tenure-track faculty. Like many other college leaders, Rochester's president has appointed diversity officials, instituted procedures to ensure that diversity goals will figure prominently in faculty searches, and encouraged members of search committees to undergo "diversity training." The officials of some schools have gone even further than their Rochester counterparts, mandating diversity training for those involved in searches and requiring that diversity officers be included in all faculty search committees. Hundreds of schools have appointed "Chief Diversity Officers," with the authority to implement diversity plans.[12] And still others have employed the services of one or another of the now-ubiquitous diversity consulting firms which will, for a hefty fee, help ensure that they do not overlook any possibilities that might help to speed them along the road to greater and greater diversity.[13]

While diversity is an important goal, at first blush the current administrative full-speed-ahead drive to add under-represented minorities and women to college faculties seems a bit off the mark. The simple, if unfortunate, fact of the matter is that in many fields there are few women and virtually no minority faculty available to be hired. In a recent year, only ten African Americans earned PhD degrees in Mathematics and only thirteen in Physics.[14] Given these numbers, it might appear that the only way to bolster the presence of minority faculty in such fields would involve a long term effort to identify and nurture math and science skills among talented minority secondary-school students. A crash program to hire minority scientists when none are being produced seems misguided, to say the least.

In the humanities and social sciences, to be sure, women and members of racial and ethnic minorities constitute a larger fraction of the graduate school population and, hence, the pool of individuals from which professors can be recruited. In these fields, though, the academic departments have been actively hiring minority faculty for a number of years. My department of eighteen full-time political science professors is currently chaired by a woman. The full-time faculty includes two African Americans, one African, six women, and one Arab-American. Two of the six women are Asian-American. By some counts, we might be considered a majority/minority department. Most of the university's other humanities and social science departments became similarly diverse long before our president and provost learned that the term did not merely refer to the mix of securities in the school's investment portfolio.

Thus, in some fields, professorial diversity cannot be achieved simply though university hiring processes, while in those fields where women and minority professors are actually available to be recruited, efforts to do so have been under way for a number of years and have been fairly successful. Why then have university presidents, provosts and other high-ranking officials suddenly, and somewhat belatedly, become outspoken diversity advocates, seemingly on a collective quest to drastically change the gender and racial balance of their faculties? The answer to this question has more to do with administrative interests than with long-standing moral commitments.

To begin with, the diversity plan has become as important an assertion of administrative leadership as the strategic plan. When they announce a bold new diversity plan, presidents and other top administrators are, in effect, averring that only they, and not department chairs or other campus luminaries, are capable of providing leadership in this important realm. An ambitious new diversity plan is likely to be endorsed by the school's liberal activists and minority faculty and staff, particularly if the administration involves these groups in the planning process. Once liberal activists and minority representatives endorse the plan, faculty members who might have doubts about the administration's ideas and intentions generally remain silent for fear of being seen as lacking proper enthusiasm for racial and gender equality. Indeed, clever administrators will make increased diversity and an imaginative diversity plan the centerpiece of their vision for the school — a fundamental value, as Rochester's president put it. By wrapping themselves and their programs in the mantle of diversity, university presidents hope to broaden their base of support on the campus and to intimidate potential critics. Administrators who are insufficiently clever to think of this tactic on their own often benefit nonetheless from the usual administrative propensity to do what everyone else is doing.

Diversity plans often have more than a symbolic significance. On many campuses, the quest for diversity has allowed administrators to intrude into and gain a greater measure of control over the faculty hiring process. Since the emergence of the tenure system, faculties, particularly at research universities, have strongly resisted even the slightest encroachments by administrators into faculty autonomy in the realm of hiring. Typically, university departments have defined their own academic needs and, subject to budgetary approval, identified, interviewed and hired professors deemed to fill those needs. Efforts by administrators to intervene in the process were almost always firmly rebuffed.

Today, under the rubric of diversity, university administrators have been able to arrogate to themselves an ever-growing role in the faculty hiring process. The rationale for this administrative encroachment into what had been a faculty domain is the idea that university departments are not well suited in terms of their own interests and sense of purpose to work diligently on behalf of diversity. According to one scholar, university departments assign too much weight to "their notion of quality, appropriate credentials, and scholarly research/productivity expectations."[15] The only solution to this departmental myopia is "leadership intervention" to set appropriate hiring standards and recruitment policies.

Such intervention has become the norm at a growing number of colleges and universities. At many schools, staffers from human resources or the diversity office play an active role in faculty searches. One modest form of intervention is diversity training — sometimes mandatory — for members of search committees. The University of Virginia, for example, recently adopted such a requirement.[16] At Hopkins, I once served on a campus-wide search committee for a senior college staffer. The deanlet who chaired the committee insisted that we undergo diversity training before we began the search and invited a well-known diversity consultant to help us understand such issues as biases in labor markets and racial stereotyping. My recollection of the training session is that the consultant seemed decidedly less conversant than the faculty members on the committee with the major issues in these fields. The consultant also seemed altogether too eager to share with us various religious and ethnic stereotypes, as he ostensibly warned us against them. Perhaps ours was an unusually poorly-prepared consultant, but there was something odd about compelling a group of professors who included some of the nation's leading authorities on race relations to listen to the rather uninformed views and banal opinions of a consultant whose credentials were markedly inferior to our own.

Some schools have moved beyond diversity training to require that all search plans be approved by diversity officials and that all search committees include human resources or diversity staffers as voting members. At one large community college in the South, for example, human resources and diversity staff screen all potential candidates for faculty positions before they can be interviewed by the search committee. At a Midwestern state college, human resources personnel organize all faculty search committees. At one Southern college, a human resources, equal opportunity staffer serves as a member of every search committee, and at a Midwestern state college, an "Inclusion Advocate" is assigned to every search committee by the human resources department. At the University of California, Berkeley, where the faculty resisted the idea of including human resources staffers on search committees, the Faculty Equity Office moved to train students, who often had a role in faculty hiring, to serve as the office's *de facto* agents on search committees.[17]

All this effort might have some value if it demonstrably resulted in enhanced faculty diversity. But, "inclusion advocates" and the like cannot make up for the absence of minority PhDs in some fields and offer little or no improvement over the faculty's own efforts in others.[18] Diversity campaigns do produce an increase in the number of diversity officials which, by administrative logic, might in and of itself be seen as evidence of a more diverse campus. Such campaigns, however, cannot produce minority physicists and mathematicians. Administrators and diversity consultants, groups with short time horizons, appear to have little interest in the longer term efforts that might actually produce minority physicists and mathematicians, dismissing the idea that such programs might be effective as "an insidious myth."[19]

But, while they do not produce much actual diversity, administrative diversity campaigns have given university officials a tool with which to attack the autonomy of the faculty recruitment and promotion process and, perhaps, the tenure system itself. My own school's Commission on Equity, Civility and Respect, created by the president to promote diversity, among its other goals recommended mandatory diversity education for search committees, recommended that faculty performance evaluations include an assessment of professors' "contribution to diversity," and, to promote diversity, encouraged university administrators to review "current policies on promotion and time related assessment of employment," i.e., the tenure system.[20] Clearly, under the rubric of diversity, administrators are seeking and finding ways to enhance their power vis-à-vis the faculty.

Ironically, but not surprisingly, one realm in which campus administrators are careful not to seek diversity is in the staffing of departments, programs and centers nominally created to study the history and culture of minority and under-represented communities. Thus, black studies programs seldom employ white faculty, women's studies programs almost never recruit male faculty and so forth. From an administrative perspective, diversity is a useful tool — not a moral or philosophical imperative. The use of that tool, moreover, requires the blessing and cooperation of campus minority communities. Accordingly, no administrator would ever question the right of a campus minority community to control a piece of academic turf from which they excluded others. Hence, their constant pursuit of academic diversity requires administrators to ignore the lack of diversity in some obvious places on their campuses.

One campus realm in which lack of diversity has become especially noteworthy in recent years is in departments or centers for Middle Eastern studies. Since the 1970s, the field of Middle Eastern studies has come to be dominated by "anti-Zionist" scholarship.[21] And, when they recruit new faculty members, academic programs and departments in this field — often funded by the Saudi Arabian government — generally give strong preference to scholars from Arab countries. Jews are not excluded completely from the field of Middle Eastern studies. Indeed, a recent president of the Middle East Studies Association (MESA) was a Jew. However, the handful of Jews employed by such departments are, almost without exception, staunchly anti-Zionist Jews, often appearing anxious to prove their ability to rise above the self-perceived limitations of their own cultural background. It almost goes without saying that university administrators ignore the absence of ethnic and ideological diversity in their schools' Middle East studies programs. Since such programs are usually allied with and supported by the left-liberal campus community, the question of diversity does not apply to them.

SPEECH AND CIVILITY CODES

Much the same story can be told about campus speech and civility codes. Since the 1980s, hundreds of colleges and universities have enacted codes proscribing forms of speech and conduct that might be seen as offensive or hostile by particular groups or designed to intimidate or harass individuals based upon their racial, religious, social, gender or other characteristics.

Administrators sometimes justify these codes by asserting that they are required by federal law or that failure to promulgate a speech or conduct code might leave a school open to suit, under federal employment or equal opportunity laws, by individuals alleging that the institution had failed in its duty to prevent the development of a hostile or harassing environment. In point of fact, however, far from requiring colleges to adopt codes, the U.S. Department of Education has actually warned schools against adopting anti-harassment codes that might infringe upon First Amendment rights.[22] And, as to the problem of litigation, one prominent attorney has pointed out that efforts by schools to enforce their codes have generated more litigation than the lack of such codes.[23]

Parallel to the case of diversity, college administrators view the regulation of speech less as a philosophical issue than a matter of political expedience. They will attempt to block speech they view as threatening to themselves or their allies while defending speakers whose views are supported by vocal campus constituencies. Thus, for example, the Duke University administration shut down a professor's website after the faculty member posted an article calling for a strong military response to the 9–11 terrorist attacks. The website had been condemned by campus activists and Islamic groups. On the other hand, when the Palestine Solidarity Movement announced that it would hold its annual conference at Duke, administrators responded to objections from Jewish and conservative organizations by strongly affirming their support for the "principle of free expression."[24] At the ensuing conference, speakers predictably denounced Zionism and the Jews and praised suicide bombers. One speaker declared that every Jewish wedding, Passover celebration and Bar Mitzvah represented a potential military target. Duke administrators congratulated themselves for having struck a blow for free speech. "It's a good thing we did here," said the university's vice president for public affairs.

As in the case of the quest for faculty diversity, speech and civility codes reflect the tacit alliance that has emerged between university administrators and activist and minority groups on the campus. The latter have sought speech, diversity and civility codes to block racist, sexist or homophobic expression and, mainly in the case of Muslim students, criticisms of Islam. African American student groups are especially eager to silence criticism of affirmative action programs and preferential racial admissions policies, viewing such criticisms as illegitimate attacks upon their very presence on the campus. Thus, for example, in 2007 African American students at Tufts filed charges against the editors of a student magazine, *The Primary Source*, for publishing a mock Christmas carol which parodied what the authors saw as the school's propensity to admit blacks with lower grades than were required of white applicants. After a hearing held against the backdrop of vehement campus protests, the editors were found guilty of harassment and of "creating a hostile learning environment."[25]

Campus administrators, for their part, are anxious to avoid trouble from vocal and sometimes militant forces. Increasingly, too, administrators have come to see speech and civility codes as management tools which might help them intimidate or silence their own critics. One cadre of campus functionaries likely to be particularly outspoken in its support for restrictions on speech consists of the bureaucrats who administer diversity, multicultural and similar campus offices. These officials tend to regard any criticism of their programs as attacks on the validity and legitimacy of their own positions in the university and will respond aggressively to even the mildest questions. I became aware of the vehemence with which the diversity bureaucracy would defend speech codes by an event on my own campus. In June 2008, I attended an open meeting to listen to the report of a presidentially-appointed commission on "equity and civility" which, among other things, supported strengthening our campus civility code. Along with several other faculty members, I spoke against the Commission's report. When we completed our comments, we were castigated, in the most uncivil terms, by administrators from the campus multicultural office who essentially accused the faculty-as-a-whole of fostering a racist and abusive climate on the campus — as now evidenced by faculty expressions of opposition to the proposed new civility code. Thus, hoping to intimidate critics and protect their own jobs, campus bureaucrats have reason to agree with campus activists that speech or civility codes can be useful devices. Of course, as Jon Gould has observed, some college administrators adopted speech codes without giving the matter much thought just because everyone else seemed to have them.[26]

The codes adopted by many schools during the 1980s and 1990s sought to prohibit forms of speech or expression deemed to be offensive by campus administrators and faculty or student activists. For example, the 1989 "policy against racism" adopted by the University of Massachusetts board of regents outlawed speech which was racist, "in any form, expressed or implied, intentional or inadvertent."[27] In a similar vein, the Syracuse University code forbade "offensive remarks," including "sexually suggestive staring, leering, sounds or gestures" and "sexual, sexist, or heterosexist remarks or jokes."[28] The University of Wisconsin outlawed "racist or discriminatory comments, epithets or other expressive behavior."[29] The University of Pennsylvania's speech code prohibited "any verbal or symbolic behavior that... insults or demeans the person or persons to whom the behavior is directed...on the basis of his or her race, color, ethnicity or national origin, such as (but not limited to) the use of slurs, epithets, hate words, demeaning jokes, or derogatory stereotypes."[30] This code figured in Penn's well-known 1993 "water buffalo" case in which the university charged a freshman, Eden Jacobowitz, with violating its speech code by allegedly shouting a racial slur at a group of fifteen black sorority members who had been loudly singing and stomping outside the window of his dorm room one night while he was trying to write a paper. Jacobowitz had yelled, "Shut up, you water buffalo!"

These early speech codes seldom passed judicial muster and in recent years, colleges and universities have generally turned from speech codes to harassment or civility codes covering students, faculty, and other members of the university community. These codes purport to be based upon federal employment and education law. Title VII of the U.S. code prohibits employment discrimination while Title IX outlaws discrimination by educational institutions receiving public funds. As interpreted by the Equal Employment Opportunity Commission, the Department of Education's Office for Civil Rights and the courts, these laws hold both employers and schools liable when their actions or failure to take action helped to bring about an environment that was hostile or harassing to women, members of minority groups or other persons.[31]

Contemporary civility and harassment codes claim to ban speech and behavior that might be deemed hostile or harassing, possibly in violation of federal law. Thus, for example, the University of Miami prohibits, "any words or acts...which cause or result in physical or emotional harm to others, or which intimidate, degrade, demean, threaten, haze or otherwise interfere with another person's rightful actions or comfort."[32] Similarly, the University of Pennsylvania's new code prohibits "any behavior, verbal or physical that stigmatizes or victimizes individuals on the basis of race, ethnic or national origin...and that has the purpose or effect of interfering with an individual's academic or work performance, and/or creates an intimidating or offensive academic, living or work environment."[33] The University of Iowa's harassment code declares that sexual harassment "occurs when somebody says or does something sexually related that you don't want them to say or do."[34] My own school's civility code declares that "rude, disrespectful behavior is unwelcome and will not be tolerated."[35]

Though nominally grounded in employment and education law, civility and harassment codes enacted by public universities have not fared well in the courts when schools have attempted to apply them in disciplinary settings rather than merely trumpet them as aspirations. In the educational context, true harassment was defined by the Supreme Court in the case of *Davis v. Monroe County Board of Education* as conduct "so severe, pervasive, and objectively offensive that it effectively bars the victim's access to an educational opportunity or benefit."[36] The expression of words, symbols or views that someone finds offensive is not harassment. Rather, it is constitutionally-protected speech. Accordingly, judges have tended to see civility and harassment codes as efforts to circumvent the First Amendment and have found them to be unconstitutional when their application has been challenged. For example, a federal judge in Pennsylvania recently ordered Shippensburg University to stop enforcing a provision of its code that declared, "the expression of one's beliefs should be communicated in a manner that does not provoke, harass, intimidate or harm another."[37]

Despite their poor record in the courts, many public universities continue to promulgate civility and harassment codes and endeavor to punish students who violate them. When students or faculty members are disciplined under even the most patently unconstitutional code they, of course, bear the burden of time, money, effort and anguish associated with vindicating their rights in court. For example, a group of San Francisco State students recently was threatened with disciplinary action under the school's harassment code when it held an anti-terrorism protest which included stepping on images of the flags used by *Hamas* and *Hezbollah,* two organizations officially classified as terrorist groups by the United States government. After a complaint from Muslim students, the anti-terrorism protestors were charged with "attempting to create a hostile environment" and "incivility" in violation of the Student Code of Conduct. Political protest and flag desecration — even of the American flag — are certainly First Amendment rights, but the students were subjected to five months of hearings until threatened action by a civil libertarian group led the school to drop its charges. Without external intervention, the students would very likely have been punished for their constitutionally-sanctioned protest.

An even more egregious violation of a student's rights by university bureaucrats enforcing the school's racial harassment code took place at Indiana University-Purdue University, Indianapolis (IUPUI) in 2008. Keith Sampson, a student working part-time as a school janitor to help finance his education, was observed reading a book entitled *Notre Dame vs the Klan: How the Fighting Irish Defeated the Ku Klux Klan,* a history of events in the 1920s when Notre Dame students confronted klansmen in South Bend,

Indiana. Sampson had obtained the book from IUPUI's library. After a co-worker complained that Sampson was reading a book on an "inflammatory topic," he was charged by the school's chief affirmative action officer with "openly reading the book related to a historically and racially abhorrent subject in the presence of your Black co-workers." Such conduct, according to this university functionary, constituted racial harassment.[38] After a number of civil libertarian groups, including Foundation for Individual Rights in Education (FIRE) and the Indiana chapter of the ACLU, intervened and the case began to receive negative publicity, the university dropped all charges, issuing a number of evasive explanations of the events in question.

Private colleges and universities are generally not bound by the First Amendment and have broad leeway to discipline students and faculty under their civility and harassment codes.[39] Thus, as mentioned above, in 2006 a Johns Hopkins student was disciplined for publishing invitations and displaying a plastic skeleton announcing his fraternity's "Halloween in the Hood" party. In 2007, a group of Tufts writers were disciplined for a satiric essay on minority admission. In 2008, a Brandeis professor was disciplined for using the term "wetback," apparently in the context of explaining the term's etymology to a class. Also in 2008, a Colorado College student was punished for posting a flyer parodying a flyer posted by the school's Feminist and Gender Studies program. If these events had taken place at public institutions, the students and faculty involved might have been able to vindicate their rights in court, but this option is probably not available to them in the private setting.

As I noted earlier, university administrators have a number of reasons to seek to regulate campus speech through civility and harassment codes. Such codes can placate campus activists and minority groups. Indeed, when they charge a student or faculty member with sexual or racial harassment, administrators are signaling to groups capable of making trouble that the school's administration is on their side. At the same time, administrators have their own agendas. The growing stratum of administrators of multicultural and diversity programs regard speech restrictions as useful and proper instruments through which to silence those who might question the legitimacy and validity of their own positions on the campus. For the more general cadre of campus functionaries, civility and harassment codes seem to be attractive means of intimidating critics of every stripe.

A recent case from Georgia is a bizarre but telling example of how these codes can be used. In 2007, T. Hayden Barnes, a student at Valdosta State University in Georgia, posted flyers and sent letters and e-mails to newspapers raising environmental and fiscal objections to his university's plan to build two large parking garages adjacent to the campus. The school's president Ronald Zaccari apparently regarded the proposed garages as an important part of his administrative legacy and took offense at the student's criticisms. In a letter slipped under Barnes's door during the night, Zaccari informed him that he had been "administratively withdrawn" from the school for his alleged violation of harassment regulations and because he presented a "clear and present danger" to the campus.[40] Only after the Foundation for Individual Rights in Education (FIRE) provided Barnes with a *pro bono* attorney who filed suit on his behalf in federal court was Barnes allowed to return to school.

When employed by public universities, virtually no civility or harassment code has been able to withstand judicial scrutiny. They all violate the First Amendment if actually employed for disciplinary purposes rather than merely to trumpet a school's values. But, despite defeats in the courts, more and more codes are written every year.[41] From the perspective of college administrators, the very fact that use of a code almost certainly will violate the constitutional rights of the student or faculty member against whom charges are brought is actually an advantage rather than a problem. Unconstitutionality is an advantage because it facilitates selective enforcement. If administrators find it politically useful to bring charges they do so, in effect telling the defendant, "so, sue me" if you don't like it. Where, on the other hand, administrators believe that bringing charges would not serve their political interests, they piously cite their own First Amendment concerns.

Recent events at the University of California, Irvine, exemplify this phenomenon. While campus administrators were quick to investigate charges of harassment and hate speech made by African Americans and women, similar allegations made by Jewish students against Muslim and Palestinian groups were ignored. When challenged, administrators were quick to cite First Amendment concerns as their reason for not taking action.[42] In a similar vein, claiming that some members of the university community might be offended, administrators at St. Louis University canceled a planned speech by conservative author David Horowitz, who had been invited by the College Republicans to speak on "Islamo-Fascism." The same school, however, did not object when a campus organization co-sponsored an appearance by professional "anti-Zionist" speaker Norman Finkelstein as part of "Palestine Awareness Week."[43] Apparently the First Amendment applied in one case but not the other.

LITTLE EICHMANNS?

It should by now be easy to understand why many university administrators often find it expedient to look the other way when allegations of antisemitism are made on their campuses. Muslim activists have been welcomed by the campus Left as fellow fighters against American imperialism. In turn, the campus Left is willing to declare that even the most blatantly antisemitic activity is actually anti-Zionist and justified by Israel's brutal treatment of the Palestinians. Called Zionists, Jews can be declared to be corrupt, manipulative, degenerate and, indeed, even to eat Arab babies! Efforts to criticize or condemn this sort of rhetoric will inevitably be denounced by campus left-liberals and activists as conspiracies against free speech. The Jews in this group, anxious to affirm their bona fides, will declare that anti-Zionism and antisemitism are not one and the same thing.[44] This argument is true in principle, but not often in practice.

To university administrators, the views of the left-liberal and even radical activist groups are important. By maintaining good relations with this community, administrators avoid disturbances and potentially enhance their own power on campus. Those who offend this community are courting trouble. Witness the case of Harvard's Larry Summers, whose problems began when, in 2002, he voiced his opposition to the anti-Israel divestment movement and declared that opposition to Israel was often antisemitic in effect if not in intent. It was after the divestment imbroglio that Summers found himself under attack from virtually all left-liberal quarters on the Harvard campus.

Given a choice between nurturing their own career interests and objecting to antisemitic, oops, anti-Zionist rhetoric, many administrators choose the former. For example, rather than risk offending the Middle East and Asian Languages and Cultures (MEALAC) department's defenders on the campus, Columbia administrators opted to conduct a rather cursory examination of the many complaints of antisemitic commentary on the part of MEALAC faculty. Though the ad hoc committee created by the administration to investigate student complaints of antisemitic intimidation was chaired by a well-respected Political Science professor, Ira Katznelson, several other members of the committee were apparently friends and close associates of the individuals accused of the conduct in question.[45] It was difficult for the complainants to believe that Columbia administrators were as serious about investigating charges of antisemitic conduct on their campus as they might have been if the accusations had involved racism, sexism or homophobia. Could anyone seriously assert that this belief was unfounded?

Benjamin Ginsberg is the David Bernstein Professor of Political Science and Director of the Center for Governmental Studies at the Johns Hopkins University. He is the author or co-author of a number of books, including *Moses of South Carolina: A Jewish Scalawag during Radical Reconstruction* (2010) and *Presidential Power: Unchecked and Unbalanced* (2007).

ENDNOTES

1   U.S. Commission on Civil Rights, *Campus Anti-Semitism*, July 2006, p. 14.

2   Kenneth L. Marcus, "Higher Education, Harassment, and First Amendment Opportunism," *William & Mary Bill of Rights Journal* (2008). Available at http://ssrn.com/abstract=1112189

3   Manfred Gerstenfeld, "2007–2008: Another Year of Global Anti-Semitism and Anti-Israelism," Jerusalem Center for Public Affairs, No. 73, 2 October 2008.

4   Jon Wiener, "Bogus Campus Anti-Semitism," *The Nation*, July 7, 2008.

5   Johns Hopkins University Office of News and Information, "News Release: University Statement on Investigation of Fraternity," Oct. 30, 2006.

6   Andy Guess, "Sending in the Class Monitor," *InsideHigherEd.com*, Nov. 9, 2007.

7   Jon B. Gould, *Speak No Evil: The Triumph of Hate Speech Regulation* (Chicago: University of Chicago Press, 2005), 90.

8   Robert McCaughey, *Stand, Columbia* (New York: Columbia University Press, 2003), chs. 15 and 19.

9   Stuart Taylor and K.C. Johnson, *Until Proven Innocent* (New York: St. Martin's, 2007).

10   Jerome Karabel, *The Chosen* (Boston: Houghton-Mifflin, 2005).

11   University of Rochester, "Diversity at the University," http://www.rochester.edu/diversity/faq.html.

12   Damon A. Williams and Katrina C. Wade-Golden, "What Is a Chief Diversity Officer?" *InsideHigherEd.com*, April 18, 2006.

13   Pauline Keyes, "New Paradigms for Diversifying Faculty and Staff in Higher Education: Uncovering Cultural Biases in the Search and Hiring Process," *Multicultural Education*, Winter 2006.

14   Alan Contreras, "Affirmative Inaction," *InsideHigherEd.com*, July 21, 2006.

15   Lisa M. Portugal, "Diversity Leadership in Higher Education," *AcademicLeadershipOnline*, February 12, 2007.

16   Anne Bromley, "Faculty Diversity Rising: Search Committees Required to Have EOP Training," *InsideUVAOnline*, August 26, 2005.

17   University of California, Berkeley, *"Efforts of the Faculty Equity Office: October 2001 to April 2002."*

18   Contreras.

19   Keyes.

20   Johns Hopkins University, "Feedback Needed on Equity, Civility and Respect Recommendations," May 5, 2008.

21 Martin Kramer, *Ivory Towers on Sand: The Failure of Middle Eastern Studies in America* (Washington Institute for Near East Policy, 2001).

22 Peter Brownfield, "Administration Deals Blow to Campus Censorship," *FoxNews.com*, September 2, 2003.

23 Harvey A. Silverglate, "Memorandum to Free Speech Advocates," University of Wisconsin, January 26, 1999.

24 Eric Adler and Jack Langer, "The Intifada Comes to Duke," *Wall Street Journal*, January 5, 2005. http://www.opinionjournal.com/extra/?id=110006102.

25 Harvey Silverglate and Jan Wolfe, "Well Shut My Mouth," *The Phoenix*, May 16, 2007.

26 Gould, 90–91.

27 Alan Kors and Harvey Silverglate, *The Shadow University* (New York: Harper, 1999), 150.

28 Kors and Silverglate, 152.

29 Kors and Silverglate, 167.

30 Kors and Silverglate, 11.

31 Donald A. Downs, *Restoring Free Speech and Liberty on Campus* (New York: Cambridge University Press, 2005), 59.

32 Kent M. Weeks and Joel D. Eckert, "Student Civility," *Lex Collegii*, Vol. 29, No. 4, Spring 2006, 2.

33 Kors and Silverglate, 10.

34 Foundation for Individual Rights in Education, "Spotlight on Speech Codes 2007," p. 11.

35 Johns Hopkins University, "Principles for Ensuring Equity, Civility and Respect for All," 2006.

36 526 U.S. 629 (1999).

37 Weeks and Eckert, 3.

38 Dorothy Rabinowitz, "American Politics Aren't Post-Racial," *Wall Street Journal*, July 7, 2008.

39 In California, state law requires private institutions to obey the First Amendment. The courts, however, have been equivocal in their application of the statute. David Bernstein, *You Can't Say That* (Washington, DC: The Cato Institute, 2003), 65–66.

40 Andy Guess, "Maybe He Shouldn't Have Spoken His Mind," *InsideHigherEd.com*, January 11, 2008.

41 Gould.

42 Kenneth L. Marcus, "Conflicts 101: Higher Education and the First Amendment," 16 *William & Mary Bill of Rights Journal* 1025 (April 2008).

43 Richard L. Cravatts, "All Campus Free Speech Is Acceptable–Except About Islam," *American Thinker*, October 9, 2009. http://www.americanthinker.com/2009/1.

44 For example, Judith Butler, "No, It's Not Anti-Semitic," *London Review of Books*, August 21, 2003. http://www.lrb.co.uk/v25/n16/butl02_.html.

45 Noah Liben, "The Columbia University Report on its Middle Eastern Department's Problems: A Methodological Paradigm for Obscuring Structural Flaws," *Jerusalem Center for Public Affairs*, April 2005. http://www.jcpa.org/JCPA/Templates/ShowPage. asp?DRIT=3&DBID=1&LNGID=1&T.

WELLESLEY COLLEGE
Antisemitism with White Gloves

Jerold S. Auerbach

Wellesley College opened in 1875 to educate young women "for the glory of God and the service of the Lord Jesus Christ." In the sylvan setting of Henry Fowle Durant's sprawling estate fifteen miles west of Boston, students learned that "Christian character" was *the most radiant crown of womanhood.*" There they engaged in "the war of Christ...against spiritual wickedness in high places." Wellesley women were encouraged to live their lives "in humble imitation of Him who *'came not to be ministered unto, but to minister'''* (*Matthew* 20:28).

Wellesley architecture reflected and reinforced Christian devotion, literally carving it in stone. The massively elegant College Hall, the first building, was designed to resemble a double Latin cross. The spacious five-story entry Centre reminded one observer of "mediaeval convents." Consistent with the founder's principles, for nearly a century every trustee, faculty member and officer was required by College statute (although one not always honored in practice) to belong to an evangelical church.

By the dawn of the twentieth century Durant's evangelical fervor had subsided. Enlightened Unitarianism took hold at Wellesley, the better to attract the daughters of proper Bostonians. But to this day, the biblical admonition from *Matthew* still serves as the inspirational College motto, enthusiastically proclaimed on ceremonial occasions such as Convocation and Commencement. Now, to be sure, it is better understood as a source of feminist independence and a call for public service.

Like its Big Brothers — Harvard, Yale and Princeton — and the other Seven Sister colleges, Wellesley designed its admission policy to cultivate and perpetuate a white Anglo-Saxon Protestant elite. This challenge became all the more imperative after World War I, when hordes of socially undesirable candidates with academically superior credentials—in a word, Jews—threatened to inundate the academic citadels of privilege. With Harvard in danger of becoming "Hebrewized," Yale fearful of being "overrun" by Jews, and Princeton anxious lest Jews "ruin [it] as they have Columbia and Pennsylvania," the solution was obvious. Just as Congress enacted immigration laws to curtail the entry of undesirables from Southern and Eastern Europe, so colleges imposed quotas to exclude Jews.

Wellesley, like other elite academic institutions, privileged its preferred applicants with an admission policy that was antisemitic at its core. To be sure, some Jewish girls were sufficiently respectable to gain admission, but in small numbers. They tended to come from wealthy and assimilated German-Jewish families with meager Jewish knowledge or identification. One alum from the Twenties recalled that she "went to church with her friends regularly"; another knew that she benefited from not "looking Jewish"; and still another, who dutifully attended the College chapel service every morning, seemed relieved that other students believed her to be Episcopalian. Questions about religious identification, designed to identify Jews, were part of the application process. So, too, were geographical distribution preferences, personal interviews, and photographs.

Occasionally, if ironically, Wellesley's prejudice deepened Jewish awareness. A member of the Class of 1928 was infuriated to discover that Jewish students had been grouped together at one end of a hallway in her dormitory. A student in the class behind resented that a dean had gathered Jewish students to inhabit "the meanest place...off the back stairs." When she complained, the dean justified the arrangement, saying: "I thought you'd all be so happy together." More than sixty years later, a Jewish alumna still remembered the oblivious freshman classmate who had complained to her: "Isn't it awful how Jews turn up everyplace and how they have horns."

Once admitted and housed in their dormitory ghettos, Jewish students confronted discrimination from the College societies that were designed, like country clubs, to enhance social life for the privileged few. "There were very few Jewish girls in the societies," a Jewish student recalled, adding: "I don't know why." Another student offered a reason: "Jews tend to look a certain way...all funny and unkempt...with big noses."

By the mid-Thirties, the College maintained precise statistics on Jewish admissions, limited to 9–11% of each entering class. As College president Mildred McAfee evasively conceded: "I presume there is a sense in which it is true that we have a quota." Then she acknowledged: "We try to keep the number [of Jewish students] within approximately 10 percent of the number of students admitted." With that number set low, the president explained, "it has not seemed to us impossible to assimilate them." In a letter to a Jewish alumna, the president politely informed her that her daughter would not be accepted because Wellesley had already taken "its Jews" for the entering class.

Wellesley's policy of discrimination was couched in President McAfee's rhetoric of respect and tolerance. Jews, she acknowledged, "are our best students." But Wellesley, after all, was "a Gentile community." Too many Jews would create problems. Just a few years earlier, a "considerably larger number" of Jewish students than usual had arrived on campus, "and an antagonism began to develop which made the Jewish students race conscious." This resulted in "bitterness." The president approved "a more searching scrutiny of the credentials of Jewish students than is true of other students" because, she claimed, limiting their presence on campus assured that Jews "can be assimilated as individuals and we can really demonstrate the possibility of Gentile and Jew living together without prejudice." Better to reject qualified students, President McAfee insisted, than "to create a condition on campus which would produce discrimination." At Wellesley, tolerance of Jews required discrimination against Jews.

During the 1930s, Nazi sympathies surfaced at Wellesley, as at other Seven Sister colleges. In May 1934, the German battle cruiser *Karlsruhe* sailed into Boston harbor flying the swastika. Local Jews protested and a Boston rabbi denounced the ship as a symbol of "hate and darkness," but Wellesley arranged a reception for the German naval cadets on board and welcomed them to the College for a dance. Wellesley *News*, the student newspaper, described them admiringly as young blond men, "immaculate in flawless black uniforms," who were "soft and sincere."

Three years later President McAfee personally invited Lilli Burger, known to be a "staunch supporter of Hitler," to join the faculty as a visiting professor. Midway through her Wellesley year (1937–38), in an interview with a student reporter, Professor Burger "fervently" praised Hitler's "great work." The American press, she added, was "exaggerat[ing] . . . the persecution of the Jews." Throughout the decade, Wellesley maintained active exchange programs with German universities, welcomed German students and, along with other American academic institutions, helped the Nazi regime to burnish Hitler's image. No refuge was provided for Jewish professors or students.

During the war years, Wellesley maintained its Jewish quota at 10 percent. This, the College continued to insist, was good for Jews because, as its president explained, "Any group characterized by identifiable physical features runs a risk of being set apart." Therefore, it was College policy "to keep the percentage of Jewish students small enough so that segregation and prejudice will be at a minimum within the College....It has seemed fairer to a tragically misused minority group to admit its members only in such numbers that they can be truly assimilated as individuals." The College would continue to "discriminate numerically," but only "in the interest of stimulating diversity" — by excluding Jews.

After World War II, when the Massachusetts legislature considered legislation prohibiting colleges from requesting information about the religion or race of applicants, President McAfee Horton testified in opposition to the proposed law. It would "do more harm than good," she asserted, "thwarting the efforts of institutions which are working to eliminate prejudice." If enacted, Wellesley would no longer be permitted to select "students whom we actively want because they represent minority groups with which we want our majority to become acquainted." Wellesley, she claimed, "needs and wants" Jewish students. But "in order to avoid segregation it is important to regulate the number of representatives of certain minority groups." Exclusion, in her persistently tortured logic, prevented discrimination.

After the Fair Educational Practices law was enacted, there was a spurt in Jewish student enrollment to 16–20% during the 1950s. But Wellesley remained, in the words of its new president Margaret Clapp, "a non-denominational Christian college to which people of all faiths were welcomed." Preferably, to be sure, not too many of them. One Jewish student from that decade recalled: "Jewish life on campus was basically non-existent." Jewish students still were "likely to be" assigned Jewish roommates. "We were," she wrote, "used to accommodating ourselves to a Christian world." The College still had barely a handful of Jews on its faculty, who preferred to remain silent on Jewish issues.

During the early Sixties, Jewish students comprised 14% of the Wellesley population, but there was a steady decline thereafter to their pre-World War quota level of 10–12%. The nationwide trend toward coeducation surely contributed to this reduction. Then, too, Jewish high-school girls may have learned where they were not wanted. Wellesley still embraced its Christian symbolism as a neutral reflection of the natural order. It held its annual Convocation ceremony and celebrated Flower Sunday (to strengthen Christian sisterhood) in the College chapel, and retained the Christian cross as the symbol of its spiritual life.

Wellesley was especially inhospitable to Orthodox Jewish students. Molly Myerowitz, admitted in 1960, encountered what she subsequently described as "the peculiarly polite yet inhumane brand of Wellesley anti-Semitism." Because her religious obligations prohibited her from working on the Jewish Sabbath and holy days, she was compelled to postpone examinations scheduled for those days. The College solution was to incarcerate her in the infirmary for the duration, without access to books or friends lest she benefit from an "advantage" denied to other students. There Miss Myerowitz was served non-kosher food that she could not eat and a nurse was assigned to accompany her to the bathroom. Unable to endure life at Wellesley beyond her sophomore year, she transferred to Radcliffe. Only years later did she finally realize that "the failure was Wellesley's and not my own."

In 1967, Professor Walter Houghton, a venerable member of the English Department, and Daniel Horowitz, a young instructor in the History Department, circulated a petition among their colleagues asking Wellesley trustees to drop the provision in College by-laws restricting the faculty to those who professed Christianity. Half the faculty signed; but the Trustees, while reaffirming their commitment to religious freedom, declined to change the by-laws.

When Wellesley began to consider coeducation, President Ruth Adams anticipated a novel Jewish problem. She worried that with young men on campus, the likelihood of Jewish weddings in the College chapel would increase. A Religion professor suggested that the presence of so many Jews might require "a Yiddish speaking corridor" in a dormitory. And, should Wellesley decide to admit young men, the College would need a Jewish chaplain who would guide the determination of "those parietal hours and sexual relations which were appropriate to the torah observances of different Jewish groups." The Jewish chaplain, he continued, should also possess "those skills necessary for the rite of circumcision." There was also the "canopy problem," the President responded, which required "experience in merchandising so that we can get full value." An even more worrisome prospect was "the ritual smashing of glassware." She wondered: "Will the floor of the chapel have to be resurfaced in order to provide the resistant surface on which such breakage can be achieved."

For nearly a century, the Department of Religion, known until 1968 as the Department of Biblical History, had been the unofficial academic custodian of Christian culture at the College. Until then, Bible study was required of every student — but Jewish scholars were deemed inherently unqualified to teach the New Testament. (No such prohibition was imposed on Christian scholars teaching the Hebrew Bible.) President Adams was informed that professors in the Religion Department were so irrationally resistant to the appointment of a Jewish scholar that it had become known as "a collection of resident preachers and campus witch doctors."

Three years later a tenured dissenter in the department rebuked the president for "the flap created because you had decided that you did not want a Jew teaching the required New Testament" course. Adams was unmoved. The alumnae, she insisted, would not tolerate a Jew teaching that subject. Not long afterward, Dean Krister Stendahl of the Harvard Divinity School resigned from the Wellesley College Board of Preachers in protest. Hostility to Jews in the Religion Department, recalled a retired member, "was so intense for so many years. It was hard to understand the depth of it." Antisemitism at Wellesley, like the chapel floor, had proven to be resilient.

In 1981 the Religion Department, true to its tradition, voted to deny tenure to Jon Levenson, an exceedingly promising—and religiously observant—scholar of the Hebrew Bible whose excellent teaching and scholarship even his prejudiced senior colleagues acknowledged. But in a fifty-four-page letter, containing elaborate hypothetical models of departmental structure designed to exclude Levenson, they insisted that his "style of interpersonal relationships" disqualified him. (To be sure, he had the temerity several years earlier to inquire of the President: "What, exactly, accounts for the abnormally low percentage of Jewish students at Wellesley?") Furthermore, they claimed, there was little interest in Jewish subjects at Wellesley.

That fall, Levenson retained as his attorney the son of a retired member of the Religion Department. With ample evidence of Jewish quotas, presidential statements that Jews were incompetent to teach the New Testament, and persistent departmental antisemitism, the lawyer carefully documented the "normal pattern of discrimination" against Jews at Wellesley. Levenson, he asserted, had been rejected only because he was a Jew. With negative publicity and litigation looming, the College Committee on Faculty Appointments, which included new president Nan Keohane, overturned the departmental decision. Levenson became the first tenured Jew in the Religion Department in the 106-year history of the College. The following year, he departed for the University of Chicago Divinity School, and then to the Harvard Divinity School where he has since become a renowned Bible scholar.

No sooner had the Levenson tenure issue faded than a litany of student complaints surfaced to provide dismaying evidence of persistent insensitivity—if not actual discrimination—toward Jews at the College. From admission to graduation, antisemitism infested virtually every corner of Wellesley life. Admissions officers systematically avoided recruitment at predominantly Jewish high schools. Professors routinely denied student requests to postpone exams and assignments scheduled on Yom Kippur, and openly expressed their displeasure when Jewish students missed class for holy day observance. College events were scheduled with blithe disregard for the Jewish calendar. In dormitory dining halls, Jewish students often confronted forbidden pork products as the only available main course — for both lunch and dinner. When one mother requested that the dietician offer simple alternatives — cottage cheese, cereal — she was told: "My dear woman, if we start providing for the dietary needs of our Jewish students, before long we shall have to provide for Indian girls who don't eat meat." President Keohane conceded "a disturbing pattern" of "insensitivity" at Wellesley toward Jews.

It was, however, more than insensitivity; it was antisemitic discrimination, a pattern sufficiently entrenched and egregious to finally attract attention from local media. Like a prim Victorian maiden, Wellesley had carefully preserved its privacy and decorum, rarely permitting antisemitism to surface as an issue inside the College, much less in public. But in September 1983 the Boston *Jewish Advocate* published a lead story documenting the long history of antisemitism at Wellesley College. Once its dirty linen began to be washed in public — with a sustained flurry of letters in response to the article — the facade of institutional denial finally began to crack.

In Academic Council — the faculty governing body — a resolution was introduced condemning and repudiating "the history and legacy" of antisemitism at Wellesley. But what seemed so self-evident and necessary to a handful of Jewish faculty members quickly became bogged down in a swamp of evasion and avoidance. Would the pattern of discrimination be perceived as institutional, or would it be reduced to the isolated acts of individuals who just happened to be College presidents, trustees, deans, and members of the faculty? Would discrimination targeting Jews be specifically identified and condemned — or would antisemitism vanish amid vapid declarations of universal tolerance? Would the burden of history be recognized, or swept under a carpet of platitudinous promises about the future?

After hours of excruciating debate stretching across three acrimonious faculty meetings, the faculty (amid thunderous administrative silence) finally decided to decide. It acknowledged and condemned the persistence of antisemitism at Wellesley, committed the College to obliterate discrimination against Jews in recruitment, admission, employment, and promotion, and declared that insensitivity toward the obligations of religiously observant Jews was impermissible. To placate universalistic colleagues, who could not tolerate condemnation of antisemitism alone, the faculty also dedicated

Wellesley College to the eradication of all forms of racial and religious discrimination.

The resolution was not a solution. But it carried significance, at least symbolically, in a college whose only official policy toward Jews had declared them to be an unwelcome presence. In response, however, the Board of Trustees dug in its heels. Jewish alumnae on the Board demonstrated that their deepest loyalty was to the college that had deemed them worthy of admission. Declining to endorse the faculty resolution, it refused to mention Jews by name. With cavalier disregard of the history of restrictive admission quotas and bias in faculty hiring, the Trustees denied that there was a history of antisemitism at Wellesley College. Instead, they fabricated and celebrated a mythical "history of dedication to diversity" — in a college where for many decades only white Christian women had been welcome. They affirmed "the moral imperative of the Founder," which, of course, was the bedrock of Christian exclusivity at Wellesley. In the end, the Trustees managed to deny what by then everyone else at the College, and many outside it, knew to be true.

President Keohane — caught between faculty and trustees — blithely asserted the compatibility of their diametrically opposed resolutions. Only a sustained torrent of public criticism, from inside and outside the College, finally nudged the Trustees to the minimum concession that antisemitism had indeed been an enduring problem at Wellesley and that it was deplorable.

So much, it seemed, for Wellesley's Jewish problem — finally confronted and presumably resolved. But during Academic Council debates it had become evident that the struggle to frame an acceptable condemnation of antisemitism had also exposed acrimonious intramural Jewish conflict among the faculty. A bemused, or indifferent, majority watched the spectacle of Jews against Jews, with every dismal stereotype from centuries of Jewish diaspora history placed on display.

There were Court Jews who reflexively aligned themselves with their Wellesley benefactors, even when it discriminated against their own people. Jewish universalists, who were passionately committed to every worthy liberal cause, could not bear to identify and condemn discrimination only against Jews. Assimilated Jews retreated behind the veil of civility and decorum that defined good manners among the Christian elite whose behavior they emulated. Self-hating Jews, inclined to identify as Jews only to legitimate their criticism of Israel, endlessly reiterated the complexity of the issue, the better to deny the reality of antisemitism. Finally, there were the Jews of silence, who could not rouse themselves to utter a word in public against antisemitism.

College administrators tried, if haltingly, to finally confront Wellesley's Jewish problem. Plans to initiate a Jewish Studies program and expand relations with nearby Brandeis University were publicized, but little came of them for nearly a decade. Indeed, the proximity of Brandeis proved a deterrent to Wellesley initiatives, as did the resistance of the Religion Department to the prospect of competition. The College paid closer attention to conflicts between the Jewish and academic calendars. It assured the availability of vegetarian, if not kosher, food in dining halls. Admissions office representatives, clearly under instruction from higher authorities, began to visit and recruit students from suburban high schools with substantial Jewish populations.

But Wellesley's Jewish problems lingered. In the English Department a young woman hired in the Eighties to teach Yiddish and Jewish literature encountered hostility to her research topics and teaching plans. Colleagues informed her, "loud and clear, that work in Yiddish wasn't valuable." Her American literature syllabus was criticized for including three Jewish authors: Saul Bellow, Cynthia Ozick, and Bernard Malamud. She was advised to eliminate the Jews, refocus on early modernism, and add Nathaniel Hawthorne and Henry James. She soon resigned her position.

By the Nineties Wellesley, like so many academic institutions, had made a strong commitment to affirmative action and multicultural diversity. The special admissions consideration that once was confined to Christian applicants now was reserved for African-American, Latina, Asian and Native-American students — and, of course, the daughters of alumnae. Young Muslim women were attracted to the gendered insularity of a women's college. A small Jewish Studies department was established. But Jewish students, with every reason to anticipate the benefits of heightened tolerance, found themselves marginalized as members of the white majority and available as scapegoats for the grievances of other minorities.

The College had signaled its new commitment to diversity twenty years earlier, when it hired Tony Martin for the budding African-American Studies department. Although still at the beginning of his career as chronicler of Marcus Garvey, the prominent Black Nationalist who had led a "Back to Africa" movement in the 1920s, Martin was quickly awarded tenure. Armed with a doctorate and a law degree, he came to rely upon litigation to rectify his grievances against those who disagreed with his sense of his own worth, challenged his imperious behavior or, eventually, disputed the integrity of his scholarship. Denied a merit salary increase, he sued the College for racial discrimination and received a settlement payment to avoid negative publicity. Criticized in print by a student journalist from MIT who exposed his angry intimidation of a Wellesley student in her dormitory, Martin sued for libel. He lost, but the distraught Wellesley student withdrew from the College.

Then, in the spring of 1993, Martin assigned to students in his African-American history class an anonymously written volume published by the Nation of Islam entitled *The Secret Relationship Between Blacks and Jews*. A farrago of false claims, it asserted that Jews, united "in an unholy coalition of kidnappers and slave makers," had played a "disproportionate" role, amounting to "monumental culpability," in slavery and the slave trade — "the black holocaust." Martin's department chairman accurately described the book as "patently and scurrilously anti-Semitic." Martin responded by calling his colleague a "handkerchief head."

To Martin, the explanation for the instant outcry against his assignment of the book was simple: "The long arm of Jewish intolerance reached into my classroom." Hallucinating a conspiracy by Jewish organizations to silence him, Martin denounced "the ongoing Jewish onslaught against Black progress." He was, he loudly proclaimed, the victim of "a classic textbook case study of organized Jewish intimidation."

In a college ruled by polite decorum, the vehement tirade of an angry black man was frightening and intimidating. Adding fuel to the fire, Martin self-published an irate tract later that year entitled *The Jewish Onslaught: Despatches [sic] from the Wellesley Battlefront*. The self-described victim of a "Jewish onslaught," he denounced allegations of his antisemitism as "a clever smokescreen for a burgeoning Jewish intolerance of truly Stalinist proportions." Hallucinating a Jewish cabal aligned against him, he noted that the Dean of the College, chair of the Board of Trustees, head of student government, "a goodly portion" of the tenured faculty, and "sundry other persons in high positions, were all Jews." Martin raged against "all the dirty Jewish tricks" used against him.

With publication of *The Jewish Onslaught*, Wellesley president Diana Walsh finally was moved to respond — as tepidly as circumstances permitted. It being Wellesley, she quickly segued from Martin's ludicrous allegation of a "Jewish onslaught" — from, that is, his antisemitic venom — to an impassioned plea for polite manners. In a letter to 40,000 alumnae, community members and parents, Walsh denounced Martin's "incendiary words, and his attempt to portray Wellesley College as a repressive institution bent on silencing him." His book, she continued, "crossed the line [between] simply unpopular or controversial argument to unnecessarily disrespectful and deeply divisive speech." But it would violate his freedom of speech, she claimed, to silence him. His tenured status would not be adversely affected. Nor would the College even censure him.

President Walsh, evidently fearful of confronting Martin, had abjectly capitulated. She ignored his rabidly antisemitic rants; she said nothing about his teaching of scurrilous lies about the role of Jews in the slave trade; and she rationalized her surrender by posing as a defender of freedom of speech, which nowhere included the freedom to teach falsehood as truth. That Martin was teaching antisemitic fabrication as historical fact did not seem to concern Walsh, who chastised him most energetically for his violations of decorum.

Away from Wellesley's manicured lawns and refined etiquette, critics of Martin and the College were less restrained. The American Historical Association declared that it "deplores any misuse of history that distorts the historical record to demonize or demean a particular racial, ethnic, or cultural group." To civil libertarian Nat Hentoff, academic freedom was irrelevant; Martin was "teaching anti-Semitism as a fact" from material that was "plain wrong." University of Chicago professor Edward Shils pointedly stated that Martin "should be removed not because of his anti-Semitic speech but because his scholarship is garbage." Even the Boston *Globe*, normally quite friendly to the College, noted that not only had President Walsh omitted any reference to antisemitism; the word "Jewish" appeared nowhere in her letter except in the title of Martin's book. Martin was evidently pleased with the Wellesley president's response. Appearing at public debates with four Nation of Islam bodyguards, he noted that the attendant publicity had spiked his speaking fees.

Martin's shoddy scholarship was not confined to Jewish subjects. Respected Wellesley classics scholar Mary Lefkowitz noticed that Martin taught a Wellesley course containing erroneous assertions, popular among Black nationalist scholars, about the presumed Afrocentric origins of ancient civilization. When she complained, the (Jewish) Dean of the College politely told her: "He has his view of ancient history, and you have yours," a display of intellectual relativism that stunned the classical scholar.

Predictably, Martin counter-attacked. Branding Lefkowitz as "a national leader of the Jewish onslaught against Afrocentrism in general and me in particular," whose "verbose rantings" and intellectual dishonesty had undermined his reputation, he sued her for malicious libel. Wellesley College was too fastidious — or fearful — to get involved. Once again, the College declined to defend academic integrity; it was, the same dean told her, "your problem." So courts, not the College, had the final word on *Martin v. Lefkowitz*. After nearly five years of costly legal proceedings, Martin's claim was dismissed. Martin had confronted Wellesley College with a test of its principles. And, a young alumna perceptively observed several years later, "it failed."

After the September 11th terrorist attacks the battleground for Jews at Wellesley shifted. President Walsh forcefully reminded the Wellesley community to show respect for Muslim students, lest they be held guilty by association with Muslim terrorists. But she said nothing to reassure Jewish students, who encountered malicious allegations, on and off campus, of Israeli responsibility for the terrorist outrages, accompanied by mendacious claims that several thousand Jews, forewarned of the attacks, had not reported for work at the World Trade Center that day. Wellesley Jewish students were hurt, apprehensive, and infuriated by administrative indifference to their legitimate concerns about intensifying antisemitism.

Not long afterward, a swastika was painted at a bus stop near the College. The Office of Religious and Spiritual Life, the center of College multicultural sensitivities, sponsored a three-faiths panel discussion about Jerusalem — which it scheduled on Yom Kippur. Blatantly antisemitic email postings by Muslim students on College conferences infuriated their Jewish classmates: an anti-Israel poem repeated centuries-old antisemitic canards about Jews as "Judas," while a photograph of three Israeli soldiers bore the caption, "Three Jewish Animals."

In characteristic Wellesley fashion, College administrators responded by bracketing egregious examples of antisemitism with "other" forms of prejudice, of which there were no recently recorded complaints. The implicit message was clear: antisemitism alone was not sufficiently offensive to warrant condemnation. This double standard made a mockery of Wellesley's oft-repeated claim of multicultural sensitivity. Nothing was heard from President Walsh about the insulting Muslim student posts. When asked explicitly whether she would speak publicly to Jewish concerns, as she had done for Muslim students, she declined to answer. The most she would say was to caution against "hateful or harmful speech" at a time of antisemitism "and other ancient hatreds." No other "ancient hatreds" were identified.

For Jewish students, Wellesley often provided their first bitter encounter with antisemitism. After Angela Davis roused a campus audience with an impassioned endorsement of the vicious hostility directed at Israel and Jews at the Durban Conference against Racism (2001), a Jewish student acknowledged, "I do not feel accepted here. I feel ignored." Rachel Isaacs, a rising leader in the Jewish student community, wrote pointedly in the College newspaper: "I did not come to Wellesley expecting to learn what it felt like to be hated or demonized because I was Jewish," while College administrators "stand idly by."

One year after September 11, Amiri Baraka — formerly militant Black activist Leroi Jones — was invited by the Africana and Arts departments, and by African-American student groups, to speak at the College. Baraka had achieved national notoriety for his poem "Somebody Blew Up America," suggesting that Israel had advance knowledge of the terrorist attacks. He wrote: "Who told 4,000 Israeli workers at the Twin Towers/To stay home that day." (The correct answer, of course, was no one.) Jewish students were outraged that College funds were spent to import antisemitism to the campus — on the Jewish Sabbath, no less. Picketing his speech, they were less concerned with displaying good manners than confronting antisemitism in their midst.

Along the way, some Jewish students realized that Wellesley Hillel, impaired by years of limited funding, unassertive rabbinical leadership, and the loyalty of its Advisory Board to the College, was part of their problem. Early in the new century a student rebellion erupted within Hillel, leading to the resignation of the incumbent rabbi. She was replaced by an amiable social director who famously complained, several years later, that "male voices" too loudly supported beleaguered Jewish students. Leaderless, powerless and uninspiring, Hillel was more likely to antagonize than attract strongly identified Jewish students. For the most important holy days — Rosh Hashanah, Yom Kippur, and Passover — Hillel often confined its energies to directing and transporting students to religious services at Brandeis, Boston University and Tufts, where they might experience genuine Jewish observance. When the organization finally roused itself to deplore an episode of antisemitism, its preferred source of authority was Ralph Waldo Emerson.

Racial, religious and ethnic animosity continued to fester. The College assertively proclaimed its commitment to multicultural sensitivity, but Jews, perceived as privileged white Americans, were excluded from its concerns. Jewish students, encountering antisemitism and the indifference of College authorities to it, often felt battered. In 2007, at the invitation of a pro-Israel Jewish student group, Nonie Darwish, the controversial founder of Arabs for Israel, spoke on campus. After Muslims in the audience raucously interrupted her defense of Israel, Darwish was forced to leave the auditorium under police protection. Yet even strongly identified Jewish students, who were deeply attached to Israel, felt the need to apologize abjectly and publicly for extending an invitation that had offended their Muslim classmates.

Jewish students dutifully internalized Wellesley's Jewish problem as their own. "We wanted to be accepted by our peers," explained a Jewish student leader. "We didn't want to rock the boat or have our classmates dislike us." The result was "a culture of fear in which the Jewish students were afraid to stand up for themselves for fear of being blacklisted or disliked by their friends and classmates." In the face of persistent hostility, another student confided: "I'm scared and confused and wonder if maybe...I'm doing something wrong by being Jewish."

Wellesley, like other academic institutions, had embraced a redefinition of "minority" that excluded Jews. The more that College administrators swept blatant antisemitism under the bland rug of "discrimination and prejudice," the more suffering they inflicted on Jewish students. "One of several reasons I don't always feel comfortable on campus is because of Wellesley's tepid response to anti-Semitism," wrote another student. "It is hard to be Jewish on campus," she continued, "because there is a general sense that Jews are not really a minority; it is assumed Jews have assimilated into White America."

Confused and even frightened by the inability of administrators and students alike to accept them as Jews, Jewish students assuaged their discomfort by internalizing their hurt. One student was astonished to discover "how lonely Jewish students were feeling." Another confided: "After banging my head against the wall, tiptoeing around, walking on eggshells avoiding stating any of my beliefs so as not to make anyone uncomfortable, to find out the fact that I am religious offends someone else was too much. It's why I hate Wellesley so much but can never leave it." Torn between their Jewish identity and their desire to belong at Wellesley, it was difficult for Jewish students to realize that when Wellesley made them feel uncomfortable, frightened or confused about being Jewish, that meant something was wrong with Wellesley, not with them.

Jewish students have paid a high price in self-esteem for Wellesley educational and career benefits. They are subtly, but powerfully, reminded that they must sacrifice or silence their Jewish identity to win the promised rewards. Deans who patrol the boundaries of multiculturalism and diversity at the College rarely include Jews in their encouragement of tolerance. Racism and Islamophobia are promptly and properly denounced for what they are; but antisemitism, blandly labeled "prejudice" or "intolerance," is routinely stripped of Jewish content.

In the Fall of 2007, a new president was installed at Wellesley College. Listening, a few months later, to a summary of the history and durability of Wellesley's Jewish problem, Kim Bottomly was astonished. She knew that Yale, which she had left to come to Wellesley, once had the same problem. But Yale, she noted, had long since confronted and eradicated it. Evidently puzzled, President Bottomly asked: "Why hasn't Wellesley?"

Jerold S. Auerbach is a professor of history at Wellesley College, where he has taught since 1971. His most recent book is *Hebron Jews: Memory and Conflict in the Land of Israel* (Lanham, MD, 2009).

BIBLIOGRAPHICAL NOTE

The most comprehensive study of antisemitism in American academic institutions, focused largely on Harvard, Yale and Princeton, is Jerome Karabel, *The Chosen* (New York, 2005). For Wellesley's evangelical origins and commitment, see Helen Lefkowitz Horowitz's perceptive *Alma Mater* (New York, 1985). Michael Rosenthal, *Nicholas Miraculous* (New York, 2006), analyzes Columbia under the imperious, and often antisemitic, reign of Nicholas Murray Butler. See also, Louise Blecher Rose, "The Secret Life of Sarah Lawrence," *Commentary* (May 1983). For academic support for Nazi Germany, at Wellesley and elsewhere, see Stephen H. Norwood, *The Third Reich in the Ivory Tower* (Cambridge, 2009). The breakthrough article publicizing the history and legacy of Wellesley antisemitism was Lawrence Harmon, "Wellesley College Struggles With Pluralism," *The Jewish Advocate* (September 29, 1983). Many responses appeared in the issues of October 6, 13, and 20. A lengthy editorial, "College on the Spot: Pluralism Questioned," appeared in *The Wellesley News* (October 21, 1983). Wellesley College Archives contains Jewish quota statistics, presidential correspondence and interviews with Jewish alumnae. For a revealing retrospective, see Molly Myerowitz Levine '64, "Annals of an Orthodox Jew at Wellesley in the '60s," *Wellesley Alumnae Magazine* (Fall, 1985). My own correspondence files with Jewish students, alumnae, faculty, College officials and administrators cover the years between 1983 and the present. My thanks to Talia Schatz '08, Anna K. Johns '09, and Professor Helen Horowitz for their perceptive comments and suggestions on an earlier draft of this essay; Professor Jon D. Levenson of the Harvard Divinity School for granting access to material in his possession; and Ian Graham, Wellesley College Archivist, for his prompt and helpful responses to my queries.

ANTISEMITISM-DENIAL
The Berkeley School

Edward Alexander

<hr>

> *"I have to be here. Berkeley is the center of the world-historical spirit."*
>
> — Michael Lerner[1]

"NO, IT'S NOT ANTISEMITIC": JUDITH BUTLER VS. LAWRENCE SUMMERS

Few contemporary literary critics have placed so much emphasis on the power of language as Judith Butler, professor of rhetoric and literature at the University of California at Berkeley. She has insisted that "Language plays an important role in shaping and attuning our common or 'natural' understanding of social and political realities."[2] Invoking Marxist thinkers, she has asserted that critics of "postmodern" style understand "only the word coined by commerce," the "commodified" truisms of the capitalist system. It is against this background of her intensely political approach to language as well as her general attitude that linguistic gestures are an adequate substitute for, if not actually a form of, political action, that we should examine her truculent forays into the campus onslaught against Israel.

Prior to the autumn of 2003 she was, like many members of Berkeley's "progressive" Jewish community, somebody who defined her "Jewishness" (not exactly Judaism) in opposition to the State of Israel, a signer of petitions harshly critical of the Jewish state. She was, for example, one of the 3,700 American Jews opposed to "occupation" (Israeli, not Syrian or Chinese or any other) who signed an "Open Letter" urging the American government to cut financial aid to Israel; later she expressed misgiving about signing that particular petition — it "was not nearly strong enough...it did not call for the end of Zionism."[3] In autumn of 2002 she requested honorary inclusion in the Campus Watch organization's listing of Middle East specialists polemicizing in their classrooms on behalf of Radical Islam and against Israel and America.

In June 2003, her name could be found on the ubiquitous "Stop the Wall Immediately" petition. The wall, signatories alleged, was "supposed to block 'terrorist attacks' but certainly won't prevent missiles and helicopters from hitting their human target." Suicide bombings, lynchings, pogroms, and roadside shootings were not terrorist attacks but only "terrorist attacks," whereas Israeli response to those so-called "terrorist attacks" injured real human targets.

But deeper currents were also stirring in Butler. She had undertaken some research into the history of Zionism and discovered that there had been "debates among Jews throughout the 19th and early 20th centuries as to whether Zionism ought to become the basis of a state."[4] From this she swiftly concluded that demanding an end to Zionism in 2003, that is, calling for politicide, was no different from taking a debater's position against Zionism fifty years before the state existed. By August 2003, Butler was belatedly moved to a classic utterance by a speech given at Harvard a year earlier, a speech that touched in her a raw nerve of anger that not even Ariel Sharon's attempts to keep suicide bombers from blowing up Israelis had been able to inflame. Lawrence H. Summers, Harvard's president, delivered to the Harvard community on September 20, 2002, a speech deploring the upsurge of antisemitism in many parts of the globe: he included synagogue bombings, physical assaults on Jews, desecration of Jewish holy places, and (this with special emphasis) denial of the right of "the Jewish state to exist." But his most immediate concern was that "at Harvard and... universities across the country" faculty-initiated petitions were calling "for the University to single out Israel among all nations as the lone country where it is inappropriate for any part of the university's endowment to be invested."[5]

One of the Harvard faculty, Professor Ruth Wisse, described the divestment petition as "corrupt and cowardly" in offering its reasons for calling on the U.S. government to stop military aid and arms sales to Israel and upon universities to divest both from Israel and from American companies selling arms to Israel. "The petition," wrote Wisse, "requires that Israel comply with certain resolutions of the UN — the terms of which it distorts to say what those resolutions do not mean"; she also pointed out that the petition says nothing of the fact that all the Arab states remain in perpetual violation of the entire UN Charter, which is based on the principle of mutual respect for the sovereignty of member states, which are to settle disputes by peaceful means.[6]

Butler had herself signed the same divestment petition at its place of origin, Berkeley, where it had circulated in February 2001. She therefore found Summers' remarks not only wrong but personally "hurtful" since they implicated Butler herself in the resurgent campus antisemitism. She could hardly have failed to notice that the Berkeley divestment petition had supplied the impetus for anti-Israel mob violence on her own campus on April 24, 2001, a few weeks after it had been circulated, and for more explicitly anti-Jewish mobs at San Francisco State University in May of the following year. (By June 2009 uniformed Berkeley thugs, in a ghoulish reenactment of Nazi "Kauf nicht bei Juden" riots against Jewish stores, were vandalizing Israeli products at Trader Joe's grocery.) Slander of Israel has provoked physical violence on many campuses, especially those (like Wayne State in Detroit or Concordia in Montreal) with a large Arab presence. Summers, aware of how ubiquitous in anti-Israel discourse is the straw man called "the defender of Israel who decries any criticism of Israeli policy as antisemitism," went out of his way in his address to separate himself from this (conjectural) figure: "I have always throughout my life been put off by those who ... conjured up images of Hitler's Kristallnacht at any disagreement with Israel." Nobody has ever discovered just who these conjurors might be, but if Summers thought he would separate himself from them by this disclaimer he was mistaken.

Despite the large role played in promoting the divestment campaign by people like Noam Chomsky, Summers chivalrously went out of his way to say that "Serious and thoughtful people are advocating and taking actions that are anti-Semitic in their effect if not their intent." To annihilate this distinction between intentional and effective antisemitism is the primary aim of Butler's counterattack. Her strategy is what logicians call the *tu quoque* (i.e., you too, or you're another) argument: Summers' accusations, says Butler, are "a blow against academic freedom, in effect, if not intent." His words have had "a chilling effect on political discourse." No evidence is (or could be) adduced for this allegation. Of one thing we can be sure: the chill did not take hold at Harvard itself, which would soon (in November) play host to Oxford University's Tom Paulin, who had urged (in yet another "criticism of Israeli policy") that Jews living in Judea/Samaria "should be shot dead," or at Columbia, where Paulin continued merrily through the autumn semester as a visiting professor, or at the *New York Review of Books*, which in October 2003 would publish Tony Judt's "Israel: The Alternative," a call for an end to the state; neither did Summers dampen the fires of Israel-hatred at the *London Review of Books* itself, which in January 2003 published 133 lines of Paulin doggerel called "On Being Dealt the Anti-Semitic Card," a versified rehearsal of Butler's "No, It's Not Anti-Semitic." If Summers' speech had a chilling effect on antisemitic clarion calls, including incitement to raw murder, one would not want to know what the fully heated versions would sound like.

Butler perfunctorily assented to Summers' recommendation that — as she artfully restated it — "every progressive person ought to challenge anti-semitism vigorously wherever it occurs," but she seemed incapable either of recognizing it in such (to her) mild "public criticisms" as economic warfare against the Jewish state or calls for its dismantling or assaults on Zionism itself or opposing any effort Israel might make to defend her population against suicide bombers. Indeed, she made it clear that she saw no difference between Jews intentionally murdered by suicide bombers (and their sponsors and despatchers) and Arabs accidentally killed by Israeli efforts to repel would-be murderers. She presented herself as offering Jews a salutary warning against crying wolf: "if the charge of anti-semitism is used to defend Israel at all costs, then its power when used against those who do discriminate against Jews — who do violence to synagogues in Europe [synagogues and Passover seders in Israel are not mentioned], wave Nazi flags or support anti-semitic organizations — is radically diluted." In trying to confute Summers' distinction between intentional and effective antisemitism, Butler calls it wildly improbable that somebody examining the divestment petitions signed by herself and her co-conspirators might take them (as hundreds on her own campus already had done), as condoning antisemitism. She therefore poses this conundrum: "We are asked to conjure a listener who attributes an intention to the speaker: so-and-so has made a public statement against the Israeli occupation, and this must mean that so-and-so hates Jews or is willing to fuel those who do." But Summers was perfectly correct in stating that one need not "hate Jews" in order to perform actions or utter words that are "antisemitic in their effect if not their intent." When Dickens wrote *Oliver Twist* he harbored no hatred of Jews and had no programmatic or conscious intention to harm them. Indeed, he said of his character Fagin that "he's such an out and outer I don't know what to make of him." Dickens did not indeed "make" Fagin, and therefore didn't know what to make *of* him. Fagin was ready-made for Dickens by the collective folklore of Christendom, which, for centuries had fixed the Jew in the role of Christ-killer, surrogate of Satan, inheritor of Judas, thief, fence, corrupter of the young; to which list of attributes Butler and her friends would now add "Zionist imperialist and occupier." Has *Oliver Twist* been antisemitic in its effect? Of course — or does Butler think that it is for their interest in Bill Sikes and Nancy and the plight of the homeless in early Victorian England that Arab publishers have long kept cheap paperback translations of the book in print?

Butler also uses the *tu quoque* "argument" in rebutting the charge of selectivity that Summers had made. Why, among all the nations on earth, has Israel alone been singled out for punishment and pariah status by the advocates of divestment and academic boycott? Where is their advocacy of divestment from China until China withdraws from Tibet, or from Morocco until that country ceases to occupy Western Sahara, or from Zimbabwe until it ceases persecuting its white citizens, or from Egypt until it stops allowing construction of tunnels for the smuggling of arms to Palestinian killers? Could the singling out of Israel possibly have anything to do with the fact that it is a Jewish country? Despite the inordinate length of her essay, Butler cannot find space to answer this question. Instead, she accuses Summers himself of biased selectivity. "If we say that the case of Israel is different, that any criticism of it is considered as an attack on Israelis, or Jews in general, then we have singled out this political allegiance from all other allegiances that are open to public debate. We have engaged in the most outrageous form of 'effective' censorship...."

Her ultimate use of the *tu quoque* strategy is to make Summers himself guilty of what he attacks. Why? Because he assumes that Jews can only be victims, conflates "Jews" with Israel, and writes as if all Jews were a single, undifferentiated group. Apparently the 1,135 Israelis murdered and the nearly 10,000 wounded (in a Jewish population of under six million) by Arab terrorists between September 27, 2000 and the time Butler published her essay were not sufficient to meet her stringent requirements for (Jewish) victim status. But if Israelis were not the victims of Palestinian aggression in the latest round of the Arab nations' interminable war to eradicate the Jewish state, why is it that Jewish schools in Tel-Aviv and Jerusalem must be protected by armed guards while Arab schools in Nazareth or Ramallah require no such safeguards? Why is it that getting on a bus in Jerusalem or going to a cafe in Haifa is a form of Russian roulette, a far more dangerous activity than prancing about as a "human shield" for Yasser Arafat?

As for the argument that nothing is antisemitic which does not explicitly target every single Jew in the world, it is jejune. After all, insists Butler, not all Jews are committed to Israel: "Some Jews have a heartfelt investment in corned beef sandwiches." But does she really think that when Josef Pfefferkorn, whose distinction between "good" and "bad" Jews became the paradigm for Jewish self-haters, urged his countrymen (in the 1520s) to "drive the old Jews out [of Germany]" he had himself in mind? When Karl Marx excoriated Jews as "the filthiest of all races," did he really mean to include himself? Do the operators of Nazi websites have trouble making "exceptions" for the writings of Chomsky or Finkelstein? Indeed, Butler's requirement of total inclusiveness would have allowed Hitler himself to say (had he so wished) of his racial policy: "No, it's not antisemitic."

Although Butler's essay is a loose, baggy monster, what it leaves out is even more blatant than what it includes. It omits history altogether, torturing a text and omitting context. Did it never occur to Butler that the divestment effort is the latest installment of the (illegal) Arab economic boycott of Israel, one prong in the Arab campaign to destroy the Jewish state? Equally egregious is the omission of context that is *de rigueur* among all those who have made Palestinophilia the touchstone of campus progressivism. The "occupation" which they constantly bemoan did not precede and cause Arab hatred and violence; it was Arab hatred and violence that led — in 1967 as later — to occupation. But the crucial omission from this essay by somebody who has relentlessly insisted on the political implications of language is the political implications of the language of the advocates of divestment. Josef Joffe has succinctly defined the linguistic difference between "criticism of Israeli policy" and antisemitism:

> "Take this statement: 'Demolishing the houses of the families of terrorists is morally wrong because it imputes guilt by association, and politically wrong because it pushes more people into the arms of Hamas.' Such a statement is neither anti-Israel nor anti-Semitic; it might even be correct. By contrast, 'the Israelis are latter-day Nazis who want to drive the Palestinians from their land in order to realize an imperialist biblical dream' inhabits a very different order of discourse, ascribing evil to an entire collective and, in its equation of Israelis and Nazis, revealing an obsessive need for moral denigration."[7]

The Harvard/MIT divestment petition that Butler championed was promoted at MIT by Chomsky, for whom the Israeli-Nazi equation is axiomatic; it was promoted at Harvard by Professor Paul Hanson, who called Israel the "pariah" state. Butler was herself one of the "first signatories" of a July 28, 2003, petition that uses the Israeli-Nazi equation beloved of nearly all denigrators of the Zionist enterprise in asserting that "concrete, barbed wire and electronic fortifications whose precedents . . . belong to the totalitarian tradition" were transforming the Israel "'defense forces'" (again the rhetorical quotation marks) and indeed "Israeli citizens themselves into a people of camp wardens."[8] And so it would seem that, for Butler, "Language plays an important role in shaping and attuning our...understanding of social and political realities" except when it happens to be the antisemitic language that (relentlessly) implies that Israel is a country ruled by a Nazi party which organizes Kristallnacht pogroms, burns books by Arabs, expels them from universities, and destroys them in death factories.

MAKING THE CASE FOR JEW-HATRED: MARTIN JAY EXPLAINS

> "There is a great temptation to explain away the intrinsically incredible by means of liberal rationalizations. In each one of us, there lurks such a liberal, wheedling us with the voice of common sense."
>
> — Hannah Arendt [9]

The academic boycotters of Israeli universities and the professorial advocates of suicide bombing of Israeli citizens are in the front lines of the defense of terror, which is the very essence of Palestinian nationalism.[10] But they themselves are supported by a rearguard of fellow-travelers, a far more numerous academic group whose defining characteristic is not fanaticism but time-serving timorousness. In the thirties, "fellow-travelers" usually referred to the intellectual friends of communism,[11] although Hitler competed with Stalin in attracting people from America and Britain who never actually joined the Nazi or Communist parties but served their purposes in the conviction that they were engaged (at a safe distance) in a noble cause. At the moment the favorite cause of peregrinating political tourists is the Palestinian movement;[12] and the reason why fellow-travelers favor this most barbaric of all movements of "national liberation" is that its adversaries are Jews, always a tempting target because of their ridiculously small numbers and their enormous image.

As a representative example of the academic fellow-traveler in the ongoing campaign to depict Israel as the center of the world's evil and make it ideologically vulnerable to terror, take the case of Martin Jay, a professor of history at University of California, Berkeley, and author of books about the Frankfurt school in Germany and "ocularcentric discourse" in France. In the Winter-Spring 2003 issue of *Salmagundi*, Jay argues, in an essay entitled "Ariel Sharon and the Rise of the New Anti-Semitism,"[13] that Jews themselves, primarily Sharon and the "fanatic settlers" (22) but also American Jews who question the infallibility of the *New York Times* and National Public Radio or protest the antics of tenured guerrillas on the campuses, are "causing" the "new" antisemitism. Jay, unlike such people as Edward Said (of whom he writes with oily sycophancy), does not deny the existence of a resurgent antisemitism, although his examples of it are vandalized synagogues and cemeteries, "tipping over a tombstone in a graveyard in Marseilles or burning torahs in a temple on Long Island [as] payback for *atrocities* [my emphasis] committed by Israeli settlers" (14); such unpleasant words as stabbings, shootings, murder — all of which have been unleashed against Jews in Europe as well as Israel — are not part of Jay's vocabulary. But his main contention is that the Jews are themselves the cause of the aggression against them. "The actions of contemporary Jews are somehow connected with the upsurge of anti-Semitism around the globe" (21), and it would be foolish to suppose that "the victims are in no way involved in unleashing the animosities they suffer" (17).

Although Jay's main concern is the (supposedly) "new" antisemitism, his heavy reliance on the thesis and even the title of Albert Lindemann's unsavory and deviously polemical book *Esau's Tears: Modern Anti-Semitism and the Rise of the Jews* (1997) suggests that he believes political antisemitism, from its inception in the nineteenth century, has been in large part the responsibility of the Jews themselves. Lindemann's book argued not merely that Jews had "social interactions" (a favorite euphemism of Jay's) with their persecutors but that they were responsible for the hatreds that eventually consumed them in Europe; antisemitism was, wherever and whenever it flared up, a response to Jewish misbehavior. According to Lindemann, the Romanians had been subjected to "mean-spirited denigration" of their country by Jews, and so it was reasonable for Romania's elite to conclude that "making life difficult" for the country's Jewish inhabitants, "legally or otherwise," was a "justifiable policy." His abstruse research into Russian history also revealed to him that whatever antisemitism existed there was "hardly a hatred without palpable or understandable cause." The 1903 Kishinev pogrom, Lindemann grudgingly admitted, did occur but was a relatively minor affair in numbers killed and wounded, which the Jews, with typical "hyperbole and mendacity," exaggerated in order to attract sympathy and money; it was a major affair only because it revealed "a rising Jewish combativeness." (As for the *Protocols of the Elders of Zion*, Lindemann apparently never heard of it, for it goes unmentioned in his nearly fifty pages on Russia.) In Germany, Jews (especially historian Heinrich Graetz) were guilty of a "steady stream of insults and withering criticism... directed at Germans"; by contrast, Hitler (who published *Mein Kampf* in 1925-27) was a "moderate" on the Jewish question prior to the mid-1930s; besides, "nearly everywhere Hitler looked at the end of the war, there were Jews who corresponded to anti-Semitic imagery." In addition to being degenerate, ugly, dirty, tribalist, racist, crooked, and sexually immoral, the Jews, as depicted by Lindemann, infuriated their neighbors by speaking Yiddish: "a nasal, whining, and crippled ghetto tongue."[14]

Although Jay is by no means in full agreement with Lindemann's thesis (as he is with that of an even cruder polemic by Paul Breines called *Tough Jews*[15]), he is intensely grateful to this courageous pioneer for breaking a "taboo" (18) on the "difficult question about the Jewish role in causing anti-Semitism," for putting it "on the table" (21). (Readers familiar with this dismal topic will be disappointed to learn that neither Lindemann nor his admirer Jay is able to explain the "Jewish role" in causing the belief, widespread among Christian theologians from St. Augustine through the seventeenth century, that Jewish males menstruate.) This is a remarkable statement to come from a historian. Washington Irving's Rip van Winkle lost touch with history for twenty years while he slept; Jay's dogmatic slumber seems to have lasted thirty-six years, since 1967, when the brief post-World War II relaxation of antisemitism came to an end.

A brief history lesson is in order here. At the end of the Second World War, old-fashioned antisemites grudgingly recognized that the Holocaust had given antisemitism a bad name, that perhaps the time was right for a temporary respite in the ideological war against the Jews. But in 1967 the Jews in Israel had the misfortune to win the war that was unleashed against them by Gamal Abdel Nasser, who had proclaimed — in a locution very much akin to Jay's style of reasoning — that "Israel's existence is itself an aggression." After their defeat, the Arabs de-emphasized their ambition to "turn the Mediterranean red with Jewish blood" and instead blamed the Middle East "conflict" on the Jews themselves for denying the Palestinians a state (something that, of course, the Arabs could have given them any time during the nineteen years that they were entirely in control of the disputed territories of "the West Bank"). Since that time, what Jay calls the "difficult question about the Jewish role in causing anti-Semitism" has not only been "on the table"; it has provided a royal feast for such heavy feeders as Alexander Cockburn, Desmond Tutu, Michael Lerner, the aforementioned Said, Patrick Buchanan, Noam Chomsky, much of the Israeli left, and scores (if not hundreds) of other scribblers.

The particular form given by nearly all these forerunners of Lindemann is, of course, blatant reversal of cause and effect in taking for granted that it is Israeli occupation that leads to Arab hatred and aggression, when every normally attentive sixth-grader knows that it is Arab hatred and aggression that lead to Israeli occupation. Jay is (characteristically) very fierce not with Lindemann for regurgitating every antisemitic slander dredged up from the bad dreams of Christendom but with Lindemann's "overheated" (18) critics (in *Commentary,* in the *American Historical Review*, in *Midstream*). In the same manner, his outrage about suicide bombings is not against the bombers or their instructors and financiers but against "American Jewish panic" (23) and "Israeli toughness" (23) in reacting to them and so perpetuating (no cliché is too stale for Jay) "the spiral of violence" (23).

Just as Jay insinuates some mild criticism of Lindemann, he also "qualifies" every now and then his insistence that the Jews themselves are to blame for antisemitism, but always in a way that only serves to make his core argument all the more flagrant. "Acknowledging this fact [that the Jewish victims are "involved in unleashing" hatred of themselves] is not 'blaming the victim,' an overly simple formula that prevents asking hard and sometimes awkward questions, but rather understanding that social interactions are never as neat as moral oppositions of good and evil" (17). Like most liberals, Jay cannot credit the full evil of the world. "In the case of the Arab war against the Jewish state," Ruth Wisse has observed, "obscuring Arab intentions requires identifying Jews as the cause of the conflict. The notion of Jewish responsibility for Arab rejectionism is almost irresistibly attractive to liberals, because the truth otherwise seems so bleak."[16] Although Jay tries to twist Hannah Arendt's well-known criticism of Sartre's foolish argument that the Jews survived in exile thanks to gentile persecution into an endorsement of his own foolish argument about Jewish responsibility for that persecution, he is himself a classic case of what Arendt called the wheedling voice of "common sense" that lurks inside every liberal, explaining away the "intrinsically incredible,"[17] such as the fact that a people would choose to define itself by its dedication to the destruction of another people.

For the benefit of Jay (and others) in bondage to the liberal dogma that "social interactions are never as neat as moral oppositions of good and evil," and at the risk of violating decorum, I should like here to quote from the description by a physicist (Dr. Pekka Sinervo of the University of Toronto) of what happens when a conventional bomb is exploded in a contained space, such as a city bus traveling through downtown Jerusalem: "A person sitting nearby would feel, momentarily, a shock wave slamming into his or her body, with an 'overpressure' of 300,000 pounds. Such a blast would crush the chest, rupture liver, spleen, heart and lungs, melt eyes, pull organs away from surrounding tissue, separate hands from arms and feet from legs. Bodies would fly through the air or be impaled on the jagged edges of crumpled metal and broken glass."[18] These are among the little "animosities," the "social interactions" that Martin Jay says Israelis, including (one assumes) the schoolchildren who usually fill these buses, have brought upon themselves.

Jay does take note of the suicide bombers, brainwashed teenage Arab versions of the Hitler Youth, by administering a little slap on the wrist to tearful Esau: "To be fair, the Palestinian leadership that encourages or winks at suicide bombers shows no less counter-productive stupidity [than Sharon taking action against suicide bombers]" (23). (The flabby syntax matches the fatuous moral equation.) Thus does Jay's labored distinction between "causation" and "legitimation" (17) or between blaming the Jewish victims and making them responsible for antisemitic aggression, turn out to be a distinction without a difference. "Tout comprendre," as the French say, "c'est tout pardonner."

But pointing out Jay's shoddy history, Orwellian logic, and addiction to worn-out clichés about settlements and "occupied territories" does not quite bring us to the quick of this ulcer. Matthew Arnold used to say that there is such a thing as conscience in intellectual affairs. An examination of the tainted character of Jay's documentation, his "evidence," reveals an intellectual conscience almost totally atrophied; for there is hardly a single reference in the essay to events in Intifada II (the Oslo War) that is not unreliable, deceptive, false. The essay starts with a reference to the "occupation of Jenin" (12), which always lurks in the background of Jay's ominous albeit vague allusions to Sharon's "heavy-handed" policies and actions (23) and "bulldozer mentality" (22). The April 2002 reoccupation of Jenin infuriated both the academic Israel-haters alluded to above (their boycott of Israeli universities and research institutes went into high gear at this point) and their fellow-travelers. As always with Jay, cause and effect are reversed, as if the actions of firefighters were to be blamed for the depredations of arsonists. The Israeli "incursion" into Jenin, for example, is treated by people like Jay as if it had nothing whatever to do with the series of suicide bombings, culminating with the Passover massacre that immediately preceded the military action. Jenin was reoccupied in April 2002 after the suicide bombing at the Park Hotel in Netanya on Passover evening, March 27. Jenin was the base of the terrorist infrastructure: most of the bombers were "educated" in Jenin, worked in Jenin, trained in Jenin, or passed through Jenin to be "blessed" before going out to kill Jews. Of some one hundred terrorists who carried out suicide bombings between October 2000 and April 2002, twenty-three were sent directly from Jenin. Prior to the Passover slaughter the supposedly tough Sharon had done little more in response to the almost daily murder of Israeli citizens than make blustery speeches and then turn the other cheek, or bulldoze or bomb empty buildings belonging to the Palestinian Authority. He had seemed far more inclined to the Christian precept "Resist Not Evil" than were the Christian ministers of Europe who were excoriating him for that "bulldozer mentality." (It does not require a powerful imagination to guess how France or Germany or America would deal with a "Jenin" that dispatched murderers to butcher French or German or American citizens on a daily basis. Of one thing we can be sure: there would have been no bulldozers for Professor Jay to complain of and also no twenty-three dead Israeli soldiers in Jenin, because the terrorist headquarters would have been obliterated by aerial bombing—and there really might have been not fifty dead Palestinians [most of them fighters] in Jenin but the "genocide of thousands," the "Jeningrad" concocted and trumpeted by Jay's favorite news media.)

Thirty Jews were killed and 140 injured at the Netanya seder table, a desecration of a holy place as flagrant as any in recent memory. But Jay's compassion is reserved for the victims of real "atrocities," such as "the cruel and vindictive destruction of the venerable olive groves under the pretext that they were hiding places for snipers" (24). Pretext? On October 30, 2002, Israel Radio reported that the terrorist who murdered two girls, ages one and fourteen, and a woman in Hermesh, exploited the olive trees that reach up to the community located between Mevo Dotan and Baka al-Gharbiya some six kilometers west of the Green Line (the 1949 armistice line between Israel and Jordan) in northern Samaria. The trees had indeed provided cover that made it possible for the killer first to reconnoiter the area in advance as an olive harvester—and then to slip under the fence to do his murderous work. Jay's congenital inability to report accurately is also apparent in his allusion to Adam Shapiro, offered as an instance of the atrocities visited by American Jews on people whose only sin is "criticism of Israeli policies" (22). He identifies Shapiro as "the idealistic…American Jewish peace activist" (22). Whatever Shapiro was, he was not a peace activist; he was a Yasser Arafat activist. A leader of the International Solidarity Movement founded by his wife, Huwaida Arraf, his "idealism" consisted of offering himself as a human shield (also breakfast companion) for Arafat in Ramallah, in the hope of making it easier for the archterrorist to murder Jewish children with impunity. His "criticism of Israeli policies" consisted of celebrating "suicide operations" as "noble" and urging that violence is a necessity of "Palestinian resistance."

One might expect that Jay would do better in reporting on Jewish misdeeds that "cause" the release of untidy emotions in antisemites when these misdeeds occur right under his nose. But in fact the most egregious example of deceptive reporting in his essay is his account of an event on his own (Berkeley) campus. It reads as follows: "When literally thousands of emails and withdrawals of substantial alumni donations to the University of California at Berkeley followed the disclosure that a course description for an English class...endorsed the Palestinian position, it becomes abundantly clear how concerted the effort has become to punish dissenters from Sharon's heavy-handed policies" (22-23). And here is the description (not provided by Jay, needless to add) of that course, taught by one Snehal Shingavi:

The Politics and Poetics of Palestinian Resistance:

> Since the inception of the intifada in September 2000, Palestinians have been fighting for their right to exist. The brutal Israeli military occupation of Palestine, an occupation that has been ongoing since 1948, has systematically displaced, killed, and maimed millions of Palestinian people. And yet, from under the brutal weight of the occupation, Palestinians have produced their own culture and poetry of resistance. This class will examine the history of the Palestinian resistance...in order to produce an understanding of the Intifada and to develop a coherent political analysis of the situation. This class takes as its starting point the right of Palestinians to fight for their own self-determination. Conservative thinkers are encouraged to seek other sections.

For Jay, this polemical balderdash, reeking of Stalinist pedagogy, a violation of the very idea of a university, and a blatant call for violence against Israelis and destruction of their state, supported by a booklist that covers the whole gamut of political opinion about Palestinian "resistance" from the omnipresent Edward Said (three separate titles) to Norman Finkelstein is nothing more than "dissent" from the policies of Sharon (who is not even mentioned in the description). The real culprit in Jay's eyes is not the puffed-up insurrectionary who conceived this obscene travesty of "an English class," but the people who have the temerity to criticize it. And somehow he knows that, in a state where millions of people consider themselves to be "conservative thinkers," all the objectors were Jews.[19]

Coming to the defense of Jews and Israel has never attracted timorous people; and to do so in a place like Berkeley, where mob rule prevented Benjamin Netanyahu (in September 2000) from giving a lecture in the city, and where cadres of Arab and leftist students can shut down campus buildings and disrupt final exams whenever the anti-Israel fit is upon them, may even require a special degree of courage. Jews who assign responsibility for anti-

Jewish aggression to Jewish misbehavior not only save themselves from the unpleasant and often dangerous task of coming to the defense of the Jews under attack but also retain the delightful charms of good conscience. Hitler's professors (to borrow the title of Max Weinreich's famous book of 1946)[20] were the first to make antisemitism both academically respectable and complicit in murder. They have now been succeeded by Arafat's professors: not only the boycotters, not only the advocates of suicide bombings, but also the fellow-travelers like Martin Jay.

Edward Alexander is professor emeritus of English, University of Washington. His books include *The Jewish Divide Over Israel* (2006) and *Lionel Trilling and Irving Howe* (2009).

ENDNOTES

A version of this article appeared in Edward Alexander and Paul Bogdanor, eds., *The Jewish Divide Over Israel: Accusers and Defenders* (New Brunswick, NJ: Transaction Publishers, 2006).

1   Quoted in David Horowitz, *Radical Son* (New York: Simon & Schuster, 1997), 176.

2   "A 'Bad' Writer Bites Back," *New York Times*, March 20, 1999.

3   "No, It Isn't Anti-Semitic," *London Review of Books*, August 21, 2003.

4   Ibid.

5   The full text of Summers' speech may be found in *Congress Monthly*, September/October 2003.

6   Ruth Wisse, "How Harvard and MIT Professors Are Planting a Seed of Malevolence," *New York Sun*, May 20, 2002.

7   Josef Joffe, "The Demons of Europe," *Commentary*, January 2004, 30.

8   "Israel and Palestine: Stop the Wall Immediately" petition.

9   Hannah Arendt, *The Origins of Totalitarianism*, 3 vols. (New York: Harcourt, Brace & World, 1951), III, 138.

10 See Edward Alexander, "The Academic Boycott of Israel: Back to 1933?" *Jerusalem Post*, January 3, 2003; "Evil Educators Defend the Indefensible," *Jerusalem Post*, January 10, 2003; and "Suicide Bombing 101," *American Spectator*, June/July 2001, 28–30.

11 See David Caute, *The Fellow-Travellers: Intellectual Friends of Communism* (New Haven: Yale University Press, 1988).

12 Martin Peretz, "Traveling With Bad Companions," *Los Angeles Times*, June 23, 2003.

13 Subsequent page references to Martin Jay's essay will be in parentheses in the text.

14 Albert Lindemann, *Esau's Tears: Modern Anti-Semitism and the Rise of the Jews* (Cambridge: Cambridge University Press, 1997), 308, 311, 291, 140–41, 496, 554.

15   Paul Breines, *Tough Jews: Political Fantasies and the Moral Dilemma of American Jewry* (New York: Basic Books, 1990).

16   Ruth R. Wisse, *If I Am Not for Myself... The Liberal Betrayal of the Jews* (New York: Free Press, 1992), 138.

17   Arendt, *Origins of Totalitarianism*, III, 138.

18   Quoted in Rosie DiManno, "Unlike Victims, Bomber Died without Pain," *Toronto Star*, June 19, 2002.

19   In a well-hidden place, n. 33, Jay acknowledges that "some of the outcry" about the course had to do with its last sentence telling Conservative thinkers to get lost; but he is confident that "the main reason for the response was the content of the course" (p. 28). Another Berkeley faculty member, who teaches in the English department, provided me with the following description of the incident, which may be instructive: I don't think that any chairman would dare disallow such a class on political grounds for fear of PC [Political Correctness] extortion. Of course, the crucial point — that such a class has nothing to do with English — doesn't even enter the picture since so many English composition classes have been politicized... that it's hard to imagine an English chair eager to defend the teaching of grammar and logic. Hence, the brazenness of the instructor who wrote that course description: without the statement that conservatives were not welcome (which is discriminatory), the pedagogy and politics of the course would have been unassailable in the current climate.

20   Max Weinreich, *Hitler's Professors: The Part of Scholarship in Germany's Crime Against the Jewish People* (New York: YIVO, 1946).

A DEADLY MUTATION
Antisemitism and Anti-Zionism in Great Britain

Robert S. Wistrich

Since the beginning of the twenty-first century, antisemitism has emerged as a serious problem in Britain, turning in just a few years from a public nuisance into something of a crisis. According to the annual report of the Community Security Trust (CST), which tracks antisemitic incidents in Britain, 2009 was the worst year of antisemitic violence, vandalism, and harassment since the group began keeping statistics in 1984. Between January and June 2009, 303 antisemitic incidents were recorded in London and 143 in Manchester, the two largest Jewish communities in the British Isles. In January 2009 alone, there were 286 incidents reported— an all-time peak in antisemitism for Great Britain. During the first six months of 2009, no less than 609 instances of antisemitism were recorded by the CST. This was all the more shocking since the previous *annual* high had been 598 antisemitic incidents in 2006.[1]

Yet Britain is unusual not simply in the frequency and severity of antisemitic incidents. Many European countries have come to associate antisemitism with the forces of the extreme Right, the radical Left, or the increasingly vocal Muslim minorities. In Britain, however, antisemitic sentiment is also a part of mainstream discourse, continually resurfacing among the academic, political, and media elites.[2] Matters have reached a point where anti-Zionism or hostility to Israel (and as a consequence, to Jews) enjoys greater tolerance in public life in England than in most countries of Western Europe. While the French state, for example, has marshaled its resources for fighting antisemitic words and actions, with greater or lesser success, in Britain the response before 2006 had been far less decisive, its public denunciations frequently unsupported by institutional or government sanction.[3] This only began to change after the publication of the British All-Party Parliamentary Inquiry into Antisemitism in 2006.

There are many possible explanations for the unusual quarter that antisemitism in Britain enjoys.[4] Whereas the efforts to combat antisemitism in France and Germany are intimately connected with the memory of the Holocaust that took place on their soil, Britain has never had to undergo a similar kind of soul-searching. At the same time, London has become a world center for Muslim antisemitism and the demonization of Jews and Israel that accompanies it. As the columnist Melanie Phillips wrote in September 2003:

> It is not an exaggeration to say that in Britain at present it is open season on both Israel and the Jews.... I no longer feel comfortable in my own country because of the poison that has welled up toward... the Jews.[5]

In a country such as Britain, with its proud history of tolerance, moderation, and multi-culturalism, this is indeed a damning indictment. Unless something significant changes, the United Kingdom risks becoming a country where radical anti-Zionism and antisemitism enjoy free rein, and where Jews feel increasingly insecure.

To understand the unique nature of British antisemitism, and the surprising degree of legitimacy it currently enjoys in the public discourse, it is important to recognize its deep roots in modern British history. While it is true that, unlike Germany, France, Russia, or Poland, Britain was not a major stronghold of antisemitism in the modern era, its liberal democratic tradition has nonetheless been far more ambivalent toward Jews than is often assumed.[6] As a result of immigration from Eastern Europe, the population of Anglo-Jewry rose from 65,000 in 1880 to 300,000 by 1914, of whom two-thirds settled in London.[7] These immigrants were at times the target of malevolent antisemitic incitement; they were seen — especially by conservatives — as breeders of anarchism, socialism, and other subversive doctrines. The 1905 Aliens Act, intended to restrict further waves of Jewish immigration, reflected this biased climate of opinion, which also found strong echoes in the British labor movement. Only a few years earlier, during the South African War (1899–1902), a left-wing, populist antisemitism had emerged in Britain, attacking wealthy Jewish capitalists and financiers for having "engineered" an imperialist war to seize the gold-rich Boer lands in order to advance the sinister interests of world Jewry. Through their presumed control of the press and high finance, this "golden international" was said to be "poisoning the wells of public information."[8]

In the first half of the twentieth century, however, Jews in Britain were associated as much with communism as with capitalism. The Russian Revolution of 1917 exacerbated fears of a world revolutionary upheaval instigated by Russian Jews purportedly engaged in a conspiracy against England.[9] This was the murky background to the popularity that the *Protocols of the Elders of Zion* initially attained in post-1918 Britain.[10]

In the aftermath of World War I, and with the establishment by the League of Nations of a British Mandate for Palestine, anti-Jewish feelings found yet another trigger. The *Morning Post*, for example, exhibited extreme hostility to the Jews and Zionism. Jews were portrayed in the early 1920s as expropriating the Palestine Arabs' land under the protective cover of British bayonets and at the expense of British taxpayers. Anti-Zionism and antisemitism became an integral part of the rhetoric used by right-wing newspapers against the Lloyd George government and British rule in Palestine.[11]

With the emergence of Oswald Mosley and his British Union of Fascists in the 1930s, a new antisemitic motif rose to the surface — one that carries a decidedly contemporary resonance. Jews were accused of trying to drag Britain into an unnecessary war with Nazi Germany.[12] Mosley's arguments combined fascist rhetoric, calls for the preservation of the Empire and for "peace with honor," and a populist appeal to lower-class antisemitic sentiment, especially pervasive in London's East End. The residues of his campaigns carried through into World War II, requiring the British government continually to demonstrate that it was not fighting a "Jew's war." During the war itself, an obsessive fear of "fifth columns" and "enemy aliens" existed alongside a perceived linkage of Jews with black-marketeering, spying, and subversion.[13] This undercurrent of antisemitism probably contributed to Britain's refusal to undertake any serious rescue effort to save the remnants of European Jewry during the Holocaust. Britain's policy of blocking Jewish immigration to Palestine beginning in 1938, and especially from the end of the war until 1948, though mainly driven by *realpolitik* and imperial strategy, cannot plausibly be detached from anti-Jewish sentiment. This would reach a climax with the advent of a Labour government in Britain in 1945.

Even after the Holocaust, antisemitic attitudes, if anything, grew worse, resonating at the highest levels of the British government. The first U.S. ambassador to Israel, James G. McDonald, writing in his diary on August 3, 1948, recorded the "blazing hatred" of Labour's Foreign Secretary Ernest Bevin for "the Jews, the Israelis, the Israeli government" as well as for American president Harry S Truman.[14] Richard Crossman, a young Labour MP who knew Bevin intimately, concluded in 1947 that British policy in Palestine was excessively influenced by "one man's determination to teach the Jews a lesson."[15] The refusal of Palestinian Jewry to conform to British plans for them had tipped the former trades union leader Bevin over into "overt anti-Semitism," he said. The Labour foreign secretary was convinced that "the Jews were organizing a world conspiracy against poor old Britain" in which the Zionists, together with the Soviet Union, would seek to bring down the Empire.[16] Jewish resistance to British rule in Palestine in the summer of 1947 would trigger anti-Jewish riots in the new postwar socialist Britain following the hanging of two British sergeants by the Irgun (the National Military Organization led by Menahem Begin). This cruel act had come in retaliation for the execution of an Irgun member by the British authorities. On August 1, 1947, mobs of youths rampaged through Jewish districts in Liverpool, Manchester, Glasgow, East London, and other cities. Jewish property was looted, synagogues attacked, and cemeteries desecrated.[17] Palestine — not for the first or last time — had become a catalyst for British hostility to Jews.

Another classic example of the ways in which anti-Zionism merged with antisemitism can be found in the person of the conservative John Bagot Glubb, the supreme commander of the Arab Legion in Israel's War of Independence in 1948. This Arabophile Englishman regarded the creation of Israel as a crime. Glubb was an unabashed antisemite, who firmly believed that the "unlikable character" of the Jews had provoked their persecution throughout history; that most Russian and East European Jews were really Khazar Turks with no connection to the promised land; that the Jews were by nature aggressive and stiff-necked; and that the "vengeful" mentality of the Jewish people had been "passed down without a break from generation to generation."[18] Since biblical times, Jews had been imbued with "the idea of a superior race," whose blood must not be contaminated "by inter-mixture with others." Not only did Jews invent the idea of the "master race," but their behavior towards Arabs was, he supposed, driven by Hitlerian politics.[19]

In a secret July 1946 memorandum, Glubb described the new Jews in Palestine as fusing the ancient, hateful Hebrew tradition with "a layer of up-to-date Eastern European fanaticism." He claimed that they had copied Nazi techniques — embracing "the theories of race, blood and soil, the terrorism of the gunmen, the inculcation of hate into the young, and the youth movements." The young Jew of Palestine, Glubb concluded, was "as hard, as narrow, as fanatical, and as bitter as the Hitler youth on whom he is modeled."[20] At least four decades before it became fashionable on the British Left, Glubb was describing Zionism as a combination of "Judaism and Nazism."

But the intellectual pioneer of the idea that Zionism is a form of Nazism in the 1950s was another eminent member of the British establishment, the renowned historian Arnold J. Toynbee. His monumental *A Study of History* unequivocally indicted the Zionists as "disciples of the Nazis;" they had even chosen "to imitate some of the evil deeds that the Nazis had committed against the Jews."[21] Ignoring the Arab determination to strangle the infant State of Israel at birth, he suggested that Jews had gratuitously murdered and expelled peaceful Arabs in a bloodthirsty and unprovoked frenzy. This, too, would eventually become a mantra of the British Left.

After the Six Day War, such comparisons became commonplace in the Soviet Union and spread more gradually in Western Europe, including Britain. One source in the Western liberal democracies was the rise of the New Left, with its dogmatic "anti-racism" that pilloried Zionist policy toward the Palestinian Arabs as "genocide" and upbraided British Jews for being reactionary accomplices of Israeli "fascism."[22]

During the Lebanon war, the far-Left Trotskyite *News Line* falsely accused the Zionists of employing "horrendous gas weapons which were once used against the Jewish people by the Nazis," and of trying to carry out a "Final Solution" against four million Palestinians.[23] Another organ of the British Left, the *Labour Herald* (co-edited by Ken Livingstone), published in 1982 a cartoon that anticipated present-day calumny down to the last detail. A bespectacled, obviously Jewish Menachem Begin, then Israel's prime minister, is shown wearing Nazi jackboots, a Death's Head insignia, and a Star of David armband, raising his right arm in a *Sieg Heil* salute over a mountain of skull bones, Lebanon lying bleeding at his feet. The headline, in Gothic script, reads: "The Final Solution."[24]

Then, as now, prominent British writers were in the vanguard of demonizing Israel, inverting the Holocaust, and spinning a web of antisemitic allusions. Best-selling children's author, Roald Dahl, for example, did not hesitate to brand Begin and Sharon in 1983 as "almost the exact carbon copies in miniature of Mr. Hitler and Mr. Goering."[25] They were "equally shortsighted," "bloodthirsty," and as deserving as their Nazi models of being arraigned by a war-crimes tribunal. "Never before in the history of mankind," Dahl proclaimed, "has a race of people switched so rapidly from being much pitied victims to barbarous murderers."[26] For good measure he added that the Jews had been "cowards" in World War II.[27]

Demonization of Jews, whether as individuals or as a collective, thus enjoys a long pedigree in broad sections of British public life. True, it has never become the mainstay of public expression, the way it was in Soviet Russia and continues to be in many Arab countries. Yet unlike the rest of Western Europe, where since the Holocaust antisemitism has become less acceptable among the educated classes, and tends to be relegated to Muslim immigrant populations or political extremists, in Great Britain demonization of Jews and especially of Israel has continued to enjoy the status of a legitimate opinion. It is especially troubling at so sensitive a moment for Europe's Jews.

Today, antisemitic expression in Britain — especially on the Left — often takes the form of virulent, disproportionate criticism of the Jewish state. It is of course the case that not all disagreement with Israeli policy can be considered antisemitic or illegitimate. But in Britain, and especially in the media, such criticism frequently leaves the bounds of civilized debate and engages in demonization, flagrant double standards, and the implicit denial of Israel's right to defend itself — thereby appropriating more traditional modes of antisemitism.

A major venue for anti-Israel views has been the state-owned British Broadcasting Corporation. While generally downplaying the jihadist motivations of militant Islam, the BBC has shown no such reticence in misrepresenting Israel's efforts at self-defense. In many current affairs programs during the Second Intifada (2000-2005), the image of a bloodthirsty, implacable Ariel Sharon would be frequently contrasted with a relatively benign Yasser Arafat, portrayed until his death as the amiable, fatherly leader of the Palestinians. In BBC interviews, Palestinian spokespeople tend to be treated to soft and respectful questioning, whereas Israelis, unless they explicitly repudiate Israeli policies, are liable to be handled far more harshly. This partiality extends to vocabulary. The BBC consistently calls Hamas and Islamic Jihad terrorists "militants" or "radicals."[28] The word "terror" is almost never used, even for the most brutal Palestinian assaults on Israeli civilians — though the network had no qualms about using the word to describe the September 11 attacks in New York and Washington, the Bali bombing, or similar terrorist assaults in Djerba, Casablanca, and Istanbul.[29] The same pattern of bias is revealed when the BBC quotes verbatim unsubstantiated Palestinian accusations — such as the harvesting of Palestinian organs by the Israeli army, and the use of poison gas or depleted uranium — while disputing the authenticity of evidence Israel might present in its own defense. Israeli sources cited by the BBC merely "allege" while Palestinians "report." This attitude was particularly apparent in the screening on *BBC Correspondent* (March 17, 2003) of "Israel's Secret Weapon," a documentary depicting Israel as a rogue regime, Ariel Sharon as a Jewish Saddam Hussein and the nuclear facility at Dimona, rather than Baghdad, as the rightful target of UN inspectors.[30] There have been many such reports over the years, almost always by left-leaning liberal journalists who tend to predominate in the media.

The prejudice is not just a matter of bias among individual editors and reporters, but appears to be a consistent pattern throughout the BBC. Media Tenor, an independent, Bonn-based research group, conducted a 2003 study which found that the BBC's Middle East coverage was 85 percent negative, 15 percent neutral, and 0 percent positive toward Israel.[31]

The Jenin affair offers a prime example of Israel-baiting in the British media. Many British journalists hailed the grossly inflated claims of 3,000 Palestinian dead after Israel's assault on the refugee camp in April 2002 as proof of a major atrocity, without any attempt at serious verification. The prominent author, A. N. Wilson, a leading columnist of the London *Evening Standard*, informed his readers that "we are talking here of massacre, and a cover-up of genocide."[32] The *Guardian* malevolently compared Israel's incursion into Jenin with al-Qaeda's attack of September 11 on New York. The Israeli action, it said, was "every bit as repellent in its particulars, no less distressing, and every bit as man-made." The incursion, it added, "already has that aura of infamy that attaches to a crime of especial notoriety."[33] The *Times*' correspondent, Janine di Giovanni, wrote that rarely had anyone seen "such deliberate destruction, such disrespect for human life."[34] Phil Reeves of the more radical *Independent* spoke of Cambodia-style "killing fields," quoting without any verification Palestinian claims of "mass murder" and wholesale "executions." His dispatch began thus: "A monstrous war crime that Israel has tried to cover up for a fortnight has finally been exposed."[35] Indeed, months after a UN investigation concluded that there was no massacre in Jenin, and even Palestinian leaders had conceded the point, BBC anchors and its website were still implying that there were doubts about what had really happened.[36]

A particularly insidious example of how easily anti-Israel defamation slides into antisemitic imagery was afforded by Dave Brown's cartoon in the *Independent*, depicting Ariel Sharon in the act of devouring the flesh of a Palestinian baby. Sharon was shown, nearly naked, wearing a Likud fig leaf, and in the background Apache helicopters fire missiles and blare, "Vote Likud."[37] This cartoon would not have looked out of place in *Der Stürmer*, but more strikingly recalls images of the medieval blood libels.[38] Nevertheless, the Press Complaints Committee in the United Kingdom dismissed all protests, and this caricature was subsequently awarded first prize in the British Political Cartoon Society's annual competition for 2003.[39]

No less disturbing was the account given by the journalist Julie Burchill in an opinion piece published November 29, 2003, which explained why she was leaving the *Guardian*: Burchill, who is not Jewish, was dismayed by the British press's "quite striking bias against the State of Israel." For all its faults, she retorted, Israel was still the "only country in that barren region that you or I, or any feminist, atheist, homosexual or trade unionist, could bear to live under."[40] Burchill's critique went beyond her own paper; she was particularly scathing about Richard Ingrams, a veteran columnist for the *Observer*, who demanded that Jewish journalists declare their racial origins when writing about the Middle East. Ingrams told his readers: "I have developed a habit when confronted by letters to the editor to look at the signature to see if the writer has a Jewish name. If so, I tend not to read it."[41]

This is not to say that the press makes no room for the occasional defense of the Israeli position — as the *Guardian*'s willingness to publish Burchill's letter attests. Rather, the problem lies more in the perception that antisemitic canards, demonization of Israel, and the implicit endorsement of terrorism against Israeli civilians are considered legitimate in British reporting and commentary. For example, in 2005, a British play called *My Name is Rachel Corrie* glorified the young American activist who was killed in the Gaza Strip in 2003 while attempting to prevent a bulldozer from destroying a home used to supply Palestinian terror networks. Instead of challenging the play's outright bias or raising the debate surrounding the play's controversial moral perspective, British theater critics hailed the play, comparing it with dramatizations of the lives of Primo Levi and Anne Frank.[42]

Whether on the Left or Right, as a result of the wholesale adoption of the Palestinian perspective and its antisemitic motifs, relatively little attention is paid to the extremist ideology, the culture of martyrdom, or the virulent antisemitism endemic in contemporary Islamism. Instead, suicide bombings against civilian targets have been explained away as a product of the general misery induced by Israel's policies. Such beliefs, for example, led Cherie Blair, wife of New Labour's prime minister, to remark at a charitable event in London in June 2002 that young Palestinians "feel they have got no hope but to blow themselves up."[43] She made the comment only hours after a Hamas suicide bomber blew up a bus packed full of Israelis, including schoolchildren — killing 19 and injuring dozens. Worse still, Jenny Tonge, a Liberal Democrat British legislator who was back-benched in 2005, after expressing sympathies for Palestinian suicide bombers and comparing Arabs in Gaza to Jews in the Warsaw Ghetto, was nominated to serve in the House of Lords.[44] In September 2006, Baroness Tonge, addressing a meeting of the Palestinian Solidarity Campaign, went one step further, declaring that the "pro-Israel lobby has got its grips on the western world, its financial grips."

Baroness Tonge included her own Liberal Democrat Party in these allegations, earning a sharp repudiation from her own Party leadership for the "clear anti-Semitic connotations" of these remarks.[45]

In the Labour Party, too, the thin boundary between antisemitism and anti-Zionism has increasingly been breached. During the eight-year incumbency of London's left-wing populist mayor, Ken Livingstone, the local politics of London began to internalize the discourse of hate. In February 2005 Livingstone angrily compared a Jewish reporter for the *Evening Standard* to a concentration camp guard. Instead of later apologizing, Livingstone criticized the reporter's employer for what he said was its history of racism, scare-mongering, and, oddly enough, antisemitism. Shortly thereafter, Livingstone published a piece in the *Guardian* claiming that Ariel Sharon "is a war criminal who should be in prison, not in office," adding that "Israel's own expansion has included ethnic cleansing." Subsequently, the Muslim Public Affairs Committee, responding to Jewish critics of the mayor, published an article in support of the mayor on its website, entitled "Zionists Want Their Pound of Flesh."[46]

Passions in London were further stirred by the 2005 election contest in the city's Bethnal Green district, the second-most Muslim area in Britain. The highly charged electoral race pitted sitting Labour MP Oona King, a black Jewish woman, against George Galloway, a former Labour MP now representing the anti-war Respect Party, a blend of far-Left and Islamist politics. After youths threw eggs at King as she honored East End Jews killed in Nazi bombing raids, one young Muslim told the *Daily Telegraph*: "We all hate her. She comes here with her Jewish friends who are killing our people and then they come to our backyards."[47] King lost by 823 votes.

After the election, the climate in London grew more hostile. On May 21, 2005, a major rally was held in Trafalgar Square, with a crowd waving Palestinian flags and anti-Israel banners despite the heavy rain. Speakers included Palestinian representatives and local Muslim leaders, but most notable was the presence of non-Muslim left-wing public figures. Jeremy Corbyn, a backbench Labour MP, called for the British government to "cease all trade with Israel," while Tony Benn, a former Labour MP, an icon of the radical Left and veteran of the British political scene, called George Bush and Ariel Sharon the "two most dangerous men in the world." Paul Mackney, president of the country's second-largest union of teachers, called for the widespread boycott of Israel by British academia, while Andrew Birgin of the Stop the War coalition demanded the dismantling of the Jewish state. "The South African apartheid state never inflicted the sort of repression that Israel is inflicting on the Palestinians," he said to cries of *Allahu akbar!* from the audience. "When there is real democracy, there will be no more Israel."[48]

The rally's most prominent speaker, however, was George Galloway, fresh from his election victory over Oona King. Galloway used the rally as an opportunity to launch an international boycott of Israel. "We will join them," he said, referring to the Palestinians, "by boycotting Israel. By boycotting Israeli goods. By picketing the stores that are selling Israeli goods." To cheers and applause, Galloway added, "It's about time that the British government made some reparations for the Balfour Declaration."[49]

Given the legitimacy that such rhetoric enjoys in Britain today, it should not surprise us to discover the emergence of efforts among the intellectual elites to convert their rhetoric of hate into action — principally through the boycotting of Jewish and Israeli products and people. It is these activities which have turned the public atmosphere in Britain into one of the most uncomfortable for Jews in all of Europe.

First came the much-publicized Mona Baker affair, which involved her removal of two Israeli colleagues from the boards of academic journals. The Egyptian-born Baker claimed to have been inspired by the boycott initiative of two left-wing Anglo-Jewish academics, Steven Rose and his wife, Hilary. Supporters of the petition included the AUT, NATFHE (the lecturers' union), and over 700 academics. Matters escalated when Andrew Wilkie, a professor of pathology at Oxford University, flatly rejected the application of an Israeli student simply because of his nationality. On June 23, 2003, Wilkie told the student that he had "a huge problem with the way that Israelis take the moral high ground from their appalling treatment in the Holocaust, and then inflict gross human rights abuses on the Palestinians."[50] Oxford promptly slapped him with two months of unpaid leave, although the same institution has failed to take any action against the poet Tom Paulin, a radical lecturer and TV personality, who published a scandalous poem in 2002 that likened the Israeli army to a "Zionist SS."[51]

Matters only worsened in April 2005 when the AUT, which had some 40,000 members, voted by sizable majorities to impose a boycott on two Israeli universities, Bar-Ilan University and the University of Haifa, in solidarity with the Palestinian cause. According to the AUT secretary general, this ban would "take the form described in the Palestinian call for academic boycott of Israeli institutions." The rushed vote was held on Passover eve, preventing most Jewish members from taking part, and opponents of the motions were denied right of reply due to "lack of time." Just before the vote, speakers addressing the AUT's executive union meeting declared Israel a "colonial apartheid state, more insidious than South Africa," and called for the "removal of this regime." While some British institutions, such as Oxford, considered action to override the ban, in general it was international pressure, rather than repercussions within British society, that made the boycott a matter of serious controversy and ultimately led to its reversal a month later.[52]

Boycotts against Jews arouse painful associations. Attempts to remove Israeli products from Selfridges, Harrods, Tesco, Marks & Spencer, and other British chains, under the slogan "Isolate the Racist Zionist State," are both a symptom and a rallying point for the resurgence of antisemitism in Britain.[53] Demonstrators collect money and signatures, sell pamphlets comparing Israeli leaders to Hitler, and shout slogans at passersby. Carol Gould offered a telling example of one such experience of a demonstration outside the Marks & Spencer on Oxford Street, London, in November 2003. Gould described how the Moroccan conductor of her double-decker bus harangued his passengers about "all Marks & Spencer money that goes to the 'Zionist murderers.'"[54] Once outside the store, she encountered "an hysterical crowd of hate-filled people," in which non-Arabs easily outnumbered those of Middle Eastern origin. One woman in religious Muslim attire was screaming, "You Jews destroyed my country, Iraq." Others shouted, "You people invented terrorism in Palestine!"; "Israel is expanding every day and will soon own the whole Middle East!" "Israel is slaughtering thousands of Palestinians every day!"[55] An elegantly dressed English businessman told Gould: "I love and revere the suicide bombers. Every time I hear of a suicide bomb going off I wish it had been eighty or ninety Jews instead of a pitiful handful."[56]

It needs to be emphasized that the old-new antisemitism in Britain is not the kind of hatred that prevailed in Europe sixty years ago. The emerging multicultural society of Great Britain will not tolerate cries of *Sieg Heil*, jackboots, or the openly racist mythology that was irrevocably stained by the Holocaust. Nor is British antisemitism "with the boots off" quite what it used to be. The classic blend of British aristocratic hauteur, bourgeois snobbery, and working-class dislike of "bloody foreigners" is no longer politically correct.

In its place we have an obsessive focus on Israel, often linked to a deep loathing for so-called American imperialism and the "neo-colonialist" West. The spearhead of this assault has been the "anti-racist" Left in Great Britain which attributes to Jews and the state of Israel all the worst sins of antisemitism: racism, ethnic cleansing, "crimes against humanity," and even genocide. This conscious attempt to "Nazify" Judaism, Zionism, and Israel deserves to be regarded as one of the most scandalous inversions in the history of the longest hatred.[57]

The continuing trend, especially visible in the liberal mainstream and on the Left (though it is also present on the Right) took full advantage of the fallout from the Gaza war at the beginning of 2009 and the many reports slamming the Israel Defense Forces for allegedly committing "war crimes." The election of Benjamin Netanyahu as Israel's prime minister and the appointment of Avigdor Lieberman as foreign minister in 2009 offered further opportunities to personalize these attacks, as did the perception of a popular new American president Barack Obama (far to the left of his predecessor) demanding a complete settlement freeze from Israel. British media hostility, especially in the *Guardian* and the *Independent*, as well as from elements of the BBC, was especially venomous throughout 2009, driving Israel's image in Britain to an all-time low.[58] The War on Want charity, which had already in 2007 advocated a world-wide boycott of Israel, organized an event in East London in July 2009 vilifying Israel as an "apartheid state" and damning it as guilty of "massive human rights abuses." It featured rabidly anti-Israel speakers like Ben White, a freelance writer who in 2002 had accused the Israeli government of ethnic cleansing, adding for good measure that he understood why people in Britain were antisemitic.[59]

Labour MP John Mann (who is not Jewish, but who chaired the British All-Party Parliamentary Groups against Antisemitism) was particularly concerned by the anti-Jewish hostility on the Left, which he found both more sinister and dishonest than the more blatant antisemitism of Muslim or far-Right extremists. Mann noted the widespread perception in the British Parliament that "Jews are rich and therefore are 'good for donations' " and the prevalence of "disgraceful and outrageous antisemitism in Parliament, including statements from those who are meant to be bastions against racism."[60]

In this context, it might be appropriate to quote briefly from an interview on British antisemitism which I gave to Manfred Gerstenfeld early in 2008 at the Jerusalem Institute of Public Affairs:

> What is interesting is that in Britain, as in much of Europe, the proclaimed anti-racism of the left-wing variety often feeds the new antisemitism — which is directed primarily against the State of Israel. Of course, if one suggests that such leftists are antisemites in disguise, they are likely to become enraged, retorting that one is "playing the antisemitic card." This has become a code-word for saying, as it were, "you are a dishonest, deceitful, manipulative Jew" or a "lover of Jews." Zionists supposedly use the "accusation of antisemitism" to disguise, to hide, to silence the

fully justified criticism of Israel and its human rights abuses. The word "criticism" in this context is misplaced — a euphemism or license for the demonization of Israel. And that in turn is a major form of antisemitism in our time.[61]

In this same interview, and subsequently, in my book *A Lethal Obsession: Anti-Semitism from Antiquity to the Global Jihad* (2010), I pointed out that Great Britain has become a European leader in several areas of anti-Zionism and antisemitism.[62] British society, for example, has played a "pioneering" role in promoting the academic isolation of Israel and trade union economic boycotts of Israeli goods; and there is no other democratic nation where jihadi radicalism, closely linked to anti-Western antisemitism, is so violent and intertwined with left-wing attitudes.

The prevalence of Trotskyite anti-Israel attitudes has been an especially significant influence on the Left since 1967, representing a particularly obtuse and dogmatic anti-Zionism. In the Trotskyite concept, Zionism has always been identified with global capitalism and since 1945 with American imperialism. In the 1970s, British Trotskyites (some of them Jewish) organized the Socialist Workers Party (SWP) into a particularly active force in demonizing Israel. They were a major factor in the huge antiwar demonstrations in London in February 2003.[63] The SWP has systematically savaged Israel as America's "attack dog" and agent in the Middle East — picking on it as the more vulnerable, isolated and easy-to-demonize surrogate for their anti-American rage. Periodically, the Trotskyites and other sections of the British Left have also presented the Israel/Jewish lobby as having a stranglehold over American foreign policy.

The theme of the omnipresent and all-powerful Jewish lobby has indeed been a leitmotif attracting much attention in the mainstream British media as well as on the British Left. The veteran Labour MP, Tom Dalyell already caused some controversy when he declared in an interview for *Vanity Fair* in 2003 that then-British Prime Minister Tony Blair was surrounded by a sinister "cabal" of Jewish advisers who had allegedly dragged him into the unpopular Iraq war. According to Dalyell, the cabal was linked to hawkish neo-conservative intellectuals (virtually a code-word for Jews influential in the Bush administration) in Washington, D.C. who supposedly masterminded the invasion of Iraq. Both President Bush and Blair, according to this far-fetched conspiracy theory, were instruments of a pro-Likud, pro-Sharon Jewish Zionist plot designed to protect Israel by forcefully removing Iraqi dictator Saddam Hussein. Dalyell bizarrely included as "Jews" the then-British Foreign Secretary Jack Straw and the New Labour spin doctor Peter Mandelson (neither of whom is actually Jewish). Under the Nazi race laws, however, their partial Jewish ancestry might possibly have qualified them for Auschwitz.[64]

The only "conspirator" in Dalyell's trio of villains who was indisputably Jewish was Blair's personal envoy to the Middle East, Lord Levy—a wealthy British Jew, New Labour's most important fundraiser and a favorite target of British media innuendo. Levy's integrity and impartiality had been fiercely attacked by, among others, the Australian-born John Pilger, a leftist pro-Palestinian crusading journalist who has never lost an opportunity to lash out at Israel's "greedy expansionism" and trampling of human rights.[65] Pilger, like many on the British Left, or in pro-Palestinian circles, as well as in the Muslim media, appears to believe that there is a dangerous Jewish/Zionist lobby that manipulates British and American foreign policy. This belief, broadly shared by a third of Britons according to a 2007 opinion survey, is periodically aired by the BBC. The most recent example, in the Channel 4 investigative series, *Dispatches*, was the screening of "Inside Britain's Israel Lobby"—aired in November 2009 and replete with repulsive innuendos about the power of pro-Israel "moneybags." Viewers were treated to infantile theories about the lobby's supposed control of the British Labour and Conservative parties and their "pro-Israel" intimidation of the British media. The documentary criticized the "pro-Israel" abuse of antisemitism to deflect criticism of the Jewish State. It contained sinister music accompanying the photos of "lobby" members blurred across British and Israeli flags.[66]

The theme of an occult Jewish/Zionist conspiracy is not, of course, new. Prior to 1948 (and during the early period of the Israeli state), the most active anti-Zionists tended, however, to be members of the British establishment—former army officers, colonial officials, Conservative politicians, Christian missionaries, and Arabists who came from elite schools. Today, on the other hand, we find a bizarre unwritten alliance of "peace" activists, left-wing radicals, anti-globalists, and Islamists spearheading the anti-Zionist forces. Many of these activists are linked to the Palestine Solidarity Campaign (PSC), which seeks to build an effective mass campaign and to organize protests that aim to isolate and delegitimize Israel. The PSC played a central role in mobilizing British opinion to divest from any companies (like the heavy machinery manufacturer Caterpillar) that have provided services, products, or technology that maintains "the occupation of the Palestinian territories."[67]

The PSC sponsors the Boycott Israeli Goods campaign, which targets agricultural and high-tech exports to Britain; and since 2005, it has offered extensive support to the anti-Zionist academics seeking to convince the AUT (the largest university teachers' union in the UK) to break all ties with Israeli universities. The PSC has also strongly backed those in the Church of England who favor divestment from Israel and it cooperates with fiercely anti-Zionist Christian groups like the Sabeel Ecumenical Liberation Theology Center headed by the Reverend Dr. Naim Ateek.[68] The PSC has, not surprisingly, developed close links with the Muslim Council of Britain (MCB), the leading organized representative body of British Muslims, and with the more radically anti-Zionist Muslim Public Affairs Committee. A closer examination of the literature, activities, and networks of the PSC confirms the view that it is more concerned to delegitimize Israel than to genuinely right any Israeli "wrong" towards the Palestinians; that its intense and even irrational hatred of Israel is more intimately connected with its opposition to a *Jewish* state than with securing a genuine peace in the Middle East.[69]

The PSC's influence on the decision of the Trades Union Congress (TUC) to promote a boycott, divestment, and sanctions campaign against Israel has been particularly striking. In collaboration with the hard Left within the TUC, they have done everything in their power to execrate Israel as a racist apartheid state. The Gaza invasion of January 2009 undoubtedly strengthened popular support for the Boycott Israel Movement in the unions, the media, among prominent NGOs, and some British politicians. The boycott drive, with its uniquely hostile treatment of the Jewish State (while ignoring massive and far graver human rights violations elsewhere), is without doubt an extreme case of double standards with clearly antisemitic implications. As Anthony Julius and Alan Dershowitz have noted, "the boycott has been an essential tool of antisemites for at least a thousand years."[70]

The essence of the boycott is to economically and politically damage the Jewish state, denying it the freedom and rights enjoyed by other nation-states. Its negative physical and psychological impact on British Jews is self-evident and palpable. While the New Labour government in Britain has opposed both the trade union and academic boycotts, it has nonetheless supported the discriminatory labeling of goods from West Bank settlements. Recently the British government also arbitrarily cancelled export licenses for Israeli warship parts.[71]

Such unfriendly acts are probably more related to the needs of British foreign policy (always mindful of its important interests in the Arab world) than to any ideological considerations. But it is worth noting that the Foreign Office under David Milliband (himself a highly assimilated Jew) does listen to influential NGOs such as Oxfam and Christian Aid and the War on Want, which have all aligned themselves with the Palestine Solidarity Campaign. The pro-Palestinian bias of the BBC and radical newspapers like the *Guardian* and the *Independent*, constantly badmouthing Israel and demonizing its settlement policy, has also contributed to current British government policy.

The anti-Zionist British Left—whether it is explicitly anti-Jewish in motivation or in its general tendency— has in effect greatly helped in *normalizing* hostility to Israel and a new level of antagonism towards Jews. Like its counterparts in Western Europe, it has made the misleading and arbitrary equation of Israel with "human rights abuse" seem almost natural and axiomatic. This has, moreover, been done under the banner of a hypocritical "anti-racism" and mindless anti-colonialism, while vehemently denying any connection to antisemitism. Such charges are usually dismissed as nothing but a "Zionist" ploy to smear critics of Israel. According to the anti-Zionist British Left the "apologists" of Israel automatically brand *all* criticism of Israel as antisemitic.

But except for a very small number of cases, this is manifestly untrue. It is rare to find anti-Zionism presented as being completely *identical* with antisemitism, though the parallels and convergences obviously exist. Left-wing, secular anti-Zionism is far more complex than that. It has many motivations, a variety of national contexts, and varying political goals. What most contemporary anti-Zionists, especially on the Left, generally agree upon is their rejection of Zionist ideology and their opposition to the State of Israel. This is not inherently or necessarily antisemitic, but in many cases it has indeed nourished anti-Jewish attitudes and practices.

While presenting Zionism as a form of racism, the British radical Left all too often stigmatizes it through an "essentialist" discourse which is highly discriminatory as well as embarrassingly monolithic.[72] Zionism is caricatured as a form of "Jewish supremacism" (a similar vocabulary exists on the far Right)— branded as a particularly ugly and vicious offshoot of the Western imperialist project. Not only is it deemed similar to European racism, Nazism, colonialism, and apartheid, but the Zionist enterprise is also defamed as being *uniquely* evil. Although the contemporary anti-Zionist movement usually sees itself as continuing the tradition of the old, pre-Holocaust Left, this language is clearly a major escalation in the direction of anti-Jewish rhetoric.[73] Of course, when Israel was founded in 1948, absorbing many Jewish refugees from Europe who had somehow survived the Holocaust, as well as Jews fleeing from pogroms in Arab lands, only the most dogmatic die-hard leftists could realistically view it as part of a Western colonialist conspiracy. The British Empire, ruled by a Labour government, was doing everything in its power in 1948 to *abort* the establishment of a Jewish state. The United States stood on the sidelines and enforced an arms embargo against Israel. It was the Soviet

Union which (for its own strategic reasons) supplied the crucial armaments that helped Israel to overcome an Arab invasion aimed at its annihilation. Communists around the world generally followed the Soviet line in supporting the Jewish State. So much for the ludicrous (if widely believed) fable of Israel as the "spoiled child" of *Western* imperialism from its very inception.

Left-wing narratives of Israel/Palestine have completely airbrushed these inconvenient facts out of the historical picture. In their one-sided and grossly distorted historiography there was, for example, no Arab ethnic cleansing of Jews from their Middle East homelands after 1945; Israel was a client state of Anglo-American imperialism from the outset; and the reality of an exterminationist antisemitism in Nazi-controlled Europe is completely sidelined. After all, that reminder might just vindicate the Zionist prognosis concerning the failure of Jewish assimilation into European society. Instead, the wretched canard of Zionist "collaboration" in the Nazi genocidal enterprise has been given a new lease of life by the contemporary British Left. Anti-Zionists can now, at their leisure, shift the perception of the Jew from that of absolute victim to the vicious propaganda myth of demonic Nazi-Zionist perpetrators. The Palestinians and Arabs in general can then be mythologized as the *victims* of Israel (and of America) rather than bearing their full share of responsibility for the Middle East conflict. The Palestinians have indeed mutated since the 1970s into the "new Jews," romanticized and even infantilized by their left-wing patrons. As a result they have become immunized from any criticism of their suicidal jihadist nihilism, which has had such a devastating effect on hopes for peace in the Middle East.

Anti-Zionism has unfortunately become not only a "lingua franca" for virtually all political extremists (on the Left as well as the far Right). It is also a feature of mainstream discourse in Great Britain. The smears against Israel have sometimes contained modern echoes of the medieval Christian blood libel (for example, that the Israel Defense Forces are an army of "child-killers"). They include soft and hard versions of the so-called Jewish conspiracy to dominate the world; they encourage fantasies about Jewish power and wild claims to the effect that Jews who are concerned with antisemitism must be acting in bad faith. This last accusation (increasingly prevalent on the British Left) amounts to suggesting that there is no real Judeophobia in Europe or the Middle East. Rather, it is the *talk about antisemitism* which is supposedly the problem — one that is being manipulated by Israel and its Zionist supporters.[74]

Antisemitism, we are told, has run its course, replaced by Islamophobia (the "real racism" of the present). This claim is highly questionable, despite the growth of the Muslim population in Western Europe today. The fears of terrorism as well as creeping "Islamization" are in fact well-founded and not merely a product of religious or racial prejudice. Nor is Jew-hatred simply a problem of the past.[75] Such claims amount to a *denial* of antisemitism as if it were a red herring. The worst form of this denial is the flirtation of radical British leftists with Holocaust inversion decked out in an anti-imperialist garb.[76] This type of Holocaust denial brackets Zionism with Hitlerism or presents the Zionist "occupation" of Palestine as a "crime against humanity" greater than that committed by Nazi Germany. It is increasingly accompanied by a "soft" version of *Protocols*-style antisemitism— which regards the "Zionist" Jews as all-powerful, occult, and malevolent masters of the cosmos.

Robert S. Wistrich holds the Neuberger chair for Modern European and Jewish History at Hebrew University in Jerusalem and is the director of the Vidal Sassoon International Center for the Study of Antisemitism at Hebrew University. Professor Wistrich in the author or editor of twenty-five books. His most recent book is *A Lethal Obsession: Anti-Semitism from Antiquity to the Global Jihad* (2010). He was one of six historians appointed by the Vatican to the Catholic-Jewish Historical Commission, charged with examining Pope Pius XII's record during the Holocaust.

ENDNOTES

1   Community Security Trust, *Antisemitic Incidents, January–June 2009* (London: Community Security Trust, 2009). See also idem, *Antisemitic Discourse in Britain in 2008* (London: Community Security Trust, 2009).

2   Efraim Sicher, *Multiculturalism, Globalization, and Antisemitism: The British Case*, ACTA series, no. 22 (Jerusalem: Vidal Sassoon International Center for the Study of Antisemitism, Hebrew University of Jerusalem, 2009).

3   *Report of the All-Party Parliamentary Inquiry into Antisemitism* (London: HMSO, 2006).

4   Robert S. Wistrich, *A Lethal Obsession: Anti-Semitism from Antiquity to the Global Jihad* (New York: Random House, 2010), 362–434.

5   Melanie Phillips, "London: A Leftist Axis of Anti-Semitism," *Hadassah Magazine*, 4 September 2003.

6   Colin Holmes, *Anti-Semitism in British Society 1876–1939* (New York: Homes & Meier, 1979).

7   Ibid.

8   See Claire Hirschfeld, "The British Left and the 'Jewish Conspiracy': A Case Study of Modern Anti-Semitism," *Jewish Social Studies* (Spring 1981): 105–107.

9   Sharman Kadish, *Bolsheviks and British Jews: The Anglo-Jewish Community, Britain, and the Russian Revolution* (London: Frank Cass, 1992).

10 Gisela Lebzelter, *Political Anti-Semitism in England 1918–1939* (London: Holmes & Meier, 1978), 13–28. The London *Times* took the *Protocols* very seriously until its correspondent in Istanbul, Philip Graves, exposed it as a forgery in August 1921. See Norman Cohn, *Warrant for Genocide* (London: Penguin, 1970), 78, 166–71.

11 See Henry Defries, *Conservative Party Attitudes to Jews, 1900–1939* (London: Frank Cass, 2001); see also the review by Rory Miller in the *Jewish Journal of Sociology* 45, nos. 1–2 (2003): 51–63.

12 See W. F. Mandle, *Anti-Semitism and the British Union of Fascists* (London: Longmans Green, 1968); Richard Thurlow, *Fascism in Britain: A History, 1918–1985* (Oxford: Blackwell, 1987).

13 Tony Kushner, *The Persistence of Prejudice: Anti-Semitism in British Society during the Second World War* (Manchester: Manchester, 1989), 78–133.

14 James G. McDonald, *My Mission in Israel, 1948–1951* (London: Gollanz, 1951), 22–24.

15 Richard Crossman, *A Nation Reborn* (London: Hamish Hamilton, 1960), 69–72.

16 Ibid.

17 *Jewish Chronicle*, 8 August 1947; see also 15, 22, and 29 Aug. reports. Most of the British press did deplore the weekend violence.

18 See Benny Morris, *The Road to Jerusalem: Glubb Pasha, Palestine, and the Jews* (London: Tauris, 2002), 23.

19 From a Glubb speech of 6 May 1949, quoted by Morris, *Road to Jerusalem*, 23.

20 Ibid., 81–82.

21 Arnold J. Toynbee, *A Study of History* (London: Oxford University Press, 1954), vol. 8, and vol. 12: 290; see also Yaacov Herzog, *A People that Dwells Alone* (London: Weidenfeld and Nicolson, 1975), 21–47. Herzog convincingly refuted Toynbee's claims in a 1961 debate at McGill University, Montreal.

22 Robert S. Wistrich, *Hitler's Apocalypse* (New York: St. Martin's, 1985), 228.

23 *The News Line*, 11, 18, 30 June, 1982, 10 July 1982.

24 *Labour Herald*, 25 June 1982, p. 7.

25 Roald Dahl, *Literary Review* (August 1983); the article was reprinted in the mass circulation *Time Out* (18–24 August 1983).

26 Dahl, *Literary Review*.

27 *New Statesman*, 26 August 1983.

28 See the 28-page critical study by Trevor Asserson and Elisheva Mironi, *The BBC and the Middle East*, www.bbcwatch.com/old.html; and a 39-page BBC Watch report on the Iraq War, also by Asserson, at www.bbcwatch.com/fullReport3.htm. Both reports indicated a marked and consistent pro-Palestinian bias.

29 See "Friends Survive Bomb Terror," www.bbc.co.uk, 14 October 2002, http://news.bbc.co.uk/1/hi/england/2328233.stm; "U.S. Urges Tunisia to Pursue Reform," www.bbc.co.uk, 2 December 2003, http://newsvote.bbc.co.uk/mpapps/pagetools/print/news.bbc.co.uk/1/hi/world/africa/3257342.stm; and "Mood of Defiance in Istanbul," www.bbc.co.uk, 21 November 2003, http://news.bbc.co.uk /1/hi/world/europe/3228422.stm.

30 See Bret Stephens, "Anti-Semitism in Three Steps," *Jerusalem Post*, 3 July 2003.

31   Tzvi Fleischer, "Beeb Outdoes Itself," *The Review* (September 2003): 8.

32   A.N. Wilson, "A Demon We Can't Afford to Ignore," *Evening Standard*, 15 April 2002; see also idem, "The Tragic Reality of Israel," *Evening Standard*, 22 October 2001. In this latter article he basically repudiated Israel's "right to exist," called it an aggressor, and claimed that "it never was a state" and was in any case doomed to failure.

33   "The Battle for Truth," *Guardian*, 17 April 2002, lead editorial. After the release of the UN report, the *Guardian* pretended that its findings confirmed "what we said last April"— namely, that "the destruction in Jenin looked and smelled like a crime." This is quite untrue. See the issue of 2 August 2002 for the paper's justification.

34   Janine di Giovanni, "Inside the Camp of the Dead," *Times*, 16 April 2002.

35   Phil Reeves, "Amid the Ruins, the Grisly Evidence of a War Crime," *Independent*, 16 April 2002. The absurdity of this comparison can be easily exposed by a few basic facts: at least 100,000 Chechens died in Russia's brutal suppression of their fight for independence since the mid-1990s. In Bosnia between 1991 and 1995, 250,000 people were killed. The documented death toll in Jenin on both sides was about 80.

36   See Greg Barrow, "Jenin Report Reflects UN Dilemma," BBC Online, 1 August 2003, http://news.bbc.co.uk/2/hi/middle _east/2166871.stm.

37   See *Independent*, 27 January 2003 (which is National Holocaust Remembrance Day in Britain). The newspaper's editor, Simon Kelner, is Jewish.

38   "Independent Cartoon Sparks Protests over 'Anti-Semitism,'" *Jewish Chronicle*, 31 January 2003.

39   Editorial, "Cartoon Jews," *Jerusalem Post*, 1 December 2003.

40   Julie Burchill, "Good, Bad and Ugly," *Guardian*, 29 November 2003. Burchill made it clear she did not swallow "the modern libel line that anti-Zionism is entirely different from anti-Semitism."

41   Ibid.

42   Yaakov Lappin, "Corrie Compared to Anne Frank," *Jerusalem Post*, 9 May 2005. Writing in the *British Theater Guide*, Philip Fisher compared the Corrie play to Anthony Sher's dramatization of the life of Holocaust survivor Primo Levi, who was deported to Auschwitz in 1944: "Like Sir Anthony Sher's 'Primo,' 'My Name is Rachel Corrie' is a remarkably moving 90-minute solo piece about human dignity and suffering. Corrie was little more than a girl and while she could be naïve, she also had a saintly aspect, meeting death with the beatific happiness of a martyr."

43   The *Independent*, 19 June 2002; and the *Guardian*, 19 June 2002, predictably defended Mrs. Blair. See also Trevor Kavanagh, *Sun*, 20 June 2002, who rubbished Mrs. Blair's remarks and denounced "the brainwashed suicide zombies [who] want to wipe the State of Israel off the map of the Middle East. . . " See also "Cherie Blair's Suicide Bomb Blunder," *Times*, 19 June 2002; and "What Cherie Really Thinks," *Daily Telegraph*, 19 June 2002, which reminded Mrs. Blair that "hope" rather than "despair" motivated the martyrs; first, the hope they would go to heaven if they murdered Jews; second, the hope they would destroy Israel; and third, the hope that their families would receive a $25,000 reward from the Iraqi and Saudi governments.

44   Michael Freund, "Fired MP Nominated to House of Lords," *Jerusalem Post*, 10 May 2005.

45 On the Tonge affair, see "UK Baroness Accused of Anti-Semitic Comments," *Jerusalem Post*, 21 September 2006, 15 October 2006, and 29 November 2006.

46 See Ken Livingstone, "This is about Israel, Not Anti-Semitism," *Guardian*, 4 March 2005; and idem, "Zionists Want their Pound of Flesh," 24 February 2005, www.mpacuk.org/content /view/369.

47 Richard Alleyne, "Jewish MP Pelted with Eggs at War Memorial," *Daily Telegraph*, 11 April 2005.

48 Yaakov Lappin, "Speakers at London Rally Call for Israel's Destruction," *Jerusalem Post*, 22 May 2005. Birgin later clarified that he was referring to Israel "in the sense that it exists now," which in his view should be replaced with a "democratic secular state in which peace can move forward."

49 Lappin, "Call for Israel's Destruction."

50 Robin Shepherd, "Blind Hatred," *Jerusalem Post*, 29 September 2004.

51 See Neil Tweedie, "Oxford Poet 'Wants US Jews Shot,'" 13 April 2002, http://news.telegraph.co.uk/news/main.jhtml?xml =news/2002/04/13/npauli13.xml&sSheet=/news/2002/04/13/ ixnewstop.html.

52 Yaakov Lappin and Talya Halkin, "Israel Fumes at UK Academics' Boycott," *Jerusalem Post*, 22 April 2005; Fania Oz-Salzberger, "Israelis Need Not Apply," *Wall Street Journal*, 8 May 2005.

53 Anat Koren, "Israeli Hate Campaign Hits London's Streets," *London Jewish News*, Supplement (September 2002). Slogans like "Do not buy from Marks & Spencer" recall the Nazi catchwords of 1933, "Don't buy from Jews."

54 "I Wish Eighty or Ninety Jews Would Die with Each Bomb," editorial, 30 November 2003, www.jewish.comment.com/cgibin/news.cgi?=11&command=shownews&newsid=569.

55 Ibid.

56 Ibid. A policewoman finally booked this individual after he screamed: "You people have been trying to acquire land across the entire globe and will soon own every nation if you are not stopped."

57 See Robert S. Wistrich, *Anti-Semitism: The Longest Hatred* (New York: Pantheon Books, 1991), where I first coined the term "the longest hatred."

58 Robin Shepherd, "New Era as British Hostility Reaches Crescendo," *Jerusalem Post*, 21 July 2009; Jenni Frazer, "Israel's Press Chief Blasts Media Critics," *Jewish Chronicle*, 19 June 2009.

59 Marcus Dysch, "Charity Plans 'Apartheid Israel' Forum," *Jewish Chronicle*, 19 June 2009.

60 "I'm shocked by MP's antisemitism. The Simon Round Interview," *Jewish Chronicle*, 13 February 2009.

61 Robert Solomon Wistrich, "Antisemitism Embedded in British Culture," *Jewish Political Affairs* (Spring 2008).

62 Wistrich, *Lethal Obsession*, 381–418.

63 Ibid., 399ff.

64 "Anti-Semitism: Tam O'Slander," *Economist*, 8 May 2003.

65 Wistrich, *Lethal Obsession*, 389–90; see also Stephen Pollard, "A Massacre of the Truth," *Guardian*, 24 September 2002.

66 "Britain's Channel 4 Exposes 'Power' of Pro-Israel Lobby," *Haaretz*, 21 November 2009. The program triggered a wave of condemnation among Anglo-Jewish representatives, who accused the BBC of stoking antisemitism.

67 Rory Miller, "British Anti-Zionism Then and Now," *Covenant* 1, no. 2 (April 2007); see http://www.covenant.idc.ac.il/en/vol1/issue2/millerprint.html, accessed 16 September 2009.

68 See Margaret Brearley, *The Anglican Church, Jews, and British Multiculturalism*, Posen Papers in Contemporary Antisemitism (Jerusalem: SICSA, 2007).

69 See Miller, "British Anti-Zionism."

70 See Anthony Julius and Alan Dershowitz, "The Contemporary Fight against Anti-Semitism," *Times Online*, 13 June 2007, http://www.timesonline.co.uk/tol/comment/columnists/guest_contributors/article 1928865.ece

71 Jeremy Sharon, "Britain's Breathtaking Double Standard," *Jerusalem Post*, 16 July 2009.

72 See David Hirsh, *Anti-Zionism and Antisemitism. Cosmopolitan Reflections*. Working Paper, Yale Initiative for the Study of Antisemitism, Yale University, 2007.

73 The seeds of this shift were pointed out by me 20 years ago in "Left-wing Anti-Zionism in Western Societies," in *Anti-Zionism and Antisemitism in the Contemporary World*, edited by Robert S. Wistrich (London: Macmillan, Institute of Jewish Affairs, 1990), 46–52.

74 *Antisemitic Discourse in Britain in 2008* (London: CST, 2009); for examples, see Johann Hari, "Israel is suppressing a secret it must face," *Independent*, 28 April 2008; and his subsequent rant, "The loathsome smearing of Israel's critics," *Independent*, 8 May 2008.

75 See Wistrich, *Lethal Obsession*, 274–361.

76 Dave Rich, "The Holocaust as an Anti-Zionist and Anti-imperialist Tool for the British Left," in Manfred Gerstenfeld, ed., *The Abuse of Holocaust Memory. Distortions and Responses* (Jerusalem: Jerusalem Center for Public Affairs, 2009), 218–230.

II

EARLIER INCARNATIONS: EXCLUDING JEWS

BRANDEIS UNIVERSITY
IN THE SHADOW OF ANTISEMITISM

Stephen J. Whitfield

Were the American Jewish community to sponsor a non-sectarian college or university, Louis Marshall predicted in 1928, the result would be an "unqualified misfortune." As a prominent civil rights attorney who came close to dominating Jewish life in that decade, Marshall feared that such an institution would signify a tribalism that tarnished the ideal of equal opportunity. A Jewish-sponsored university would suggest surrender to bigotry, and would provide the sort of haven that might justify exclusion elsewhere in the American academy.[1] His opposition was so reverberant that a span of exactly two decades was needed before Brandeis University could be created. But its origins cannot be understood without placing the 1920s into the foreground. During the "tribal Twenties," a long shadow of discrimination was cast upon the hiring and admissions policies of leading colleges and universities, and Ivy League institutions erected higher barriers than ever before. They would not be effectively breached until after the Second World War. During that period, momentum continued to gather for a Jewish-sponsored university that could forbid any discrimination against Jews, either in admissions or in hiring. The formation of Brandeis University would guarantee that at least one institution of higher learning would be bereft of antisemitism.

To be sure, the 1920s was hardly the first decade to be disfigured by the snobbery and bigotry and discrimination that the academic culture of the elite took for granted. But during that decade, when the children of Eastern European immigrants first began submitting massive numbers of college applications, "the Jewish problem" seemed to become especially acute. The increase in Jewish applicants for admissions — and the different tenor and tempo that Jewish students injected into campus life — stirred anxiety among the elites, who took their own control over the dominant institutions of the nation for granted. This land was *their* land. The dean of Yale College complained that "a few years ago every single scholarship of any value was won by a Jew.... We cannot allow that to go on." Worried, he privately asked the director of admissions about an incoming freshman class: "How many Jews among them? And are there any coons?" On its application forms, the Ivy League commonly asked for the mother's maiden name and her place of birth, for the candidate's religious preference and for a photograph. The Jewish quota at Columbia College remained so stringent that, in 1935, despite his excellent grades and scientific promise, Richard Feynman's application was rejected.[2] He would have to try his luck elsewhere. Feynman eventually won a Nobel Prize and became perhaps the most accomplished and admired physicist of the second half of the century.

In posting the "No Trespassing" signs, the Ivy League failed to make the liberal criterion of individual merit a maximal value. Columbia College narrowed the funnel even for admissions to graduate school. Clifton Fadiman '25 was told not to bother to apply for graduate work in English at Columbia; and the explanation was blunt: "We have room for only one Jew, and we have chosen Mr. Trilling." (Fadiman chose the alternative of journalism, reviewing books for the *New Yorker* and helping to shape the nation's mostly "middle-brow" culture at the Book-of-the-Month Club.) And even after Columbia's Department of English elevated Lionel Trilling into the first Jew it hired permanently, a senior colleague warned against the impulse to interpret the promotion as "a wedge to open the English department to more Jews."[3]

Antisemitism was so rampant — and not only in the Ivy League — that even Jews lucky enough to find jobs had to scrape off the barnacles of negative stereotypes. In 1931 a mathematician at the University of Chicago described a mathematical astronomer as "one of the few men of Jewish decent [*sic*] who does not get on your nerves and really behaves like a gentile to a satisfactory degree." This characterization was intended as a letter of *recommendation*. In 1946 the metaphysician Paul Weiss, a CCNY graduate, became a full professor at Yale, the first in the history of the College. Highly praised by Alfred North Whitehead, Weiss inevitably emitted the danger signal that another recommender noted. It was difficult for "men...like Weiss [who] have been brought out of the lowliest social conditions to know how to behave in a society of genuine equality where it is not necessary to assert oneself."[4] (Among the elect, what are deemed virtues like initiative and ambition might seem "pushy" when done by Jews, or "uppity" when done by blacks.) W.E.B. Du Bois, a scholar and activist who knew something about prejudice, expressed his concern in 1947. "Only the Jews among us, as a class, carefully select and support talent and genius among the young," he asserted. But academic policies were imperiling that proclivity, Du Bois warned, and "jealousy of the gifted Jew...is closing doors of opportunity."[5]

Brandeis University was founded only a year after his observation, but history played a trick on this particular remedy for academic antisemitism. In the immediate postwar period, bigotry was dramatically disappearing throughout the nation. In 1948, for example, *Shelley* v. *Kraemer* invalidated restrictive real estate covenants. That case the U. S. Supreme Court decided only a year after the publication of novelist Laura Z. Hobson's best-selling exposé of such genteel antisemitism, *Gentleman's Agreement*, which was adapted that same year into an Oscar-winning film. (Judicial invalidation of discrimination in housing contracts did not of course finally and forever end the practice of "gentlemen's agreements.") In 1947 a Presidential commission also released *To Secure These Rights*, which favored the abolition of religious and racial discrimination. Such practices could no longer be squared with democratic principles. Among the authors of the report was Rabbi Roland Gittelsohn of Boston's Temple Israel. In the immediate wake of the revelation of the Holocaust, which laid bare the lethal historical terminus of Judaeophobia, this phenomenon was vanishing from American society.[6]

But the scars could not be quickly healed. They were exemplified by the initial role that Albert Einstein played in the creation of Brandeis University. Growing up in Munich, he had experienced antisemitism; and after he graduated from the Swiss Federal Polytechnic, an academic post in "the German-speaking countries" could not be found because of "the antisemitism...which is as unpleasant as it is a hindrance." A full appreciation of the relevance of his Jewish identity came to Einstein, however, only after moving to Berlin.[7]

Arriving at the Institute for Advanced Study in 1933, the most illustrious refugee from the Third Reich quickly realized how institutions like Princeton University promulgated a quota system to suppress the proportion of Jewish undergraduates. By March 1935 Einstein was writing to Justice Louis D. Brandeis about the need to grasp how bigotry required the establishment of a Jewish-sponsored institution of higher learning. The "ever-increasing negative attitude" that American gentiles were demonstrating would "push us out from the more desirable intellectual fields unless we succeed in obtaining a certain independence." The "adherence to a narrow-minded ritual education" that Einstein associated with New York's Rabbi Isaac Elchanan

Theological Seminary and Yeshiva College meant that Yeshiva University (its name after 1945) offered no solution.[8] Unaffiliated with any religious denomination or with rabbinical studies, a new university had to be secular, he argued, and would provide "many of our gifted youth...the cultural and professional education they are longing for" but are "denied" "under present circumstances."[9]

In 1946 Rabbi Israel Goldstein of New York's Congregation B'nai Jeshurun enlisted Einstein's endorsement in gathering a group of Jewish businessmen and attorneys in New York and Boston to form such a university. Goldstein had just finished serving as president of the Synagogue Council of America and as president of the Zionist Organization of America and devoted eight months to the founding of a non-sectarian institution that the Jewish community would sponsor.[10] By then the fears of an earlier generation of assimilationists, who denounced the "ghettoization" that such an institution might betoken, had receded. Objections this time came from Zionists like Chaim Weizmann, who sensed the diversion of support for Israel and for its Hebrew University in particular. "I was astonished to hear a few months ago that someone wants to establish a Jewish university in America," Weizmann remarked in May 1947. "I raise my voice in warning: Do not waste the strength of the Jewish people. There is no substitute for Zion."[11]

The most renowned Zionist in the Diaspora nevertheless praised the new endeavor as a prospective refuge from antisemitism, and added: "I would do anything in my power to help in the creation and guidance of such an institute," Einstein promised. "It would always be near to my heart."[12] He had long sought to apply humanitarian and even pacifist ideals to the messy and intractable complications of politics, and it would have made sense to name the new university for him. But he refused. Einstein had reached the United States less than a decade-and-a-half earlier, and had become a citizen as recently as 1940. He was not even comfortable in English. (With the polyglot director of the Institute for Advanced Study, J. Robert Oppenheimer, Einstein usually conversed in German.)

Rabbi Goldstein's choice to serve as president proved to be an inspired one.[13] Abram L. Sachar, an historian of Jewry, had served for roughly two decades as national director of the Hillel Foundation, and agreed to come out of retirement for so pioneering a task. He would not be the first Jew to serve as the president of a non-sectarian institution of higher learning; Paul Klapper had become president of Queens College eleven years earlier (and later joined the Brandeis Board of Trustees). Sachar happened not to be an innovative, paradigm-busting scholar. But he could spot greatness in other academicians — or in potential academicians. Martin Peretz '59, who became editor-in-chief and publisher of *The New Republic*, claimed that "Sachar had an uncanny sense of intellectual quality; he couldn't quite sing himself but he knew good singing when he heard it." Sachar became a master builder, and proved to be so tenacious and ingenious at soliciting funds that he became in effect the solicitor-general of the American Jewish community. The challenge was formidable. Brandeis would be neither a small college nor a large university, but a small university, which risked very high operating costs. At the beginning no institution in the nation's system of higher education was subjected to a larger unit cost than Brandeis.[14]

Yet Sachar managed to transform an act of faith into a fact. By 1953 the university had set "a regional speed record," getting full accreditation from the New England Association of Colleges and Secondary Schools. With Mach 2 speed Brandeis also got a charter for a Phi Beta Kappa chapter — in 1961, after only thirteen years, faster than any college or university had managed since the birth of the national liberal arts honor society in 1776. Sachar made such achievements possible. "Without him there could have been not just no Brandeis as we know it," one former professor wrote in 1970, "but very possibly no surviving Brandeis at all. If pre-eminent for raising money," Sachar deserved to "be remembered for what he raised it for."[15]

He had to do it, however, without Einstein's support. Because of hints of the assimilationist tendencies that the physicist deplored, he wanted nothing further to do with the new university, even refusing to accept an honorary degree from Brandeis.[16] (Louis D. Brandeis had never accepted honorary degrees anyway.) Einstein's fears were exaggerated. No one associated with the genesis of the institution could have ignored the background of bigotry that spurred the formation of Brandeis University, nor could they have failed to invoke Jewish values such as appreciation of learning as a justification for communal sponsorship. The niche that the university occupied was recognized as special. As the author of *Sufferance is the Badge* (1939), Sachar described the tenacity of antisemitism. He was hardly ignorant of the phenomenon, and the press commonly noted the non-discriminatory admissions policy that Brandeis adopted. The point of the new "Jewish-sponsored secular university," the *New York Times* declared as early as 1946, was the refreshing promise of being "open to students and faculty members of all races and religions."[17]

The nation's leading black magazine certainly appreciated such a pledge, during an era when liberals tended to see prejudice against minorities as indivisible. "America's newest university," *Ebony* proclaimed in 1952, "operates on a set of democratic principles which could easily serve as goals for every other university in the United States. There are no quotas limiting students of any religion and no racial barriers at Brandeis University." Rabbi Goldstein did not expect Brandeis to harbor every Jewish student or instructor who had ever been victimized or who feared the sting of prejudice. But he did foresee the "moral value" of an institution that projected radiant democratic ideals, which older colleges and universities might therefore emulate.[18] Sachar preferred, however, to highlight the eagerness of American Jewry to join the philanthropic procession that had begun with the denominational backing of the great religious seminaries of colonial New England. He tended to emphasize the positive contribution to American higher education that the Jewish community was about to make. A historically marginalized minority within Christendom could now be expected to enhance higher education in the United States.[19]

But in the first decade and a half or so, the university drew upon the cultural capital that Germany had so spectacularly generated prior to the *Walpurgisnacht*. Even more than the native-born talent whom Sachar recruited for the faculty, German Jewish refugees became pivotal to the early life of the university. Transporting *Bildung* to Brandeis, they exemplified the higher learning that had adorned the *Kaiserreich* and the Weimar Republic. The academic culture that Germany had achieved before the bonfires of the books in 1933 left more than mere vestiges at Brandeis, but was instead integral to its academic distinction. It is well-known that German Jewry did not die a natural death. But elements of Weimar culture would miraculously endure — at the Hebrew University of Jerusalem, in New York at the Leo Baeck Institute and at the New School for Social Research, on the Committee on Social Thought at the University of Chicago. With Judaic scholars Nahum Glatzer, Simon Rawidowicz, and Alexander Altmann, with philosophers Rudolf Kayser, Aron Gurewitsch, and Herbert Marcuse, and with sociologist Lewis Coser, all of whom were German-born or German-trained, Brandeis University belongs on that roster.[20]

In hiring faculty, Sachar was indifferent to the formalities of academic certification. Space permits mention of only two examples.

Liberals loved Eleanor Roosevelt — for the same reason that she provoked exceptional suspicion and scorn at the other end of the political spectrum. In the late 1930s the First Lady had shown such friendliness to young radicals that the FBI put her under surveillance. Her file eventually ran to four thousand pages. Needless to say, she was as much of a Bolshevik as were her successors, like Bess Truman or Mamie Eisenhower. The Ku Klux Klan even put a price on her head, which made her undoubtedly the only First Lady or former First Lady ever to attract a bounty for an assassin. When no longer in the White House, Eleanor Roosevelt joined the board of the NAACP, which led some newspapers to refuse to carry her syndicated column, *My Day*.[21] Her carefully calibrated but unambiguously progressive stances helped facilitate the seemingly inconceivable day when one of her successors in the White House would be Michelle Obama.

One effect of Eleanor Roosevelt's progressive reputation was the appeal that she exerted among American Jews (and vice versa). Having fully overcome the snobbery and exclusivity of the stratum into which she was born, she agreed to join the Brandeis Board of Trustees. Her interest in contributing to the welfare of the university was not thereby depleted. Because the widow of President Roosevelt had served as a delegate to the first session of the United Nations, held in London, and because she had also chaired the committee drafting the Universal Declaration of Human Rights, why not enlist her to teach a seminar on international law and organization in the Department of Politics? "She was not an intellectual force," Sachar acknowledged. "Her immense appeal was moral."[22]

Joined by political scientist Lawrence H. Fuchs, she proved herself to be a very dedicated teacher. Though a septuagenarian, she once phoned Fuchs during a blizzard to reassure him that she would still somehow make it to their seminar. "I didn't have the heart to tell her that classes had been called off," he recalled. "So I called all of our fifteen students, and I got most [of them] to show up." Fuchs drew the logical inference: "This was typical of her sense of service."[23] But what rank should such a personage hold? She refused the designation of "Professor," she told Sachar, because "I have no college degree." The modest rank of "Lecturer" was agreed upon, as was her salary of $6,500. The faculty roster in the university catalog listed full professors first, then associate professors, on down to the rank that the former First Lady held. There her name appeared, alphabetically and democratically, near the bottom.[24]

The first woman to hold a fulltime faculty position lacked a doctorate, and could not have come from a more divergent background than Eleanor Roosevelt. Born in Bern in 1899, Marie Syrkin had lived in four countries (Switzerland, Germany, Italy, and France) before she was five years old. Such was the cosmopolitan and peripatetic existence of Zionist publicists and theoreticians like her father, Nachman Syrkin. The family reached New York in 1908; and she soon added English to her command of Russian, Yiddish, German, and French. Educated at Cornell with bachelor's and master's degrees, Syrkin belonged to the group that her biographer, Carole Kessner, dubbed "the 'other' New York intellectuals." They were, unlike the circle around the *Partisan Review*, "nominatively, not nominally, Jews." They were Jews who were thinkers and writers and critics, rather than intellectuals who happened to be Jews. The "other" New York intellectuals included the Zionist and Yiddishist journalist Maurice Samuel, to whom Syrkin was very briefly married, as well as her third husband, the poet Charles Reznikoff. Like her, they sought to cultivate an American Jewish culture rather than escape from it.[25] As an editor of the Labor Zionist monthly, *Jewish Frontier*, Syrkin wrote an editorial as early as November 1942, that reported the "avowed object" of Nazi policy as "the extermination of a whole people. It is a policy of systematic murder of innocent civilians which in its ferocity, its dimensions[,] and its organization is unique in the history of mankind."[26]

Divorced from biochemist Aaron Bodansky, bearing the primary responsibility of raising their son, married to a writer who tried to consolidate a career as a scenarist across the continent, Syrkin became a New York City public school teacher and the author of *Your School, Your Children* (1944). She wrote an early postwar account of the Jewish resistance in Nazi-occupied Europe (*Blessed is the Match*), and was 51 years old when Sachar hired her in 1950 to join the Brandeis faculty. Holding the rank of assistant professor, at an initial salary of $5,500, Syrkin was the first and for a while the only female professor on campus.[27] The topics of her courses were innovative. She may have been the first faculty member at any university to offer a course in American Jewish literature. The birth of that flourishing and much-honored literary category is usually dated from 1953, when Saul Bellow published *The Adventures of Augie March*, which won the National Book Award. That was three years after Syrkin's arrival on campus. Syrkin may also have been the first academic in the United States to offer a course on "The Literature of the Holocaust."[28]

Imaginative as she was as a teacher, Syrkin was not — strictly speaking — a scholar. In 1955 her biography of her friend Golda Meir appeared. But it lacked footnotes, or a bibliography, or even an index. Five years later Syrkin's next book was published, but it was not in the field of literature, as though in defiance of the disciplinary expectations of her colleagues. It was about and by her father: *Nachman Syrkin: Socialist Zionist: A Biographical Memoir and Selected Essays*. Six years later she retired from Brandeis, at the age of 67. She died in 1988. As a Zionist activist and polemicist, Marie Syrkin might have been more logically a candidate for the field of Judaic Studies rather than for the department of literature. But her Hebrew was weak; and she always regretted her failure to pick up that language. Not learning that sixth language is also, in part, why she was able to teach at Brandeis; she was reluctant to make *aliyah*.[29]

The multi-disciplinary ideal that the new university championed was incarnated in the first chairman of the School of Social Science. Max Lerner had been born in Minsk in 1902, and came to the United States in 1907. A stellar graduate of Yale College in 1923, with a major in English, Lerner wanted to teach that subject. But his favorite professor, a Chaucer specialist, was blunt: "As a Jew, you'll never get a teaching post in literature at any Ivy League college."[30] Lerner decided to switch to the social sciences, and four years later earned a doctorate from the Brookings Graduate School of Economics and Government. He soon carved out a conspicuous career as a public intellectual, combining political journalism (the *Nation*, *PM*, the *New York Post*) with teaching (Sarah Lawrence, Williams), prior to his appointment at Brandeis in 1949. Lerner began chairing the School of Social Science two years later, and was appointed to the first named chair in the university. He also enjoyed Sachar's active support as a recruiter. Lerner persuaded sociologists Coser and Philip Rieff to leave the University of Chicago, for example, and got psychologist Abraham Maslow to leave Brooklyn College. It was Lerner who hired Fuchs. All agreed to come to an unaccredited university.[31]

"We social science majors were especially privileged," Sandy Lakoff '53, a future political scientist, recalled. "We read Max Weber with Lew Coser, Freud with Philip Rieff, [and] Kant with Aron Gurwitsch... [We read] Burckhardt on the Renaissance... and Marx with practically everyone."[32] There was a contagion of energy and ambition. In 1954, after Maslow had finished *Motivation and Personality*, Lerner ran into him and asked what he had been working on. Maslow mentioned having just written a book on values and the higher life. Lerner was dubious: "Plato already wrote that book, Abe." "Yes, Max," the humanistic psychologist replied, "but I know more than Plato did." When minds were sharp, elbows had to be as well. At one meeting of the Department of Fine Arts, its first member, the painter Mitchell Siporin, once carried on so lengthy a monologue that the chairperson suggested that the art historians also have a chance to speak. "Fine," Siporin replied, barely missing a beat. "I will speak as an art historian."[33] Gentility was evidently for Gentiles.

The liberalism that pervaded the university and that sought a more open and inclusive society was inseparable from an opposition to antisemitism, which seems to have affected virtually all the Jews of that generation.

As dean of the graduate school and then dean of the faculty, Leonard W. Levy played an early and important role in the evolution of Brandeis. But his ascent almost didn't happen. While working on his doctorate in American history at Columbia, he had been recommended for an opening at Yale, which turned him down. The historian George W. Pierson simply informed the author of the letter of recommendation, Henry Steele Commager, that a person of "Levy's background" could not be considered for a position at Yale. (By "background," Pierson presumably was not referring to Levy's military service in the recent war.) Many years later, Pierson ran into Levy at the airport in Williamsburg, Virginia, and, without introducing himself, shook Levy's hand and declared: "Young man, I once did you a grave injustice." Pierson then turned around and walked away. The first chair of the School of Science, then the first dean of the faculty, was Saul G. Cohen, who had been a star in Harvard's Department of Chemistry during the Great Depression. But opportunities did not beckon merely because of the economic distress that afflicted the nation. Though he had graduated *summa cum laude*, he "had been discouraged from pursuing graduate studies." At Harvard, Cohen recalled, he was "the only instructor in chemistry there [in that era] whose three-year appointment was ended in four months, and the only National Research Fellow who had not even been interviewed for an appropriate university faculty appointment." Private industry was about equally unpromising. Jews were unwelcome in the industrial research departments of most of the major companies, such as DuPont, Monsanto, and AT&T.[34]

One solution to the pressure of discrimination was for Jews to found their own companies, which is what Edwin H. Land did in seeking to realize his dream of instant photography. The Polaroid Corporation is how Cohen landed on his feet. He became Chief Supervisor of Chemistry at the new company, and managed to lick the problem that had eluded Land himself, which was how to make the image stable. By solving it, Cohen ensured that the cameras could go into production; and their phenomenal sales, beginning at Jordan Marsh department store in 1948, would make Land the wealthiest scientist on the planet. But Cohen could get a chance at academe, which had been his vocational dream, in part because of Land's dearest friend, Julius Silver, the chief counsel of Polaroid, as well as the nephew of Rabbi Israel Goldstein. It was Silver who was decisive in securing for the fledgling Board of Trustees the legal foundation of the new university.[35]

Any effort to assess the significance of the first phase of the history of the university must come to terms with Ludwig Lewisohn. On the initial faculty of thirteen, he was the only full professor and was the best-known as well.[36] Through him ran the currents that this essay seeks to track: the shadow of antisemitism that instigated the establishment of a Jewish-sponsored university, the cultural authority of Germany before the irrevocable pollution of Nazism; and the struggle to determine how a religious and ethnic legacy might be defined and implemented in a secular institution. The course of Lewisohn's career touched on all these themes. Born in Berlin in 1882, he and his family immigrated when he was eight — far too early to have permitted participation in Weimar culture. But he lived long enough to have achieved a fame that almost none of his Brandeis contemporaries on the initial faculty could then match. Lewisohn died on the last day of 1955,[37] and quickly vanished from the public memory of American Jewry.

He was raised in rural South Carolina and then in Charleston. His precocity was evident. At the age of fifteen, Lewisohn entered the College of Charleston and graduated four years later with a master's degree. But he was unable to win a fellowship that would have enabled him to pursue a doctorate successfully. He nevertheless left for New York, where he entered graduate school, but gave up after repeated warnings that he would not secure an academic position in English, at least in part because he was a Jew. "The mental alertness of his race," one of his professors at Columbia declared, was better deployed outside the classroom, for which Lewisohn's "alien spirit" and "an incomplete acceptance of the ideas of the English-speaking peoples" were ill-suited.[38] So he switched to German, which was his native language, and taught it at the University of Wisconsin (1910-11) and then at the Ohio State University beginning the following year. But because of his opposition to his adopted land's entry into the Great War, and because his birthplace aroused the suspicions of super-patriots, Lewisohn was fired in 1917. It was hard enough trying to gain traction as a Jew in academe, and his admiration for the *Kultur* of the Fatherland seemed to seal his fate.[39]

By the 1920s antisemitism had made Lewisohn a Jew who sharply criticized the assimilationist proclivities that he himself had so recently shared. A chasm separated Jews from others, he believed; and though he could observe the intensifying antisemitism in the United States, he never seriously contemplated *aliyah*. But Zionism was the logical destination that his dramatic self-discovery was propelling him toward. Books like *Upstream* (1922) and *The Island Within* (1928) were signs along that journey. The associate editor of the *Nation* became an editor of *New Palestine*. But the journalist and polemicist probably achieved his greatest fame as a novelist. *The Case of Mr. Crump* (1926) was not only praised by Freud, but boasted a preface by Thomas Mann. In 1949, when *The Case of Mr. Crump* was republished as a drugstore paperback, a steamier, pulp-fiction title was substituted: *The Tyranny of Sex*.[40]

At Brandeis, Lewisohn taught comparative literature. Though he authored nearly three dozen books that included critical studies of French, English, and American writing,[41] it was Germany that got the most-favored-nation treatment. For him German thought, German music, German poetry, and German scholarship represented the "highest and heavenliest realm in the domain of Western culture."[42] The translator of Rilke, Hauptmann, Brod, and Werfel, among others, Lewisohn became the first member of the faculty to publish a book — a thousand-page biography — while at Brandeis. It should come as no surprise that the subject of Lewisohn's heroic scholarship was the incarnation of the *Bildung* that German Jewry so famously prized, the writer-in-residence of the very town that gave the German experiment in republican rule its name after the defeat in the Great War: Goethe. At Brandeis Lewisohn even offered a course devoted exclusively to *Faust*.[43] He was thus ineluctably pulled back into the Enlightenment, when the German states first addressed the Jewish question. The process that began by asking whether Jews were fit to enter the salons ended a century and a half later by concluding that Jews were not fit to inhabit the earth.

Lewisohn loved Brandeis as a refuge from the casual antisemitism that blotted other campuses, and his very presence served as testimony to what an earlier generation had confronted. Nowhere else, "outside the state of Israel," were there "no anti-Semitic tensions, whether real or fancied."[44] (He did not consider the rabbinical seminaries.) Three decades after his eviction from the Big Ten, Lewisohn acknowledged that it was "a little queer...to be involved...in education and its problems again," but somehow it seemed "ever so natural." To be a teacher again, he felt, "is a good calling." Indeed he came to express his appreciation to Brandeis: "Fundamentally I have nothing but gratitude for its having been founded and being built....It has given me a place and a task for my later years more appropriate and fruitful than anything else I could have hoped for. I like teaching."[45]

By the time Lewisohn came to Brandeis, however, he had already spent many years picking at the scabs of bitterness and jealousy, while nevertheless nursing the faith that posterity would eventually elevate his work above Steinbeck's, for example. Lewisohn was also puzzled that Faulkner and Hemingway had gotten greater acclaim for books that were no better than his own. Endowed with a prickly personality, Lewisohn was firmly set in his opinions, which were fiercely high-brow. Eleanor Roosevelt was "full of goodness, no doubt," he conceded. "But every problem really begins where her thinking ends." Though an unobservant Jew, Lewisohn was obsessed with the danger of back-sliding; and of the seventy faculty members in 1951, the forty-nine whom he estimated to be Jewish included some who were succumbing to assimilation. His judgments could be acerbic. Max Lerner was "very charming, intellectually agile, cultivated, sensitive, good-humored. All that." Then Lewisohn went in for the kill, because Lerner did not realize that leftism was a delusion, a false alternative to Jewish authenticity. A victim of "Utopian escapist hopes," Lerner possessed a mind "filled with tripe. Just tripe."[46]

The intensity of Lewisohn's Jewish nationalism alienated him from an academic community that was way to his left, that tended to express the ideal of social justice in universalist terms. The historic struggle that had bewitched so many Jews to try to repair the world was worse than a mere distraction from the continuation of a distinct people under modern conditions. The fight for economic equality, from "the young Marx and [Ferdinand] Lassalle on through all the Jewish socialist leaders in Europe," Lewisohn wrote, had ended in the death camps.[47] The historical logic that he proposed would have been far more applicable to the Soviet slave labor camps than to Nazism, which deliberately repudiated the rationalist ideals of the Enlightenment. But he hoped that political radicalism had been discredited, and sensed among Brandeis undergraduates in the early 1950s "a certain mildness" that betokened the end of ideology. That dispassionate stance also meant a comfort with American society that Lewisohn could not share. His students did not seem alienated, and their "unselfconscious feeling of being at home on the American scene" bothered him. Those with the most intense ambitions, he happily noted, did seem to gravitate toward Jewish studies, however.[48]

The opening ceremonies for the founding of the university lasted for three days in October 1948. Sachar was of course the featured speaker. But Lewisohn was designated to represent the faculty, and soon became a foe of the president. Sachar wanted to see Brandeis assume its place among other non-sectarian institutions that had spun off from religious communities. Lewisohn insisted upon the divergences — "psychologically, morally, intellectually" — that Jews had historically demonstrated from their neighbors, and expected Brandeis to be the next link in the "Jewish tradition and the Jewish faith — which have never wholly yielded to the follies and the cruelties of a pagan and unredeemed world." He added that "we have always guarded the sacred flame of disinterested learning, of learning for its own sake — of learning for two things alone — consecration and wisdom."[49] But the ideological gap with his president could not be closed. Like the overwhelming majority of his co-religionists, Sachar sought the satisfactions of inclusion and respect, rather than the cultivation of difference. He believed that academic excellence would ensure civic parity and that intellectual achievement would be a way of repaying America for its many blessings. The particularity that

Lewisohn championed, Sachar saw as a step backward, into a parochialism to which few in the Jewish community subscribed.

Lewisohn therefore came to loathe "Sachar's spiritual degradation," his purported refusal to invest the university with a serious and demanding Jewish character. When the founding president was quoted in *Time* as hoping that Brandeis would not be "just another little school, but a symbol of what the Jewish people want to contribute in the intellectual world," Lewisohn sniffed shame rather than pride. He cared only for Brandeis to make a major contribution to the *Jewish* world, and believed that Sachar was pursuing a "silly and futile pretense" of downplaying the gulf between Jew and Gentile. Fortunately Lewisohn did not live long enough to read in *Time* the president's claim that Brandeis was "no more Jewish than Princeton is Presbyterian." It should be added that Sachar's refusal to honor Lewisohn as much as he considered proper also generated resentment, leaving Lewisohn feeling "unhoused, homeless, alone" — an odd complaint against a founding president who after all *found* Lewisohn a home and gave him a job.[50] But their conflict over the definition of a Jewish-sponsored, nonsectarian institution, their competing claims over the status of a minority in American society, remains unresolved.

Stephen J. Whitfield holds the Max Richter Chair in American Civilization at Brandeis University, where he has taught since 1972. He is the author, most recently, of *In Search of American Jewish Culture* (1999) and the editor, most recently, of *A Companion to Twentieth-Century America* (2004). Professor Whitfield is currently writing a political history of Brandeis University.

ENDNOTES

1   Quoted in Morton Rosenstock, *Louis Marshall, Defender of Jewish Rights* (Detroit: Wayne State University Press, 1965), 255.

2   Quoted in Marcia Graham Synnott, *The Half-Opened Door: Discrimination and Admissions at Harvard, Yale, and Princeton, 1900–1970* (Westport, CT: Greenwood, 1979), 17, 141; John Gribben and Mary Gribben, *Richard Feynman: A Life in Science* (London: Penguin, 1998), 22.

3   Quoted in Alexander Bloom, *Prodigal Sons: The New York Intellectuals and Their World* (New York: Oxford University Press, 1986), 30; Susanne Klingenstein, *Jews in the American Academy, 1900-1940: The Dynamics of Intellectual Assimilation* (New Haven: Yale University Press, 1991), 112; Diana Trilling, "Lionel Trilling: A Jew at Columbia," in Lionel Trilling, *Speaking of Literature and Society*, ed. Diana Trilling (New York: Harcourt Brace Jovanovich, 1980), 428.

4   Quoted in Nathan Reingold, "Refugee Mathematicians in the United States, 1933–1941: Reception and Reaction," in *The Muses Flee Hitler: Cultural Transfer and Adaptation, 1930–1945*, eds. Jarrell C. Jackman and Carla M. Borden (Washington, D.C.: Smithsonian Institution Press, 1983), 211, and in Dan A. Oren, *Joining the Club: A History of Jews and Yale*, 2nd ed. (New Haven, CT: Yale University Press, 2000), 281–84.

5   W.E. Burghardt Du Bois, *The World and Africa: An Inquiry into the Part Which Africa Has Played in World History* (New York: Viking, 1947), 253; Ange-Marie Hancock, "Du Bois, Race, and Diversity," in *The Cambridge Companion to Du Bois*, ed. Shamoon Zamir (New York: Cambridge University Press, 2008), 99; Lewis S. Feuer, "The Stages in the Social History of Jewish Professors in American Colleges and Universities," *American Jewish History* 71 (June 1982), 458–60, 462.

6   Edward S. Shapiro, *A Time for Healing: American Jewry since World War II* (Baltimore: Johns Hopkins University Press, 1992), 8-10; Leonard Dinnerstein, *Uneasy at Home: Antisemitism and the American Jewish Experience* (New York: Columbia University Press, 1987), 178–96.

7   Silvan S. Schweber, *Einstein and Oppenheimer: The Meaning of Genius* (Cambridge, MA: Harvard University Press, 2008), 102.

8   Quoted in Jamie Sayen, *Einstein in America: The Scientist's Conscience in the Age of Hitler and Hiroshima* (New York: Crown, 1985), 240; Israel Goldstein, *Brandeis University: Chapter of Its Founding* (New York: Bloch, 1951), 4.

9   Quoted in Goldstein, *Brandeis University*, 28.

10   Goldstein, *Brandeis University*, vii, 11, and *My World as a Jew: The Memoirs of Israel Goldstein* (New York: Herzl Press, 1984), I, 172, 173.

11   Quoted in Simon Rawidowicz, "Only from Zion: A Chapter in the Prehistory of Brandeis University" (1948), in *Israel: The Ever-Dying People and Other Essays*, ed. Benjamin C.I. Ravid (Rutherford, NJ: Fairleigh Dickinson University Press, 1986), 241; Abram L. Sachar, "Foreword" to Simon Rawidowicz, *Studies in Jewish Thought*, ed. Nahum N. Glatzer (Philadelphia: Jewish Publication Society of America, 1974), vii.

12   Quoted in Schweber, *Einstein and Oppenheimer*, 108.

13   Goldstein, *Brandeis University*, 56, 94, 96, 110, 115, and *My World as a Jew*, 182, 184; Schweber, *Einstein and Oppenheimer*, 130.

14   Martin Peretz, "Frank Manuel: An Appreciation," in *In the Presence of the Past*, eds. R.T. Bienvenu and M. Feingold (Dordrecht, Netherlands: Kluwer Academic Publishers, 1991), 5; "Builder in a Hurry," *Time* 90 (September 29, 1967), 64; David Hackett Fischer, "The Brandeis Idea: Variations on an American Theme," *Brandeis Review* 19 (Fall-Winter, 1998), 27.

15   Richard M. Freeland, *Academia's Golden Age: Universities in Massachusetts, 1945–1970* (New York: Oxford University Press, 1992), 190; Louis Kronenberger, *No Whippings, No Gold Watches: The Saga of a Writer and His Jobs* (Boston: Little, Brown, 1970), 247.

16   Sayen, *Einstein in America*, 241–44.

17   "The Jews Are Hosts," *Time* 68 (November 19, 1956), 58–59; Freeland, *Academia's Golden Age*, 188–90; "Topics of The Times: Church and College in America," *New York Times*, August 21, 1946, 26; Goldstein, *Brandeis University*, 83.

18   "Brandeis University: New Jewish-Founded School in Massachusetts Preaches and Practices Democracy," *Ebony* 7 (February 1952), 59; *From the Beginning: A Picture History of the First Four Decades of Brandeis University*, ed. Susan Pasternack (Waltham, MA: Brandeis University, 1988), 133; Goldstein, *Brandeis University*, 6, and *My World as a Jew*, 173.

19   Freeland, *Academia's Golden Age*, 192, 211–12.

20   Harry Zohn, "Brandeis University: German-Jewish Lecturers," [Association of Jewish Refugees in Great Britain] *AJR Information* 12 (April 1957), 10.

21   Lawrence H. Fuchs, "The Senator and the Lady," *American Heritage* 25 (October 1974), 83; Amanda Ripley, "The Relentless Mrs. Roosevelt," *Time* 173 (July 6, 2009), 45, 46.

22   Abram L. Sachar, *The Many Lives of Eleanor Roosevelt: An Affectionate Portrait*, Ford Hall Forum Lecture, 1963, n. p. (copy in Robert D. Farber University Archives, Brandeis University).

23   Quoted in Hannah Agran, "Just a Year Short of Half a Century," *Justice*, April 16, 2002, 15; Fuchs, "Senator and the Lady," 57.

24   Quoted in Abram L. Sachar, *A Host at Last* (Boston: Little, Brown, 1976), 48; Joseph P. Lash, *Eleanor: The Years Alone* (New York: Signet, 1973), 298, 299; Sachar, *Many Lives of Eleanor Roosevelt*, n. p.

25   Carole S. Kessner, ed., Introduction to *The "Other" New York Intellectuals* (New York: New York University Press, 1994), 10, and "Marie Syrkin: An Exemplary Life," in ibid., 52–53, 55–56, 58.

26   Quoted in Kessner, "Marie Syrkin," in *"Other" New York Intellectuals*, 61.

27   Carole S. Kessner, *Marie Syrkin: Values Beyond the Self* (Hanover, NH: University Press of New England, 2008), 396.

28   Kessner, *Marie Syrkin*, 399, 400.

29   Kessner, *Marie Syrkin*, 404, and "Marie Syrkin," in *"Other" New York Intellectuals*, 53.

30   Quoted in Sanford Lakoff, *Max Lerner: Pilgrim in the Promised Land* (Chicago: University of Chicago Press, 1998), 30.

31   Lakoff, *Max Lerner*, 153, 159; "Appointed," [Boston] *Jewish Advocate*, January 25, 1951, in "Faculty Hiring, Individual Faculty: Max Lerner Folder," George Alpert Collection, Robert D. Farber University Archives, Brandeis University; Edward Hoffman, *The Right to be Human: A Biography of Abraham Maslow* (New York: St. Martin's, 1988), 193–96.

32   Quoted in Pasternack, ed., *From the Beginning*, 42.

33   Quoted in Hoffman, *Right to be Human*, 205–6, and in Karen Klein, "The Creative Arts at Brandeis," *Brandeis Review* 19 (Fall-Winter, 1998), 38.

34   Leonard W. Levy, *A Bookish Life: The Memoir of a Writer* (Ashland, OR: Gazelle Books, 2003), 30; Saul G. Cohen, *Memoirs of Saul G. Cohen: Scientist, Inventor, Educator* (Newton, MA: Montefiore Press, 2008), 165, 221.

35   Cohen, *Memoirs of Saul G. Cohen*, 166, 167, 188, 190, 204, 207, 213; Goldstein, *Brandeis University*, viii, 20.

36   Pasternack, ed., *From the Beginning*, 7; Zohn, "Brandeis University," 10.

37   Ralph Melnick, *The Life and Work of Ludwig Lewisohn: "A Touch of Wildness"* (Detroit: Wayne State University Press, 1998), I, 13–16; Klingenstein, *Jews in the American Academy*, 88–98.

38   Quoted in Melnick, *Life and Work of Ludwig Lewisohn*, I, 299–300.

39   Melnick, *Life and Work of Ludwig Lewisohn*, I, 209–10, 216–17.

40   Ralph Melnick, *The Life and Work of Ludwig Lewisohn: "This Dark and Desperate Age"* (Detroit: Wayne State University Press, 1998), II, 388, 518; Klingenstein, *Jews in the American Academy*, 97–98.

41   Melnick, *Life and Work of Ludwig Lewisohn*, II, 373.

42   Quoted in Melnick, *Life and Work of Ludwig Lewisohn*, II, 394, 436, 456.

43   Melnick, *Life and Work of Ludwig Lewisohn*, II, 365–68, 442.

44   Quoted in Melnick, *Life and Work of Ludwig Lewisohn*, II, 439, 450; Ludwig Lewisohn in Oscar Handlin, David Riesman, Lionel Trilling et al., "Seven Professors Look at the Jewish Student," *Commentary* 12 (December 1951), 529–531.

45   Quoted in Melnick, *Life and Work of Ludwig Lewisohn*, II, 381, 475; Klingenstein, *Jews in the American Academy*, 133–34.

46   Quoted in Melnick, *Life and Work of Ludwig Lewisohn*, II, 394, 397, 410–11, 432, 510; Lewisohn in Handlin et al., "Seven Professors," 529.

47   Quoted in Melnick, *Life and Work of Ludwig Lewisohn*, II, 434–35.

48   Lewisohn in Handlin et al, "Seven Professors," 529.

49   Quoted in Melnick, *Life and Work of Ludwig Lewisohn*, II, 357–58, 359–60, 379.

50   Quoted in Melnick, *Life and Work of Ludwig Lewisohn*, II, 376, 379, 490, and in "Builder in a Hurry," *Time*, 64; "University with a Mission," *Time*, 60.

"OBJECTIONABLE TRAITS"
Antisemitism and the Hiring of Jewish Psychologists, 1920–1950

Andrew S. Winston

By the second and third decades of the 1900s, many children of the great East European Jewish migration to America entered universities, especially in eastern, urban areas. Despite the explicit or secret quotas instituted by the 1920s, a substantial number of Jewish students completed undergraduate work and entered graduate programs at Columbia, Harvard, Yale, and elsewhere. Many showed promise as researchers and aspired to an academic career. The generally homogeneous, Anglo-Saxon faculties were faced with a set of problems: Were some Jews acceptable? Did most have "objectionable traits"? Could they be placed? Or, to save face for all, could they be persuaded to change career plans before, during, or after completing graduate study? What should be said in a letter of recommendation? The management of these "difficulties" provides an important window on the history of antisemitism in American academia.

Psychology, occupying a middle ground between the humanities and the sciences, was still struggling to establish its identity as a scientific discipline in post-World War I America. As proponents of the new scientific means of assessing human beings for the army, school, and industry, psychologists of the interwar period were careful to justify their hiring decisions on "objective" grounds. During this time, Jews would come to play an important role in the emergence of modern psychology.[1] Thus the hiring of Jewish psychologists has particular historiographic significance. This chapter addresses the ways in which American psychologists generally supported, occasionally objected to, or resigned themselves to the exclusion of Jews from the discipline, particularly at Harvard and Columbia University. Their discursive practices, also common in other disciplines, show how exclusion could be managed with a veneer of politeness and the appearance of academic respectability.

JEWISH ENROLLMENT AT COLUMBIA
AND THE "EASTERN EUROPEAN HEBREWS"

In New York City, the Jewish population rose from an estimated 80,000 or under 9% in 1870 to 1.4 million or nearly 28% by 1915.[2] In contrast to the predominately German and Sephardic Jews who had arrived earlier, the immigrants of the 1880s and 1890s tended to be from Russia, Poland, Romania, and other areas of Eastern Europe. By 1909–10, the Jewish enrollment at Columbia University had reached 11.37%, rising to 32.7% in 1918–19.[3] Discussions of the "Jewish problem" began early on, and administrators began to see Jewish enrollment as a threat. In 1914, Dean Frederick Keppel described the problem:

> By far the majority of the Jewish students who do come to Columbia are desirable students in every way. What most people regard as a racial problem is really a social problem. The Jews who have had the advantages of decent social surroundings for a generation or two are entirely satisfactory companions... their presence in the classroom is distinctly desirable. There are indeed, Jewish students of another type who have not had the social advantages of their more fortunate fellows.[4]

In private correspondence, Keppel noted that "ill prepared and uncultured Jews" were transferring to Columbia from City College.[5] These "uncultured Jews" were not likely to be the children of the established, assimilated German Jews, but the children of the Eastern European Jews of the Lower East Side. They were described in the popular press, in religious tracts, in fiction, and in academic works with a long list of "objectionable traits": they were covetous, criminal, dishonest, crude, carping, greedy, speculative, ostentatious, materialistic, ugly, unclean, ill-mannered, clannish, self-defensive, cowardly, unpatriotic, and unwilling to assimilate.[6]

In his widely read *The Old World in the New* (1914), reproduced in part in the *Century* magazine, University of Wisconsin sociologist E. A. Ross made some positive remarks about family life and social spirit among Jews. But he went on to describe East European Jews as generally immoral, unethical, and criminal due to their "inborn love of money-making."[7] They were "slippery" businessmen who were likely to burn a property to collect insurance, declare bankruptcy to avoid debts, and were prone to "pursue Gentile girls." With their "monstrous and repulsive love of gain," Jews used their "shove and wile" to achieve a position of "prosperous parasitism."[8]

Ross also argued that Jewish interest in education merely reflected acquisitiveness. Jews were not brighter than other groups, merely more hardworking, or in modern terms, "overachievers."[9] This theme was also a major concern at Columbia, as indicated by Dean Hawkes in 1918:

> We have honestly attempted to eliminate the lowest grade of applicant and it turns out that a good many of the low grade men are New York City Jews. It is a fact that boys of foreign parentage, who have no background in many cases attempt to educate themselves beyond their intelligence. Their accomplishment is over 100% of their ability on account of their tremendous energy and ambition.[10]

Increased applications allowed President Butler to argue that Columbia College had reached the limit of its facilities, and a new selection process was introduced based on "personality" and "promise" as well as academic record.[11] By 1919, applicants were required to submit letters of recommendation and a photograph, indicate religious affiliation, be interviewed if possible, and take an intelligence test.[12] So strong was the belief that Jews were "overacheivers" that it was thought that an intelligence test would eliminate many Jewish applicants. Similar screening efforts at other schools, including explicit or secret quotas, soon followed.[13] Jewish enrollment at Columbia declined after 1919 to 18–20% in 1924, rose again during the early 1930s, and declined to 10–12%, a level that many universities ultimately found "comfortable." At Harvard, President Lowell was unable to institute a quota, but by 1925 was able to change the selection criteria to emphasize "character and fitness." Harvard's Jewish enrollment had risen from 4.35% in 1908–09 to 27.6% in 1920–30, but fell to 16.05% by 1934–35.

By the late 1800s and early 1900s it was clear that placing Jews in faculty positions would be problematic if not impossible. Particularly in English literature, where an Anglo-Saxon background was deemed essential, Jewish graduate students since the early 1900s were politely counselled to shift career plans or leave the program.[14] At the turn of the century, the founding members of psychology considered some Jews acceptable, but their numbers were very small. Still, the seventh and ninth presidents of the American Psychological Association (APA), Hugo Münsterberg and Joseph Jastrow, were known to be of Jewish origin. Not all reaction was positive; James McKeen Cattell, the head of psychology at Columbia and editor of *Science,* wrote to Columbia President Seth Low that Jastrow "had the merits and defects of the Jewish race to a very marked degree."[15] William James treated Jewish graduate students at Harvard, such as Boris Sidis and Morris Cohen, well, although he did not believe it was possible to place them in academic positions. G. Stanley Hall was encouraging to his Jewish graduate students at Clark, and hired at least three Jewish faculty.[16]

While some leading psychologists held liberal views with regard to Jews, by the early 1920s the general societal climate had changed considerably. Fueled by popular accounts of the mental, moral, and social deficiencies of the Eastern European Jews, descriptions linking Jews to Bolshevism, the increased popularity of racial theory, and the spread of international Jewish conspiracy theories by Henry Ford and others, open discrimination against Jews in all realms of employment became a common feature of American life. Jewish faculty were rare and generally unwelcome; according to Leonard Dinnerstein, total Jewish liberal arts and sciences faculty in American universities numbered less than 100 during the mid-1920s.[17]

LETTERS OF RECOMMENDATION[18]

Letters for Jewish psychologists reveal commonly held conceptions of "Jewish traits" that were used to separate Jews into socially acceptable and unacceptable categories, an important distinction in the 1920s through the 1940s. As a matter of academic obligation, it was thought necessary to state whether the candidate was, or might be, a Jew, and had the "objectionable traits" commonly expected in Jews. These "traits" were often unspecified or described in vague terms such as "personal unpleasantness," suggesting a shared understanding of the dangers in admitting Jews to the socioculturally homogeneous professoriate.

By 1925, leading Harvard psychologist Edwin G. Boring (1886–1968) was well established at Harvard as the chair of the de facto "Psychology Department," which had not yet been separated from philosophy.[19] A major figure in American psychology, Boring felt a special responsibility for placing graduate students, and his letters of reference were careful and detailed. In a letter to Stanford psychologist Lewis Terman, he described 10 candidates, noting that there were substantial openings that year. Ranked last was Gilbert Joseph Rich, who received his PhD under Boring's mentor, E.B. Titchener at Cornell:

> You would get a good and enthusiastic worker cheap in Dr. G.J. Rich at the University of Pittsburgh, but I most emphatically do not recommend him, because he has some of the personal unpleasantnesses that are usually associated with Jews.[20]

Boring was somewhat milder regarding Rich when he gave evaluations of ten possible candidates to Stevenson Smith of the University of Washington. He stated that Rich had not received a permanent post at Pittsburgh "because of his race" and was therefore studying medicine.[21] Boring added that Rich had "many good points, and if race is not final with you, there is time for me to write you fully about him."

The nexus between issues of antisemitism and collegiality is illuminated by examining the contrasting cases of Abraham Aaron Roback and Kurt Lewin. These cases help us understand how the personal characteristics of the "bad Jew" were seen as bound up with Jewish identity, which was often, but not universally, conceived as racial. This conception may be set against the "good Jew" or "noble Jew," a literary figure dating at least from Gotthold Lessing's *Nathan der Weise* of 1799. The "good Jew," through some combination of heredity, background, and experience, had escaped the "defects" of Jewishness, and might be an acceptable colleague.

ROBACK AND "DEFENSIVE AGGRESSIVENESS"

On April 22, 1925, Boring answered a request from J.H. White at Pittsburgh to recommend candidates for an opening. Boring described 12 candidates; fifth was A.A. Roback, a 1917 Harvard PhD and prolific scholar: "Dr. A.A. Roback... is a Jew with some of the defects of his race, although much better than Rich. He certainly ought to place somewhere."[22] To R. H. Wheeler of the University of Kansas, he ranked Roback fifth of eight, and noted that he "has not placed because he is a Jew, and his inferiority sometimes expresses itself in aggression."[23] In the same letter, Boring implied that there were important distinctions among Jews: he placed Nathaniel Hirsch above Roback, noting that Hirsch "is a Jew but doesn't show it much." When Madison Bentley asked Boring to recommend someone for a one-year appointment, he specified that the candidate "should fit without friction of adjustment into the work of the department." Boring recommended three candidates and added:

> If you did not specify an anti-friction surface, I should suggest the eminent Roback, who remains perpetually unplaced. Why not? He knows psychology. What matter if he knows more than you, and tells you so every day?[24]

Thus Roback was perceived as "aggressive" and likely to disrupt collegial harmony. Not all the Harvard faculty agreed. Herbert Langfeld, who moved to Princeton in 1924, referred to Roback as "a Jew of the best sort," implying that there were Jews who were not.[25] Boring noted that Roback had "some of the defensive aggressiveness that one so often finds in Jews."[26] Although Boring used the term "race" for Jews, as was the common practice, he did not support an hereditary interpretation of the "problem":

> As a psychologist I do not myself believe that there is any inherited Jewish temperament. It seems rather that the basis for the common prejudice against the race is a psychological result of the prejudice: Jews find themselves discriminated against and seek to combat what they feel to be an unjust social inferiority by an aggressiveness which increases rather than diminishes the prejudice.[27]

When describing E.G. Wever and Karl Zener for a position at Pittsburgh, Boring noted that "they are both good 100% Nordics, and in discussing them one discusses merits rather than defects (which is perhaps a bit unusual)."[28] Nordic character was contrasted with the presumed defects of Jews: in parallel letters to William J. Robbins of the National Research Council, sent three weeks apart, Boring recommended two candidates for Biological Science Fellowships. One was presented as a "pleasant agreeable 'Nordic'" with "no eccentricities or defects of personality," and the other described as "...a Jew. He is a fairly tactful Jew, with a personality which stresses intellectual enthusiasm to such an extent that one is likely to forget the little deferential mannerisms."[29] Jewishness might be counted as a special defect and enumerated along with other defects. For a nonacademic research position with Carney Landis, Boring described a brilliant young woman as "having certain obvious defects for the normal academic job.... She is a Jewess. She is not beautiful. Her voice is very bad." Landis judged her "overqualified" and did not hire her.[30]

So strong was the obligation to identify Jews that it might override other obligations or principles. Thus Karl Dallenbach wrote to Boring regarding a fellowship candidate, "I suppose it is un-American to report that he is of Jewish extraction, but since this is a personal letter I think I should in fairness to you and to him mention the fact."[31] Dallenbach's candid admission suggests that the practices regarding Jews were not universally considered appropriate. Like others, Boring used the contrastive conjunction, "he is a Jew, *but...*" followed by a description of how the personality traits expected in Jews were absent in this particular case. Other psychologists used similar constructions: regarding Abraham Maslow, Hulsey Cason wrote to Robert Yerkes, "Although he is a Jew, I can assure you that he does not have *any* of the objectionable characteristics for which the race is famous." Clark Hull was initially less positive about Maslow: "He is definitely Jewish, with the characteristic Jewish eagerness," but softened this assessment a few sentences later by noting that "his personality is rather attractive."[32] Nearly identical phrases were used in other disciplines. If any sign of the "objectionable traits" were present, it was important to note that the person might *not* be a Jew.[33] Boring repeatedly denied that H.E. Israel was a Jew and offered his observations of Israel's interpersonal behavior in support. Shortly after Boring's assurances, Israel obtained a permanent post at Smith College. Similar assurances were required for Harry Helson, whose personal characteristics, such as talkativeness, raised suspicions.[34]

Even when Boring did *not* identify a candidate as a Jew, antisemitism was sufficiently strong in some departments that suspicion of Jewishness might override his recommendations. J.S. Moore wrote to Boring to complain that his department at Western Reserve had missed the opportunity to hire Harry DeSilva because:

> ...the K.K.K.'s in our Faculty feared he might be a Jew (!), or even a Catholic (!!), though pretty sure he was not a negro (!!!), so we lost him. My good colleagues are excellent and lovable persons, but sometimes a little trying! They do not care what kind of a Protestant a man is, or if he has no religion at all (as is the case with most of them), but a Jew or a Catholic are anathema.[35]

Given this context, the case of Roback was particularly problematic. Roback was widely known to be a very "difficult" person with both his family and colleagues. Yet Boring continued to respect Roback's prodigious intellect ("He has really an excellent head") and wide-ranging knowledge. Despite an enormous scholarly output, Roback did not obtain a permanent academic appointment until he joined the faculty at Emerson College in the late 1940s.[36] Although Boring expressed the wish that "we could find a place where his brains counted for more than his personality," he could not realistically have considered this possible, especially after the onset of the Depression.[37]

KURT LEWIN
AND THE MITIGATION OF THE "DEFECT"

In terms of the social perception of character, the case of noted social psychologist Kurt Lewin contrasts sharply with that of Roback.[38] Boring first met Lewin at the 1929 International Congress (held at Yale University) and invited him to Cambridge. His favorable early impression and positive reports from Germany encouraged Boring to recommend Lewin to Lewis Terman as a replacement for Walter Miles: "Just at present I should say that Lewin is the best young foreigner.... If you could move him it would be a distinguished appointment." Two months later, he continued: "Lewin is anything but self-important after the German manner; he seems like a youngster, a pleasant youngster who wants you to like him."[39]

"Is Lewin a Jew?" asked Terman.[40] Boring responded that he was uncertain, and called up his wife to discuss the issue. He wrote to Terman:

> ...we talked about it at length just now, and our collected judgment is that he probably is a Jew—though God forbid we impute any damning attribution to him if it be false. Köhler's crowd has tended to be Jewish and Köhler himself has been a suspect. Lewin was so jolly and gay with us that we never thought of such a thing. I don't think that anyone could say that he was obviously Jewish in appearance.[41]

Boring was still uncertain until Carroll Pratt, Boring's colleague at Harvard, returned from Germany with more information, which Boring passed on to Terman:

> In the first place Lewin is a Jew. Pratt was astonished when I said I had been in doubt. Also the wife is a Jew and their child, who has figured in some of the movies of Lewin's child psychology, is "a perfect little Yid."[42]

Although the disturbing characterization of Lewin's child is probably Pratt's rather than Boring's, it illustrates how the entire family of the job candidate might enter into the assessment.

Terman made it clear that he had no difficulties with Jews who did *not* show any of the "objectionable traits usually ascribed to Jews." His observation that if Lewin was a Jew, it would not necessarily be "fatal" for hiring him, suggests the possibility of exemption for a Jew with acceptable characteristics. Whatever reservations Terman may have had about Lewin were apparently dispelled after Lewin spent the summer and fall of 1932 at Stanford. By 1933, when it was clear that he should not stay in Germany after the dismissal of Jewish faculty there, Lewin was able to enlist the help of both Boring and Terman in finding a position in America. Boring sent out 26 letters to prominent psychologists, asking about temporary employment. Boring did not expect much help, and the response bore out his fears, as he reported to Terman:

> From my twenty-six letters I have had thirteen replies and no immediate suggestions. There are vague things, like Tolman's suggestion that I find a rich Jew in Boston to pay him a salary, presumably while at Harvard. Nafe says Wheeler might help him, but Wheeler says Nothing.[43]

Lewin's extraordinary personal qualities helped to mitigate the "defect" of Jewishness. But even Lewin's charm was insufficient to produce an offer of a permanent academic appointment in a psychology department.[44]

Although Lewin was extraordinarily well-liked, apparently he did not have *all* of the qualities desired in a colleague. Terman noted to Boring that "Lewin is more like a mid-western American in personality and lacks the poise and dignity that distinguish Köhler and Koffka."[45] Lewin's informal, enthusiastic and expressive manner was not the repertoire of stern formality of a proper German professor, a persona developed to near-comic proportions by Hugo Münsterberg at Harvard. Eric Trist recalled Lewin "gesticulating and talking excitedly" to Frederic Bartlett on a visit to Cambridge in August, 1933.[46] Even in America, "gesticulating excitedly" was not considered the demeanor of an ideal colleague, and was consistent with common stereotypes of Jews.[47]

Boring's efforts to help Lewin were undoubtedly sincere. He was equally sincere in his attempts to help Saul Rosenzweig (PhD Harvard, 1932) and Jerome D. Frank (PhD Harvard, 1934), while identifying both as Jews for some positions but not for others.[48] As the Depression deepened, Boring despaired of helping anyone find a position, a situation that did not change until the post-war boom in psychology. In 1936–37, Heinz Werner had a visiting professorship at Harvard, but in April 1937 Boring wrote to Lewin:

> I am distressed and worried about Werner...what in the world am I to do about Werner, since there is no other job for him here when Allport shall have come back and resumed his entire salary?[49]

Thus Boring lent his influence and effort for individual Jewish psychologists, while *usually* satisfying his obligation for "full disclosure." With émigré scholars as Lewin and Werner, the task of finding employment was doubly difficult. The success of émigrés in finding suitable academic employment was highly variable.[50] In cases such as that of Werner, who did not receive a regular faculty appointment until the 1947 invitation to Clark, it is not possible to assess the relative contributions of the Depression, foreignness, and Jewishness. Foreign-born Jewish women such as Charlotte Bühler suffered triple marginalization, and it is not surprising that they fared particularly poorly in the search for academic jobs.[51]

ROBERT S. WOODWORTH'S LETTERS
OF REFERENCE IN THE 1930S

In the early twentieth century, Columbia University was more important than Harvard as a training ground for new psychologists, producing APA presidents, heads of departments and prominent researchers.[52] Many Columbia graduate students were supervised by Robert S. Woodworth, administrative head of psychology from 1911 to 1926 and APA president in 1914.[53] A letter of reference from Robert S. Woodworth carried considerable weight, particularly during the difficult job market of the Depression.[54] One 1939 letter to Sidney Pressey began:

> Dr. Aaron Nadel who is a candidate for a position with you is, as his name indicates, a Jew, but I am sure you would find him a very satisfactory colleague...cooperative and eager to fit into the group.[55]

A year later, he wrote to Gladys Tallman regarding another of his students:

> Dr. Heinz Ansbacher wishes to offer himself as a candidate for one of your Fellowships. I know him quite well and would recommend him heartily. Among our Jewish graduates he has about the best social background....I have never seen any objectionable traits.[56]

Like Boring, Woodworth felt obliged to indicate the candidate's group membership. But early in his career, Woodworth warned against drawing conclusions based on group averages. In *Science* in 1910, he argued against the popular concept of *type*, such as a "typical Englishman or Frenchman." Woodworth continued to promote a balanced view of nature and nurture for intelligence and personality. In the 1934 edition of his introductory psychology textbook, he argued that the continuous distribution of characteristics made dichotomized categorizations of personality "bad science."[57] During this period, Woodworth encouraged research on racial differences that contradicted prevailing racial theories. This research was carried out by one of his Jewish graduate students, Otto Klineberg, who later joined the Columbia faculty.[58]

In his published work, Woodworth did not discuss Jews *per se*. But in his lecture notes of the 1930s, under the topic of "Race Problems," Woodworth kept a page of quotations from Albert Einstein's 1934 *The World As I See It*, describing the distinct nature of Jewish identity. In his comments, Woodworth referred to Jewry as a "worldwide institution," and a "nation," and it is in this context that the difficulty arises:

>...It is the attempt to perpetuate this institution, this nation within other nations, that creates the Jewish Problem. Can a modus vivendi be worked out which will enable the Jews to maintain their solidarity as an institutionalized group, "sticking together," and "helping each other" as against outsiders, and which will be acceptable to mankind as a whole?[59]

Thus Jews were categorized as a clannish "race," and were at least partly to blame for the "Jewish Problem." Woodworth's notes continued under "Social Science and Social Welfare":

>...the Jews...are determined to maintain their group solidarity while intermingled with gentile populations. Though opposed to "patriotism" of the localized nations, and strong supporters of internationalism, they are extremely loyal to their own group and patriotic in this sense. Must this tendency be accepted as basic in a theory of general welfare? Can a theory of maximum human welfare be worked out that accepts this situation as fundamental? If so, what concessions are necessary from the gentile populations and can they be persuaded to make them? If it is not so, can the Jews be persuaded to abandon their long tradition of being a "separate people" and allow themselves to be merged in the general population?[60]

Here Woodworth introduced themes that are often found in antisemitic discourse since the Civil War. The stereotype of Jews as "unpatriotic" was epitomized by songs and jingles describing efforts of Jews to avoid service during both World Wars. In contrast to true Americans, the Jews were said to suffer from "internationalism," a term that carried connotations of Bolshevism and, in the 1920s, the more sinister connotations portrayed in Henry Ford's "The International Jew."[61] The necessity for Jews to disappear by "merging" is one of the oldest themes of Christian-Jewish relations, rooted in the view that Jews must accept Christ and be forgiven to complete the mission of Christianity. But Woodworth placed his own seemingly even-handed stamp on the issue, by asserting that either or both groups must compromise in order to resolve intergroup tension. Thus Woodworth occasionally ignored his own 1910 warning on group generalizations, and did so with an absence of data, which was uncharacteristic of his scholarship.

"IMPOSSIBLE TO PLACE YOU"

In a 1994 interview, Heinz Ansbacher, a graduate student under Wood-worth in the mid-1930s, reported that Woodworth showed no signs of antisemitism toward him, and that they never discussed how being Jewish might affect Ansbacher's job opportunities. He was, however, not surprised that Woodworth would identify him as a Jew in letters.[62] Otto Klineberg described Woodworth as "a constant source of help and encouragement."[63] But Woodworth was not always encouraging. The unpublished diary of Daniel Harris, who received his PhD at Columbia in 1931, notes in his entry for November 22, 1934, that "about May 1929, I had gotten a severe blow when Woodworth told me I couldn't be his assistant in survey the following year because I was Jewish and that I shouldn't be too hopeful in an academic career."[64]

This pattern was repeated elsewhere. Theodore Sarbin reported that in 1937 at Ohio State, Harold E. Burtt, the longtime chair of the department, called him in to discuss his progress:

> He wanted me to know that it would be virtually impossible to place me in an academic job because I was Jewish, even though it was the department's policy to find academic jobs for all its doctoral students. To his knowledge, only two or three members of the APA were Jewish. He went on to assure me that, personally, he was not prejudiced, but departments of psychology in universities and colleges recruited mainly gentile, white males, especially since jobs were scarce in the middle of the Great Depression. He wanted me to know the facts and not to labor under any illusions about becoming an academic. Because he was interested in my welfare, he urged me to consider other options.[65]

It is the face-saving expression of interest in the *student's* welfare, and the denial of personal bias, that are particularly noteworthy. However, the recommendation to abandon academic aspirations was not always suspiciously for the benefit of the advisor; sometimes this guidance came from Jewish psychologists who had themselves experienced employment difficulties. Heinz Ansbacher recalled that Morris Viteles, the eminent industrial psychologist, advised him that an academic job would be "impossible;" nevertheless, Ansbacher ultimately secured a tenured position at the University of Vermont.[66]

Some warnings came even before graduate study began: Boring warned Jacob Levine that he had been unable to place some of his best students because they were Jewish and that if Levine came to Harvard, it should be for "an intellectual adventure" with no hope of academic employment.[67] Much of the correspondence of the period implied that Jews could be reliably identified. The issue was, however, by no means so clear, as the correspondence of both Woodworth and Boring reveals. There was, as indicated above, a reliance on names and appearance, and when this strategy failed, one asked one's colleagues. For example, Woodworth wrote to Dashiell regarding Harry B. Gertwagen: "You may wish to know whether he is Jewish. Nobody here seems to know. I should judge, rather, that he is rather of straight German ancestry."[68]

In the face of these ambiguities of identification, many Jewish students were confronted with a classic dilemma of life outside the ghetto: to pass or not to pass as a gentile. As Seymour Sarason put it, "When in 1938 I applied for admission to graduate school, the knotty question was whether or not I would lie about being Jewish."[69] Some, after suffering substantial and obvious discrimination, chose to change their names. Isadore Krechevsky, later David Krech, found that he would not even be considered for a position at the University Heights campus of NYU, an incident that much angered his supervisor, E. C. Tolman.[70] In Europe, conversion to Christianity helped to open the gates of academia for some, as it may have for Hugo Münsterberg, who converted to Protestantism when a young man in Germany.[71] But there was always the danger that the stigma might not be so easily shed. Münsterberg, generally known and vilified during World War I as a German, was still referred to as "a very offensive German Jew" by President Butler of Columbia.[72]

For others, the choice was obvious: find a career in the youthful and as yet amorphous field of pre-World War II clinical psychology, where antisemitism seemed less of an issue than in academe, and the possibilities for employment seemed better.[73] Many Jewish psychologists from Columbia, such as Aaron Nadel and David B. Klein, took this path during the 1930s, as did a number of psychologists from Harvard. But even in clinical psychology, the presence of Jews caused concern. In 1945, the premier issue of the *Journal of Clinical Psychology* carried an editorial by Frederick Thorne. After a lengthy review of recent developments in the field, Thorne urged that the discipline avoid:

> undue representation of any one racial group among those accepted for training. Perhaps because of long racial experience with suffering and personality problems, certain groups of students show an unusual interest and propensity for psychological science.... While disclaiming racial intolerance, it nevertheless seems unwise to allow any one group to dominate or take over any clinical specialty as has occurred in several instances. The importance of clinical psychology is so great for the total population that the profession should not be exploited in the interests of any one group in such a manner that the public acceptance of the whole program is jeopardized.[74]

Identification of this "one group" was hardly necessary. This fear of Jewish "domination" echoes the fear expressed thirty years earlier that Columbia University would be "overrun" with Jews and resonated with older fears that the presence of Jews in any but very small numbers is cause for alarm and for the invocation of exclusionary social policies. What had changed by 1946 was that Thorne's editorial was met with vigorous protest. Woodworth defended Thorne, a former Columbia graduate student, while Boring rejected Thorne's position completely.

"IT SIMPLY CANNOT BE HELPED"

Boring felt his "hands tied" in the case of his Jewish graduate students. Leo Hurvich, who received his PhD in 1937, was repeatedly rejected for academic positions. The extent of the problem is indicated by a letter Boring received from Samuel Fernberger, whom Boring had known since graduate school. Fernberger, known to be Jewish by his colleagues, served as APA secretary and treasurer. On May 4, Boring wrote to Fernberger recommending Hurvich for a one-year position at the University of Pennsylvania, noting: "of course he is a Jew. I do not think that we have a trace of anti-semitism here in the Department anywhere, except as against the great problem of placing Jews."[75] Fernberger replied on May 20:

> Both Twitmeyer and I are convinced that he is the best person available for this particular job and that he has better qualifications and interests than we could have hoped for. But I am extremely sorry to say that we cannot ask him to come.... We cannot ask him simply and solely because of his Jewish background. And you will realize the situation when you remember that Viteles and I are both in the Department. We simply, as a department cannot afford to take on another even for an annual appointment...it simply cannot be helped no matter how much we all regret the situation.[76]

Thus Fernberger and Viteles, both Jews, could "not afford" another Jew in the department. Given the commonly held stereotype that Jews would "stick together" and hire other Jews, it is likely that they feared such accusations from colleagues and administrators.[77]

Boring continued the discussion of Hurvich's case in a letter to Calvin S. Hall at Western Reserve the next year. He noted, "You get to a stage where you hesitate to recommend him again because you feel sure that people will refuse him and you might as well spend your time on a more potentially acceptable man."[78] He listed three reasons why Jews were rejected:

(1) They do not appoint Jews because they are Jews. Word magic.

(2) They do not appoint difficult personalities, and that includes competent bright men who, because of frustration, are too aggressive. The incidence of that personality is higher among bright competent Jews than among burght (sic) competent gentiles because (1) and (2) constitute a vicious circle, the two working by mutual catalysis in the world at large.

(3) They do not appoint Jews or encourage them into graduate work because they are afraid of the difficulty of placement after the present job is done.

Boring implied that only (1) was genuine antisemitism and argued that some faculty at Harvard fell into this category, while other faculty, such as R.B. Perry, "like Jews per se and lean over in favor of them."[79] He did not require any systematic evidence that bright Jews were more likely to be aggressive, despite his dedicated empiricist stance on psychological issues. Nor did Boring sense the terrible bind created by his assumption of a correlation between talent and aggressiveness in Jews: those who most deserved an academic appointment on intellectual grounds were, by implication, most likely to deserve exclusion on personal grounds. Given the importance of achieving a favorable ranking in Boring's letters, it would have required extraordinary social skills for a Jewish graduate student to demonstrate intellectual superiority over other students while at the same time appearing sufficiently modest and unaggressive.

Once the student was admitted to graduate work, there is no evidence that Boring ever discussed these aspects of the search for employment. Leo Hurvich recalled no discussions with Boring on antisemitism and his job prospects (personal communication, May 22, 1997). In the 1940s, Hurvich was told by a friend at another institution that Boring had written he was a "likeable Jew," and he was at least pleased that Boring viewed him positively, which was not discernable from Boring's restrained interactions. Hurvich was not a member of the "aggressive group," such as Roback and Rich, and Boring viewed Hurvich's treatment as completely unfair.

It might be thought that by 1941, Hurvich and others would not have faced the barriers of the previous two decades. But general antisemitism in America continued to increase during the 1930s *and* during World War II. Opinion polls during this period suggested that two thirds of Americans believed Jews to be "mercenary, clannish, pushy, crude, and domineering."[80]

Although Nazi persecution created some sympathy, the proportion of survey respondents who believed that Jews "had too much power" or "are a menace to Americans" increased substantially during the war. In academia, Jews remained associated not only with "objectionable traits" but with political radicalism, a most unwelcome attribute to university administrators who scrutinized new faculty appointments.

The general climate for hiring Jews changed substantially in the late 1940s, and general antisemitism continued to decline (but not disappear) in the 1950s and 1960s.[81] It is often said that collective guilt over the Holocaust made discrimination in hiring unfashionable, but supply and demand also played a significant role. In academia, the situation changed quite suddenly, and Boring could now write to C. A. Dickinson of the University of Maine that jobs were plentiful and candidates in short supply.

In this postwar climate, so many Jews were hired and achieved prominence in psychology that the history of earlier discrimination could easily be forgotten. This relaxation of barriers was general in academia, and occurred even for the teaching of English literature and American history, areas for which an Anglo-Saxon background was previously considered an absolute necessity. However, Boring continued to identify Jews in letters in the 1940s and early 1950s. When recommending Silvan Tomkins for a job at UCLA, Boring wrote:

> Tomkins is a Jew. I am sure of that, although I never think about it except when I am writing letters of this sort. He has been a delightful person to have in the laboratory, a keen well-informed man with a good sense of humor. He has recently been married, not to a Jewess. I think he has some outside means.[82]

Concerns over Jews continued at other universities. David Bakan received his PhD at Ohio State in 1948, but not without difficulty. Bakan recalled that noted philosopher and Vienna Circle member Gustav Bergmann objected to his marriage:

> Bergmann was a refugee who was deeply wounded in his soul by the Nazis. I have seen many such people but Bergmann's injury was the worst I have seen. He had become profoundly anti-Jewish. He renounced his Judaism.... His view was that the only way the Jews could prevent repetition of their various historical persecutions was in a relentless assimilation. This meant that no Jew should ever marry a Jew. Millie and I became of great interest to him. We should not be married. He told her how she had a great career ahead of her as a philosopher, and that being married to me was impedance.[83]

Bakan's supervisor, noted learning theorist Kenneth Spence, tried to dissuade him from pursuing an academic career. After taking his PhD written exam, Bakan noted:

> Weeks went by but I heard nothing. A kind of strange silence began to surround me. Finally, I approached Spence and asked. He told that I had done very well. However, he decided not to enter the results in the record, and that I would be asked to leave. He also told me that he had hoped I would fail the exam and that would have been that. Furthermore, he told me that I was only at the 85th percentile of graduate students, and that was not enough. As a Jew I would have to be at the 95th percentile. It was true that they had given a number of degrees to Jews but, he said, that was all the more reason, because of the saturation, he did not want to give the impression that he was turning out too many Jewish PhDs. He told me how sorry he was.[84]

By the early 1950s, the statement "…is a Jew," had become much less acceptable. In some circles, Jewish identity was flagged in a less direct way. Letters sometimes mentioned the candidate's need to take time off for religious holidays. Such an approach permitted the writer and recipient to treat the problem as a practical barrier, rather than an issue of hiring Jews *per se*. In 1953, Boring recommended a student for graduate study who "did excellent work against certain handicaps, that is to say, he missed all of the Saturday discussions in the course because of religious scruples about working on Saturday…" The word "Jew" does not appear.[85]

CONCLUSIONS

The letters discussed here reveal and exemplify the discursive production of "The Jew" as a social object. This abstracted conception served a variety of functions. As a prototype against which candidates might be assessed, it provided the means to judge the degree of "Jewishness" and thereby the degree of unsuitability of the candidate. When socially undesirable traits or habits were noticed, such as loudness, aggressiveness, excessive talk, or argumentativeness, these actions could then be interpreted as the unfortunate but expected characteristics of the race. The belief that there were indeed exceptions to the pattern of objectionable Jewish traits, those who by some combination of nature and social experience had escaped this stain, allowed a face-saving self-assessment for those making the selection. As long as a few socially acceptable, highly assimilated Jews were permitted, then the judgment could be said to rest on the candidate's social behavior, deemed relevant for successful work with both students and colleagues. If exclusion was based on personal attributes, it could not be said to be based on the general condemnation of Jews as religion or race. And if the Jewish graduate student *chose* a career in clinical or industrial psychology, then bias could be more readily denied.

The selection processes from graduate school on would have favored those assimilated Jews with no involvement in Jewish observance or Jewish community life. As Jerome Bruner noted in his autobiography:

> ...to the idealistic young Jew who 'makes it' at Harvard, another symptom may be added to the Harvard disease. If he does not have a good immune system, he turns into a simulated Wasp: Wasp wife, Wasp tastes, even Wasp sports.[86]

The personal cost of concealing Jewish identity, a very common feature of life through the 1950s, can only be guessed. For many who had been reared in secularized American families, there was little to conceal.

David Hollinger argued that it was the influx of secularized Jews into postwar academia that transformed so many disciplines. For Hollinger, this process was part of the "de-Christianization" and secularization of American intellectual life and the decline of the Protestant hegemony.[87] But in psychology, some features of this change had already taken place. The prominent psychologists of the early twentieth century were already highly secularized; many had abandoned plans to enter the ministry or rejected religion altogether. These psychologists sought a universalistic description of human life which transcended cultural and historical particulars. By contrast, A.A. Roback, with his deep commitment to Yiddish culture and Jewish organizations, represented the kind of "parochial Jew" who would be seen as unsuitable for the new science of behavior. While even secularized Jews were denied entry in the 1930s, their "cosmopolitanism" would be an asset for their acceptance in the 1950s.

For some historians, particularly John Higham, the increasing resistance to Jewish entry into academia during the 1920s and 1930s and diminished opposition after the war are simply part of the more general history of competition among immigrant groups, arriving at different times and under different economic climates, advancing in status at different rates.[88] Higham located the problem of antisemitism as a theme within American nativism, i.e., militantly defensive nationalism aroused by the belief that alien elements were intruding and threatening the life of the nation. Nativism, he argued, would surge and recede according to the social and economic crises facing society, and racial nativism was a variation of this theme. From this perspective, the increasing interest of many psychologists in "race psychology" from the early 1900s to the early 1930s was part of this general trend. Thus many psychologists were particularly likely to see Jews in racial terms, and to think of their "objectionable traits" within that framework.[89] The case of E.G. Boring shows that it was not necessary to take a hereditary position on alleged Jewish traits in order to participate in a system of identification and exclusion. As American psychologists shifted away from instinct theories and race psychology in the 1930s, biological interpretations of Jewish characteristics were less likely, but the perceived threat of Jews to academic group harmony remained.

Although attuned to the alleged "objectionable traits" of Jews, E.G. Boring and Robert S. Woodworth were not bigots. Boring was a sponsor of the 1938 Harvard Committee to Aid German Student Refugees, whose pamphlet was subtitled: "Harvard's Book for Religious, Racial, and Political Tolerance: Expressing Opposition to Nazi Persecution."[90] A person of Boring's character, convictions, and Quaker background could never think of himself as antisemitic. Woodworth viewed himself as an opponent of rigid racial categorization and hierarchies. Nevertheless, both shared some of the prevailing stereotypes and antisemitic discursive practices of the times. To use Kuklick's characterization of the Harvard philosophers in the early 20th century, "they participated in, and therefore in some measure reinforced, a vicious system of prejudice."[91] This system was not confined to academic psychology or philosophy. The grammatical form of the letters of reference, "he is a Jew, but...," was remarkably constant across disciplines, and the presence or absence of "offensive traits" was usually noted.[92] As Peter Novick observed, the use of the formulation "offensive traits which some people associate with his race" allowed the writer to both embrace and distance himself from the stereotype.

These practices did not imply personal animosity toward Jews, nor is such participation incompatible with helping individual Jews or having Jewish friends. Both Boring and Woodworth believed they could do little about their perceived collegial obligation to identify Jews or about the discrimination their students faced. But Woodworth and Boring were respected leaders of twentieth century academic psychology. Both had a great deal of institutional and informal power and prestige. It is not presentist to suggest that they could have protested or refused to participate in the conventions of disclosure without damage to their well-established careers. They chose not to.

Andrew Winston is a professor of psychology at the University of Guelph. He is the editor of *Defining Difference: Race and Racism in the History of Psychology* (2004) and past executive officer of Cheiron: the International Society for the History of Behavioral and Social Sciences. His recent research is on the history of scientific racism and the use of psychological research by neo-Nazi groups.

ENDNOTES

Portions of this chapter are based on Andrew S. Winston, "'As his name indicates': R. S. Woodworth's letters of reference and employment for Jewish psychologists in the 1930s," *Journal of the History of the Behavioral Sciences* 32 (1996): 30–43, copyright © 1996 by Wiley Periodicals, Inc, adapted with permission; and from Andrew S. Winston, "'The defects of his race:' E.G. Boring and antisemitism in American psychology, 1923–1953." *History of Psychology* 1 (1998): 27–51, copyright © 1998 by the American Psychological Association, adapted with permission.

1. See, e.g., Andrew R. Heinze, *Jews and the American Soul* (Princeton: Princeton University Press, 2004).

2. Marcia Graham Synnott, "Anti-Semitism and American Universities: Did Quotas Follow the Jews?" in David A. Gerber, ed., *Anti-Semitism in American History* (Urbana: University of Illinois Press, 1986), p. 271.

3. Synnott, "Anti-Semitism and American Universities," p. 241. During the same period, Jewish enrollment at the Columbia College of Physicians and Surgeons increased from 18 percent to approximately 50 percent, p. 253. See also Harold S. Wechsler, *The Qualified Student: A History of Selective College Admission in America* (New York: John Wiley, 1977), p. 170.

4. Frederick P. Keppel, *Columbia* (New York: Oxford University Press, 1914), pp. 179–181. If Dean Keppel's language seemed cautious, it was for at least two reasons: this volume served as a promotional device, designed to portray the school in the most desirable light to "the best families." Such families would be reassured to know that Jewish enrollment was declining, even if the figures suggested otherwise. In addition, Columbia had been grateful for the substantial contributions of some of New York's wealthy Jews, such as Jacob Schiff, and it would not do for the dean to express any stronger antisemitism.

5. Wechsler, *The Qualified Student*, pp. 151–152.

6. Leonard Dinnerstein, *Antisemitism in America* (New York: Oxford University Press, 1994); Michael Dobkowski, *The Tarnished Dream: the Basis of American Anti-Semitism* (Westport, CT: Greenwood Press, 1979). On the earlier history of distinctions between German and Eastern European Jews, see Sander Gilman, *Jewish Self-Hatred: Anti-Semitism and the Hidden Language of the Jews* (Baltimore, MD: Johns Hopkins, 1986).

7. Edward A. Ross, *The Old World in the New* (New York: Century Co., 1914).

8. Edward A. Ross, "The Hebrews of Eastern Europe in America," *The Century Magazine* 88 (September, 1914): 785–792. On Ross, see Dinnerstein, *Antisemitism in America*,

ch. 4, and Dorothy Ross, *The Origins of American Social Science* (Cambridge: Cambridge University Press, 1991) for a discussion of Ross's general importance. On the later softening of Ross's nativism, see Heinze, *Jews and the American Soul,* p. 357.

9   Ross, "The Hebrews of Eastern Europe," p. 790. According to Ross, the apparent cases of outstanding achievement were thought to reflect high variability among Jews. A similar argument was made in 1923 by Carl Brigham to conclude that the World War I army IQ data "disproved the popular belief that the Jew is highly intelligent." See Brigham, *A Study of American Intelligence* (Princeton: Princeton University Press, 1923), p. 190. To arrive at this conclusion, Brigham assumed that half the army recruits who were born in Russia must be Jewish.

10 Herbert Hawkes to E. B. Wilson, June 16, 1922, quoted in Wechsler, *The Qualified Student*, p. 161. The notion that Jews were interested in education for financial rather than intellectual gain, as mentioned by Ross, was echoed by Dean Keppel of Columbia: "The Jew more than any other group looks upon the college course from the point of view of an investment." See Frederick P. Keppel, *The Undergraduate and his College* (New York: Houghton Mifflin Company, 1917), p. 83. Earlier, Keppel argued that the Pulitzer scholarships should give preference to students interested in a career in journalism. He noted that this move would help the new School of Journalism and "might also give us a larger proportion of Gentiles among the scholars; for Journalism is not sufficiently lucrative a profession to be particularly attractive to the Jew." Frederick Keppel to Nicholas M. Butler, January 27, 1912. Quoted in Wechsler, *The Qualified Student*, p. 94.

11 For a detailed discussion of Butler's later silence regarding the Nazi regime and his failure to allow student protest at Columbia, see Stephen H. Norwood, *The Third Reich in the Ivory Tower: Complicity and Conflict on American Campuses* (New York: Cambridge University Press, 2009).

12 Wechsler, *The Qualified Student*, p. 155–156.

13 See Marcia Synott, *The Half-Opened Door: Discrimination and Admissions at Harvard, Yale, and Princeton, 1900-1970* (Westport CT: Greenwood Press, 1979). See also Dan Oren, *Joining the Club: A History of Jews and Yale* (New Haven: Yale University Press, 1985).

14 Ludwig Lewisohn, the noted man of letters, described in his autobiography how he was denied a fellowship after receiving his master's degree in English literature at Columbia in 1903. He was advised that because he was a Jew, "While we shall be glad to do anything we can for you, therefore I cannot help feeling that the chances are going to be greatly against you." See Lewisohn, *Up Stream: An American Chronicle* (New York: Boni & Liveright, 1922), p. 122, quoted in Susanne Klingenstein, *Jews in the American Academy 1990-1949: The Dynamics of Intellectual Assimilation* (New Haven: Yale University Press, 1991), pp. 97–98. The person who advised Lewisohn to change career plans was probably Brender Matthews, who believed that only those of Anglo-Saxon descent could properly teach English literature.

The experience of Lionel Trilling in 1936 was similar to that of Lewisohn, in that he was told by the head of the English department at Columbia that there was no future for him there despite his outstanding work. But under the advice of Columbia philosopher Sidney Hook, Trilling did not "go gently," and instead directly confronted the chair over the potential antisemitism involved in the decision. Trilling's career at Columbia was rescued, and he went on to a record of brilliant scholarship. When he became the first Jew to occupy a tenure-track position in English Literature, a colleague noted that he hoped Trilling would not use this event as "a wedge to open the English Department to more Jews." Thus Robert S. Woodworth's conception that Jews would "stick together" was apparently shared by other colleagues. See Sidney Hook, "Anti-Semitism in the Academy: Some Pages of the Past," *Midstream* 25 (January 1979): 49-54; Diana Trilling, "Lionel Trilling, a Jew at Columbia," *Commentary* 67 (March 1979): 40–46.

15 Quoted in Michael Sokal, "G. Stanley Hall and the Institutional Character of Psychology at Clark, 1889-1920," *Journal of the History of the Behavioral Sciences* 26 (1990): 114–124. For information on antisemitism directed at Jastrow, see Arthur L. Blumenthal, "The Intrepid Joseph Jastrow," in Gregory A. Kimble, M. Wertheimer & Charlotte White, eds., *Portraits of Pioneers in Psychology* (Washington: American Psychological Association, 1991), pp. 75–87.

16 Blumenthal, "The Intrepid Joseph Jastrow;" Matthew Hale, Jr., *Human Science and Social Order: Hugo Münsterberg and the Origins of Applied Psychology* (Philadelphia: Temple University Press, 1980); Michael Sokal, "G. Stanley Hall and the Institutional Character of Psychology at Clark, 1889–1920." While the reasons for Hall's tolerance are undoubtedly complex, it is likely that his feelings toward Jews were influenced by the very positive experiences he had as a young tutor to the children of the Seligman family of New York. The tolerance of G. Stanley Hall and William James, who were instrumental in founding the APA, may help explain why Jews could be elected APA presidents.

17 Dinnerstein, *Antisemitism in America.*

18 All Boring correspondence is from the E.G. Boring Papers, Harvard University Archives, and is cited with permission of Harvard University Archives. All Woodworth correspondence is from the Robert S. Woodworth Papers, Columbia University Rare Book and Manuscript Library, and is cited with permission of Columbia University.

19 For biographical information on Boring, see E.G. Boring, *Psychologist at Large: An Autobiography and Selected Essays* (New York: Basic Books, 1961); Julian Jaynes, "Edwin Garrigues Boring: 1889–1968," *Journal of the History of the Behavioral Sciences* 5 (1969): 99–112; Saul Rosenzweig, "E.G. Boring and the Zeitgeist: *Eruditione gesta beavit*," *Journal of Psychology* 75 (1970): 59–71; Andrew S. Winston, "Edwin Garrigues Boring," in Alan E. Kazdin, ed., *Encyclopedia of Psychology*, vol. 1 (Washington, DC: American Psychological Association; New York: Oxford University Press, 2000).

20 E.G. Boring to Lewis Terman, February 1, 1923.

21 E.G. Boring to Stevenson Smith, May 7, 1925. Rich took an MD in 1928 and later joined the staff of the Boston Psychopathic Hospital.

22 E.G. Boring to J.H. White, April 22, 1925.

23 E.G. Boring to R.H. Wheeler, December 18, 1926.

24 Madison Bentley to E.G. Boring, March 26, 1926; E.G. Boring to Madison Bentley, March 29, 1926.

25 Herbert Langfeld to President Foster, August 9, 1919. Quoted in Eugene Taylor, "Abraham Aaron Roback," in J.A. Garraty, ed., *American National Biography* (New York: Oxford University Press, 1999). Langfeld was generally thought to be a Jewish convert to Christianity, and Boring later maintained that although Langfeld was among his best friends, he did not know whether he was a Jew.

26 E.G. Boring to Stevenson Smith, May 7, 1925.

27 E.G. Boring to Erving Betts, May 5, 1925.

28 E.G. Boring to J.H. White, April 24, 1926.

29 E.G. Boring to William J. Robbins, Nov. 25, 1931; E.G. Boring to William J. Robbins, December 17, 1931.The fact that Boring placed "Nordic" in quotes in 1931 but not in 1926 is likely significant. It suggests either that by 1931 Boring no longer thought of "Nordic" as a biological category or that he wanted to distance himself slightly from the more extreme uses of the term, as in the work of Madison Grant.

30 E.G. Boring to Carney Landis, October 5, 1935. For a discussion of the careers of Jewish women psychologists, see Elizabeth Johnston and Anne Johnson, "Searching for the Second Generation of American Women Psychologists," *History of Psychology* 11(1) (2008): 40–72.

31 K. Dallenbach to E.G. Boring, March 12, 1934.

32 Hulsey Cason to R.M. Yerkes, March 7, 1932; Clark Hull to R.M. Yerkes, February 25, 1932. Robert M. Yerkes Papers, Yale University.

33 See Bruce Kuklick, *The Rise of American Philosophy: Cambridge, Massachusetts 1869–1930* (New Haven: Yale University Press, 1977), p. 456 for similar assurances given by Harvard philosopher C.I. Lewis in 1930.

34 E.G. Boring to Madison Bentley, March 29, 1926; E.G. Boring to J.H. White, April 24, 1926; E.G. Boring to Madison Bentley, July 27, 1925.

35 J.H. Moore to E.G. Boring, May 26, 1928. Although this is the only letter I have seen mentioning discrimination against Catholics in academic psychology, this topic is certainly worthy of further investigation.

36 According to his *New York Times* obituary (June 8, 1965), Roback had 1700 published articles and texts, a figure that undoubtedly included his many magazine articles. Many of these works were on Jewish culture. Thus Roback's Jewish identity was never, and could never be, concealed or in doubt.

37 E.G. Boring to Stevenson Smith, May 7, 1925.

38 On Lewin, see Albert Marrow, *The Practical Theorist: the Life and Work of Kurt Lewin* (New York: Basic Books, 1969).

39 E.G. Boring to Lewis Terman, May 18, 1931; E.G. Boring to Lewis Terman, July 31, 1931.

40 Lewis Terman to E.G. Boring, August 13, 1931.

41 E.G. Boring to Lewis Terman, August 18, 1931.

42 E.G. Boring to Lewis Terman, October 6, 1931.

43 E.G. Boring to Lewis Terman, April 17, 1933.

44 According to Mitchell Ash, "Cultural Contexts and Scientific Change in Psychology: Kurt Lewin in Iowa," *American Psychologist* 47 (1992): 198–207, the fact that Lewin's appointments were not in psychology should *not* be taken as evidence of discrimination. Ash argued that Lewin's positions at Cornell and Iowa offered "far better funding, contact with socially relevant research issues, access to facilities, such as laboratory schools, and support from doctoral students and co-workers than he might have had at many university departments" (p. 200). But the School of Home Economics at Cornell was a "radical change" in intellectual environment (T. Dembo, quoted in Marrow, p. 74), and hardly the expected place for an academic from the Faculty of Philosophy at Berlin. I have been unable to find evidence that Lewin, despite his extraordinary reputation, ever received an offer of permanent, tenure-stream employment from a psychology department. Lewin's daughter, Miriam Lewin (personal communication, September 16, 1996) could not recall any such offers.

45 Lewis Terman to E.G. Boring, November 25, 1934.

46 Marrow, *The Practical Theorist.*

47 For a useful discussion of the role of politeness and decorum in the history of Christian — Jewish relations, see J.M. Cuddihy, *The Ordeal of Civility: Freud, Marx, Lévi-Strauss and the Jewish Struggle with Modernity* (New York: Basic Books, 1974).

48 For a variety of reasons, J.D. Frank left psychology, took an MD, and began a successful career in psychiatry (personal communication, June 20, 1995). Rosenzweig, a noted clinical psychologist, remained on cordial terms with Boring until Boring's death (Rosenzweig, personal communication, July 30, 1995).

49 E.G. Boring to Kurt Lewin, April 20, 1937.

50 M.G. Ash, "Emigré Psychologists after 1933: The Cultural Coding of Scientific and Professional Practices," in M.G. Ash and A. Söllner, eds., *Forced Migration and Scientific Change: Emigré German-Speaking Scientists and Scholars after 1933* (New York: Cambridge University Press, 1996), pp. 117–138; J. Mandler and G. Mandler, "The Diaspora of Experimental Psychology: The Gestaltists and Others," in D. Fleming and B. Bailyn, eds., *The Intellectual Migration: Europe and America, 1930–1960* (Cambridge, MA: Harvard University Press, 1969), pp. 371–419; M.M. Sokal, "The Gestalt Psychologists in Behaviorist America," *American Historical Review* 89 (1984): 1240–1263; A. Wellek, "The Impact of the German Immigration on the Development of American Psychology," *Journal of the History of the Behavioral Sciences* 4 (1968): 207–229; Lewis A. Coser, *Refugee Scholars in America: Their Impact and Their Experiences* (New Haven: Yale University Press, 1984).

51 Charlotte Bühler was of Jewish origin although she had been reared as a Protestant. See Coser, *Refugee Scholars in America*, pp. 39–40.

52 R.S. Harper, "Tables of American Doctorates in Psychology," *American Journal of Psychology* 62 (1949): 579–587.

53 For information on Woodworth see Andrew S. Winston, "Robert Sessions Woodworth and the Creation of an Eclectic Psychology," in D.A. Dewsbury, L.T. Benjamin, Jr., and M. Wertheimer, eds., *Portraits of Pioneers in Psychology*, vol. VI (Washington, DC: American Psychological Association / Lawrence Erlbaum, 2006), pp. 50–66; Albert Poffenberger, "Robert Sessions Woodworth, 1869–1962," *American Journal of Psychology* 75 (1962): 677–689. See also Woodworth's autobiography, in Carl

Murchison, ed., *The History of Psychology in Autobiography,* vol. II (New York: Russel & Russel, 1930), pp. 359–380.

54   For a discussion of the job market from 1929–1933, see Albert Poffenberger, "Report on Supply and Demand for Psychologists Presented by the Committee on the Ph.D. in Psychology," *Psychological Bulletin* 30 (1933): 648–653. On the impact of the Depression on the history of psychology, see Lorenz J. Finison, "Unemployment, Politics, and the History of Organized Psychology," *American Psychologist* 31 (1976): 747–755.

55   Robert S. Woodworth to Sidney Pressey, February 14, 1939.

56   Robert S. Woodworth to Gladys Tallman, March 31, 1940.

57   Robert S. Woodworth, "Racial Differences in Mental Traits," *Science* 31 (1910): 171–186 and Robert S. Woodworth, *Psychology,* 3rd. ed. (New York: Henry Holt, 1934), p. 89.

58   See Otto Klineberg, *Race Differences* (New York: Harper, 1945). For a discussion by Klineberg of Woodworth's views of race and national character, see Otto Klineberg, "Culture and Personality," in G.S. Seward & J.P. Seward, eds., *Current Psychological Issues: Essays in Honor of Robert S. Woodworth* (New York: Henry Holt, 1958), pp. 329–354.

59   Robert S. Woodworth, "Race Problems," Robert S. Woodworth Papers, Columbia University.

60   Robert S. Woodworth, "Social Science and Social Welfare," undated notes, Robert S. Woodworth Papers, Columbia University Archives.

61   Dearborn *Independent*, "The International Jew: The World's Problem," May 22, 1920. See Dinnerstein, *Antisemitism in America*, pp. 80–83.

62   Interview with Heinz Ansbacher, Burlington VT, November 29, 1994. Ansbacher recalls that when he was hired at the University of Vermont, he was told that there was a letter identifying him as a Jew, but the letter recommended he be appointed nevertheless.

63   Otto Klineberg, in Gardner Lindzey, ed. *A History of Psychology in Autobiography,* vol. VI (Englewood Cliffs, NJ: Prentice Hall, 1974), pp. 163–182.

64   Daniel Harris, transcribed diary of 1922–1934. Copy provided by Prof. Benjamin Harris, University of New Hampshire.

65   Theodore R. Sarbin, "Steps to the Narratory Principle: an Autobiographical Essay," in D. John Lee, ed., *Life and Story: Autobiographies for a Narrative Psychology* (Wesport, CT: Praeger, 1994), p. 36.

66   Interview with Heinz Ansbacher, Burlington, VT, November 19, 1994.

67   Personal Communication, Jacob Levine, December 9, 1994. This letter is also discussed in Seymour B. Sarason, *The Making of a Psychologist: An Autobiography* (San Francisco: Jossey-Bass, 1988), pp. 126–127 and in Sarason's "Jewishness, Blackishness, and the Nature-Nurture Controversy," *American Psychologist* 28 (1973): 962–971.

68   Robert S. Woodworth to John F. Dashiell, February 25, 1939.

69   Sarason, "Jewishness, Blackishness, and the Nature-Nurture Controversy," p. 965.

70 David Krech, in Gardner Lindzey, ed., *A History of Psychology in Autobiography*, vol. VI (Englewood Cliffs: Prentice Hall, 1974), p. 242. Changing names to improve chances of employment was a ubiquitous practice for all occupations. For a discussion of the case of Josiah Morse, formerly Josiah Moses, see Sokal, "G. Stanley Hall," p. 121. See also Nicole B. Barenbaum, "American Jews and Psychology," in Stephen H. Norwood and Eunice G. Pollack, eds., *Encyclopedia of American Jewish History*, vol. 2 (Santa Barbara, CA: ABC-CLIO, 2008), pp. 707–710.

71 See Matthew Hale, Jr., *Human Science and Social Order: Hugo Münsterberg and the Origins of Applied Psychology* (Philadelphia: Temple University Press, 1980), p. 19.

72 See Wechsler, *The Qualified Student*, p. 179.

73 According to Sarason, "No one ever said it to me, but from my earliest days at Clark I concluded that if you got your doctorate in psychology and you were Jewish, you became a clinical psychologist.... It was a conclusion based on very hard data!" See *The Making of an American Psychologist*, p. 126.

74 "The Field of Clinical Psychology: Past, Present and Future," Editorial, *Journal of Clinical Psychology* 1 (1945), p. 13. For a recent, thorough analysis of the Thorne incident, see Benjamin Harris, "Jewish Quotas in Clinical Psychology?: *The Journal of Clinical Psychology* and the Scandal of 1945," *Review of General Psychology* 13 (2009): 252–261.

75 E.G. Boring to Samuel Fernberger, May 4, 1940.

76 Samuel Fernberger to E.G. Boring, May 20, 1940. Although rejected by the University of Pennsylvania in 1940, Hurvich was hired there as a full professor in 1962.

77 Refusal of Jews to hire Jews, although not common, did occur in a wide range of employment settings during the 1920s and 1930s, generally out of fear that the hiring would provoke an antisemitic reaction. Some Jews even supported immigration restrictions and college quotas in hopes of reducing antisemitism and encouraging rapid integration. Jews were advised to "remain circumspect in their public behavior, to draw no attention to themselves as Jews." Dinnerstein, *Antisemitism in America*, p. 123.

78 E.G. Boring to Calvin S. Hall, July 4, 1941.

79 E.G. Boring to Calvin S. Hall, July 4, 1941. Despite Boring's assessment, Perry had been known to write exactly the same kind of letters as described here, stating that the candidate had "none of the unpleasant characteristics which are supposed to be characteristic of the race" (Perry, 1911, cited in Kuklick, *The Rise of American Philosophy*, p. 456).

80 E.S. Shapiro, *A Time for Healing: American Jewry since World War II* (Baltimore, MD: Johns Hopkins University Press, 1992).

81 Dinnerstein, *Antisemitism in America*; Shapiro, *A Time for Healing*.

82 E.G. Boring to Roy Dorcus, March 12, 1946.

83 David Bakan, "Reflections on My Years in Psychology," in L.P. Mos, ed., *History of Psychology in Autobiography* (New York: Springer, 2009), p. 55.

84 Bakan, "Reflections," p. 56.

85 E.G. Boring to Boston University Graduate School, April 17, 1953.

86 Jerome Bruner, *In Search of Mind: Essays in Autobiography* (New York: Harper & Row, 1983).

87 David Hollinger, *Science, Jews, and Secular Culture: Studies in Mid-Twentieth Century American Intellectual History* (Princeton, NJ: Princeton University Press, 1996).

88 John Higham, *Strangers in the Land* (New Brunswick, NJ: Rutgers University Press, 1955); John Higham, *Send These to Me: Jews and Other Immigrants in Urban America* (New York: Atheneum, 1975). For a valuable set of critiques and comments on *Strangers in the Land,* see *American Jewish History* (December 1986).

89 On the transformation of Jews into "Whites," see Eric Goldstein, *The Price of Whiteness: Jews, Race, and American Identity* (Princeton, NJ: Princeton University Press, 2008).

90 On the generally weak response of Harvard to the Nazi regime, see Norwood, *The Third Reich in the Ivory Tower.*

91 Kuklick, *The Rise of American Philosophy,* pp. 456–457, referred specifically to letters written by Ralph Barton Perry, James Woods, Ernest Hocking, and C.I. Lewis.

92 Historian Oscar Handlin was said in 1935 to have "none of the offensive traits which some people associate with his race." Richard Leopold was "of course a Jew, but since he is a Princeton graduate, you may be reasonably certain he is not of the offensive type." Quoted in Peter Novick, *That Noble Dream: The "Objectivity Question" and the American Historical Profession* (New York: Cambridge University Press, 1988), p. 173. For antisemitism in economics, see Melvin W. Reder, "The Anti-Semitism of Some Eminent Economists," *History of Political Economy* 32 (2000): 833–856.

MERITOCRACY AND ITS LIMITS
Harvard, Yale and Columbia Law Schools before the Second World War

Henry D. Fetter

The record of discrimination against Jews in elite institutions of American higher education before World War II has been well-documented. The imposition of quotas, whether formal or informal, to restrict Jews' undergraduate enrollment, the bar to appointment to faculty positions especially in the humanities, the strict limitation on Jews' admission to medical schools, all characterized an era when Jews' academic ability and ambition were consistently frustrated by discriminatory barriers.[1] Similarly, the leaders of the legal profession resented, resisted and made determined efforts to limit the increasing number of Jewish (and other ethnic minority) lawyers, and entry into the most prestigious law firms was almost entirely foreclosed, even to the most outstanding Jewish law school graduates.[2]

One countervailing trend to the prevailing discriminatory ethos shared by the upper reaches of both academia and the bar can be found— in that era's law schools. Although by no means free of the discrimination that pervaded much of academia at the time, elite law schools were notable for their incipient embrace of a meritocratic ethos. In an overview of the position of Jews at Yale, Dan Oren wrote, "On the eve of the Second World War Jews were excluded in parts of Yale College. In the graduate school they were isolated. In the medical school they were limited."[3] Indeed, this was the position of Jews in academia in general at the time. The law school at Yale, and elsewhere in the upper ranks of academia, notably at Harvard, constituted an exception to that exclusionary state of affairs. This essay will trace the law schools' early commitment to a meritocratic ideal, which made them the advance guard of values that would in time transform the place of Jewish students and faculty in the American college and university. That ideal was, however, often compromised in practice and this essay will consider the limits of that meritocratic commitment. The conclusion will suggest why and how the elite law schools came to play that pioneering role.

JEWISH LAW STUDENTS:
ACADEMIC OPPORTUNITIES

By the early 1900s, the Jewish presence at top law schools was significant enough to elicit intolerant comment. En route to flunking out of Harvard Law School, future Democratic presidential candidate Adlai Stevenson was evidently unable to keep up with what he described as "the display of erudition not to mention the thirsty intellects of the semitic element."[4] When Franklin Roosevelt began his studies at Columbia Law School in 1904, where there were about 20 Jewish students in a class of 74, fiancée Eleanor (another future liberal icon) anxiously inquired "whether you found any old acquaintances or had only Jew Gentlemen to work with."[5]

While an (unannounced) quota cut the Jewish presence at Harvard College from over 20 percent in the early 1920s to between 10 and 16 percent until World War II, the leading scholar of the quota issue found no evidence that Harvard's law school, with an estimated Jewish enrollment of 14 percent in 1922, imposed a similar quota.[6] Although in 1928 Columbia Law School adopted a selective admissions policy expressly designed to recruit students "from all classes and all sections" of the country, it did not, in practice, significantly reduce the school's number of Jewish students, though they were largely drawn from the New York area. "Anyone entering [the law school building] at noon might suppose it almost entirely Jewish," one observer reported at the time.[7] A 1935 survey found that almost 35 percent of Columbia law students were Jewish.[8]

The elite law schools were not, however, free of the kinds of social exclusion and discrimination that characterized the Ivy League colleges of the era. For example, Laura Kalman, Abe Fortas's biographer, writes that at Yale Law School the future Supreme Court Justice's "religion remained a handicap." "Jews were not admitted to the Corbey Court eating club and pressure was placed on Gentiles who roomed with Jews to make other housing arrangements."[9] However, "the school that excluded Jews socially was one that they frequently dominated academically for Yale Law School was a meritocracy."[10] Though no doubt in idealized form, Felix Frankfurter portrayed the prevailing ethos, at Harvard Law School— and throughout elite legal academia generally— as a dominating atmosphere, first of professionalism, and what I think is an indispensable quality of true professionalism, the democratic spirit. What mattered was excellence in your profession to which your father or your face was equally irrelevant. And so rich man, poor man were just irrelevant titles to the equation of human relations. The thing that mattered was what you did professionally.... [A]fter the first year...the very good men were defined by the fact that they got on the *Harvard Law Review*. This was determined entirely on the basis of your work as a student by examinations at the end of the year....All this big talk about 'leadership' and character, and all the other things that are non-ascertainable, but usually are high-falutin' expressions of personal likes or dislikes, or class, or color, or religious partialities or antipathies — they were all out.[11]

It was a system of rewards within which Frankfurter (who had arrived in the United States at age 12 not knowing a word of English and made his way upwards through City College to Harvard Law School, where he graduated first in his class) proved able to make his mark and have his abilities recognized, despite the handicaps of diminutive stature, immigrant status, and Jewish parentage. Expressing an idealized, but not misplaced, vision of the school's self-image, Frankfurter, extrapolating from his own experience, asserted that

the *Harvard Law Review* in particular and the Harvard Law School in general are to me the most complete practices in democracy that I have ever known anything about.... If somebody whom the rest of the fellows may dislike has shown the mettle that is his in open competition, that's that. If he hasn't shown it, it doesn't matter whether he is one of the nicest fellows in the world, and that his father is Secretary of State.[12]

Laura Kalman's more objective portrayal of Yale Law School in the New Deal era nonetheless confirms the essentials of Frankfurter's paean:

The word 'meritocracy' would not become popular until the 1950s, but the concept of an aristocracy of intellect underlay selective admissions at Yale, and the New Deal.... [A]fter matriculation, performance on examinations proved all important. Though parentage and golfing skills might prove as significant as grades in determining the graduate's success in private practice, meritocrats and New Dealers envisaged a world in which academic performance accounted for placement in university and government.... New Dealers and meritocrats believed that the best faculty and government positions belonged to those with the strongest records.[13]

Recalling the "ferocious competitiveness" of the Harvard Law School he attended in the 1930s, David Riesman[14] wrote that "competition for grades which determined Law Review which in turn determined placement was unabashed; and since papers were read and graded by numbers, anonymously, faculty members...could not play favorites."[15] In their 1931 survey of antisemitism in American society, education and the professions, Heywood Broun and George Britt found that, compared to other professional schools, the law schools displayed markedly less intolerance towards Jewish applicants and students:

> Even the day law schools, the best ones in the land, welcome qualified students without objection to religious variations.... Columbia has twice the percentage of Jews in its law school as in medicine.... Columbia University which demands a passport photograph with applications to enter the college or the College of Physicians and Surgeons has no such requirement for the law school. [The Jewish applicant] will be admitted there, or he may go to Harvard or Yale. He may choose from the most famous law schools in the country. And in the school he will be treated quite fairly. There will be a number of Jewish professors and instructors.... He will get a chance purely on merit for a place on the cherished Columbia or Harvard *Law Review* or the Yale *Law Journal*, the magazine staff composed of the fifteen men with the highest grades in the class.[16]

"With their keen minds, ambition and knack for passing examinations," Jewish law students, Broun and Britt wrote, "proved their ability to get excellent grades." As a result, often half the members or more of the law reviews at Yale, Harvard and Columbia were Jewish.[17] At Columbia, "the Law Review board of editors whose members are automatically chosen from the scholastically highest in the class is usually Jewish in the majority; and of the last nine editors-in-chief, six have been Jews."[18]

JEWISH LAW STUDENTS:
CAREER OBSTACLES

If the law schools constituted an exception to the barriers to Jewish ambition and achievement that remained — and were being fortified — within the university at large in the first half of the twentieth century, that was not the case with respect to the legal profession itself. One graduate remembered Harvard Law School's "sense of meritocracy and fair competition" as "very important" precisely "because there was a lot of anti-Semitism and racism in the legal world."[19] The antisemitic line in the legal profession was drawn not in the admissions process or classroom, but when Jewish law graduates, including the *Law Review* high achievers, sought employment commensurate with their credentials and with the career paths open to their non-Jewish colleagues.

In the spring of 1936, when a number of Jewish *Harvard Law Review* editors were unable to find employment, even Felix Frankfurter — who, upon his own graduation, had made a point of beginning his legal career at a firm that had never employed a Jewish lawyer — was moved to question whether Jews should pursue a legal education at Harvard at all. Since "none of the so-called desirable firms will take a Jew," he "wonder[ed] whether this School shouldn't tell Jewish students that they go through...at their own risk of ever having an opportunity of entering the best law offices."[20] As Broun and Britt were told, "ninety percent of the big firms won't take a Jew under any circumstances."[21]

Even the few major firms that occasionally hired a Jewish lawyer were hardly immune to less than enlightened attitudes. Intending to praise a Jewish lawyer at his own firm, a partner noted that he was "devoid of every known quality which we in New York mean when we call a man 'Jewy.'"[22] Thurman Arnold, the Yale law school professor who was most active in trying to place Jewish students, made sure to inform prospective employers in one case that the candidates he recommended had "no traces of those characteristics that one associates with Hebrews," or that they were without "Jewish characteristics" in another.[23]

Well into the post World War II era, Jewish lawyers faced discrimination at large law firms. Even as "conscious and actively exclusionary policies" declined, a 1964 study conducted by the *Yale Law Journal* concluded that "discrimination, both present and past, has left its mark on the employment profile." "The legacies of earlier exclusionary policies tend to perpetuate the disadvantages of Jewish entrants to this market."[24]

JEWS ON THE FACULTY:
RECOGNITION AND RESISTANCE

Law school teaching was an alternative career path to private practice or government service for Jewish law students. Those with outstanding academic records were potentially qualified for faculty positions, which elite schools invariably limited to graduates with top grades and law review service. (When Harvard sought to identify potential new faculty members in the mid-1940s a list was prepared of recent Harvard Law School students who had graduated with an "A" average.)[25] From a current perspective, when Jews often comprise around half the faculty at a top law school, Jews' opportunities to teach in the inter-war period may merit the description of being "no better–and perhaps worse" than they were in private practice.[26] However, compared to the hiring situation then prevailing in other departments of the university, they were promising.

As Broun and Britt pointed out, the Jewish law student at the time could expect to encounter a number of Jewish professors.[27] In his study of Jews at Yale, Dan Oren observed that "in sharp contrast to the exclusiveness of the college faculty was the law school." Leon Tulin, son-in-law of Rabbi Stephen S. Wise, taught at the law school in the 1920s, and Abe Fortas was on the faculty in the 1930s. A number of Jewish professors, including constitutional law scholar Herbert Wechsler and anti-trust authority Milton Handler, held faculty positions at Columbia Law School.[28]

Felix Frankfurter had first joined the Harvard Law School faculty in 1914. After service in the administration of Woodrow Wilson, he returned to the law school, the only Jew on the faculty.[29] During his teaching career, there were Harvard Law School professors who pushed for an "Americanization" campaign, which would have reduced the number of Jewish students and awarded financial aid based on considerations other than academic merit, and who seemed, according to Law School dean Roscoe Pound, "determined to cut off Jews wherever possible," and were "very intolerant" about "orthodox Jews who can't take examinations on Saturday."[30] Still, it was not the faculty (despite the views of some) who were primarily responsible for Frankfurter's singular status. During his tenure, faculty proposed Jewish appointees, but they were blocked by university president A. Lawrence Lowell. Notably, Lowell had also been instrumental in imposing — in the face of heated opposition from Frankfurter among others — an informal, but effective, quota on the number of Jewish undergraduates at Harvard College.[31]

In the late 1920s Frankfurter waged a determined battle for the appointment of one of his outstanding Jewish students, Nathan Margold, to the faculty. He wrote Law School dean Pound, "The issue I wish to raise in the Margold case is whether or not he is to be considered on the merits — in the light of his professional equipment, his character and his qualities — or whether the fact that he is a Jew is to be taken into account."[32]

After Margold had served as an instructor for one year, the Law School faculty, with only two dissenting votes, recommended Margold's appointment as an assistant professor. However, President Lowell vetoed the appointment.

Led by Dean Pound, the faculty then voted not to challenge Lowell.[33] Pound was prone to disparaging remarks about the character of Jews and other ethnic minorities, who he claimed "furnish nearly all our cases of nervous breakdown." "Jews and Italians furnished nine tenths of the cases of stage fright" in contrast to "your Simon pure Yankee or your man from Dixie [who was not] affected in that fashion,"[34] Pound alleged. Frankfurter could only rebuke one of his more liberal colleagues who had sided with Pound, writing that there could be no doubt "that [Margold] was not rejected on the merits, that the rule of reason did not prevail."

In the course of the Margold controversy, Frankfurter had written to Dean Pound that "the objection that is now raised against Margold is that he is a Jew....You are reported to have stated...that Margold cannot be added to the Faculty because Bettman, Friendly and Glueck are possibilities, and that would make too many Jews on the Faculty! So far as I am able to ascertain, there has been no enunciation of any policy that would lead one to know how many Jews would make too many on the faculty!"[35] Policy or not, Frankfurter remained Harvard's only Jewish law professor until his appointment to the Supreme Court in 1939. By then, Lowell was no longer university president and Pound had been replaced as dean by Frankfurter protegé James Landis. Shortly after Frankfurter left, Paul Freund and Milton Katz were appointed professors of law, a belated triumph for the new Justice's meritocratic convictions.[36]

The reform programs of the New Deal played an important, if somewhat indirect, role in opening up faculty positions to Jews. Turning discrimination to advantage, Jewish law school graduates, shut out from employment opportunities in the private sector, became key legal staffers for the government agencies that proliferated in the 1930s.[37] President Roosevelt himself identified the likely legal recruits to his administration, asking a supporter to "dig me up fifteen or twenty youthful Abraham Lincolns from Manhattan and the Bronx to choose from.... They must be liberal from belief and not by lip service.... They must know what life in a tenement means."[38] The resulting Jewish legal presence in the expanding federal government of the New Deal era was so conspicuous that Adlai Stevenson, then working for the Agricultural Adjustment Administration, worried that "there is a little feeling that the Jews are getting too prominent...many of them are autocratic and the effect on the public — the industries that crowd our rooms all day — is bad."[39]

As Jerold Auerbach noted in his study of Jewish social mobility within the legal profession, "For many young Jewish lawyers with the proper academic certification the New Deal offered a unique opportunity for upward professional and social mobility."[40] "The New Deal needed legal talent and Jews needed the jobs that the New Deal provided."[41] Whatever the impact of his Jewish colleagues on Stevenson's sensibilities, the experience they gained in novel fields of law provided them with unique qualifications for academic appointments, as law schools were compelled to offer new courses based on recent innovations in government policy, including administrative, labor and securities law.[42]

As the defeat of Frankfurter's effort to secure a teaching position for Margold demonstrated, the path to a law school faculty appointment for Jews frequently remained a difficult and contested one. Instances of blatant discrimination occurred regularly.[43] Certainly the frequency of Jewish faculty appointments lagged well behind the numbers who were fully qualified and credentialed. Recommendations of outstanding Jewish students for faculty positions routinely included the assurance that "I do not regard him as forward or pushing.... I should have no hesitation in saying that such Jewish characteristics as he possesses are not a handicap."[44] Even at apparently accommodating Yale, consideration of Jerome Frank, a prominent Jewish New Dealer and leading exponent of legal realism, for a professorship in 1935 elicited significant opposition. The eminent contracts law professor Arthur Corbin protested to the president of the university in terms that, in the assessment of university historian Gaddis Smith, "blended political considerations, anti-Semitic prejudice, and concern for Yale's image."[45] "Personally," Corbin wrote, "I think that the time has come when our new faculty appointments should not be drawn exclusively from employees of the present national administration. This applies *particularly* to those who are extreme radicals by race, color or nationality."[46] In a similar spirit, Corbin, opposing the appointment of scholars fleeing from Nazism, also warned that "the service this school can render will be rapidly reduced if we appear to become an asylum for the oppressed of less tolerant nations." This attitude was shared by Yale President James Rowland Angell when he rebuffed the Law School dean's effort to attract Ernst Levy ("the most distinguished Romanist in the world," in the dean's judgment) to the faculty after he was removed from his professorship as a "non-Aryan" in Nazi Germany.[47]

Concerns about the appointment of Jewish faculty persisted into the World War II era. As the war drew to a close, Harvard Law School embarked on an effort to upgrade its faculty and position itself to sustain its leading place in the hierarchy of legal education. To that end, an offer was made to Harry Shulman, a leading scholar of labor law at Yale Law School whose candidacy for dean of that school had been blocked on religious grounds a few years earlier. However, before reaching out to Shulman, Harvard Law School Dean James Landis felt compelled to note "one further comment on Shulman that I think is not without relevance," that

> he is, of course, Jewish. In discussion the other day in Washington…in regard to Shulman I raised this issue in order to get the reaction of men outside the School on adding another person of Jewish extraction to our faculty. The answer came quickly from a source that set my own fears at rest….He said in substance that in calling Shulman we were calling a person of known capacity and known distinction and that the fact that he was a Jew did not disturb him and would not disturb others….Because of that we all went ahead in our consideration of Shulman without any reference to that issue.[48]

Shulman rejected Harvard's offer and stayed at Yale, but thereafter, Morton Keller and Phyllis Keller note, "Concern over the number of Jews on the faculty rapidly diminished as (or because) the number of Jews on the faculty rapidly increased."[49] Harvard law professors may not have been free from prejudice, the Kellers observe, but they shared a powerful "sense of belonging to a *brüderbund,* defined by the mysterious science of the law and the ties of HLS faculty membership."[50]

THE DEANSHIP BARRIER

A controversy over the appointment of a new dean of Yale Law School in 1939 highlighted the limits to that law school's relatively open faculty-hiring policy. Harry Shulman, a graduate of Brown University and Harvard Law School, who had served as a law clerk to Supreme Court Justice Brandeis, had been appointed to the Yale Law School faculty in 1930. Born in Russia, Shulman's "'unabashed' identification as a Jew had little adverse effect upon his popularity within the law school."[51] Not only was he well-liked by the students, Shulman emerged as the preferred choice of most of his fellow professors to succeed Charles Clark as dean, after the initial leading candidates (former law professor and current Securities and Exchange Commission chairman William Douglas and Dean Acheson) became unavailable.[52] Distinguished federal judge Learned Hand and top law professors at other schools also strongly supported Shulman.[53]

However, following soundings among alumni and the legal establishment, Yale president Charles Seymour was dissuaded from appointing Shulman.[54] After conferring with new Supreme Court Justice Douglas, Seymour wrote,

"I gathered that Douglas would regard Shulman as a wise appointment provided the University was willing to take the widespread and unfair criticism which would certainly result throughout the country and especially among our Yale College alumni."[55] Acting Dean Ashbel Green Gulliver was named dean instead and Seymour fobbed off his rejection of Shulman by appointing him to a prestigious Sterling professorship, somewhat disingenuously telling him "that one factor that has bulked very much in my own mind has been the importance of your scholarly work and the necessity of making it possible for you to push this forward under the most favorable conditions."[56] Supreme Court Justice Frankfurter, who had taught Shulman at Harvard and strongly supported his candidacy, complained to Yale's provost that Shulman's religion was the only possible objection to his appointment and should not derail it.[57] Oren concludes, "Shulman was the clear favorite, but his Jewish background *alone* held him back."[58] According to Kalman, "although two-thirds of the faculty ultimately pressed for Shulman's selection, they probably would have worked harder…if Shulman had not been Jewish."[59]

An echo of the Shulman controversy at Yale occurred in 1946 when Erwin Griswold and Milton Katz were the leading candidates to succeed Landis as dean of Harvard Law School. Writing to university president James Conant, the outgoing dean reported, "I was…delighted and very proud with the attitude of the faculty with regard to the Jewish problem. It became clear that the suggestion of a Jew like Katz for the deanship would create no internal problem whatever." However, much as had been the case with respect to Shulman's mooted deanship at Yale, significant concern among the school's alumni focused on Katz's Jewishness, and, whether or not that was decisive, Griswold was appointed.[60]

In 1954, Shulman would finally be appointed dean of Yale Law School. The religious issue which, though not openly acknowledged, had undermined Shulman's candidacy in 1939, was expressly faced this time around and was even cited as a reason *not* to block the appointment. Writing to the president of Yale, law professor emeritus Arthur Corbin, while continuing to give credence to the type of concerns about Jewishness that he had expressed earlier, now averred that "certain supposed objections to Harry's appointment should be disregarded….He is a Jew, and was law clerk to Justice Brandeis. His associates know that he has none of the supposed disagreeable characteristics that anti-Semites like to dwell upon. His character and personality are sufficient rebuttal. He can be depended upon to give a fair and unbiased administration and one that all Yale men will respect."[61] Shulman's appointment evidently dispelled any lingering concerns about a Jew serving as dean. Although his tenure was cut short by his sudden death in 1955, thereafter the deanship was held by four Jewish professors in succession — Eugene Rostow, Louis Pollak, Abraham Goldstein and Harry Wellington.[62]

WHY MERITOCRACY?

A number of considerations contributed to the acceptance of meritocratic values by elite law schools in advance of the academy and the legal profession in general. First, Louis Brandeis's outstanding career at the bar and on the bench has often been cited as having played a significant role in making elite law schools more hospitable to Jews than the larger institutions in which they were located. The relative readiness of top law schools to appoint Jews to faculty positions was encouraged by Brandeis's preeminence as a lawyer and Supreme Court Justice. Harvard Law School Dean Landis's evaluation of Brandeis — "the greatest [Supreme Court Justice] excepting perhaps Marshall and Holmes" — was (and is) widely shared.[63] Perhaps even more important in validating the potential excellence of Jewish legal scholars within the grade-driven law school milieu was a widespread tradition crediting Brandeis with the highest marks in the history of Harvard Law School.[64] Brandeis's intellect made an enduring impression on his classmates and teachers; in 1883, after several years teaching part-time, he was offered an assistant professorship at Harvard (which he declined in favor of private practice), a remarkable opportunity for a Jew at that time.[65] Brandeis thus served as a "role model" not so much for those aspiring Jewish law students and lawyers who wished to follow in his path, but for the faculty members and administrators who would determine the extent to which other Jews would have the academic opportunities that Brandeis had enjoyed.

Second, the grades-driven ethos that permeated the ranks of elite legal education provided Jewish law students with the chance to thrive. The "case method" introduced by Dean Christopher Columbus Langdell at Harvard Law School in the 1870s, and thereafter adopted at all leading law schools, considered law to be a science akin to chemistry or biology. An emphasis on the objective measure of student performance — numerical grades on anonymously read examination papers — flowed naturally from the scientific ambitions that inspired Langdell's approach to the study of law. No one better expressed the focus on grades, and the exceedingly fine distinctions they entailed as the overriding measure of merit, than Frankfurter: "If one fellow got 76 and another 76.5, there's no use saying, 'The 76 man is better.' Maybe so, but how do you know he's better?"[66]

Ironically, Harvard's relaxed admissions policy — a college transcript was not required until 1925, and after 1927 all graduates in the top three-quarters of their class were eligible for admission[67] — which made it possible for virtually anyone of means to be accepted, contributed to the premium that was placed on test scores. The relaxed admission standards that made it easy for almost anyone from a "good family" to enter situated the school within established society's network of social exclusiveness and economic elitism.[68] However, it also had the (perhaps unintended) effect of emphasizing academic merit within the school itself. The winnowing process, whereby almost half the first-year students were flunked out, put a premium on scores on anonymously graded tests, which rewarded achievement regardless of religion or social standing.[69] "The risk of failure was real; the prizes for the successful were proportionately great," the historian of Harvard Law School writes.[70] Thus, for those Jewish students able to gain (i.e. afford) admission, a pathway to recognition and reward based on performance alone was made available.

Third, that the law remained a relatively open profession in which barriers to entry were lower than in medicine made quotas more difficult to maintain.[71] Leaders of the bar made strenuous efforts to exclude aspiring Jewish and other minority lawyers by raising standards for law school accreditation and for admission to the bar.[72] However, these attempts fell short of their sweeping objectives. Night law schools continued to operate, aspiring lawyers continued the long-standing tradition of preparing for the bar, not by attending duly accredited schools, but by "reading law" in an attorney's office, and ethnic minorities exerted political pressure to secure access to legal careers for their constituents. Outstanding Jewish law students could not be entirely excluded from the bar; better for both schools and students to provide opportunities for them within the established educational order.

CONCLUSION

During his time as a professor at Harvard Law School, Frankfurter repeatedly insisted that "the great thing about the School when I was a student was that Skull & Bones, Hasty Pudding, an H, family fortune, skin, creed — nothing particularly mattered, except scholarship and character objectively ascertained."[73] Although in the decades before the Second World War law school practice often fell short of this ideal, the meritocratic creed that Frankfurter voiced was more prevalent in the elite law schools than in the colleges from which their students came, or the practice of law into which they graduated. The law schools provided a middle passage in which the meritocratic ideal, albeit not fully realized, might be nurtured in between educational and real world realms where it was hardly acknowledged and where social exclusiveness and religious intolerance continued to flourish. "Since the days of Brandeis," George Packer, son of Professor Herbert Packer, a poor Jewish boy from the New Haven area who had graduated from Yale Law School after World War II military service and later taught at Stanford Law School, wrote in his family biography, "the law schools had generally functioned as meritocracies, and so they became pathways of Jewish success before medical schools and English departments opened their doors."[74]

Harvard Law School, as it emerged from World War II, has been described as "the leading meritocratic institution within America's leading meritocratic university,"[75] an endorsement that must, however, be qualified by recognition that resistance to meritocracy persisted both in the law school, and even more especially, in the university as a whole. Although in the post-World War II era, an "old boys network" that compromised the commitment to meritocracy continued to play a role in law school hiring,[76] the process of opening up faculty positions to the best credentialed "was evident in the law schools before the college and other departments. By the 1950s, the Yale law faculty included many Jews, while the Yale College faculty, where the old boys congregated, still possessed few."[77] Where the law schools led, the universities that housed them would follow. "In the 1960s, Harvard College came in some respects to resemble the Harvard Law School of earlier decades" in its commitment to meritocracy, writes one-time Harvard law student David Riesman who had later become a Harvard University social sciences professor.[78] It is significant that in the aftermath of World War II, it was considered necessary and desirable to establish a liberal arts university (Brandeis) and a medical school (Albert Einstein) under Jewish auspices, but not a law school.

In 1971, conversation at a dinner party turned to the recent appointment of Albert Sacks as dean of Harvard Law School. Noting that the law schools at Harvard, Yale, Columbia, Penn, Boalt (Berkeley) and UCLA now all had Jewish deans, one guest joked that the "Harvard trustees had been willing to appoint a WASP but couldn't find one who was qualified."[79] By then, Jews made up almost 40 percent of elite law school faculties.[80] Though it may have been a joke, it marked the culmination of the law schools' embrace of the meritocratic values that, despite much travail and struggle, had fostered an unusually hospitable environment for Jewish achievement and recognition at a time when antisemitic prejudice was prevalent in the wider academic and professional worlds.

Henry D. Fetter is a graduate of Harvard Law School and holds degrees in history from Harvard College and the University of California, Berkeley. He is a contributor to the *Encyclopedia of American Jewish History* and has been awarded the Kerr History Prize by the New York State Historical Society. He has published several articles on the United States and the birth of Israel in *Israel Affairs*.

ENDNOTES

1. Marcia Graham Synnott, *The Half-Opened Door: Discrimination and Admissions at Harvard, Yale, and Princeton, 1900–1970* (Westport, CT: Greenwood Press, 1979); Jerome Karabel, *The Chosen* (Boston: Houghton Mifflin Company, 2005); Heywood Broun and George Britt, *Christians Only: A Study in Prejudice* (New York: Vanguard Press, 1931). For a case study of medical school discrimination, see Dan A. Oren, *Joining the Club: A History of Jews and Yale* (New Haven: Yale University Press, 1985), pp. 136–155. Antisemitism in medical education and training was dramatized by Clifford Odets, "Waiting for Lefty," in *Six Plays* (New York: Modern Library, 1939), pp. 25–29 (Scene V: "Interne Episode").

2. The legal profession's discriminatory practices have been documented in a series of works by Jerold S. Auerbach: "From Rags to Robes: The Legal Profession, Social Mobility and the American Jewish Experience," *American Jewish Historical Quarterly* 66:2 (December 1976): 250–253; *Unequal Justice: Lawyers and Social Change in Modern America* (New York: Oxford University Press, 1976), pp. 40–73, 102–130; "Enmity and Amity: Law Teachers and Practitioners, 1900–1922," *Perspectives in American History* V (1971): 551–601. A contemporary account is provided in Broun and Britt, *Christians Only*.

3. Oren, *Joining the Club*, p. 155.

4. John Bartlow Martin, *Adlai Stevenson of Illinois* (Garden City, NY: Doubleday & Company, 1976), p. 71.

5. Joseph Lash, *Eleanor and Franklin* (New York: New American Library, 1971), p. 198. Eleanor's inbred antisemitism would persist. Upon first meeting Felix Frankfurter in 1918, she reported to her mother-in-law that he was "an interesting little man but very jew," p. 295.

6. Synnott, *Half-Opened Door*, pp. 97, 112.

7. Harold S. Wechsler, *The Qualified Student: A History of Selective College Admission in America* (New York: Wiley, 1977), pp. 171–172.

8. Marcia Graham Synnott, "Anti-Semitism and American Universities: Did Quotas Follow the Jews?" in David A. Gerber, ed., *Anti-Semitism in American History* (Urbana: University of Illinois Press, 1986), p. 258.

9. Laura Kalman, *Abe Fortas: A Biography*, (New Haven: Yale University Press, 1990), p. 14.

10. Kalman, *Fortas*, p. 15.

11. Harlan Phillips, ed., *Felix Frankfurter Reminisces* (New York: Reynal & Company, 1960), pp. 26–27.

12 *Felix Frankfurter Reminisces*, p. 27. For doubts about the validity of Frankfurter's perspective, and a view of Frankfurter as "the conspicuous exception, not the prototypical product of a democratic meritocracy," see Auerbach, "From Rags to Robes," p. 253.

13 Laura Kalman, *Yale Law School and the Sixties* (Chapel Hill: University of North Carolina Press, 2005), p. 38.

14 David Riesman, "Educational Reform at Harvard," in Seymour Martin Lipset and David Riesman, *Education and Politics at Harvard* (New York: McGraw-Hill, 1975), p. 330.

15 Riesman, "Educational Reform at Harvard," p. 330.

16 Broun and Britt, *Christians Only*, pp. 162–165.

17 Ibid., pp. 164, 168.

18 Quoted in Wechsler, *Qualified Student*, p. 172.

19 W. Joseph Peck quoted in Geoffrey Kabaservice, *The Guardians: Kingman Brewster, His Circle, and the Rise of the Liberal Establishment* (New York: Henry Holt, 2004), p. 129.

20 Frankfurter quoted in Auerbach, *Unequal Justice*, p. 186.

21 Broun and Britt, *Christians Only*, pp. 164–173.

22 Auerbach, *Unequal Justice*, p. 186.

23 Quoted in Kalman, *Fortas*, p. 14; Auerbach, "From Rags to Robes," p. 265.

24 "The Jewish Law Student and New York Jobs — Discriminatory Effects of Law Firm Hiring Practices," *Yale Law Journal* 73 (1964), pp. 625, 657. The study was financed by the Anti-Defamation League of B'nai B'rith. The study found that "a Gentile had about the same advantage over a Jew with equal class standing as he did over a Gentile a third of a class below him," p. 657.

25 Morton Keller and Phyllis Keller, *Making Harvard Modern: The Rise of America's University* (New York: Oxford University Press, 2001), p. 114.

26 Auerbach, *Unequal Justice*, pp. 186–187.

27 Broun and Britt, *Christians Only*, p. 163.

28 See Julius Goebel, Jr., ed., *A History of the School of Law, Columbia University* (New York: Columbia University Press, 1955), pp. 321, 326.

29 Seymour Martin Lipset, "Politics at Harvard," in Lipset and Riesman, *Education and Politics at Harvard*, p. 149; Charles Silberman, *A Certain People: American Jews and Their Lives Today* (New York: Summit Books, 1985), p. 100.

30 Michael E. Parrish, *Felix Frankfurter and His Times: The Reform Years* (New York: The Free Press, 1982), p. 156. On Frankfurter's strong opposition to Pound's accepting an honorary degree from Nazi Germany's ambassador at the law school, see Stephen H. Norwood, *The Third Reich in the Ivory Tower: Complicity and Conflict on American Campuses* (New York: Cambridge University Press, 2009), pp. 56–57.

31 Donald A. Ritchie, *James M. Landis: Dean of the Regulators* (Cambridge: Harvard University Press, 1980), p. 33. On Lowell's advocacy of a Jewish quota, and Frankfurter's opposition, see Synnott, *Half-Opened Door*, pp. 58–106; Parrish, *Frankfurter and His Times*, pp. 155–156.

32 H.N. Hirsch, *The Enigma of Felix Frankfurter* (New York: Basic Books, 1981), p. 96.

33 Parrish, *Frankfurter and His Times*, p. 156.

34 Quoted in Parrish, *Frankfurter and His Times*, p. 157.

35 Hirsch, *Enigma of Felix Frankfurter*, p. 96.

36 Ritchie, *Landis*, p. 89. An unsuccessful offer was also made to former Frankfurter student and prominent New Deal lawyer Benjamin Cohen.

37 Auerbach, *Unequal Justice*, pp. 185–188.

38 Quoted in Auerbach, *Unequal Justice*, p. 187.

39 Quoted in Auerbach, *Unequal Justice*, p. 188.

40 Auerbach, "From Rags to Robes," p. 265.

41 Auerbach, "From Rags to Robes," p. 266.

42 Leonard Dinnerstein, *Antisemitism in America* (New York: Oxford University Press, 1994), p. 144 (citing an oral history interview with Paul Freund). For the impact of the New Deal on the law school curriculum, see Robert Stevens, "Two Cheers for 1870: The American Law School," *Perspectives in American History* V (1971), p. 487.

43 See Auerbach, *Unequal Justice*, p. 187.

44 Dean James M. Landis of Harvard quoted in Auerbach, *Unequal Justice*, p. 187.

45 Gaddis Smith, "Politics and the Law School," in Anthony T. Kronman, ed., *History of the Yale Law School* (New Haven: Yale University Press, 2004), pp. 142–143.

46 Quoted in Laura Kalman, *Legal Realism at Yale 1927–1960* (Chapel Hill: University of North Carolina Press, 1986), p. 138. Frank was not appointed.

47 Smith, "Politics and the Law School," p. 143. Levy left Germany in 1936 and accepted a position at the University of Washington.

48 Landis to Conant, March 10, 1945, quoted in Keller and Keller, *Making Harvard Modern*, p. 115.

49 Keller and Keller, *Making Harvard Modern*, p. 115.

50 Ibid., p. 116.

51 Oren, *Joining the Club*, p. 126. The account of the Shulman deanship controversy is drawn from Oren, *Joining the Club* and Kalman, *Legal Realism at Yale*.

52 Douglas was appointed to the Supreme Court and Acheson declined to accept the deanship. Kalman, *Legal Realism at Yale*, pp. 140–141.

53 Oren, *Joining the Club*, p. 126.

54 Kalman, *Legal Realism at Yale*, p. 143; Oren, *Joining the Club*, p. 126.

55 Quoted in Oren, *Joining the Club*, p. 127.

56 Quoted in Oren, *Joining the Club*, p. 127.

57 Kalman, *Legal Realism at Yale*, p. 143. Kalman's assessment is that "Frankfurter was wrong. It was not only Shulman's religion that damaged him but his Harvard affiliation as well," p. 142.

58 Oren, *Joining the Club*, p. 127.

59 Kalman, *Legal Realism at Yale*, p. 143.

60 Keller and Keller, *Making Harvard Modern*, pp. 115–116. Albert Sacks would become Harvard Law School's first Jewish dean in 1971.

61 Corbin to A. Whitney Griswold, December 7, 1953, quoted in Oren, *Joining the Club*, p. 270.

62 Oren, *Joining the Club*, pp. 27–271; Geoffrey Kabaservice, "Eugene Rostow" in Roger K. Newman, ed., *Yale Biographical Dictionary of American Law* (New Haven: Yale University Press, 2009), p. 470.

63 Ritchie, *Landis*, p. 23.

64 On the example set by Brandeis, see Oren, *Joining the Club*, p. 125; on Brandeis's academic record, see Arthur E. Sutherland, *The Law at Harvard: A History of Ideas and Men 1817–1967* (Cambridge: Harvard University Press, 1967), p. 198.

65 Melvin I. Urofsky, *Louis D. Brandeis* (New York: Pantheon Books, 2009), pp. 30–31, 80–81.

66 Sutherland, *The Law at Harvard*, pp. 174–176; *Felix Frankfurter Reminisces*, p. 27.

67 Kabaservice, *The Guardians*, p. 129.

68 Auerbach, "From Rags to Robes," p. 253; Auerbach, "Enmity and Amity," pp. 598–599; Auerbach, *Unequal Justice*, pp. 28–29.

69 Stevens, "Two Cheers for 1870," pp. 488–489; Sutherland, *The Law at Harvard*, pp. 221, 248–250.

70 Sutherland, *The Law at Harvard*, p. 249.

71 Carey McWilliams, *A Mask for Privilege* (Boston: Little Brown, 1948), p. 133.

72 Auerbach, *Unequal Justice*, pp. 102–129.

73 Parrish, *Frankfurter*, p. 156.

74 George Packer, *Blood of the Liberals* (New York: Farrar, Straus and Giroux, 2000) (pb. ed.), p. 144.

75 Kabaservice, *The Guardians*, p. 129.

76 Ibid., p. 130.

77 Kalman, *Yale Law School and the Sixties*, p. 38.

78 Riesman, "Educational Reform," pp. 330–331.

79 Silberman, *A Certain People*, p. 100.

80 Ibid., p. 99.

THE EDUCATIONAL CRUSADE
OF GEORGE W. ARMSTRONG

Edward S. Shapiro

In October 1949 George Washington Armstrong, a Fort Worth, Texas oilman and Mississippi land baron, publicly offered a seemingly princely gift to tiny Jefferson Military College (JMC) in Washington, Mississippi, a small town in southwest Mississippi a few miles from Natchez. The gift was conditioned among other things on teaching the doctrine of racial supremacy and not admitting Jews as students.[1] This was among the most blatant examples of antisemitism in the history of American education. A couple of years later Armstrong made a similar offer to Piedmont College, a small church-related college in Georgia. These offers were not accompanied by any of the euphemisms which had previously accompanied efforts to limit the Jewish presence in academia, such as the need to geographically balance the undergraduate student body or the inability of prospective Jewish graduate students, the children of poor urban immigrants, to comprehend the genius of American history and English literature.

Armstrong and his proposed gifts to JMC and Piedmont College are not discussed in any of the standard histories of American antisemitism, even though he was one of America's most prominent antisemites during the 1930s and 1940s. He had long been on the radar of Jewish organizations combating antisemitism, and the two proposals were widely covered in the press, including the *New York Times*.[2] Leonard Dinnerstein's *Uneasy at Home: Antisemitism and the American Jewish Experience* (1987) and *Antisemitism in America* (1994) do not mention Armstrong, and there is only one reference to him, and none to his proposed contributions, in Michael Dobkowski's *The Tarnished Dream: The Basis of American Anti-Semitism* (1979).

The local and national response to Armstrong's offer to Jefferson Military College, coming just four years after the end of World War II and five years prior to the outlawing of school segregation by the Supreme Court in the Brown decision, throws light on American attitudes toward antisemitism in the wake of the Holocaust, the changing racial attitudes in the Deep South during the post-war years, and the strategies adopted by Jews in fighting antisemitism. At first glance the Mississippi of the 1940s might appear to be a congenial place for a person such as Armstrong. W. J. Cash's classic *The Mind of the South* (1941) argued that antisemitism was part of the "savage ideal" that lay at the heart of southern identity, and no state was more southern than Mississippi. For much of the 1940s it was represented by two of the most notorious antisemites ever to sit in Congress—Congressman John E. Rankin and Senator Theodore G. Bilbo. Rankin accused Jews of attempting "to destroy Christianity and everything that is based on Christian principles. They are now trying to undermine and destroy America. God save our country from such a fate," he told his fellow Congressmen. Bilbo warned those whom he called New York Jewish "Kikes" that they faced deportation to Palestine if they continued their agitation on behalf of civil rights for blacks and the mongrelization of the South.[3]

Thus if there was any place in the Union that one could assume would be sympathetic to someone of Armstrong's ilk it would have been Mississippi. But here, as well as in other aspects of the history of Armstrong's gift, including its size, the response of the institution's board of trustees, and even the nature of Jefferson Military College itself, the story is more surprising and complicated than it might appear at first glance. First of all, Jefferson Military College was not a college but a military preparatory boarding school for boys eight to eighteen years old. Such schools were found throughout the South, but few had a history as old and as illustrious as that of JMC. Chartered by the territorial government of Mississippi in 1802 during the administration of Thomas Jefferson and named for the third President, it became fully operational in 1811.

JMC's charter stated that its trustees should

> take effectual care that students of all denominations may, and shall be admitted to equal advantages of a liberal education, and to the emoluments and honors of the college, and they shall receive a like fair and generous treatment, during their residence therein.

A guide to the school published around the time of the Armstrong controversy a century and a half later noted, "Each year there are cadets of different faiths and no cadet receives any interference with his own religion. The daily service in chapel is so arranged as to fit the needs of all cadets." In this spirit, the school had admitted Jewish students and it even had had Jewish trustees. But the guide also stated that "a wholesome Christian influence prevails" at JMC and that "on Sundays each cadet attends the church of his choice." This ambiguity as to the limits of the school's religious latitudinarianism would surface in 1949 when Armstrong announced his willingness to help the school financially.[4]

The administration and graduates of JMC took pride in its history. The Mississippi trial of Aaron Burr for treason in 1807 supposedly occurred on its campus under two giant oak trees; Andrew Jackson camped here during the War of 1812; the Mississippi statehood convention of 1817 met in a church that later became part of the school's campus; Lafayette reviewed the school's cadets in 1825; and federal troops were stationed on the campus from July 1863 to July 1866. The artist and naturalist John James Audubon taught at JMC during the 1820s, and its graduates included Jefferson Davis, the future president of the Confederacy.

JMC's students came primarily from the South and Latin America, a fact that would influence the conditions that Armstrong attached to his gift. For about a century the school had flourished, sending its graduates off to a variety of military academies and southern universities. By 1949, however, it was in serious financial straits. There had even been a question as to whether it would open for the fall semester. It did, but its enrollment had dropped to under fifty, it had only seven faculty members, and its physical plant was in a state of disrepair. One recent superintendent had been killed when he was blown up by a boiler he was repairing, and two recent fires had seriously damaged the main dormitory. Routine maintenance such as painting had been put off because of a lack of funds. There was little money in the bank, and some persons associated with JMC were not certain whether the school could meet its fiscal obligations and finish out the academic year. Any offer of financial relief would certainly receive a careful hearing by its board of trustees, even one with noxious conditions which seemingly violated its charter.[5]

Armstrong's relationship to JMC stemmed from his ownership of thirty-eight plantations in southwest Mississippi near Natchez. Here he lived the life of an ante-bellum planter-intellectual — raising cattle and cotton, reading, writing antisemitic tracts, and corresponding with virtually all of the leading American antisemitic figures of the 1930s and 1940s. By the mid-1940s, Armstrong was a source of funds for George Van Horn Moseley, Gerald L.

K. Smith, and other prominent antisemites. Armstrong, however, had bigger goals in mind than simply sending checks to fund the antisemitic activities of others. The financial difficulties of JMC provided him the opportunity to put into practice his grandiose ambitions, which included the transformation of JMC into a full-fledged university committed to the teaching of antisemitism and white supremacy.

Armstrong, a graduate of the University of Texas law school, had accumulated a fortune in Texas from oil and gas, steel, ranching, banking, real estate, flour milling, ginning and exporting of cotton, public power, and the practice of law. He was one of the most prominent Texas businessmen of the early twentieth century and had served as president of both the Texas Chamber of Commerce and the Associated Industries of Texas. He was also a prominent figure in Democratic state politics in Texas. In 1917 he purchased the first of his Mississippi plantations, and in 1925 he bought a plantation named Woodstock, located twelve miles south of Natchez. Here he spent much of his time during the 1930s and 1940s, punctuated by a return to Texas in 1932 in order to run in the Texas Democratic Party primary for governor. His platform condemned the Federal Reserve System and the gold standard, and supported the establishment of a state currency system and the revival of a Populist alliance of southern Democrats and western progressive Republicans against Wall Street. His campaigns in the Democratic Party primary and as an independent gubernatorial candidate garnered little support.

Armstrong detested the New Deal and Roosevelt. In 1943 he urged that FDR be impeached and the white South divorce itself "from the eastern wing of the party dominated by aliens and negroes and political bosses with their corruption, and...form a new party with the people of the western and middle states." Eight years earlier he had described Roosevelt's "Jew Deal" as "a deliberate and well managed campaign to destroy State sovereignty and our Constitutional form of government. This is the program of the Zionist Jewish conspiracy."[6]

Why Armstrong ever became an antisemite and a racist in the first place remains a mystery. His privately printed autobiography is of limited help in this regard. He had few if any social or business contacts with Jews or blacks while growing up in Texas. The autobiography does note, however, the influence of his father, a Confederate veteran, Methodist minister, and one of the founders of Texas Wesleyan University. The father was deeply religious and intolerant of deviance from Protestant religious orthodoxy. "With him right was right and wrong was wrong, and the Bible was the one and only standard of right and wrong," Armstrong recalled. "There was no middle ground and no compromise. If he ever sinned it was the sin of intolerance of evil." Religion dominated family life with daily prayer sessions in the morning and at night. Perhaps here was the source of Armstrong's own intolerance and revulsion from ambiguity and complexity. His father saw himself as an intellectual and writer (one of his publications was a book titled *Romanism vs. Protestantism*). Armstrong also became interested in intellectual matters. From an early age, he said in his memoirs, he also had wanted "to influence people through my writing."[7]

But if Armstrong's authoritarianism and intolerance can be traced to his early years, this still does not explain why he focused on Jews (and blacks) rather than on Roman Catholics, Mexican Americans, or Asians in the decades after World War I. Here again his autobiography is silent, although there is a clue in his bankruptcy in 1923, which stemmed from the death of cattle on his plantations due to tick fever.[8] He attributed his inability to borrow money to avoid bankruptcy to the machinations of New York bankers, the newly instituted Federal Reserve System, the gold standard, and the international financial system, all frequent targets of western and southern monetary radicals during the Populist-Progressive period. Armstrong had been interested in the money question even before his bankruptcy, and his first book, *The Crime of '20: An Official Story of Frenzied Finance*, which appeared in 1920, attacked the Federal Reserve System. Further reading and his bankruptcy broadened his understanding of monetary issues, particularly their "Jewish origin." It was helpful in this regard that Felix M. Warburg of Kuhn, Loeb & Company, the son-in-law of Jacob Schiff, had been a leading advocate of the Federal Reserve System.[9]

A staple of antisemitic literature in the early twentieth century was the claim that Jewish international bankers, particularly the Rothschild interests, were responsible for the world's economic ills. This made sense to the unsophisticated and provincial Armstrong, and his mission for the last three decades of his life was unmasking the machinations of Jewish financiers, including those of the J. P. Morgan investment house, which Armstrong believed to be a Jewish bank. This struggle against Jewish international finance gave purpose and meaning to his life, provided him with the key that unlocked many of the world's mysteries, and supplied him with the topic that could bring him the intellectual acclaim and influence he craved. Until his death in 1954 Armstrong's monomania regarding Jewish financiers would shape his understanding of national and international politics and was reflected in the titles of many of his pamphlets and books. They include *To*

Hell With Wall Street, The Story of the Dynasty of the Money Trust in America, The Mighty Rothschild Power, Rothschild Money Trust, The Zionists, Third Zionist War, Zionist Wall Street, and *The Reign of the Elders.*

Armstrong was an antisemitic crank, but a dangerous one because of his wealth and intellectual pretensions. His antisemitism was extreme in its crudity and resistance to common sense, encased in a veneer of fake scholarship and gullibility, most notably exhibited in his taking at face value the notorious forgery *Protocols of the Elders of Zion* and his use of fake quotes from Benjamin Franklin and George Washington. His ignorance of Jews and American politics was breathtaking. He asserted that Woodrow Wilson, Dwight Eisenhower, Franklin Roosevelt, and Harry Truman were Jews, that Jews ruled the British Empire at the very time when the British government was enforcing the White Paper restricting Jewish immigration to Palestine, and that Jews were responsible for the American entry into both world wars even though not a single Jew had a significant policy-making position in the War Department and State Department in 1917 and 1941. He wrote that Lincoln was murdered by the Jew John Wilkes Booth; Jews murdered William McKinley, Warren Harding, Huey Long, and Archduke Ferdinand; Douglas Fairbanks, Jr. and Ethel Merman were Jews; the Rothschild family owned half the wealth of the world, and America's fifteen million Jews owned four-fifths of the wealth in the United States.[10] Jews, Armstrong claimed, dominated America's newspapers, magazines, cinema, radio networks, railroads, principal industries, both political parties, and naturally the Roosevelt administration.[11]

Armstrong emphasized the connection between Jews and communism. He wrote that Jews controlled the Soviet Union at the same time that Stalin was conducting an antisemitic and anti-Zionist campaign. In *The March of Bolshevism*, Armstrong said that Kuhn, Loeb & Company had financed the Russian revolution, and that the communist type of Jew "crucified Christ and…overthrew the Russian Czar and…is now seeking to undermine and destroy our constitutional form of government." The source of Armstrong's insights regarding Jews, he declared, was Jesus, overlooking the fact that Jesus himself was a Jew. Jesus, Armstrong wrote in his memoirs, was an antisemite and had provided him "the intelligence and the experience to understand the subject of money and the sinister control of it, and the will and courage to expose the evil." With a few exceptions, Jews were traitors and should be banished from America or executed and their property confiscated.[12]

Particularly venomous were Armstrong's comments regarding World War II and the Holocaust. These first came out in his 1940 book *The Rothschild*

Money Trust, which he dedicated to a rogue's gallery of American antisemites, including Henry Ford, the Rev. Charles E. Coughlin, William Dudley Pelley, George Van Horn Moseley, and Gerald B. Winrod. They were, Armstrong wrote,

> patriots who despite calumny and persecution, have boldly proclaimed the truth regarding the Jewish menace....If our country is saved from revolution and our republican form of government is preserved it will be due largely to the educational work of these brave men.

In this same book Armstrong said that Hitler "abhorred" war, and he blamed the outbreak of the conflict in 1939 entirely on the British and French, who were fighting on behalf of their Jewish masters. Hitler was merely trying to liberate the German people from the clutches of their Jewish oppressors. The Jews "have had a great picnic and very rich picking, and they are now paying for their fun."[13]

During the war Armstrong disseminated seditious hate literature which, among other things, accused Bernard Baruch, Felix Frankfurter, Samuel Rosenman, and Roosevelt of engineering the Pearl Harbor attack. His 1950 book *The Zionists* praised Hitler for waging war "according to the rules of civilized warfare," said that the German dictator was a better man than Roosevelt or Churchill, and that he did not seek war but merely wanted the return of Germany's pre-World War I possessions by peaceful agreement. Armstrong described the Nuremberg trials as a frame-up and the mass murder of Jews as "alleged crimes." None of the defendants at Nuremberg were guilty of war crimes, he claimed. Rather, they were persecuted by a pro-Zionist court "for the offense of being opposed to Zionism and communism." If anyone should have been put on trial it should have been Henry Morgenthau and Felix Frankfurter.[14]

A theme common to Armstrong and other antisemites, particularly in the South, was the role that Jews had had in promoting racial integration and the "mongrelization" of the races. He proudly announced that he was a white supremacist, declared that no black was his equal, and called for the repeal of the first sections of the Fourteenth and Fifteenth Amendments to the Constitution, which guaranteed citizenship to blacks and forbade anyone from being denied the vote on the basis of race. Blacks, as well as Asians and immigrants, he argued, should not be allowed to vote, hold office, have any interest in a newspaper, radio station or movie studio, or belong to any secret organization. Blacks, he declared, are not my equal nor are their children the equals of my children or grandchildren. I am superior by blood and inheritance to any and every man of African of Asiatic ancestry. The Anglo-Saxon race is superior to every other race. We are God's chosen people. Through us God has created this Christian civilization which we enjoy, and our forefathers founded this Christian government without the help of Jews or negroes. If that is bigotry then I am a bigot, but I regard it as pride of blood and ancestry.[15]

Despite his early anti-Catholicism, Armstrong by the 1930s was advising the Ku Klux Klan to welcome Roman Catholics into its ranks and to concentrate its fire on blacks and Jews.[16]

It is unlikely that the JMC's board of trustees were unfamiliar with Armstrong's extreme views regarding Jews and blacks. Nevertheless, they initiated the contacts that led to his financial assistance. In January and February 1949, Stanley M. Murphy, the chairman of the school's executive committee, wrote to one of Armstrong's sons, Allen Jack Armstrong, regarding the school's desperate financial straits and its plans to become a college that "could be unique in its character" if sufficient funding could be found. "Mr. Armstrong, knowing your father's inclination and knowing that he is a champion for Jefferson Democracy, it is hoped that he will visualize the possibilities of Jefferson Military College and see fit to support this institution." At first the school suggested a $7,500 loan, later modified to a loan of $6,500, to be used for repairs and school equipment.[17] George Armstrong responded affirmatively to the latter request and loaned the school $6,500 with the understanding that he would not demand payment of interest or principal. The school then named Allen Armstrong to its board of trustees, selected him as chairman of its executive committee, and appointed him the school's business manager.

In late October 1949 Armstrong's foundation announced that it was offering a major gift to JMC which, it was widely estimated, could be worth as much as $50,000,000. As was true of much of the story of the Armstrong gift, the $50,000,000 figure was a fantasy. $50,000,000 in 1949 was the equivalent of $475,000,000 in 2010. This would have been an unprecedented figure in the history of fund-raising by American educational institutions, and few Americans, and Armstrong was certainly not among them, had the resources for such a gift. Many of Armstrong's business ventures were doing poorly in the late 1940s, and persons familiar with Armstrong's finances believed his financial resources were a fraction of what the press assumed them to be.[18]

At times Armstrong refused to attach any precise monetary figure to his proposed gift. The $50,000,000 figure, he said, was pure speculation. But on other occasions he used the $50,000,000 figure himself, and he even said that the gift could be worth more than that. But neither he nor anyone else could be certain of its value. He proposed giving to JMC the surface title to twenty-eight of his plantations totaling twenty-six thousand acres of land, in addition to one-half of his six-tenths mineral rights in an additional forty-two thousand acres. The remaining four-tenths were owned by members of the Armstrong family and Armstrong's foundation. It was not clear how much oil and gas the plantations contained, and it was impossible to predict the future value of either of these commodities or the price which the school would receive should it decide to sell some of the land. At the time of the gift there were only three functioning oil wells on all his land in Mississippi. Nevertheless, the figure of $50,000,000 stuck and was frequently used in the many newspaper and magazine accounts of the gift.[19]

It was not the amount of the gift that brought notoriety to JMC and Armstrong but the conditions he attached to it. First of all he insisted that the school's board of fifteen trustees be replaced by a new board of five persons, three of whom he would appoint, with the other two selected by the outgoing board. Armstrong's nominees were Allen Armstrong, United States Attorney Joseph E. Brown, and George Van Horn Moseley. Allen Armstrong was a racist and antisemite himself, and Brown saw nothing inappropriate about the proposed gift. "If a Jew embraces the Christian faith," he remarked, "he can attend just as well as any other Christian."[20]

Of the three, Moseley was undoubtedly the vilest. For years Armstrong had sent Moseley a monthly stipend, undoubtedly in appreciation for Moseley's continuing fidelity to the antisemitic cause.[21] The depth of Moseley's antisemitism is indicated by a speech he gave in 1938 at Tulane University in New Orleans before a group of medical reservists in which he stated that he would allow refugees from Nazi Germany to be admitted into the United States provided they all agreed to be sterilized. The United States, he said on other occasions, must immediately begin "selective breeding, sterilization, the elimination of the unfit, and the elimination of those types which are inimical to the general welfare of the nation," and there is little doubt as to whom Moseley regarded as particularly unfit. The Jew, he exclaimed, would always be a "human outcast." Writing about Jews "is like writing about something loathsome, such as syphilis." Moseley admired Nazi Germany for its antisemitism and declared that Nazism and fascism were perfectly compatible with American values and institutions. During the war he said that Jews were receiving their just desserts, and that the most humane solution to the Jewish problem was "breeding all Jewish blood out of the human race."[22] Armstrong wanted Moseley to become chairman of JMC's board of trustees.[23]

The involvement of Moseley, however, was not the most noteworthy aspect of the Armstrong gift. This, rather, was his announced objective of using the gift to promote white supremacy and antisemitism. Under the terms of the gift, both blacks and Jews would be forbidden from attending the school. The issue of blacks attending JMC was a moot point since the segregation laws of Mississippi precluded school integration, and the school's trustees were fervent segregationists. But the issue of Jews attending JMC was not moot since Jews were presumably white, although not in the eyes of Armstrong. Armstrong also demanded that white supremacy become the regnant ideology of the school and be emphasized in its promotional literature.

Armstrong asserted that since blacks and Jews had their own schools, white Christians also had the right to have schools of their own. He was simply seeking equality for white Christians, he lamely argued, and not discriminating against blacks and Jews. Armstrong's definition of "white Christians" was very elastic. He excluded Asians as racially inferior but included Latin Americans, perhaps because there had been a Latin American presence at the school for decades. Also, although most Latin Americans were not Protestants, they at least were Christians, but this was not true of Asians. It was irrelevant to Armstrong that "Latin Americans," "Anglo-Saxons," or "white Christians" were not recognized by anthropologists or other social scientists as legitimate racial categories.

Within a few weeks of offering the small loan to JMC, Armstrong enlarged his focus and broached the possibility of a major gift of land and mineral rights to the JMC board of trustees. He wrote to Murphy on February 14, 1949, outlining the proposed gift and his conditions.[24] Two weeks later the board wrote Armstrong that it had unanimously accepted his proposal, including all of his conditions. The board expressed "its genuine appreciation to you for your selflessness and magnanimity in making it possible to re-create an institution that has been so long associated with American principles of democracy." The proposed gift was a "noble deed," and, the board hoped, "will provide the spark and the impetus that shall build a monument which the entire United States shall cherish and...future generations shall pay homage and respect to your name."[25] The next day Murphy wrote to Armstrong confirming the board's decision. Ironically, this letter was written on the stationery of Murphy's insurance company, which was located in the Levy Building in downtown Natchez.[26] And on October 20, 1949, during the final discussions of the board regarding the gift, Murphy wrote to Armstrong of the board's gratitude. "May your name ever be perpetuated, not only through the institution which you are endowing, but through the men and women who are taught the principles of Constitutional Government!"[27] At no time prior to the announcement of the acceptance of the gift in late October did the board of trustees object to any of Armstrong's conditions. In fact, F.R. Blankenstein, a Roman Catholic of German background, agreed to resign from the school's board of directors if it thought his Jewish-sounding name complicated negotiations between the board and Armstrong over his gift.

Nor was the general JMC community ignorant of Armstrong's plans for the school. Allen Armstrong had outlined his father's thinking in a commencement speech he gave at the end of the 1948-1949 school year. He first described the land and mineral rights which were to be conveyed to the school. This, he avowed, would, at a minimum, provide millions of dollars to the school. But this gift, he warned, was predicated on the school remaining faithful to the "traditions of the South." These included opposition to political collectivism in any form, constitutional government, "true democracy," states rights, free enterprise, and "belief in the Christian faith and in the supremacy of the Anglo-Saxon and Latin races over those of African or Asiatic origin with their false gods and ideologies."[28]

On Monday, October 24, 1949, Allen Armstrong formally announced that JMC had accepted Armstrong's gift, including the provisos that it would teach the superiority of the Anglo-Saxon and Latin-American races and that no one of Asian or African origin would be admitted as a student or even be employed by the school. The younger Armstrong anticipated that his father's gift would enable JMC to evolve into a junior college and then into a university, and he promised that similar gifts to other schools were being contemplated. He specifically mentioned Belhaven College in Jackson, Mississippi, a Presbyterian institution, and Texas Wesleyan in Fort Worth as possible recipients.[29]

Although he realized that the conditions of the gift might arouse opposition in some quarters, Allen Armstrong did not anticipate any obstacles to consummating the gift. In fact he was already planning a gala ceremony in November or December celebrating it. Possible speakers at this event included Fielding Wright, the governor of Mississippi and the Dixiecrat vice-presidential nominee in 1948.[30] There was good reason for Armstrong's confidence. The school's trustees had never expressed any reservations about the gift. They had, in contrast, predicted the Armstrong gift would transform JMC into "the finest military institution in the South, if not the entire nation," and that eventually it would become "a great university."[31]

But, much to its surprise, the board was now confronted with a public relations disaster. Northerners and Southerners, Jews and Gentiles alike, were outraged both by the gift and the school's acceptance of it. Southerners in particular had reason to be angry and embarrassed since Armstrong had seemingly substantiated the widespread stereotype of the South as benighted and bigoted. Dozens of newspaper editorials throughout the country strongly condemned Armstrong for his bigotry and severely censured the school for accepting his gift. The Boston *Globe* of October 26 said Armstrong's offer was "a startling reminder that there is plenty of un-Americanism to combat here in this country," while the St. Louis *Dispatch* that same day described it as "$50,000,000 worth of ignorance." Jewish organizations naturally strongly condemned Armstrong's gift. The Anti-Defamation League of B'nai B'rith compared it to "Hitler's technique of using educational institutions to spread Nazi religious and racial doctrines."[32]

Radio commentators and newspaper columnists, most notably Walter Winchell and Drew Pearson, also criticized JMC and Armstrong. In his radio program of October 30, Winchell called Armstrong's gift a "slimy deal" and described Armstrong as a "miserable old man." "The greatest service this unspeakable bigot could perform is to create a foundation for the education of himself," Winchell said, "or build a modern mental institution and reside in it, until he drops dead."[33]

Armstrong immediately protested to the American Broadcasting Company. He demanded a transcript of Winchell's comments as well as fifteen minutes of free air time to answer him. This should be provided gratis by the Kaiser-Frazer Corporation, the automobile manufacturer and Winchell's sponsor. ABC rejected both of these requests.[34] Armstrong also complained to the Federal Communications Commission regarding Winchell's supposed misuse of the airways and threatened to sue for slander if he was not granted his fifteen minutes of fame. Neither ABC nor the FCC offered any relief to Armstrong, and Armstrong did not carry through on his threat to sue although he did consult with a couple of attorneys.[35] On October 30, Pearson also denounced Armstrong over the radio. Armstrong responded by writing a twenty-page pamphlet titled *The Truth About My Alleged $50,000,000 Donation* in which he claimed that Winchell's original name was "Lipschitz," described Winchell and Pearson as "public enemies," said they had spread "malicious lies" about him, and charged they were inspired by the Non-Sectarian Anti-Nazi League and were agents of the Zionist-financial conspiracy.[36]

In the evening of October 27, JMC's trustees announced that they could not assent to Armstrong's demands to exclude Jewish and Asian students, to restrict the faculty to white Christians, and to incorporate the doctrine of racial superiority in its teaching. They claimed that Armstrong had never made clear the conditions which he attached to the gift; they expressed surprise that Armstrong actually wanted to exclude Jews from the school; and they professed ignorance regarding the racial views of Armstrong and Moseley. This is hardly credible. Armstrong had clearly enunciated his objectives to the trustees when they initially approached him for the loan in January 1949. He told the school then that he was "interested in financing a first class university" on his Whitehall Plantation provided that the provision in the 1802 charter guaranteeing admittance of applicants from all religious denominations be deleted. This would weed out Jews. He also said at this time that he wanted the school to exclude Asians and Africans as students.[37]

The trustees claimed that the misunderstanding with Armstrong was partially due to semantics. Armstrong, the board pointed out, at times had said that he wanted the school to remain "primarily" an institution for white Christians, while at other times he used the word "exclusively." But there could have been little doubt about his ultimate intentions. The trustees chose to hear what they wanted to hear. The board also claimed that Allen Armstrong had announced the school's acceptance of the gift without its authorization. But there was nothing in the board's actions over the previous nine months that would have led Allen Armstrong to believe that the board opposed George Armstrong's intentions.

Murphy issued a statement absolving the board of blame for this "complete misunderstanding." For the board, the sticking points were antisemitism and the teaching of white supremacy, not the exclusion of Asians, Africans, or American blacks from the student body or the appointment of Moseley to a new board of trustees. Armstrong's antisemitism, Murphy said, was "utterly foreign to the thinking of all the members of the board." "There are some things money cannot buy," he continued. "There is not enough money in the world to make us go through with a philosophy of education based on religious bias or anti-Semitic feeling." Of course the trustees had been eager to do precisely that a few weeks earlier. In addition, the board announced that racial supremacy would never be taught at the school, although the school would continue admitting only white students. To admit "colored" students, the board asserted, was simply "unthinkable."[38]

On October 29, after learning of the school's change of heart, Armstrong withdrew his gift. He also said he would not demand repayment of the one-year loan so that JMC could finish the scholastic year. The board also rejected this, and in February 1950 it paid off the loan, including interest. Armstrong concluded that the board had caved in to Jewish pressure. He said that he planned to transfer the assets that would have gone to JMC to the Judge Armstrong Foundation, established three years earlier, which, he declared, "was under attack by the Truman New Deal Administration." This referred to the government's effort to remove the foundation's tax exemption as a charitable organization. Armstrong also mentioned that he hoped to establish a university either in Mississippi or Texas, to be named the Judge Armstrong University, and that he was not opposed to the Jewish and Negro races. "But I am opposed to mongrelization." He also reiterated his opposition to the Fourteenth and Fifteenth Amendments.[39]

JMC won plaudits throughout the nation for its rejection of the Armstrong gift and its courageous stand in behalf of religious tolerance and fair play. The New York *Herald Tribune* of October 31, 1949, said the school had shown its "spunk" by rejecting Armstrong's riches. "Let us trust that temptation is rejected as boldly elsewhere." Southern newspapers praised JMC's stand. The Greenville (Mississippi) *Times* called Armstrong "a fool" with money. The *News and Courier* of Charleston, South Carolina and the *News and Observer* of Raleigh, North Carolina complimented JMC for not agreeing to teach the anti-Christian and un-American doctrine of racial superiority.[40] Elliott Trimble, the editor of the Natchez *Democrat* and JMC's public relations counsel, wrote that the school's board deserved the congratulations of all Americans for rejecting a gift that was "inimical to American freedom and ideas."[41]

Five months earlier, a June 4, 1949 editorial in the Natchez *Democrat* titled "Logical Expansion" had described Armstrong's proposed gift as "ambitious" and "inspiring." "We can think of ... no better cause for financial aid," it stated. But the paper sang a different tune in late October. Now it praised JMC's rejection of the gift in an October 29 editorial titled "New Day Ahead." Americans could breathe "a sigh of relief" now that the school had unequivocally rejected Armstrong's "abhorred philosophy" of antisemitism and white supremacy. The board of trustees, the paper said, had never planned to do otherwise. "This was not a new policy ... for at no time ... has the reverse been true — news stories and broadcasts to the contrary." The proper response for lovers of democracy and freedom, the paper advised, would be to send checks to the school. As far as those who had slandered the trustees as racists, "LET THEM NOW PRAISE THE SAME TRUSTEES WHOM

THEY HAVE ACCUSED OF ADVOCATING THE TEACHING OF RACIAL SUPERIORITY WHEN IN FACT NOTHING COULD BE FARTHER FROM THE TRUTH" (capitals in original). Evidently the paper believed that the rejection of racial superiority referred only to non-Christian students and teachers. Left unsaid was the school's continuing ban on black students and teachers, which, of course, conformed to the laws of Mississippi mandating segregation in the state's schools.

Praise in the press, while welcome, did not alleviate JMC's desperate financial straits and the fear that the school would have to close before the end of the academic year. In early November the school launched a "Save Jefferson" and "Dollars for Democracy" financial campaign to raise $100,000. Checks poured in from throughout the country, including one for $5,000 from Nathan J. Klein, a wealthy Houston Jewish ice cream manufacturer, so that the school could repay its debt to Armstrong. JMC even received contributions from blacks, though the school would not have admitted any of their children. The fund-raising campaign was a limited success, and less than $40,000 was raised.[42] This money alleviated the short-term fiscal troubles of JMC and removed the threat of imminent financial collapse. But it did not resolve the bleak long-term fiscal situation of JMC due to shrinking enrollment and lack of an endowment. The school would ultimately close its doors in 1964, the same year that Congress passed its historic civil rights law.

Armstrong and his foundation, the Judge Armstrong Foundation, were well-known to American Jewish defense organizations. Beginning in 1947, the American Jewish Committee's (AJC) Legal and Investigative Division had attempted to get the Internal Revenue Service (IRS) to revoke the tax-exempt status of the foundation on the basis that it had violated its charter by engaging in political activities and spreading hateful propaganda. The foundation had been established in November 1945, ostensibly for charitable, religious, and educational purposes, and Moseley was one of its trustees. In reality, as the AJC pointed out several times to the IRS, the bulk of the foundation's grants underwrote the publication and distribution of Armstrong's antisemitic and racist tracts. The IRS, the AJC maintained, should not be in the business of encouraging religious and racial bigotry. The IRS agreed, and on December 8, 1949 it rescinded the foundation's tax-exempt status.[43] Armstrong then transferred the assets he had been planning to give to JMC to a new foundation with the innocent-sounding name Texas Educational Association (TEA).[44]

Armstrong, a true believer, was not discouraged by the JMC fiasco or the revocation of his foundation's tax-exempt status. He received overtures from a few small church-related colleges in the Deep South for funds. Nothing came of these or of his plans to establish a university in Fort Worth or Port Arthur. This would be named for himself and only accept white Christian students. At the time of the JMC flap a controversy arose over a $5,000,000 gift which Armstrong had supposedly offered to Southern Methodist University in Dallas provided it "disassociate itself from Jews," including not admitting any Jewish students. Rev. W. Harrison Baker, a member of the SMU board of trustees, claimed Armstrong had made such an offer and, when it was rejected by Dr. Umphrey Lee, the university's president, he demanded that the board discharge Lee and reconsider his proposal. Armstrong strenuously denied that he had made any such offer, and Lee confirmed this. Armstrong said he would never have made such an offer because of SMU's involvement in interfaith work, particularly its sponsorship of a lecture series at Temple Emanu-El, a Dallas synagogue. This was an "unholy alliance," Armstrong said, because Jews are not Methodists. "They are *anti-Christ*." (italics in original)[45]

There was no doubt, however, regarding Armstrong's interest in 1950 in making a gift to Texas Wesleyan College (TWC) in Forth Worth. The previous year Armstrong had announced plans to donate eight hundred and twenty-six acres of land adjacent to Port Arthur, Texas, which he valued at over one million dollars, to TWC. Nothing came of this proposal, which had been prompted in part by estate tax considerations.[46] The 1950 gift was much different. TWC had announced its intention of hiring Texas Congressman Martin Dies, the chairman of the House Committee on Un-American Activities, to teach courses in government and to give speeches throughout the country. Dr. Law Sone, TWC's president, asked Allen Armstrong whether his father's foundation would pay part of Dies' salary and expenses, and the younger Armstrong conveyed the request to his father. George Armstrong was enthusiastic and agreed to pay $1,000 per month for three years. Within a few days, however, he withdrew the offer. The problem was Sone's chairmanship of the Fort Worth campaign for "Brotherhood Week," and his invitation to Dies to speak in Fort Worth on behalf of this cause. Armstrong told Moseley that he could not support any Zionist program such as Brotherhood Week and was skeptical of Dies since he had become a pawn of the Jews. He did not foreclose the possibility of funding a position in government at TWC, but only if an appropriate person was hired. His candidates included such noxious antisemites as Merwin K. Hart and Gerald L. K. Smith.[47]

In March 1951 Armstrong was in the news again when the press reported that the board of trustees of Piedmont College in Demorest, Georgia had been receiving since January of that year a monthly check of $500 from the

Texas Educational Association.[48] The critics of the monthly gifts focused on Moseley since he lived at the Biltmore Hotel in Atlanta, only seventy-five miles from Demorest, was president of the TEA and controlled its funds, and had visited the Piedmont campus. Hoping to tap the foundation's money, the college had honored Moseley at a student-faculty banquet in November 1950. It is unlikely that the college was aware of Moseley's outlook when it solicited the TEA, along with over a thousand other foundations and individuals, for financial aid. But once the college accepted TEA's money, it dug in its heels in. While Moseley was notorious because of his attacks on Jews, blacks, and democracy and his sympathy for Nazi Germany, his chief critic on campus was a war hero, English professor Hoyt E. Bowen. Bowen had been a naval combat pilot and was wounded during World War II.[49]

The furor over the monthly gifts lasted nearly a year and resulted in the firing of David Eddy, the school's treasurer, and the failure to renew the contracts of A.R. Van Cleave, the college's dean, and Bowen. All three men had protested the TEA as undemocratic, anti-Christian, and un-American, but the trustees and James E. Walter, the college's president, accused the protesters of being insubordinate. Walter stated that Piedmont's policy was "to accept money without strings or qualifications for purposes of Christian higher education" and that the actions of the dissenters were harmful to this goal of Christian education. Piedmont had been founded in 1897 as a Congregational institution, Walter was a Congregational minister, and the school retained ties to the church. The college's critics argued rather that the Christian character of the college was being polluted by its association with Armstrong and Moseley.[50]

Eddy responded in March 1951 by gathering the signatures of over one hundred students demanding the resignation of Walter "to spare the college...the necessity of our washing still more of your dirty linen in public."[51] That same month sixteen members of the faculty called on the college to reject any money from TEA, and students voted 114-14 for Walter's resignation and the return of all TEA money. Two months later during commencement festivities the alumni voted 25-3 that it no longer had any confidence in the Walter administration and that he should be dismissed. The board of trustees, in response, denied that it could be bought off by a mere $6,000 per year or that any strings were attached to the gift. They instead focused on the college's dire financial situation and what good things Piedmont could do with Armstrong's tainted money. As one trustee put it, the only tainted aspect of Armstrong's money was that it "taint enough."[52]

The school's stance was strongly condemned in editorials and letters-to-the-editor in newspapers in Atlanta and Chattanooga. The Anti-Defamation League considered bringing pressure to remove the college's tax exemption and accreditation and offered its services to the American Association of University Professors in any action it might take against the college for violating the academic freedom of Bowen.[53] In February 1952 the college's board reaffirmed its acceptance of TEA's monthly stipends. Trustee Josephine Wilkins, a former Georgia state president of the League of Women Voters, promptly resigned over "a vital issue of principle," namely the racism and antisemitism of Armstrong and Moseley. Within a year, however, the issue was moot since the TEA had stopped supporting Piedmont. Various bodies within the Congregational Church had demanded Walter's resignation, and its National Board of Home Missions had cut off its annual contribution to Piedmont as long as it accepted money from the TEA. The mayor and city council of Demorest even passed a unanimous resolution calling for Walter's removal "in the name of civil responsibility, quality education of our youth and Christian unity in our community."[54] Walter remained as president. The Piedmont College controversy was the last chapter in Armstrong's crusade to purify American higher education. He died five months after the Supreme Court in the *Brown* decision of May 1954 outlawed racial segregation in the nation's schools.

CODA

On July 14, 1996, the *New York Times* carried the wedding announcement of Christine Mitchell Armstrong, the daughter of George W. Armstrong 3rd of Natchez, Mississippi. A graduate of the University of Texas, she worked as an analyst at the investment banking firm Lehman Brothers in New York. Lehman Brothers had been established in the nineteenth century by a family of German Jews living in Alabama, and, according to antisemites, was an important part of the Jewish financial conspiracy controlling the American economy. The groom was Benjamin Edward Nickoll of Beverly Hills, California. Nickoll was a bond trader at Morgan Stanley & Company, and his father was chairman of a commercial finance company in Los Angeles. The marriage took place in Salisbury, Connecticut with Rev. James Petty, a Church of Christ minister, and Rabbi Joel S. Goor officiating. George Armstrong's warning about the power of Jewish finance and Jewish "mongrelization" had seemingly come to pass. But he could not have anticipated that it would occur in his own family within four generations. Nor could he have predicted the establishment of the Armstrong Nickoll Foundation which, along with foundations with Jewish sounding names such as the Horace W. Goldsmith Foundation, the Litowitz Foundation, and the Slifka Foundation, contributed to the capital campaign of a Shakespeare theater in Brooklyn, New York, home to the largest Jewish population in the United States as well as to one of the largest black ghettos. But by the date of the wedding George W. Armstrong had been dead for over four decades, and the retrograde impulses which he personified were of interest only to historians.[55]

Edward Shapiro received his B.A. from Georgetown University (1959) and his PhD in history from Harvard University (1968). He taught at Seton Hall University for three decades. His books include *A Time for Healing: American Jewry since World War II* (1992), *We Are Many: Reflections on American Jewish History and Identity* (2005), and *Crown Heights: Blacks, Jews, and the 1991 Brooklyn Riot* (2006).

ENDNOTES

1   The public library of Natchez bears the name "George W. Armstrong" and is, ironically, directly across the street from Temple B'nai Israel, the city's synagogue.

2   See, for example, "Memorandum on GEORGE W. ARMSTRONG," July 18, 1947, Armstrong File, American Jewish Committee Library, New York.

3   For Rankin and Bilbo, see Edward S. Shapiro, "Anti-Semitism Mississippi Style," in *Anti-Semitism in American History*, ed. David A. Gerber (Urbana: University of Illinois Press, 1986), 129–51. Armstrong dedicated his 1947 book *World Empire* to Rankin.

4   "Tullis Heads Effort to Save Jefferson Military College," New Orleans *Times Picayune*, December 12, 1949; *Jefferson Military College: Preparatory Schools for Boys 8–18* (undated), p. 5. A copy of this guide to the school is in the George W. Armstrong Papers, Special Collections, University of Texas at Arlington Library, Arlington, TX.

5   "Virtue Triumphs: School Refuses to teach Bigotry for $50 Million," *Life*, November 14, 1949, 108–111; Charles F. Sudduth, "Jefferson Military College: A Brief History," http://www.mississippidays.com/jmc. JMC struggled on until 1964 when the state of Mississippi took over the school and paid off its debts of $66,000. "Governor Johnson Confident State Will Acquire Jefferson," Natchez (Mississippi) *Democrat*, May 30, 1964.

6   *Memoirs of George W. Armstrong* (Austin, TX: Steck, 1958), 152–61, 311, 318.

7   Armstrong, *Memoirs*, 20, 62. Armstrong's father had been the chaplain of his Confederate regiment and a circuit-riding minister. His two brothers were also Methodist ministers.

8   "Judge Armstrong of Natchez Only Living Man for Whom Oil Field in State Has Been Named," Jackson (Mississippi) *Daily News*, October 20, 1949.

9   Armstrong, *Memoirs*, 113.

10 The American Jewish population was, in fact, less than 1/3 of the fifteen million figure claimed by Armstrong. It is likely that Henry Ford was the source of Armstrong's idea that John Wilkes Booth was Jewish.

11 In *The Zionists* (1950), 91, Armstrong claimed that the fortune of Franklin Roosevelt stemmed from a Jewish ancestor involved in the opium trade.

12 Armstrong, *The March of Bolshevism* (1945), 17, 29; Armstrong, *Memoirs*, 204, 365.

13 Armstrong, *The Rothschild Money Trust* (1940), 78-80.

14 Armstrong, *The Zionists*, 107–14. The extent of Armstrong's ignorance is revealed by his use of the word "Israeli" when referring to the Jewish state rather than "Israel."

15 Armstrong, *Memoirs*, 187, 200. Armstrong's contempt toward blacks is indicated by his refusal in his autobiography and elsewhere to capitalize "Negro."

16 Armstrong to Samuel W. Roper, 7 September 1951, Gerald L. K. Smith Papers, Bentley Historical Library, University of Michigan, Ann Arbor, MI.

17 Stanley M. Murphy to Allen J. Armstrong, 2 January 1949, 24 January 1949, 2 February 1949, Jefferson Military College Papers, Mississippi Department of Archives and History, Jackson, Mississippi.

18 R. Gordon Grantham, a Jackson, Mississippi attorney, was one of those who was skeptical regarding Armstrong's wealth and the value of his proposed gift to JMC. Grantham to Jacob Spolansky, 5 November 1949, Armstrong File, American Jewish Committee Library. See also "Personal History and Background of George W. Armstrong, Sr.," 1–4, 12, *ibid*. This document concluded that Armstrong's net wealth barely exceeded a million dollars.

19 Among the publications that used the fifty million dollar figure were the *New York Times*, *Life*, Fort Worth *Star-Telegram*, San Antonio *Express*, Dallas *Morning News*, Houston *Post*, Oklahoma City *Times*, and Memphis *Commercial Appeal*. The headline in the *New York Times* of October 26, 1949 proclaimed, "Little School Accepts 50 Million to Champion White Supremacy." For examples of Armstrong's use of the $50,000,000 figure see his letter in the Natchez *Democrat* of May 8, 1949 and his letter to Congressman John E. Rankin, 16 July 1949, Armstrong Papers.

20 "College Offered 50 Million to Teach Race Superiority," Fort Worth *Star-Telegram*, October 26, 1949.

21 For Armstrong's financial support of Moseley, see George Van Horn Moseley to Y. Q. McCammon, 5 May 1952, Armstrong Papers.

22 These quotes are from Joseph W. Bendersky, *The "Jewish Threat": Anti-Semitic Politics of the U.S. Army* (New York: Basic Books, 2000), 21–22, 38, 203, 249–58. Moseley wrote the introduction to Armstrong's memoirs. On pages 85-86 of the memoirs is a November 29, 1949 letter by James H. Sheldon, chairman of the Non-Sectarian Anti-Nazi League. It quoted from a speech Moseley gave the preceding month in St. Louis at a meeting of antisemites. "I have only one thing to say about the Jews," Moseley reportedly said. "As for me, the whole tribe should be eliminated from the human race." Moseley never denied saying this. Moseley remains a model for American antisemites, and their web sites continue to quote him. His son, Col. George

Van Horn Moseley, Jr., commanded the 502nd Parachute Infantry Regiment of the 101st Airborne Division during the parachute drop into Normandy on the evening of June 5–6, 1944. He broke his ankle during the drop, and for a day or so commanded the regiment from a wheelbarrow. Moseley was part of the composite character played by John Wayne in the movie "The Longest Day." Wayne leads his troops while in a wheelbarrow, but his character is named Benjamin Vandervoort. Lt. Col. Benjamin H. Vandervoort commanded the 505th Parachute Infantry Regiment of the 82nd Airborne Division during the Normandy invasion. It is possible that the movie used the name Vandervoort rather than Moseley because of the senior Moseley's reputation.

23 Armstrong to Moseley, 18 June 1949, Armstrong Papers.

24 Armstrong to Stanley Murphy, 14 February 1949, Jefferson Military College Papers.

25 Trustees of Jefferson College to Armstrong, 28 February 1949, Jefferson Military College Papers.

26 Murphy to Armstrong, 1 March 1949, Armstrong Papers.

27 The letters of Stewart and Murphy are reprinted in Armstrong, *Memoirs*, 196–97.

28 Allen J. Armstrong, "Excerpts From Jefferson Military College 1949 Commencement Address," Armstrong Papers.

29 "School Gets Five-Tenths of Armstrong Minerals in State: Policy Revealed," Natchez *Democrat*, October 25, 1949.

30 Allen Armstrong to George W. Armstrong Jr., 25 October 1949, Armstrong Papers.

31 Announcement of the Board of Trustees of Jefferson Military College on the occasion of the Armstrong gift, Armstrong Papers. This document is untitled and undated.

32 "George W. Armstrong," *The Facts*, November, 1949, 4. *The Facts* was a monthly publication of the Anti-Defamation League of B'nai B'rith.

33 There is a transcript of the Winchell broadcast in the Armstrong Papers.

34 Mark Woods to Armstrong, 9 December 1949, Armstrong Papers. Woods was president of ABC.

35 Armstrong to Moseley, 21 December 1949, and Mark Woods to Wayne Coy, 23 November 1949, Armstrong Papers. Coy was the chairman of the FCC. Armstrong later changed his demand to two ten-minute segments and the right to purchase a five-minute slot for as long as ABC aired the Winchell show. Armstrong to Woods, 12 December 1949, Armstrong Papers. Winchell continued his attacks on Armstrong in his newspaper column. See, for example, his column in the Chicago *Herald-American*, December 5, 1949 and December 12, 1949. There is no mention of the Armstrong-Winchell confrontation in Neal Gabler, *Winchell: Gossip, Power and the Culture of Celebrity* (New York: Alfred A. Knopf, 1994).

36 One version of this pamphlet is reprinted in Armstrong, *Memoirs*, 183-204. Another version is found in the Gerald L. K. Smith Papers. It was common for other American anti-Semites, including Congressman John Rankin, to claim Winchell's original name was Lipschitz, perhaps because of its scatological association. Reputable encyclopedias and biographical dictionaries give the original name as Weinschel,

Winchel, Wincheles, or Winschel. The standard biography of Winchell, Gabler's *Winchell: Gossip, Power, and the Culture of Celebrity*, does not discuss the Armstrong-Winchell hullabaloo.

37 Armstrong to Murphy, 26 January 1949, Jefferson Military College Papers. Armstrong also wrote to others of his plans for an "Armstrong University," his wish that the offensive section in JMC's charter be deleted, and his hope that the first sections of the Fourteenth and Fifteenth Amendments to the Constitution be repealed. Armstrong to W.C. Wells, 3rd, 26 January 1949, *ibid*.

38 "Chronological Statement of Events with reference to Proposal of Judge George W. Armstrong to Endow Jefferson Military College and the Ultimate Rejection of the Offer;" "Statement with Reference to Endowment of Jefferson College;" George Armstrong to Murphy, 28 October 1949, Jefferson Military College Papers; "George W. Armstrong," 3–4.

39 "$50,000,000 Endowment Offer to Jefferson Is Withdrawn by Oil Man," Jackson *Daily News*, October 29, 1949; Allen Armstrong to George Armstrong, 21 October 949, Armstrong Papers. Allen Armstrong agreed with his father that Jewish influence had caused JMC to reject his father's gift. Allen J. Armstrong to Moseley, 1 November 1949, Armstrong Papers. A typescript copy of George W. Armstrong's statement is in the Armstrong Papers. In November, 1894 Armstrong was elected a county judge of Tarrant County. He served two terms, and was defeated for renomination in 1898. Armstrong liked the title of "Judge," and his family and friends frequently referred to him as such.

40 "Things Money Can't Buy — Murphy," Natchez (Mississippi) *Times*, October 28, 1949.

41 Elliott Trimble, "The 8th Column," Natchez *Democrat*, October 30, 1949.

42 "Jefferson to Launch Its 148th Year with Faith in the Future," Natchez *Times*, September 10, 1950. Approximately ninety percent of the funds raised by the school in the aftermath of the Armstrong controversy came from Jews, according to a report by the school's endowment fund committee to its board of trustees. A copy of this report is in the Jefferson Military College Papers.

43 "Armstrong Exemption Revoked," *New York Times*, December 9, 1949; E.I. McLarney to Judge Armstrong Foundation, 9 December 1949, Armstrong Papers. McLarney was the deputy director of the Internal Revenue Service, and his letter informed the foundation of the revocation of its tax-exempt status. For the involvement of the American Jewish Committee in the revoking of the foundation's tax-exempt status, see McLarney to George J. Mintzer, 22 December 1947, and John Slawson to George Kellman, 12 December 1949, Armstrong File. The American Jewish Congress opposed the attempt to deprive the Armstrong Foundation of its tax-exempt status, perhaps because of civil libertarian concerns.

44 George W. Armstrong to Thompson, Walker, Smith & Shannon, 7 November 1949; Moseley to Armstrong, 17 July 1951; Y. Q. McCammon to Armstrong, 15 August 1952, Armstrong Papers. McCammon, a nephew of Armstrong, was also his accountant.

45 George W. Armstrong to H.A. Boaz, 18 October 1949, and Armstrong to Umphrey Lee, 16 June 1949, Armstrong Papers; Armstrong, *Memoirs*, 192; "SMU Shuns Endowment to Bar Jews," Dallas *Morning News*, October 28, 1949.

46 In January 1949 the Fort Worth National Bank, following Armstrong's instructions, had a trust officer draw up an estate plan which provided for the creation of a perpetual trust for the benefit of Texas Wesleyan College. The bank estimated that Armstrong's estate was worth approximately eight million dollars. For the details of this plan, see R.E. Harding to Armstrong, 24 January 1949, Armstrong Papers. Harding was the president of Fort Worth National Bank.

47 Allen Armstrong to Moseley, 24 February 1950 and George Armstrong to Moseley, 27 February, 1950, Gerald L.K. Smith Papers.

48 At this time Piedmont's enrollment was approximately three hundred and thirty-five full- and part-time students, and it had a faculty of twenty-three.

49 See, for example, Bowen's letter in the Atlanta *Constitution*, May 28, 1951.

50 Celestine Sibley, "Students Hit Firing of 2 at Piedmont: College Rift Laid to Moseley Gifts," Atlanta *Constitution*, March 3, 1951; Davenport Steward, "Piedmont College Group Fights Grant: Students and Faculty to Ask Return of $1,500 to Moseley's Texas Association," *Atlanta Journal*, March 4, 1951.

51 "College Ousts Official: Piedmont in Georgia Continues to Accept Protested Gifts," *New York Times*, March 21, 1951; "Piedmont Uprising," *Time*, April 2, 1951, 68.

52 Phil Curtiss, "The $500-a-Month Sellout," *ADL Bulletin*, April 1952, 5, 8; "Alumni Challenge Piedmont President," *New York Times*, June 4, 1951.

53 Isaiah Terman to Milton Kulick, 26 March 1951; Terman to George Kellman, 26 April 1951; Theodore Leskes to Ralph E. Himstead, March 26, 1951, Armstrong File. Himstead was the general secretary of the American Association of University Professors.

54 "School Takes Fund Despite Race Bias: Piedmont College in Georgia Refuses to Disown Group That Gives $500 Monthly," *New York Times*, February 20, 1952; Moseley to George W. Armstrong, 26 February 1953, Armstrong Papers; "College With a Hate Endowment," *ADL Bulletin*, June 1953, 6.

55 "Weddings: B. E. Nickoll, Christine Armstrong," *New York Times*, July 14, 1996. For the contribution of the Armstrong-Nickoll Foundation, see http://www.tfana.org/capital/support_meetourdonors.html.

III
_____

THE LEFT, BLACKS, JEWS AND ANTISEMITISM

OLD WINE IN NEW BOTTLES
Antisemitism in the American Far Left, 1917–1973

Stephen H. Norwood

USING ANTISEMITIC STEREOTYPES
TO DEMONIZE ISRAEL, 1967–1973

During the late 1960s and early 1970s, the American far left repeatedly denounced Israel as a criminal regime resembling Nazi Germany and enthusiastically endorsed the Arab guerilla movement's campaign to eradicate the Jewish state. This was a period, bounded by two wars that threatened Israel with destruction, in which the far left devoted particular attention to the Arab-Israeli conflict. Leading far left publications joined the Arab guerillas in charging that Israel was aggressively racist and expansionist.

To support these claims, the far left often invoked long-standing antisemitic stereotypes, both economic and theological. It attributed to Jews enormous financial power and an arrogance and sense of superiority that drove them to exploit and dominate other peoples. In a three-part series published in 1969 on what it called "The History of Middle East Liberation Struggle," *New Left Notes*, newspaper of the Students for a Democratic Society (SDS), declared that the Jews' "Chosen people" concept gives Israel "the right to expand and expand." Like Nazi Germany, the Jewish state would "not contain itself within any set borders." It explained that the "architects of Zionism were mainly bourgeois Jewish intellectuals" and that the movement's early sponsors were "leaders in ... world imperialism" like wealthy Jewish banker Edmond de Rothschild, who wanted to create a Jewish homeland in Palestine to promote "his own financial interests."[1]

The Black Panther Party, which identified as Marxist-Leninist, made similar charges rooted in a tradition of economic antisemitism dating to medieval Europe. For the Black Panthers the core of the Middle East conflict was a war between heroic Palestinian guerillas and "Israeli Pigs." They referred to Zionism as "Kosher Nationalism." In 1973 the Black Panther Party newspaper approvingly quoted South African Pan-Africanist David Sibeko, who charged that since its creation in 1948, Israel had sustained itself on "the blood and wealth" that "Zionist Jews" extracted from South Africa. He claimed that South Africa's gold mines were "owned by Zionists." Using the term "Zionist" to mean "Jew," a technique popularized decades before by right-wing antisemites, Sibeko declared that "the Zionists" had "assume[d] superiority in the take-over" of South Africa's industries. He dismissed as a "red herring" the argument that a Jewish state was needed because of the existence of antisemitism; it was part of a scheme to "cover up imperialism's designs against Africa [and its] rich resources."[2]

The Student Non-Violent Coordinating Committee (SNCC), which in 1966 had expelled its white members, a sizeable proportion of whom were Jewish, and positioned itself on the far left of the African-American movement, made similar charges. Shortly after the Six-Day War in 1967 it published an article in its newsletter entitled "The Palestine Problem" that compared Israel to Nazi Germany and accused it of committing "atrocities" against the Palestinians. The article was accompanied by a blurred photograph that purported to show Israelis shooting Arab prisoners lined up against a wall. The caption read, "This is the Gaza Strip, Palestine, not Dachau, Germany." According to SNCC, the Jewish state had been established "through terror, force, and massacres." The "Zionists" had committed mass slaughter, indiscriminately murdering and mutilating Arab men, women, and children.

SNCC's article implied that the Zionists' primary motivation had been the lust for wealth. It declared that "the famous European Jews, the Rothschilds," who had "long controlled the wealth of many European nations," had conspired with the British to create the state of Israel. Like the Black Panther Party, SNCC claimed that the Rothschilds controlled "much of Africa's mineral wealth."[3]

The Trotskyist newspaper the *Militant*, organ of the Socialist Workers Party (SWP), insisted that the SNCC article was not antisemitic and accused Jews who had denounced it of "chauvinist hysteria." It claimed that SNCC had presented "well-known fact" in "defense of the Arab nations," which faced "imperialist-backed invasion by the Zionists."[4]

The *Militant* had itself claimed that the Jewish state was created as a beachhead for Western imperialism to economically exploit the Middle East. It declared that Israel owed its prosperity to sizeable financial contributions from American Jews and to West German Holocaust reparations payments, in addition to U.S. government aid.[5]

SDS published two contrasting letters on the SNCC controversy in *New Left Notes*, but did not take a position as an organization or otherwise address the issue of antisemitism. Itzhak Epstein asked the SDS National Council to adopt a resolution expressing regret about SNCC's "recent inclination towards racism in general and antisemitism in particular." He wanted SDS to maintain a fraternal relationship with SNCC, and called on the two organizations to engage "in a mutual dialogue on racism and antisemitism." Michael Meeropol, son of the executed atom spies Julius and Ethel Rosenberg, responded by accusing Epstein of "hav[ing] bought the lies of the Establishment Press about SNCC." He called Epstein's proposed resolution patronizing and declared that SDS had no right "to charge SNCC with a trend towards racism." Meeropol suggested instead a resolution that would reaffirm SDS's "continuing support for the revolutionary program of SNCC."[6]

The radical pacifist Daniel Berrigan, one of the most prominent figures in the anti-Vietnam War movement, drew on both theological and economic antisemitism in an address condemning Israel before the Association of Arab University Graduates during the Yom Kippur War in October 1973. The Jesuit priest invoked the hoary image of the demonic Jew in the Christian Bible. Berrigan denounced Israel as a racist "settler-state" that used the Hebrew Bible to justify its "crimes against humanity." He claimed that a generation after the Holocaust, Israel had embraced a Nazi-style ideology "aimed at proving its racial superiority to the people [the Arabs] it has crushed." Blinded by "the blood myths of divine election," Israel had "closed her sacred books" and become morally bankrupt. Like Nazi Germany, Israel created ghettoes and disenfranchised peoples; its citizens existed "for the well-being of the state." The Jewish state had become "an Orwellian transplant," a totalitarian society "taken bodily from Big Brother's bloody heart."

Berrigan castigated Israel's American Jewish backers for abandoning the prophetic tradition centered on social justice. He accused them of ignoring what he called the "Asian holocaust," his term for the American military effort in Vietnam.[7] Here Berrigan raised a standard claim of the far left, that the Holocaust was not unique.

David Dellinger, another leader of the anti-Vietnam War movement and long-time pacifist, strongly supported Berrigan's tirade against Israel and her American Jewish supporters. He acknowledged that it had precipitated a storm of criticism from prominent liberals and conservatives. But Dellinger declared that this was because of a "taboo against serious public criticism of

Israel": "It was almost impossible . . . to speak truth to power grown arrogant." Here Dellinger raised a hackneyed charge long leveled by conservative anti-Zionists, that American Jews had the power to suppress public debate about Zionism and Israel because they controlled the mass media.[8]

Shortly after the Six-Day War the far left underground newspaper the Berkeley Barb had also depicted the Jewish state as Pharaoh's Egypt, a monstrous Goliath contemptuous of the Jewish ethical tradition. The top panel of its cartoon showed an ancient Egyptian commander in a chariot leading spear-bearing warriors against fleeing Hebrews. The bottom panel depicted Israeli jets marked with the Star of David, along with tanks and infantry, pursuing retreating Arabs.[9]

Drawing a parallel between Israel and Nazi Germany was the most dramatic way to make the Jewish state appear demonic. In 1970 Mike Klonsky, leader of SDS's Revolutionary Youth Movement II faction, equated what he called Israel's "continuous attacks on the Arab people" with the Nazis' annihilation of the Jews. During the Yom Kippur War the Maoist Progressive Labor Party published a lengthy statement in the UCLA student newspaper calling Israel "a Nazi state" and denouncing Zionism as a "racist atrocity." The Weatherman newspaper Fire even claimed that Nazi antisemitic propaganda was directly modeled on "Zionist writings."[10] Far left groups repeatedly referred to Israel's campaign to defend itself against fourteen Arab nations during the Six-Day War as a "blitzkrieg," suggesting a parallel with the Wehrmacht's conquest of Poland in 1939 and its Western offensive in the spring of 1940.[11] The Black Panther Party called Israeli soldiers "fascist storm troopers," and charged that Israel's victory in the Six-Day War resulted in Arab refugees being forced into "modern concentration camps."[12]

The far left repeatedly made this analogy while remaining silent about the sizeable numbers of Nazi war criminals harbored by such Arab governments as Egypt's and Syria's, which placed many of them in high political and military positions. It ignored the collaboration of Arab heads of state like Egypt's Anwar Sadat with the Hitler regime during World War II. Nor did far left groups mention the participation of former Wehrmacht troops in the Arab military effort during Israel's War of Independence, a charge that American Communists had leveled against the Arabs in 1948.[13]

The far left's denigration of Israel was shaped in part by its trivialization of antisemitism, which it considered a non-issue. During the period from 1967 to 1973 its leaders and press never denounced antisemitism anywhere in the world.[14] The far left made many attempts, however, to refute charges that it existed in Arab countries and among black nationalists. Following the lead of the Arab guerilla groups, the American far left of the late 1960s and early 1970s not only ignored the pervasive and centuries-old antisemitism in the Middle East, but denied that it had ever been significant there, or in the Islamic tradition. In this sense it replicated the Communist Party's decades-long insistence that no antisemitism existed in the Soviet Union. To do otherwise would bolster arguments for a Jewish state.

Adhering rigidly to a narrow economic analysis, the far left could never properly assess or understand antisemitism. It ignored the highly important role of Christian and Islamic theology in forming, shaping, and sustaining antisemitism. For the far left antisemitism was merely a device employed by the ruling class to maintain control by preventing the working masses from uniting against it. As the *Militant* explained, Zionism, as part of a ruling class divide-and-conquer strategy, "pits the Jewish people against those [the Arab masses] who should be their natural allies."[15]

American far left groups echoed Palestinian guerilla spokesmen like Yassir Arafat, leader of Al Fatah, whom *New Left Notes* quoted in 1969 as stating that "Arabs have never discriminated against the Jews." Similarly in 1968 the *Militant* quoted an Al Fatah "commando" who declared: "Before 1948 we lived in peace with Jewish people." Only the creation of Israel had disrupted harmonious relations.[16] The *Militant* claimed after the Six-Day War that Israel had raised the issue of Arab antisemitism "to divert attention from the virulent anti-Arab racism the Zionists have pumped into the Israeli masses."[17] During the Yom Kippur War, when Israel came very close to being overrun by invading Arab armies, which launched a surprise attack on the holiest day of the Jewish calendar, the *Militant* stated that Arab "hostility to Jews came about as a result of the crimes of Zionism."[18] The Black Panther Party similarly ridiculed the notion that a Jewish state was needed to protect Jews from extermination. It maintained that Arabs and Jews had "lived in complete friendship until the advent of Zionism."[19]

The far left's proposed solution to the Arab-Israeli conflict, that Israel be dismantled and replaced with a state of Muslims, Christians, and Jews, with an Arab majority and Jewish minority, assumed not only the insignificance of Arab antisemitism but the speciousness of Jewish claims to be a people with valid national aspirations. The Palestinian guerilla movement also claimed that Jews were merely a religious group, not a people. As Al Fatah's chief public information officer put it in 1969: "Judaism is a religion...and it cannot construct a national identity."[20] The SWP rejected as "false to the core" the notion that Jews had "a right to a state of their own or to self-determination of any kind."[21] The Weatherman organ *Fire*, to delegitimize the Jewish claim to a homeland in Palestine, described the ancient Hebrews as "invaders," whose subsequent "occupation" of "Judaea" was "intermittent and unstable." Anticipating the claims of the rabidly antisemitic Nation of Islam and Christian Identity movements that contemporary Jews were "imposters," *Fire* asserted that "Zionist racial theory" connecting "modern European-American Jews" to the ancient Hebrews was "demonstrably false."[22] The Black Panther Party claimed that the ancient Hebrews were late-comers to the region and remained there only 100 years, whereas "the Palestinians" maintained "their continuous residence in Palestine until they were expelled by the Zionists in 1948."[23]

Fire even suggested that Zionism bore significant responsibility for the annihilation of Europe's Jews during the Holocaust. Quoting British historian Arnold Toynbee that "Zionism and anti-Semitism are expressions of an identical point of view," *Fire* argued that the Zionists propagandized that the Jews were an alien people who could never be integrated into the nations in which they lived. This intensified prejudice against Jews, so that in Eastern Europe, where Jews were inclined toward Zionism, hardly anyone objected to their slaughter during the Holocaust. *Fire* claimed that in Western Europe, by contrast, where Jews had acculturated and "were distinguished by religion only," the surrounding gentile population made "concerted efforts" to rescue them. Weatherman even suggested a moral equivalency between "organized Jewry" and the Nazis, alleging that the former's willing "collaboration" with those committing mass genocide was almost "universal." Without this collaboration, the Holocaust would have been impossible: "there would have been chaos or an impossibly severe drain on German manpower." Facing two enemies — "the Nazi authorities and the Jewish authorities" — the victims were doomed.[24]

Portraying Israel as a racist, genocidal settler-state similar to Nazi Germany led far left groups to justify or excuse the most brutal acts of terrorism against its population. At its 1971 convention the SWP declared, "We unconditionally support the struggles of the Arab peoples against the state of Israel." A 1973 column in the *Militant* called "By any Means Necessary" implied that any act of violence the Palestinian terrorists committed in the effort to destroy Israel was excusable.[25] Weatherman leader Eric Mann declared in 1970 that "Israeli embassies, tourist offices, airlines and Zionist fund-raising and social affairs are important targets for whatever action is decided to be appropriate."[26]

Such was the reasoning that shaped the far left's reaction to the massacre of Israeli athletes by Palestinian terrorists at the Munich Olympics in 1972. The *Militant* expressed concern that the public outcry against the kidnapping and murder of the Olympic athletes made "the criminal [Israel] look like the victim."[27] The Black Panther Party justified the murder of the athletes, comparing it to the prison uprising at the Attica penitentiary: "the same events unfolded: desperate, disenfranchised men take other men as hostages in order to command the attention of the world to their plight." It absolved the Palestinian terrorists of responsibility for the murders at Munich, blaming the authorities instead: "In Munich, as in Attica...heads of state did not hesitate to condemn the athletes to death to hide from the world the unbearable suffering of the Palestinians."[28]

Many on the far left openly endorsed the hijacking of airplanes, which risked large numbers of civilian lives, as a legitimate way for the Palestinians to publicize their cause. In 1970, the *Black Panther* reprinted an article entitled "The Sky's the Limit" that glorified the hijacking by members of the Popular Front for the Liberation of Palestine of a TWA passenger plane flying from Rome to Athens. The hijackers took hand grenades into the cockpit and ordered the pilots to fly to Damascus, Syria. SDS's *New Left Notes* also supported Palestinian terrorist attacks on Israeli airliners as one of the "requirements of total war, of resistance to the [Israeli] occupier."[29]

During the period from 1968 to 1973 the far left did express some discomfort with the frequent calls from Arabs for a jihad, or Muslim holy war, against Israel and the Jews, and the boasts of such Arab leaders as Egyptian dictator Gamal Abdel Nasser that the Arabs would drive the Jews of Israel "into the sea," a euphemism for genocide. Believing that class interest fundamentally shaped the outlook of the Arab masses, these groups dismissed religious and cultural factors, including radical Islamic theology, as of only superficial importance. SDS stated that the calls for jihad against the Jews were merely a desperate tactic of "the Arab bourgeoisie" to deflect the anger of the Arab working masses from "their own throats." *New Left Notes* called this "the non-progressive element of the Palestinian liberation struggle."[30]

Shortly after the Six-Day War, the *Militant* admitted that "The Egyptian and other Arab leaders....ha[d] called for a 'jihad' or holy war against Israel." It considered such appeals unwise. They would cause "the Israeli Jewish masses to fear that a successful Arab struggle against Zionism would result in the extermination or suppression of the Jews in the Middle East."[31] Calls for jihad would discourage Israeli workers from joining their Arab counterparts in a class war to dismantle Israel and establish a revolutionary bi-national state with an Arab majority, which the SWP advocated as the solution for the Arab-Israeli conflict.

Although they acknowledged that Arab heads of state called for driving the Jews of Israel into the sea, the far left organizations never thought through the implications of denying Israel the right to defend itself against attacks that could annihilate its population. On the very rare occasions when far left newspapers addressed the issue, they simply characterized Arab threats to wipe out Israel's Jews as meaningless bombast. Typical was the claim of the communist weekly *National Guardian* shortly after the Six-Day War, during which it had strongly backed the Arabs. The *National Guardian* had been founded by Stalinist supporters of the Progressive Party in October 1948. In 1967 its circulation probably surpassed that of any other American far left newspaper. Responding to the question posed by several readers, "Has not Nasser threatened to destroy Israel?" the *National Guardian* declared, "Unbiased observers tend to view the reckless but essentially empty threats to exterminate Israel as internal propaganda directed to the Cairo radio audience, unsupported by Egypt's actual military preparations."[32]

Of course, the *National Guardian*'s answer implied that the Cairo masses indeed harbored genocidal intentions toward Israel's Jews, for why else would the Nasser dictatorship mobilize the populace in this way? The far left, which vehemently denied the existence of Arab antisemitism, assumed that Islamic theology barely affected the Arab masses. It made no mention of Islam's concept of *dhimmitude*, which placed Jews in Muslim countries in an inferior position and status; of the implications of Muslim *sharia* law for Jews and women; of the numerous and horrific antisemitic pogroms in the Muslim world, including those in Baghdad in 1941 and in Tripoli, Cairo, and Alexandria in 1945; and of the forced expulsion of nearly all Jews from Arab countries after 1948, destroying centuries-old Jewish communities. Nor did the far left express any concern about how Jews' rights or existence could be safeguarded in an Arab-dominated "Palestine," or what the implications would be for women, who were subjugated, often brutally, in much of the Arab world.

PROMOTING A "SOCIALISM OF FOOLS": ROOTS OF FAR LEFT ANTISEMITISM

The far left's outlook toward Jews and its understanding of antisemitism can be traced back to early Marxian paradigms. Karl Marx set the tone for the far left's assessment of the Jewish role in society in his 1844 essay "On the Jewish Question," in which he employed both Christian theological and economic antisemitic stereotypes in denigrating Jews and Judaism. Asserting that "Money is the jealous god of Israel, in face of which no other god may exist," Marx combined Christian and pagan contempt for the Jewish concept of God.[33] Early Christians depicted the Jewish God as devoid of compassion, envious and wrathful. They portrayed the Temple as permeated with money-changing and had Judas, whose name resembles Judaism in any language, betray Jesus for thirty pieces of silver. Idol-worshiping, polytheistic pagans, unable to grasp the oneness and invisibility of the Jewish God, contended that the Jews worshiped not a deity in their Temple, but some material object. Money was such a material object. In accusing the Jews of permitting no other God to exist besides money, Marx was mocking their monotheism.

Marx's depiction of Judaism as nakedly materialistic and "anti-social" strongly resembled that of Christian theologians. Employing the antisemitic stereotype of the Jew as unscrupulous money lender and petty trader, Marx claimed that "huckstering" was the Jew's "worldly religion." Invoking a nefarious image of Jewish conspiracy and power that resonated with the Christian Bible's deicide accusation, Marx argued that by helping to stimulate the rise of capitalism Jews had not only "acquired financial power" but had infected the world with their commercial spirit, so that "the Christians [themselves] have become Jews." Socialist revolution, by eliminating "huckstering" and its "preconditions" (a capitalist economy and social relations), would, however, render the Jews "*impossible.*"[34]

During the late nineteenth and early twentieth centuries, European socialists—both Jews and gentiles—commonly held that Jewish identity was not worth preserving. The Jews were an "anachronistic sect" fated to disappear with the decline of petty capitalism.[35] There was therefore no point in supporting the Jewish national aspirations advanced by either modern Zionism or Bundism, the competing movements, themselves strongly influenced by socialism, that were emerging during the late 1890s. Most socialists of the period, not only those on the far left, considered the Zionist goal of reestablishing a Jewish homeland in Palestine as unfeasible, dismissing it as utopian. They did not believe it would be possible to stimulate sufficient Jewish emigration to a land so undeveloped and lacking in natural resources. Jewish communities established there would be easily annihilated by hostile Arabs. Nor could most socialists accept the Bund's goal of achieving cultural autonomy for Jews within Eastern Europe. Russian Marxist George Plekhanov, highly influential in the European socialist movement before World War I, derided the Bundists simply as "Zionists suffering from sea-sickness." Most socialists during the late nineteenth and early twentieth centuries, and nearly all on the far left, favored assimilation as the solution to what they called the "Jewish Question."[36]

Bolshevik theoreticians addressing this subject, notably V. I. Lenin, Leon Trotsky, and Josef Stalin, strongly opposed both Bundism and Zionism. By separating Jewish workers from their gentile counterparts, they argued, Bundism and Zionism impeded the effort to forge an inclusive revolutionary socialist alliance that would eliminate antisemitism — and with it, Jewish identity — merely by overthrowing capitalism. Lenin derided the idea that Jews possessed a national culture as only "a slogan of the rabbis and the bourgeoisie."[37]

The most influential work outlining the Communist position that Jews did not compose a national group was Josef Stalin's 1913 essay "Marxism and the National Question." Stalin argued that because Jews were physically dispersed, even within the countries they inhabited, and were culturally diverse, they did not constitute a national group. Moreover, the Jews were not involved in agriculture, which he believed bound other peoples together. The Bund encouraged Jewish workers to observe what Stalin considered anachronistic "ancient Hebrew holidays." This isolated them from their gentile counterparts, who otherwise would be their allies. Socialists should instead encourage Jewish assimilation. Stalin was confident that "semi-Asiatic" Russia would follow the path of Germany. Germany was "already Europe," and its Jews were rapidly assimilating. As a result, Stalin asserted, attempts to infringe on Jewish rights in Germany never escalated into pogroms. Germany was well on the way to solving the Jewish Question.[38]

European socialists formally condemned antisemitism, but at the same time many believed it could sometimes prove useful in raising socialist consciousness among the working masses. August Bebel, one of German socialism's leading theoreticians during the late nineteenth century, referred to antisemitism as "the socialism of fools." He argued that working-class antagonism toward Jewish merchants and financiers was misdirected because the liberation of the proletariat could only be accomplished through the overthrow of the entire bourgeoisie, not merely a small section of it.[39] Those who considered Jews in the bourgeoisie to be the working-class movement's primary adversary were therefore not advocating true socialism. Nonetheless, many socialists believed that denunciations of Jewish businessmen or bankers might at least instill in workers an abhorrence of capitalism. Exposure to socialist agitation and propaganda could then propel the workers to expand the focus of their antagonism to include all capitalists, not just the relatively small minority who happened to be Jews.[40]

This conviction all too often led the far left to ignore, and sometimes even to encourage, outbursts of severe antisemitism in the working and lower classes in Europe, the United States, and the Middle East. In Hungary in the period immediately following World War II, the Communists who controlled the government bore significant responsibility for sparking antisemitic pogroms at Kunmadaras in May 1946 and at Miskolc two months later. Fully aware that much of the Hungarian population stereotyped Jews as "hucksters" bent on economically exploiting gentiles, the Communist press repeatedly called for "violent action against black marketers [and] profiteers."[41] Pogromists at Kunmadaras, who killed two Jews and inflicted injuries requiring hospitalization on seventy-eight others, acted out of concern that Holocaust survivors, rendered destitute, would ask for the return of their property. The 100 Jews who survived the Kunmadaras pogrom fled to Budapest for safety.[42]

The Hungarian Communist press incited the populace against the Jews by explicitly associating them with profiteering and even by invoking the blood libel. Next to the Magyarized names of arrested Jewish black marketers it sometimes published their original Jewish names. The Communists also urged "the toiling people" to "take revenge on the 'bloodsuckers,'" old coded language that suggested that Jews were parasites who did not engage in productive labor.[43] The term "bloodsucker" was linked with the persistent medieval Christian fantasy that Jews kidnapped innocent Christian children, most commonly around Easter, to mock Jesus and to extract blood to mix with Passover matzoh.

Hungarian Communist Party head Mátyás Rákosi sparked the Miskolc pogrom by declaring that currency speculators should be hanged. Local workers lynched one alleged black marketer and mortally wounded another, both Jews, although they were already under arrest. However, they released another accused black marketer, who was not Jewish. The Miskolc pogromists received no punishment.[44] The American Communist Party publications ignored the Communist role in these pogroms, part of a larger pattern of denial of antisemitism in the Soviet bloc.

Similarly, from 1964 to 1968, when riots erupted in the black ghettos of many American cities, the American far left also overlooked, and sometimes encouraged, the overt antisemitism and the destruction of Jewish stores. Far left groups identified the riots as "ghetto rebellions." When SNCC program director Ralph Featherstone gave classic expression to the "socialism of fools" by proclaiming that "it is the Jews who are doing the exploiting of black people in the ghettos," none of the far left groups publicly denounced him.[45]

Featherstone referred not to big manufacturers or financiers but only to the owners of "the little corner groceries." In condemning these Jewish petty entrepreneurs, he ignored that insurance companies required them to pay unusually high premiums to operate in dangerous neighborhoods. And that many gentile businessmen avoided these neighborhoods altogether because of their disdain for blacks and their greater access to more affluent sections of the city. Moreover, prices in these corner groceries were also affected by the relatively high rate of shoplifting. Reinforcing his antisemitic message, the SNCC official compared American Jewish grocers' "gouging" of ghetto blacks to "the oppression of Arabs by the Israelis."[46]

THE COMMUNIST RESPONSE TO THE 1929 POGROMS: PRECEDENT FOR THE AMERICAN FAR LEFT'S POST-1967 SUPPORT FOR PALESTINIAN TERRORISM

The American Communist Party's (CP) support for the anti-Jewish pogroms Arab mobs unleashed in Palestine during late August 1929 set a precedent for the far left's backing of, or excusing, Palestinian terrorist attacks against Jews during the 1960s and subsequent decades. Much of the CP propaganda on behalf of what it alleged was a "revolutionary Arab uprising" was as viciously antisemitic as that issued by the Black Panthers or SDS during the late 1960s and early 1970s.

Aroused by the virulently antisemitic harangues of the grand mufti of Jerusalem, Haj Amin al-Husseini, Arab mobs armed with swords and axes, knives, sledgehammers, iron bars, and stones, screaming "Allah is Great… Kill the Jews!" attacked Jews in Hebron, Jerusalem, Safed, Haifa, Jaffa, and even Tel Aviv, as well as many Jewish agricultural settlements. They broke into Jewish homes and stores and massacred Jewish men and women — including the elderly — and children, some of them less than five years old. The Arabs' savagery was unrestrained. The pogromists beheaded some of their victims with axes and chopped off hands. They gouged out the eyes of a Jewish pharmacist in Hebron while he was still alive and then murdered him. The attackers castrated two rabbis there and killed them, and burned another rabbi alive. They raped Jewish women. An Arab, noticing a Jewish girl with stab wounds writhing on the ground, sliced open her abdomen. The pogromists looted Jewish houses and stores before setting them on fire. They burned down the Jewish orphanage at Safed and desecrated synagogues. Arab policemen, sympathetic to the pogromists, did little or nothing to intercede.[47]

The pogroms inflicted massive damage to the Yishuv (the Jewish community in Palestine) — at least 133 Jews were killed and 399 wounded.[48]

Entire Jewish settlements and neighborhoods were permanently destroyed. Hebron, "the most ancient Jewish community in Palestine," was "virtually extinguished."[49] Many of the murdered Jews in Hebron were orthodox students at the Slobodka Rabbinical College, which was attacked on the Sabbath. Rooms there were "strewn with arms, legs, and noses," which Arabs had amputated from their Jewish victims.[50] British forces, arriving from Egypt several days after the pogroms had begun, forced Jews to evacuate agricultural settlements where they had determined to make a stand, after which "the Arabs came in and looted and pillaged and smashed to their hearts' content." A few days after the pogroms had subsided, the *New York Times* estimated that the pogroms had created 9,200 Jewish refugees, of whom 4,200 had been left absolutely destitute.[51]

Although hostile to Zionism, the American CP's Yiddish newspaper *Morgen Freiheit* at first called the violent outbreaks in Palestine anti-Jewish pogroms. It assigned "final responsibility," however, to the "British imperialists," arguing that had the British authorities wished to do so they could have suppressed the violence. But "Zionist leaders" were also partly to blame, according to *Morgen Freiheit*, because their "anti-Arab policy" had sparked resentment among the masses.[52]

The CP secretariat almost immediately condemned *Morgen Freiheit*'s position as "counterrevolutionary." It informed *Morgen Freiheit* that it had seriously erred in viewing the violent outbreaks as a "race" war, rather than as a "class" war launched by "expropriated Arab peasants" against "British imperialism" and its "Zionist agents." The British used the Zionist movement to confiscate Arab land and gain control of Palestine's "rich" chemical resources. The Zionists flooded the labor market by encouraging Jewish immigration to Palestine, thereby depressing wage levels. Parasitic Jewish capitalists established large fruit plantations on the land of displaced Arab peasants, sharing with their British masters the profits they extracted from Arab and Jewish workers employed at "starvation rates."[53] The CP was emphatic that "Palestine is an Arab country."[54]

Reacting to pressure from the CP secretariat, which following Moscow's instructions, the *Morgen Freiheit* now joined the CP's English-language newspaper, the *Daily Worker*, in a campaign of vituperation against the "Zionist-Fascists" who had "provoked the Arab uprising." During the years from 1928 to 1935, the "Third Period" in world Communist policy, the Comintern assumed that capitalism was entering its final stage of crisis, and adopted an ultra-leftist posture to hasten its collapse. (The Comintern was the Soviet-controlled international organization of Communist parties.)

Thus *Morgen Freiheit* proclaimed, "The Arab uprising is spreading throughout the entire Middle East." Foreshadowing the charges of "criminality" that such groups as the Black Panthers and SDS later directed against Israel, the CP denounced Zionists as "murderers" engaged in "frightful campaigns of land robbery." The CP staged rallies in New York and other major cities to build support for "the Arabian masses in their struggle against British imperialism and its Zionist allies."[55] In the late twentieth and early twenty-first century the denunciations would undergo a slight change, with Zionists now identified as "agents of American imperialism."

Incredibly, the American Communist press accused the Jews of the Yishuv of joining with the "British imperialists" to carry out pogroms against the Arabs, issuing such headlines as "Zionists Slaughter Arab Men, Women, and Children."[56] The *Daily Worker* denied the reports of Arab atrocities against Jews as fabrications by "Zionist" physicians.[57] The CP defamed the Jewish Legion, the first Jewish army created since the Romans crushed Bar Kochba's uprising in 135 CE. Formed to fight with the British in Palestine during World War I, the Jewish Legion had been a tremendous source of inspiration to Jews around the world, for centuries defenseless against antisemitic attack. The *Daily Worker* denounced the Jewish Legion as "fascists" and "dupes of British imperialism" (for having fought on the Allied side in World War I). *Morgen Freiheit* accused its veterans in Palestine of carrying out pogroms against the Arabs.[58]

Most shocking were the *Daily Worker*'s blatantly antisemitic cartoons that accompanied reports of the conflict. Invoking the Christian deicide accusation, one depicted a huge cross, with a Star of David on top of the vertical bar and the words "For Arabs" on the horizontal bar. Another showed a smiling fat man, labeled Zionist, holding a cigar, leaning back comfortably in an armchair, the proverbial capitalist, with bodies hanging above him.[59]

The CP's support for what *Morgen Freiheit* editor Melech Epstein later called "fanatical Arab nationalism" and terrorism against Jews seriously damaged its standing in the Jewish community. Epstein commented that "the harm done was irreparable."[60]

AMERICAN COMMUNISTS' CONVOLUTED RESPONSES TO NAZISM AND ANTISEMITISM, 1933–1945

From January 30, 1933, when Adolf Hitler assumed power in Germany, until the end of World War II, the Communist Party, the most influential American far left group of the time, made several sudden and substantive shifts in its positions on Nazism and antisemitism. These changes were necessitated by the sharp fluctuations in the Comintern's positions. During the early period of Nazi rule, which coincided with the last years of the Third Period, the Communists made no attempt to cooperate with the mainstream American Jewish and labor groups that organized massive street demonstrations and rallies against Nazi antisemitism. Assuming that capitalism was entering its death throes, the CP considered anyone to its right to be allies of a decaying bourgeoisie that would turn to fascism to protect its class interests. To stimulate a revolutionary consciousness the CP preferred to stage or join dramatic confrontations to protest Nazi officials' speaking engagements in the United States and the arrival of German vessels in U.S. ports. Most of these protest actions resulted in clashes with the police and arrests. To be sure, such demonstrations proved valuable in making Americans more aware of Nazi barbarism.[61] But in its anti-Nazi agitation, the CP emphasized the Hitler regime's imprisonment of German Communists and trade union opponents rather than Nazi antisemitism.

The CP distanced itself from the Jewish community by refusing to support the boycott of German goods, extending the damage created by its Palestine policy in 1929.[62] Initiated by the Jewish War Veterans of the United States in March 1933, almost immediately after the Nazis came to power, it was endorsed in May by Samuel Untermyer's American League for the Defense of Jewish Rights and in August by the American Jewish Congress. The American Federation of Labor (AFL) declared its enthusiastic support for the boycott at its convention in October, where it strongly condemned the Nazi persecution of Jews. By the end of 1933, Jews at the grassroots were extensively involved in promoting the boycott.[63]

Following the Kremlin's lead, the CP characterized the boycott as a "scheme" of the "bourgeoisie" to "capture the German market" in the United States. Ignoring massive grassroots Jewish and labor support for the boycott, the CP depicted it as a conspiracy by American corporate business to enlarge its market share by preventing German concerns from selling to American consumers. The Communists' main motive in opposing the boycott was probably its Third Period reluctance to cooperate in any way with mainstream Jewish organizations or with the AFL. Melech Epstein, editor of the *Morgen Freiheit* when it condemned the boycott, later asserted that Kremlin opposition was influenced by a "huge new credit" that the Nazi government had extended for Soviet orders of German goods.[64]

In explaining Hitler's rise to power the CP typically advanced a simplistic class analysis that greatly deemphasized the role of antisemitism in Nazi ideology. The most widely distributed Communist work on the subject published in the United States, R. Palme Dutt's *Fascism and Social Revolution* (1935), subtitled *A Study of the Economics and Politics of the Extreme Stages of Capitalism in Decay*, presented Nazism as a maneuver by a desperate ruling class, confronted with the imminent collapse of the bourgeois economic system, to "hold down the workers" and "maintain its power." According to Dutt, modern antisemitism emerged when capitalism was "tottering," and it intensified "in proportion as the class struggle" grew "acute." Modern antisemitism was "directly inspired and stimulated from above" (that is, by the ruling class) to divide and undermine a growing proletarian movement. Like the far left of the 1960s, the Communists of the 1930s ignored the deep theological and cultural roots of antisemitism in the Christian and Islamic worlds.[65]

The CP made a dramatic shift in position in 1935 when the Comintern, alarmed by a remilitarizing and increasingly menacing Nazi Germany, encouraged Communists to join socialists and liberals in building a Popular Front against fascism. To enhance its security against German attack, the Soviet Union also tried to forge stronger ties with the western democracies.

The effort to build a broad anti-Nazi coalition led the CP to devote more serious attention to antisemitism. The Nazis, after all, were virulent antisemites. The CP remained hostile to Zionism (a movement banned in the Soviet Union) but did not fully back the Arabs in their violent uprising of 1936 to 1939 against Jewish immigration to Palestine.[66] But the Communists now presented themselves as the most ardent and dependable opponent of the Nazis. The CP was prominent in the formation and leadership of the Abraham Lincoln Brigade, sent to Spain to defend the republican government in the first armed confrontation with fascism. The Communists also repeatedly proclaimed that the Soviet Union was the first nation in the world to make antisemitism illegal. A. B. Magil, a CP leader, claimed to be the first to expose the antisemitism of the radio priest Charles Coughlin, in a 1935 pamphlet.[67]

The signing of the Molotov-von Ribbentrop Non-Aggression Pact between the Soviet Union and Nazi Germany in August 1939 caused Communists to completely reassess their position on Nazism and once again to downplay the issue of antisemitism. Since 1935, the Communists had urgently appealed to the western democracies to take immediate measures to block Nazism's advance. In an abrupt about-face, the Communists now denied that any significant difference existed between the democracies and the fascist powers. They were merely a clash between imperialist coalitions competing to control world markets.

The Non-Aggression Pact opened the way for Nazi Germany to invade Poland, endangering the very existence of Europe's largest Jewish population. Wehrmacht troops rode into Poland on trains marked with crude antisemitic caricatures and the slogan "We're off to Poland — to thrash the Jews."[68]

Yet the Communists immediately mobilized to prevent U.S. intervention in a war against Nazi Germany. Vehemently opposed to supplying Britain with war materiel, they lobbied against President Roosevelt's Lend-Lease legislation. Communist-led unions staged strikes designed to halt production of tanks at Milwaukee's Allis-Chalmers plant and aircraft at North American Aviation in California. The CP coined a new slogan, "The Yanks Are Not Coming!" and established a front group, the American Peace Mobilization (APM), to "Keep America Out of the Imperialist War!"[69]

In August 1940, during the Battle of Britain, when Germany had conquered nearly all of non-Soviet Europe, U.S. Congressman Vito Marcantonio (Bronx, New York), an APM leader and fellow traveler of the CP, declared, "This is a rotten, big business war between a bunch of Nazis in Germany and a bunch of Nazis in England."[70] Denying that there was even a "slight difference" between Britain and Hitler's Germany, Marcantonio insisted that nothing in Europe "warrant[ed] the shedding of the blood of one American boy."[71] Neither Marcantonio nor the CP displayed any concern about the implications for European Jewry of a Nazi conquest of Britain, which appeared very possible, even imminent, in the summer of 1940.

Following the CP line, in April 1941 Rep. Marcantonio rejected an appeal from Rabbi Stephen S. Wise to join the American Palestine Committee, which was then engaged in a desperate effort to help Jews in Nazi-occupied Europe escape to Palestine. Marcantonio explained that he was refusing because of "the position which your committee has taken on [supporting] aid to Britain."[72]

The American Jewish community's outrage over the Molotov-von Ribbentrop Pact was "volcanic." In New York's heavily Jewish garment district workers confronted Communists with mock Nazi salutes and calls of "Heil Hitler!" All across the city Jews hurled the taunt "Communazi" at the Communists.[73]

When Nazi Germany invaded the Soviet Union on June 22, 1941, the CP immediately swung back to a Popular Front position, making victory over Hitler its central priority. It devoted its energies to mobilizing support for the war effort. Having downplayed antisemitism as an issue after the Molotov-von Ribbentrop Pact, the CP now made combating it a focus of its war work. It considered the intensification of domestic antisemitism during the war a threat to the national unity needed to achieve victory over the Axis.

The CP backed the appeals by the American Jewish Congress and the Anti-Defamation League for the city and state authorities in Boston and New York to stop the epidemic of street assaults on Jews by Irish-American youth who had been inspired by the Coughlinite Christian Front.[74]

When Massachusetts CP chairman Otis Hood ran for the Boston School Committee during World War II, he made the authorities' indifference to the violent assaults on Boston's Jews a major issue in his campaign, and called for the city public school system to initiate an educational campaign to combat antisemitism. Yet Hood's understanding of antisemitism was marred by the simplistic analysis Communists favored. When asked later about why antisemitism was "so rife in Boston," he explained only that the "ruling class" used it to divide the working class.[75]

Peter V. Cacchione, a CP member who served on the New York City Council during World War II, repeatedly raised the need to aggressively combat antisemitism in the city. He pressured New York City commissioner of investigation William B. Herlands to immediately make public the information he had on the antisemitic violence in New York City so as to arouse public opinion against it, and make it possible to swiftly punish the perpetrators.[76] Cacchione twice introduced a resolution in the City Council calling on New York's mayor to discharge Brooklyn patrolman James Drew, known as an "avowed anti-Semite and distributor of pro-Nazi literature." He also called for exposing "every other anti-Semite on the [New York City police] force."[77] Cacchione brought to public attention the case of a Brooklyn public school teacher who made antisemitic comments in the classroom, explaining that it was "no rare incident." He declared, "It is high time that the Board of Education began to take steps to weed out such fascist-minded people from our schools."[78]

U.S. Representative Marcantonio became similarly involved in the campaign against domestic antisemitism. In July 1944, he made two radio broadcasts denouncing antisemitism to refute propaganda that Italian Fascists were circulating in New York City's Italian-American community that World War II was "a Jewish war," and that Jews were shirking military service. He also attacked the antisemitic policies of the Mussolini dictatorship. During the war Marcantonio supported a campaign for federal legislation to outlaw antisemitism, to which the CP devoted significant effort in the immediate postwar period.[79]

The Stalin regime created a Jewish Anti-Fascist Committee to help raise funds in the West for armaments, food, and supplies for the Soviet war effort, but otherwise rarely mentioned the plight of the Jews. The Soviets did save many Jews by evacuating them from areas overrun by Axis forces into the interior of Russia. A considerable number of the evacuated Jews, however, were transported in box cars to labor camps in Siberia and East Asia, where many died. Soviet reluctance to display public concern for the Jews during the Holocaust was partly due to the Stalin regime's antisemitism. The regime also feared that doing so would play into the hands of the invading Nazis, who exploited the endemic antisemitism in Russia, the Ukraine, Belorussia, and the Baltic states to win over a sizeable proportion of the population. During the war the Soviet press and radio almost never reported the annihilation of Jews. On the few occasions that they did refer to mass killings, as Isaac Deutscher noted, they "mentioned them in such a manner that no one could guess that the Jews provided the main contingent of victims."[80]

Over a decade after the war, Alexander Bittelman, the American CP official primarily responsible for Jewish affairs during World War II, expressed profound regret for his "tragic failure" to realize that Nazism was "the special mortal enemy of the Jews as Jews." He recognized that the Jewish people's experience during World War II was unique, because it alone was targeted for total annihilation. Looking back, Bittelman believed that he and other "leading Jews" had "failed to arouse our people everywhere to the grave menace confronting their very physical existence." Bittelman wished that he, and by implication, all Communists, had urged the Jews to arm themselves and to fight the Nazis "as Jews."[81]

A NEW SENSITIVITY TO THE JEWISH PLIGHT, 1945–1949

Following the sharp shift in Comintern policy during the years immediately following World War II, the CP abandoned its decades-long hard-line opposition to Zionism and in May 1947 threw its support behind partitioning Palestine into a Jewish and an Arab state. The abrupt reversal occurred largely because the Kremlin believed that the Zionists' struggle to dislodge the British in Palestine and create a Jewish state would hasten the collapse of the British Empire and allow the Soviets to gain a foothold in the Middle East.

Expecting class conflict to intensify in the West, the Communists discarded the Popular Front strategy and adopted a more strident and sectarian approach. In early 1947, the CP magazine *Jewish Life* compared the situation in the United States to Germany's shortly before the Nazis came to power. It predicted that "a major economic crisis" was imminent. Big business would exploit the crisis to assume control over the state. The large manufacturers and financiers would disseminate antisemitic and racist propaganda to confuse and divide the working class, allowing them to install a fascist dictatorship to maintain their profits.[82] Promoted by William Z. Foster, who became CP chairman in 1945, this apocalyptic perspective became known in the party as "the five minutes to midnight line."[83] As in the Third Period, the CP rejected alliances with socialists, often even conflating them with fascists.

The new outlook differed significantly from that of the Third Period on issues involving Jews and antisemitism. With the onset of the Cold War, antisemitism became a weapon the Communists used to discredit the West. They repeatedly cited the horrendous treatment of Holocaust survivors in the displaced persons (DP) camps in the Western occupation zones of Germany, and the rapid release of Nazi war criminals by the Americans and the British. Earl Harrison, dispatched by President Truman in the summer of 1945 to observe conditions at the DP camps, reported to the White House that "We seem to be treating the Jews as the Nazis treated them, except that we do not exterminate them."[84]

In June 1946, CP chairman Foster compared the camps for Jewish DPs with Nazi concentration camps. The Western powers had become the new fascists. Foster declared that it was no surprise that "American imperialism is quite content to put Nazis in charge of displaced persons" and "allow American soldiers to be infected with Nazi ideology."[85]

The CP's outrage at Western treatment of DPs even caused it to abandon its longstanding contempt for Judaism during the immediate postwar period. In October 1945, the *Daily Worker* printed an appeal by a U.S. army medical corps officer for people to donate Jewish religious articles, including Tallith and Tephillin, and Hebrew religious books to the DPs.[86]

The CP argued that Britain's harshly punitive measures against the Haganah and the Irgun in Palestine, and antisemitic comments by British Foreign Secretary Ernest Bevin, tore the "mask" of liberalism "from the face" of the Labour government, revealing its nakedly repressive, neo-fascist character. When Bevin commented at a British Labour conference in June 1946 that Americans were calling on Britain to admit 100,000 displaced Jews to Palestine because "they did not want too many of them in New York," the *Daily Worker* denounced him as antisemitic. It approvingly quoted New York mayor William O'Dwyer's comparison of Bevin to prewar fascist demagogue Joe McWilliams. Breaking with the wartime Soviet approach of minimizing the Jewish identity of those murdered in the Holocaust, the *Daily Worker* editorialized that the "anti-Semitic jibe" voiced by the "so-called 'labor leader'" Bevin was "filled with malice toward a people whose sufferings have surpassed imagination."[87] Joseph Starobin, a CP leader, stated that no issue more clearly revealed the "fraudulent character of 'Socialism' as interpreted by Social Democrats" than Palestine. The "British mis-leaders of labor," callous toward Jewish refugees trapped in Europe, indifferent to the "fate of the heroic Jewish community" there, concerned themselves only with promoting "imperialist interests."[88]

The CP accused the U.S. government of favoring the entry into their country of displaced persons from Eastern Europe sympathetic to fascism, while barring admission to Jewish Holocaust survivors. It charged that many of the non-Jewish DPs accorded priority immigration status had served in the Nazi armies or with antisemitic partisan units that had slaughtered Jews. Some had been guards in death camps. The CP forcefully denounced as antisemitic the Wiley-Revercomb bill, passed by the U.S. Senate in 1948, which required that half the visas allotted to DPs go to persons with agricultural skills. This eliminated most Jews, few of whom had been permitted to work on the land prior to the Holocaust. The *Daily Worker* editorialized that the bill would admit Nazi "beasts" into the United States, while shutting out their homeless victims.[89]

Although silent about Nazi war criminals granted positions of authority in Soviet-dominated areas, the *Daily Worker* repeatedly charged U.S. and British authorities with excessive leniency toward those in their occupation zones. In April 1949 the *Daily Worker* denounced an American tribunal in Nuremberg for granting light prison sentences, rather than the death penalty, to "19 Nazi leaders directly responsible for the organized murder of millions of Jews and other anti-fascists."[90]

In New York City, Communist protestors disrupted a speech by General Lucius D. Clay, former U.S. Military governor in Germany, by shouting "Let's ask General Clay about Ilse Koch and the human skin!" Known as the "Beast of Buchenwald," Koch, the camp commandant's wife, was convicted of committing atrocities against inmates. Witnesses charged that she had prisoners with tattoos murdered so their skin could be made into lampshades. Yet General Clay had reduced her life sentence to only four years. Even the *New York Times* ridiculed the U.S. army's implication that Frau Koch "was merely a good wife who brought her husband his slippers and saw that he was well fed after a hard day at his butcher's office."[91]

Unwilling to criticize the Soviet bloc, the CP remained silent about East Germany's leniency toward former Nazis, some of whom assumed important governmental posts. By contrast, very few Jews in East Germany ever occupied major positions. Although in the late 1950s West Germany agreed to pay reparations to Holocaust survivors, East Germany never did. East Germany followed the Soviets in refusing to acknowledge the centrality of Jewish suffering during the Holocaust or how deeply rooted antisemitism was among European workers and peasants. The Soviets and the Communist parties in their satellites considered Nazism primarily a movement big business used to protect its profits and maintain control over labor. They viewed Jews as only one among a multitude of groups that the Nazis oppressed. Indeed, when referring to those murdered by the Nazis, Soviet bloc Communists used the amorphous term "victims of fascism," making no specific mention of Jews.

The American CP never questioned the purge, arrest, and imprisonment of East German Communist Party Central Committee member Paul Merker because the regime disapproved of his "writings and actions on behalf of the Jews." During World War II, Merker had taken refuge with a small number of other German Communists in Mexico City, where he published articles that placed antisemitism and "the Jewish catastrophe at the center of the anti-fascist struggle." In contrast, most of those who assumed leadership of the East German Communist regime in 1945 had spent the war years in Moscow, and were minimally concerned with antisemitism. When they came to power, they focused on "establish[ing] their legitimacy as *German* leaders," distancing themselves from Jews.[92] The *New York Times* reported after Merker's arrest that the East German regime had charged him with "such 'heinous' crimes as having favored restoration to German Jews of property confiscated from them by the Hitler regime."[93]

Abandoning assimilationism, in 1946 the CP founded a new magazine, *Jewish Life*, specifically devoted to Jewish affairs and culture. In the inaugural issue, the editors announced that it was dedicated to "reviving and spreading the progressive Jewish culture and tradition." They went so far as to denounce assimilationism as "bourgeois."[94]

Reviewing Hollywood's "Gentleman's Agreement" (1947), *Jewish Life* praised the film for demonstrating that there was considerable antisemitism among mainstream Americans, but expressed irritation that it did not present any character with a well-defined Jewish identity. *Jewish Life* complained that "the conception of the American Jew that prevails in the film is epitomized by the Jewish scientist, Dr. Lieberman, who advances the assimilationist thesis that the only difference between the Jew and non-Jew is religious, and that the non-religious Jew is one only because he is pressed to make this identification by persecution."[95]

To promote a "progressive" secular Jewish culture, the CP established a School of Jewish Studies in New York City in 1945. This was a time when

American colleges and universities devoted almost no attention to Jewish studies. The School's curriculum consisted mostly of courses on Jewish history and literature, many of them taught by prominent CP members, including Alexander Bittelman and A. B. Magil. The emphasis was on exploring and celebrating how Jewish culture had influenced Jews to assume a prominent role in improving conditions for all humanity. In a striking departure from Communist assimilationism, the School encouraged its students to study Jewish languages, offering not only Yiddish, but Hebrew, which Communists had always scornfully associated with rabbis and Zionists.[96]

In the fall of 1945, the CP became significantly engaged in demonstrations demanding the immediate abrogation of the 1939 British White Paper, to permit unrestricted Jewish immigration to Palestine. Most of these protest actions were led by mainstream Jewish or labor groups. Following the Soviet line, the American CP from 1945 to mid-1947 favored making Palestine a homeland for Jews, but did not officially call for establishing a Jewish state there. Like the Soviets, it advocated a bi-national state in which Jewish minority rights would be guaranteed. On several occasions during this period, however, the *Daily Worker* gave tacit support to creating a Jewish state. Supporting unrestricted Jewish immigration brought the CP into direct conflict with the Arab nations. The CP strongly condemned the Arab leadership as reactionary feudalists who had collaborated with the Nazis during World War II.

In October 1945, the *Daily Worker* praised the 250,000 who participated in a massive rally against the White Paper in New York City for their contribution to the "heroic struggle to rebuild the national life of the Jewish people and to restore dignity and honor to the broken remnants of European Jewry." The demonstration was conducted under the auspices of pro-Zionist Jewish organizations. The *Daily Worker* backed the demonstrators' pledge to fight for unrestricted Jewish immigration to Palestine, which they made "with a tremendous swelling shout." It quoted approvingly the chairman of the New York state Congress of Industrial Organizations (CIO), who told the rally that "The spokesmen of the Arab League [representing the Arab nations] all speak with the accents of fascists."[97]

In a November 1945 editorial, the *Daily Worker* declared that Arab consent should not be required for Jewish immigration to Palestine. In the same issue, it endorsed the statement of Zionist leaders Rabbi Stephen S. Wise and Dr. Abba Hillel Silver that surviving European Jews had nowhere to go but Palestine. While President Truman and the British Atlee government dithered, the hungry and homeless Holocaust survivors faced "a winter of hardship and death."[98]

Increasing Jewry's desperate plight were the Anglo-American abandonment of de-Nazification efforts in Germany and indifference toward savage Arab pogroms against Jewish communities in North Africa. In the fall of 1945 the *Daily Worker* published articles on the Arab killing of more than 100 Jews and the wounding of several hundred more in Tripolitania, Libya, and the massacre of at least ten Jews and wounding of 350 in Alexandria, Egypt. It reported that in Palestine, British military patrols were inciting a "wave of terror" against the Yishuv, while the Atlee government permitted "Arab leaders who openly supported Hitler" to return there. The "heroic Jewish colonists around Jerusalem" were arming to defend themselves, "in the face of...heavy British armor." The conservative Chicago *Tribune* commented angrily that the "current communist line, laid down by the *Daily Worker* and followed obediently by other communist and communist-front publications [is]...Stir up the Jews on the Palestine issue....Fan the fires of hatred of the Germans."[99]

In 1946 the CP established a new front group, the American Jewish Labor Council (AJLC), to mobilize support for unrestricted immigration to Palestine and, after the Soviet Union swung behind partition in 1947, for a Jewish state. The AJLC also pledged to fight antisemitism in the United States, which it declared was reaching a level parallel to Germany's on the eve of Hitler's accession to power.[100]

In May 1947, as the United Nations (UN) opened debate over the future of the British Mandate, the Soviets signaled a major policy shift when Foreign Minister Andrei Gromyko declared that if Arab-Jewish tensions rendered a bi-national state unviable, his government was prepared to support the partition of Palestine into an Arab and a Jewish state. Gromyko asserted that having failed to protect the Jews from the "Fascist hangmen," the Western European nations had forfeited any right to oppose a Jewish state. A Hebrew newspaper hailed Gromyko's speech as "the Soviet Balfour Declaration."[101]

CP publications found the Arab delegates' rhetoric during the debate deeply offensive. *Jewish Life* published an article by Soviet Yiddish writer Itzik Feffer that condemned the Arabs for spreading "anti-Semitic poison" at the UN. Feffer noted that the heir of Grand Mufti Haj Amin al-Husseini, Muslim leader in Jerusalem and a passionate supporter of Hitler during World War II, had rejected any cooperation with Jews in Palestine on the grounds that they had killed Jesus. He maintained that contemporary Jews were descended from Mongolians. The Syrian delegate similarly claimed that contemporary Jews had no connection to Biblical Jews.[102]

The American Communists and others with pro-Soviet sympathies applauded Zionist efforts to break the British blockade of Palestine, established to bar entry to Jewish immigrants. In a series of articles for *PM*, a left-wing New York tabloid then friendly to the Soviets, I. F. Stone provided a first-hand account of "illegal" Jewish immigration and published the *PM* articles as a book, *Underground to Palestine* (1946), concluding that "full support of the so-called illegal immigration is a moral obligation." European Jewry's only hope lay in "filling the waters of Palestine with so many illegal boats that the pressure on the British and the conscience of the world becomes unbearable."[103]

CP publications denounced Britain's deportation to Germany of over 4,500 Jewish passengers on the *Exodus 1947*, seized by the Royal Navy as it approached Haifa, calling it a crime against the Jewish people and against humanity. The British transferred the *Exodus 1947* passengers into the caged holds of three other ships for transport to France. When the captured Jews refused to disembark in France and the French government would not cooperate in removing them, the British transported the Jews to Hamburg, Germany, in their occupation zone. The British confined the Jews in two former concentration camps behind barbed wire. *Jewish Life* condemned as "callous, crass cruelty" Britain's returning the "suffering Jews once more to the land of the crematorium and the gas chamber." The AJLC urged British union seamen not to serve on ships returning the *Exodus 1947* Jews to Germany.[104]

During the fall of 1947, the American CP contrasted Soviet support for partition with the U.S. government's "evasive" stand. Shortly before the UN General Assembly voted on partition in November, Gromyko declared that the Holocaust survivors' homelessness and the Jews' long historical connection to Palestine justified establishing a Jewish state there. *Jewish Life* praised the Soviets for treating Jewish aspirations with "dignity and respect," but criticized the United States for displaying uncertainty about partition.[105] In the UN General Assembly on November 29, 1947, the entire Soviet bloc joined the United States in voting for partition.

The CP's enthusiasm for a Jewish state was reflected in the highly influential role it assumed in Henry Wallace's Progressive Party presidential campaign in 1948. Wallace was easily the candidate most supportive of Israel immediately before and during its War of Independence, which began in the spring of 1948, early in the presidential campaign. In March 1948 Wallace charged that President Truman, beholden to the fiercely pro-Arab oil corporations, was doing nothing to protect the Yishuv: he "talks Jewish and acts Arab."[106] He compared the U.S. government's embargo on arms shipments to the Yishuv to its refusal to send weapons to the embattled Loyalists during the Spanish Civil War.[107]

As the Arab nations prepared to launch a full-scale war against the Jews in Palestine, the CP organized demonstrations of solidarity with the Yishuv. In March 1948, at least 10,000 members of Communist-dominated trade unions in New York City's fur and garment district marched through a driving rainstorm to protest what they claimed was the U.S. refusal to proceed with the UN decision to partition Palestine. The Communist-edited newspaper *Union Voice* reported that the demonstrators "thunder[ed] a demand that should have echoed all the way to the White House: 'Two-Four-Six-Eight, We Demand a Jewish State.'"[108]

Shortly after the New York march, a new CP front group, the United Committee to Save the Jewish State and the United Nations, brought 5,400 protestors, mostly members of Communist-dominated trade unions, to Washington, D.C., to rally for a Jewish state in Palestine and to picket the White House. U.S. Representative Leo Isacson of the Communist-led ALP declared that President Truman's embargo on the sale of arms to the Yishuv was "deliberately imposed for the massacre of the Jews."[109]

After Israel declared itself a state on May 15, 1948, the CP celebrated its determination to defend itself against six invading Arab armies. In June 1948, the *Daily Worker* quoted a passionate statement of support for Israel by Lorna Wingate, widow of the legendary (non-Jewish) British officer Orde Wingate, who in the 1930s had determined to transform the Haganah, largely confined to guarding Jewish settlements, into a highly-trained striking force prepared to take the attack to the Arabs. The mother of a four-year-old son, Lorna Wingate declared: "If I had gold and money, I would contribute them for the war which my husband foresaw. Not having them, I decided to send you my son to be educated in Israel and to be a loyal son of both Israel and Britain." In the same issue, the *Daily Worker* used a page-one photograph to document an Arab atrocity against the Haganah. It showed two soldiers next to a rock pile marked by a Star of David, the grave of twenty-nine Haganah fighters killed in the attack on the Arab fortress of Nebi Yusha. The caption stated that the Arabs had decapitated each of the slain Haganah soldiers.[110]

Communist-led trade unions in New York City mobilized their members to assist the Haganah forces. David Livingston, vice-president of Local 65 of the Warehouse Workers Union, CIO, declared, "We want to send arms and men, if necessary, to aid the Haganah in halting the British-supported Arab invasion."[111] The AJLC appealed for funds to purchase ambulances for the Haganah.[112]

The CP expressed pride in the Soviet bloc's shipments of desperately needed armaments to the Haganah. When the well-equipped Arab armies launched their invasion to wipe out the Jewish settlements, the Jews were at an enormous disadvantage. In 1947 the Haganah had no cannons or anti-tank weapons, only one heavy machine gun, and no air force or navy. The United States continued to maintain an arms embargo. With Soviet approval, Communist Czechoslovakia supplied the Haganah with weapons, although at a significant cost. Even though mostly obsolete, these weapons proved of considerable benefit to the Israelis. Jewish volunteers from around the world traveled to Czechoslovakia to be trained to pilot fighter planes manufactured there. Czechoslovakia ignored a U.S. State Department protest against sending weapons to the Haganah. When Austrian frontier police detected a shipment of Czech arms bound for Palestine, Soviet soldiers prevented them from confiscating it.[113]

Unlike the CP, the American Trotskyists remained consistently hostile to a Jewish state in Palestine. Compared to the CP, their influence was minuscule. According to the SWP, Palestine's Jews had to be made to understand that "the expulsion of imperialism from the Middle East" would be achieved "only through the Arab revolution and under the leadership of the Arab workers' movement." The Jews would have to become reconciled to residing in a state with an Arab majority. The SWP condemned the Haganah for pursuing what it called "the chauvinist and class-collaboration policies of Zionism," such as promoting "continued Jewish immigration." The Trotskyists insisted that no Jewish immigration to Palestine be permitted "against the wishes of the Arab masses." Like SDS and the Black Panthers twenty years later, the SWP equated the Zionists with the Nazis, accusing them of advocating "Jewish 'master race' poison." When Israel's War of Independence began, the *Militant* editorialized that "a Jewish state in Palestine and the Jewish war for this end is reactionary and bankrupt."[114]

On the campuses of the late 1940s, supporters of Zionism and Israel dominated the discourse on the Middle East conflict. Besides the highly active student Zionist organizations, the campus groups most supportive of the Jewish state were the Progressive Party's university branches, in which Communists were prominent. The Intercollegiate Zionist Federation of America (IZFA), which in 1948 had chapters on over 100 campuses, sponsored numerous lectures by supporters of Israel, including persons engaged in breaking the British naval blockade of Palestine, such as crewmen from the *Exodus 1947*.

Speakers on campus presented Israel as the progressive, democratic force in the Middle East, and condemned Arab authoritarianism, intolerance, and reaction. Lecturing at Harvard, R.H.S. Crossman, British Labour Party

M.P., declared that the Yishuv constituted "a tremendous, model socialist experiment." Its success would doom "every Arab feudal regime in the Middle East." During the 1948 war, the Harvard *Crimson* editorialized that when the Arab League had launched its reactionary "Holy War against the infant state of Israel, the entire civilized world shuddered." It warned that the Arabs had "dedicated themselves to the complete extermination of the new Jewish nation," in short, a second Holocaust.[115]

In November 1949, Rudolph Augarten, Harvard class of 1949, spoke about his experiences as a fighter pilot in the fledgling Israeli air corps during the War of Independence, when he shot down four Egyptian planes. Already a seasoned fighter pilot, having flown 101 missions over Germany during World War II, Augarten left Harvard immediately after final exams in the spring of 1948 for Czechoslovakia. There he was trained to fly the Messerschmidts manufactured at the Skoda works outside Prague. He arrived in Israel in July. In December 1947 the Harvard *Crimson* interviewed three other Harvard students, one of them a former marine, who were preparing to fight in defense of the Jewish state when the Arabs launched their Holy War.[116]

During the late 1940s, when World War II veterans comprised a significant proportion of university enrollments, the American Veterans Committee (AVC), founded after the war as a progressive alternative to the American Legion and the Veterans of Foreign Wars, strongly backed Israel on the campus. At Harvard in February 1948, the AVC co-sponsored with the Harvard and Radcliffe Zionist Societies a lecture supporting partition by Rev. David Hunter, who had toured Palestine the previous summer and found the Arabs to be "deeply anti-Semitic." Hunter reported that the Arabs believed the Jews to be of "diabolical design."[117]

Among the presidential campaigns on the campuses, Henry Wallace's gave Israel the most emphasis and the most ardent support, even though President Truman and Governor Dewey also backed a Jewish state. The College Progressive Party chapters denounced Truman for failing to accord Israel *de jure* recognition, which the Soviet Union had extended, and for maintaining an arms embargo against Israel.[118]

Organized campus opposition to the UN partition plan and support for the Arab war effort in 1948 were confined to a small number of college administrators and faculty members, all hostile to the Left. The most notable were Virginia Gildersleeve, dean of Barnard College, and the Rev. Henry Sloane Coffin, president emeritus of Union Theological Seminary. Chair and vice-chair, respectively, of the pro-Arab League Committee for Justice and Peace in the Holy Land, they used code language favored by antisemites in their anti-Zionist tirades. Gildersleeve, the Committee's chair, charged that fear of the "Jewish vote" had caused politicians to "bully" the Arabs into admitting a "huge influx of alien foreigners" [her term for Jews] into Palestine. Like the far left of the 1960s, Gildersleeve, Coffin, and the other leaders of the Committee denied the significance of Arab antisemitism. During the 1948 War of Independence, they charged that American Zionists, by standing up for Jewish rights in Palestine, were "encouraging antisemitism and endangering the Nation's unity."[119]

At Harvard, William Yandell Elliott, Leroy B. Williams Professor of Government, directly linked Zionism with Communism in a lecture denouncing the partition plan before the university's United Nations Council. If a Jewish state were established in Palestine, it would be one "celebrating the virtues" of Karl Marx. Elliott warned of the danger of allowing 100,000 Jews from Eastern Europe into Palestine, a plan President Truman supported, because they came "from carefully indoctrinated countries," and would bring Communism with them.[120]

Throughout Israel's War of Independence and in its immediate aftermath, American Communists and their fellow travelers remained strongly committed to the Jewish state. In an article equating the CP and Progressive Party platforms, the *New York Times* in late July 1948 quoted the CP's platform as calling for "full support to the new Jewish state, Israel." The Progressive Party demanded "Immediate recognition of Israel, admission to the United Nations, [and] lifting by Presidential proclamation of arms embargo." It asked the United States to "take the lead in calling for economic and diplomatic sanctions against nations guilty of or abetting aggression against Israel." The Progressive Party supported the Soviets in rejecting the proposal by UN mediator Count Folke Bernadotte that required Israel to relinquish the Negev, awarded to it under the UN partition plan. In October 1948 Henry Wallace declared that the "oil monopoly that rules both Truman and Dewey" was causing them to "stab Israel in the back." He claimed that the Democratic and Republican presidential delegation to the UN was pressuring Israel to give up the Negev.[121]

The newly-founded Stalinist weekly *National Guardian* asserted that the Arab nations and the oil corporations feared the destabilizing influence of democratic and prosperous Israel, "which by its example would give ideas" to the Arab masses throughout the Middle East. The *National Guardian* reported that Palestine's Arabs had not taken part in the 1948 war against Israel, having benefited from rising living standards because of the Jewish presence. The 300,000 refugees who fled their homes in Palestine did so "under the urging of the ex-Mufti, Haj Amin el-Husseini," expecting "to return behind triumphant Arab armies." The *National Guardian* predicted that the Arab nations would refuse to admit the refugees, fearing that they would resent the lower living standards there.[122]

TAKING CONSPIRATORIAL ANTISEMITISM
TO A NEW LEVEL

In yet another abrupt shift, the Soviet Union in late 1948 and 1949 began virulent attacks on Israel and Jewish culture, unleashing a torrent of antisemitic propaganda that drew on centuries-old conspiracy fantasies. Like the Nazis, for whom the Jews were the primary force behind both capitalism and Communism, the Soviets leveled contradictory charges, denouncing the Jews both for "bourgeois nationalism," their term for Zionism, and as "cosmopolites" (internationalists). During the next several years, Jewish emigration from the Soviet bloc was for all intents and purposes terminated, Soviet Yiddish writers were murdered by the state, and Yiddish culture was permanently destroyed.

The Soviets initiated the new antisemitic campaign in the fall of 1948 with an article by Jewish writer Ilya Ehrenburg, a Stalin protégé, in which he denounced Zionists as "mystics" and Israel as "bourgeois." Echoing the argument Stalin advanced in 1913, Ehrenburg denied that "there was any affinity between Jews in different countries."[123] Thus Jews could not be considered a people.

The Kremlin almost simultaneously denounced Soviet Jewish writers and intellectuals as "cosmopolites," incapable of displaying national allegiance. The Nazis had used the same word as an antisemitic slur, to make the same charge. Soviet Jews were thus condemned as both nationalists (Zionists) and internationalists (cosmopolites). The Kremlin alleged that both Zionists and cosmopolites promoted the interests of "American imperialism."[124]

As in the period of the Molotov-von Ribbentrop Pact, when the CP refused to consider the implications of refusing to back Britain against Nazi Germany, American Communists heatedly disputed charges that the new Soviet Jewish policy was antisemitic. The *Daily Worker* declared that charges of Soviet antisemitism were "a complete fabrication, a cruel cheat," noting that antisemitism was illegal in the Soviet Union.[125]

The *Daily Worker* even defended the blatantly antisemitic practice of the Soviet press of printing their "original Jewish names" beside the names of Soviet intellectuals whose writings it denounced as "decadent [and] bourgeois." According to the *Daily Worker*, when a writer used a "pseudonym," it was common in the Soviet Union to print "his or her original family name" next to it.[126]

In January 1953 the *National Guardian* justified the ban the Soviet Union and the "People's Democracies" had imposed on Jewish emigration to Israel on the grounds that Israel had moved into the Western orbit. Israel was hypocritical in protesting the ban because it "never tried to impose [its] salvation on the Jews of the West," where the Communists claimed antisemitism was rife. Its real motivation was to weaken the "People's Democracies" by hiring away their "skilled labor and technical experts."[127]

Soviet bloc antisemitism reached its peak of intensity during the Slansky show trials of fourteen leaders of Czechoslovakia's CP, eleven of them of Jewish origin, in Prague in late 1952, and with the arrests in January 1953 of nine Soviet physicians, six of them Jewish, charged with murdering high Soviet officials. As Peter Meyer noted in *Commentary*, "the Prague trial with its lurid tale of a 'Zionist conspiracy' recalled the Czarist-invented and Nazi-popularized legend of the Elders of Zion," while the accusation against the physicians "harked back to the Middle Ages with their charges of Jewish poisonings and ritual murder."[128] Yet the American CP and its fellow travelers insisted that the defendants were guilty.

The Slansky trial was foreshadowed by that of László Rajk, a longtime (non-Jewish) leader of the Hungarian Communist Party, the first postwar Soviet bloc show trial in which defendants were accused of participating in a "worldwide Zionist conspiracy." Rajk, the lead defendant, was Hungary's former Minister of Foreign Affairs and Minister of the Interior, and a Spanish Civil War veteran. This "Judas" and his accomplices, also high-level Hungarian Communists, were alleged to have wallowed in the "ideological sink" of "Trotskyism, fascism, Zionism, and anti-sovietism." They were forced to confess to having conspired with Yugoslavia's Tito regime, the U.S. Office of Strategic Services (OSS), and "world Zionism" to overthrow the Hungarian Communist government. Rajk and other defendants were hanged. Although the Trotskyists had always been fiercely hostile to Zionism, the trial concluded with a defendant confessing to having been a member of a "Trotskyite Zionist movement." The *Daily Worker* endorsed the prosecutors' accusations linking "the Zionists" with the "American espionage attempts to overthrow the people's governments."[129]

The Slansky trial in Czechoslovakia in November 1952 provided the clearest illustration yet of state-sponsored antisemitism in the Soviet bloc. The fourteen defendants were charged with participating in a "Jewish nationalist-Zionist-imperialist conspiracy" to wreck the economy, overthrow the government and restore capitalism. The indictment explicitly identified eleven of them as "of Jewish origin." For defendants who bore Czech-sounding surnames, the indictment listed in parentheses their original Jewish names: for example, Rudolf Slansky (Salzmann), Andre Simone (Otto Katz), Ludvik Frejka (Ludwig Freund). Prosecutors repeatedly mentioned the defendants' Jewish background during the trial and associated Jews with the accumulation of money. The indictment attached to the name of each of the eleven such designations as "son of a big merchant" and "son of a manufacturer." The prosecution accused defendants of arranging export deals from which Czech Jewish émigrés and "other Zionists" collected enormous "usurer's profits."[130]

As in *The Protocols of the Elders of Zion*, an early twentieth century forgery of the czarist secret police that depicted a Jewish cabal concocting a plot to take over the world, the Prague prosecutors charged that the "Zionist-imperialist" scheme to seize control of Czechoslovakia originated at a closed-doors conference in Washington, D.C., in 1947. Allegedly participating were President Truman, U.S. Under Secretary of State Dean Acheson, former U.S. Secretary of the Treasury Henry Morgenthau, Jr. (who was Jewish), and David Ben-Gurion and Moshe Sharett, at the time of the Slansky trial Israel's Prime Minister and Foreign Minister respectively. The prosecutors charged that in exchange for U.S. support for Israel, "Zionist organizations" would carry out espionage and economic sabotage within Czechoslovakia.[131]

In fact, Rudolf Slansky and other defendants in the Slansky trials were made to utter statements that closely resembled those in the *Protocols*. Protocol 10 called on the conspirators to place in high posts persons who had "in their past some dark, undiscovered stain." Fearing exposure, such persons "will be trustworthy agents for the accomplishment of our plans." Defendants were forced to confess that they had kept secret their service to the Gestapo or Leon Trotsky, or both. Protocols 20 through 22 outlined how conspirators could wreak havoc by manipulating foreign loans and investments. Defendant Evzen Loebl confessed that he had arranged for Czechoslovakia to borrow money from Western capitalist nations "at exorbitant rates of interest," severely damaging his nation's economy.[132]

The prosecutors identified as important conspirators Jews prominent in Western business and finance, such as Bernard Baruch and Baron Rothschild. They also named Georges Mandel, a Jewish hero of the French Resistance arrested by the Vichy regime and murdered by order of the Gestapo in 1944.[133]

In denouncing the defendants, Czechoslovakia's Communist Party chairman Klement Gottwald and the prosecution drew on antisemitic passages in the Christian Bible. Because the accused initially denied their guilt, Gottwald called them "stiff-necked," a term Christian theologians used to describe Jews' "stubborn" refusal to recognize Jesus as the messiah. Invoking demonic imagery from the Christian Bible, the prosecutor declared that "the verdict of judges must fall like an iron fist on this nest of snakes." Gottwald similarly described the defendants as "a ball of snakes." The gospel of Matthew had Jesus denounce Jewish leaders as "Serpents, broods of vipers."[134] In the Christian Bible, serpents were the devil's instruments, placed among humans to promote evil.

Long periods of torture and threats against the defendants' families extracted "groveling confessions" and "fantastic tales." Slansky told the court that to conceal the "Zionist-imperialist plot" he had proposed "a campaign . . . against anti-Semitism" and then denounced "the people who pointed to the hostile activities of Zionists" as antisemites. This too appeared lifted from Protocol 9, which called on conspirators to accuse those who challenged their activities of antisemitism. This suggested that antisemitism was "the creature of Jewish plotting, purposefully conceived, organized and spread by Jews themselves to camouflage their world-wide conspiracy." Eleven of the defendants were hanged, and the others sentenced to prison terms.[135]

To establish a direct link between the defendants and Israel, the Czechoslovak government arrested in Prague Mordechai Oren, a leader of Israel's pro-Soviet Mapam party, and charged him as the courier transmitting instructions from leaders of the "worldwide Jewish conspiracy" in Israel to the Slansky group. The court sentenced Oren to fifteen years in prison. Oren had declared that Israeli workers would never agree to fight against the Soviet Union.[136] Prague radio accompanied its broadcast of Oren's "confession" with blatantly antisemitic invective, describing him as having "the dwarfed figure and typical face of the international apache."[137]

Although the antisemitic character of the Slansky trial was obvious, the *Daily Worker* proclaimed that the witnesses had destroyed "the smokescreen of antisemitism" created by Western "pro-war organs" and "produced unassailable factual evidence of the guilt of the defendants." In his pamphlet "The Truth About the Prague Trial," *Jewish Life* editor Louis Harap insisted that Zionism, a form of "bourgeois nationalism," naturally served the interests of the "owning class." This explained Israel's "subservience to Washington, the leader in world capitalism." Embracing America's "anti-Soviet global policy," Israel eagerly joined its "espionage and sabotage conspiracies" in Czechoslovakia. *Jewish Life* also published an article charging that the OSS had "explicit instructions to concentrate on work with the Jews." Applying the antisemitic stereotype of Jews as disloyal profiteers, the article accused the "conspirators" of "trad[ing] on their positions as 'victims of fascism' to export millions of dollars of goods out of a country which is recovering from war damage."[138]

Similarly, a *National Guardian* editorial complained that because most of the defendants were Jewish, "the whole noisy machinery of the U.S. government and press and radio" made "a big Thing out of 'anti-Semitism behind the Iron Curtain.'" It was, however, preposterous to charge a Soviet bloc nation with antisemitism. These nations had "abolished the economic basis of racism in any form" and made antisemitism illegal.[139]

In a lecture at Columbia University Morris Schappes, a *Jewish Life* editor and Lecturer in Jewish History at the CP's Jefferson School of Social Science, called the Slansky Trial "a service to the American people." He accused the American press of falsely injecting the issue of antisemitism. The defendants were convicted because they were "U.S. intelligence agents." There was, in fact, "no anti-Semitic movement in Eastern Europe." There was only antagonism towards ideas that were "contrary to the interests of the working class," including "bourgeois nationalist doctrines" such as Zionism.[140]

Responding to Schappes, a speaker at another Columbia forum, sponsored by the IZFA and Students for Democratic Action, asserted that the Soviets had used the Slansky trial to mobilize neo-Nazi elements in Germany behind them, a view widely held in the West. The trial was also designed to solidify Soviet control over Eastern Europe, where antisemitism was endemic, and to appeal to the Arab world.[141]

In January 1953, the Kremlin imprisoned nine physicians, six of them Jewish, who treated Soviet leaders, on charges of having murdered two high party officials, one by poisoning, on the orders of American and British intelligence and the American Joint Distribution Service. Denounced as "devils in white" and "fiends in human form," they were also accused of conspiring to undermine Soviet defenses by murdering military leaders.[142] In medieval Christian belief, demons ("fiends") serving Satan were capable of assuming human or animal guise. The charges of a "doctors' plot" drew on the medieval antisemitic fantasy that demonic Jews poisoned wells to deliberately spread plague among Christians, and the longstanding libel that Jews' allegiance was to a nefarious international conspiracy, never to the country in which they lived. In the *Daily Worker*, Joseph Clark insisted that the Kremlin had not attacked the "plotters" as Jews, but as "bourgeois nationalists." Johnny Gates, editor-in-chief of the *Daily Worker* until leaving the CP in 1957, recalled that although the charge about "an international

'Zionist conspiracy' to poison the Soviet leaders" was "fantastic," he had "accepted it as gospel truth."[143]

Following the Slansky trial and the doctors' plot, the CP lashed out at Jewish trade union leaders who had been long-time party members or sympathizers but continued to support Israel and promote Jewish culture after the switch in party line. In March 1953, the *Daily Worker* denounced Arthur Osman, a founder and president of what was then the largely Jewish Distributive, Processing, and Allied Workers, District 65 in New York City, for publishing an article in District 65's *Union Voice* that declared: "we as Jews are justifiably incensed at the insults and slanders leveled at us in Prague and in Moscow." Osman called on each Jewish member to "renew his efforts to raise funds for [the] United Jewish Appeal, and do everything else he possibly can to enable more Jews to emigrate to Israel."[144]

Like the prosecutors at the Slansky trial, the *Daily Worker* in its attack on the trade union "renegades" invoked images of sinister Jewish conspiracy and criminality. It called Soviet antisemitism a "hoax" that the AJCommittee "concocted and organized" at a secret meeting in 1947 and "fed to the press." The *Daily Worker* sneered: "Now that Osman discloses himself as a Zionist, he has forgotten entirely the theory of the class struggle he upheld for many years."[145]

Similarly, the CP's theoretical journal *Political Affairs* made use of the antisemitic stereotype of the Jewish huckster in a lengthy diatribe against "opportunism" in District 65. The union represented workers in New York's dry goods industry, where both employees and employers were Jewish and often worked together. Such conditions had led a once "fighting militant union" to collaborate with management and adopt its petty bourgeois outlook. The prevailing "atmosphere of shady dealing and black marketing" encouraged everyone "to rook whomever you can for as much as you can." "The powerful pressure of Zionism" further "obscure[d] class lines." The union joined with management to raise funds for Israel and for Jewish charities, retarding the development of proletarian consciousness among the workers.[146]

1956: SHOCK AND DISARRAY

When Khrushchev's February 1956 secret speech at the twentieth Congress of the Communist Party of the Soviet Union (CPSU) denouncing Stalin's crimes became available in the United States in June, there were rumblings of dissatisfaction within the American CP over Soviet unwillingness to acknowledge the severe damage that had been inflicted on Jewish cultural institutions in the USSR. The Suez war late that year deeply split the CP, contributing to the departure of many leaders and a significant proportion of the membership, distressed by Soviet hostility to Israel and revelations about Soviet antisemitism.

Many Communists and their fellow travelers continued to support the Kremlin position that there was no official Soviet antisemitism. Shortly after Americans learned of Khrushchev's secret speech, the *National Guardian* provided a platform for Ekaterina Furtseva, a member of the CPSU Central Committee, to deny "emphatically that there had ever been any suppression of Jewish culture or repression of the Jewish people" in the Soviet Union. She explained that when Jews became too heavily concentrated in particular departments, the government shifted them to other "equally good" positions in the bureaucracy. Such transfers, a clear indication of government Jewish quotas, were "in accordance with Lenin's principles on the national problem."[147]

However, not long after Khrushchev's speech, questions about Soviet Jewish policy were voiced within the CP. *Daily Worker* foreign editor Joseph Clark sharply criticized *Pravda* for deleting from an article by CP general secretary Eugene Dennis his charge that Stalin had killed "more than a score of Jewish cultural figures." Clark asked for an explanation from the Soviet leadership "about the physical annihilation of the top Soviet writers and poets in the late 1940s." *Morgen Freiheit*'s editors, while refusing to acknowledge that the Soviet regime was antisemitic, complained that under Stalin's leadership Yiddish culture had been "liquidated."[148]

Unlike the American far left in 1967 and after, the CP during the 1956 Suez war reiterated that Israel had a right to exist and to engage in reprisal raids against Arab fedayeen, who had repeatedly attacked its population from bases in Egypt. (This was why Israel had joined the British and French attack on Egypt.) The *Daily Worker* called the fedayeen "marauders." A.B. Magil in the *Daily Worker* recalled the Egyptian aerial bombardment of defenseless Jewish civilians during the 1948 War of Independence, and the "heroism of the people of Israel who, aided by Czechoslovak arms . . . hurled back the armies of five Arab states." The *Daily Worker* editors condemned the Arab states' refusal to recognize Israel, their vow to exterminate the Jewish state, their border raids against it, and Egypt's barring Israeli ships from the Suez Canal.[149]

At the same time the CP justified Nasser's nationalization of the Suez Canal and condemned the British and French attack. It considered the Nasser government a progressive anti-colonialist force. The CP acknowledged that Israel had "legitimate grievances" against Egypt, but this did not justify "its aggression" with Britain and France. It urged the Big Four (the U.S., Soviet

Union, Britain, and France) to persuade the Arab countries to negotiate with Israel, hoping that this would result in recognition of the Jewish state and Israeli access to the Canal.[150]

The CP remained similarly optimistic about the prospects for a revitalization of Jewish culture in the Soviet Union. In a March 1957 resolution on "Jews of the USSR," the New York state CP convention denounced current charges of official Soviet antisemitism as "slander." It acknowledged that many Soviet Jewish writers and artists had been "unjustly and secretly executed" and the Yiddish press and theater disbanded. The convention did not accept the Soviets' argument that Jewish acculturation and assimilation rendered the restoration of Soviet Jewish cultural life and institutions unnecessary. But the resolution concluded by expressing faith that the Soviets would abandon Stalin's "Great Russian chauvinism" and support secular Jewish culture.[151]

Soviet antisemitism was a primary reason for the departure from the CP of a sizeable proportion of its membership, including party leaders and *Daily Worker* staff. Johnny Gates, *Daily Worker* editor-in-chief until he left the CP in 1957, recorded his anger over the Soviet government's suppression of Yiddish culture and murder of Soviet Jewish writers in his 1958 autobiography. He denounced its refusal to support the resuscitation of Yiddish literature, theater, and education. Rejecting as "spurious" the Kremlin's explanation that there was no reason to offer support because Soviet Jews favored assimilation, Gates pointed out that "the Jewish people were never consulted on the matter." Failing to vigorously protest Soviet Jewish policy revealed the American CP's "moral and political bankruptcy." Gates concluded: "For centuries the Jewish question has been the acid test of the...humanity of societies...the failure on this score by the Soviet Union...is the most shameful blot on its record."[152]

Novelist Howard Fast, the only writer in the CP with a significant readership among the American public, left the party in 1957 largely for the same reasons. That year he wrote: "The whole Soviet attitude on the Jewish question is compounded of ignorance...and latent anti-Semitism." Fast noted: "To this date, no explanation of the utter destruction of Yiddish culture in the Soviet Union has been forthcoming, much less some comprehensible account of why the cream of Jewish writers and critics were put to death." He characterized the Soviet refusal to grant exit visas to Jews as "the mass imprisonment of a people."[153]

During the 1956 Suez War, unlike in 1948, the far left had almost no presence on campus. McCarthyism had severely hobbled the far left. The CP was in disarray, as a sizeable proportion of its membership was leaving or preparing to leave because of Khrushchev's revelations about Stalin, anger over persisting Soviet antisemitism and hostility to Israel, and the November 1956 Soviet invasion of Hungary. The Trotskyists, a tiny splinter group, had almost no campus chapters. Nor did the Suez crisis elicit the fierce campus confrontations and riots between supporters and opponents of the British-French-Israeli offensive that occurred at British universities.

Although there were some on the campuses who cheered Nasser's nationalization of the Suez Canal as an assertion of Afro-Asian independence, most continued to view Israel as the progressive force in the Middle East. Symposia on the Suez War were held on major university campuses. Several speakers denounced Nasser as a Fascist, noting his authoritarianism, determination to destroy Israel, and the protection he extended to Nazi war criminals, many of whom occupied high Egyptian government and military positions.[154] Indeed, early in the Sinai campaign, the Israeli army revealed that captured Egyptian officers carried with them as "standard equipment" a paperback Arabic translation of Adolf Hitler's *Mein Kampf*.[155] Arab students and a few Arab faculty members sometimes defended Egypt's position in these symposia, but the campus alliance between Arab student organizations and the far left, highly significant after 1967, had yet to be forged.

SOVIET JEWRY:
OFF THE AGENDA

Although the Soviet destruction of Yiddish culture and murder of prominent Jewish writers caused severe distress among many Communists and drove many from the party, the far left of the 1960s was never much concerned about the oppression of Soviet Jews.[156] In 1965 former CP member William Mandel, longtime Soviet affairs commentator on the leftist Radio Pacifica system and a mentor for many young radicals, told the Berkeley *Barb* that he opposed a vigil against Soviet persecution of Jews that Jewish campus and community groups had recently staged at Oakland City Hall. Voicing a view common on the far left, Mandel declared that such protests against Soviet policy would be acceptable only "when [America's] hands are clean." At the time, according to Mandel, "the overriding moral questions" for Americans were "what are we doing to Vietnam and about Watts."[157]

Although Mandel, who was prominent in Berkeley's countercultural left, had resigned from the CP in 1957, his naiveté about Soviet intentions appeared unshaken. In 1949, he gave one of the principal addresses praising

Stalin at the National Council of American-Soviet Friendship celebration of the dictator's seventieth birthday.[158] Mandel now claimed that there was no official antisemitism in the Soviet Union, only isolated acts by individuals, which the Soviet government actively combated. Americans who spoke out for Soviet Jewry were hypocrites: their vigils "only serve[d] to revive the cold war." He asked the participants in the Oakland vigil for Soviet Jewry to explain what they were doing to protest against the Vietnam War and conditions in the Watts ghetto.[159] Of course, the Hitler regime had similarly claimed that Americans had no right to criticize Nazi persecution of Jews in Germany because minorities experienced discrimination in the United States.

THE SIX-DAY WAR:
THE FAR LEFT MARGINALIZED

In the years immediately following the Six-Day War, the far left, by then largely campus-based, made Israel a major focus of antagonism. Hostility toward Israel became a central defining issue for the far left, as the nation's leading liberals staunchly backed Israel. In its first issue after the outbreak of the Six-Day War, the *Militant* denounced two of the nation's most prominent opponents of the Vietnam War, Eugene McCarthy and Wayne Morse, as "pro-Israel hawks." It complained that numerous critics of the Vietnam War had signed an appeal in the *New York Times* calling on the United States to break Egypt's blockade of the Gulf of Aqaba, which denied Israel access to the Indian Ocean. The *Militant* also condemned Martin Luther King, Jr. for signing what it called a "bellicose" statement backing Israel on the eve of the Six-Day War.[160]

The far left increasingly gave priority to supporting the Arab effort against Israel as the United States reduced its troop commitment in Vietnam after 1969. However, the withdrawal of U.S. forces from Southeast Asia, completed in January 1973, eliminated the issue that had most energized the far left, causing its ranks to shrink precipitously. The far left was also severely debilitated in the late 1960s and early 1970s by its stridency, dogmatism, and bitter factionalism, reminiscent of the CP's Third Period.

During the Six-Day War, which occurred toward the very end of the universities' spring semester in June 1967, campus sentiment strongly favored Israel, and the far left was marginalized and largely unnoticed. Indeed, William Mandel declared about a week after the war ended: "It is appalling to me that the anti-imperialist groups in America have so far not organized one single meeting in defense of the Arabs."[161] Students viewed Israel as the progressive beacon in the Middle East. Stephen Lerner, executive editor of the Harvard *Crimson*, wrote shortly after the Six-Day War: "Thousands of Jews all over the world reacted to this war in the same way that an earlier generation of idealists had reacted to the Spanish Civil War."[162]

PROPAGANDIZING FOR THE PALESTINIAN GUERILLAS: FROM THE SIX-DAY WAR THROUGH THE YOM KIPPUR WAR

The far left enthusiastically championed the Palestinian guerilla movement, which emerged as a well-publicized force after the Six-Day War, because of its unrelenting determination to destroy Israel. The far left feared that the Arab states' shock at their catastrophic military defeat in June 1967 might weaken their commitment to wage war against Israel. The *National Guardian* published an article by an Arab complaining that Egypt after the Suez War had "abandoned its policy of encouraging commando raids" against Israel. The author denounced Egypt for permitting the UN to place personnel near the Straits of Tiran, reopening them to Israeli shipping. Although far left youth seemed solidly in the Arab camp, the author noted that "latent pro-Israeli sympathies...exist among much of the older readership of the *Guardian*." During the Yom Kippur War, the *Militant* asserted that the only solution to the Middle East crisis was "the overthrow of the Zionist state of Israel and the return of Palestine to the Palestinians," but complained that "this course is rejected by Cairo and Damascus."[163]

After the Six-Day War, the SWP and its youth arm, the Young Socialist Alliance (YSA), devoted considerable energy to attacking the CP, which was no longer a significant part of the American left after 1956, as not sufficiently hostile to Israel. In 1966, the CP in a "Draft Resolution on the Jewish Question" had softened somewhat its antagonism toward maintaining Jewish identity and grudgingly acknowledged Israel's right to exist. Lucy Dawidowicz, analyzing the draft resolution for the AJCommittee, noted the absence of the pejorative term "bourgeois nationalism," the CP's euphemism for Zionism during the early 1950s. In another noticeable shift, the CP resolution found it "understandable" and justifiable that an American Jewish Communist might "feel kinship with Jews throughout the world." Its "full fury" was directed against "national nihilism," a "'left sectarian' deviation" that "rejects the continued distinct existence and role of the Jewish people." Dawidowicz believed that the CP's new positive emphasis on Jewish identity was related to current Soviet charges that the People's Republic of China was oppressing its ethnic minorities.[164]

The Trotskyists boasted that, unlike the Communists, they had "struggle[d] ceaselessly against Zionist colonialism" ever since partition in 1947. In 1973, the *Militant* published an article from the Belgian Trotskyist newspaper *La Gauche* that denounced the Soviet Union for taking the lead in extending *de jure* recognition to Israel and for permitting Czechoslovakia to send weapons to the Haganah in 1948. The Soviets were therefore "fully responsible for the tragedy of the Palestinian people." During the Yom Kippur War, the *Militant* derided the CP's Pacific Coast weekly *People's World* for declaring that "the path for peace" in the Middle East included "guarantees for Israeli existence." The *Militant* denounced the CP for supporting a Soviet-backed cease-fire. It proclaimed that the Palestinian guerillas "will continue fighting no matter what Egypt and Syria accept."[165]

In 1970, the SWP's Pathfinder Press published the first U.S. edition of *The Jewish Question* (1946), an anti-Zionist screed by Belgian Trotskyist Abram Leon that explained medieval and modern antisemitism as rooted in abhorrence of Jewish usury. Many far leftists of the early 1970s were attracted to Leon's combination of anti-Zionist invective and the crude economic antisemitism popularized by black militant groups like SNCC and the Panthers. Leon argued that the Jewish population had been widely dispersed across the Middle East, North Africa, and the Mediterranean long before 70 CE, with Judaea containing only the "smallest" and "least vital part." This appealed to radicals who wanted to de-legitimize the Jewish claim to a homeland in Israel. Leon declared that Jews in antiquity were privileged. Anti-Jewish prejudice stemmed from the natural antagonism people engaged in production harbored toward merchants. Contemporary scholars, however, believe that economic antisemitism was not a feature of the ancient world. Most Jews were poor, eking out a living as artisans, laborers, or farmers.[166]

Leon similarly explained medieval antisemitism as rooted in resentment over Jews' usury. The English nobility, angry over "the extremely high rates of interest," which caused them to lose property, "avenge[d] itself by organizing massacres of the Jews." Leon ignored medieval Christian theology as a significant source of anti-Jewish prejudice. As a capitalist economy developed, the kings no longer considered the Jews' money-lending services essential and turned against them. Becoming petty usurers for the masses, the Jews incurred their wrath, sparking pogroms. As the emerging capitalist economy absorbed the non-Jewish population, it rejected usury, identified only with the Jews. As a consequence, the Jewish population was expelled from Western Europe, a process complete by the end of the fifteenth century. But the Jews moved to Eastern Europe, where they thrived as tradesmen.[167]

Leon went beyond previous Marxist writers in declaring that medieval prohibitions against Jews owning land or working as artisans or in certain commercial pursuits were "a fable." He asserted that Jews were psychologically drawn to money-lending. Leon claimed that in Western Germany, where the largest Ashkenazic communities were located, Jews "enjoyed the same civil rights" as Christians. Guilds that excluded Jews were not motivated by "religious animosity or racial hatred." They did not want Jews because they considered usury and peddling dishonest.[168]

Leon asserted that Eastern European antisemitism resulted from peasant resentment of the Jews' role in usury and as the lords' agents in extracting wealth from those who worked the land. This was the cause of the horrific Chmielnicki massacres of 100,000 Jews in the Ukraine in 1648 and 1649.[169]

Oddly enough, although Leon was writing during the Holocaust, and was himself murdered in Auschwitz, he devoted almost no attention to it, or to Nazi Germany's policies before the war. Leon ascribed the refusal of the world's nations to admit Jewish refugees to the inability of decaying capitalist societies to absorb any immigrants.[170]

Shortly after the Six-Day War, far left and Arab student groups began working together to defame Israel on campus and promote support for the Palestinian guerillas. Arab students took the initiative in forging an alliance with the far left by approaching campus radicals at the SDS national convention in Ann Arbor, Michigan, during the summer of 1967. In September 1970, speakers from the YSA and the Organization of Arab Students (OAS) participated in a week of anti-Israel rallies and "teach-ins" at George Washington University and the University of Maryland. That December, OAS members and representatives of Palestinian guerilla groups appeared on Middle East discussion panels at the YSA national convention. This far left alliance with Arab student organizations came to full fruition during the 1973 Yom Kippur War, when the far left and Arab student groups jointly sponsored anti-Israel forums and rallies at numerous universities.[171]

During the Yom Kippur War, pro-Israel activism on the major campuses overshadowed efforts by far left groups and the Arab student organizations with which they allied. While the Arab student population was growing on American campuses, the far left groups steadily diminished in size and influence during the early 1970s. At Columbia the student newspaper, the *Spectator*, reported that campus Jewish organizations reacted immediately to the Arab attack by raising a sizeable amount of money for Israel. During the war's first week, Jewish students staged a campus rally and a symposium (attended by almost 200 students) to demonstrate solidarity with embattled

Israel. By contrast, Arab students at Columbia whom the *Spectator* contacted "said they were not planning any immediate actions to express support for the Arab position." The *Spectator* reported that "the Arab-India Club, which has represented Arab students, [is] currently inactive." Organized Columbia student involvement on behalf of the Arab war effort appears to have been confined to an off-campus demonstration involving about 100 participants, which included "a small contingent" from the Barnard-Columbia Attica Brigade, a Maoist splinter that supported the Palestinian guerillas.[172]

The situation was similar at Harvard, where Israel also commanded more support than the Arabs, and the far left-Arab student alliance staged its major demonstration off campus, at Boston's Government Center. Arab and far left opponents of Israel were among about 100 persons who attended the rally. The radicals participating, not all of whom were affiliated with area universities, were from the SWP and the Spartacist-Revolutionary Communist Youth Organization, a Trotskyist splinter group.[173]

The UCLA student newspaper commented that a majority of students on that campus appeared to back Israel in the Yom Kippur War. Four hundred people attended a rally sponsored by UCLA's Student Zionist Alliance (SZA). Arab and Iranian students briefly interrupted the proceedings by loudly chanting "Down with Zionism." By contrast, a YSA rally "to express solidarity with the Arabs" attracted only "a sparse, disinterested crowd." YSA's keynote speaker labeled Israel a dictatorship and denounced the Soviet Union for supplying the Arabs with only "token amounts of war materiel."[174]

CONCLUSION

The far left of the late 1960s and early 1970s, composed largely of youth, in contrast to earlier radical cohorts, did not acknowledge antisemitism as a problem worth addressing, either in the United States or elsewhere. Where Jews were concerned, it was dogmatically assimilationist. It shared none of the ambivalence toward secular Jewish culture or toward Israel expressed by some older Communists. The young radicals of the late 1960s and early 1970s were unaware of or indifferent to the intense and steadily increasing antisemitism of the decades preceding 1945. When they were educated during the 1950s and 1960s, American schools devoted almost no attention to antisemitism, the Holocaust, or any aspect of the Jewish experience. Unlike previous generations of American radicals, this far left cohort was profoundly influenced by a stridently anti-Zionist black nationalist movement whose rhetoric was often antisemitic.

The leading Marxist theoretical treatises on the "Jewish Question" denied that Jews were a people and dismissed their national aspirations as reactionary. They asserted that Jewish identity largely derived from involvement in an archaic petty capitalism which modern economic development was steadily undermining. Assimilation would draw Jewish workers into a natural alliance with their gentile counterparts by eliminating confusing and meaningless cultural differences, as well as unpleasant personality traits Jews had developed through long involvement in "hucksterism."

On the far left only the CP ever drifted from single-minded fixation on assimilation, and then only temporarily, during periods when promoting secular Jewish identity conformed to Soviet interests. Adherence to the Soviet line often caused the CP to willingly and enthusiastically embrace positions very damaging to Jews. It did so even when suddenly required to reverse its stand. This occurred in August and September 1929 when the CP endorsed the Arab slaughter of Jews in Palestine and published virulently antisemitic cartoons. The Comintern's ultra-left Third Period sectarianism during the early years of Nazi rule, which required the CP to refuse cooperation with socialists and liberals, caused it even to denounce the boycott of German goods. The signing of the Molotov-von Ribbentrop Pact, which placed Europe's largest Jewish population in imminent danger of annihilation, led the CP to sabotage efforts to assist Britain, the sole remaining obstacle to Nazi Germany's gaining long-term control over Europe.

To be sure, in backing partition and Israel during the War of Independence, the CP differed from the Trotskyists, who remained consistently hostile to Israel, and the far left of the late 1960s and early 1970s, which gave ardent support to the Arab military and terrorist forces determined to eradicate the Jewish state. The CP carefully adhered to the twisting Soviet line, however, and began to decrease its support for Israel in 1949.

During the early 1950s, the CP aggressively defended Soviet bloc show trials in which prosecutors, drawing on the *Protocols of the Elders of Zion*, linked defendants to a sinister "world Zionist" conspiracy and used antisemitic invective. The CP refused to challenge the prosecutors' bizarre conspiracy theories and use of vicious economic and theological antisemitic stereotypes. For years, CP leaders loudly denied clear evidence of Soviet antisemitism.

Khrushchev's secret speech in 1956 denouncing Stalin's crimes, which did not address antisemitism, came as a jolt to many American Communists, causing them to think more critically about the Soviet record. During 1956–57 some of them finally admitted that they had deceived themselves in denying that antisemitism was official Soviet policy. Many American Communists left the party in 1956 and 1957 after at last acknowledging the Kremlin's total destruction of the Soviet Union's Yiddish cultural institutions and murder of its leading Jewish writers and poets. This was the case with top leaders like Johnny Gates and the party's most prominent writer, Howard Fast.

These lessons were lost on the far left of the late 1960s and early 1970s. White radicals of this cohort imitated or remained indifferent to the antisemitic invective spewed out by the Black Panther Party, SNCC in its Black Power phase, and Malcolm X, an SWP icon whose writings and speeches strongly influenced many campus radicals. The far left of the late 1960s and early 1970s, in a tradition dating to the young Karl Marx, advanced crude stereotypes of the Jewish huckster, the amoral bloodsucker, drawn from medieval economic antisemitism and Christian theology. Unlike some Communists of the preceding generation, it never considered Israel a progressive beacon in a reactionary Middle East. It did not even express ambivalence about Israel. The younger radicals accepted Palestinian guerilla claims that the Jews were merely a religious group and not a people. Like the CP during the 1929 Arab pogroms, this far left demonized Zionism, condemning Israel with increasing fervor after 1967 and calling for its destruction. Largely uninformed about the Holocaust and Islamist theology, and contemptuous of democracy, the youthful far left remained unconcerned about what would result from Israel's destruction. Purporting to favor modern secular values and equality of peoples, it naively backed forces that, if successful, would replace Israel with an Arab-dominated dictatorship unwilling to extend rights to minorities and women. Any Jews who survived the genocide accompanying Arab military victory would undoubtedly be subjected to an official policy of brutal antisemitism. This far left shared the naiveté of its predecessors about the intentions of authoritarian regimes and movements. There was a striking continuity since Marx's time in the far left's embrace of negative stereotypes of Jews and contempt for Jewish culture and national aspirations. Such an outlook pervaded the far left of the late 1960s and early 1970s, although some radicals active in earlier decades had, at least temporarily, rejected it.

Stephen H. Norwood is Professor of History at the University of Oklahoma. His most recent book, *The Third Reich in the Ivory Tower: Complicity and Conflict on American Campuses* (Cambridge University Press, 2009), was a Finalist for the 2009 National Jewish Book Award in Holocaust Studies. He is co-editor (with Eunice G. Pollack) of the two-volume *Encyclopedia of American Jewish History* (2008).

ENDNOTES

1 *New Left Notes*, February 28, 1969.

2 *Black Panther*, January 4 and August 30, 1969, and November 10, 1973.

3 *New York Times*, August 15, 1967; Los Angeles *Times*, August 15, 1967; Clayborne Carson, *In Struggle: SNCC and the Black Awakening of the 1960s* (Cambridge, MA: Harvard University Press, 1981), 267-269. The article was written at the request of the SNCC Central Committee by the newsletter's editor, Ethel Minor, a former member of the virulently antisemitic Nation of Islam. Carson, *In Struggle*, 267.

4 *Militant*, September 4, 1967.

5 *Ibid.*, July 10, 1967.

6 *New Left Notes*, September 11 and October 2, 1967.

7 Daniel Berrigan, "The Middle East: Sane Conduct?" *Liberation*, February 1974, 10–13.

8 David Dellinger, "The Berrigan Debate: Bringing It All Back Home," *Liberation*, February 1974, 6.

9 Berkeley *Barb*, June 16–22, 1967.

10 *New York Times*, August 14, 1970; UCLA *Daily Bruin*, October 18, 1973; *Fire*, November 21, 1969.

11 *Militant*, June 26, 1967; *Fire*, November 21, 1969; *Black Panther*, October 20, 1973.

12 *Black Panther*, August 30, 1969 and November 16, 1968.

13 *Union Voice*, February 15, 1948.

14 Nathan Glazer, "Jewish Interests and the New Left" in Mordecai S. Chertoff, ed., *The New Left and the Jews* (New York: Pitman, 1971), 160.

15 *Militant*, October 26, 1973.

16 *New Left Notes*, April 17, 1969; *Militant*, September 20, 1968.

17 *Militant*, November 2, 1973 and June 19, 1967.

18 Ibid., October 26, 1973.

19 *Black Panther*, November 24, 1973. See also issues of January 4 and August 9, 1969 for similar statements.

20 Washington *Post*, March 8, 1969.

21 Anti-Defamation League of B'nai B'rith [hereafter, ADL], "Danger on the Left," *Facts*, November 1972, box 3, Julius Bernstein Papers, Tamiment Library [hereafter, TL], New York University [hereafter, NYU].

22 *Fire*, November 21, 1969. *Fire*'s article was reprinted from Tricontinental, part of Cuba's propaganda service.

23 *Black Panther*, November 3, 1973.

24 *Fire*, November 21, 1969.

25 *Militant*, October 26 and November 2, 1973.

26 Seymour Martin Lipset, "The Socialism of Fools," *New York Times Sunday Magazine*, January 3, 1971, 26.

27 ADL, "Danger on the Left."

28   *Black Panther*, September 30, 1972. The Black Panthers claimed that "heads of state" were responsible because West German authorities ordered police sharpshooters to fire on the terrorists. During the shooting the terrorists murdered the Israeli hostages.

29   *New Left Notes*, March 7, 1969.

30   Ibid., March 13, 1969.

31   *Militant*, June 19, 1967.

32   *National Guardian*, July 29, 1967.

33   Karl Marx, "On the Jewish Question" in Karl Marx and Frederick Engels, *Collected Works*, vol. 3 (New York: International Publishers, 1975), 172.

34   *Ibid.*, 170, 174.

35   See Walter Laqueur, *The Changing Face of Anti-Semitism: From Ancient Times to the Present Day* (New York: Oxford University Press, 2006), 172-73.

36   Walter Laqueur, *A History of Zionism* (New York: Schocken Books, 1972), 417, 419.

37   Robert S. Wistrich, "Marxism and Jewish Nationalism: The Theoretical Roots of Confrontation" in Wistrich, ed., *The Left Against Zion: Communism, Israel, and the Middle East* (London: Vallentine, Mitchell, 1979), 12.

38   Josef Stalin, *Marxism and the National and Colonial Question* (New York: International Publishers, 1934), 35–37, 39, 42–43.

39   Isaac Deutscher, *The Non-Jewish Jew and Other Essays* (New York: Oxford University Press, 1968), 65.

40   Lipset, "Socialism of Fools," 34.

41   István Deák, "Jews and Communism: The Hungarian Case" in Jonathan Frankel and Dan Diner, eds., *Dark Times, Dire Decisions: Jews and Communism, Studies in Contemporary Jewry* XX (2004): 38–61.

42   Deák, "Jews and Communism," 49; Washington *Post*, May 24, 1946; *New York Times*, July 19, 1946.

43   Deák, "Jews and Communism," 49. Rákosi and the other three top leaders of Hungary's Communist government were of Jewish origin but nonetheless held antisemitic views.

44   Ibid., 49; *New York Times*, August 2, 1946.

45   Los Angeles *Times*, August 15, 1967.

46   Ibid.

47   Jerold S. Auerbach, *Hebron Jews: Memory and Conflict in the Land of Israel* (Lanham, MD: Rowman & Littlefield, 2009), 66, 68–72; Howard M. Sachar, *A History of Israel From the Rise of Zionism to Our Time* (New York: Alfred A. Knopf, 1996), 173–174; *New York Times*, August 26, 28 and September 1, 1929; Chicago *Tribune*, August 29, 1929.

48   Sachar, *History of Israel*, 174.

49   Auerbach, *Hebron Jews*, 75.

50   Chicago *Tribune*, August 29, 1929.

51   Atlanta *Constitution*, October 17, 1929 and *New York Times*, September 8, 1929.

52   Melech Epstein, *The Jew and Communism: The Story of Early Communist Victories and Ultimate Defeats in the Jewish Community, U.S.A., 1919–1941* (New York: Trade Union Sponsoring Committee, 1959), 223–224; *Daily Worker*, August 30, 1929.

53   *Daily Worker*, August 24 and 30, 1929; Epstein, *The Jew and Communism*, 224–225.

54   *Daily Worker*, September 3, 1929.

55   Epstein, *The Jew and Communism*, 225–227, 231–32; *Daily Worker*, August 29, 1929. In an interview published in February 1934, Leon Trotsky, exiled by Stalin from the Soviet Union, was asked to comment on the official Communist characterization of the "Jewish-Arab events in 1929 in Palestine as the revolutionary uprising of the oppressed Arab masses." Afforded an opportunity to condemn the antisemitic slaughter, Trotsky dodged the issue, responding that he was not sufficiently "familiar with the facts to venture a definite opinion." He stated that he would need to study the matter further to determine how best to assess the involvement of "national liberationists (anti-imperialists) and reactionary Mohammedans and anti-Semitic pogromists." Like most Communists, Trotsky believed that "the Arabian-Jewish" conflict could be solved only through a proletarian revolution carried out by the working classes of both peoples acting in alliance. Leon Trotsky, "On the 'Jewish Problem'" [February 1934] in Leon Trotsky, *Leon Trotsky on the Jewish Question* (New York: Pathfinder Press, 1970), 18.

56   Epstein, *The Jew and Communism*, 226–227; *Daily Worker*, September 4, 1929.

57   *Daily Worker*, September 25, 1929.

58   Ibid., August 29 and 30 and September 4, 1929; Epstein, *The Jew and Communism*, 226.

59   Ibid., September 4 and 5, 1929.

60   Epstein, *The Jew and Communism*, 225, 233.

61   Communists had a significant role in the street protests on Beacon Hill in Boston against Hitler emissary Friedrich Schoenemann when he spoke at Ford Hall Forum in November 1933; in the demonstration in Charlestown's City Square against the visit to Boston of the German battle cruiser *Karlsruhe*, which sailed into port flying the swastika flag in May 1934; in the protests in Harvard Yard and in Harvard Square against the warm reception the Harvard University administration extended to Hitler's foreign press chief, Ernst Hanfstaengl in June 1934; and the demonstrations the next year against the arrival in New York of the German passenger liner *Bremen*. Each of these protest actions climaxed in fights with the police and in arrests. Stephen H. Norwood, *The Third Reich in the Ivory Tower: Complicity and Conflict on American Campuses* (New York: Cambridge University Press, 2009), 27–28, 42–55, 76–77, 83–85.

62   Epstein, *The Jew and Communism*, 286.

63   Norwood, *The Third Reich in the Ivory Tower*, 12, 14–15, 18–19, 26–27.

64   Epstein, *The Jew and Communism*, 286.

65   R. Palme Dutt, *Fascism and Social Revolution: A Study of the Economics and Politics of the Extreme Stages of Capitalism in Decay* (New York: International Publishers, 1935), 203–04, 213.

66   Harvey Klehr, *The Heyday of American Communism: The Depression Decade* (New York: Basic Books, 1984), 479; Nathan Glazer, *The Social Basis of American Communism* (Westport, CT: Greenwood Press 1974 [1961]), 153.

67 A.B. Magil, interview by Alan Thompson, January 5, 1994, New York City, Oral History of the American Left Collection [hereafter, OHAL], TL, NYU; A. B. Magil, *The Truth About Father Coughlin* (New York: Workers Library, 1935).

68 Martin Gilbert, *The Holocaust: A History of the Jews of Europe During the Second World War* (New York: Henry Holt, 1985), 84.

69 Daniel Bell, *Marxian Socialism in the United States* (Princeton: Princeton University Press, 1967 [1952]), 184; Epstein, *The Jew and Communism*, 359.

70 "Quotations," Speech of Vito Marcantonio before Brooklyn Community Peace Congress, August 14, 1940 in International Labor Defense, "War-Conscription-Civil Liberties," box 44, Vito Marcantonio Papers, New York Public Library [hereafter, NYPL].

71 "Quotations," Speech of Marcantonio before Brooklyn Community Peace Congress.

72 Emanuel Neumann to Vito Marcantonio, March 7, 1941 and Marcantonio to Neumann, April 19, 1941, box 3, Marcantonio Papers, NYPL.

73 Epstein, *The Jew and Communism*, 349, 361.

74 Stephen H. Norwood, "Marauding Youth and the Christian Front: Antisemitic Violence in Boston and New York During World War II," *American Jewish History* 91 (June 2003): 233–267.

75 Otis Hood, interview by B. Schecter, March 24, 1981, Boston, MA, OHAL, TL, NYU.

76 Councilman Peter V. Cacchione to William B. Herlands, October 21, 1943, roll 2, Peter V. Cacchione Papers, TL, NYU.

77 "Councilman Cacchione's Statement on the Drew Case," January 12, 1944, roll 2 and Councilman Peter V. Cacchione, "It Happened at City Hall: The Fight Grows Sharper," February 20, 1944, roll 1, Cacchione Papers, TL, NYU.

78 Cacchione, "It Happened at City Hall: The Fight Grows Sharper."

79 Leonard E. Golditch to Congressman Vito Marcantonio, June 20, 1944, box 3, Marcantonio Papers, NYPL.

80 Arkady Vaksberg, *Stalin Against the Jews* (New York: Alfred A. Knopf, 1994), 117–119; Deutscher, *Stalin*, 605–06; Epstein, *The Jew and Communism*, 374–375.

81 Alexander Bittlelman, "My Return to Jewish Life," 571, n.d., box 1, Alexander Bittelman papers, TL, NYU.

82 Editorial, "Anti-Communism, Anti-Semitism, and America," *Jewish Life*, February 1947, 3.

83 Maurice Isserman, *If I Had a Hammer: The Death of the Old Left and the Birth of the New* (New York: Basic Books, 1987), 6.

84 I.F. Stone, *Underground to Palestine* (New York: Pantheon Books, 1978 [1946]), 4; D.D. Guttenplan, *American Radical: The Life and Times of I.F. Stone* (New York: Farrar, Straus and Giroux, 2009), 207.

85 *Daily Worker*, June 22, 1946.

86 Ibid., October 9, 1945.

87 Ibid., June 13 and 14, 1946.

88   Ibid., June 15, 1946.

89   Ibid., June 9 and 10, 1948; *New York Times*, May 29 and June 4, 1948.

90   *Daily Worker*, April 15, 1949.

91   *New York Times*, September 17, 18, and 21 and October 18, 1948 and May 25, 1950.

92   Jeffrey Herf, "East German Communists and the Jewish Question: The Case of Paul Merker," *Journal of Contemporary History* 29 (October 1994): 627–633.

93   *New York Times*, January 8, 1953.

94   "Jewish Life," *Jewish Life*, November 1946, 3.

95   Louis Harap, "Breaking Down the Gentleman's Agreement," *Jewish Life*, January 1948, 29. Voicing the party line that antisemitism was a symptom of American "imperialist aggression," Harap criticized the film for failing to connect it to "the broader socio-economic drive for an 'American Century.'"

96   *Daily Worker*, October 12, 17, and 24, 1945.

97   Ibid., October 25, 1945.

98   Ibid., November 15, 1945.

99   Ibid., November 3, 5, 10, and 15, 1945; *New York Times*, November 3, 1945; Chicago *Tribune*, February 17, 1947.

100   *Daily Worker*, June 17, 1946.

101   Ibid., May 15, 1947; *New York Times*, May 16, 1947.

102   Itzik Feffer, "Gromyko's Ray of Light," *Jewish Life*, September 1947, 11; *Daily Worker*, May 15, 1947.

103   Stone, *Underground to Palestine*, 223–224.

104   "Barbaric Act," *Jewish Life*, October 1947, 4; *Daily Worker*, July 31, 1947; *New York Times*, August 31, 1947; Jon and David Kimche, *The Secret Roads: The "Illegal" Migration of a People, 1938–1948* (New York: Farrar, Straus and Cudahy, 1955), 187–192.

105   Arnold Krammer, *The Forgotten Friendship: Israel and the Soviet Bloc, 1947–1953* (Urbana: University of Illinois Press, 1974), 20–21; Moses Miller, "The Fate of Palestine in the Balance," *Jewish Life*, November 1947, 3–4; *Daily Worker*, October 14, 1947.

106   *New York Times*, March 7, 1948.

107   Henry Wallace, "Palestine: Civilization on Trial," *New Republic*, February 16, 1948, reel 44, Henry A. Wallace Papers, University of Iowa Library, Iowa City, IA.

108   *New York Times*, March 12, 1948; *Union Voice*, March 28, 1948.

109   Washington *Post*, April 16, 1948; *Union Voice*, April 25, 1948.

110   *Daily Worker*, June 4, 1948.

111   *New York Times*, June 1, 1948.

112   *Union Voice*, June 20, July 4, and September 26, 1948.

113   Krammer, *Forgotten Friendship*, 54–55, 62–63, 68, 70, 90, 123; *New York Times*, November 6 and 8, December 14 and 20, 1948.

114   *Militant*, July 27 and August 3, 1946; January 25, May 24 and September 8, 1947; and May 31, 1948.

115   Harvard *Crimson*, November 1, 1946 and November 16, 1948.

116   Ibid., November 10, 1949 and December 2, 1947.

117   Ibid., February 26, 1948; *Washington Square College Bulletin*, November 23, 1948.

118   Columbia *Spectator*, October 14, 1948.

119   Norwood, *The Third Reich in the Ivory Tower*, 130; *New York Times*, November 21, 1947 and June 18 and November 29, 1948.

120   Harvard *Crimson*, February 18, 1948.

121   *New York Times*, July 28 and October 29, 1948; Chicago *Tribune*, July 12, 1948.

122   *National Guardian*, January 10, 1949.

123   *New York Times*, September 22, 1948.

124   Walter Bedell Smith, *My Three Years in Moscow* (Philadelphia and New York: J.B. Lippincott, 1950), 273–74; *New York Times*, March 27, 1949.

125   *Daily Worker*, January 19 and 25 and February 16, 1953.

126   Ibid., May 12, 1949.

127   *National Guardian*, January 8 and March 5, 1953.

128   Peter Meyer, "Soviet Anti-Semitism in High Gear," *Commentary*, February 1953, 116.

129   Paul Lendvai, *Anti-Semitism Without Jews: Communist Eastern Europe* (Garden City, NY: Doubleday, 1971), 307–308; London *Times*, June 20, 1949; Chicago *Tribune*, June 20 and October 16, 1949; *New York Times*, September 20, 1949; *Daily Worker*, September 20, 1949.

130   Peter Meyer, "Stalin Follows in Hitler's Footsteps," *Commentary*, January 1953, 1; Lendvai, *Anti-Semitism Without Jews*, 244; Manchester *Guardian*, November 27, 1952.

131   Lendvai, *Anti-Semitism Without Jews*, 245; Joseph L. Lichten to Lester J. Waldman, December 1, 1952, roll 188, Jewish Labor Committee Papers, TL, NYU.

132   "*The Protocols* and the Purge Trial: A Report of the Anti-Defamation League of B'nai B'rith Analyzing the Prague Purge Trial and Communist Propaganda Use of an Infamous Forgery: *The Protocols of the Learned Elders of Zion*," box 22, Bernstein Papers, TL, NYU.

133   *The Anti-Semitic Nature of the Czechoslovak Trial* (New York: Library of Jewish Information, American Jewish Committee, n.d.), box 22, Bernstein Papers, TL, NYU.

134   Klement Gottwald, "The Prague Treason Trials," *Political Affairs* 32 (February 1953): 46, 49; Harvard *Crimson*, December 8, 1952; Matthew 23: 1–3, 33–34 in *The Jerusalem Bible* (Garden City, NY: Doubleday, 1966).

135   *New York Times*, November 22 and 23 and December 4, 1952; *The Anti-Semitic Nature* and "The Protocols and the Purge Trial."

136   *New York Times*, March 24 and November 23, 1952; Herbert Felix, "Mordechai Oren Returns," *New Leader*, June 25, 1956, 13.

137   Felix, "Mordechai Oren Returns," 13.

138   *Daily Worker*, November 30, 1952; Louis Harap, "The Truth About the Prague Trials" (New York: Jewish Life, 1953), 11; Eleanor Wheeler, "Why So Many Jews at Trial?" *Jewish Life*, March 1953, 17.

139   *National Guardian*, January 22, 1953.

140   Columbia *Spectator*, March 5, 1953.

141 Ibid., March 27, 1953; George Lichtheim, "Will Soviet Anti-Semitism Teach the Lesson?" *Commentary*, March 1953, 225; *New York Times*, November 28, 1952.

142 J.B. Salsberg, "Talks With Soviet Leaders on the Jewish Question," *Jewish Life*, February 1957, 37; Deutscher, *The Non-Jewish Jew*, 82; *National Guardian*, January 22, 1953.

143 *Daily Worker*, January 19, 1953; John Gates, *The Story of an American Communist* (New York: Thomas Nelson & Sons, 1958), 152.

144 *Union Voice*, February 22, 1953; *Daily Worker*, March 2, 1953.

145 *Daily Worker*, March 2, 1953.

146 Alex H. Kendrick and Jerome Golden, "Lessons of the Struggle Against Opportunism in District 65," *Political Affairs* 32 (June 1953): 27–28, 33.

147 *National Guardian*, June 25, 1956.

148 *New York Times*, July 3 and September 17, 1956.

149 *Daily Worker*, October 31, November 1, 2, 6, and 11, 1956.

150 Ibid., October 31, November 2 and 11, 1956.

151 "CP Resolution on Jews of the USSR," *Jewish Life*, May 1957, 28–30.

152 Gates, *Story of an American Communist*, 163.

153 Howard Fast, *The Naked God: The Writer and the Communist Party* (New York: Frederick A. Praeger, 1957), 126.

154 See, for example, *Square Journal* (New York University), November 9, 1956 and *Daily Californian* (University of California at Berkeley), November 15, 1956.

155 Martin Gilbert, *Israel: A History* (New York: HarperCollins, 2008 [1998]), 325.

156 The SWP, which had on occasion charged the Kremlin with antisemitism in an effort to discredit Stalinism, challenged the Soviet government's denial of charges of antisemitism during the early 1960s. In 1963 it praised dissident Soviet poet Yevgeny Yevtushenko's poem "Babi Yar" and noted that "Stalin and his government apparatus engaged in a particularly vicious anti-Semitic campaign in the years 1947–1953." Yevtushenko's poem denounced the Soviet failure to erect a memorial to the more than 33,000 Jews whom the Germans and their Ukrainian sympathizers slaughtered in two days in September 1941 at the Babi Yar ravine near Kiev. Soviet guides refused to take tourists visiting Kiev to Babi Yar, where the murdered Jews lay buried in a mass grave. The city of Kiev used part of the ravine as a garbage dump, and its municipal council made plans in 1962 to build a sports center on the site. Soviet premier Khrushchev condemned Yevtushenko for placing "undue stress on Jews." *Militant*, December 30, 1963; *New York Times*, February 8, 1962, January 12 and March 11, 1963.

157 Berkeley *Barb*, September 24, 1965.

158 *New York Times*, December 21, 1949.

159 Berkeley *Barb*, September 24, 1965.

160 *Militant*, June 12 and 19, 1967.

161 Berkeley *Barb*, June 16–22, 1967.

162 Harvard *Crimson*, June 5 and August 11, 1967.

163 *National Guardian*, June 3, 1967; *Militant*, October 26, 1973.

164 Lucy Dawidowicz, "American Communists Zigzag Again," American Jewish Committee Information Service, August 25, 1966, box 7, Bernstein Papers, TL, NYU.

165 *Militant*, June 15 and November 2, 1973.

166 Abram Leon, *The Jewish Question: A Marxist Interpretation* (New York: Pathfinder Press, 1970), 71–72, 95–96; Shaye J. D. Cohen, "'Anti-Semitism' in Antiquity: The Problem of Definition" in David Berger, ed., *History and Hate: The Dimensions of Anti-Semitism* (Philadelphia: Jewish Publication Society, 1986), 44. Cohen notes that "No ancient text assigns an economic motive to the hatred of Jews."

167 Leon, *The Jewish Question*, 82–83, 145–46, 152–53, 160, 171–73.

168 Ibid., 141.

169 Ibid., 192.

170 Ibid., 250.

171 ADL, "Danger on the Left," box 3, Bernstein Papers, TL, NYU; *Militant*, September 4, 1967 and October 26 and November 2, 1973; UCLA *Daily Bruin*, October 17, 1973.

172 Columbia *Spectator*, October 9, 10, 11 and 17, 1973.

173 Harvard *Crimson*, October 26, 1973.

174 UCLA *Daily Bruin*, October 9, 15, and 17, 1973.

AFRICAN AMERICANS AND
THE LEGITIMIZATION OF ANTISEMITISM
ON THE CAMPUS

Eunice G. Pollack

From the mid-1960s, antisemitism and anti-Zionism increasingly became part of the fabric of American campus life — and conflicts. For three decades, it was African-American student organizations that shaped the antisemitic and anti-Zionist discourse, before Arab- and Muslim-American groups on campus assumed the lead near the turn of the century. By characterizing antisemitic and anti-Zionist rhetoric simply as protected campus speech or even essential parts of students' re-education, a number of black student organizations (BSOs), often sympathetic to black nationalist views, and black studies programs foreshadowed and, in effect, prepared the way for the Muslim student unions (MSUs) and Middle East studies departments' academic assaults on Israel and Jews. Many of the patterns that characterized campus conflicts of the early twenty-first century had been forged and hardened in the earlier period — where speakers invited by BSOs leveled their patently false charges, followed by preemptive denials that the claims could be antisemitic; administrators often equivocated, minimized the menace, or offered exercises in role-playing and courses in tolerance; faculty pandered to the students, and only rarely provided accurate data, context or informed argument to counter the allegations and invective. Indeed, MSUs and PSOs (Palestinian student organizations) drew expressly on the experiences of the BSOs as they sought to lure students to their cause. Earlier, students had rushed to defend the BSO speakers, in an effort to prove they were not racists. Similarly, the new leaders convinced other students to ally with them by characterizing Israel as an apartheid state where Jews ghettoized people of color and discriminated against them. "Pro-Israel Jews," they taught, were only "celebrating the triumph of racism and ethnic cleansing in Palestine."[1]

Many of the speakers whom black student groups featured again and again and who attracted overflow audiences and developed large, adulatory followings on campus were nationalists, whose rants offered up a combination of classical antisemitism and anti-Zionism. Although there are those who maintain that anti-Zionism need not be antisemitic, in the preachings of representatives of black nationalist groups, often antisemitism and anti-Zionism were seamlessly merged. The virulent anti-Zionism of the Nation of Islam (NOI), for example, had deep roots in its extremely negative ideology about Jews. It is not surprising that it was Malcolm X, a leading figure in the NOI for seventeen years, and who counted himself a strong anti-Zionist, whom Louis Farrakhan, head of the NOI since 1977, credited with promoting the *Protocols of the Learned Elders of Zion* and putting it on blacks' essential "reading list." Indeed, Farrakhan explained that it was the *Protocols*' revelations of Jews' conspiracy to take over the world that led "Brother Malcolm" to understand and expose the real motives that underlay Jews' involvement in "the NAACP and the civil rights movement," as well as Israel's goals in the Middle East. The NOI and several other militant groups that promoted black nationalism and black power in these years sought both to de-legitimize Jews as a progressive group and Israel as a Jewish state.[2]

Although the NOI and others who shared its perspective now obsessively focused their rage on Israel and on Jews, earlier the central villains of the NOI narrative were whites — both Christians and Jews. Even in the 1990s, the NOI's most popular provocateur on campus routinely began his harangues by declaiming that he was not going to play "pin the tail on the donkey," but "pin the tail on the honky," a pejorative term for whites. He invariably proceeded, however, to pin the tail — and horns — on the Jew — literally demonizing the Jewish state and Jews. If earlier it was whites who had erected an apartheid state, now it was Zionist Jews who formed an apartheid nation, and later, built an apartheid wall. Farrakhan often claimed that it was the American "white man" who "made a nigger. You educated niggers to be niggers." But he now attributed the responsibility for the condition of blacks solely to Jews. "You'll never succeed," Farrakhan warned, not because of whites, but "because of Jews.... They're plotting against us even as we speak." Repeatedly stressed by the nationalists, it was a lesson absorbed by the many black youth influenced by them. As one eighteen-year-old stated categorically, "Behind every hurdle that the Afro-American has yet to jump stands the Jew" barring the way. Formerly the NOI emphasized that it was the insidious whites who used "tricknology" to dominate blacks. But now it was the Jews — the Zionists — who were deceiving them. When in 1996 two journalists wrote about how they had bought the freedom of blacks who had been captured by Arab slavers in the Sudan, the *Final Call*, the NOI organ, dismissed the reports as fabrications because they appeared in the Baltimore *Sun*. "The *Sun* is a Zionist Jewish daily," it claimed. "Don't let the Zionists get away with damn lies." Formerly it was whites who were condemned for slavery and the slave trade. But in 1991, having learned of the Elders of Zion's relentless drive to subjugate or enslave the peoples of the world, the NOI changed the players, reassigning the "dominant" role to Jews. Jews were now responsible for the expulsion of blacks from their African homeland—and Zionist Jews for driving Palestinian Arabs from their homes.[3]

Although the NOI had long held not only whites but Christianity responsible for the subjugation of black people, increasingly its spokespeople would refocus attention on the culpability of Judaism and Jews. W.D. Fard, the founder of the Nation of Islam, had identified Christianity as a "dirty religion," but a half century later, it was Judaism to which Farrakhan attached the founder's exact words. The NOI characterized the Christian bible as the "Poison Book" and Christianity as an unholy conspiracy, designed to obscure the fact that Jesus was black and had been sent by Allah to teach the truths of Islam. Worse, Christianity maintained that its followers were capable of goodness, which was inconceivable because whites had been artificially formed by the evil, "big-headed scientist" Yacub as a "devil race." They were the exact opposite of the naturally created Original Man, the black man, righteous man, who had been "the maker, the owner, the cream of the planet Earth." These teachings were central to the NOI's foundation narrative and could never be disavowed, but its spokesmen now drew attention to the pernicious Hebrew bible and the "Babylonian Talmud," which, they alleged, invented racism, the consequence of the punishment of the descendants of Ham. (No matter that blacks were the descendants of Cush, not Ham, and this was the interpretation of Muslims, not Jews.) The NOI had revealed the Christian's true nature and now was determined to expose the Satanic Jew and Jewish state, craftily obscured behind a progressive disguise, just as the *Protocols* taught.[4]

Even as Christianity began its retreat from two millennia of Judaeophobia, of linking Jews and Satan, the Nation of Islam and some other black nationalists clung to the old image and language, while providing their own spin. At Vatican II the Catholic Church had at last taken a momentous step away from its central teachings about the traitorous Jews, but a prominent black nationalist, with a "Bachelor of Sacred Theology degree," revived the view of the "perfidious" Jew, who now "educationally castrated" "our black children" and "mentally poisoned" them — sacrificing the innocent once again. The NOI persisted in hurling the old Christian accusations at Jews, shrieking, "Jesus was right. You're nothing but liars. The Book of Revelation is right. You're from the Synagogue of Satan!" But the Nation did not have to draw on Christian images to portray the treacherous Jew. From its beginnings, NOI theology taught that it was Jews who handed Jesus over to bounty hunters, who skewered him with a knife. The Jews hated Jesus because he knew their origins as white devils and knew that before Allah sent Musa (Moses), they, unlike the blacks, had been savages, barely human, at best wearing animal skins and living in caves. But the Nation and its acolytes now extrapolated from there. With Farrakhan storming that the Jews "were the killer of all the prophets," he and others now charged that they had killed all the more recent black liberators as well. The *Protocols*, after all, had exposed Jews' intention to undermine societies by assassinating their leaders. Jews — and the Jewish state — were truly the agents of Satan. (That it was Farrakhan who was allegedly involved in the assassination of Malcolm X underscores the ease with which he rid himself of guilt by projecting his own evil onto Jews.) It followed that Jews were responsible for the ignominious state of the black ghettos, and Israel for the instability of the world. Notably, the shift of the narrative away from the white devils or the Christian conspiracy to the Satanic Jews had greatly expanded the nationalists' audience and even their appeal.[5]

Mainstream scholars have recently described the historical experience of Jews in America as one of "whitening." In their model, Jews became increasingly indistinguishable from other European immigrant groups, as they all Americanized by demeaning — and distancing themselves from — blacks. Many of the black nationalists, by contrast, insisted on Jewish difference, Jewish exceptionalism, singling them out for special opprobrium, vilifying — "blackening" — them and the Jewish state.

Those nationalists who were black separatists, such as the NOI, used antisemitism, in part, to sabotage the integrationist, civil rights movement — Malcolm X dubbed the 1963 March on Washington the "Farce on Washington" — by smearing the Jews, who played so prominent a role in it. Paradoxically, some black students who had embraced the Nation's antisemitic message saw it as integrating them, Americanizing them. As one eighteen-year-old girl, writing in the catalogue of the Metropolitan Museum of Art's exhibit "Harlem on my Mind," concluded, "Our contempt for the Jews makes us feel more completely American in sharing a national prejudice."[6] I.e., it was antisemitism that had "whitened" her. If racism had "whitened" European Americans, it was antisemitism that was "whitening" African Americans.

Many of the nationalists, pan-Africanists and other black militants who became iconic figures on campus expressed both antisemitic and anti-Zionist worldviews, albeit in various combinations. To be sure, a large number of commentators have denied that there are any distinctions between the two phenomena. For the essayist Cynthia Ozick, "the term anti-Zionism — like its predecessor, anti-Semitism — is born in mendacity," is a "cover-up" for the old hatred of Jews. Ozick asks, "To what other people has the morally and politically diseased phrase, 'the right to exist,' been applied?" Similarly, to the historian Gil Troy, "Zionophobia" is of a piece with the long history of antisemitism, just the latest form of scapegoating Jews. "Jews were saddled with the sins of the capitalist and the communist, just as Israel today is saddled with the West's alleged sins." And he points to the many parallels between the earlier and more recent movements: "the obsessive, disproportionate hysteria, the demonization, the delegitimization, the odious comparisons...." Others, however, perceive them as separate — and unequal — belief systems, with anti-Zionism stripped of much of the stigma attached to antisemitism. Indeed, the sociologist Glen Lowry attributes the embrace by many African Americans of an "anti-Israel" posture to their anti-Western view, but does not link this to antisemitism: "The experience of constant rejection makes blacks feel in but not of the West and thus highly susceptible to the 'fundamentally anti-West'" movements in the Third World, including anti-Zionism. By contrast, the literary scholar Edward Alexander, though not responding to Lowry, dismisses as "utterly fanciful" any effort "to locate the origins...of American black anti-Semitism in adherence to Third World ideology. The Jew-hatred was a cause, not an effect, of 'Palestinianism,'" he concludes.[7] I.e., antisemitism was the independent variable.

Most of the new black nationalists, pan-Africanists and black militants propounded a mix of anti-Zionist and earlier antisemitic views, the strands often wound so tightly together that one could not locate the beginnings, their roots. For the poet and playwright LeRoi Jones, who would become Amiri Baraka, however, the path to anti-Zionism can be traced. Jones' early antisemitism is well-documented, some of which has even been acknowledged by him. There was the call to "rip[ ] off" "joosh enterprises," there were the people referred to as "jew-slick," and the harrowing: "I got the extermination blues, jewboys/ So come for the rent jewboys/...I got something for you, gonna give it to my brothers so they'll know what your whole story is, then one day, jewboys, we all.../ gonna put it on you all at once." But in 1980, in a cover story in New York's *Village Voice*, entitled "Confessions of a Former Anti-Semite," Baraka apologized, after a fashion, and identified antisemitism as a "wasteland" that he had now left behind. At the end of the long confession, the reader could understand why — as he announced his re-birth as an anti-Zionist. His explanation of his transformation left little doubt, however, about the vessel into which he had poured his Jew-hatred. "Anti-Semitism," he had discovered, "is as ugly an idea and as deadly as white racism — and Zionism. No progressive person could ever uphold any of these ideas."[8]

Apparently, few people read beyond the title or to the end, and in 2000 the governor of New Jersey appointed Baraka the state's poet laureate. Indeed, Gerald Stern, the first person who had been awarded the title, and who later remarked, "I'm sensitive as a Jew," had nominated him. His "confession" in the *Voice* had convinced him that Baraka had "repented for his sins." Thus, he was stunned by Baraka's new poem: "Who knew the World Trade Center was gonna get bombed/ Who told 4,000 Israeli workers at the twin towers/ To stay home that day/ Why did Sharon stay away." As Stern averred, "'Israeli' is a code word for 'Jew' and he knows that too." The publisher of the African-American paper the *Amsterdam News* praised it as an "epic poem . . . that will live for as long as there is value attached to poetry." The Newark *Star Ledger* disagreed: "Of poets one hates to be critical/ But not when they're anti-Semitical."[9]

The precise etiology of many others' anti-Zionism was not so clear, but the footprint of antisemitism at or near its core was unmistakable. The nationalists and militants sought — and found — the evil Jew everywhere, "pimping the world," in an NOI spokesperson's pithy charge, robbing people of color of their "birthright" wherever they were. For many, all Jewish wealth was wrung from "the blood of us." The Black Panthers, who were increasingly celebrated and romanticized on campus — Huey Newton, their "minister of defense," even conducted a symposium at Yale with the noted psychologist Erik Erikson — were virulent anti-Zionists and antisemites, both for much the same reason. Thus the Jews' only right to the "Zionist fascist state" was a "robber's right." They pictured the "Zionist Puppet State of Imperialism" as an "eye-patched pig" with a Star of David wand, "sucking greedily at nursing bottles filled with dollar signs," which were held by its smiling pig masters, including the United States — and from a platform in Jordan in 1970, a Panther delegation called for the elimination of the "Zionist entity."

The only difference between the Jews of Israel and the "Zionist exploit[ers]" and occupiers of the ghettos "here in Babylon," as they termed the U.S., was that Jews in America did not serve a higher imperial power. Here the puppets were the black "Uncle Toms," in league with the white or Jew. The Jews in America — like the arrogant Jews in Israel — always dominated — and sacrificed — the people of color. Influenced by the *Protocols*, which conflated

Jews' conspiracy to conquer the world with the rebirth of the Zionist movement, the Panthers always referred to American Jews — whom they saw as colonizing the black ghettos — as "Zionists." Thus a "Zionist judge" sentenced Huey Newton; another "Zionist judge" sentenced Bobby Seale, the only black member of the Chicago 8 conspiracy trial, "to four years for contempt" of court, while he "allowed the other Zionists [his codefendants] to go free." Moreover, "the other Zionists" on trial "did sacrifice Bobby Seale" for their own pernicious ends — "to gain publicity." In America, the Jews sacrificed black leaders, just as in Israel, in the Holy Land, they had sacrificed the original savior. A Panther's poem, which promised to "kill [ ] every Jew we see/ Jew-Land, NOT another day should pass/ Really, Without a foot up Israel's ass," it was "Really, Cause that's where Christ was crucified." Their antisemitism and anti-Zionism were inextricably entwined.[10]

Stokely Carmichael (who would later change his name to Kwame Ture), prime minister of the Black Panther Party and before that, head of SNCC (Student Non-Violent [changed to National in 1969] Coordinating Committee), was a pan-Africanist and a genocidal anti-Zionist, who vehemently — and disingenuously — denied his antisemitism. ("I am not now, have never been, nor can ever be anti-Semitic or anti-Judaic. However I am, and will be, unto death, anti-Zionist," he wrote in his memoir.) At a speech he gave at the University of Maryland in 1986, Ture announced, "The only good Zionist is a dead Zionist." In response to protests organized by Jewish students, who demanded that he not be paid his $700 honorarium, the Black Student Union, which had sponsored the talk, refused to apologize, vowing, "If we have to pay him out of our pockets, we'll pay him." For its part, the administration assured the students that it welcomed speakers "of all viewpoints," and would not withhold his fee. The call for the death of Jews had become only another "viewpoint." In the wake of Ture's ringing battle cry, a swastika — that threatening symbol of genocide — was painted on the Jewish student newspaper's door. Earlier, in 1970, Ture had famously declared, "I have never admired a white man, but the greatest of them, to my mind, was Hitler." I.e., the greatest of white men was the one who pursued the genocide of Jews. Strangely enough, he also indirectly honored another would-be leader of genocide, this one directed against "colonized people of color," as the infamous battle charge he had adapted was that of the Indian fighter and cavalryman General Phil Sheridan — "the only good Indian is . . . ."

To Carmichael (or Ture), "Zionists" were colonizing or suppressing black people — East and West. As he had explained in 1967, "the same Zionists that exploit the Arabs also exploit us in this country." Like the Panthers he led, he had learned from the *Protocols* that Zionists were everywhere, bent on subjugating the non-Jewish peoples of the world. To be sure, at that time the American inner cities were ablaze and the Middle East had just exploded in the Six Day War — but Carmichael had never altered his view. Clearly, he wanted a lot of Jews dead. The next year, at a national convention of "Arab students" held at the University of Michigan, Carmichael promised that "we will fight to wipe it (Zionism) out wherever it exists, be it in the ghetto of the United States or in the Middle East." Here he may have been calling for "wiping out" Zionism, but significantly, he never suggested how to do it without killing — or wiping out — Jews. Few people were surprised when after his call for "dead Zionists" at the University of Maryland, "several Jewish students received telephone threats" and "anti-*Jewish* pamphlets" were pushed under the student union door. Despite his obsession with the evil Jews, Carmichael would deny that he was antisemitic — he was not even "anti-Judaic," he said. But as the Synagogue Council of America pointed out, "the classical defense of the anti-Semite always was the Jew was singled out not for his Jewishness but for 'objective' sins attributed to him."[11]

Carmichael attached to Zionism the labels that antisemites had long applied to Judaism and Jews, as he denounced "Zionist aggression," the "trickery of Zionism," the "evil of Zionism." SNCC, which he led, also appropriated classical antisemitic imagery and deployed it in its cause. Almost any threat to the black man could now be traced to Zionists. When heavyweight champion Muhammad Ali was sentenced for refusing induction into the U.S. Army, it was Moshe Dayan SNCC pictured, dollar sign and Star of David in his hand, holding the looped rope — that lethal symbol of lynching — that was choking him.

But Carmichael's pan-Africanism added another dimension to the view of the Zionist or Jew. To Carmichael, when the Six Day War ended with Israel in control of the Sinai, Zionists had seized the black homeland. Zionists owned the ghetto and now had robbed the diaspora blacks of their motherland as well. Trying to convince American blacks to share his sense of the expansionist Zionist menace, Carmichael declaimed, "We have got to be for the Arabs. We are Africans wherever we are." Israel "is moving to take over Egypt. Egypt is our motherland — it's in Africa.... Egypt belongs to us since four thousand years ago." Like many black nationalists and pan-Africanists, Carmichael conflated the Arab lands with all of Africa, some nationalist ideologies positing that they had been black societies from earliest times.

In effect, some of the new black nationalists were calling for a crusade — that would restore the motherland to them. Some now sought to reverse the

Jews' foundation narrative. If Yahweh had once caused the Hebrews' Egyptian oppressors to drown, it was now the Egyptians (or to some, Allah) who would obliterate the "Zionist entity" by driving the Jews into the sea. To Carmichael, the "so-called state of Israel" was illegitimate — the Zionists were not the descendants of the original black inhabitants of the land. In any case, it was an "unjust and immoral state." Why should it continue to exist? Notably, it was Carmichael who at Madison Square Garden in 1985 would deliver the opening address for Louis Farrakhan, who presided over what some likened to a Nuremberg rally, where "the audience greeted each anti-Semitic thrust by rising to its feet, cheering, arms outstretched at 45-degree angles, fist clenched."[12]

Although ever-increasing numbers of black militants became staunch anti-Zionists in the years framed by the Six Day War and the Yom Kippur War, the Nation of Islam had been at least latently anti-Zionist from the time of its founding and the shaping of its ideology by W.D. Fard in the early 1930s. Indeed, Fard's mythology promised to de-victimize blacks by literally demonizing and dehumanizing whites and demonizing, animalizing — or expunging — Jews. In the Nation's cosmology, the Jews could only be usurpers in Palestine — the people most others consider Jews are "imposter Jews," who, from their origins, were only a "European strain of people." The Jews of Palestine — the indigenous Jews — were a black people. NOI members continue to recognize the founder's teachings as gospel and Farrakhan could dismiss those who labeled him an anti-Semite as "not Semites themselves," but "Jews that adopted the faith of Judaism up in Europe.... They have nothing to do with the Middle East — they're Europeans...not Semitic people. Their origin is *not* Palestine." According to the Nation's theology, it was only the blacks — the "Original People" — who had settled and created the illustrious civilization of the Middle East. As Khalid Muhammad, cleaving to the teachings of the Nation's founder, instructed his rapt listeners, the blacks had built great universities while the "Johnny-come-lately Jews" were still "crawl[ing] around on all fours in the caves and hills of Europe, eatin' juniper roots and eatin' each other."

Thus in 1956, Elijah Muhammad, who would lead the NOI from the time of Fard's "disappearance" in 1933 until his death in 1975, was elated when Egypt's president Gamel Abdel Nasser stood up to the white imperialist powers, nationalized the Suez Canal, placing it for the first time under the "complete jurisdiction" of what the NOI considered "an African nation," and closed it to Israeli shipping. In 1959, when Malcolm X went to Egypt and Mecca to prepare for Elijah Muhammad's visit later in the year, he informed his hosts that the "millions of colored people in America" "would be completely in sympathy with the Arab cause" because they are "related to the Arabs by blood." According to the NOI belief system, the Arabs and the blacks, the founders of North African societies, were one. It is not at all clear, however, as the cultural critic Stanley Crouch observed, that "many color-conscious Arabs would [ ] welcome ... this racial consanguinity," pointing, for example, to "Libyan leader Muammar Gadhafi's contemptuous writings about sub-Saharan Africa." Still, binding them together was the shared hatred of Israel. At their meeting, Muhammad explained to Nasser that the NOI was the perfect vehicle for "propagating the Arab cause against Israel in the U.S." The false Jews had, after all, "swindled us, [they] have stolen our birthright," as a later minister of information of the NOI declaimed.

The Arabs and the NOI shared another enemy as well. The apocalypse foretold in Fard's narrative would begin with the annihilation of the white devils not only in the United States, but Britain. This was in retribution for Britain's having drawn up the Balfour Declaration, which promised Palestine to the "false Jews." Devised by Fard in the 1930s, before the establishment of the State of Israel, now it would no longer be Britain that should be destroyed first.[13]

Malcolm X belonged to the Nation of Islam for seventeen years, leaving less than a year before his assassination on February 21, 1965, and accepted much of its worldview. But even after he had left the Nation, and increasingly became an orthodox Muslim, classical Christian antisemitic images continued to pervade his repeated statements about Jews. He portrayed them as parasites, preying on the innocent black people, from whom they extracted their wealth, the pound of flesh, which they used to build the Jewish state. Again and again he roused his audiences by telling them of all the Jewish owners of the stores in their neighborhoods who are "robbing you deaf, dumb and blind" — a vivid image of the usurious Jew. "It's Jews right here in Harlem," he went on, "that run these whiskey stores that get you drunk." (In singling out Jews as responsible for drunkenness, Malcolm X may also have been influenced by Protocol 6, which revealed this to be a favored technique used by the Elders of Zion in their quest for control of workers.) "It's Jews that run these run-down stores that sell you bad food," he continued. I.e., once again, it is Jews who are poisoning them. "In fact," he informed them, "the Jews control about 80 percent of the economy in most Negro communities across the country." The Jews, in effect, control the black world.

His audiences could not fail to understand Malcolm's allusions as over and over he spoke of the Jew as bloodsucker, drawing on the most lethal image of Christian antisemitism. Jewish blood lust was causing the murder of innocents once again. He taught that Jews "sap the very life-blood of the so-called Negroes [in America] to maintain the state of Israel." "Israel," he explained, "is just an international poorhouse which is maintained by money sucked from the poor suckers in America." He pictured the Jewish merchants fleeing after dark every night "with another bag of money *drained* out of the ghetto." And then there were the absentee landlords — all apparently Jews. Like Malcolm, drawing heavily on the Christian gospels, Farrakhan ratcheted up the rhetoric — and the threat — only a notch when, fittingly, on the NOI Savior's Day (2005), he railed, "Jewish people don't have no hands that are free from the blood of us." The original alleged crime had apparently been passed down even unto the current generation of Jews, who were now focused on sacrificing, on bleeding, the blacks.[14]

Once again drawing on — and updating — antisemitic themes with which his audiences had been familiar since childhood, Malcolm X warned them of the cunning, duplicitous Jew. The Jews, he told them, want you to believe they are progressive, but "You can find a whole lot of them who are Nazis."[15] The Jews only pose as their allies, "claim to be friends of the American black man," but "so many Jews actually were hypocrites." His audience could not fail to recognize his barely veiled identification of Jews as Pharisees, which the dictionary still defines as "one pretending to be highly moral or virtuous without actually being so." He acknowledged that Jews were "among all other whites the most active...in the Negro civil rights movement. But...I knew that the Jew played these roles for a very careful strategic reason: the more prejudice in America could be focused upon the Negro, then the more the white Gentiles' prejudice would keep diverted off the Jew." (In fact, their involvement in the movement intensified antagonism toward "the Jew.")[16] He goes on, determined to expose the crafty Jew, claiming (incorrectly) that "so often in the North the quickest segregationists were Jews themselves." Ultimately, such arguments would lead his successors in the NOI to disclose the "*Secret Relationship between Blacks and Jews*" — that Jews dominated the Atlantic slave trade. (As leading scholars have shown, they had only a "very marginal" role.) If Jews' wealth now "came...out of the back of every Black brother in the ghetto," as one militant put it, earlier Jewish wealth had been stripped from the backs of the slaves.[17]

As part of the effort to de-victimize blacks, the NOI had turned the traditional (white) historical narrative on its head. Now Malcolm X determined that he also had to rewrite the recent historical record of the Jews. Black suffering had to be placed at the center of the American and world narratives — not the experience of the Jews. While characterizing Jews as deceitful, Malcolm X conjured up grossly inflated figures that diminished the Holocaust, now overshadowed by the dimensions of the Atlantic slave trade. Cannily invoking images of manipulative Jews, he pictured them "always running around here trying to get you sympathetic for them…make you cry crocodile tears over what happened to him in Germany." (The Holocaust was not, of course, confined to Germany.)

In response, "You tell him what happened to you right here. You haven't got no time to cry no tears for no Jew." And now he introduced his audience to the new American foundation narrative he had fashioned that would supposedly liberate them: "Why, they only killed 6 million Jews, only 6 million Jews were killed by Hitler. Uncle Sam killed 100 million black people, bringing them here, yeah 100 million, 100 million. Don't let no Jew get up in your face and make you cry for him. Ask him what happened when our forefathers were brought over here as slaves — 100 million black people were taken from Africa." Occasionally, even in the same oration, the 100 million had been brought to "the Western hemisphere," but more often, he taught his riveted and credulous listeners that they were brought "to this country." "One hundred million of us were kidnapped and brought to this country — 100 million. Now everybody's getting wet-eyed over a handful of Jews…. What about our hundred million?" Of the 100 million, Malcolm X claimed 80 million had been "murdered," "butchered," "mutilated," "and these Jews got the audacity to run around here and want you to cry for them." The Holocaust had now been replaced at center stage, and the black holocaust would have an Adolph Eichmann too: "If Jews were justified in grabbing Eichmann and putting the gas to him (he was, in fact, hanged), then God is justified in grabbing Uncle Sam and putting the gas to him."[18]

Malcolm X had formulated the new nationalist liturgy — and for his legions of followers it became the gospel truth. The Atlantic slave trade had in fact involved between 10 and 12 million Africans, and only 6 percent of them were brought "to this country" — six hundred thousand to seven hundred twenty thousand. Rather than 80 million dead in the Middle Passage, the death toll has been estimated at between 1.2 and 2.6 million. And since the Atlantic slave trade long preceded the founding of the country and the U.S. ended it about two decades later in 1808, it was far more than "Uncle Sam" who was at fault. But none of this mattered. Stokely Carmichael charged in 1968 that "a hundred million niggers [had] been killed during the trip from Africa to America," and so African Americans were owed a homeland more than Jews. He proposed that Zionists "take the land from their home state of Germany [sic]," not from the Arabs in the Middle East. More recently, in

2005, Malcolm X's namesake, Malik Zulu Shabazz, national chairman of the New Black Panther Party for Defense, has raised the stakes by 50 percent, declaiming before a room filled to capacity at Carnegie Mellon University: "You say you lost 6 million? We lost 150 million." Like most other antisemites and anti-Zionists, they minimized the suffering of the Jews.

According to the adherents of the new nationalists' bible, there was no need "to cry no tears for no Jew — cry tears for yourself." For some, there was also no need for a Jewish state — because antisemitism and the victimization of the Jews were confined to four years (in some versions, six), while blacks have been subjected to "400 years of lynchings" here. With the new paradigm, which trained a lens only on the suffering of non-whites — with this sleight-of-hand — two millennia of the oppression of Jews by the world's oldest and longest hatred were erased. After Khalid Muhammad, along with two academic supporters of the Nation, were taken to the Holocaust Memorial Museum in Washington, D.C. in 1994, they remained "unimpressed." As the minister of information remarked, "They had piles of shoes....We didn't even have shoes." Notably, his audiences knew so little of the history of Jews that when he informed Howard University students that Jews were never "stripped of their names, culture, religion, land, and family, like black people were," no one dissented. It seemed credible to them.[19]

The new nationalists also employed the methods used by antisemites down through the ages (and more recently, by anti-Zionists as well) to handle parts of themselves (or their societies) that they need to disavow by attaching them — projecting them — instead onto the Jew (or the Jewish state). Thus Malcolm X taught that Jews did not deserve his followers' sympathy for the Holocaust because they "brought it on themselves." Jews bear the responsibility for the annihilation. Without Jews' cooperation with the Nazis, the Holocaust could never have taken place. As Carmichael put it, "The Jews were the ones carrying out the orders so the Nazis could say it's not us, it's the Jews, and then they pulled the Uncle Tom Jews up." He called on black people to "check out the difference between us and the Jews when the Nazis started to commit genocide against them." Although this egregious comparison has had long legs among the many admirers of Malcolm X over the last half century, they almost never even mention all the black Africans who facilitated the Atlantic slave trade — who staged the raids to capture the slaves and who brought them overland to the white slave traders waiting on the coast. It is without them, the African slavers, that the Atlantic slave trade may not have taken place.[20]

A counter narrative of America and of the world, forged on the campus, generally told from the black nationalist point of view, was increasingly embraced by African-American students after the martyrdoms of Malcolm X and Martin Luther King, Jr. Black spokesmen told the students, "Our presence must mean revolutionary kinds of changes in these institutions" and urged them not to "be fooled by the special claims of the 'great universities' to the sources of wisdom, objectivity and truth." Students, "sens[ing] the bankruptcy of American higher education," must effect "the total reorganization of university knowledge and curriculum from a Black perspective."

Charged with the critical and heady mission of transforming knowledge, and repeatedly warned that Euro-Americans, and especially Jews, had intentionally falsified the historical record, the students provided platforms for an endless parade of black nationalists, many of them charlatans, whom they wildly applauded for teaching them "heterodoxy." Indeed, the students bestowed on Farrakhan and Khalid Muhammad the title of "Dr." though neither had a college degree. To them, they were the real educators, the trusted authorities, bearers of the hidden historical truth. The students learned that works by Euro-Americans would only keep them in "mental slavery," a phrase repeated again and again. The much celebrated Africanist John Henrik Clarke explicitly cautioned students away from a volume on slavery by "Brion Davis Brion" — tellingly reversing the name of the Pulitzer-prize winning scholar and past-president of the Organization of American Historians, David Brion Davis — which could not compare with works by a black author. Those shaping the new narrative incessantly reminded their audiences and readers that the information they imparted would never appear in the European-Americans' or Jews' texts. Indeed, Malcolm X, alerted by Protocol 9 that the Elders of Zion only "foster an illusory belief in freedom of the press," taught that "liberal Jews" prevented the re-broadcasting of televised interviews in which he dared expose the dimensions of Jews' domination and exploitation of black communities. Thus it was only the NOI that would publish *The Secret Relationship between Blacks and Jews*, exposing what the Jews did not want them to know. As Leonard Jeffries, chair of the African American studies department at the City College of New York, and known for the paradigm dividing the world into "sun people" and melanin-deficient "ice people," proclaimed, "We have now redefined reality, and that's real power."[21]

At the center of the new reality was often the iniquitous Jew. Clarke introduced Christopher Columbus as "a willful murder[er] and a liar," "an organizer of rape of Indian women, a slave trader, a reactionary religious fanatic, and the personal director of a campaign of mass murder of defenseless peoples" — and a Jew. *All* who financed his voyage were "Jewish bankers." Columbus has "so much dirt" attached to his name that there may even have been "two Columbuses" — presumably both Jews. Others taught that *all* the conquistadores were Jews. And the NOI instructed, against all the evidence, that not only did Jews dominate the slave trade, but the Inquisitors ("reformers") expelled the Jews from Spain because they were slave traders. When a speaker presented an informed account of the very marginal role of Jews in the slave trade, students simply dismissed his comments as the false teachings of the "devil" — i.e., of a Jew. At a press conference in February 1994, Farrakhan announced that 75 percent of the slaves in the South were owned by Jews (the figure is closer to 0.2 percent). Incredibly, the NAACP's director of communications remarked that Farrakhan "*may* have exaggerated the historical fact," but that is "a matter for academics to debate."

Students now prepared papers and wrote articles exposing the demonic Jew at the center of their new narrative. In conclusion, one student wrote, "Caucasian Jews" continue to "defile and trash and defecate on the rest of the world."[22] Impressed by the black nationalist magic, the students were framing a new past, viewed through an antisemitic lens.

Eunice G. Pollack received her PhD in history from Columbia University, 1999 and has been a professor of history and Jewish studies at the University of North Texas since 2001. Her publications include articles on antisemitism and on the inner life. Most recently, she co-edited (with Stephen H. Norwood) the *Encyclopedia of American Jewish History*, 2 vols. (2008), winner of the American Library Association's Editor's Choice Award. She is the editor of the interdisciplinary series Antisemitism in America for Academic Studies Press. She originated and wrote (with David Brion Davis and Seymour Drescher) the American Historical Association's resolution and statement on Jews and Slavery (1995).

ENDNOTES

[1]   *MetroWest Jewish News*, September 19, 2002; *Arab American News*, August 30 — September 5, 2008. Arab-American protestors, condemning Israel, would even co-opt the civil rights anthem "We Shall Overcome." *Stanford Daily*, June 3, 2010.

[2]   "Unedited Interview with Minister Farrakhan," FinalCall.com, September 1, 2007.

[3]   *Jewish Bulletin of Northern California*, May 16, 1997; *Daily Pennsylvanian*, March 28, 1995; "Black Antisemitism," *American Jewish Year Book*, 1969, 76–78. For the

Protocols, see Benjamin W. Segal, *A Lie and A Libel: the History of the Protocols of the Elders of Zion*, Richard S. Levy, translator and editor (Lincoln: University of Nebraska Press, 1995 [1926]), 59.

4   Claude Andrew Clegg III, *An Original Man: The Life and Times of Elijah Muhammad* (New York: St. Martin's Press, 1997); Jewish Telegraphic Agency, April 26, 1994; *Daily Pennsylvanian*, March 28, 1995.

5   Leo Blond, "Black Anti-Semitism in New York City," *Phi Delta Kappan*, November 1968, 176–177; Khalid Abdul Muhammad, quoted in Paul Berman, "The Other and the Almost the Same," *Society*, September 1994; Segal, *A Lie and A Libel*, 80; Stephen Eric Bronner, *A Rumor about the Jews: Antisemitism, Conspiracy, and the Protocols of the Elders of Zion* (New York: Oxford University Press, 2003).
    In 2005, the *Final Call* interviewed Ashahed Muhammad, author of a new book, *The Synagogue of Satan*. A correspondent for the NOI online newspaper and executive director of an institute that sends speakers to campuses, Muhammad explained that the Synagogue of Satan consists of "media manipulators," "the swindlers who rule the economic realm with impunity," and those whose "goal" is the "continuance of global domination." He assured his interviewer, however, that he "would never advocate hatred of adherents to Judaism. The book is not about that at all." FinalCall.com, November 7, 2005.

6   FinalCall.com, September 24, 2002; "Black Antisemitism," 78.

7   Cynthia Ozick, "The Mirror of Anti-Semitism," *New York Jewish Week*, May 13, 1994; Gil Troy, "The Ivory Tower: Understanding Zionophobia," *Forward*, November 22, 2002; Lowry quoted in Washington *Post*, December 29, 1985; Edward Alexander, "Multiculturalists and Anti-Semitism," *Society* (September — October 1994): 58–59.

8   Amiri Baraka, "Confessions of a Former Anti-Semite," *Village Voice*, December 17–23, 1980.

9   Suzy Hansen, "Amiri Baraka Stands by his Words," www.salon.com/books/feature/2002/10/17/baraka; *Forward*, March 7, 2003.
    Notably, the *Protocols* had revealed the Elders of Zion's plans to "blow whole cities to kingdom come, including state offices, archives..." See Segal, *A Lie and A Libel*, 93.
    The timing of Baraka's very public rejection of his past antisemitism may be linked to his frustration that his application to teach at Rutgers University in Newark, his hometown — he had applied repeatedly over the past four years — had been "turned [ ] down again last year [and] the reason given to insiders was that I was considered an anti-Semite." He knew, however, that was not really why "Rutgers, the South Africa of American universities," had rejected him, and apparently, he would now be able to call its bluff. After all, "If that [antisemitism] were a barrier to employment in English departments, then such departments throughout the country would be cleaned out overnight." Baraka could recognize antisemites — we are surrounded by them — but he is not, or is no longer, one of them.

10 *Jewish Bulletin of Northern California*, May 16, 1997; www.adl.org; Robert G. Weisbord and Richard Kazarian, Jr., *Israel in the Black American Perspective* (Westport, CN: Greenwood Press, 1985), 42–44; *New York Times*, August 14, 1970, August 24,

1970; Stephen H. Norwood, Letter to the Editor, *Chronicle of Higher Education*, April 6, 2007.

11   Washington *Post*, February 15, 1986, March 2, 1986; *New York Times*, August 21, 1968, April 14, 1970; Chicago *Daily Defender*, February 17, 1970; Eric J. Sundquist, *Strangers in the Land: Blacks, Jews, Post-Holocaust America* (Cambridge, MA: Harvard University Press, 2005), 317; Weisbord and Kazarian, *Israel in the Black American Perspective*, 36.

12   Weisbord and Kazarian, *Israel in the Black American Perspective*, 35–37; *New York Times*, August 15, 1967; Sundquist, *Strangers in the Land*, 158–159, 330–334; Julius Lester, quoted in Leonard Dinnerstein, *Antisemitism in America* (New York: Oxford University Press, 1994), 221.

13   Quotes from: Weisbord and Kazarian, *Israel in the Black American Perspective*, 45–47; Harold Brackman, "Zionism in Black and White: Part II, 1948–2010," *Midstream*, March 2010; Khalid Abdul Muhammad, quoted in Anti-Defamation League, full-page advertisement, *New York Times*, January 16, 1994; Stanley Crouch, "Farrakhan, 1985 to 1996: The Consistency of Calypso Louis," in Amy Alexander, ed., *The Farrakhan Factor: African-American Writers on Leadership, Nationhood, and Minister Louis Farrakhan* (New York: Grove Press, 1998), 267; Sundquist, *Strangers in the Land*, 139; Clegg, *An Original Man*, 41–67, 123–25; *Jewish Chronicle*, February 24, 2005; Malcolm X (with Alex Haley), *Autobiography of Malcolm X* (New York: Grove Press, 1964), 278.

14   Notably, Malcolm X's father had been a Baptist minister and at times Malcolm had attended Seventh Day Adventists' meetings with his mother. Malcolm X (with Alex Haley), *Autobiography*, 16–17. "Malcolm X Exposes White Liberal Jews," YouTube video of Malcolm X speech; Bronner, *A Rumor about the Jews*, 18; Sundquist, *Strangers in the Land*, 337, 396; Weisbord and Kazarian, *Israel in the Black American Perspective*, 45–46; www.adl.org.

15   By labeling Jews "Nazis" and making this particularly invidious analogy, Malcolm X was setting an American precedent that would later be widely applied by campus antisemites to Israeli Jews.

16   Similarly, the *Protocols* stressed that the Elders promoted and dominated social movements, not out of an interest in supporting social justice, but only in an effort to create social chaos.

17   Malcolm X (with Alex Haley), *Autobiography*, 372–373; *Webster's New World Dictionary: College Edition*; Eunice G. Pollack, "African American Antisemitism in the 1990s," in Stephen H. Norwood and Eunice G. Pollack, eds., *Encyclopedia of American Jewish History* (Santa Barbara, CA: ABC-CLIO, 2008), I: 195–200; Weisbord and Kazarian, *Israel in the Black American Perspective*, 45. See too: Washington *Post*, March 19, 1987.

18   "Malcolm X Exposes White Liberal Jews;" Peter Goldman, *The Death and Life of Malcolm X* (New York: Harper and Row, 1973), 15.

19   Sundquist, *Strangers in the Land*, 333, 439; *Jewish Chronicle*, February 24, 2005; Alex Haley, "Interview with Malcolm X," *Playboy*, May 1963; Jewish Telegraphic Agency, April 26, 1994; Howard University *Hilltop* (1994).

20 Malcolm X quoted in Goldman, *Death and Life of Malcolm X*, 15; Sundquist, *Strangers in the Land*, 337.

21 Dr. Vincent Harding, "Black Students and the 'Impossible Revolution,' Part I," *Ebony*, August 1969, 141-148; James Turner, "Black Students and their Changing Perspective," *Ebony*, August 1969, 135-138; Pollack, "African American Antisemitism in the 1990s," 195–200; Dr. John Henrik Clarke, with an introduction by Leonard Jeffries, *Christopher Columbus & the Afrikan Holocaust: Slavery and the Rise of European Capitalism* (Brooklyn, NY: A & B Books, 1992), 1, 5, 22-23; Jewish Telegraphic Agency, April 26, 1994; "Malcolm X Exposes White Liberal Jews;" Bronner, *A Rumor about the Jews*, 20, 63.

22 Clarke, *Christopher Columbus & the Afrikan Holocaust*, 10–11, 21–29, 79–80; David Walter Leinweber, "An Historian Critiques the Book *The Secret Relationship between Blacks and Jews*," www.h-net/org/~antis/papers/occasional.papers.html; *New York Times*, February 4, 1994; Berman, "The Other and the Almost the Same;" Pollack, "African American Antisemitism in the 1990s," 195–200; *Uhuru na Mazungumzo*, Spring 1995.

BLUSHING PROFESSORS
Jews Who Hate Israel

Edward Alexander

> "Jewish boys and girls, children of the generation that saw Auschwitz, hate democratic Israel and celebrate as 'revolutionary' the Egyptian dictatorship. Some of them pretend to be indifferent to the anti-Jewish insinuations of the Black Panthers; a few go so far as to collect money for Al Fatah, which pledges to take Tel Aviv. About this, I cannot say more; it is simply too painful."
> — Irving Howe, 1970[1]

Those "Jewish boys and girls" who made Howe's heart sink in 1970 are now, many of them, well-established figures in the academic and journalistic worlds, tigers of wrath who became tenured insurrectionaries or established editors or columnists for the *New Yorker* and *New York Times*. To Howe, who (it should be remembered) was himself not only a lifelong socialist but also a lifelong non- (but not anti-) Zionist, there was something indecent about young Jews, a mere quarter century after the Holocaust, not only acquiescing in but actively supporting a program of politicide against the Jewish state. Three decades later, those same Jews would deride anyone who dared to mention the Holocaust in relation to Israel's constant burden of peril — Thomas Friedman's glib vulgarities about Israel as "Yad Vashem with an Air Force" being the best-known example. Indeed, they would cast Israel itself as the aggressor, pretending (as Friedman himself usually did) that it was the "occupation" that led to Arab hatred and violence and not Arab hatred and aggression that led to occupation.

Take the case of Professor Joel Beinin. In the late sixties he was an undergraduate at Princeton University, where — so he later claimed — he was "repressed" by the established professoriat, prevented from doing his senior thesis on the post-1948 Palestinian national movement, officially because it was too "modern" a topic, but actually because of his passionately anti-Israel views. "Professors in Princeton's Department of Near Eastern Studies who were critical of Israel," he has alleged, "rarely expressed their views to students." In 1970 he moved from Princeton to Harvard, where he completed an MA, but was rejected for its doctoral program in Middle East Studies — rejected, so he claims, for his expression of pro-Arab views during the Yom Kippur War. And so he moved west to Michigan. There too he was forced to write his thesis about Egypt rather than the Palestinian working class because of his "fear that those who held the then dominant views in the field of Middle Eastern Studies would use their power to...impede the advancement of those with unorthodox views."[2] Not that he was bashful about expressing his anti-Israel and Marxist views. One student of the young instructor at Ann Arbor recalls the following scene from the early eighties: "One day, at a particular forum, [Beinin] gave what I can only describe as a kind of beer-hall speech. Shouting and pumping his fist, he admonished the Arabs to forget any negotiating with Israel and to stay true to pure radicalism."[3]

Several decades later, Beinin, now a professor of history at Stanford, would become president of the Middle East Studies Association (MESA). He took office in November 2001, a few weeks after the massacres of 9/11. But MESA's official statement about 9/11 avoided using the words "terror," "terrorism," and "terrorists"; it reluctantly admitted that crimes had been committed but opposed the use of force — "misguided retaliation" — against the "criminals." The organization of 2,600 academics now presided over by the once "repressed" Beinin had not planned a single panel on terrorism until after the World Trade Center and Pentagon massacres, which they proceeded — with the full blessing of Beinin himself — to blame on America and Israel.[4]

In his presidential address, Beinin made the obligatory allusion to his childhood study of the Mishnah to establish his Jewish credentials. This — or so he thought — permitted him to allege that all critics of MESA were "neo-conservative true believers with links to the Israeli right" and to attack the president of Harvard University, Lawrence Summers, for posing a "grave threat to academic freedom" by describing the campaign to boycott Israel as antisemitic. He also complained that perpetrators of the killings at Sabra and Shatila had never been brought to justice, and implied that Ariel Sharon had arranged for the murder of Elie Hobeika, a potential witness against him in the (aborted) show trial of Sharon planned in Belgium. (In September 1982 Lebanese Christian Phalangists killed over 400 people in the towns and camps of Sabra and Shatila. Sharon and the IDF, then occupying part of Lebanon, were accused [falsely] of collaborating with the Phalangist killers.) Journalists covering the conference at which Beinin was crowned head of the whole Middle Eastern Studies establishment observed that the professors of Middle East Studies called "terrorism" a racist term, but that if the typical MESA member were forced at gunpoint to offer a definition of terrorism, he would likely reply: "Whatever Israel does."[5] By December 2004 Beinin, addressing another cadre of academic leftists, declared that "In my view, the state of Israel has already lost any moral justification for its existence." For his uneasiness about sharing the planet with a Jewish state, he gave two reasons, apparently of equal weight. The first was that "Israel oppresses the Palestinians"; the second was that "its claim to represent all Jews throughout the world endangers even Jews who totally reject Zionism or are severe critics of Israeli policies" (i.e., Joel Beinin).[6]

Another of those "Jewish boys and girls" whose hostility to Israel shocked Howe in 1970 was Michael Lerner. In the fall of 1969 Lerner commenced his open battle with what he called "the Jewish establishment" of "fat cats and conformists" in an article entitled "Jewish New Leftism at Berkeley" in *Judaism* magazine. It followed the ancient pattern of blaming Jews for the violence unleashed against them. "Black anti-Semitism," wrote Lerner, "is a tremendous disgrace to Jews; for this is not an anti-Semitism rooted in ... hatred of the Christkillers but rather one rooted in the concrete fact of oppression by Jews of blacks in the ghetto ... in part an earned anti-Semitism." Lest antisemites (Jewish as well as gentile) be confused about the location of their rightful targets, he added that "The synagogue as currently established will have to be smashed." As for the anti-Zionism of many young Jews (again, those "boys and girls"), it was "irrational in its conclusions [that Israel should be destroyed]," but "I know it to be correct in its fundamental impulses."[7]

After a short-lived (indeed disastrous) academic career, Lerner turned to leftwing journalism and founded *Tikkun* magazine, which had two declared purposes: one was to pull down *Commentary* magazine, the other "to mend, repair, and transform the world." But what brought him to national prominence was the zeal with which he argued the Palestinian cause within the Jewish community. When the (first) intifada (1987-1993) was well on its bloody course it was hard to watch American television or read the American press for very long without becoming aware that Lerner himself had become, if not quite the Jewish establishment, then the omnipresent, gentile-appointed voice of the Jewish community. Nevertheless his anti-establishment rhetoric remained very much what it had been in 1969-70. On February 24, 1989, the *New York Times* afforded him space to hold forth on the way in which the voice of progressive Jews like himself, "the silenced majority" who were "appalled by Israel's brutal repression of the Palestinian uprising," had been "stifled" by the "establishment leadership." Rarely had a stifled voice been heard by so many millions. As he had done in 1969, but now far more absurdly, he adopted the pose of a lonely knight, a sensitive soul sallying forth to confront a mob of thick-skinned conformist louts who would eat him alive if only they could. Here was a rotund beard-plucker of vaguely rabbinic appearance (in later years he would actually become a "rabbi" of sorts) who could always be relied on to blame Israel rather than the Arabs for the absence of peace, and to liken Israeli defense against Palestinian Arab violence in the intifada to "medieval Christian mobs...organizing pogroms against the whole Jewish community."[8]

When the second intifada ("the Oslo War") commenced in 2000, Lerner, long since dislodged from his role as the Clintons' White House Rasputin, again donned the antique robes of biblical prophet and defined his moral purity in opposition to the State of Israel. Yes, he wrote in the *Nation* in May 2002, Palestinian suicide bombings and lynchings and pogroms were "immoral," but Israel was not justified in protecting itself against them because it too was ethically impure: "Israeli treatment of Palestinians has been immoral and outrageous." Besides, Israeli military response to Arab terror was bad for the Jews, in Berkeley and other centers of prophetic morality: it had caused "a frightening upsurge in anti-Semitism." During the Iraq war he behaved true to form. In October 2005 he invited Cindy Sheehan, the professional grieving mother, to address his congregation in San Francisco on Yom Kippur. Sheehan had for weeks been haranguing President Bush with the antisemitic slogans of the day; "You get Israel out of Palestine;" "my son was killed for a neoconservative agenda to benefit Israel." Once again, Lerner showed how nothing antisemitic is entirely alien to him.

II

Where, one asks, did the Joel Beinins and Michael Lerners and scores just like them come from? Jewish intellectuals, to an even greater extent than Jews at large, have long assumed that Judaism follows an arrow-straight course from Sinai to liberal and leftist politics. So long as the existence of the State of Israel was in harmony with liberal ideals, it could be supported or at least accepted by the majority of Jewish liberals, especially in the wake of the Holocaust. Prior to the Holocaust, Jewish liberals were deeply divided about Zionism. Lionel Trilling, for example, recalled that he and the other editors of *Menorah Journal*, a precursor of *Commentary*, "were inclined to be skeptical about Zionism and even opposed to it, and during the violence that flared up in 1929 some of us were on principle pro-Arab."[9] But the June 1967 war, or rather its aftermath, required them to choose between liberal pieties and defense of the beleaguered Jewish state. Prior to the war, there were no "occupied territories;" for nineteen years the so-called West Bank had been entirely in the hands of the Arabs, theirs to do with whatever they liked (and what they liked did *not* include an independent Palestinian Arab state). Nevertheless, in the months leading up to the war, the Arabs had vowed to "turn the Mediterranean red with Jewish blood" and Egypt's Nasser had declared that "Israel's existence is itself an aggression." The Arab nations appeared to be, as indeed they were, imperialist and racist aggressors bent on conquering the .06 of the Middle East that they did not control. But, after suffering a catastrophic defeat, the Arabs showed that their inferiority to the Jews on the battlefield could be overcome by their superiority in the war of ideas. They ceased speaking of their desire to reduce Israel to sandy wastes and instead redefined their struggle as the search for a haven for homeless Palestinian Arabs. Ruth Wisse has argued that this transformation of their rhetoric of opposition to Israel from the Right to the Left was a calculated appeal to liberals, not least to Jewish liberals. It shrewdly recognized that Israel's attractiveness to liberals — as a tiny, besieged, socialist country with (very aggressive) labor unions and women's rights — ended with its victory in the Six Day War.[10]

If ideological liberals became unsympathetic to the fate of the Jews in the Middle East because it contradicted their sanguine view of the world, the tenacity of the Arabs' rejection of Israel and their campaign — aggressively and adroitly pursued in the schools and universities, in the churches, in the news media, in the publishing houses, in the professional organizations — to destroy Israel's moral image was bound to cause the mass defection of Jewish liberals too from Israel. For Jewish liberals had the additional motive of seeking to escape from the negative role in which they were being cast by the alleged misdeeds of Israel.

Careful readers of broadsides against Israel by Jewish intellectuals will note the frequency with which they mention the shame and embarrassment endured at cocktail parties or faculty lounges, so much so that they help one to understand the frequency with which Jewish prayer begs that "we shall not be shamed, nor humiliated."[11] Thus Berkeley history professor Martin Jay's notorious essay blaming Ariel Sharon for the rise of the new antisemitism begins as follows: "'No one since Hitler,' my dinner partner [another Jewish academic 'proudly identified with his Jewish heritage'] heatedly contended, 'has done as much damage to the Jews as Ariel Sharon.'...This stunning accusation [was] made during a gracious faculty soiree in Princeton...."[12] One hears from countless Jewish accusers and prosecutors of Israel about how much they blush, how grievously they suffer from — embarrassment. The executive director of a group called Jews for Peace in Palestine and Israel complains that "there are many American Jews who are flat-out embarrassed" by Israeli actions. Jacqueline Rose, "appalled at what the Israeli nation perpetrated in my name" and wishing to live "in a world in which we did not have to be ashamed of shame," hopes to cure her shame-sickness by destroying its cause: Israel. Professor Tony Judt is perhaps the most famous victim of this newest entry in the nosology of social diseases. "Today," he wrote in his highly publicized essay (in the *New York Review of Books*) calling for an end to Israel, "non-Israeli Jews feel themselves once again exposed to criticism and vulnerable to attack for things they didn't do.... The behavior of a self-described Jewish state affects the way everyone else looks at Jews.... The depressing truth is that Israel today is bad for the Jews."[13] About this astonishing passage (very similar to the aforementioned cry of self-pity from Beinin) Leon Wieseltier has written: "Bad for the Jews! This is the parodic formula for a ludicrous degree of Jewish insecurity, an almost comic infirmity.... The behavior of the self-described Jewish state seems to have affected the way everyone else looks at *him*. I detect the scars of dinners and conferences."[14] In a later essay in the *Nation* (January 2005), Judt expatiated further on the embarrassment factor, especially the great question of how people look or are looked *at*. He exhorted Germans, French, and "others" to "comfortably condemn Israel without an uneasy conscience" so that they "can look their Muslim fellow citizens in the face." While the Jews in Israel worry about suicide bombers, Tony Judt worries about how to conciliate (or perhaps join) their apologists. While the Jews in Israel have for over sixty years been forced daily to defend their lives, Jewish intellectuals who have never been called on to defend anything more than a dissertation find sustained exertion on behalf of Israel too great a burden to bear. As Bernard Harrison, the shrewd critic of the "new" antisemitism, has observed: "While plenty of intellectuals...have blushed at the crimes or inadequacies of their respective nations, very few...have proved ready to blush merely at *having* a nation. In practice, the one people whose very national *identity* has been widely held to constitute, in its objectionable 'particularism,' a standing offence against the ideal of Universal Man, is the Jews."[15] And so, by a cruel irony, the Jews who try desperately to evade the (supposed) moral taint of defending harsh Israeli measures of self-defense have found themselves, in this age of suicide bombers, playing the role of accessories to murder, advocates of "genocidal liberalism," accomplices of Iran's president Ahmadinejad, exhorting the mob to remove "this disgraceful blot [Israel] from the Islamic world."

III

Howe, speculating on the spiritual ancestry of those "Jewish boys and girls" mentioned above, thought that he saw in the anti-Israel vehemence of the Jewish branch of the New Left the pampered suburban descendants of the Jewish anarchists of the 1880s who had ostentatiously eaten ham sandwiches at their Yom Kippur balls; the cold indifference of prominent American Jewish intellectuals to the plight of their European brethren during the Holocaust is also well-documented. But both those *fin de siècle* exhibitionists and the "New York (Jewish) Intellectuals" of the thirties and forties were themselves the latest representatives of a long-standing tradition of violent dissociation, brazenly assuming postures of hatred and contempt for their fathers. Such Jewish intellectuals have long played a crucial role in the Jewish world, especially during periods of persecution. Indeed, they have made such large contributions to the theology of religious Jew-hatred and the politics of modern antisemitism that both might fairly be called offspring of the Judeo-Christian tradition, a hideous progeny elaborately traced in Sander Gilman's book, *Jewish Self-Hatred*. At the very end of his book, Gilman suggested the need for a sequel: "One of the most recent forms of Jewish self-hatred is the virulent opposition to the existence of the State of Israel.... The older European form seems no longer to have validity."[16]

Of all the Jewish self-haters portrayed by Gilman, the one most relevant to consideration of the current bumper crop of Jewish enemies of Israel is Karl Marx. Although only a minority of the Jewish prosecutors of Israel are orthodox, unrepentant Marxists, almost all of them identify with the political left and take Karl Marx as an exemplar of wisdom on a large range of issues, including the Jewish one. For that reason alone, Marx's relation to both Judaism and Jewishness is worth recalling. Marx was converted to Lutheranism at age six, a year after his father had joined the Lutheran church. For his mother's tardiness in converting (she did not do so until age 38, when her father, a rabbi, died) as well as for other "despised remnants of [her] Judaic practice," Marx never forgave her. Throughout his career he mocked the "Jewish" character of his various rivals for revolutionary leadership in the Communist and working-class movements. Moses Hess was "Moysi the communist rabbi," Eduard Bernstein, "the little Jew Bernstein." The choicest epithets were reserved for Ferdinand Lassalle (himself a Jewish antisemite of formidable derangement): "It is now completely clear to me," wrote Marx to Engels, "that, as his cranial formation and hair show, he is a descendant of the Negroes who attached themselves to the march of Moses out of Egypt (assuming his mother or grandmother on the paternal side had not crossed with a nigger)....The pushiness of this fellow is also nigger-like." Nor did one have to be a socialist rival to arouse Marx's anti-Jewish spleen: Moses Mendelssohn, he wrote to Engels, was a "shit-windbag;" Polish Jews, the "filthiest of all races."[17] None of which has kept Marx from being drafted (along with the even more vituperative Jewish antisemite Karl Kraus) into the pantheon of Diaspora Jewish all-stars by such accusers of Israel as the high-minded and high mandarin George Steiner.

These accusers play a crucial role in the current upsurge of antisemitism, the likes of which we have not seen since the Hitler era. Although most of the anti-Jewish physical violence in Europe today is the work of cadres drawn from the fifteen to twenty million Muslims now living there, the verbal violence there and in North America is the work primarily of leftists and liberals, of strugglers against racism, of the learned classes. Because such people usually pride themselves on their rejection of anything smacking of racism and prejudice, they must cast the Israelis themselves as the new Nazis in order to make antisemitism, which had (so to speak) been given a bad name by the Holocaust, again "respectable," but under the new name of anti-Zionism. This explains their ubiquitous exploitation of the Israeli-Nazi equation (which originated in British circles in the Middle East as far back as 1941). The disproportionate influence of Jewish accusers depends in large part on the fact that they demonize Israel precisely as Jews; indeed, since religion and tradition count for little in most of them, it is the demonization of Israel that *makes* them Jews. For them the old wisecrack (first used in a short story by the Hebrew writer Haim Hazaz in 1942) that "When a man can no longer be a Jew, he becomes a Zionist" no longer applies; rather they embody a new reality: "When a man can no longer be a Jew, he becomes an anti-Zionist." By declaring themselves in favor of Jewish powerlessness — which according to Steiner, for example, "made us [Jews] the princes of life" as opposed to the Israelis, who torture and humiliate Palestinian Arabs[18] — they announce, with a vanity at once personal and ethnic, both their virtue and their "Jewishness." They have apparently forgotten what the powerlessness of virtue (and the supposed virtue of powerlessness) ended in for European Jewry. The existence of Israel also affords them the opportunity to formulate policy — from the safety of Maryland or Manhattan — for a country in which most of them do not live and whose burdens they do not bear. Thomas Friedman, that self-appointed diplomat from Chelm, planted in James Baker's brain the idea of publicly asking Prime Minister Shamir to phone him when he really wanted to pursue peace, and later found himself magically in harmony (and collusion) with the potentates of Saudi Arabia over how to solve the Israel problem; Jerome Segal, a "research scholar" at the University of Maryland, became a (self-described) Jewish "advisor" to the PLO. Moreover, by a colossal irony, the policy formulations of those Jews who themselves contend that Israel should not exist at all invariably rest on the premise that Israel can afford unlimited concessions of territory and easing of security because the Palestinian Arabs recognize Israel's "right to exist."

IV

But what then shall we say of those *Israeli* intellectuals who have turned against their own country? Most of them do not live in Maryland or Manhattan, and it was to them, or at least to their parents and grandparents, that Hazaz's quip applied. *They* do not want to be identified either as Zionists or as Jews, and their fierce diatribes against their own country express a double emptiness. It has been well described by the Israeli novelist Aharon Appelfeld, condescendingly referred to, because of his preoccupation with the Holocaust, as "the Jew" by many of his trendier Israeli literary colleagues:

> Today the Jewish people [in Israel] are waging two existential wars simultaneously. One for the body, against the Arabs, and a second for the soul, against itself. The identification of Judaism with a religion from which people are trying to dissociate themselves is creating a very serious vacuum here. The result is a black hole of identity. That is why there is a deep recoil from everything Jewish. But without some sort of Jewish identity, we will not be able to exist....A society without true roots is a society without a future.[19]

The special contribution of Israeli accusers of Israel to the larger campaign against their country has been their compulsive promotion, with countless variations on the theme, of the Israeli-Nazi equation. The Israeli novelist Aharon Megged observed in an explosive essay in 1994 that this uniquely spiteful (and obscenely licentious) equation was already, *in Israel itself*, the dominant idea of "*thousands* [emphasis added] of articles and reports in the press, hundreds of poems...dozens of documentary and feature films, exhibitions and paintings and photos."[20] Indeed, even Noam Chomsky, in a rare fit of (needless) modesty, in 2003 expressed his indebtedness to the late Israeli philosopher Yeshayahu Leibowitz for this "insight."[21] Megged went still farther in his severe judgment of his fellow writers and thinkers: "Since the Six Day War, and at an increasing pace, we have witnessed a phenomenon which probably has no parallel in history: an emotional and moral identification by the majority of Israel's intelligentsia with people openly committed to our annihilation." Once the academic boycott of Israel, an attempt by (mostly British) haters of Israel to translate the fifty-seven-year-old Arab economic boycott of Israel into intellectual form, got under way in April 2002, it produced tragicomic episodes of staggering dimensions: Israelis like Oren Yiftachel of Ben-Gurion University, who had for years castigated his own country as blacker than Gehenna and the pit of hell, now hoist on his own petard, or like Ilan Pappe of Haifa University calling for a British boycott of his own university — and himself.[22]

V

To the new antisemitism Jewish progressives are indispensable because they are ever at the ready to declare that what might seem antisemitic to untutored minds is really nothing more than "criticism of Israeli policy." After all, who should know better than Jews whether something is antisemitic or not? Antisemitism-denial (a term coined by Gabriel Schoenfeld)[23] has become the predictable response of Jewish haters of Israel to all of the following: demonization of Israel as the center of the world's evil; calls for its abolition or destruction; economic or academic warfare against it; burning of synagogues or murder of Jews in Istanbul or Buenos Aires; allegations of Jewish control of American foreign policy.

Jewish experts in antisemitism-denial are now omnipresent. A Jewish (also Israeli) Dr. Pangloss named Amitai Etzioni assures the readers of the *Chronicle of Higher Education* that "calls to destroy Israel, or to throw it into the Mediterranean Sea...are not evidence of hatred of Jews" but merely "reflect a quarrel with the State of Israel"; moreover, apart from "the troubling exception of Iran's trial in 2000 of thirteen Jews who supposedly spied for Israel," Jews in Iran have as much religious freedom as Muslims.[24] Another Jewish academic named Andrew Bush breaks new ground in the field of euphemism (at Vassar College) by defining Intifada II, in the course of which Palestinian Arab suicide bombers, pogromists, and lynch mobs slaughtered a thousand people (most of them Israeli Jews) and wounded 10,000 more, as "a critique of Zionism."[25] The most fully articulated example of antisemitism-denial — was the August 2003 essay in the Israelophobic *London Review of Books* by University of California feminist Judith Butler entitled "No, it's not anti-semitic," a broadside against Harvard University president Lawrence H. Summers for his speech of September 20, 2002, deploring the upsurge of antisemitism in many parts of the globe.

But the gold standard in Jewish antisemitism-denial has been established by Noam Chomsky, not a surprising achievement for the person who previously earned laurels for his collaboration with and support for neo-Nazi Holocaust deniers. "Anti-Semitism," he declared in 2002, "is no longer a problem, fortunately. It's raised, but it's raised because privileged people want to make sure they have total control, not just 98 % control. That's why anti-Semitism is becoming an issue."[26] Is it, one wonders, because of such delicate perceptions about the Jews or because of his seething hatred of America that, according to Larissa MacFarquhar of the *New Yorker*, "Wherever he goes, [Chomsky] is sought after by mainstream politicians and the mainstream press, and when he speaks it is to audiences of thousands, sometimes tens of thousands."[27] As Chomsky's charming observation suggests, the line between antisemitism-denial and antisemitism — the unadorned thing itself — is a fine one.

Many Jewish prosecutors of Israel resemble medieval apostates who confided to their new Christian co-religionists that Jews made Passover matzohs out of Christian blood, or desecrated the Host, or that the males among them menstruated. They compete successfully with the Alexander Cockburns and Ward Churchills in the extravagance of their accusations. Writers in Lerner's journal *Tikkun* warn of Jewish "conspirators" who run the U.S. government on behalf of "Jewish interests" and — as if this were not explicit enough — refer to "the industrial sized grain of truth" in the *Protocols of the Learned Elders of Zion*, the early twentieth-century Czarist police forgery purporting to describe a conspiratorial meeting held at the founding of the Zionist movement in 1897.[28] The *Protocols* have fueled antisemitic violence for a century. But Jewish endorsement of them is something new. So too is explicit endorsement of violence against Jews by other Jews, exemplified by the *ne plus ultra* of unabashed Jewish antisemitism, Professor Michael Neumann of Trent University in Canada. Speculating, in a 2003 interview, on the best strategy "to help the Palestinians," Neumann proposes the following:

> If an effective strategy means that some truths about the Jews don't have to come to light, I don't care. If an effective strategy means encouraging reasonable anti-Semitism, or reasonable hostility to Jews, I also don't care. If it means encouraging vicious, racist anti-Semitism, or the destruction of the state of Israel, I still don't care.... To regard any shedding of Jewish blood as a world-shattering calamity...is racism, pure and simple; the valuing of one race's blood over all others.[29]

Earlier, in Cockburn's *Counterpunch* of June 4, 2002, Neumann had announced that "we should almost never take anti-Semitism seriously, and maybe we should have some fun with it."

Lower than the fun-loving Neumann in this sea of bloodlust it might seem impossible to sink. But wait: there is still Chomsky's acolyte Professor Norman Finkelstein, who thinks "the honorable thing now [December 2001] is to show solidarity with Hezbollah,"[30] there is also England's Jacqueline Rose, who not only regurgitates the standard clichés about Palestinian mass murderers as "people driven to extremes," but rhapsodizes about bonding with Islamist fanatics, lashes out against "those wishing to denigrate suicide bombers and their culture," and declares that "culture" superior to the Jewish culture of a butchered Israeli teenager — Malki Roth — who had addressed a Rosh Hashanah letter to God expressing the hope she would live another year and that the Messiah would arrive.[31] "In the lowest deep," as Milton's Satan observes, "a lower deep."

VI

The solution to their predicament which most of the Jewish "self-haters" studied by Sander Gilman chose was conversion to Christianity. In the modern world, however, the contradiction between liberal pieties and the intellectual defense of Israel is very rarely resolved by apostasy. Two possible (potential) exceptions to this generalization might be such "theological" Israel-haters as Daniel Boyarin, the Berkeley professor (of Talmud!) and the wandering "liberation theologian," Marc Ellis. Boyarin, once an Israeli, now identifies himself as a Jew "destined by fate, psychology, personal history, or whatever, to be drawn to Christianity." Second to nobody in his hatred and denunciation of Israel, Boyarin adds his very own complaint to the endless list of accusations against the Jewish state: "My Judaism may be dying at Nablus, Daheishe, Beteen" — i.e., places that the Israeli army has entered to pursue Muslim fanatics who have massacred Jews. Boyarin seems to threaten to turn Christian if the Israeli government refuses to dance to his tune and return Jews to the subordinate position that he, like Saint Augustine, believes to be their special destiny.[32] Ellis spends Yom Kippur publicly confessing the sins of (other) Jews against Palestinian Arabs in front of a Christian audience at the (Protestant) Union Theological Seminary. But if conversion to Christianity is no longer, as in Europe it almost always was, required of Jews eager to play a special role as accusers of Jews (as they did in the forced debates of the Middle Ages, for example) the supersessionist Christian worldview nevertheless lurks in the recesses of their brains. The mental universe of Israel's fiercest Jewish accusers is permeated by a messianic utopianism that depicts Israel as the Devil's very own experiment station, the one stumbling block impeding the arrival of a post-national new heaven and new earth, the one nation in the world whose "right to exist" is considered a legitimate subject of debate.[33]

Carlyle used to observe that people can live without heaven, but not without hell or the Devil. For such Jewish demonizers of Israel as the Chomskys, the Finkelsteins, the Ellises, the Butlers, the three Roses of England (Steven and Hilary, originators of the academic boycott of Israeli teachers and researchers, who publicly renounced their "right of return" to a Jewish country, and the aforementioned Jacqueline, busily elucidating reasons why Israel ought not to exist),[34] Israel is hell on earth, the lair of Satan. What Paul Berman said in *Terror and Liberalism* about the failure of liberalism's angelic sociology in the face of suicide bombers has been still truer of the prodigious "explainers" in the ranks of Jewish liberals:

> Each new act of murder and suicide testified to how oppressive were the Israelis. Palestinian terror, in this view, was the measure of Israeli guilt. The more grotesque the terror, the deeper the guilt....And even Nazism struck many of Israel's critics as much too pale an explanation for the horrific nature of Israeli action. For the pathos of suicide terror is limitless, and if Palestinian teenagers were blowing themselves up in acts of random murder, a rational explanation was going to require ever more extreme tropes, beyond even Nazism.[35]

The desperate search for these "extreme tropes" is everywhere evident in the way that Jews who hate Israel exhaust themselves in the attempt to find language adequate to express their visceral loathing. Jacqueline Rose calls Zionism itself "defiled," "demonic," "deadly," "corrupt," responsible for the ruin of Judaism's moral mission to the world (a subject about which she knows and cares exactly nothing) and for much of the misery of the world itself. Butler promotes a petition ("Stop the Wall Immediately") that calls all the citizens of Israel "a people of [concentration] camp wardens." Chomsky would be rendered virtually speechless if deprived of the epithet "Nazi" for Israel; but he is outdone by his late collaborator Israel Shahak and by his chief disciple Norman Finkelstein, the dream-Jews of the world's antisemites. For Finkelstein (like most of Edward Said's Jewish acolytes) not only are the Israelis *worse* than the Nazis,[36] but Jews who do not stand against Israel are morally worse than Germans who did not oppose Hitler: "The Germans could point in extenuation to the severity of penalties for speaking out against the crimes of state. What excuse do *we* have?"[37]

This frenzied rhetoric expresses a utopian messianism (ostensibly secular) that plays an enormous role in Jewish intellectuals' disparagements of Israel. Among its earliest exponents was George Steiner, that distinctly British citizen of the world. Starting in the late sixties, this self-proclaimed wanderer, outsider, *luftmensch*, and exile offered himself as the embodiment of what a Jew should be — especially if, while constantly discoursing on the fate of the Jews, that Jew refused to learn Hebrew or to read (even in translation) anything written by Yiddish and Hebrew writers on the subject in question. Writing with his characteristic mixture of innocence and corruption, Steiner constantly asked: "Might the Christian West and Islam live more humanely, more at ease with themselves, if the Jewish problem were indeed 'resolved' (that *endlösung* or 'final solution')? Would the sum of obsessive hatred, of pain, in Europe, in the Middle East, tomorrow, it may be, in Argentina, in South Africa, be diminished?"[38] If only Israel and indeed the Jews themselves would disappear, everyone from China to Peru might inhabit Eldorado. In his lucubrations on "the redefinition of culture," Steiner always found it more convenient to locate the cause of Nazism in the psychic damage mankind had inherited from Moses than in certain easily identifiable German and Christian traditions, and more safe to blame the helpless Jewish victims than such formidable institutions as the Vatican and Stalinism, to say nothing of National Socialism itself.

Professor Peter Novick became wildly popular (if not quite as much so as Finkelstein) in Germany because he published a book in 1999 deploring American Jews' supposed "obsession" with the Holocaust, an obsession he blamed — naturally — on Israel and Zionism. The very word "Holocaust," he argued, was an alien import from Israel at the time of the Eichmann trial. The campaign to "vilify" Hannah Arendt for her Eichmann book was also, he says (still more absurdly), orchestrated from Israel.[39]

At no point does it occur to Novick, who knows about as much of the inner life of Jews as Jacqueline Rose does, that a European Jewish survivor of the camps might have *wanted* to emigrate to Palestine, or that American Jews might have *instinctively* responded to the trauma of the Yom Kippur War by remembering the Holocaust even without the tentacles of the Zionist propaganda machine taking possession of their brains. If not for their Zionist-induced Holocaust memories, Novick argues, the American Jewish community would be hard at work feeding the hungry, and so the millions of innocent children round the world would not today be dying of starvation.

Tony Judt (d. 2010), yet another utopian enemy of Israel, does not pretend to worry about the demise of American Jewish liberalism; he is too obsessed with the need to eliminate Israel altogether to bother with such parochial concerns. He merely argues that the problems of the Middle East and by extension of the whole world would be solved by demolishing the Jewish state, which he presents as the sole "anachronism" of "a world that has moved on, a world of individual rights, open frontiers, and international law."[40] Judt is untroubled by anachronism in the strenuous attempt of Israel's Muslim neighbors to restore the world of the eighth century: clitorectomy, jihad, beheadings, murder, torture, dismemberment. It is much easier for him to envision the realization of utopia by the elimination of Israel than by the arduous business of bringing democracy to Arab countries and throwing back the tide of militant Islam. If, after the Stalin and Hitler revolutions (and *1984* and *Animal Farm*), one needed additional demonstrations that utopianism expresses not love but hatred, the febrile lucubrations of the Steiners, the Judts, and the Novicks about Israel provide them in abundance. And just where does this notion that Jewish collective existence is an obsolete anachronism originate but in Christianity? John Henry Newman, the great figure of Anglo- and then, from 1845, Roman-Catholicism, inherited from the first and second century Alexandrian theologians Clement and Origen his assumption that "In the fullness of time...Judaism had come to nought." Newman wrote this in his *Apologia Pro Vita Sua* in 1864, over three thousand years after Judaism was born; Steiner, Judt, and Novick consigned Israel to the dustheap of history less than sixty years after it was created.

VII

The Jewish professors and intellectuals who promote the "new" (though also very old) antisemitism are not merely "critics of Israel" or of Israeli policies, but explicit advocates of Israel's removal from the family of nations. They work, and with a demonic energy, to besmirch, vilify, blacken, and delegitimize the world's only Jewish state so as to render it both morally and politically vulnerable to the onslaught of its (numerous) enemies. In a now familiar ideological scam, Jews like Tony Judt and George Soros have claimed that any criticism of their blatant and licentious calumnies of Israel as continuous with the ancient themes of antisemitism is an attempt to stifle debate and shut down free speech. On the contrary, so far from insisting that Israel should be immune from criticism for what it does or does not do, its defenders have argued that even if it did *everything* wrong it would not deserve to be made a pariah nation whose "right to exist" is open to debate, any more than the Jews of Europe deserved to be made a pariah people whose "right to live" was contingent upon the willingness of Germans to share the earth with them.

And just what is this Israel whose erasure promises — to the Steiners and Judts and Chomskys and Finkelsteins and Roses — the best of all possible worlds? Even less extreme figures like Martin Jay take it for granted that Israel is a society that falls far short of the prophetic standards they have established for it, indeed a "failed" society. Of this smug, spiteful, and by now almost fixed epithet, Edward Luttwak wrote in spring of 2004:

> That is an interesting way of describing a state that from 1948 till the present has advanced from poverty to a GDP per capita in the European range, even while its population increased tenfold. Very few states have done better (Ireland, Singapore) and for all their virtues, they would not pretend to compete with Israel in scientific research or overall cultural achievement, however that may be judged. But of course Israel's greatest achievement has been to restore the broken morale of Jews worldwide by winning its wars and battles against all comers — although I do understand that some are repelled by that very thing, seemingly viewing an incapacity to fight, if only to protect oneself from violence, as a positive moral attribute in itself. Such people see great virtue even in plain cowardice. They would no doubt find a weak and defeated and thus nonexistent Israel altogether more attractive.[41]

"Cowardice" is the word that springs to mind most often as the suitable epithet for Israel's Jewish enemies. This is not only because coming to the defense of this tiny and beleaguered nation (or of the Jews themselves) has never been an exercise for the timid, but also because of the abundant accolades these accusatory Jews have received for their *courage* from persons not exactly famous as discerning judges of character. "I deeply sympathize with you," said the late Yasser Arafat to the Jewish "critics" of Israel in 1975, "and with the numerous other Jewish dissenters who have raised their voice with courage and dedication to save the adherents of the Jewish faith from the pitfalls and dangers of Zionism. The heavy price you are all paying for your courageous positions sets you apart as symbols of courage and moral integrity, in a troubled world...."[42] Vying with Arafat in admiration for the "courage" of Jewish enemies of Israel is the American Nazi leader David Duke:

> Unexpectedly, I found that there are a number of Jews who dare to expose the truth about Zionism and Jewish supremacism. A much-persecuted and slandered group, they are just as appalled as I was about

the intolerant and hateful strains of Judaism that had arisen in the Jewish community and the Zionist state. They have included Americans such as Alfred Lilienthal, Noam Chomsky, Norman Finkelstein, and a courageous Jew in Israel, the late Dr. Israel Shahak. These scholars have dared to stand up against Jewish intolerance.[43]

I began these reflections with Irving Howe's cry of pain at the spectacle of young Jews wallowing in hatred of Israel. Although a non-Zionist, Howe understood the difference between debating the desirability of a Jewish state a hundred years ago and doing so half a century after the destruction of European Jewry — "the six million" — and the establishment, at tremendous human cost, of a living society of (now) nearly six million people. He was also a man of great moral intelligence and decency, able to recognize, despite deep-seated ideological prejudices, that the foundation of the state of Israel was one of the few redeeming acts of a century of blood and shame, "perhaps the most remarkable assertion a martyred people has ever made."[44]

Edward Alexander's books include *The Jewish Wars: Reflections by One of the Belligerents* (1996), *Irving Howe: Socialist, Critic, Jew* (1998), and *Robert B. Heilman: His Life in Letters* (2009).

ENDNOTES

A version of this article appeared in Edward Alexander and Paul Bogdanor, eds., *The Jewish Divide Over Israel: Accusers and Defenders* (New Brunswick, NJ: Transaction Publishers, 2006).

1. "Political Terrorism: Hysteria on the Left," *New York Times Magazine*, April 12, 1970.

2. Joel Beinin, MESA Presidential Address, November 24, 2001.

3. Jay Nordlinger, "Impromptus," *National Review Online*, November 20, 2001.

4. Martin Kramer, "Terrorism? What Terrorism?!" *Wall Street Journal*, November 15, 2001.

5. See Franklin Foer, "San Francisco Dispatch: Disoriented," *New Republic*, December 3, 2001.

6. Message sent December 2, 2004 by Joel Beinin to the "alef" (academic left) list (alef@list.haifa.ac.il).

7. Michael Lerner, "Jewish New Leftism at Berkeley," *Judaism*, Fall 1969, 474–76.

8. Quoted in Hershel Shanks, "Michael: His Magazine and His Movement," *Moment*, June 1990, 33.

9. *The Last Decade: Essays and Reviews: 1965–75* (New York: Harcourt Brace Jovanovich, 1979), 11.

10 Ruth R. Wisse, *If I Am Not for Myself... The Liberal Betrayal of the Jews* (New York: Free Press, 1992). On this topic, see also Fiamma Nirenstein, *The Liberal Anti-Semites: The New Face of an Ancient Hatred* (Milan: Rizzoli, 2004).

11 Second blessing in the daily prayer book before the morning Shema.

12 Martin Jay, "Ariel Sharon and the Rise of the New Anti-Semitism," *Salmagundi*, Winter-Spring 2003, 12.

13 Jacqueline Rose, *The Question of Zion* (Princeton, NJ: Princeton University Press, 2005), xvi, 144; Tony Judt, "Israel: The Alternative," *New York Review of Books*, October 23, 2003.

14 "Israel, Palestine, and the Return of the Bi-National Fantasy: What Is Not to be Done," *New Republic*, October 27, 2003.

15 Bernard Harrison, "Blushing Intellectuals," *Israel Affairs* 14 (January 2008), 135; David Frum, "The Alternative," *National Review Online*, October 14, 2003.

16 *Jewish Self-Hatred: Anti-Semitism and the Hidden Language of the Jews* (Baltimore: Johns Hopkins University Press, 1986), 391.

17 Frank E. Manuel, *A Requiem for Karl Marx* (Cambridge, MA: Harvard University Press, 1995), 15.

18 Quoted in Stuart Schoffman, "Mental Borders," *Jerusalem Report*, February 21, 2005.

19 Interview with Ari Shavit, "A Jewish Soul," *Ha'aretz*, February 13, 2004.

20 Aharon Megged, "The Israeli Suicide Drive," *Jerusalem Post International Edition*, July 2, 1994.

21 Quoted in Larissa MacFarquhar, "The Devil's Accountant," *New Yorker*, March 31, 2003, 74.

22 See the discussion of the case of Yiftachel in Edward Alexander, "Hitler's Professors, Arafat's Professors," *Judaism*, Winter/Spring 2003, and Pappe's letter in the *Guardian* of April 20, 2005.

23 *The Return of Anti-Semitism* (San Francisco: Encounter Books, 2004).

24 Amitai Etzioni, "Harsh Lessons in Incivility," *Chronicle of Higher Education*, November 1, 2002.

25 Andrew Bush, "Postzionism and Its Neighbors," *Judaism*, Winter/Spring 2003, 111.

26 Noam Chomsky, Speech to the Scottish Palestine Solidarity Campaign (delivered by live video from MIT), October 11, 2002; published as "Anti-Semitism, Zionism and the Palestinians," *Variant* (a Scottish arts magazine), Winter 2002.

27 "The Devil's Accountant," *New Yorker*, 67.

28 Paul Buhle, "The Civil Liberties Crisis and the Threat of 'Too Much Democracy,'" *Tikkun*, May 2003.

29 See Jonathan Kay, "Trent University's Problem Professor," *National Post*, August 9, 2003.

30 Letter to (Beirut) *Daily Star*, December 2001, posted at http://www.normanfinkelstein.com.

31 "Deadly Embrace," *London Review of Books*, November 4, 2004.

32   "Interrogate My Love," in *Wrestling with Zion*, ed. Tony Kushner and Alisa Solomon (New York: Grove Press, 2003), 198, 202. See also Jay M. Harris, "A Radical Jew," *Commentary*, June 1995.

33   As an example of the perfect ease with which "progressive" Jewish minds take up the question of whether the Jewish state should exist at all, as if it were the most natural question in the world, take Scott Simon, long-time host of National Public Radio, in June 2004, interviewing a strident "critic of Israel" named Richard Ben Cramer: "Is there," asked Simon, "still a need for the state of Israel?" Cramer, author of a book excoriating Israel, thought not.

34   See the discussion of Rose's *The Question of Zion* in Alvin Rosenfeld, "A Poisonous Perspective," *New Leader* (May/June 2005) and Benjamin Balint, "What Zion is Not," *Weekly Standard*, November 14, 2005.

35   *Terror and Liberalism* (New York: W. W. Norton, 2003), 134, 137.

36   "I can't imagine," Finkelstein has said, "why Israel's apologists would be offended by a comparison with the Gestapo. I would think that, for them, it is like Lee Iacocca being told that Chrysler is using Toyota tactics." Quoted in John Dirlik, "Canadian Jewish Organizations Charged with Stifling Campus Debate," *Washington Report on Middle East Affairs*, May/June 1992.

37   *Image and Reality of the Israel-Palestine Conflict* (London: Verso, 1995), 4.

38   *Errata: An Examined Life* (London: Weidenfeld and Nicolson, 1997), 52.

39   *The Holocaust in American Life* (Boston: Houghton Mifflin, 1999), 207.

40   Tony Judt, "Israel: The Alternative," *New York Review of Books*, October 23, 2003. The most thorough demolition of the utopian fantasy that not just the Middle East but the whole world would be at peace if Israel disappeared is Josef Joffe's "A World Without Israel," *Foreign Affairs*, January/February 2005.

41   Letters, *London Review of Books*, March/April 2004.

42   Public statement of January 31, 1975. See Ruth R. Wisse, "Israel and the Intellectuals: A Failure of Nerve?" *Commentary*, May 1988, 19.

43   http://www.davidduke.com/index.php?p=148.

44   *A Margin of Hope* (New York: Harcourt Brace Jovanovich, 1982), 276.

IV

STUDENT ASSOCIATIONS
AND ANTISEMITISM

CAMPUS WAR, 1977
The Year that Jewish Societies were Banned

Dave Rich

When does anti-Israel political campaigning become antisemitic? This short question lies at the heart of contemporary disputes about antisemitism, anti-Zionism, free speech and the impact of public discourse about Israel on diaspora Jewish life. As much as this is a current issue, though, it is certainly not new. In the 1970s Jewish students fought a series of political battles on British university campuses against radical groups who sought to restrict, or even completely outlaw, their right to organize any pro-Israel or Zionist activities. This article will examine these campus battles and identify what they can teach us about the relationship — practical as much as theoretical — between anti-Zionism and antisemitism.

THE NATIONAL UNION OF STUDENTS

Since the late 1960s student political factions in Britain have consisted, in the main, of the student wings of various left wing and far left political parties. By the mid-1970s, most of the factions operating within the National Union of Students (NUS) divided into two political coalitions. The Broad Left included the National Organisation of Labour Students (NOLS — the student wing of the Labour Party), student activists from the Communist Party of Great Britain, the Union of Liberal Students or Young Liberals (part of the Liberal Party),[1] and others who sympathized with a general left wing politics. Further to the left — often described as 'ultra-left' to distinguish them from the 'far left' Communist students — sat the Trotskyite National Organisation of International Socialist Students (NOISS) — the student wing of the International Socialists (IS) — and the Socialist Students Alliance

(SSA), controlled by the International Marxist Group (IMG). In addition to these political factions there were, and still are, several single-issue groups active within student politics, both locally in individual students unions and on a national level within NUS. The most relevant of these are the Union of Jewish Students (UJS), formed in 1974; and the UK branch of the General Union of Palestinian Students (GUPS), an international Palestinian student organization politically aligned, and at times organizationally linked, to the Palestine Liberation Organization (PLO), and within that to Fatah.[2] Islamist groups which supported the Muslim Brotherhood or the South Asian Jamaat-e-Islami, familiar on contemporary campuses, were almost entirely absent at that time, although Iranian pro-Khomeini activity appeared at the end of the 1970s.

Few of the factions active in student politics showed much interest in the Israel/Palestine conflict at the start of the 1970s. The energy they put into international issues was mainly focused on supporting liberation struggles in South Africa; other African countries such as Mozambique and Angola; Chile after the 1973 coup; and, closer to home, Greece and Portugal. All this took place within a general Cold War opposition to America and NATO, although the far left was far from uniformly pro-Moscow.

As the years passed after 1967 with Israel still in possession of the territories conquered in the Six Day War and starting in earnest to build settlements there, pressure grew within NUS to adopt a policy that would place support for the Palestinians alongside student support for other national liberation struggles. In May 1973 three representatives of NUS attended an International Conference of European and Arab Youth in Tripoli, Libya, organized and fully paid for by the Revolutionary Council of the Libyan Arab Republic. There were over 200 delegates from 55 countries at the conference, including a host of liberation movements. The PLO was present in large numbers; the ANC from South Africa; the South Vietnamese NLF; the Namibian SWAPO; the MPLA from Angola and others. Certain consistent themes emerged during the conference: that Zionism was a racist system, allied to imperialism; that Israel, the West Bank and Gaza should be replaced by a single state, which would give equal rights to all its citizens, irrespective of religion or ethnicity; that armed struggle is the only way to achieve this; that Zionism is distinct from Judaism, and Jews should be encouraged to campaign against Zionism; and that there should be no relations with Zionism or Israel. The NUS delegation held a side meeting with the leader of the GUPS delegation, Nabil Oulailat, to discuss ways to develop a policy for NUS on "the Palestinian question."[3]

FREE PALESTINE AND THE YOUNG LIBERALS

The NUS officials were among a party of over 20 British delegates at the conference from a range of organizations. According to the NUS report, "The British delegation was organized and led by 'Free Palestine' which is the official organ of the PLO in Britain."[4] *Free Palestine* was a monthly newspaper which had been launched in 1968 by a group of Palestinians and other Arab supporters in London. It followed the PLO line closely, although it tended to support Fatah rather than any of the smaller Palestinian factions, but NUS overstated the case in calling it an official organ of the PLO. Rather, its role in organizing the British end of the Libyan-funded conference hints at a wider, and less reliable, range of financial backers, including various individual supporters and Arab governments. Although only a small-circulation newspaper, its target audience was firmly mainstream: it had little contact with the far left, focussing its efforts on influencing MPs, journalists and other mainstream opinion formers. *Free Palestine*'s efforts to court NUS fit perfectly within this strategy of targeting mainstream opinion. Louis Eaks, the editor of the newspaper, followed up the contacts made for the Libyan conference by arranging for *Free Palestine* to have a stall at the national NUS conference that autumn.

Eaks had been chairman of the Young Liberals (YL or 'the YLs') from 1969 to 1970, and he continued to be active in the Liberal Party while editing *Free Palestine*. Peter Hain, chairman of the YLs from 1971 to 1973 before later joining the Labour Party, where he would serve in the governments of both Tony Blair and Gordon Brown, was an occasional contributor to *Free Palestine*, as was Peter Hellyer, the YL International vice-chairman from 1968 to 1970. All three of the *Free Palestine* delegates at the International Youth Conference in Libya in 1973 were former Young Liberal activists.[5] This connection between the YLs and pro-Palestinian activism was not a coincidence. In a far cry from the Zionism of David Lloyd George, the YLs were the first organization on the British left to take up the Palestinian cause, and the first to call for Zionists to be excluded from mainstream political structures.

The Liberal Party at all levels was intimately involved in campaigning against South African apartheid, which opened doors to a world of national liberation movements and Third World post-colonial leaders. The first contacts between the YLs and the PLO were at an Afro-Asian Peoples Solidarity Organisation conference in Cairo in January 1969 which Peter Hellyer attended, although the YLs' interest in the issue predated that trip. For Hellyer, support for the Palestinians was a natural extension of his anti-apartheid activities.

While opposition to South African apartheid was a core value for the YLs and not remotely controversial within the party, the relentless promotion of anti-Zionism by Eaks and his followers was very divisive, both within the YLs and with the party leadership. Their connections to Libya were an open secret and put off many of their colleagues. However, a pro-Palestinian position was formally adopted as policy at the YLs national conference in Skegness in March 1970, where Eaks had invited a member of Fatah as a guest speaker. The policy was rather confused: it supported Fatah's call for a single state of Palestine, but also called for ceasefire lines to be respected and the belligerent nations to enter negotiations. But most significant for the purposes of this essay, the new policy:

> ...called for the Israeli Young Liberals and Independent Young Liberals of Israel to be expelled from the Liberal International and the World Federation of Liberal and Radical Youth unless they accepted the principle of a secular Palestinian state.[6]

WHITHER THE LEFT?

By the early 1970s it was generally accepted across the far left that Zionism was a racist ideology and that Israel was comparable to apartheid South Africa, but the issue was a low priority compared to Vietnam or South Africa and was not featured regularly on the pages of far left newspapers. This started to change in October 1973 when war broke out between Israel, Egypt and Syria (which were aided by troops from several other Arab countries.) The signing of a peace treaty ending the Vietnam War in January 1973 had left a campaigning vacuum which the Middle East could conveniently fill.

The approach of the far left, however, limited its ability to gain support amongst Palestinians and other Arabs in Britain. Calls for unity between the Israeli and Palestinian working classes, grounded in Marxist ideology, bore little relation to the facts on the ground and did not appeal to the majority of Palestinians, who viewed their cause as a simple national liberation struggle. For pressure groups like *Free Palestine*, the doctrinaire sects of the far left were a sideshow to the main strategy of influencing mainstream opinion in Parliament and elsewhere. In addition, the ultra-left considered many of the Arab students and other activists, often quite correctly, to be bourgeois and capitalist; in return, Arab students viewed the ultra–left with suspicion, again correctly, as opportunistic. According to Peter Hellyer, "the difference between analysing the issue as one of 'national liberation' and as one where a Marxist class struggle analysis was required was pretty fundamental."[7]

NO PLATFORM FOR RACISTS AND FASCISTS

In April 1974, at their national conference, NUS voted to deny access to any individual or organization deemed to be racist or fascist. What became known as the 'No Platform' policy, though amended several times since, had two main planks: "to refuse any assistance (financial or otherwise) to openly racist or fascist organisations...and to deny them a platform," and "to prevent any member of these organisations, or individuals known to espouse similar views from speaking in colleges by whatever means are necessary (including disruption of the meeting)."[8]

The new policy instantly caused an uproar and condemnation poured down on NUS from all sides, including from within the student movement. What outraged so many was not just the restriction on free speech, but the implicit threat of violence in the promise to enforce it "by whatever means are necessary." NUS president John Randall explained, "We are not going to send round a heavy squad to break up meetings....What we intend to do is to deny platforms to the apostles of racial hatred,"[9] but few were listening. Groups on the ultra-left, using as broad a definition of 'racist' as possible, took the new policy as a mandate to disrupt meetings on campus of a wide range of speakers whom they disliked, including Conservative MPs associated with the Monday Club.

These disruptions only increased the pressure on NUS to change the policy and the union called an emergency conference in London in June to review their new position. In a highly-charged debate the No Platform policy was retained, but without the mandate to disrupt "by whatever means are necessary" racist or fascist activity on campus. A further clarification from the NUS executive was accepted: "As a point of principle students' unions should not allow a platform to members of organised fascist, racialist groupings on its campus."[10]

Even before the No Platform policy was passed, there had been signs that anti-Zionist students sought to restrict campus Zionist activities on the grounds that they were racist. In 1973, Birmingham Polytechnic Students Union discussed—and rejected—a motion "to prevent Jewish societies from functioning on campus."[11] In February 1974, North London Polytechnic had passed a motion calling for the NUS Executive to "campaign against any Zionist societies or propaganda on campus" and for Students Unions to "prevent Zionists advertising in their publications."[12] An almost identical motion was submitted to the NUS Technical Colleges Conference the same year. In time, opposition to the No Platform policy within the student movement subsided and it was adopted widely by individual Students Unions. There was disagreement amongst pro-Palestinian campaigners over whether it should be applied to Zionists, but those who argued that Zionism's underlying premise was racist could now cite the NUS policy as grounds for exclusion. In February 1975, Coventry Polytechnic passed a motion which resolved "To sever all connections existing between the N.U.S. and Zionist groups and organisations."[13]

At the NUS national conference in April 1975, the Union of Jewish Students, which had been formed the previous year, applied to join NUS as a "recognised student organisation." The then NUS president Charles Clarke, later to become Home Secretary under Tony Blair:

> ...explained that in the Executive's view, certain clauses of the constitution of the Union of Jewish Students in the United Kingdom and Eire, who had applied to join, were contrary to the aims of NUS.[14]

UJS were separately told that they could not join NUS as they were "racially exclusive." This was apparently based on the misconception that only Jews could join UJS, which, it was thought, contradicted the obligations of NUS to act "without regard to race, religion or creed."[15] When the matter was put to a vote UJS gained a majority, but not the two-thirds majority needed for admission. Sue Slipman, then a member of the Communist Party of Great Britain and part of the Broad Left in NUS, was on the NUS Executive at that time. She remembers the Executive being divided over the question of admitting UJS, but feels that "nobody saw where excluding UJS from national conference would lead, in terms of setting an example for individual Students Unions."[16]

If the No Platform policy is one half of the story of how some Jewish Societies came to be banned at British universities, the other half came at the end of 1975 when the United Nations General Assembly passed Resolution 3379, "that Zionism is a form of racism and racial discrimination."[17] The UN vote brought political coherence to a general anti-Israel position, which was, by then, widespread within student politics, and lent respectability to the idea that Zionism was a form of racism that should be banned. The only catch was that the student organizations supporting Zionism were Jewish societies. The theoretical distinction that anti-Zionists tried to observe between Zionists and Jews did not reflect the reality on most campuses. Slipman saw this as "a most peculiar Alice in Wonderland kind of time," which came about "more by accident than design." Combining the No Platform policy with the UN vote to justify banning Jewish societies was perfectly logical, but "no one got the irony that banning Jewish societies is in itself a racist act."[18]

A RABBI IS BANNED IN SALFORD

The beginning of 1977 saw a rash of motions at Students Unions around the country equating Zionism with racism. Many of these did not explicitly call for Zionist activities on campus to be banned, but that was a logical implication that could not be ignored. Still, the idea that a ban on Zionist activities meant restrictions being placed on Jewish societies would not have occurred to everybody. Students Union politics were often the preserve of a small number of political hacks and rarely engaged the interest of the wider student body. Many Jewish societies were not involved in political activities and had no mention of Israel or Zionism in their constitution, even though most of their members would have considered themselves Zionists. Therefore Students Union activists, from within their political bubble, may not have realized the potential for Jewish societies to fall victim to a ban on Zionism. On the other hand, Jewish societies and UJS were keenly sensitive to the possibility that a policy equating Zionism with racism opened the door to exactly that consequence.

Many of the motions in the early part of 1977 were the result of 'Palestine Week' events which were held on several campuses, often featuring an exhibit and speakers provided by a relatively new group, the British Anti-Zionist Organisation (BAZO). With a strong presence in Scotland and supporters elsewhere around the country, BAZO's approach was very much targeted at the rebuttal of pro-Israel views and suppression of Zionist activity. University campuses were a key part of BAZO's strategy. An article written in October 1976 for use in student newspapers made it clear that the plan was not just to present the Palestinian case, but to remove the Zionist argument entirely from the stage:

> Continuous national exposure of Zionist ideology has reduced its base among the student population to the point where its (few) spokesmen are demoralised, dwindling in number and hardly visible on the campuses....We must reach into the other sectors and classes in our society if we are to ensure the complete elimination of an effective Zionist base in Britain.[19]

Jewish anti-Zionists were prominent in BAZO and they frequently promoted Jewish and Israeli anti-Zionist speakers, including Akiva Orr, Moshe Machover and Alfred Lilienthal. They also worked closely with GUPS, whose president, Mohammed Abu-Koash, spoke alongside Orr and BAZO Chairman Norman Temple at several BAZO-organized events in the early part of 1977.

In March, Jewish students at the University of Manchester Institute of Science and Technology (UMIST) were granted a high court writ against the proposers of a motion equating Zionism with racism, put forward by the Palestinian Society, on the basis that the UMIST constitution included a clause preventing discussion of "political and sectarian matters."[20] Soon after, UJS's worst fears were realized at nearby Salford University, which had passed a policy equating Zionism with racism the previous October. A Palestine Week had recently been held at which Louis Eaks and Akiva Orr had spoken. The Jewish Society applied to hold an Israel Week, but was told that it could not include any political activities. After a failed appeal to the High Court by the Jewish Society, the Students Union announced that the Israel Week could go ahead as a cultural event. However, after hearing the first speaker, an Israeli diplomat, address a meeting of 250 people without any disruption, the Students Union promptly banned a meeting planned for the following day at which a local rabbi was due to give a talk on Judaism and Zionism. It would be alright for him to talk about the differences between Judaism and Zionism, UJS was told, but not the links between them. The Jewish Society was also prevented from setting up a bookstall to distribute Zionist leaflets. A Students Union meeting subsequently reaffirmed Salford's 'Zionism equals racism' policy, despite the presence of NUS president Charles Clarke, who warned that NUS opposed any restrictions being placed on Jewish societies. NUS, though, did not have the power to enforce its policies on individual Students Unions, which often jealously guarded their autonomy against perceived interference from the national union with which they were affiliated.

By this stage the issue had reached the attention of the national media. An editorial in the *Times Higher Education Supplement* commented:

> ...the line between Judaism and Zionism is a fine one and Jewish societies cannot reasonably be expected to commit themselves to anti-Zionism. The unions where the anti-Zionist motions have been passed are themselves confused about their attitudes to Jewish societies. At Salford, there is no objection as long as the society's role is cultural rather than political. Nobody, however, seems sure where to draw the line.
>
> There is a long, passionately upheld student tradition of opposition to racism and the present policy of the National Union of Students is to deny a platform to those they think are fascists and racists.... Students Unions, however, must see that opposition to racism and the exclusion of fellow students from the union are very different matters.[21]

Similar conflicts were cropping up elsewhere. At Essex University, a motion was passed in May equating Zionism with racism. The atmosphere became so heated that both sides nearly came to blows. University College Swansea and University College Bangor both demanded an apology from Charles Clarke after he named them among six Students Unions that refused to allow Zionists a platform; not because Clarke was wrong (he wasn't), but because, they insisted, they did not discriminate against Jewish students, but only against Zionism. At Bristol University, a motion was proposed by the Palestinian Students Society to "sever all connections existing between this Union and Zionist groups and organisations," and "To expel Zionist student bodies affiliated to this Union."[22]

Jewish students were certainly not alone in opposing such moves. On May 7, the Federation of Conservative Students, Union of Liberal Students, National Organisation of Labour Students and the Communist Party National Student Committee issued a joint statement condemning all attempts to ban Zionism from Students Unions.

JUDO AT YORK

In January 1977, York University Students Union passed a lengthy motion on Palestine which included a call "to sever all connections between NUS and Zionist groups and organisations."[23] The motion was proposed by Richard Burden, then the president of York Students Union and a former Young Liberal, now the Labour MP for Birmingham Northfield. Burden was astonished to find that the Jewish Society now expected to be banned. In an example of the profound cultural ignorance which blinded many anti-Zionist activists to the impact that banning Zionism would have on most Jewish students, it had simply not occurred to Burden that a policy to "sever all connections between NUS and Zionist groups and organisations" would affect the Jewish society. "Of course we are not going to ban you," Burden told the Jewish Society. "Why on earth would we?"[24]

The matter went to the Students Union Council (of which Burden was a member), which had the final say on the registration and funding of societies. The Council ruled that the Jewish Society was not Zionist, despite the Society insisting to the contrary, and could therefore continue to receive Union funds. The Jewish Society at York was very small—perhaps 30 or 40 members—but worked closely with UJS, which was developing a taste for confrontation and was not prepared to let the new policy stand unchallenged. They seized the initiative by amending the Jewish Society constitution to include a clause explicitly supporting Zionism. Burden felt as if he were being set up, and he was not entirely wrong. According to Avi Linden, the Israel Officer for UJS at the time, "We used the official banning of the Jewish societies as a judo move. If someone wanted to ban us then they had to take the negative consequences." The issue went back to the Union Council, which ruled in June that the change to the Jewish Society's constitution could not be ignored. Burden did not personally support No Platform, but it was union policy and had to be applied. The Council issued a statement which reiterated its support for a Jewish Society, but said that it could not "continue to recognise or fund an organisation, one of whose explicit aims is to mobilise support for the Zionist State of Israel."25

With the benefit of hindsight, Burden views this as a rather naïve move. "If I had the political experience then that I have now, I would have recommended that we take no action: you don't leap into the trap that somebody is setting for you." But nobody on the Union Council saw the bigger picture and recognition of the Jewish Society was withdrawn. The intention was not to apply a strict No Platform policy to Zionists — they could still express their opinions and hold events in the union — but they could not be supported with Union funds. The fact that the Jewish Society would also not appear in the annual Freshers' Guide or have a stall at the Freshers' Fayre blurred this distinction somewhat. Conscious that it was not satisfactory for the Union Council to make this decision alone, a Union General Meeting was called for the following week to settle the matter.

Two motions were proposed to the new meeting. One, from Burden and Tim Lunn, the Students Union vice-president, reaffirmed the union policy equating Zionism with racism and called on the union:

> To refuse to support, fund or recognise any organisation whose constitutional purpose is support of Zionist Israel and to refuse to support or fund any activities supporting Zionist Israel.26

An opposing motion called for the reinstatement of the Jewish Society, endorsed its right to express its support for Zionism and Israel, removed the equation of Zionism with racism and called for a two state solution in the Middle East. This second motion passed by 124 votes to 103. The ban on the Jewish society had lasted exactly one week and the official policy of York University Students Union now recognised Zionism as "an expression of the nationhood of the Jewish people."27

The whole episode was a chastening experience for Burden, who learned some important political lessons very quickly. "The whole debate misrepresented pro-Palestinian activism and led up blind alleys," he feels now. Underpinning the whole debate was an inability on both sides to listen to their opponents:

> People on both sides need to recognise and validate the deeply-held beliefs and collective memory of the other side. Palestinians need to appreciate the Jewish collective memory of existential threats, going back centuries. Israelis should understand the Palestinian collective memory of the Naqba. This doesn't happen enough.... If people, especially Jews, feel threatened, then they feel threatened and you should reach out to them and have a dialogue. You should try to be careful about the use of terminology, not leave room for misinterpretation and avoid words and actions that run the risk of being counterproductive. This also applies to people making allegations of antisemitism. It doesn't mean that there are subjects you must not discuss, but you have to consider the impact your words will have, and how they might get used in a way you don't intend.[28]

THE RACE TO NUS

By 1977, NUS was the last remaining Students Union in Europe not to have a policy on Israel/Palestine. When students returned to their university campuses in the autumn, all sides in the argument knew that the race was on to prepare for the NUS conference in December, where the national union would finally adopt a policy on the issue. *The Observer* set the scene:

> With the new academic year under way, Arab and Jewish students have wasted little time in resuming their bitter squabbling on the campuses of Britain.... The confrontation is expected to become increasingly intense in the run-up to the National Union of Students annual conference in December, where it is now almost certain that the Middle East will be debated.
>
> The outcome of that debate is likely to determine a firm NUS policy on Zionism. Many Jewish students fear that if the vote goes against them, there will be an outbreak of anti-Semitism leading to the victimisation of Jews in universities and colleges.[29]

First out of the blocks was the Socialist Workers Student Organisation (SWSO — formerly the National Organisation of International Socialist Students)[30] at the School of Oriental and African Studies (SOAS) in London, supported by Arab and African student societies there, which successfully passed a motion to "refuse money and facilities to societies whose aim is to propagate Zionism and organise support for the state of Israel."[31] SOAS Students Union officers insisted that the motion did not relate to the Jewish Society, only to union funding for an explicitly Zionist society. Attempting to prove the point, SWSO with the Arab and African Societies tabled an amendment to the policy they had created, allowing an Israeli Society to be formed but restricting its activities and denying it union financing. By December, the union executive had ruled that the Jewish Society was indeed Zionist, and could not receive union funds.

Similar motions were being debated in Students Unions up and down the country. At North London Polytechnic, a motion from SWSO was passed ordering that there should be "no material aid for Zionist propaganda," although acknowledging that "Jewish students have to (sic) right to organise in Jewish Societies."[32] One of the speakers quoted *The Protocols of the Elders of Zion* during the debate.[33] The 20-strong Jewish Society was disbanded not long after. At North East London Polytechnic, a motion proposed by SWSO was passed which denied funds or facilities to any organization supporting Israel, and prevented any Zionist speakers from being invited onto campus. At Hatfield Polytechnic a motion was passed equating Zionism with racism, while affirming "the right of Jewish societies to organise along cultural, religious and social lines."[34] Their political rights are notably absent from that list, although an amendment to offer support to any colleges that cut off funding from Zionist societies was defeated. At Middlesex Polytechnic a motion was narrowly passed which equated Zionism with racism, but like many such motions it stopped short of explicitly invoking the No Platform policy.

Not every student body was prepared to put the logical conclusion of such a policy down on paper, but without clarification to the contrary, everybody understood that once Zionists were branded as racists, there was nothing to stop a Students Union from cutting them off. Anyway, there were other ways in which these debates made Zionist activity more difficult: at Middlesex, antisemitic graffiti began appearing on posters and Jewish students received threatening phone calls.[35] At Leeds University, a female Jewish student was punched in the face by a Palestinian student before a debate, which was eventually won by the Jewish Society.[36]

The victory in Leeds was one of several that suggested UJS was finding its feet as a political force around the country. Jewish Societies won debates in Bristol, Cambridge, Hull and Liverpool, while at Warwick University a coalition of the Jewish Society, Conservative, Labour, Liberal and Communist students overturned a three-year-old policy equating Zionism with racism, in the face of opposition from Palestinian and Trotskyite students. At Sheffield University, the 45-member Jewish Society won a debate attended by over 1,000 people, largely due to a coalition with Christian students and a sophisticated propaganda campaign. The most symbolic victory came at Salford University, which had been the first to enforce restrictions on its Jewish Society. A proposal by Dave Glanz, a Jewish member of SWSO, to maintain the existing ban on the use of union facilities by Zionist groups or individuals was overturned (although the policy defining Zionism as racist was maintained) and the Jewish Society was permitted to extend its constitution to allow it to take part in political activities.

CREDIT AND BLAME

What had begun as a few isolated debates on university campuses had now become a major issue, filling the editorial columns and letters pages of national newspapers. UJS at that point received little funding from the wider Jewish community and, with the arrogance of youth, were quite happy to fight the battles on their own. They often had little choice: few in the Jewish community establishment considered student politics to be of great importance, often advising Jewish students not to get involved in debates about the Middle East, but rather to vacate the floor entirely. Jewish student activists who were enjoying the thrill of political battle had little patience with that attitude. David Cesarani, then the UJS political officer, viewed the communal leadership as "a liability.... Slow to respond is putting it mildly. The leadership of the community was sclerotic and when it did act, incompetent."[37] Despite this, UJS did try to enlist outside help. In November 1977 Moshe Foreman, the UJS chairman, briefed a gathering of Labour MPs, including four ministers. Soon after, Eric Moonman, Labour MP for Basildon, led an adjournment debate in the House of Commons on the efforts to ban Jewish societies and the associated intimidation and abuse of Jewish students who wanted to defend Israel. Moonman was a member of the Select Committee on Race Relations and had been increasingly brought into Jewish community affairs by Lord Fisher, president of the Board of Deputies. The debate was largely a rhetorical exercise, but it placed the Jewish community's concerns on the statute book and garnered coverage in several national newspapers.

Moonman became increasingly popular with Jewish students and he began touring campuses to speak at Jewish Society meetings. Their energy and commitment certainly impressed him and his talks, in turn, boosted their morale. UJS showed their appreciation by electing him honorary vice-president for 1978. From his perspective outside of the student bubble, Moonman had little doubt that the campaigns to ban Jewish societies would eventually fail. "Even the supporters of the Palestinians [in Parliament] could see that banning Jewish societies was wrong. It was taken as a given. The lack of wider political support meant that they were always going to lose the political battle in the end."[38]

With the issue now firmly in the spotlight, one question being asked continually was whether any political faction or pressure group was behind the drive to ban Zionists — and therefore Jewish Societies — from operating on university campuses. Many pointed the finger at BAZO, and not just their opponents. *Free Palestine*, for one, was under the impression that BAZO was involved, writing in a review of the first two years of BAZO's work:

> The organisation was established at a founding conference in Glasgow in October 1975 to spearhead a campaign specifically to challenge Zionism and those organisations which promote or represent it. Its political position was greatly enhanced by the decision of the United Nations General Assembly to define Zionism as a form of racism, and this stand by the world community acted to strengthen BAZO's campaign in British universities to bar explicitly Zionist groups under the National Union of Students ruling that no platform should be provided by university facilities to racists.[39]

Although not particularly influential within NUS at a national level, BAZO was active on several campuses around the country and was a constant thorn in the side of UJS. BAZO had a very confrontational approach. It promoted the idea that Zionists collaborated with the Nazis during the Second World War, while at the same time comparing Israel to Nazi Germany. Richard Burden joined BAZO after he left York, but found it to be overly aggressive and its material full of dense diatribes. Even its name seemed unnecessarily negative: Burden suggested changing it from British Anti-Zionist Organisation to 'Palestine Solidarity,' as it should be trying to help Palestinians rather than arguing over the nature of Zionism. As a compromise, it was added as a suffix: BAZO became the British Anti-Zionist Organisation — Palestine Solidarity (BAZO — PS).[40]

Yet for all its hardline campaigning, even BAZO was unsure whether banning Jewish societies was the right thing to do. In a letter to *Socialist Challenge* (the newspaper of the IMG) in August 1977, BAZO insisted that it did not support banning pro-Zionist Jewish societies from campus, and had not done so "for a number of months."[41] UJS activists at the time did not consider BAZO to be responsible for an organized conspiracy as such, but held it at least indirectly responsible. "If you pour petrol all over a building," asks Avi Linden, "how can you avoid being responsible for the conflagration even if you do not actually light the match?"[42]

On the wider left, the International Socialists, now going under the new name of the Socialist Workers Party, were most supportive of the bans on Zionists. Richard Burden remembers them having "a very literal approach to the question of 'Zionism equals racism equals No Platform.'"[43] The ultra-left groups would always look for ways to distinguish themselves from the moderate left and the SWP in particular was quite predictable and opportunistic in this regard. Sue Slipman remembers the idea of banning Zionists as "something that was talked about and adopted organically as a general ultra-left position... nobody spoke out against it so a conspiracy of silence allowed it to gain momentum." This was not a matter of principle, but the SWP trying to "inject revolutionary zeal" into every issue that came along.[44] In June 1977 the SWP paper *Socialist Worker* reported:

> Students in York are demanding that recognition of the Jewish Society by the Union Council be withheld until they change their explicit support for Zionism. Members of York NOISS, the student organisation of that supports (sic) the Socialist Workers Party, have declared: 'We support unconditionally the right of the Jewish Society to exist as a cultural and religious body within the students union. We support unconditionally the right of all people of all races to live in and participate freely in a secular state in Palestine.
>
> 'It is because we oppose all racism that we oppose an openly Zionist and racist Jewish society.'[45]

However, this remained a more localized phenomenon, with SWP activists proposing and supporting motions on their particular campus rather than following a centralized campaign from the party leadership. By October, the SWP felt the need to defend themselves against allegations that they were behind the banning of Jewish societies. As they never missed an opportunity to point out, several of their activists were themselves Jewish, including people who were promoting the bans on Students Union funding for pro-Zionist activities. In any case, they argued, they did not support restricting the rights of Jewish students; they were just opposed to the use of union funds to promote Israel and Zionism. Support was frequently voiced for the cultural and religious rights of Jewish societies, as if this mitigated circumscribing their political rights.

There was disagreement within the SWP about how to approach the issue. Andy Strouthous, an NOISS member on the NUS Executive, endorsed a policy to deny union funds to Zionists, adding that "pro-Israel government meetings should be treated like the one in Salford last term"[46] (i.e. banned). Not so, replied the SWP's Alex Callinicos two weeks later: NOISS does not have a policy of physically preventing Zionists from meeting on campus, but it does argue that Students Union money and facilities should not be provided for the purpose.[47] Dave Glanz, who had led the NOISS anti-Zionist campaign at Salford University, wrote an NOISS Bulletin which stated:

> We believe that clubs and societies etc. established in colleges which have the promotion of Zionism or Israel as part of their objectives are inevitably promoting racialism...we will campaign for this Union to refuse money and facilities when they aim to propagate Zionism and support the state of Israel.[48]

The SWP was effectively trying to separate the two parts of the No Platform policy that NUS had adopted three years earlier: no union funds or facilities for Zionism, but no disruption of their meetings either. Although they may have seen this as a compromise, their approach neglected the practical and emotional impact of denying Jewish societies funding for their activities unless they agreed not to promote Israel or Zionism in any way. This is without even considering the historic echoes of placing limits on Jewish behavior, if those Jews want to be accepted into the wider society.

NUS TAKES CONTROL

From a situation at the start of 1977 where this issue was at the periphery of NUS's vision, the leadership of the national union suddenly found themselves confronting a situation that threatened to get out of control. Nobody knew quite how they had got there, but there was a sense at the time that the bannings were gathering enough momentum to become the dominant position within NUS, however unlikely that appears with hindsight. It was increasingly clear that the NUS leadership had to establish a policy on Israel/Palestine and set some limits on how the issue would be fought out on British campuses.

In June, GUPS invited NUS to send a delegation to visit Palestinians in various Arab countries. When UJS heard about the offer they insisted that Israel be included in the trip, so in late August four members of the NUS leadership set off for two weeks in Lebanon and Israel: Trevor Phillips, NUS national secretary and delegation leader; David Aaronovitch, vice-president

(Education); Eddie Longworth from the NUS Executive; and Colin Talbot, from the NUS Executive and NUS International Committee. The trip was paid for and the itineraries organized by GUPS and UJS. The composition of the delegation was carefully balanced: Phillips and Aaronovitch were both from the Broad Left, Longworth was a Conservative and Talbot from the Trotskyite Socialist Students Alliance.

The itinerary was similarly constructed to cover every angle. The group started off in Lebanon, which was in total chaos. The detritus of war was everywhere and basic order had completely broken down. A visit to an orphanage in Shatila refugee camp, full of children traumatized by the civil war, was profoundly disturbing. The group then flew to Israel via Cyprus. The Israeli leg of the tour was organized by the Ministry of Foreign Affairs and fronted by the National Union of Israeli Students. Talbot was particularly impressed by their meeting with Golda Meir, by then almost eighty and no longer in office. Meir had obviously been very well briefed: she totally ignored Longworth, who was already pro-Israel, and Talbot, who as a Trotskyite was a lost cause, and concentrated all her efforts on persuading the other two of Israel's case.

The whole experience left a deep impression on all the participants. Talbot found it "incredibly emotional. One week we were in Shatila refugee camp seeing orphans from the Lebanese civil war, then seven days later we were at Yad Vashem." Phillips found it humbling: "The Palestinians were absolutely under the cosh [under pressure], while Israel was also caught in a desperate trap." Too many people on the outside, Phillips felt, presumed to tell both sides how to resolve their conflict.

The delegation wrote a report on their return, to be used as the basis for NUS to debate a policy on the Middle East at their conference in December. For Aaronovitch, the sole aim was to take the heat out of the issue: "We were a national Students Union, not a branch of the UN." Aaronovitch, Phillips and Longworth endorsed a proposal for two states, one Israeli and one Palestinian; that the PLO should be recognized as the representative body of the Palestinians; and that Zionism is not racism and is a legitimate expression of Jewish nationhood.

Talbot dissented from the recognition of Zionism and Israel, and wrote a minority report condemning Zionism as racist and endorsing a single-state solution. Talbot's report also included a recommendation that:

> We should not place any bureaucratic or administrative measures in the way of an open and democratic debate, including any restrictions on the rights of the Zionists.

This reflected the position of the SSA and its parent body the IMG, which opposed the bans. It satisfied Talbot, who "always felt very uneasy about the bannings. The logic was clear but it was taking you to places where I didn't want to be." Now a professor at Manchester Business School, Talbot has changed his views on many things, including the existence of Israel. He left the IMG in the early 1980s, having been a member since 1972.[49]

Having amassed their evidence in the Middle East, NUS now turned to matters at home. In October a meeting of the NUS Executive voted, by 11 votes to 3, to propose that NUS adopt powers to suspend Students Unions which ban their Jewish society. This would require an amendment to the NUS constitution, which could only be granted by vote at NUS conference that December. Once the argument was won within the NUS Executive their strong leadership gave a welcome boost to UJS's growing ability to win debates, and the momentum started to shift. At Hull University, the International Socialists Society withdrew a motion that proposed withdrawing union funds and facilities from Zionist groups. At Teesside Polytechnic, where Lewis Davies was President of the Students Union, an anti-Zionist motion was withdrawn by the proposers specifically because of the new threat of suspension from NUS. At Lancaster University, where there was an existing policy that did not allow the distribution of Zionist material on campus, Labour students proposed lifting the ban, again citing the warning from NUS.[50] Motions equating Zionism with racism were defeated at Leicester University, Sunderland Polytechnic and Aberdeen University. Motions condemning Students Unions that ban Jewish societies were passed at Leicester and at Exeter University, while the existing anti-Zionist policy at North East London Polytechnic was overturned.

Most significantly, GUPS, while criticising NUS for threatening to suspend Students Unions, announced that they opposed any bans being placed on Zionist student activity. GUPS included some relatively moderate people and one of the key aims of the NUS strategy had been to draw them away from the bannings. At the same time, Sue Slipman and others were in constant contact with UJS and the Board of Deputies of British Jews. UJS in particular felt beleaguered and frustrated. They had been warning for some time of the possibility of Jewish societies being banned, and felt, with some justification, that they had been ignored. The efforts of NUS to bring both sides together bore fruit on the eve of the NUS conference, when they brokered parallel statements from UJS and GUPS which called for debates to take place "within a free and open atmosphere," and insisted that "No limitations on the rights of Jewish or Palestinian students or Jewish or

Palestinian societies, whether they are religious, political or social groupings, should be contemplated."[51]

The NUS conference saw the successful conclusion of the NUS leadership's strategy. The Middle East delegation's report was presented to the conference and accepted; a motion was passed recognizing that "Both the Palestinians and the Jews have a right to national self-determination ... [which are] not necessarily mutually exclusive;"[52] powers were granted to suspend member unions that banned their Jewish society; and, after several failed efforts by the NUS leadership, the entire No Platform policy was rescinded. The *Times Higher Education Supplement* breathed a sigh of relief:

> The student year culminated in a triumph for moderation, as the new model National Union of Students met in December to ditch the extremist policies which had brought the union into disrepute and undermined the important educational campaigns the NUS was keen to wage.

> At a Blackpool conference this month, the NUS agreed by a narrow margin to overturn its 'no platform' policy which had barred from campuses anyone loosely labelled racist or fascist. The same conference also voted to take steps to remove the spectre of Jewish students being discriminated against because of their allegiance with Jewish societies and the Zionist cause.[53]

ANTI-ZIONISM AND ANTISEMITISM

This is, in large part, a story of unintended consequences. None of the people involved with banning Zionists from university campuses would have considered him or herself to be antisemitic. For the most part they acted, they sincerely believed, in the cause of anti-racism and out of sympathy and support for the Palestinians. Yet then as now, on every campus, the majority of ordinary Jewish students supported Israel and Zionism at some very basic, emotional level. It was Jewish societies that wanted to include the promotion of Israel and Zionism in their aims and objectives, and were consequently being denied the union funds and facilities provided to every other society. The theoretical question of whether or not it is antisemitic to describe Zionism as intrinsically racist divides many people. What UJS repeatedly did was demonstrate that, whatever the theoretical argument, translating that view into action opens the door to the marginalization of, and discrimination against, the majority of Jews. Whether or not this sort of disproportionately negative impact on Jews can be described as antisemitic, on a lot of campuses it left the relatively few Jews feeling isolated, intimidated and discriminated against.

This essay began by asking when anti-Israel political campaigning becomes antisemitic. However, even to describe these events as antisemitic requires some qualification. Antisemitism is often understood to mean a direct hatred of Jews or a desire to do them physical harm, and clearly neither motivation played much, if any, part in this story. The campaigns of the far left against Zionism were probably informed to some degree by prejudices about Jews that have punctuated the history of the left, but this is a story of a more insidious, but very British, form of antisemitism: that of partial exclusion, conditional acceptance to mainstream society, restrictions placed on what Jews can or should say and do if they want to be treated normally.

Yet a more profound factor was probably the fact that the campaign was framed from the outset as anti-Zionist rather than pro-Palestinian. Anti-Zionism is by its nature abstract, negative and potentially limitless. It fits the liberation politics of the student world — where everything is black and white and maturity and nuance are rare qualities — and provides a platform for the revolutionary agitation so beloved by Trotskyite groups. It is dehumanizing and leaves little room for compromise or dialogue. It is a world away from offering practical help to Palestinians. Richard Burden's realization of the need to listen to and understand your political opponents' fears and concerns is an important lesson to come out of this story. Another is that Jews, like all minorities, sometimes need to fight to establish their place in society. Bans on campus Zionism did not disappear after 1977 and continued to occur until the mid-1980s, but never reached the same pitch as they did that year. After the NUS conference in December 1977, UJS had one simple comment to make:

> All that happened was that the national union decided that Jews have as many rights as anyone else. And that, after all, was all we ever wanted.[54]

Dave Rich is deputy directory of communications for the UK-based Community Security Trust. He has contributed chapters to Zach Levey and Elie Podeh, eds., *Britain and the Middle East: From Imperial Power to Junior Partner* (2008); Manfred Gerstenfeld, ed., *The Abuse of Holocaust Memory: Distortions and Responses* (2009); Barry Rubin, ed., *The Muslim Brotherhood: The Organization and Policies of a Global Islamist Movement* (2010).

ENDNOTES

[1] The Liberal Party had two youth organizations with overlapping memberships and areas of activity: the Union of Liberal Students and the National League of Young

Liberals. 'Young Liberals' was often used as a generic name for both student and non-student youth activity. The Liberal Party is the forerunner of today's Liberal Democrats.

2   GUPS was formed as an international body in Cairo in 1959; the UK and Ireland branch was formed in the late 1960s.

3   International Conference of European and Arab Youth, NUSUK Delegation Report, May 1973.

4   NUSUK Delegation Report.

5   The Delegates list names Louis Eaks, "Helluer" and "J Fogg" as the three Free Palestine delegates. "Helluer" refers to Peter Hellyer who has confirmed to the author that he was present at the confererence; "J Fogg" almost certainly refers to Liberals for Palestine founder Nicholas Fogg. None of the British delegates at the conference were of Palestinian or Arab origin.

6   "Young Liberals reject extreme pro-Arab," *Jewish Chronicle*, April 3, 1970.

7   Peter Hellyer, correspondence with the author, December 26, 2009.

8   "Dialectics of freedom," *Patterns of Prejudice* 8:1 May/June 1974.

9   "Dialectics of freedom."

10   "Dialectics of freedom."

11   "Llandudno and after," *Jewish Chronicle*, April 18, 1975.

12   Policy on Palestine and Zionism, North London Polytechnic SU Handbook 1977–78.

13   Motion on Palestine, February 1975. Copies of this and all other motions quoted in this essay are in the possession of the author.

14   "Minutes and Summary of Proceedings," NUS April Conference, Llandudno 1975.

15   "Llandudno and after."

16   Sue Slipman, interview with the author, January 5, 2010.

17   Full text available at http://daccess-dds-ny.un.org/doc/RESOLUTION/GEN/NR0/000/92/IMG/NR000092.pdf?OpenElement (accessed February 5, 2010).

18   Avi Linden, correspondence with the author, November 26, 2009.

19   George Mitchell, "Statement on the struggle against Zionism in Britain," published in *BAZO Infobulletin* October 1976.

20   "Students issue a writ," *Jewish Chronicle*, March 18, 1977.

21   "Anti-Zionism on campus," *Times Higher Education Supplement*, April 29, 1977.

22   Hani Salaman, motion on Palestine, May 11, 1977. It is not known if this motion was passed.

23   Richard Burden, Phil Harris & Steve Andrew, motion on Palestine, undated. As well as becoming union policy at York, this motion was submitted (but not discussed) to NUS conference in April 1977, hence the references to NUS rather than York Students Union in the actual text.

24   This and all subsequent quotes by Richard Burden are from an interview with the author, January 12, 2010.

25   "Students' Jewish Society 'racialist'," *Yorkshire Evening Press*, June 16, 1977.

26   Richard Burden & Tim Lunn, motion for Union General Meeting, June 22, 1977.

27   Alan Newland & Steve Crook, motion for Union General Meeting, June 22, 1977.

28   Burden, January 12, 2010.

29   Iain Murray, "Students 'at war'," *The Observer*, October 16, 1977.

30   During this period, the student wing of the Socialist Workers Party was referred to both under its old name, the National Organisation of International Socialist Students (NOISS), and its new name, the Socialist Workers Student Organisation (SWSO).

31   Assif Shameen, "SOAS bans Zionists," *Sennet*, October 19, 1977.

32   Policy text, Middle East, 1977.

33   John Izbicki, "Left-wingers put student gag on Zionism," *Daily Telegraph*, November 18, 1977.

34   N. Rahimtulla & M. Ayyad, motion on Palestine, November 28, 1977.

35   "Middle East text for students," *Guardian*, November 25, 1977.

36   "Violence erupts in campus war," *Jewish Chronicle*, November 25, 1977.

37   David Cesarani, correspondence with the author, November 12, 2009.

38   Eric Moonman, interview with the author, December 11, 2009.

39   "BAZO enters third year of campaigning," *Free Palestine*, November 1977.

40   Burden, January 12, 2010.

41   BAZO Information Bulletin, November 17, 1978.

42   Linden, November 14, 2009.

43   Burden, January 12, 2010.

44   Slipman, January 5, 2010.

45   "Israel uses torture," *Socialist Worker*, June 25, 1977.

46   "NO to anti-semitism NO to Israel as well," *Socialist Worker*, October 29, 1977.

47   Alex Callinicos, "Argue with Zionists," *Socialist Worker*, November 12, 1977.

48   Dave Glanz, *NOISS Bulletin* November 1977; "Zionism: A Racist Ideology," *Agitator*, December 1977.

49   Interviews with the author: Phillips, December 14, 2009; Aaronovitch, December 22, 2009; Talbot, January 12, 2010.

50   It is not known if this new policy was passed.

51   Annabel Ferriman, "Move to end students' Jewish-Arab conflict," *The Times*, December 2, 1977.

52   Paul Infield, "NUS Conference 1977—What Really Happened," *UJS Journal*, December 1977.

53   Peter David, "NUS strides along middle of the road," *Times Higher Education Supplement*, December 30, 1977.

54   Infield, "NUS Conference 1977."

THE IRONY OF IT ALL
Antisemitism, Anti-Zionism, and Intimidation on South African University Campuses

Gregg Rickman

"Don't expect me to put up with your Jewish identity," warned Harvard Professor Farid Esack, Nelson Mandela's former Gender Equality Commissioner, "if it involves a relationship of marginalization, subjugation and expulsion of other people."[1] Esack's discussion centered on the Muslim trope, Zionism equals Apartheid. This narrative pervades the Muslim-Jewish debate in South Africa today, dominating the lives of Jewish students on university campuses there.

With overt denunciations and discrimination against Jews considered unacceptable since the Holocaust, anti-Zionism has become the new mode of antisemitism. This is particularly clear on South African university campuses. As one Jewish student wrote, indicating the extent of the problem Jewish students in South Africa face today, "A significant portion of our resource[s] ... goes to defending Israel on campus."[2] So consistent and strident is the anti-Zionist propaganda used to harass Jewish students that the line is very often crossed into overt antisemitism. Jewish students are confronted with "apartheid walls," physical threats from union activists, calls for boycotts of Israel, and campus visits by Leila Khaled, celebrated by the Witwatersrand University Palestine Solidarity Committee as a "two-time plane hijacker and Palestinian activist."[3]

Over a century before, the ancestors of many of these Jewish students had come to South Africa, fleeing from just this sort of harassment. They were escaping pogroms and harsh antisemitic restrictive legislation in the Russian Empire. One emigrant explained why he left for South Africa:

> We had fantasies about South Africa. For most of us, living as we were in dire poverty and squalor, it was a fantastic world where the streets were paved with gold and we would live in marble halls with magnificent candelabra, dining at tables laden with viands of the most appetizing variety and taste.[4]

The first three Jewish families had arrived in 1820 with the initial influx of British settlers; followed by seventeen more Jews, in 1841 they formed the first Jewish congregation in Cape Town. The discovery of diamonds and later gold, combined with the increasing number of pogroms and intensification of antisemitism in the Russian Empire, led to the further migration of Jews to South Africa. By 1880, there were some 4,000 Jews in South Africa. By the turn of the twentieth century there were over 38,000. By 1936, there were over 90,000 Jews; and by 1980, more than 117,000.[5] The Jewish community now had established roots and a significant presence in South Africa. Yet the country would undergo a profound transformation.

Apartheid, the political system that subjugated black Africans and consigned them to second-class status, finally began its demise in February 1990 when President F. W. de Klerk released Nelson Mandela from prison, where he had been confined for twenty-seven years. A year later Mandela was elected president of the African National Congress (ANC). In 1992 a whites-only referendum approved the reform process and on April 27, 1994, South Africa held its first democratic elections. The end of Apartheid brought the end of white minority rule, but it also changed the tone of the political culture. The ANC, the ruling party, owed deep debts of gratitude to its international supporters, among them Palestinians and other Arabs. This allegiance would figure prominently in the treatment Jewish students later faced in South Africa.

SOUTH AFRICA'S UNIVERSITIES

Apartheid had characterized South Africa's university campuses. Black students were only allowed to go to certain universities. Other universities, in direct contravention of the law, permitted black students to attend. Some liberal universities openly confronted Apartheid. Their oppositional stance developed into support for the ANC. Their student representative councils (SRC) began representing various elements of the ANC and the left generally. On many campuses the SRCs are now controlled by the Progressive Youth Alliance (PYA), which is a combination of the ANC youth league, the Young Communist League and the South African Congress of Student Organizations.[6]

JEWISH STUDENTS

The South African Union of Jewish Students (SAUJS), representing at any given time some 2,000 university students, was established in 1976, succeeding the South African Federation of Jewish Student Associations. According to the SAUJS, in 2009 there were 800-1,000 Jewish student members at Witwatersrand University, 500-600 at the University of Cape Town, and 200-300 at the University of Johannesburg, with the rest in private schools or not in school at the time.[7]

MUSLIM STUDENTS

Estimates of the number of Muslim students on South African campuses vary. According to some, there are about 4,000 Muslims at Witwatersrand University. It is estimated that about 300 are members of the Muslim Students Association (MSA). The University of Cape Town, the University of Durban Westville, and the University of Johannesburg also have sizeable Muslim student populations.[8]

More general estimates indicate that there may be as many as 25,000 Muslim students on South African university campuses, about seven times the number of Jewish students. However, according to the South African Board of Jewish Deputies, many of the Muslims attend universities where there are few or no Jewish students by choice, such as Durban-Westville and the University of the Western Cape.[9]

PATTERNS AND PRACTICES OF HARASSMENT
AND INTIMIDATION

Although it is often said that universities reflect the broader society, in few countries is this clearer than South Africa. As one commentator suggested, the government is itself a sponsor of anti-Zionism. Indeed, the pro-Palestinian, anti-Israel bent of the South African government is omnipresent on campus, adding to the palpably hostile climate experienced by Jewish students, as it, in effect, licenses the actions of Muslim student associations that spread anti-Israel/anti-Zionist hatred and antisemitism.

Jewish students on university campuses are not only outnumbered, but also outmaneuvered. A former Witwatersrand student said that she "lost sleep" trying to keep up with the relentless barrage of anti-Israel propaganda and intimidation issuing from Muslim student groups, which often crossed the line into antisemitism. Jews were, she explained, "always put back on their heels" by the ferocity of their campaigns.[10] Organizations such as the Muslim Students Association and the Palestine Solidarity Committee (PSC) and their other student supporters are in the forefront of the propaganda campaigns. Their focus always involves two issues: a sustained effort to link contemporary Israeli actions and policies with those of historical Apartheid and endless comparisons of Israel and Nazi Germany.

The Muslim Students Association originated in 1969 as the Cape Muslim Students Association (CMSA). In 1974, the CMSA became the MSA, which became dedicated to coordinating—and motivating—Muslim students' actions. The MSA grew in popularity and chapters appeared in a number of secondary schools as well as universities. According to information gathered by the South African Board of Jewish Deputies and others, the MSA's aim is to bring Muslim students into a single ideological movement, centered on Islam.

The Palestine Solidarity Committee was formed in 1998, much later than the MSA, and was initiated, in part, by trade union activists, who themselves instigate a number of anti-Zionist, and even antisemitic, actions on university campuses. Following the 2000 Intifada, the PSC became increasingly radicalized, concentrating its activities on establishing parallels between the practices of South Africa under Apartheid and Israel. As one of the PSC's flyers put it, its main focus "has been the drawing of parallels between the South African and Israeli apartheids as well as the parallels between the South African and Palestinian liberation struggles."[11] The Committee often promotes the Palestinian cause in South Africa, denouncing the Jewish settlements, backing academic and cultural boycotts of Israel and supporting campaigns to divest from, and impose sanctions on, the Jewish state. The PSC also strongly endorsed the 2001 World Conference against Racism, Racial Discrimination, Xenophobia and Related Intolerance, the Durban Conference, which was the platform from which the first salvos of a renewed and virulent form of antisemitism were launched in the twenty-first century. Conference delegates were supposed to discuss trafficking in women, migration, and discrimination due to gender, race, and origin. Instead, the conference was hijacked. Jewish delegates were greeted in conference sessions by shouts of "Jew, Jew, Jew" and calls to take responsibility for killing Jesus. Copies of the *Protocols of the Learned Elders of Zion* were sold and vile anti-Semitic cartoons were handed out.

If the strategies for these groups' antisemitism are the comparisons of Israel to Apartheid South Africa and Nazi Germany, their tactics are the use of classical antisemitic canards, Communist slogans, and the misappropriation of the Holocaust and its terminology to harass, intimidate, and threaten. At times the tactics skate along the divide between antisemitism and anti-Zionism. At other times, they cross over into overt antisemitic behavior and claims.

To understand where the line between criticism of Israel ends and antisemitism begins, we should refer to the discussions and definitions of the European Monitoring Center on Racism and Xenophobia of December 2006. These definitions were adopted as US policy in the State Department report on *Contemporary Global Anti-Semitism* (March 2008):

> Comparing contemporary Israeli policy to that of the Nazis is increasingly commonplace. Anti-Semitism couched as criticism of Zionism or Israel often escapes condemnation since it can be more subtle than traditional forms of anti-Semitism, and promoting anti-Semitic attitudes may not be the conscious intent of the purveyor. Israel's policies and practices must be subject to responsible criticism and scrutiny to the same degree as those of any other country. At the same time, those criticizing Israel have a responsibility to consider the effect their actions may have in prompting hatred of Jews. At times hostility toward Israel has translated into physical violence directed at Jews in general...
>
> Examples of the ways in which anti-Semitism manifests itself with regard to the state of Israel, taking into account the overall context, could include:
> - Denying the Jewish people their right to self-determination...
> - Applying double standards by requiring of it a behavior not expected or demanded of any other democratic nation.
> - Using the symbols and images associated with classic anti-Semitism (e.g., claims of Jews killing Jesus or blood libel) to characterize Israel or Israelis.
> - Drawing comparisons of contemporary Israeli policy to that of the Nazis.
> - Holding Jews collectively responsible for actions of the state of Israel.[12]

These examples make it easier to recognize when criticism of Israel becomes antisemitism.

The antisemitic roots and implications of the Israel–Apartheid allegations should also be underscored. As Gideon Shimoni, former head of the Hebrew University's Institute of Contemporary Jewry, explained:

> ...when Israel cooperated with the South African government, after about 1973, the Israel=apartheid equation was deployed in the international forum as a propaganda sub-theme of the notorious 'Zionism is Racism' slander. More recently the 'Israel-is-an-apartheid state' mantra has subsumed and largely superseded the defamatory 'Zionism is Racism' slogan.[13]

We will now consider how these strategies have been used against Jewish students in South Africa.

STRATEGIES

Muslim student groups on campus engage in provocative actions and publicity stunts that are designed to drive a wedge between Jews and Israel and to discredit supporters of the Jewish state. These groups promote the union movement, which, in turn, castigates Israel and threatens Jews in general and Jewish students in particular. They use "lawfare" tactics or legal maneuvers, suing their critics in South African courts, to intimidate and silence them.

In driving a wedge between Jews and Israel, Muslim student groups revived a tactic used by Communist movements — clouding the issue, for example, by labeling some Jews "Refuseniks," which originally referred to Soviet Jews to whom the Communist government had denied exit visas. Thus, when "Shministim" — Israeli 12th graders who refused to join the Israeli Army — visited South Africa in October 2009, they were referred to as "Refuseniks." They were celebrated on the South African website Amandla Intifada, whose symbol, a clenched fist, is prominently featured in PSC advertisements.[14]

Another device they used can be seen in the "Gaza Document." South African Muslim attorneys assembled what they called evidence, photographs and statements detailing the activities of South African Jewish volunteers and participants in the Israeli Army's "Operation Cast Lead" in Gaza, December 2008 — January 2009. Muslim students circulated the document widely on campuses. They portrayed South African Jewry as a collective, co-responsible for what they describe as Israel's unwarranted brutality against the Palestinians. Once again using "lawfare," they sought to have participants in Operation Cast Lead arrested upon their return to South Africa.

Muslim groups sponsor talks by Jewish critics of Israel, such as columnist and media commentator Steven Friedman, whom they pointedly describe as "a well known and observant Jew." They use his Jewishness to maintain that his motives and criticism of Israel cannot be questioned, and by extension, to discredit those Jews who defend Israel's actions.[15] They also promote the comic strips of Jewish, anti-Zionist critic "Zapiro," who uses his comics to denigrate Israel and Jews.[16]

In August 2009, Norman Finkelstein, author of *The Holocaust Industry*, was also invited to speak on several South African university campuses. Just

as the PSC does with its featured speakers, Finkelstein touts his parents' status as Holocaust survivors to bolster his credentials and lend credibility to his claims that Jewish world leaders use the Holocaust for purposes of financial gain and as a cover for Israel's ostensibly illegal acts against the Palestinians.[17]

Similarly, Muslim student groups tout eighty-five-year-old American "peace activist" and Holocaust survivor Hedy Epstein as a fellow-champion of the Palestinian cause. The Wits PSC of South Africa newsletter (March 2006) featured her poem, "When I see the word Palestine."[18] Like Finkelstein, Epstein offers the students a Jewishly credentialed spokesperson who shares and parrots their views.

The remarks of South African parliamentarian and former intelligence minister Ronnie Kasrils, a long-time virulent opponent of Israel, are repeatedly featured in the Wits PSC newsletters. He regularly speaks on campuses, where he is lauded for his stands on the issues which the PSC also promotes, such as his denunciation of the "monstrous Zionist plot to violently dispossess the Palestinian people of their land and rights."[19]

In March 2008 when Jewish students proposed a "Cook for Peace" event on campuses, the MSA responded by issuing a press release decrying the

Jewish students union's support for Israel's policies. Once again seeking to drive a wedge between Jewish students and Israel, the MSA declared:

> The South African Union of Jewish Students (SAUJS) have [sic] never recognized the plight of the Palestinians. By its own admission on a statement to be found on its website, SAUJS in fact supports Zionism. Many prominent people have spoken out against the action of Zionist Israel and the defiant manner in which they defy all initiatives of peace, including the Honorable Desmond Tutu.... [U]ntil such time that SAUJS affirms their recognition of the injustices perpetrated against the Palestinians by the Israeli government, we, the Muslim Students of South Africa, undertake not to participate in their farcical Cook for "Peace."[20]

Seeking to capitalize on useful propaganda appearing in the press, the Witwatersrand PSC newsletter also took advantage of a letter by an avowed "Christian Zionist," Johan Pieter Coetzee of Johannesburg, which was published in the *South African Jewish Report*, May 18, 2007. There Coetzee described an "embarrassing debate" that reputedly occurred, but was unsubstantiated, between the SAUJS and the PSC on May 4, 2007:

> First of all, the Jewish students handled themselves in a manner that seemed extremely unprepared, disorganized, and indeed unintelligent, while the speakers from the Palestinian Solidarity Committee (while I do not agree with their sentiment) were very knowledgeable and managed to have a massive impact on the crowd that sat before them.[21]

The strategy of the PSC is to continually insist that Jewish students support Israel's supposed Apartheid and Nazi-like policies. How they promote the strategy is what caused the Jewish student to "lose sleep."

TACTICS

The pro-Palestinian events staged by Muslim students on campuses across South Africa have brought them considerable notoriety. The tactics they have used, however, in the end served to undermine their cause by exposing their base of support and ideological origins.

These groups choose from a menu of tactics that intimidate and threaten Jews. The latest and most flagrant form of intimidation was revealed in a speech by Bongani Masuku of the Congress of South African Trade Unions (COSATU) at a rally organized by the PSC at Witwatersrand University on March 5, 2009. Alleging hate speech, the South African Board of Jewish

Deputies filed a complaint with the South African Human Rights Commission, in which it objected to Masuku's statements and provocative actions. In the words of the Commission's findings of guilt against him, Masuku "uttered numerous anti-semitic remarks which were seen to have incited violence and hatred amongst the students who were present." Masuku had told his audience that:

> COSATU has got members here even on this campus; we can make sure that for that side it will be hell;
> COSATU is with you, we will do everything to make sure that whether it's at Wits University, whether it's at Orange Grove, anyone who does not support equality and dignity, who does not support the rights of other people must face the consequences even if it means that we will do something that may necessarily cause what is regarded as harm;
> ...The following things are going to apply: any South African family who sends its son or daughter to be part of the Israeli Defence Force must not blame us if something happens to them with immediate effect...

The Commission also found that Masuku had written a letter to Anthony Posner (who identifies himself as "an anti-anti-zionist") in which he advised,

> ...all who have not accepted or woken up to the reality that we now live in a democratic South Africa where racism or promotion of it is a crime, are free to leave the country. I repeat whether Jew or whomsoever does so, must not just be encouraged but forced to leave, for such a crime is so heinous it can't be tolerated...[22]

With this as background, the Commission's findings were clear: Masuku had committed the crime of hate speech. The Commission concluded:

> 1. On the day in question Mr. Masuku was speaking to students who included both Jewish Zionists and Palestinian supporters. There appeared to already have been noted tension between these two groups. Therefore by Mr. Masuku making those remarks he surely intended to incite violence and hatred that was already potentially imminent amongst these two groups. COSATU members of Palestinian supporters present at this rally could easily have been incited to hate, and even attack their Jewish counterparts. This is exactly what Section 16(2) of the Constitution seeks to prevent.
> 2. Mr. Masuku's heated statements made amidst an already tense audience appeared to advocate hatred against Jews and all other supporters of Israel. This is inciting violence based on religion, an area which freedom of expression does not protect.[23]

Other forms of harassment and intimidation on university campuses have included the following:

- People arriving to attend the Limmud seminar (on Jewish learning) at Witwatersrand University on August 9, 2009 were subjected to continual verbal abuse by protestors calling them "Nazis," "Baby killers" and "Hitler's grandchildren."
- In May 2008, three cases of antisemitic graffiti on University of the Witwatersrand – East Campus: "Jews must die," "The Holocaust is exaggerated by 5 million" and "Israel was formed under the fictitious assumption that the Jews are G-d's chosen people and as such are allowed to violate human rights with impunity."
- On May 13, 2008, a wall 4 meters long by 2 meters high was spray painted with the slogan "1948 — What you say? Palestinian Nakba or Israeli Celebrations" — "Wits PSC www.psc.za.org" Pens were left for people to add their comments. A notice posted on the wall stated that the remarks do not necessarily reflect the views of the University.

  Initial comments written on the wall included:
  o 1948 = Dispossession for the Palestinian people
  o Creation of refugee camps
  o Nakba = catastrophe 4 Palestinians

  The next day comments continued to be written on the wall, including,
  o Israel celebrates death
  o The Zionist cancer will end
  o Zionism = Racism
  o Zionism = Nazi
  o In 1948, two Apartheid regimes were formally established!! Today one of them still exists...
  o We are not truly free until the Palestinians are free — Nelson Mandela
  o Star of David = Swastika

- In October 2008, the PSC ran a 'Torture Campaign,' graphically acting out scenes of Palestinians purportedly being tortured by Israeli soldiers.
- On December 2, 2007, in an academic seminar sponsored by the Iranian government and held at the University of South Africa in Pretoria, an ANC Member of Parliament cited the *Protocols of the Elders of Zion* as a credible historic document and implied that the historicity of the Holocaust was a matter of debate. The MP confirmed that she had asked

a Jewish delegate to the conference, "Are the *Protocols* still relevant to you in today's times?" Another delegate reportedly questioned the authenticity of the Holocaust, citing Iranian President Ahmadinejad's dismissal of it as "a myth."[24]

Muslim students' newspapers and events are also pervaded with Soviet-style terminology that is used to perpetuate the ideas of revolution and liberation. The students endlessly glorify those they deem to be engaging in acts of "liberation" and "resistance." In terms reminiscent of earlier Soviet support for liberation movements around the world, including that of the Palestinians, they extend the term "liberation" to the fight against what they define as racism. In March 2006 the PSC at Witwatersrand University explained that: "We, students of a post-apartheid regime see it as our responsibility to stand with all those who are still engaged with liberating themselves from racist paradigms"[25] — and those "paradigms" apparently include Israel's response to Palestinians.

Rachel Corrie (1979–2003)

Thus Muslim students handed out flyers commemorating the anniversary of American "peace activist" Rachel Corrie's death in the Gaza Strip in 2003. Presenting her as a resister and fighter for liberation and against racism, the flyer declared, "This year marks the 5th year since her murder and the 60th year of the Nakba (Catastrophe) of Israeli occupation of Palestine."[26] Thus they define the "occupation" as including the State of Israel, since before 1967 Jordan held the West Bank and Egypt, the Gaza strip.

References to Israel as a "belligerent occupying power," a "colonialist power," and part of a larger effort directed against the Palestinian people are commonplace. Yumna Mahomed, writing in the PSC Witwatersrand newsletter, explained, "As Israel and its global backers in Canada, the US and Europe tighten the economic stranglehold on the Palestinian people and while the Israeli military continues its daily assault on Palestinian life, our collective responsibility in isolating the Israeli apartheid regime is becoming ever more crucial."[27] These terms echo those of earlier Soviet propaganda efforts.

Muslim students also insidiously co-opt the terminology of the Holocaust for their own purposes. Zapiro's cartoon is typical of the abuse of the Holocaust analogy. Campus events cry out: "Holocaust Victims threatening a new and even bigger Holocaust."[28] Equally offensive is the Muslim groups' cynical appropriation of the term "Never Again," which Jews embraced following the Holocaust, applying it to Israel's supposed current actions against the Palestinians.[29]

ANTI-ZIONISM BECOMES ANTISEMITISM

Despite all the obvious conflation of anti-Israelism/anti-Zionism and antisemitism, Muslim students deny any connection. "Zionists," they say, "are guilty of using the word 'anti-Semite' too freely to label everyone who criticized Israel and Zionism but this undermines those who suffer under truly anti-Semitic conditions."[30] This is the typical pattern of denial — and intentional distortion of meaning — by those who espouse antisemitism under the guise of anti-Zionism. They vehemently proclaim that they agree that it is wrong to hate "a religion" and that labeling them "anti-Semitic" is only "a scare tactic" to silence them.[31] But in the process of denouncing the critics who dare to call them antisemites, they further reveal themselves as such.

Consulting the definitions drawn up by the European Monitoring Center on Racism and Xenophobia and adopted by the United States Government, one can see how South Africa's Muslim student groups have repeatedly crossed the line between "criticism of Israel" and antisemitism, particularly by:

- Denying the Jewish people their right to self-determination
- Using the symbols and images associated with classic antisemitism to characterize Israel or Israelis
- Drawing comparisons of contemporary Israeli policy to that of the Nazis
- Holding Jews collectively responsible for actions of the state of Israel.

When Muslim students characterize the creation of Israel only as the "Nakba" (Arabic for catastrophe), that is denying Israel's right to self-determination. When Muslim students declare Israel to be part of a global conspiracy aligned with the United States and other world powers to "tighten the economic stranglehold on the Palestinians," that is using the symbols and images associated with classic antisemitism. When Muslim students design posters declaring that Holocaust victims are perpetrating an even larger Holocaust, that is drawing comparisons of Israeli policy to that of the Nazis. And when Muslim students work to publicly call on the South African Union of Jewish Students to denounce Zionism and Israeli policy, that is holding Jews collectively responsible for actions of the state of Israel.

Muslim students vehemently deny they are antisemitic, but the atmosphere they have created for their fellow Jewish students betrays precisely that — and this is the irony of it all. For the descendants of Russian Jews who envisioned South Africa's streets "paved with gold," Muslim students are turning the land into one resembling the Russian Empire they fled.

Gregg J. Rickman, Ph.D, served as the first U.S. Special Envoy to Monitor and Combat Anti-Semitism from 2006–2009. He is a Senior Fellow for the Study and Combat of Anti-Semitism at the Institute on Religion and Policy in Washington, DC; a Visiting Fellow at The Yale Initiative for the Interdisciplinary Study of Antisemitism at Yale University; and a Research Scholar at the Initiative on Anti-Semitism and Anti-Israelism of the Institute for Jewish & Community Research in San Francisco.

ENDNOTES

1   Farhana Ismail, "Harvard Professor Parallels Zionism and Apartheid," *Wits Palestine Solidarity Committee of South Africa* (henceforth, *WPSCSA*) *Quarterly Newsletter*, Issue 2.2, Block 2 (July 2007), p. 1, reprinted in the *Vuvzela Newspaper* (May 17, 2007).

2 South African Jewish Students Union, "South African Universities: A context," December 2009, p. 2.

3 Natasha Vally, "A Year of Solidarity," *WPSCSA Quarterly Newsletter*, Issue 4, Block 4 (December 2006), p. 1.

4 Moishe Levin, *From Vilna to Johannesburg* (Johannesburg: Beacon, 1965), p. 51, quoted in Gwynne Schrire, *From Eastern Europe to South Africa: Memories of An Epic Journey, 1880–1937*, Jacob Gitlin Library, Western Province Zionist Council, Cape Town, South Africa, p. 6.

5 David Saks, *South African Jewry, A Contemporary Portrait*, Institute of the World Jewish Congress, Policy Study No. 25, 2003, p. 5.

6 "South African Universities: A context," December 2009, p. 1.

7 Email from the South African Union of Jewish Students to the author, December 10, 2009.

8 Ibid.

9 Email from the South African Board of Jewish Deputies to the author, December 8, 2009.

10 Author's discussion with a former Witwatersrand student, Johannesburg, South Africa, March 24, 2008.

11 International Israeli Apartheid Week flyer, Wits Palestine Solidarity Committee, 2008.

12 State Department report to the United States Congress, *Contemporary Global Anti-Semitism*, March 2008, pp. 6–7.

13 Gideon Shimoni, "Deconstructing Apartheid Accusations Against Israel," *Middle East Strategic Information*, March 24, 2008. http://mesi.org.uk/ViewArticle.aspx?ArticleId=106

14 "Israeli Conscientious Objectors visit South Africa," Website of Amandla Intifada, November 15, 2009. http://sayeddhansay.wordpress.com/2009/11/15/israeli-conscientious-objectors-visit-south-africa/

15 Natasha Vally, "A Year of Solidarity," *WPSCSA Quarterly Newsletter*.

16 Cartoon of Jonathan Shapiro, *Cape Times*, March 12, 2008.

17 "Norman Finkelstein in South Africa, Everything you need to know about Professor Norman G. Finkelstein's visit to South Africa." http://normanfinkelsteininsouthafrica.wordpress.com/about/

18 Hedy Epstein, "When I see the word Palestine," *WPSCSA Quarterly Newsletter*, Issue 1, Block 1 (March 2006), p. 2.

19 *WPSCSA Quarterly Newsletter*, Issue 2.2, Block 2 (July 2007).

20 "In the Matter of 'Cook for Peace' to be held on Sunday 16 March at the University of Johannesburg," MSA press release, March 15, 2008.

21 "To the Organisers and Participants, Israel Apartheid Week, Message of Ronnie Kasrils, M.P.," reprinted in the *WPSCSA Quarterly Newsletter*, Issue 2.1, Block 1 (2007), p. 1.

22 Letter of Ms. Ursula Nyar, Legal Officer, Gauteng Provincial Office, South African Human Rights Commission to Bongani Masuku, International Relations Secretary COSATU, December 3, 2009, pp. 2–3.

23 Ibid, pp. 8–9.

24 South African Jewish Board of Deputies, "Antisemitism Reports Relating To Incidents On South African University Campuses, 2006–2009."

25 "Why the need," WPSCSA Quarterly Newsletter, Issue 1, Block 1 (March 2006), p. 2.

26 "Visibility Campaign," campus handout, Witwatersrand University, March 19, 2008.

27 Yumna Mahomed, "Israel Apartheid Week 2007," WPSCSA Quarterly Newsletter, Issue 2.1, Block 1 (2007), p. 1.

28 Report by the South African Jewish Board of Deputies, 2008.

29 Ibid.

30 Yumna Mohamed, "De-constructing Anti-Semitism," WPSCSA Quarterly Newsletter, Issue 4, Block 4 (December 2006), p. 1.

31 Ibid.

ANTISEMITISM
IN THE ACADEMIC VOICE

Kenneth Lasson

Universities perceive themselves as places of culture in a chaotic world, as protectors of reasoned discourse, peaceful havens where learned professors roam orderly quadrangles, pondering higher thoughts. The real world of higher education is not quite so wonderful. Among the abuses of the academic enterprise that have been taking place in American universities over the past several decades are failures of intellectual rigor — failures of facts, common sense, and logic — often presented in the academic voice. Instead of a community of scholars thirsting for knowledge in sylvan tranquility, we are confronted with academics promoting narrow political agendas, many of them — in England and Europe but in elite American universities as well — quick to voice strident opposition to the Jewish State.

Although the number of overt antisemitic incidents has declined markedly in the United States over the past few years, there has been a significant increase in anti-Zionist rhetoric and activity on campuses around the country. Although antisemitism and anti-Zionism are distinct concepts, currently they are often confluent. Anti-Zionism, in its narrowest dimension an argument against the political realization of the State of Israel, has been transformed into a catchword for antisemitism, a cloak behind which bigots often hide. Recently a number of academics have used this cover for their antisemitic views.[1] This essay examines how the relationship between antisemitism and anti-Zionism plays out on contemporary university campuses.

THE HISTORICAL BACKDROP

Antisemitism is not a new phenomenon in the academy. It can be traced to Karl Marx, the father of modern leftist thought, whose essay *On the Jewish*

Question was a virulent attack on Jews. To Marx, the profane basis of Judaism was "practical need," self-interest; the worldly cult of the Jew was "huckstering;" his worldly god, "Money." In emancipating itself from huckstering and money — and thereby from real and practical Judaism — our age would emancipate itself, he contended. The emancipation of the Jew is the emancipation of mankind from Judaism.[2] Marx was a classic antisemite, not unlike those who fabricated *The Protocols of the Elders of Zion*, who see the world captured and destroyed by Jewish values, practices and conspiracies. The message is that all would be well if the world were rid of the Jews.[3]

Some scholars offer a psychological explanation for Marx's antipathy to Jewry. He could not shed being branded a Jew, although he did not consider himself one. His father, who had changed his name from Herschel Levi to Heinrich Marx, converted to Christianity and had his children baptized as well.[4]

Other forebears of the modern Jewish left were hostile to Israel and often to Jews as well. Jewish members of the Communist Party drew a line between themselves and the larger Jewish community — even though they had to form their own branch of the party, which was openly antisemitic at times.[5]

Whatever their political leanings — Left or Right — those who demonize Israel or Jews have often relied on the Big Lie. Israel has long stood accused of conducting a brutal occupation of lands inhabited by indigenous, peace-seeking Arabs, though the evidence is overwhelming that these characterizations have no substantial basis in fact. Instead, they are a manifestation of the truth-twisting tactic made notorious by Nazi propagandists during World War II.[6]

Israel's "occupation" began subsequent to its 1967 victory in the Six Day War, when Jews began to resettle the Biblical areas of Judea and Samaria, which had been under Jordanian control since 1948. Initially, Arab reactions were positive. Jews regularly visited Arab towns and villages and employed and assisted the residents; the Arab living-standard improved significantly as per-capita income rose and modern infrastructures were developed. Tourism flourished. Arabs and Jews worked and shopped together in Haifa, Ramallah, and Bethlehem. Roadblocks were virtually unknown.[7]

These relationships were dramatically altered with the signing of the Oslo Accords of 1993. Emboldened by the promise of a Palestinian state in Judea, Samaria, and Gaza, Arab extremists demanded the removal of all Jewish communities in their midst, claiming the lands as exclusively their own. In 1994, Israel granted the Palestinian Authority autonomous control of the major Arab cities and towns in these territories.[8]

At this time, however, a new rallying cry — "End the Occupation" — was introduced. Few questioned the incongruity that Jews would be branded occupiers of Judea, the province historically named for its Jewish residents. No one considered it odd that Jews were now accused of occupying parts of Jerusalem, known since the dawn of history as a Jewish city. In fact, Jews — not Arabs — were sovereign in Judea, Samaria, Jerusalem, and the lands west of the Jordan River for a thousand years.[9]

Nowhere did the Big Lie become more popular than in the universities, where scores of anti-Zionist professors developed myths to denigrate Israel as an occupier, specifically as a brutal occupier of Arab lands. They claim that Israel's military has responded to Arab resistance with cruelty and insensitivity, purposely setting up humiliating checkpoints in order to harass innocent Arabs. They ignore the fact that no other army has been confronted daily — and for so extended a period — with more suicide bombers, deadly ambushes, drive-by shootings, kidnappings, and rock-throwing interspersed with rifle fire. Other democratic nations recognize the Israel Defense Forces as models of humane behavior, thoroughly trained to respect the sanctity of life and to demonstrate an individual and collective morality, which greatly exceeds that of other armed forces.[10]

ANTISEMITISM AND ANTI-ZIONISM
ON CONTEMPORARY CAMPUSES
Statistics and Narratives

According to the Anti-Defamation League (ADL), since 2002 there has been an average of 88 antisemitic incidents each year on American university campuses.[11] These numbers include only the reported and documented incidents. Many acts remain unreported out of fear, intimidation, or embarrassment.[12]

The most overt antisemitism experienced by college students appears in the form of harassment and intimidation, ranging from minor physical contact (such as spitting) to extreme violence involving lethal weapons. Such attacks can be traced back at least fifteen years. In March 1995 two Jewish students at the University of Pennsylvania were walking near campus when they were confronted by two students shouting derogatory epithets at them. One harasser went into a house and returned with a shotgun, with which he threatened them. The police and university officials questioned the perpetrators and confiscated several weapons, though the students ultimately decided not to press charges.[13]

Such bigotry has continued on American campuses in the twenty-first century. The University of California at Irvine (UCI) boasts a student body of about 24,000, of which 1,000 are Jewish. Since at least 2002 a pattern of antisemitism has emerged on the campus, which includes destruction of property, physical threats, and violence. In 2002, an article in a UCI student publication stressed that Jews are genetically inferior to non-Jews. The same year, posters appeared on campus depicting the Star of David dripping with blood and equating the traditional Jewish symbol with the swastika.[14] In 2003, a Holocaust memorial on campus, which was supposed to stay up for a week, was destroyed after the first night. While a candlelight vigil commemorating the victims of the Holocaust was being held on campus, Jewish students found that a swastika had been carved into a nearby table.[15]

In February 2004, a Jewish student who spoke and understood Arabic was walking inside an academic building wearing a "United We Stand" pin with an imprint of the American and Israeli flags. An Arab student who spotted the pin shouted "Ee Bakh al Yahud" — "Slaughter the Jews." The two began a heated dialogue, which ended with the Jewish student being surrounded and threatened. Later, while walking across campus wearing a yarmulke and carrying a prayer book, the same student was subjected to obscene gestures, ethnic slurs, and threatening language. He left the university soon after to study elsewhere.[16]

UCI is hardly the only university to experience such harassment.[17] The same month Arab and Muslim students at San Francisco State University (SFSU) staged an anti-Israel rally featuring posters of soup cans marked "Made in Israel," the contents labeled "Palestinian Children Meat;" pictured on the bottom of the can were a baby, its stomach sliced open, and the words "according to Jewish Rites under American license."[18]

Pro-Palestinian rallies at SFSU have often served as sites where supposed anti-Zionism has readily merged into overt antisemitism. In May 2002, four hundred Jewish students, attempting to engage in dialogue with Palestinian students, held a "Sit-in for Peace in the Middle East." At the rally, students voiced support for Israel and hope for a peaceful settlement. When the event concluded and about thirty of the Jewish students were cleaning up, pro-Palestinian students surrounded them, screaming, "Hitler didn't finish the job," "Fuck the Jews," and "Die racist pigs." Responding to the incident, university and city police formed a barrier between the Jewish and pro-Palestinian students, eventually funneling the Jewish students out of the plaza. Yitzhak Santis, director of Middle East Affairs for the Jewish Community Relations Council in San Francisco, who attended the rally, stated that he felt very threatened by these acts. Karen Alexander was "convinced that if the police had not been present there would have been violence" (San Francisco *Dispatch*, June 14, 2002).[19]

The most prevalent form of harassment may be psychological intimidation, often expressed through acts of vandalism. In February 2006, "kike" was painted on the front porch of a Jewish fraternity house at the University of California, Berkeley. Later the same year other American universities reported similar incidents.[20] A more extreme example occurred near Brown University in 2008. Yossi Knafo, an emissary from the Jewish Agency of Israel, was in his kitchen when firebombs were thrown at his building, burning the exterior. Although Knafo escaped unharmed, the incident had a profound effect on students; the Hillel house was locked down, and a police officer had to be stationed outside. In an open dialogue with campus officials, students explained that they felt unsafe and vulnerable.[21]

The frequency of anti-Zionist incidents tends to increase directly with the intensity of negative reports about Israel. During the intifada of the 1980s, expressions of anti-Zionism rose sharply, reflecting the perceived evils perpetrated by the Israeli army against Palestinians. During the 1988-89 school year, the University of Michigan student newspaper regularly published anti-Israel statements, including several editorials censuring a Jewish student group that was calling attention to Arab terrorism.[22]

The incidence of anti-Zionist invective declined after the 1991 Gulf War and the election of a Labor government in Israel in 1992; similarly, a period of relative tranquility followed the assassination of Israeli prime minister Yitzhak Rabin in November 1995. There were, however, a number of exceptions. On the Monday after Rabin's assassination, California State (Fresno) University's *Daily Collegian* carried an article by Hadi Yazdanpanah that venomously attacked Israel and Jews. The author attributed numerous quotes to anonymous students, including, "When they [the Jews] disobeyed G-d, they broke the covenant; from that point on it's no longer their land."[23]

In the early years of the twenty-first century, as Yasser Arafat refused to abide by the Oslo Accords and the second intifada began, the frequency of anti-Zionist/antisemitic incidents increased once again. At UCI a registered student group initiated what would become an annual "Anti-Zionist Week," "Zionist Awareness Week," and "Israel Awareness Week." The message was always the same, with speeches and harangues repeatedly insisting that an insidious Jewish lobby controls the U.S. Government, that the Jews use the media to "brainwash" others, and that Jews need to be "rehabilitated" from the "psychosis" that exists in their community.[24]

Such events have left many Jewish students feeling alienated and marginalized, afraid to identify themselves as Jews or supporters of the Jewish state. In 2002, a female graduate student wrote a letter to the UCI Chancellor, explaining:

> Not only do I feel scared to walk around proudly as a Jewish person on the UC Irvine campus, I am terrified for anyone to find out. Today I felt threatened that if students knew that I am Jewish and that I support a Jewish state, I would be attacked physically. It is my right to walk around this campus and not fear other students and hear condemnation from them. It is my right for my government to protect me from harm from others. It is my right as a citizen who pays tuition and taxes to be protected from such harm....YOU may claim the first amendment. I claim the right to be safe and secure. You cannot use the first amendment as an argument against my safety. MY SAFETY SUPERSEDES FIRST AMENDMENT RIGHTS.[25]

The same year a construction site for new dormitories at UC, Santa Barbara was defaced with anti-Israel/antisemitic graffiti, including "Anti Zion/Nuke Israel," "God Hates Jews," and "Burn the Torah." At the University of Colorado, Boulder, anti-Zionist/antisemitic messages, including "Your Tax Dollars are Paying to Kill Palestinian Children," were scrawled on sidewalks across campus on the first day of the planned observance of Holocaust Awareness Week. The next day at UC Berkeley, seventy-nine pro-Palestinian protesters were arrested after storming into a university hall in an attempt to disrupt a Holocaust Remembrance Day commemoration. Following a pro-Israel rally at SFSU, Jewish students, faculty, and campus visitors were verbally assaulted and threatened. A group of pro-Palestinian counter-demonstrators hurled epithets at the crowd, including, "Go back to Russia" and "Hitler did not finish the job."[26]

Many similar demonstrations have occurred on California campuses. In September 2008, a pro-Israel poster at a bus-stop at UC Berkeley was defaced with antisemitic graffiti, including swastikas.[27] In May 2009, a massive "Apartheid Wall" was erected at UC Irvine, displaying inflammatory photographs and accusing Israel of deliberately targeting Palestinian children.[28] Graffiti smeared on a building at UC Santa Cruz screamed that Jews were behind the 9/11 attacks.[29]

Similar incidents occurred on other campuses around the country in 2008, including at Anna Maria College (where swastikas and "white power" were drawn on hallway walls); Baylor University (swastikas appeared near the dorm room of a student who had recently converted to Judaism); Illinois State University (KKK fliers distributed on campus); Middlesex County (NJ) College (antisemitic graffiti); Rowan University (swastikas and "Hitler is awesome" painted on dormitory); Rutgers University (antisemitic graffiti); Saint Xavier University (neo-Nazi group demonstrated outside building where Holocaust survivor Elie Wiesel was lecturing); Seton Hall University (numerous antisemitic and racial slurs on restroom walls); Temple University (two individuals physically assaulted and subjected to antisemitic taunts); University of North Carolina (Jewish student harassed by new roommate, who claimed that Jews control world's banking and entertainment industries); University of North Dakota (student taunted with antisemitic slurs, then shot at with pellet gun); and University of Oregon (Holocaust denier David Irving addressed students at event sponsored by Pacifica Forum).[30]

Although anti-Israel activity is not necessarily antisemitic, when the Jewish state is accused of war crimes for responding forcefully to terrorist bombardments of its citizens — as in the incursion into Gaza, Operation Cast Lead — the antisemitic sentiment is clear. As Abraham Foxman, national director of the Anti-Defamation League, puts it: "Sixty years after the Holocaust, we are watching one layer after another of the constraints against anti-Semitism, which arose as a result of the murder of six million, being peeled away. The world is losing its shame about anti-Semitism. As a result, anti-Semitism is becoming more acceptable in more and more circles."[31]

ANTISEMITISM IN THE CLASSROOM

Antisemitism in the academy is not limited to outsiders or students, but often emanates from faculty as well. As the ADL puts it, "From behind their lecterns at respected institutions of higher learning, under the cover of pseudo-scholarship, they try to make bigotry sound respectable." These professors have not only turned their classrooms into breeding grounds for ethnic hatred, but have also been rewarded with lucrative lecture fees.[32]

Leonard Jeffries, former head of the Black Studies Department at the City College of New York (CCNY), began teaching in 1972, but only achieved national notoriety when he announced in class that "rich Jews who financed the development of Europe also financed the slave trade."[33]

More controversy ensued in 1991 following a speech Jeffries gave at the Empire State Black Arts and Cultural Festival in Albany, where he declared that "rich Jews" financed the slave trade and control the film industry, using it to project a negative stereotype of blacks. He also attacked Diane Ravitch, a member of the task force he was on to fight racism in the public school curriculum — she was then Assistant U.S. Secretary of Education — describing her as a "sophisticated Texas Jew," "a debonair racist," and "Miss Daisy."[34]

Jeffries was a featured speaker at the antisemitic, anti-white, Black Holocaust Nationhood Conference held in Washington D.C., October 14 and 15, 1995. Jeffries, a tenured professor, still teaches at CCNY and still lectures at colleges and universities around the country.[35]

OUTSIDE THE CLASSROOM

The intense antipathy toward Israel on American campuses shocked an Arab-Israeli journalist touring the United States to promote peaceful dialogue about the Middle East conflict. In March 2009 Khaled Abu Toameh often found himself confronted by hostile audiences, who told him that Israel has no right to exist, that its "apartheid system" is worse than the one that had existed in South Africa, and that Israel launched Operation Cast Lead only because Hamas was signaling that it was interested in making peace (and not because of the rockets that Hamas and its affiliates repeatedly directed at Israeli communities).[36]

He was informed that all the talk about financial corruption in the Palestinian Authority was "Zionist propaganda," and that Yasser Arafat had done wonderful things for his people, including the establishment of schools, hospitals and universities.[37] Toameh regarded his hecklers as "hard-line activists/thugs:"

> If these folks really cared about the Palestinians, they would be campaigning for good government and for the promotion of values of democracy and freedom in the West Bank and Gaza Strip. Their hatred for Israel and what it stands for has blinded them to a point where they no longer care about the real interests of the Palestinians, namely the need to end the anarchy and lawlessness, and to dismantle all the armed gangs that are responsible for the death of hundreds of innocent Palestinians over the past few years. The majority of these activists openly admit that they have never visited Israel or the Palestinian territories. They don't know — and don't want to know — that Jews and Arabs here are still doing business together and studying together and meeting with each other on a daily basis because they are destined to live together in this part of the world.[38]

Toameh concluded that what is happening on the U.S. campuses is less about supporting the Palestinians than about promoting hatred for the Jewish state — that it is not about ending the "occupation" but about ending the existence of Israel.[39]

A significant part of the anti-Israel lobbying and instruction on campus appears to be funded by an Iranian front organization, which supports pro-Iranian anti-Zionist professors. For example, hundreds of thousands of dollars have been donated to fund Middle East studies and Persian studies at Columbia University and Rutgers, where courses are taught by academics who openly express sympathy for the terrorist groups Hezbollah and Hamas.[40]

A recent report by the Reut Institute, a Tel Aviv-based think-tank, describes a "new battlefield" in which a new front of individuals and academic and human rights groups — "Hubs of Delegitimization" — has formed, which focus their attacks on Israel's political legitimacy, depicting it as a pariah state, and mobilizing its Arab minority in the struggle.[41]

The report distinguishes between "soft critics" of Israel and "hard-core delegitimizers," the latter seeking to blur any distinction between criticism of Israeli policy and the legitimacy of the Jewish State. In the massive effort to demonize Israel, the groups often support an "all-or-nothing" strategy, holding that boycotts are the only option.[42]

ACADEMIC BOYCOTTS OF ISRAEL

In the United States, more than a few campuses have become hotbeds of anti-Israel activism. In February 2006, campuses all over North America commemorated "Israel Apartheid Week." This followed a campaign that originated in Great Britain, whose largest academic association voted several times over the past five years to encourage a boycott of Israeli universities and faculty over what it called Israel's "apartheid" policies toward Palestinians. It stated that union members should refuse to cooperate with Israeli academics who do not "disassociate themselves from such policies."[43] A "silent boycott" by some may be in effect. In 2006, for example, Bar-Ilan University made public a letter in which a British professor refused to write for an Israeli academic journal because of what he called the "brutal and illegal expansionism and the slow-motion ethnic cleansing" perpetrated by the Israeli government.[44]

Although many countries routinely apply a double-standard toward Israel, the academic and scientific boycotts being urged against the Jewish state are still jolting and dismaying. In his ascent to power Adolph Hitler was highly successful among university professors, many of whom were drawn into the higher echelons of the Nazi party and participated in its gruesome excesses. Mussolini too had a large following of intellectuals, not all of them Italian. So did Stalin and Mao Tze-tung.[45]

Students are increasingly confronted by curricula manipulated by pseudo-scholarly extremists. Principles of academic freedom and the universality of science have not prevented such noxious campaigns. The quest for "balance" raises problems of its own. How much balance? Must Holocaust studies be balanced by Holocaust denial? Should evolution be balanced by "intelligent design?" Does the obligation cover every point taught in a course, or only major disputes? Who should enforce the norm?

The current campaign against Israeli scholars began in April 2002 in England. Its specific goals were to inhibit Israeli scholars from obtaining outside grants; to persuade academic institutions to sever relations with Israeli universities and faculty; to convince academics not to visit Israel and not to invite Israelis to conferences; to prevent the publication of articles by Israeli scholars and to refuse to review their work; to deny recommendations to students who wished to study in Israel; to promote universities' divestment of Israeli securities and American suppliers of weapons to Israel; and in some cases to expel Jewish organizations from campus.[46]

Over 700 academics ultimately signed the boycott petition — most of them British, but a number from other European countries as well.[47] There were, however, swift condemnations of the various boycott/divestment campaigns against Israel — most notably by then-president of Harvard, Lawrence Summers; Judith Rodin, president of the University of Pennsylvania; and Lee Bollinger, president of Columbia University. They pointed out that many countries involved in the Middle East conflict have been aggressors and yet calls for divestment against them have been absent.[48] This raises the possibility that the real motivation behind boycott and divestment campaigns against Israel is anti-Zionism, which, many point out, is a razor-thin line away from antisemitism.

Although the campaigns have many supporters, Middle Eastern and Islamic studies faculty are often in the lead. Prominent academics in the field make antisemitic statements. Columbia University students reported intimidation and hostility by faculty members in the Department of Middle East and Asian Languages and Cultures (MEALAC), at least part of whose funding comes from the United Arab Emirates. In one incident, Professor Joseph Massad allegedly challenged an Israeli student, "How many Palestinians have you killed?" He told a class that "the Palestinian is the new Jew, and the Jew is the new Nazi." According to another account, he repeated 24 times in a half-hour period that "Israel is a racist Jewish apartheid oppressive state." He allegedly yelled at a Jewish student, "I will not have anybody here deny Israeli atrocities." More than a third of MEALAC faculty signed a petition calling for the university to divest from companies doing business with Israel. The department chair, Hamid Dabashi, refers openly to Israel's "brutal massacres" of innocent Palestinians.[49]

In 2005 the academic boycotts were pressed anew in Great Britain and elsewhere. Despite the fact that in 2002 Prime Minister Tony Blair privately told the Chief Rabbi of Great Britain, Jonathan Sacks, that the government would not tolerate a boycott of Israel, the university establishment continues in that direction.[50]

DIVESTMENT CAMPAIGNS

A new incarnation of the anti-Israel boycott is the university divestment campaign — similar to the one directed earlier at South Africa's apartheid regime. This one demands that universities divest from companies that do business with Israel.

A University of California student group "Students for Justice in Palestine" launched the organized divestment campaign. Since then, many campuses have followed suit. At least two major universities — the University of California and the University of Michigan — have hosted divestment conferences. In 2002 faculty at Harvard and the Massachusetts Institute of Technology began an ongoing divestment campaign.[51]

Faculty supporters of divestment and academic/scientific boycotts often chafe at the charge that they are antisemitic. A Harvard professor told a reporter that he was "definitely hostile to the aggressive eye-for-an-eye, tooth-for-a-tooth policies of the current Israeli leadership," but that he didn't "consider himself antisemitic at all."[52]

A number of Jewish professors have also joined the divestiture/boycott movement. No matter the provocation, they insist that Israel must always respond humanely and nonviolently. Given the actual situation, this amounts to asking Jews only to be victims.

ISRAEL AS AN "APARTHEID STATE"

The number of campuses hosting an "Israel Apartheid Week" has been increasing every year since 2006.[53] According to the organizers of the events, the aim is "to contribute to this chorus of international opposition to Israeli apartheid... [and] an end to the occupation and colonization of all Arab lands — including the Golan Heights, the Occupied West Bank,... East

Jerusalem and the Gaza Strip — and dismantling the Wall, and the protection of Palestinian refugees' right to return to their homes and properties."[54]

As Martin Luther King, Jr., said shortly before he was assassinated, "When people criticize Zionists, they mean Jews. You are talking antisemitism."[55] What would he have said about the comparisons being made between modern Israel and apartheid South Africa? The fundamental differences should be evident, but many distortions are promulgated by the Palestinians and circulated by the media. Although academic boycotts were virtually unknown before the campaign against apartheid in South Africa — where they were used largely at the behest of that country's own scholars as a means of pressuring the minority white government — there was never an attempt to cut off all South African academics from international discourse with their peers.

The campaign to equate Israel with apartheid South Africa overlooks incontrovertible facts:

- Israel's Declaration of Independence (1948) announced that the state "will ensure equality of social and political rights to all its inhabitants irrespective of religion, race or sex."
- Israeli Arabs attend and lecture in every Israeli university. Moreover, an overwhelming majority of Israeli Arabs have consistently stated that they would prefer to remain in Israel rather than join a future Palestinian state.
- Israeli-Arabs serve in the Knesset and can serve in the army, if they wish. An Arab justice (Salim Joubran) holds a seat on Israel's Supreme Court. Even diplomatic positions are open to Israeli Arabs, who have held posts in the United States, South America, Finland, and elsewhere.[56]

No such exercises in democracy occurred in apartheid South Africa. Why are there no boycotts of Muslim countries, where academic freedom doesn't exist or is under constant attack, as in Syria, Egypt, Iran, and Saudi Arabia? Is it because the boycotters' real goal is the elimination of Israel, which they condemn as a "colonial apartheid state, more insidious than South Africa"?

No one has proposed that Chinese scholars be boycotted over what their government is doing to the Tibetans, or Russian scholars for their actions against Chechnya, or Indonesians for their treatment of civilians in East Timor. Indeed a number of countries today — including China, Russia, Turkey, Iraq, Spain, even France — control disputed land and rule over people seeking independence. Those pushing for academic boycotts against Israel should be asked why the United Nations has passed hundreds of resolutions censuring Israel — but few condemning known terrorist organizations or states.

Other countries have treated Arabs much more harshly. Jordan killed more Palestinians in a single month (an estimated four thousand, in September 1970) than Israel ever has; Kuwait expelled 300,000 Palestinians during the Persian Gulf War. On the other hand, no Arab country has contributed to the Palestinians' humanitarian needs nearly as much as the United States and Israel have.[57]

Today some 90,000 slaves serve the ruling class in Mauritania. In Sudan, Arab northerners raid southern villages, killing the men and capturing the women and children, to be sold into slavery. Where was the academic outcry against slavery in 2007? Where are the protests against Saudi Arabian apartheid, where women, Christians, Jews, and Hindus are denied equal rights?

HOLOCAUST DENIAL

Promoters of Holocaust denial, another form of antisemitism, have specifically targeted American university students.[58] Using campus newspapers, videos, DVDs, and the Internet, they seek to initiate a "debate" over whether the Holocaust happened. These self-styled intellectuals are able to disseminate their message by presenting their work as legitimate academic inquiry. Student editors eager to demonstrate their commitment to free speech and the airing of controversial ideas have facilitated the dissemination of their views. Thus they allow deniers to reach impressionable students, who are forming their own perceptions of the past, and often have little knowledge of the Holocaust.[59]

Holocaust deniers claim to be legitimate historical "revisionists" seeking to uncover the truth behind what they term the greatest hoax of the twentieth century. They score propaganda points merely by convincing students that the existence of the Holocaust is debatable.

Holocaust denial emerged as an organized movement in 1979 when Willis Carto's Liberty Lobby, the nation's largest antisemitic organization at the time, established the Institute for Historical Review (IHR), which enables professors with limited credentials in history and other antisemites to engage in pseudo-academic efforts to deny the Holocaust. Through the IHR and his own company, Noontide Press, Carto helped publish books on white racialism, including Francis Parker Yockey's *Imperium* and David Hoggan's *The Myth of the Six Million*, two of the first books to deny the Holocaust.[60]

The IHR had its biggest impact on campuses under its Media Projects Director, Bradley Smith, who heads the Committee for Open Debate on the Holocaust. In 1991, Smith bought a full-page advertisement in *The Daily*

Northwestern, the student publication of Northwestern University. The ad looked like a newspaper article and was headlined "The Holocaust Story: How Much is False? The Case for Open Debate." In it, Smith argued that the "Holocaust lobby" prevents scholars from thoroughly examining the "orthodox Holocaust story." He alleged that there was no proof that Jews were gassed at Auschwitz, and that the piles of corpses photographed at Bergen-Belsen resulted from disease and starvation, not from a Nazi plan to murder Jews. Smith made his case in the academic voice — not using blatantly antisemitic terms, but a seemingly thoughtful, rational argument intended to provoke serious academic consideration.[61]

Smith's advertisement in *The Daily Northwestern* sparked a flurry of opinion pieces, letters to the editor, and on-campus lectures and forums. These activities, in turn, resulted in wider media coverage in the Chicago area. Emboldened, Smith submitted his ads/essays to other university newspapers, beginning with that of the University of Michigan. In the next year, they appeared in more than a third of the sixty campus papers to which they were submitted.[62]

Smith launched another campaign during the 1993-94 school year, challenging the authenticity of the newly opened U.S. Holocaust Memorial Museum and attacking Deborah Lipstadt's book *Denying the Holocaust: The Growing Assault on Truth and Memory*. Smith charged that Professor Lipstadt, and others like her, work to suppress "revisionist" research, and he called for an end to their "fascist behavior."[63]

By the end of that academic year, Smith's ad had appeared in thirty-two campus newspapers, including *The Justice*, the student publication of predominantly Jewish Brandeis University. The ad, which cost $130, caused a media frenzy, including coverage in the *New York Times*, Washington *Post*, and *Time*. The check for the ad was not cashed, but was donated to the U.S. Holocaust Memorial Museum — which refused to cash it.[64]

In mid-April 1995, Smith began another ad campaign, deploying the same advertisement he used the year before. The ad was distributed on or right after Yom Hashoah (Holocaust Remembrance Day), near the end of the academic year. Although only seventeen school newspapers printed it, the timing almost precluded an effective response.[65]

Smith has continued to be active over the last decade. In September 2009, the Harvard *Crimson* published one of his ads, which raised questions about General Eisenhower's account of World War II and the existence of Nazi gas chambers. The ad was quickly criticized and the student editor issued an apology for printing it.[66]

AMERICAN VOICES, OUT OF THE WILDERNESS

Some academic leaders of anti-Zionist and antisemitic campaigns have openly embraced terrorists. In May 2006, famed MIT professor of linguistics Noam Chomsky began an eight-day visit to Lebanon where he met with leaders of the terrorist organization Hezbollah. There he received a hero's welcome and effectively acted as a propagandist for the group, repeating its rhetoric and lies on Lebanese television, including Hezbollah's Al Manar TV.[67]

Chomsky expressed support for arming Hezbollah, in direct contradiction to UN Security Council resolution 1559. He said, "Hezbollah's insistence on keeping its arms is justified.... I think [Hezbollah leader Sheikh Hassan] Nasrallah has a reasoned argument and [a] persuasive argument that they [the arms] should be in the hands of Hezbollah as a deterrent to potential aggression, and there is plenty of background reasons for that."[68] Little more than a month after Chomsky left Lebanon, Hezbollah used its arms to launch an attack on Israel.

Although born to Jewish parents, Chomsky embraces Nasrallah, who calls Jews the "grandsons of apes and pigs." Hezbollah's ideology, rooted in a fundamentalist and antisemitic interpretation of Islam, has been described as the "direct ideological heir of the Nazis."[69] Chomsky's statements and actions typify those of what some call "the unholy alliance between Islamic extremists and secular radicals in the West." Chomsky, who describes the United States as "one of the leading terrorist states," claims that the attacks of 9/11 pale in comparison to the terror America perpetrated, for example, in the 1973 coup that overthrew Chilean president Allende.[70]

For decades Chomsky has used his celebrity as a prominent linguist to support militant organizations, including not only Hezbollah and Hamas, but also the Khmer Rouge in Cambodia, and murderous dictators such as Slobodan Milosevic in Serbia. He minimizes the atrocities and murders these groups have committed, while implicating those he perpetually depicts as the guilty parties — the United States and Israel.[71]

The Israel Lobby by University of Chicago professor John Mearsheimer and Harvard professor Stephen Walt has had an impact in part because the authors were considered respected scholars. Yet the book presents a conspiratorial view of history in which the "Israel lobby" is seen to have a "stranglehold" on American foreign policy, the American media, think tanks, and academia. Alan Dershowitz, professor of law at Harvard, observes that the authors often wrench quotations out of context, misstate or omit important facts, and frequently rely on embarrassingly weak logic. Dershowitz asks why, in light of such errors and a lack of originality, Mearsheimer and Walt chose to publish a paper and then a book that do not meet their usual scholarly standards — especially given the likelihood that the book's charges, recycled under their imprimatur as prominent scholars, would be featured, as they have been, on extremist websites.[72]

Mearshimer and Walt write, "[T]he United States has a terrorism problem in good part because it is so closely allied with Israel, not the other way around. There is no question, for example, that many Al Qaeda leaders, including Bin Laden, are motivated by Israel's presence in Jerusalem and the plight of the Palestinians."[73] In fact, Bin Laden was motivated by the presence of American troops in Saudi Arabia, which had asked the United States to defend the Arabian Peninsula against Iraqi aggression prior to the first Gulf War. It was America's ties to, and defense of, an Arab state — from which fifteen of the nineteen hijackers originated — and not the Jewish state, that precipitated the 9/11 attack. Prior to 9/11, Israel was barely on Bin Laden's radar screen. Nor does Israel's supposed domination of American public life explain terrorist massacres in Bali, Madrid, London, and elsewhere. Europe, after all, is praised for being more immune to manipulation by the lobby.[74]

Mearsheimer and Walt claim that "contrary to popular belief, the Zionists had larger, better-equipped, and better-led forces [than the Arabs] during Israel's War of Independence." The authors are trying to persuade readers that despite multiple attempts by the Arab world to eliminate the Jewish state and its inhabitants, Israel has never been in serious danger. On the contrary, the invading Arab armies — trained professional militaries — possessed armor and a steep manpower advantage, whereas Israel "had few heavy weapons and no artillery, armored vehicles," and only a few, outdated planes. Although accounts of the numbers of soldiers and armaments in the 1948 war vary greatly, one estimate shows the Arab armies with ten times more aircraft than Israel at the time.[75]

Jimmy Carter's bestselling book *Palestine: Peace Not Apartheid* is similarly replete with errors. Although many of the facts on which its premise rests are demonstrably false, anti-Israel academics endorse Carter's assertions as truth.[76]

The Providence *Journal* called Carter's book "a scathingly anti-Israel polemic," which "absurdly [charges] that Israel engages in 'worse instances of apartness, or apartheid, than we witnessed even in South Africa.'" The editors question how a former president can lack any sense of balance. "Carter blames minuscule Israel, bordered by enemies who desire its annihilation, for the failure of peace with the Palestinians, while skimming over the latter's terrorist attacks and their refusal to recognize even Israel's right to exist."[77]

The Atlanta *Journal Constitution* suggests that when so many former Carter loyalists feel they must divorce themselves from his legacy because of the positions he takes in his book, the rest of us should surely take notice.[78]

In the *New York Times*, Dennis Ross, former U.S. ambassador to Israel, wrote:

> ...Mr. Carter's presentation badly misrepresents the Middle East proposals advanced by president Bill Clinton in 2000, and in so doing undermines, in a small but important way, efforts to bring peace to the region....the reader is left to conclude that the Clinton proposals must have been so ambiguous and unfair that Yasir Arafat, the Palestinian leader, was justified in rejecting them. But that is simply untrue.[79]

The *Times'* Ethan Bronner called Carter's work:

> ...a strange little book about the Arab-Israeli conflict from a major public figure. It is premised on the notion that Americans too often get only one side of the story, one uncritically sympathetic to Israel, so someone with authority and knowledge needs to offer a fuller picture. Fine idea. The problem is that in this book Jimmy Carter does not do so. Instead, he simply offers a narrative that is largely unsympathetic to Israel. Israeli bad faith fills the pages. Hollow statements by Israel's enemies are presented without comment. Broader regional developments go largely unexamined. In other words, whether or not Carter is right that most Americans have a distorted view of the conflict, his contribution is to offer a distortion of his own.[80]

Writing in the Washington *Post*, Jeffrey Goldberg observes that Carter places the blame for the hundred-year war between Arab and Jew almost entirely on Israel, and manufactures sins "to hang around the necks of Jews when no sins have actually been committed."[81]

REMEDIES

Although the First Amendment guarantees freedom of speech and should protect the individual as well as the idea of academic freedom on campuses, there are constitutional remedies for the problems of antisemitism. Principal among them is the right to recognize antisemitism when it occurs and to condemn it vociferously. Indeed, the American Association of University Professors (AAUP) endorsed college and university administrators' condemnation of hateful and bigoted speech and conduct.[82] Failure to speak out sends a message that such hatred is tolerable or acceptable.[83]

Universities must encourage vigorous debate and academic freedom "while also promoting the values of respect, tolerance, diversity and inclusiveness," and ensuring that they have systems in place that continually monitor the situation on campus.[84]

Title VI, 42 U.S.C. §2000d et seq., of the federal Civil Rights Act of 1964 requires recipients of federal funding to ensure that their programs are free from harassment, intimidation, and discrimination on the basis of race, color, and national origin. In order to receive funding from the U.S. Department of Education, colleges and universities must comply with Title VI. The Office for Civil Rights (OCR) in the Department of Education is charged with ensuring that they are in compliance. Historically, OCR's interpretation of Title VI did not protect against antisemitism on the ground that the law did not cover religious discrimination. This policy was changed in 2004 when the OCR confirmed that Jewish students are protected under Title VI. This decision was based on the understanding that being "Jewish" is not simply a religious characteristic; it is also an ethnic characteristic, describing a people who share not only a religion, but also a common ancestry, history, heritage, and culture. The decision to include Jews under Title VI is in line with the U.S. Supreme Court's decision in *Shaare Tefila Congregation v. Cobb*, where the protections under the Civil Rights Act of 1866 were extended to Jews.[85]

In October 2004, the Zionist Organization of America filed a complaint with OCR under Title VI on behalf of Jewish students at UCI, arguing that the university had long been aware of a hostile and intimidating environment for Jewish students, but did not take adequate steps to protect them. Despite an abundance of data provided by ZOA, OCR found "insufficient evidence to support the complainant's allegation that the University failed to respond promptly and effectively to complaints by Jewish students that they were harassed and subjected to a hostile environment."[86]

How then can academic and scientific boycotts against Israel best be confronted and condemned? One recommendation would be to exercise some self-restraint. Instead of crying "Nazi" every time the Israel Defense Forces does something with which an academic disagrees, or urging a boycott of Israeli academics, or signing petitions encouraging soldiers to desert their units, or calling on European powers to intervene immediately to save the Palestinians from "genocide," one could proceed cautiously, speaking in more measured tones and carefully ascertaining the facts.[87]

Israel's defenders could also endeavor to drive a wedge between soft- and hard-core critics of the state, between human-rights groups like Oxfam that take issue with Israeli policy and radical Islamists who deny the state's legitimacy.[88]

It is the obligation of academics to recognize or refute — not ignore — claims that have no basis. Scholars should not only accept their responsibility to be informed and aware, but the obligation to respond when logic, fact, and history are being ignored, flagrantly distorted, or denied. Not only are the principles of academic freedom and the universality of science at stake, but so are democratic values.

Academics should not allow history and logic to be rendered meaningless by twisted "human rights" rhetoric — whether it emanates from a former president of the United States who receives substantial sums of money from Arab governments or from a professor making antisemitic claims in the academic voice.

Kenneth Lasson is Professor of Law, University of Baltimore. He thanks his research assistant, Itamar Ezaoui, for his diligent work on this project.

ENDNOTES

1   The most notorious recent example is John Mearsheimer and Stephen Walt, *The Israel Lobby and U.S. Foreign Policy* (New York: Farrar, Straus & Giroux, 2007). See also http://www.independent.co.uk/opinion/commentators/rupert-cornwell-out-of-america-464069.html

2   Sally F. Zerker, "Anti-Zionist Jewish Leftists Are Part of a Line Stretching Back to Marx," *Canadian Jewish News*, November 26, 2009. Zerker is professor emeritus at York University in Canada.

3   Ibid.

4   Karl Marx was six years old when he was converted to Christianity. Ibid.

5   Ibid.

6   Adolf Hitler used the Big Lie as a propaganda tool in *Mein Kampf* (1925). To be effective, he wrote, it "must be so colossal that no one would believe that someone could have the impudence to distort the truth so infamously." He explained that "in the big lie there is always a certain force of credibility; because the broad masses of a nation are always more easily corrupted in the deeper strata of their emotional nature than consciously or voluntarily." Joseph Goebbels, Nazi Minister of Propaganda, understood that the false claim must not only be colossal, but must contain a kernel of truth and must be repeated with great frequency. In the Middle East today the kernel of truth is that Israel "occupies" Judea, Samaria, and Jerusalem — but in the same way as it occupies Tel Aviv and Haifa, or the United States occupies Miami and Los Angeles with their minority Latino populations, or Canada occupies Quebec, with its minority French population. *See* http://www.israelnationalnews.com/Articles/Article.aspx/7656. *See also* Israel Frederick Krantz, "On Campus: Defending the University Means Winning the Ideological War," *ISRAFAX* 266, August 23, 2009.

7   Ibid.

8   Ibid.

9   It was not until the late 19th and early 20th century that the majority of Arabs living west of the Jordan River migrated to the area. During those years, the land was part of the Ottoman Empire, and subsequently, until the founding of the state of Israel, it was under the control of the British Empire. Following Israel's War of Independence, Egypt occupied Gaza, Jordan occupied the West Bank, and Syria, the Golan Heights. Neither Egypt nor Jordan helped the Palestinians to create their own homeland.

10 *See* http://www.youtube.com/watch?v=zW5VaxxBhCw; *See also* http://www. jewishvirtuallibrary.org/jsource/Society_&_Culture/IDF_ethics.html

11 The number of incidents are: 2002: 106, 2003: 68, 2004: 74, 2005: 98, 2006: 88, 2007: 94, 2008: 85. Email from Emily Friedman, assistant director ADL, Washington, D.C.

12 Ibid.

13 One of the perpetrators was "voluntarily separated" from the university. http://www. adl.org/sih/SIH-print.asp

14 Ibid.

15 U.S. Commission on Civil Rights, "Briefing Report on Campus Antisemitism" (2006), p. 14.

16 At least one other student has also left UCI because of the hostile environment on campus. Ibid.

17 In April 2002, a Jewish student at Illinois State University was asked to sign a petition in support of Palestinians; when he asked whether it also addressed the issue of suicide bombings, an organizer of the petition told him it addressed how to blow off the Jewish student's head. http://www.adl.org/CAMPUS/campus_incidents.asp

18 Ibid.

19 U.S. Commission on Civil Rights, "Briefing Report," p. 14.

20 At the University of Northern Colorado "Fucking Jews" was written on a Jewish student's dormitory room door. At Ramapo College, New Jersey, a professor found swastikas and the words "Die, Jew Bitch" written on her board. At State University of New York, Albany, students found swastikas and "KKK" painted on the walls near a lecture center. http://www.antisemitism.org.il/eng/adl

21 http://www.browndailyherald.com/2.12235/hillel-staffer-moving-on-after-attack-1.1670469

22 http://www.adl.org/sih/SIH-print.asp

23 Ibid.

24 U.S. Commission on Civil Rights, "Briefing Report," p. 15.

25 (Emphasis in original). Notably, the chancellor never responded. An administrator who did respond, suggested that the student visit the Counseling Center to help her "work on her feelings." Ibid.

26 http://www.adl.org/CAMPUS/campus_incidents.asp

27 Email from Emily Friedman, November 16, 2009.

28 Photos of Anne Frank were used to compare her fate at the hand of the Nazis with what is happening to Palestinians today. http://www.standwithus.com/app/iNews/view_n.asp?ID=1033

29   Ibid.

30   http://www.adl.org/main_Extremism/pacifica+forum.htm

31   www.adl.org/main_Anti_Semitism_Domestic/Indiana_Achievement_Address.html

32   http://www.jewishvirtuallibrary.org/jsource/anti-semitism/Black_student_groups.html

33   The comment was reported in the *New York Times*. Ibid.

34   http://www.archive.org/details/OurSacredMission

35   Jeffries' notoriety first led to the shortening of his term as head of African-American studies from three years to one; he was then removed as chair and later, the department was dissolved. http://www.nytimes.com/1993/08/05/nyregion/judge-reinstates-jeffries-as-head-of-black-studies-for-city-college.html. Jeffries sued the school, and a federal jury found that his First Amendment rights had been violated; he was restored as chair and awarded $400,000 in damages. On appeal the federal appeals court upheld the verdict, but removed the damages. However, a month later, the U.S. Supreme Court ruled in another case, Waters v. Churchill, that a government agency may punish an employee for speech if the agency shows "reasonable predictions of disruption." 114 S.Ct. 1878, 511 U.S. 661 (1994). Using this new decision, the New York State Attorney General, G. Oliver Koppell, appealed Jeffries' case to the Supreme Court. In November 1994, the high court ordered the court of appeals to reconsider its findings, which it did in April 1995, when it reversed its earlier decision, upholding the dismissal. *See also* Jeffries v. Harleston, 52 F.3d 9 (2nd Cir. 1995).

36   http://www.hudsonny.org/2009/03/on-campus-the-pro-palestinians-real-agenda.php

37   Ibid.

38   Ibid.

39   Ibid.

40   The Alavi Foundation, which recently had up to $650 million seized by United States federal law enforcement, donated $100,000 to Columbia University in 2007. In 2009 Britain's director of the Brunel Centre for Intelligence and Security Studies reported that up to 48 British universities have been infiltrated by Muslim fundamentalists, heavily financed by major Muslim groups, to the tune of more than a quarter billion Sterling. www.IsraelNationalNews.com (quoting news reports by the New York *Post* and *New York Times*).

41   Jerusalem *Post*, December 25, 2009.

42   Ibid.

43   "Israel Apartheid Week" has been celebrated worldwide every year since. *See* http://apartheidweek.org/en/history

44   *See* http://www.phyllis-chesler.com/176/ivory-tower-fascists

45   *See, e.g.,* A. James Gregor, *Mussolini's Intellectuals* (Princeton, NJ: Princeton University Press, 2004).

46   Jerusalem *Post*, December 15, 2002.

47   Bill L.Turpen, "Reflections on the Academic Boycott Against Israel," *Washington Report on Middle East Affairs*, March 1, 2003 at p. 58.

48   Lawrence H. Summers, "Address at Morning Prayers," September 17, 2002; http://www.ajc.org. *See also* Edward Alexander, "Pushing Divestment on American Campuses," Jerusalem *Post*, May 12, 2004. In November 2002, seventy U.S. medical professors, twelve of whom were from Harvard, held an international conference in Jerusalem to protest the divestment campaign and other anti-Israel activities on American campuses. Jerusalem *Post*, November 18, 2002.

49   *See* Notebook, "A Not So Academic Debate," *New Republic*, January 24, 2005, and Editorial, *The Bollinger Committee*, New York *Sun*, December 10, 2004.

50   *The Daily Telegraph*, November 17, 2002.

51   *See* Report of the Third North American Conference of the Palestine Solidarity Movement, Rutgers University - New Brunswick, New Jersey (October 10-12, 2003), at http://www.divestmentconference.com. *See also, Time,* October 7, 2002.

52   *See* Boston *Globe*, September 20, 2002, quoting Peter Ashton, a research professor of forestry.

53   *See* note 51. "Israel Apartheid Week," report of the ADL, available at http://www.adl.org/main_Anti_Israel/israeli_apartheid_week_2009.htm?Multi_page_sections=sHeading_1_

54   *See*, e.g., "About Israeli Apartheid Week," available at http://apartheidweek.org/en/about

55   Seymour Martin Lipset, "The Socialism of Fools: The Left, the Jews and Israel," *Encounter*, December 1969, p. 24.

56   http://www.honestreporting.com/SSI/main/send2friend.asp?site=www.honestreporting.com&title=Distorting%20Israeli%20Arab%20Reality&url=Distorting_Israeli_Arab_Reality.asp

57   *Thirty Trucks Loaded with Food Enter the Gaza Strip*, Infopod, GLOBAL NEWS WIRE, March 12, 2003.

58   *See* Kenneth Lasson, "Holocaust Denial and the First Amendment: The Quest for Truth in a Free Society," *George Mason Law Review* 6 (1997), p. 35.

59   Ibid.

60   http://www.adl.org/Holocaust/carto.asp.

61   *See* Kenneth Lasson, "Defending Truth: Legal and Psychological Aspects of Holocaust Denial," *Current Psychology* (November 2007).

62   Ibid.

63   Ibid.

64   Ibid.

65   Ibid.

66   CNN.com (September 10, 2009); http://edition.cnn.com/2009/US/09/09/massachusetts.harvard.holocaust/index.html.

67   *See* Tzvi Fleischer, "The Far Left and Radical Islamic International Alliance," *Australian*, June 8, 2006.

68   *Forward*, May 19, 2006.

69   *See* Jeffrey Goldberg, "In the Party of God: Are Terrorists in Lebanon Preparing for a Larger War?" *New Yorker*, October 14, 2002.

70 Alan Taylor, "Noam Chomsky...Still Furious At 76," *Sunday Herald*, March 20, 2005.

71 *See* Mark Lewis, "Nonfiction Chronicle," *New York Times*, November 20, 2005 (commenting on critique of Chomsky by Alan Dershowitz).

72 *See* Nicholas Rostow, "Wall of Reason: Alan Dershowitz v. the International Court of Justice," *Albany Law Review* (June 2008): 953ff.

73 "The Israel Problem," *London Review of Books*, March 26, 2006; http://www.camera. org/index.asp?x_context=7&x_issue=35&x_article=1099; New York *Sun*, March 20, 2006.

74 Ibid.

75 Ibid.

76 *See* http://zionism-israel.com/israel_news/2007/02/everything-you-wanted-to-know-about.html. Mearsheimer and Walt seem to adopt Carter's views. *See* http://www.americanthinker.com/2006/03/stephen_walts_war_with_israel.html

77 Editorial, Providence *Journal*, January 2, 2007.

78 Editorial, Atlanta *Journal Constitution*, January 14, 2007.

79 Dennis Ross, "Don't Play with Maps," *New York Times*, January 9, 2007.

80 Ethan Bronner, "Jews, Arabs and Jimmy Carter," *New York Times*, January 7, 2007.

81 Jeffrey Goldberg, "What Would Jimmy Do?" Washington *Post*, December 10, 2006.

82 Seth Frantzman, "Terra Incognita: The (Ir)responsibility of the Academy," Jerusalem *Post*, November 16, 2009. Founded in 1915, the AAUP is comprised of faculty, librarians and academic professionals at two- and four-year accredited public and private colleges and universities. Its mission is "developing the standards and procedures that maintain quality in education and academic freedom in this country's colleges and universities."

83 Frantzman, "Terra Incognita."

84 Ibid.

85 481 U.S. 615 (1987).

86 The ZOA has indicated it will continue to fight for the students at UCI and across American campuses through an appeal of the OCR decision. Title VI is usually used to fight discriminatory practices during admission, and not for a student's protection against racial discrimination or bias. Its use in this manner could depend largely on ZOA's appeal of the UCI decision. http://www.zoa.org/sitedocuments/pressrelease_view.asp?pressreleaseID=264

87 Frantzman, "Terra Incognita."

88 *See* Reut Study, note 41 and accompanying text.

V

YOUTH CULTURE
AND ANTISEMITISM

BAD RAP
Public Enemy and Jewish Enmity

Glenn C. Altschuler and Robert O. Summers

Sponsored by the Black Students Organization of Columbia University as part of Black History Month, the talk on American education by "Professor Griff," a member of the rap group Public Enemy, on February 11, 1990, was an invitation to a confrontation. After all, eight months earlier, Griff had told David Mills of the Washington *Times* that Jews were responsible for "the majority of wickedness that goes on across the globe, [they] have a grip on America, [and] a history of killing black men."[1]

And so, even before Griff addressed the audience of four hundred men and women in Altschul Auditorium, community activist Lisa Williamson sought to defend him. Antisemitism, she claimed, was the "McCarthyism of the '90s." And the decision of the Columbia Board of Managers to withdraw funds from Black History Month "demonstrates whites' use of economic power to control blacks.... If you take away your pittance for a celebration that should occur year round because we are your historical mothers and fathers, you can keep it. You can keep it and you can choke on it."

Outside the hall, eighteen speakers — and fifteen hundred listeners — held a protest rally. Awi Federgruen, a professor in Columbia's Business School, declared that he would not take guidance on the subject of education "or any other subject from a man whose daily preoccupation consists of the foundation and publication of the most slanderous and bigotrous [sic] statements we've seen this century." Federgruen had had enough: "We have stood by silently and passively as we watched waves of pogroms roll through Eastern Europe. Enough as we stood passively and silently in the years 1933 to 1945 as we saw six million die!...Enough!"[2]

As even their enemies acknowledged, Professor Griff (Richard Griffin), the "Minister of Information," who didn't sing or write songs, and Public Enemy had eviscerated notions of rap and hip hop culture as a passing inner-city musical fad. Inheritors of disparate strands of the Black Power movement, the group had captured the attention of young people with monologues — and diatribes — about race, society, and politics in the Age of Ronald Reagan. With record sales of more than a million for their second album, *It Takes a Nation of Millions to Hold Us Back*, Public Enemy had a legitimate claim on the title of "the most extreme group to achieve sustained commercial success" in rap.[3] "When PE was on top," rapper Ice T recognized, "you rode the tip" (Iceberg, Sire Records). With their incendiary lyrics — and in their public appearances — they were laying bare the gulf between blacks and Jews in late twentieth century America.

Rap's birth in the 1970s coincided with a new round of white flight to the suburbs and the decay of inner city black neighborhoods, rife with crime, failing schools, unemployment, and grotesquely inadequate social services. Along with Graffiti art and the dance form known as b-boying (the other main elements of "hip hop culture"), rap music emerged as a way to express outrage at economic, educational, and social oppression in the United States.

Best understood as "the creative intelligence" of the black street culture, hip hop took its inspiration from the house parties of the boogie-down Bronx, where DJ Kool Herc' spun break beats, samples, and loops to which dancers and break boys responded on the dance floor.[4] Eventually the spoken word artist or "MC" (taken from Master of Ceremonies) rapped a modern griot narrative over the top of mixes created by DJs' simultaneous spinning of many records and beats. Before long, hip hop culture spread across the continent — from West coast to East coast, down south to south side — and throughout the world.[5]

From the earliest rappers, GrandMaster Flash and the Furious Five, Kurtis Blow, Sugar Hill Gang, Run DMC, and Fat Boys in the late '70s, to the proliferation of artists in the '80s, rap lyrics struck political chords, implicitly or explicitly, addressing racism and social justice with a distinctive voice and through a new cultural medium that accentuated the commercially appealing aesthetic of the urban b-boy look and combined it with funk, rock, and rhythm-and-blues-based beats. The street "cred" (credibility), the look, the rawness of the presentation, the ingenuity, and the energy of hip hop made it the music of choice not only for black youth, but for non-blacks as well, especially those young men and women who felt starved for "authenticity," left out of or oppressed by America's political economy, or adrift in an ocean of material possessions and blandness. Freshly articulated, imagined, and invented visions of what it meant to be black in the United States found audiences eager to deride, degrade, and disrespect authority, tradition, middle-class mores, and race-based hierarchies. Whether it was the proto-gangsta West coast street realism of NWA, or the hippy hop imagination of De la Soul, the smooth delivery and style of Juice crew member Big Daddy Kane, or the "dirty south" nastiness of 2 Live Crew, rap appealed, appalled, scathed, subverted — and sold.

Out of Long Island, New York, circa 1986, came a catalyzing force appropriating the hip hop form for a take-no-prisoners discourse on Black Power politics, Nation of Islam ideology, economic self-determination, black identity, autonomy, and education: the "prophets of rage," Public Enemy. If Bobby Seale and Huey P. Newton, co-founders of the Black Panther Party for Self-Defense, considered themselves the children of Malcolm X, then Chuck D (Carlton Ridenhour), Flavor Flav (William J. Drayton, Jr.), Terminator X (Norman Rogers), and Professor Griff might well be regarded as Malcolm's grandchildren. Choice cuts from each of their albums provided "a Black Man's perspective...on Black America."[6] Behind dense mixes and hard funk beats arranged by "The Bomb Squad" (Hank and Keith Shocklee and Eric "Vietnam" Sadler), Chuck D issued virulent attacks on racism and called on blacks to do whatever it took to lift themselves up.

By virtually all accounts, Public Enemy was a charismatic group. Lead singer Chuck D, one critic wrote, "bounced about the stage in an Oakland Raiders cap and jacket, moving with the side-step shuffle and wiry intensity of a prize-fighter. He spat out his dense, militant rhymes and percussive outbursts, which he acted out with shadowboxing punches." Riding out "the thick, hypnotic rhythm track manipulated by DJ Terminator X," his voice had a "spellbinding authority" akin to Elvis Presley and James Brown.[7]

In four albums, released between 1987 and 1991 — *Yo! Bum Rush the Show* (Def Jam), *It Takes a Nation of Millions to Hold Us Back* (Def Jam), *Fear of a Black Planet* (Def Jam), and *Apocalypse 91: The Enemy Strikes Back* (Def Jam) — Public Enemy dominated the political rap landscape. Dubbed by Chuck D "the CNN" of news for the black community (Chuck D, Yusuf Jah), the group was controversial, in your face, and eager to stir the pot with a "white man with his foot on our necks" consciousness.

No subject was off limits to them. Public Enemy had something to say about the "N-word" ("I don't wann be called yo Niga"); the controversies surrounding the establishment of Martin Luther King's birthday as a national holiday ("By the time I get to Arizona"); what every American needs to know about slavery ("Can't Truss It"); the definition(s) of black ownership ("Bring the Noise"); the ravages of crack cocaine and alcohol on black families ("Night of the Living Base Heads/One Million Bottle Bags"); black consciousness ("Rightstarter: Message to a Black Man"); Nation of Islam leader Louis Farrakhan ("Don't Believe the Hype"); the racial biases of the mass media ("She Watch Channel Zero"); police, ambulance, and emergency services in the inner city ("9-11 Is A Joke"); the criminal justice system ("Black Steel in the Hour of Chaos").

Public Enemy emerged at a tense time in the tangled and turbulent relationship between blacks and Jews. With the rise of black nationalism and black pride in the 1960s, Jews, who had played a prominent role in the civil rights movement, from the founding of the NAACP through Martin Luther King's March on Washington and Freedom Summer, were singled out for criticism by militants and excluded from their organizations. The charge that Jewish merchants made windfall profits circulated widely in inner-city neighborhoods. Blacks clashed with teachers, administrators, and union officials, many of them Jewish, over control of the public schools in Ocean Hill-Brownsville (in Brooklyn) and in cities across the nation. They fought with Jews, who had been victimized by quotas throughout the first half of the twentieth century, over affirmative action. And many blacks supported a Palestinian state, condemning Israel as a colonialist power, contemptuous of human rights.

Black leaders with "street cred" in the 1980s exhibited enmity for Jews. In January 1984, during his campaign for the presidential nomination of the Democratic Party, Jesse Jackson referred to Jews as "Hymies" and New York City as "Hymietown" during a conversation with Washington *Post* reporter Milton Coleman. After denying that he made the remarks, and then accusing Jews of conspiring to defeat him, Jackson apologized in a speech to Jewish leaders in Manchester, New Hampshire.

Not surprisingly, Louis Farrakhan, the leader of the Nation of Islam, was among Jackson's most vehement defenders. Already on record with remarks favorable to Adolf Hitler, assertions that Judaism was "a gutter religion," and claims that Muslims were the true chosen people, Minister Farrakhan praised Jackson for meeting with Yassir Arafat, chairman of the Palestine Liberation Organization. Jews hated Jackson, he insisted, because he extended his hand to American Indians, Mexican Americans, Arab Americans, and anyone who was poor: "When you attack him, you attack the millions that are lining up with him. You're attacking all of us."[8]

Enter Professor Griff. In May 1989 Public Enemy's "Minister of Information" proved to reporter David Mills and the readers of the Washington *Times* that he wasn't anything like the typical entertainer, who "goes out there talking about girls." No, he'd let it all hang out. Endorsing allegations of artistic control and exploitation of black singers and songwriters by white (and Jewish) managers, producers, and executives throughout the twentieth century, Griff opined that "ninety percent of the business is operated by Jews."[9]

Since he was working with Jews in Def Jam, Public Enemy's record company, RUSH management, its booking agency, and a Jewish publicist, manager, photographer, and art director, Griff added, with uncharacteristic understatement, that "Chuck D doesn't know how Def Jam Records will react to this story. A lot of people are not ready for the truth."

And then Griff tossed a few more Molotov cocktails. "Jews are wicked," he told Mills, "and we can prove this." Their wickedness included, but was by no means limited to, culpability in the slave trade. Griff would later acknowledge that his information came from *The International Jew*, a rant by Henry Ford, a rabid anti-Semite. When told that Ford's claims were unsubstantiated, incorrect or fabricated, Griff stuck to his guns: "I'm sorry....It's in the book."[10]

The publication of the Washington *Times* piece ignited a firestorm in the mass media — and Public Enemy scrambled to respond. In a release sent to retailers by CBS (which distributed PE's label, Def Jam), Chuck D insisted "We aren't anti-Jewish. We are pro-black, pro-black culture, and pro human race....We aren't here to offend anybody, but to offend that system that works against blacks 24 hours a day, 365 days a year." And, in what critic Armond White called "a rap show trying to smooth white feathers,"[11] Chuck D held a press conference to explain that Griff had been asked to leave the group because his comments "are not in line with Public Enemy's program at all."[12] Assured by Def Jam president Russell Simmons that the other members of the group did not share Griff's views, CBS seemed pleased. "The group recognized the problem quickly," a spokesperson claimed, "acted on it swiftly, and they made the right decision in eliminating the cause of the problem."[13]

Although these moves appeared to defuse the backlash, which included a boycott organized by the Jewish Defense League, Chuck D was not done. Indicating that CBS was refusing to release PE's next project, he told MTV's Kurt Loder he was disbanding the group: "It's our way of boycotting the music industry....We got sandbagged. There was a conflict between the group's idea of how to discipline Griff and the industry's idea of how to discipline Griff."

A few days later, however, Russell Simmons denied that CBS had applied pressure, and indicated that PE would disband for "an indefinite period" to reassess its plans for the future. Reports circulated that the group might sign a multimillion dollar contract with MCA.[14]

With these fits and starts, Public Enemy was responding to fierce cross pressures. Although many blacks agreed with Juan Williams, the distinguished reporter, critic, and intellectual who was appalled by rap music's "ugly trend: racism, sexism, and gay bashing,"[15] a significant number of Public Enemy's fans, according to journalist Marcus Reeves, saw the apology and Griff's dismissal as "a devastating defeat: further proof that whites — and in this case, Jews — were still pulling the strings."[16] In July, at the Slave Theater in Bedford-Stuyvesant, a day before the release of Spike Lee's film *Do The Right Thing* (which featured Public Enemy's rap "Fight the Power"), Al Sharpton gave voice to their concerns. Flanked by bodyguards from the Nation of Islam's Fruit of Islam, Sharpton shouted that the charge of black antisemitism "was just a tactic [and] this ain't no haven of justice. Spike Lee told the real deed.... Public Enemy put the message to music!"[17] Apparently, *Billboard* reported that Sharpton was considering a counter-boycott by Public Enemy supporters of CBS products.[18]

Responding to its core constituents, Public Enemy effected a re-organization as deft as Flavor Flav's switching out the trademark clocks around his neck. In August, Chuck D repeated that "Griff's statements were wrong." Emphasizing that Griff's real beef was "with Israel and its involvement in South Africa, which hurts his people, black people," Chuck D said that his colleague "wasn't clear in his thinking and he wasn't 100 percent right." No longer "Minister of Information," Griff had been appointed Public Enemy's "supreme allied chief of community relations," with special responsibilities for local youth programs. "He's definitely going to talk — you can't tell any man to be quiet, this is America," Chuck D acknowledged, then hastened to add, "but he won't be dealing with any kind of major media. He's going to tell black kids to be the best they can be."[19]

Representatives of Jewish groups were outraged. By firing and then re-hiring Professor Griff, fumed Abraham Foxman, the national director of the Anti-Defamation League of B'nai B'rith, "the rap group Public Enemy has engaged in a repugnant charade characterized by cynicism and disdain for the public. A leopard doesn't change its spots, and exposing America's youth to Griff's unadulterated anti-Semitism can only exacerbate already existing tensions within our society." Rabbi Abraham Cooper of the Simon Wiesenthal Center agreed. Conceding that Chuck D did not share Griff's prejudices,

Cooper claimed that "the issue is that you have an unreviled [sic] bigot who is not going to pay the price....When individuals in the black community cannot or will not speak out against bigotry when it emanates from one of their own, they are actually helping the forces of racism in America."[20]

As critics fired away, a few rappers circled the wagons around Public Enemy. Ice T (Tracy Morrow) was the most prominent among them. A rapper from the streets of South Central Los Angeles, by way of Newark and Summit, New Jersey, Ice T, the self-appointed "creator of the crime rhyme," was a rising star, with a gold album in 1987 and another in '88. In October 1989, he released Iceberg/Freedom of Speech, which included "This One's For Me," a rap riff on Professor Griff.

Without endorsing or condemning Griff's comments, or Public Enemy's "re-organization," Ice T called on all his "brothers" to "help my man out." When "PE was on the top," he rapped, "you rode the tip/ But now they got problems and you suckers run/ Who's Chuck's real friends, does he really have one?/ You yell PE this, PE that/ Fist in the air, proud to be black/ Now they got static and you run like punks./ I ain't heard an MC stand up for him once."

Rap rivals should be ashamed of themselves, Ice T added, if they were waiting in the wings, hoping for Public Enemy to fall so they could fill the group's shoes: "That's what the matter with black people anyway/We ain't down with nothin, I don't care what you say/yell or lie, don't even bother/ How low will a brother go for a dollar."

For Ice T, Public Enemy's service to the community outweighed any antisemitism, hatred or holes in their thinking. And, most importantly, blacks stand behind — and in front of — their own people: "YouknowwhatI'msayin? Griff is my man, I don't care WHAT he said/ YouknowwhatI'msayin?/ And I ain't gon' let them go out like that/ YouknowwhatI'msayin? Chuck, Ice got your back/ Anybody out there's got problems with Public Enemy, come talk to me" (Iceberg, Sire Records).

And so, with this invocation of free speech, the controversy began to die down, as controversies inevitably do. Until Public Enemy decided — and clearly it was a conscious decision — to blow oxygen onto the cinders. Just in time for Christmas, the group released a single, "Welcome to the Terrordome." An "aggressive sonic collage," the rap had something to say about the murder of Yusuf Hawkins in Bensonhurst, riots in Virginia Beach, the assault on the Central Park jogger, Malcolm X and Huey Newton. With two lines, Public Enemy went on record, so to speak, about its views of Jews. As they "told the rab to get off the rag," PE asserted "Crucifixion ain't no fiction/ So-called chosen, frozen/ Apologies made to whoever pleases/ Still they got me like Jesus."[21]

This time, Chuck D's claim that the lines "weren't meant to be offensive and are being misinterpreted by people who don't understand rap language," didn't pass the smell test. Jeffrey Sinensky, director of the civil rights division of the Anti-Defamation League, condemned the song's "blatantly anti-Semitic lyrics, including the repulsive and historically discredited charge of deicide on the part of Jews." The dismissal of Griff, Sinensky added, was a sham. "I think it's fair to say we understand the language of bigotry only too well. Despite Chuck D's effort to put the most favorable cast on his words, it's only too clear to us what is intended."[22] Rabbi Cooper, who had given Chuck D a tour of the Museum of Tolerance in the aftermath of the Washington *Times* interview, called the rap "a slap in the face to every Jew."[23] Several Jewish organizations called on all Americans to boycott Public Enemy's records and stop attending their concerts.[24] Russell Simmons might, legitimately, warn against censorship ("chopping up records is not what I do"), but a diminishing number of people, black and white, agreed with him that "Public Enemy has done a lot more good than harm."[25]

Adding insult to insult, just before his lecture at Columbia, Professor Griff had an altercation with Jewish rapper Michael MC "Serch" Berrin at Def Jam's New York offices, which ended with the epithet "Jew Bastard." Aware of the damage "Griff's wildest imaginary Jewish conspiracy theories" were doing to Public Enemy, Simmons banned Griff from the premises — and Public Enemy dropped him. For a while.[26]

A bit bloodied, Griff remained unbowed. As his appearance at Columbia University approached, students, staff, and faculty disagreed about whether he should have been invited at all. And whether his critics should boycott the event. The Columbia Board of Managers, a student group that sponsors public events, withdrew financial support, leaders indicated, because the Black Students Organization had implied that poet Maya Angelou would be the speaker, informing them about Griff a mere week before the lecture was scheduled to take place. "Columbia has a disciplinary statute saying any speech that denigrates another because of race, religion or sexual orientation will be dealt with in the most severe manner," said David Mlodinoff, president of the Board of Managers. "I thought co-sponsorship would make me partially responsible." Acknowledging that inviting Griff was a mistake, Jack Greenberg, dean of Columbia College, told students that withdrawing money for the talk was also unwise: "The best way to handle this is just to leave him alone." Nonetheless, three petitions protesting Columbia's support of the event, by the senior class, the Council of Jewish Organizations, and an ad hoc student group, garnered thousands of signatures.

Griff's supporters weighed in as well. Citing free speech, the Columbia College Student Council decided not to rescind the $9,000 appropriation it had earmarked for the Black Students Organization to use at its discretion for Black History Month. And the BSO defended its choice, reminding students, faculty, and staff of the popularity of Public Enemy. Griff would speak on education, Alethia Jones, a junior from Brooklyn and the president of the BSO, insisted: "We want to hear him on that." Hector Carter, chairman of the group's political committee, added that the BSO did not necessarily endorse Griff's comments on Jews: "We're not saying, 'yes, he's right,' or 'no, he's wrong.'"[27]

A few students tried to put Columbia on the defensive. In a letter to the editor of the school's newspaper, one of them proclaimed "If you are so concerned with equality and justice for all, and if you are all concerned about creating divisions on this campus, where are your letters of protest concerning Columbia's curriculum which forces students of African descent to study Western Civilization (the very civilization that has oppressed those of African descent for hundreds of years)."[28]

Griff tried to be conciliatory — after his own fashion. He offered to meet with officers of the Columbia Board of Managers. But he indicated that he would tell them "I have to break up the old relationship between blacks and Jews. No more master and slave relationship, no more landlord and tenant, no more employee-employer relationship. We are mature. It's 1990 and we should get together at the bargaining table."[29]

As members of the Columbia University community filed into Altschul Auditorium, protestors on 118th Street greeted them with chants of "Black Rights yes, bigotry, no" and "Jews united will never be defeated." Black members of the New Alliance Party responded with "No more Zionists, no more lies. Black leadership is on the rise." At Columbia, Dean Greenberg told the crowd, "we must rededicate ourselves to fighting racism."[30]

Inside the hall, Griff let it all hang out in a talk that lasted about thirty minutes. "The American educational system is designed to support a supremacist white elite government," he asserted. It "suppresses the nature of the black man." Columbia's curriculum, like those of colleges and universities throughout the nation, was designed to "brainwash" blacks. Convinced that "this integrating stuff" wouldn't work, Griff told blacks "We have to be separate. As long as you're connected with the slavemaster, it won't do you any good." As if to clinch his case, he charged that AIDS had been invented by Jews and (somehow) injected into black Africans.

Perhaps because sponsors of the event informed audience members that any questions not specifically related to the topic of black education would be "deemed irrelevant and have to be rephrased," the exchanges following the talk were anything but hostile. When Griffin was done, Rebecca Grant, a spokeswoman for the BSO, announced that "The views expressed by Richard Griffin are not necessarily those of the Black Students Organization"—and the event ended without an untoward incident.[31]

Weeks later, Public Enemy released *Fear of A Black Planet*. The album included "Welcome to the Terrordome" and a brief shout-out in between tracks to Ice T for "This One For Me." Proving that there's no such thing as bad publicity, another round of mass media condemnation may have helped the album, which debuted at number ten on the *Billboard* charts, and went on to become the group's best seller.

1991 proved to be an even better year for antisemitic rappers. Two months after race riots in the Crown Heights section of Brooklyn, which began when a car driven by a member of the Lubavitcher sect struck and killed Gavin Cato, a seven-year-old black; continued with the revenge murder of Yankel Rosenbaum, a graduate student from Australia; and lasted, with spasms of rock throwing and looting, for three days, Ice Cube, another rising rap star, who had just left NWA, released *Death Certificate*. Ice Cube excoriated blacks for trying to be like whites or Jews, demanding that they ask themselves "who are they equal to." To make sure Jews didn't break up "black crews," he advised, "Get rid of that Devil real simple, put a bullet to his temple." This "unabashed espousal of violence" against Jews, Timothy White, editor of *Billboard*, informed his readers, "crosses the line that divides art from the advocacy of crime"—and, for the first time in the magazine's history, he asked record stores not to carry it.[32]

Death Certificate debuted on the R&B Hip Hop chart at number one, was number two on *Billboard*'s chart, and sold over two million copies. The timing seemed perfect for Ice Cube to gush about the latest Nation of Islam publication, *The Secret Relationship Between Blacks and Jews*, a compendium of conspiracy theories.

And, then, mysteriously, tensions between blacks and Jews began to recede. Or, to be more precise, the mass media moved on. As did the ever opportunistic rappers. Dr. Dre, another former member of NWA, and Snoop Dog, his protégé, introduced "gangsta rap"—and Ice T capitalized on it before moving "actor" in front of "rapper" in his resume. They glorified street life, smoking weed, violence, and "booty," be it women or cash money. MTV, a fledgling outlet in the 1980s, now cool-hunted black culture and featured rappers. In the 1990s a much less political, though no less controversial, rap went mainstream, with artists from Coolio, Cypress Hill, Queen Latifah, L.L. Cool J, Salt 'N' Pepa, DMX, Outkast, Tupac Shakur, to the Notorious B.I.G., Wu Tang Clan, Puff Daddy, 50 cent, Jay-Z and the Fugees raking in huge revenues for record companies, management companies, and themselves.

"We don't even give a damn about no grammy," Flavor Flav declared, defiantly. And group members may have meant it. For a time. In any event, Public Enemy was slow to remove Jew-baiting from its repertoire. In the summer of 1999, the rappers mocked Stephen Spielberg's film *Schindler's List*, with a single, "Swindlers Lust." Among the finger-in-the-eye lyrics was Chuck D's rap: "More dollars more cents for the Big Six/ Another million led to bled claimin' they innocence/ Is it any wonder why blacks folks goin' under?" Having rejoined the group, Professor Griff contributed a rant about stolen knowledge, to which Chuck D responded, "Laughin' all the way to the bank/ Remember dem own the banks/ And dem goddam tanks/ Now what company do I thank?/ Ain't this a bitch heard they owned slaves/ and a ship that sank."

Chuck D insisted that "Swindlers Lust" was not antisemitic: "The song is anti-music industry, directed at an industry, not a people." The release got a rise out of the Anti-Defamation League. But just about nobody was paying attention to what seemed like a summer re-run. The *New York Times* buried the story on its back pages.

Public Enemy, of course, didn't invent antisemitism. But the group and other rappers did play a role in spreading it and giving it authority and credibility. Hip hop culture, for better and worse, re-cycles the anxieties, aspirations, fears, phobias, and fantasies of the black street. Like so many young people, white and black, alas, rappers don't know (or care) all that much about history. Community activist Richard Greene has noted "the bitter irony" of black teens and twenty-somethings who were — and are — "growin' up on their own out there.... So when they see a Lubavitcher, they don't know the difference between 'Heil Hitler' and whatever else....You ask 'em who Hitler was, and half of 'em wouldn't even know — three quarters of them wouldn't even know.... Just like they don't know who Frederick Douglass was, or Booker T., or Mary McCleod Bethune."[33]

Rappers revised, rewrote, and recycled "history," shining a demonic light on race, racism, and the exploitation of black people. And, then, as businessmen attuned to the mainstream market do — and beat reporters must — they moved on to another hot topic.

Glenn C. Altschuler is The Thomas and Dorothy Litwin Professor of American Studies at Cornell University.

Robert O. Summers teaches Social Studies at Washington-Lee High School in Arlington, Virginia.

ENDNOTES

1   David Mills, "The Hard Rap on Public Enemy," Washington *Times*, May 22, 1989.

2   Columbia *Spectator*, February 12, 1990.

3   Gaby Alter, "Classic Tracks: Public Enemy's 'Fight the Power'" *Mixonline* November 1, 2006.

4   The break beat referred to the break in the record where all instrumentation dropped out except the drumbeat. A sample was a piece of a song added to a mix of other samples, while a loop was a sample repeated at regular intervals.

5   Freshest Kids: A History of the B-Boy, QD3 Entertainment (2002).

6   Richard Harrington, "Public Enemy's Rap Record Stirs Jewish Protests," Washington *Post*, December 29, 1989.

7   Geoffrey Himes, "Topical Public Enemy," Washington *Post*, July 4, 1990.

8   February 25, 1984: http://www.finalcall.com/perspectives/rift.html.

9   Mills, "Hard Rap."

10 Ibid. See also: Jeff Chang, *Can't Stop Won't Stop: A History of the Hip Hop Generation* (New York: St. Martin's Press, 2005).

11 Chang, *Can't Stop.*

12 Adam Sexton, ed., *Rap on Rap: Straight-Up Talk on Hip Hop Culture* (New York: Dell Publishing, 1995), p. 246.

13 Melinda Newman, "Public Enemy Ousts Member Over Remarks," *Billboard*, July 1, 1989.

14 Richard Harrington, "The End of Public Enemy?" Washington *Post*, June 28, 1990.

15 Juan Williams, "Fighting Words," Washington *Post*, October 15, 1989.

16 Marcus Reeves, *Somebody Scream! Rap Music's Rise to Prominence in the Aftershock of Black Power* (New York: Faber and Faber, 2008), p. 82.

17 Micha Morrison, "The World According to Spike Lee," *National Review*, August 4, 1989.

18 Janine McAdams, "Public Enemy Disbands Amid Controversy," *Billboard*, July 8, 1989.

19 Jon Pareles, "Jewish Groups Angered by Rappers' New Start," *New York Times*, August 12, 1989; Jon Pareles, "Public Enemy Rap Group Reorganizes After Anti-Semitic Comments," *New York Times*, August 11, 1989.

20 Ibid.

21 Harrington, "Public Enemy's Rap Record."

22 Ibid.

23 *People* magazine, March 5, 1990.

24 Chang, *Can't Stop*, p. 295.

25 Jon Pareles, "Public Enemy, Loud and Angry, Is Far From Its Own Best Friend," *New York Times*, December 26, 1989.

26 *People* magazine, March 5, 1990.

27 James Barron, "Speech Invitation Divides Columbia," *New York Times*, February 8, 1990.

28 Columbia *Spectator*, February 12, 1990.

29 Barron, "Speech Invitation Divides."

30 Columbia *Spectator*, February 12, 1990.

31 "At Columbia, 1,500 Protest Appearance by Rap Group Artist," *New York Times*, February 12, 1990.

32 Chang, *Can't Stop*, pp. 343, 347, 349.

33 Henry Goldschmidt, *Race and Religion among the Chosen Peoples of Crown Heights* (New Brunswick, NJ: Rutgers University Press, 2006), p. 64.

ONLINE ANTISEMITISM
The Internet and the Campus

Andre Oboler

The Internet plays a significant role in the spread of information, and misinformation, on the campus and in student communities. Antisemitic conspiracy theories, stereotyping, imagery, and motifs are shared and reused around the globe. Hateful lies not only spread, but grow. The hate is then expressed in bullying, intimidation, discriminatory policies and occasionally violent outbursts. The campus, along with the school yard, stands on the front line between a developing culture of hate on the internet and the values of tolerance and multiculturalism that society wishes to instill in youth.

The Internet opens gateways between different communities and cultures. It is a vital source of information for a campus environment that prides itself on openness and rigorous debate. The campus, however, must remain a safe environment. Unlike the internet, the debate on campus must be conducted honestly and in good faith. Not everything on the internet is appropriate for the campus. Not every argument found online should be treated as valid and of equal weight. In an honest debate inappropriate and potentially dangerous propaganda should not be shared. When online hate is brought onto the campus, it must be exposed, rebutted and rejected.

My efforts to combat internet antisemitism began on a campus in the United Kingdom (UK). I was in a meeting of the student government when otherwise reasonable representatives began spouting hate. They were not antisemites, they were dedicated student advocates. The hate was embedded in their arguments, in the analogies they used, and "factual information" they provided. These activists had done their own research. An internet search gave them the same hateful content on multiple sites. The online repetition of an antisemitic lie adds neither truth nor credibility. Nor does a source-ranking in search engine results add veracity. Unfortunately, once someone has made the effort to discover and verify these lies, explaining the hateful nature of the content is an uphill battle.

Today there is a nexus between antisemitism on the campus and on the internet. Social media sites like Facebook publicly identify participants by their institution. Students create and join groups that promote antisemitism, which can bring their institution into disrepute. Friendship groups from school provide a network through which hateful content can readily spread. The internet, which operates in a fairly value-free environment, allows casual antisemitism to grow. It is the campus where this antisemitism is likely to manifest itself first, but it is also the campus which provides the best place to respond.

This essay examines the nature of internet-based antisemitism, the growth of Antisemitism 2.0, and the online antisemitism that is most likely to influence youth and the campus environment. It conducts two case studies of online antisemitism. It then considers how to manage and mitigate the influence of online antisemitism.

CAMPUS USE OF THE INTERNET

Students' use of the internet is fairly universal today. Data from late 2009 suggest that 93% of Americans aged 18 to 29 use the internet.[1] The same survey demonstrates that the figure must be higher for those in college as education is a significant indicator of internet usage.

Given the rapid rate of change, it is difficult to present a snapshot of the volume or the purposes of internet usage. Expressed broadly, however, the most-visited sites today are search engines or social media sites, as shown by the top eleven internet destinations (Figure 1). The social media sites are gaining increasing dominance and Twitter, in particular, continues to grow. In 2007, 20% of all web requests on the residential network at the University of Bristol, servicing 4,700 students in dormitories, were for Facebook.[2] The next four most popular websites, which included YouTube, together accounted for the next 10% of requests. Since then, Facebook has grown from 20 million unique visitors a month to almost 120 million.[3] In the United States Facebook's market penetration is even higher. As Mike Richwalsky explains, "College students today in the US live and breathe Facebook all day long."[4]

Students are clearly using the internet. Perhaps to a greater extent than others, they are using it to find information through search engines and sites like Wikipedia, and to interact with people they know and those they meet

Percent of all internet users, March 13, 2010

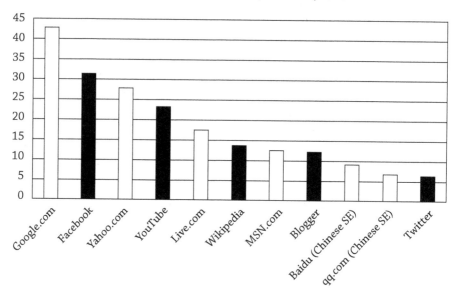

Figure 1. Top 11 Internet sites March 13, 2010.
Graph is compiled based on data from Alexa.com

online with similar interests. Students use the internet to organize, share, protest, and inform.

When it comes to academic work, students generally recognize that a glance at Wikipedia or the first few results offered by Google is not enough. However, for less formal, personal research, this is the common approach. It is this research that informs views expressed in campus debate, student meetings, and conversations with friends.

Informal research can also inform students' decisions online — to sign a petition, join an online protest group or share information with friends. In the online world links to the sources from which one obtained the information are often included in the communication. These links can be shared via private messages, through instant messengers like MSN, or publicly through forums or platforms such as Twitter or Facebook. Links are also included in comments to YouTube videos or responses to blog posts. Although this can be productive when the sources are credible, it also allows the spread of rumors, lies and deliberate propaganda.

DEEP ANTISEMITISM

Much of the antisemitic material that is regularly reproduced online contains "deep antisemitism," that is, an underlying link to classical antisemitic motifs. On the internet "deep antisemitism" generally relies on at least some republishing of existing material.

Some of the regularly republished antisemitic material was uploaded or posted in an organized effort to spread hatred of the Jewish people. Other material uses antisemitism to promote a number of political or ideological agendas. The information is disseminated through search engines and links to related material. Students who fail to recognize the hateful nature of the material can inadvertently play a role in spreading it. Others, however, intentionally spread this material to bully other students, as was the case in "Punch a Jew in the Face Day" on Facebook, which involved a school in Australia.[5] Still others have a political agenda they consider so important that it overrides all other concerns. Such student groups may deliberately spread antisemitic content and then express outrage at any complaints, as occurs in pro-Palestinian campaigns' abuse of Holocaust Memorial Day and Holocaust remembrance generally.

Not everyone recognizes the nature of this material. Although some sources of hate literature are well-known, much of it arrives with no indication of its source. Antisemitic articles are often reposted online without reference to the original sources. Sometimes this material is also reproduced in hardcopy and distributed on campus or in student gatherings, again without indicating its source. In some cases it is not students but faculty who spread or accept the antisemitic tracts.[6] A search on part of the text will often reveal its source, or its use and promotion by recognized antisemitic groups.

Ignorance is no excuse for the spread of antisemitism. When antisemitic material is encountered on the campus, one should first locate its original online source. When the intent is not to encourage antisemitism, a rational discussion may quickly resolve the problem. Similarly, when antisemitic material is encountered online, reporting the material or alerting online administrators may yield the fastest solution. In both cases, one should state the nature of the problem, the source of the material, and the justification for considering it racist, all preferably in confidence. When this fails, public exposure is the best response, informing the public about what is distributed, where it comes from, and which groups circulate it. Most groups on campus prefer not to have a reputation of spreading material known to be racist or from a well-known racist source.

The next section examines three websites that host antisemitic content: Stormfront, JewWatch, and MPACUK. These sites represent three different approaches to the website spread of online antisemitism.

ANTISEMITIC WEBSITES

One of the earliest dedicated hate sites was stormfront.org, a U.S.-based white supremacist site established in 1995.[7,8] At the beginning of February 2010, stormfront.org had over 189,000 registered users (an 18% increase in eleven months) and over 6,807,000 posts (an increase of 23% over the same period).[9]

Stormfront is the central online meeting place for the white supremacist movement. It was established, and continues to act, as a broad church despite the rivalries of competing movements. Lorraine Bowman-Grieve described Stormfront as a "community of like-minded individuals...[that] has developed a network of support for themselves and others that gives them legitimacy and allows them to further justify their ideological beliefs and actions both on an individual and group level."[10]

Community discussions occur in different sections of the site. There are sections on cultural, theological and ideological issues, spaces for regional discussion, and places where current events and news are posted and discussed.[11] The site also plays a significant role in promoting literature that supports white supremacists' views, defining the movement, and outlining "threats" to it. The content includes antisemitic libels, especially conspiracy theories.

Stormfront is self-censoring. Overt threats tend to be removed, helping the site stay on the right side of U.S. law. Despite this, the site breaches laws in countries such as Germany and France, which ban Nazism and Holocaust denial — a common feature on the site. Search results from the localized versions of Google, like Google.de and Google.fr, have omitted references to Stormfront.org since 2002.[12]

Another well-known antisemitic website is JewWatch.com.[13] Unlike Stormfront, JewWatch focuses on providing published information rather than circulating information through an interactive community. JewWatch contains a large number of pages that are well-optimized and regularly appear in search results. The site specializes in conspiracy theories, promoting the idea that Jews control the media, banks and national governments. In 2005 Missouri Attorney General Jay Nixon described it as "nothing more than a racist hate site."[14] Between 1999 and October 2006 the site ran under the slogan "Keeping a Close Watch on Jewish Communities & Organizations Worldwide."[15] Now it identifies itself as providing a "Scholarly Library of Facts about Domestic & Worldwide Zionist Criminality."[16] These "facts" are organized into sections on "Zionist Occupied Governments," "Jewish Mind Control Mechanisms," "Jewish Banking & Financial Manipulations" and other "scholarly" topics. The shift from making claims directly about Jews to hurling accusations against Zionists and Israel came after JewWatch changed ownership, but it also reflects a general increase in the "New Antisemitism" in online discussions.

Secondary slogans on JewWatch have attempted to establish the site's credibility as an educational tool and research archive. An early strap line read, "Jew Watch is a Not-For-Profit Library for private study, scholarship, or research."[17] This was later expanded, adding, "This is NOT a hate site. This is a scholarly research archive of articles."[18] In 2006 another strap line was added: "Frank Weltner, M.A. English & Certified Librarian Presents His Famous Scholarly Library of Factual Links Known Around the World."[19] From October 4 the site began to claim "The Jew Watch Project Is The Internet's Largest Scholarly Collection of Articles on Jewish History" and that it was a "Free Educational Library for Private Study, Scholarship, and Research."[20] The original purpose of the claim to be an educational site was likely in order to follow "fair use" provisions of U.S. copyright law for the many articles from the press that JewWatch reproduces, and to which it adds commentary. Over time the claim shifted to make the site look more like a respectable authority. The contents, however, remain the same, leaving little doubt about its nature.

Awareness of Jew Watch remains high due to the circulation of an e-mail claiming that Google will remove the site from its listings if 50,000 people sign the petition requesting this.[21] The e-mail circulates every few months, and though originally legitimate, it has been out-of-date since 2004. Today the e-mail can best be described as spam and unintentional advertising for JewWatch, a good reason not to forward it as requested. An online version of the same petition now has over 625,000 signatures.[22] In 2004 Google responded by noting that the high rank of JewWatch was due simply to the search engine algorithm and not to a deliberate decision at Google. Google also stated that it would not alter the results. Google made one concession, however, placing a link at the top of the search results to a page explaining its position.[23] This statement only appears on Google.com; other Google sites, like Google.de and Google.fr, omitted JewWatch from the search results in the same manner as discussed above with regard to Stormfront.org.[24]

There is also an increasing number of Islamist antisemitic sites and Muslim community sites that adopt an antisemitic narrative. This is not surprising, given that antisemitism is mainstream in many parts of the Arab world.[25] For example, MPACUK.org, website of the Muslim Public Affairs Committee in the UK, known for its extremist rhetoric and anti-semitic content[26] and for its direct impact on campuses, is another example of the use of a forum. MPACUK promotes the idea of a worldwide Zionist conspiracy and reproduces articles originally published on neo-Nazi and Holocaust denial websites.[27] In 2004, however, MPACUK and its student branch IPAC were banned from campuses in the UK under the National Union of Students' (NUS) No Platform Policy.[28] Passed (and updated) by an NUS congress of delegates from student unions across the country, the NUS enforces the "no platform policy" for its national events and appearances by its officers. Most student unions have also adopted the policy locally. The ban is well-placed, since Asghar Bukhari, co-founder and spokesperson of MPAC, recently used Facebook to demonize Jews and call for violent jihad.[29]

Sites like Stormfront.org and JewWatch.com allow antisemites to organize and share information. Given the wealth of information exposing these sites, their impact on campus is now negligible. Even websites such as MPAC regard JewWatch.com as a step too far and have closed forum threads that reference JewWatch.[30]

SUPPORTIVE SITES

A second class of sites, run by Jews, provides selective support to conspiracy theories and antisemitic websites. By writing and speaking "as a Jew," these sites convey a certain authority. Such sites are often used as references on campus, where they are considered a more reliable authority than Jewish classmates or staff.

Perhaps the most well-known of such sites are those of Neturei Karta, a sect within the Ultra Orthodox Jewish community, numbering a couple of thousand people, and the Satmar, numbering around 100,000.[31] Both oppose the existence of the State of Israel, claiming the Torah teaches that "Jews shall not use human force to bring about the establishment of a Jewish state before the coming of the universally accepted Moshiach."[32] This view is rejected by the vast majority of Ultra Orthodox Jews as well as the Modern Orthodox, Conservative and Liberal streams of Judaism. Together, Neturei Karta and the Satmar account for less than 1% of the Jewish population.[33]

The Satmar and Neturei Karta differ largely in their methods. Neturei Karta has a history of publicly lending "Jewish support" to antisemites in press conferences, conferences and through the media. In the 1970s it supported the PLO when its members were committing terrorist acts against Jews around the world, and more recently it has supported Mahmoud Ahmadinejad, the president of Iran, who has called for the destruction of Israel, the Iranian Holocaust denial conference (2006), and Iran's nuclear program.[34] Their actions and statements, supporting those who are trying to destroy the Jewish state, have been sharply condemned by Jewish communities worldwide, including the Satmar.[35]

Both Neturei Karta and the Satmar run websites that claim that "real Jews" are opposed to Zionism and Israel, including Neturei Karta International (www.nkusa.org), True Torah Jews Against Zionism (www. jewsagainstzionism.com), and Jews not Zionists (www.jewsnotzionists. org). The latter site opens with the claim, "Contrary to common perception, Jewish anti-Zionism is not restricted exclusively to the well known Jewish anti-Zionist movements such as Satmar and Neturei Karta." It mentions the Satmar and Neturei Karta to link to the above sites. By writing "We, the staff at www.jewsnotzionists.org" it gives the impression that it is independent of the Satmar and Neturei Karta. The domain registration, however, indicates that it is registered to "Rabbi Yisroel Weiss" of "Neturei Karta International."[36]

Such websites provide support for antisemitic sites that claim only to be attacking "Zionists," not "Jews." One of the best examples of such an antisemitic site is www.serendipity.li/zionism.htm, which claims that "Zionists are experts at propaganda, disinformation, denying facts and outright lying," and "Zionism seeks to dominate all of Palestine and the Middle East by means of violence and the threat of violence...to maximize its influence in world affairs...principally by means of control of the government of the USA." Here are encapsulated conspiracy theories of Jewish control of world governments, accusations of colonial expansionism, the stereotype of the lying and conniving Jew, and the accusation that Jews are experts at "propaganda" and "disinformation"—perhaps a reference to media control or to the claim that the Holocaust is a myth.

Serendipity also offers articles on topics such as "Jewish power" and its understanding of the distinction between antisemitism and anti-Zionism. It reproduces articles by Ken Livingstone, Patrick J. Buchanan, John Mearsheimer and Stephen Walt, and Gilad Atzmon. The site, which ranks high in a search on Zionism, states that "Zionism should not be equated with Judaism....There are some Jews who are totally opposed to Zionism," and then links to Jews Against Zionism and an article on the Neturei Karta International site. It encourages its readers to regard any accusation of antisemitism as an illegitimate effort to silence their views. This makes it harder to educate those who have undertaken their own research, as they have been instructed to dismiss any who challenge them.

ANTISEMITISM 2.0

Antisemitism 2.0 is "the use of online social networking and content collaboration to share demonization [of Jews], conspiracy theories, Holocaust denial, and classical antisemitic motifs with a view to creating social acceptability for such content."[37] Antisemitism 2.0 works to weaken society's immunity to the spread of hate, and often boldly asserts, counter to all evidence, that the group or its content is not racist. Antisemitism 2.0 is presented as one opinion among many, and argues explicitly or implicitly that there is a right to share "controversial" content.

Labeling Antisemitism 2.0 as nothing more than "controversial" speech serves to increase its social acceptability. People need not agree with the views expressed, but only recognize that they are legitimate views. To facilitate this, those posting the content often add disclaimers. The disclaimers suggest there is no intention to discriminate, that any problems that result are only part of the fallout to be expected from any contentious political discussion and, as such, should be excused. The distinction is one found in criminal law, which requires a *mens rea* (guilty mind) to accompany the *actus reus* (guilty act). In the case of Antisemitism 2.0, the disclaimer itself is an indication of the guilty mind. Such disclaimers seem to exist only in the presence of racist content.

Disclaimers also present a pre-emptive strike against those who would criticize a group, channel, or item. They serve, in particular, as a challenge to platform administrators. They say, "We don't trust you. We know our rights. Are you one of those fascists who would take away our rights?" Holding freedom of expression sacrosanct, a platform administrator responds defensively, backing away. This appeal to moral values, in order to spread racism, is similar to that of fascist political parties who campaign under a banner of freedom of speech with the ultimate goal of removing such freedoms.

THE DANGER OF ANTISEMITISM 2.0:
A SHIFT IN VALUES

The danger of Antisemitism 2.0 derives above all from the way it threatens values. Sixty years of civil rights progress is being undone online. We risk being returned to a world where people do not stand up against hate. Opposition to antisemitism and racism generally is seen not as an intrinsic societal value, but as the equivalent of a political or religious value. Some may share it, others may not. In such an environment hate can flourish.

Students today spend a significant part of their lives in an online world. With instant messaging and web browsing now available on cell phones, there are few times when students are not connected to the online world. Hence, the values of the online world are infiltrating the real world.

This can be seen, at the corporate policy level, in the social acceptability of Holocaust denial. In 2009 Facebook declared that Holocaust denial would not be banned under the provision against hateful content in its terms of service.[38] A statement by Facebook spokesperson Barry Schnitt demonstrates what can result from the spread of Antisemitism 2.0. He explained that the company abhors Nazi ideals and finds Holocaust denial "repulsive and ignorant," but added, Facebook wants "to be a place where ideas, even controversial ideas, can be discussed." Thus Antisemitism 2.0 can gain immunity even when the content is recognized as dangerous propaganda.[39] Though it has not publicly reversed its position, after a public outcry and media attention, Facebook seems to be removing Holocaust denial and pro-Nazi content from its platform. However, its silence indicates that Facebook is still uncomfortable with taking a moral stand, even with regard to content that countries (and the United Nations) have recognized as dangerous and outlawed.[40]

The UK's Report of the All-Party Parliamentary Inquiry into Anti-semitism drew a line between political expression and racism when it concluded, "whilst many have pointed out that criticism of Israel or Zionism is not necessarily antisemitic the converse is also true: it is never acceptable to mask hurtful racial generalisations by claiming the right to legitimate political discourse."[41] This is essentially Schnitt's mistake. The argument is not about free speech, as Facebook had already taken a position prohibiting hateful content. The question was whether the claim that the speech was political should override the prohibition and allow its hateful nature to be ignored. According to UK lawmakers, such an exception was never acceptable.

The online climate that is conducive to racism affects not only Jews but other minority groups. Conall McDevitt, a member of Ireland's Legislative Assembly, highlighted Facebook-based racism against the Roma community in Belfast. In early 2010 he wrote, "What is worrying about these online groups is that so many young people seem not to realise they are being racist. That it has become acceptable to treat members of minority communities in such a racist way is a terrible indictment of us all."[42] McDevitt correctly identified the problem as one of values. The students involved see nothing wrong with their views or behavior. This is another example of Antisemitism 2.0 — more generally, of Hate 2.0 — where racist behavior is made socially acceptable.

I will now examine two cases in depth. The first is a YouTube clip, a song intended to expose how easy it is to get Americans to go along with antisemitism, but which has instead become a lightning rod for antisemitic comments. The second is a Holocaust denial group that Facebook recently shut down.

CASE ONE:
A YOUTUBE LIGHTNING ROD FOR ANTISEMITISM

The song "In my Country there is problem," more commonly known after its refrain as "throw the Jew down the well," was originally recorded by Jewish comedian Sacha Baron Cohen for Da Ali G show (season 2, episode 3). The song is featured in "Borat's Guide to the USA (Part 2)" and on the soundtrack to the 2006 film "Borat." Copies of the clip are available on YouTube as well as other music and video sites. The most popular copy on YouTube has received around 3.5 million views.

The clip features Baron Cohen, as the antisemitic character Borat, singing in an Arizona bar. The song starts with a lament about the transport in Kazakhstan that ends with "throw transport down the well." It then rapidly descends into antisemitic lyrics, and the bar's patrons are shown clapping and singing along to the chorus "throw the Jew down the well." The antisemitic nature of the lyrics is clear and draws on classical antisemitism. The second verse is "In my country there is problem / And that problem is the Jew / They take everybody money / And they never give it back." The reference is to the stereotype of the "rich Jew" and perhaps to the classical stereotype of the Jewish money lender and banker. The chorus calls for throwing the Jew down the well, instructing: "You must grab him by his horns." The third verse makes further use of demonization, warning, "be careful of his teeth," and advises, "You must grab him by his money," again drawing on the stereotype of the greedy Jew.

The song is clearly a satire. Baron Cohen has defended the use of his antisemitic character Borat. He explained to *Rolling Stone* that by being antisemitic, Borat "lets people lower their guard and expose their own prejudice, whether it's anti-Semitism or an acceptance of anti-Semitism."[43] In a press release the Anti-Defamation League (ADL) acknowledged that there was "no malevolence on the part of Sacha Baron Cohen, who is himself proudly Jewish" and sought "to use humor to unmask the absurd and irrational side of anti-Semitism and other phobias born of ignorance and fear."[44] It did, however, express concern that "the audience may not always be sophisticated enough to get the joke, and that some may even find it reinforcing their bigotry."[45] The ADL's concern was well-grounded. The main YouTube video serves as a lightning rod attracting antisemitic comments.

EXAMINING THE COMMENTS ON YOUTUBE

Consider the comments on the most popular copy of the video,[46] looking first at a sample of those posted in the six-hour period immediately before the page was examined. This exposes the content posted before there was a reasonable opportunity for review and moderation by YouTube. A random sample of the most recent posts made a month later shows similar problematic content.

The initial examination highlights seven users. Three post racist jokes. Bobman717: "what's the difference between jews and boy scouts? Boy Scouts come back from there [sic] camps." MADgAmER476: "how did copper wire get invented? 2 jews fighting over a penny." Their listed age is 25, but in their description they state they are 15. Baxxynufc asks, "how do you get a jew on a bus? throw a penny on. how do you get a jew off the bus? tell them hitler is driving." He gives his age as 20 and location as the UK. This is the "light-hearted" face of antisemitism.

The jokes are interspersed between the racist comments of four other users. Constipatedclown writes, "Dear Jews, EAT SHIT AND DIE. yours truly, THE UNIVERSE." Constipatedclown's profile says she is a 20-year-old Canadian. On her channel comments she writes, "one jew is too many jews, and a good jew is a dead jew. 6 Million wasn't nearly enough." Gr1Mf4nD4nG0 writes, "I had no problem with jews, i've never even seen one face to face, but when you find out they control all the media and banks you start to understand why hitler wanted to kill them. they are parasites." Gr1Mf4nD4nG0 gives her/his age as 30 and location as the UK. Pebsykid puts the hate much more succinctly: "Kill all Jews." Pebsykid is 23, from the USA.

SlavicFront88 is the only clear white supremacist. He is from Russia, age 20. His channel is "14/88," doubtless a reference to David Lane's "Fourteen Words," a slogan of the white supremacist movement,[47] and the neo-Nazi shorthand for Heil Hitler (88 [HH]).[48] He writes, "Fuck jews!!!! :D throw the jew down the well!" His profile is more alarming than his comment.

Table 1. YouTube Accounts

Account	Registered	Active one month later?
bobman717	February 2008	Yes
constipatedclown	August 2007	Yes
Gr1Mf4nD4nG0	December 2007	Yes
Pebsykid	July 2006	Yes
MADgAmER476	July 2008	Yes
Baxxynufc	August 2008	Yes
SlavicFront88	November 2009	Yes

This six-hour period is not unique. Going back another eighteen hours, FatsoJetson writes, "cause they are not ethnically jewish they have a hidden history. orthodox jews are the real jews. The rest are the remnant of a eastern European empire who adopted Judaism as its religion," a reference to the Khazar myth.[49] FatsoJetson's profile includes conspiracy-related pictures, aliens, a diagram of a suitcase bomb, and a Neturei Karta member holding a sign reading "End of Zionism = Peace." He gives his country as Ireland and age as 27. More astonishing is leevi1234 who posts a poem, "From a Jew's face / The wicked Devil speaks to us, / The Devil who, in every country, /Is known as an evil plague. // Would we from the Jew be free, / Again be cheerful and happy,/ Then must youth / fight with us / To get rid of the Jewish Devil." The poem is taken from an antisemitic children's book *Der Giftpilz* by Julius Streicher, publisher of the Nazi newspaper *Der Stürmer.*[50]

This examination shows the sort of hate that "throw the Jew down the well" by Sacha Baron Cohen attracts. The question then is, should a lighting rod for hate be allowed? If so, who should take responsibility for the resulting outpouring of hate?

TAKING RESPONSIBILITY:
RESPONDING TO ONLINE VIDEO INCITEMENT

As Sacha Baron Cohen explained, the problem is both those who are antisemitic and those who do not express antisemitic sentiments, but are willing to accept them. YouTube falls into the latter category when it allows and facilitates such comments. This very popular video clearly has a history of attracting such comments. YouTube could mitigate the damage by indicating the satirical nature of the clip at the top of the page. Or it could monitor the comments on this and other "hate lightning rods" more vigilantly. However, an extreme solution may be in order. Perhaps the ADL is right, and despite his intentions, Baron Cohen's work is doing more harm than good. In such circumstances perhaps it should be removed from YouTube, either by Google (which owns YouTube) on its own initiative, or at Baron Cohen's request.

Recently the issue of corporate responsibility for hosting online videos ended up in court. Three executives of Google (YouTube's parent company) were taken to court in Italy. They were found guilty of the violation of privacy after a video was posted in 2006 showing a group of students bullying a teenager with Down syndrome while other students looked on. The video remained on Google Video for two months.[51] A statement from Google described the video as "totally reprehensible" and claimed that it "took it down within hours of being notified by the Italian police."[52] Companies must be allowed time to identify problematic content and respond, but the time should be measured as the two months since the video was posted (and became particularly popular), not the number of hours between the time the police contacted Google and it removed the video.

If Google enables anyone to become a publisher easily and quickly, it has a responsibility to make it equally easy for people to report abuses and have their complaint handled quickly. Google's responsibility may begin only when the first complaint is made, and a couple of weeks might be a reasonable time to review a case with few complaints. When something becomes viral, however, as in this case, the response must be faster; there is no technological reason why Google cannot prioritize its response rate based on time since the first complaint, time from when the video was posted until the first complaint, popularity of the video, and volume of complaints.

There are also lessons for those producing or publishing YouTube clips on racism for educational or journalistic purposes. These videos should contain subtitles with full explanations to ensure the educational message is not lost or separated from the content, which might otherwise make hate look acceptable. This also applies to satire and to translations of antisemitic television shows from the Arab world. The main problem on YouTube is hate that is posted intentionally. It is easy to find content on YouTube praising Hitler, denying the Holocaust, and attacking Jews. Getting YouTube to respond should not require a resort to law enforcement.

CASE TWO:
FACEBOOK HOLOCAUST "REVISIONISM"

Holocaust Revisionism, a Holocaust denial group on Facebook, had 881 members. Created around June 7, 2009, Facebook shut it down in late January 2010. Its removal seems to be part of a wider — unannounced — cleanup effort that Facebook has undertaken.[53] This was after much criticism had been directed at Facebook, which had, in effect, declared that Holocaust denial was not hateful.[54]

Holocaust Revisionism follows the pattern of other Antisemitism 2.0 groups.[55] It includes an info box stating, "This is NOT an anti-Semite group, nor is it to be a group to hate JEWS. Our objective is to show you a [sic] aspect of History that is often misunderstood." The description calls the Holocaust a "highly debatable aspect of history." It declares that there are "many holes in the official story that mainstream historians cannot account for" and that there are "numerous reputable historians who have been persecuted and thrown in prison all for voicing their opinion on this aspect of history." The call to action is: "This MUST stop, it is an abhorrent human rights violation to imprison someone for voicing an opinion on history."

The UN General Assembly disagrees. It resolved in 2007 that it "Condemns without any reservation any denial of the Holocaust" and "Urges all Member States unreservedly to reject any denial of the Holocaust as a historical event, either in full or in part, or any activities to this end."[56] The UN, governments and academic experts take a hard line because Holocaust denial is both racist and potentially dangerous. Historian Deborah Lipstadt called it a "clear and future danger" and noted that "the time to rise to action is when it's not yet a clear and present danger."[57]

Deborah Butler points out its racist nature: "Denial of the Holocaust is often accompanied by the allegation that the historical account of the Holocaust is a Jewish fabrication for financial gain,"[58] and even when this is absent, it is implied. Thus Holocaust denial is also a "considerable insult to the Jewish people."

Frank Knopfelmacher explained the danger of Holocaust denial as a group-libel "which exceeds in ferocity and depth of malice anything that has happened in the field of ethnic animadversion in this country at least since World War II."[59] The deniers intend to imply "that the Jewish people are witting and, rarely, unwitting accomplices in a conspiracy to extort, to lie and to kill, in order to acquire a counterfeit crown of martyrdom to be used for personal and political gain."[60] It is this implication that incites hatred and even violence against Jews and the Jewish community.

EXAMINING THE COMMENTS ON FACEBOOK

I examined all comments in the denial group until the week before the group was removed. Many of the comments echo the classic denier approaches. Cherissa Cutts asks why "In Canada you can go to jail for doubting the holocaust happened" but not for doubting the moon landing? "Welcome to zionist run Canada," she concludes. Wotan Griffiths also writes of Jewish control of governments: "Wont be long before this group is closed due to the will of zog…death to zog [Zionist Occupation Government]." Ray Loy declares "The real Holocaust was in Dresden Germany," referring to the allied bombing there. Andreas TerrorMachine leaves a one-word comment, "Holocash." The comments often link to further antisemitic material on websites and in social media or help organize the deniers.

Elijah Wilson announces in this group that he has set up an official Toben fan club and has e-mailed Frederick Toben for his thoughts on this. He provides the link and encourages others to join. Elsewhere Wilson links to a Google Video page with a clip by professional Holocaust denier Mark Weber[61] discussing the situation of fellow denier Ernst Zundel. Another user, Charles Fink, links to "A letter from Ernst Zundel" posted at David Duke's website. John Preben links to a dedicated website for Holocaust denial videos, advising, "Here you guys will find the most of Holocaust revisionism movies." Natasha Volker, the group's creator, links to Jewwatch, commenting, "A good one. Jew Watch — Jewish Holocaust — Media Lies — Frauds — Hoaxes."

John Paul Cupp, addressing the online organizing in Facebook, cheers, "This is a great upsurge in anti-Zionist and anti-hollowcause agitation. We just went from 42 when I joined a couple of days ago to 500." He offers to direct people to unlisted Facebook groups that are being created by the Far Right to aid its efforts to organize: "If anyone wants to join the red-brown united front let me know and I will send you an invite since it is invite only for security reasons but even as a secure group reaching 300 within 3 weeks!

Hail Vicotry [sic], smash Zionism!" The implication is that what we see is just the surface.

The group also contains other forms of blatant antisemitism. Christian Conn Lind links to a website called "Jews killed Jesus," which features replacement theology. It declares, "The Jews have been milking the holocaust for every penny it's worth. They have no shame!" and justifies the Holocaust as the Jews' rightful punishment for rejecting Christ. Lind comments, "Ha ha this is so good. The gentile world is still liveing [sic] the greatest hoax of all times, but these days more dramatically than ever perhaps?" Elsewhere he declares, "Too bad the ashkenazium southern whites did not end up in rockefellers eugenic programs at the turn of the century."

The group is also used to share information. Sena Bowman writes, "All those who haven't read it....It will give you all the fuel needed to out debate any sympathizer....Did Six Million Really Die? Don't recall the authors name though." Another poster promptly supplied the author's name. Another user declares, "Holocaust is just another jewish shield, which they can use against anyone who tries to oppose them. But the truth is different, Hitler believed that they could be changed if they work honestly, so he sent them to the work places....Half of them died, the rest tried to corrupt the german soldiers by offering them money...." This user's name is a Russian phrase and the "about section" reads "14/88 Russian Roulette." Perhaps a friend of the YouTube user SlavicFront88?

Ra'd Jundallah may be the most worrisome user, as he links to a Russian Islamic site and invites people to join the "World Antizionist Congress" (WAC). Here Islamism meets the Far Right and Holocaust denial. WAC is "opposed to Zionist-Imperialist expansion throughout the world in general and Zionist barbarism in Palestine in particular." The user's info box declares, "Allah is our objective. The Prophet is our leader. Qur'an is our law. Jihad is our way. Dying in the way of Allah is our highest hope." Amazingly, he has 4,388 friends. It looks more like a well-organized (and perhaps, government-funded) project than that of an individual.

SYSTEMATIC RESPONSE:
A NEED FOR POLICY DEVELOPMENT

The Facebook group "Holocaust Revisionism" exposes the link between Holocaust denial and other forms of antisemitism. It serves as an example of why such groups are dangerous and of their role in rapidly organizing a community of hate.

When an entire group is dedicated to hate, Facebook must take the initial responsibility for handling complaints and determining if it should be shut down. Although Facebook seems to have begun doing this, there are no statistics on how many groups they have examined or the percentage of these that have been shut down. Such groups may return immediately, but by removing hate groups and accounts that spread hate, the cost of using Facebook to organize for hate is increased. This reduces the antisemites' effectiveness and might ultimately force them off the platform altogether.

When confronting blatant hate in the comments, it may be more effective to close the accounts of those posting the hate before shutting down the group as a whole. Where an innocent group is collecting hate, initial reports of complaints should be redirected to the group's administrator. Facebook should step in only if there is no response within a given period. There will, of course, be administrators who shelter hate. If complaints persist, at some point Facebook should undertake an audit of the administrator, which could result in a loss of administrative privileges. Requiring an account to be registered for twelve months before it can administer a group would greatly increase the incentive to moderate a group responsibly. Giving administrators the ability to refer complaints about which they are uncertain to an elected group of reviewer-volunteers or to Facebook staff would also help manage the role. An administrator who refers everything could be dismissed as ineffective.

CONCLUSIONS

The internet, particularly Web 2.0, provides great opportunities to communicate, share, coordinate, and organize, but also extends these advantages to those wishing to spread hate. Combined with an online culture where anything goes, the internet can provide a platform for the nurture and growth of antisemitism.

Antisemitism is often based on misinformation and propaganda, such as conspiracy theories. Well-known hate sites provide a ready source of such material. Knowing these sites and recognizing their contents when reproduced on other sites or on campus would help in quickly identifying propaganda.

Popular social media sites like Facebook and YouTube can encourage antisemitism. Efforts to expose such antisemitism must be conducted and presented carefully lest they themselves end up promoting hate. Hateful content in social media should be reported to the platform providers, who should be encouraged to do more than they have done to date.

Countering antisemitism online does not stop with reporting those who spread hate. Educational campaigns are needed, both online and on campus, to encourage students not just to stand by when hate is displayed. In many countries antisemitism is illegal. Even in the U.S., the first amendment limits government censorship. It does not prevent companies like Google and Facebook from deciding that they want a hate-free platform. They are free to implement their own policies to ban or remove hate, but this will only happen across all platforms if internet users demand it. The public must take a stand against hate.

The problem exists online because laws, processes, community understanding and values have not kept up with technology. Recognition of the problem must start on the campus. The response must involve both experts and student activists. And recognition alone cannot solve the problem. Students must be trained, equipped and provided with strategies and expert help if they are to play a role in reducing online antisemitism. Monitoring, training and coordination need to improve.

Combating online antisemitism is one of the major challenges in the fight against all forms of antisemitism and hate. It is perhaps the fight we are least equipped to handle, as many experts on antisemitism are not technologically savvy. There is also a reluctance to recognize younger experts, including those on campus. Given the urgency of the problem, the community and NGOs focused on antisemitism must embrace change. Young people must also accept the challenge. It cannot be left to others.

Dr. Andre Oboler is CEO of Zionism On The Web, Director of the Community Internet Engagement Project at the Zionist Federation of Australia and a consultant for the Anti-Defamation Commission (Australia). He was co-chair of the working group on Online Antisemitism for the 2009 Global Forum to Combat Antisemitism.

ENDNOTES

[1] Lee Rainie, Internet, broadband, and cell phone statistics, The Pew Research Center's Internet & American Life Project, January 5, 2010 http://www.pewinternet.org/~/media//Files/Reports/2010/PIP_December09_update.pdf

2   Nick Skelton and Paul Seward, "A Download a Day Helps you Work, Rest and Play —
    What Students Want From the Network," Networkshop 35, The University of Exeter,
    April 3-5, 2007, JANET(UK). Video of presentation and slides seen 01/26/2010
    at http://www.webarchive.ja.net/services/events/networkshop/Networkshop35/
    programmethur.html

3   Andrew Lipsman, 2009: Another Strong Year for Facebook, comScore, January 21,
    2010 http://blog.comscore.com/2010/01/strong_year_for_facebook.html

4   Mike Richwalsky, Facebook Usage by US Colleges and Universities, UK Web Focus,
    July 1, 2009. Seen 2/14/2010 at http://ukwebfocus.wordpress.com/2009/07/01/
    facebook-usage-by-us-colleges-and-universities/

5   JIDF, "International Punch a Jew In The Face Day" Event Launched on Facebook, JIDF
    Website, December 12, 2009. Seen 2/14/2010 at http://www.thejidf.org/2009/12/
    international-punch-jew-in-face-day.html

6   David Hirsh, "Michael Cushman and the Jew-free UCU Congress," Engage, May 28,
    2009. Seen 01/26/2010 at http://engageonline.wordpress.com/2009/05/28/michael-
    cushman-and-the-jew-free-ucu-congress/

7   Jessie Daniels, Cyber Racism – White supremacy Online and the New Attack on Civil
    Rights (Rowman & Littlefield Publishers Inc., 2009), p. 42.

8   T.K. Kim, "Electronic Storm: Stormfront grows a thriving neo-Nazi community,"
    Intelligence Report, Summer 2005. Seen 1/10/2010 at http://www.splcenter.org/
    intel/intelreport/article.jsp?aid=551

9   Data for February 2010 seen on 2/01/2010 at http://www.stormfront.org/
    forum/. Data for March 2009 are taken from Lorraine Bowman-Grieve, "Exploring
    'Stormfront': A Virtual Community of the Radical Right," Studies in Conflict &
    Terrorism 32:11 (2009), p. 996.

10 Bowman-Grieve, p. 999.

11 Bowman-Grieve, p. 997.

12 Jonathan Zittrain and Benjamin Edelman, Localized Google search result exclusions,
    Berkman Center for Internet & Society, Harvard Law School, October 26, 2002. Seen
    on 1/10/2010 at http://cyber.law.harvard.edu/filtering/google/

13 Zionism on the Web, Profile: JewWatch. Seen 1/16/2010 at http://www.
    zionismontheweb.org/antizionism/jewwatch.htm

14 Missouri Attorney General's Office, Nixon sues author of racist Internet Web site for
    deceptively soliciting funds in the name of hurricane relief, September 7, 2005. Seen
    1/16/2010 at http://ago.mo.gov/newsreleases/2005/090705.htm

15 See Archive of JewWatch from February 25, 1999 at http://web.archive.org/
    web/19990225082456/http://jewwatch.com/ and Archive of JewWatch from
    September 6, 2006 at http://web.archive.org/web/20060906232943/http://www.
    jewwatch.com/. Archives seen 1/16/2010.

16 JewWatch home page, seen 1/16/2010 at http://www.jewwatch.com/

[17] See Archive of JewWatch from May 19, 2000, seen 1/16/2010 at http://web.archive. org/web/20000519225621/http://jewwatch.com/

[18] See Archive of JewWatch from September 5, 2005, seen 1/16/2010 at http://web. archive.org/web/20050905221012/http://www.jewwatch.com/

[19] See Archive of JewWatch from January 13, 2006, seen 1/16/2010 at http://web. archive.org/web/20060113051535/http://www.jewwatch.com/

[20] See Archive of JewWatch from October 4, 2006, seen 1/16/2010 at http://web. archive.org/web/20061004233412/http://www.jewwatch.com/

[21] snopes.com: Google Search for 'Jew,' Snopes.com, September 6, 2007. Seen 1/16/2010 at http://www.snopes.com/politics/religion/google.asp

[22] Remove JewWatch.com from the Google Search Engine! — Signatures, Petitions Online. Seen 1/16/2010 at http://www.petitiononline.com/mod_perl/signed. cgi?rjw23

[23] http://www.google.com/explanation.html

[24] A live comparison between Google.com and Google.de on a search for the word "jew" can be seen at http://www.chillingeffects.org/search-comparator/search. php?se=google.de&q1=jew

[25] Richard Cohen, "Where Anti-Semitism Is Mainstream," Washington Post, June 16, 2009.

[26] All-Party Parliamentary Group Against Antisemitism.

[27] All-Party Parliamentary Group Against Antisemitism, Report of the All-Party Parliamentary Inquiry into Antisemitism, UK Parliament, September 2006, p. 29. Seen 1/10/2010 at http://www.thepcaa.org/Report.pdf

[28] All-Party Parliamentary Group Against Antisemitism.

[29] "Muslim Public Affairs Committee UK Spokesman Glorifies Terror, Centre for Social Cohesion Reveals," The Centre for Social Cohesion, December 19, 2008. Seen 1/10/2010 at http://www.socialcohesion.co.uk/files/1231430557_1.pdf

[30] http://forum.mpacuk.org/showthread.php?t=33822 seen 1/10/2010.

[31] Shlomo Shamir, "Satmars: Jews at Iran Holocaust conference 'reckless outcasts'," Haaretz, December 16, 2006. Seen 1/31/2010 at http://www.haaretz.com/hasen/ spages/801717.html

[32] Neturei Karta, What is the Neturei Karta? Neturei Karta International, December 13, 2002. Seen 1/31/2010 at http://www.nkusa.org/aboutus/index.cfm

[33] Against Zionism not Jews, Anti-Zionism Resource Center at Zionism on the Web. Seen 01/32/2010 at http://www.zionismontheweb.org/antizionism/Against_ Zionists_not_Jews.htm

[34] Assaf Uni, "Neturei Karta delegate to Iranian Holocaust conference: I pray for Israel's destruction 'in peaceful ways'," Haaretz, January 1, 2007. See 1/21/2010 at http:// www.haaretz.com/hasen/spages/810100.html

35 Shamir, "Satmars."

36 Whois.net. Seen 1/31/2010 at http://www.whois.net/whois/jewsnotzionists.org

37 Andre Oboler, "Online Antisemitism 2.0. Social Antisemitism on the Social Web," *Post-Holocaust and Anti-Semitism Series*, No. 67, April 1, 2008. Jerusalem Center for Public Affairs (JCPA).

38 Andre Oboler, "Facebook, Holocaust Denial, and Anti-Semitism 2.0," *Post-Holocaust and Anti-Semitism Series*, No. 86, September 15, 2009, JCPA.

39 Brian Cuban, "The Cuban Revolution" (May 2009), www.briancuban.com/facebook-holocaust-denial-should-be-discussed-openly.

40 Oboler, "Facebook, Holocaust Denial, and Anti-Semitism 2.0."

41 Report of the All-Party Parliamentary Inquiry into Antisemitism. Seen 1/17/2010 at http://thepcaa.org/Report.pdf

42 "SDLP slams racist Facebook group," *Inside Ireland*, February 12, 2010. Seen 2/15/2010 at http://www.insideireland.ie/index.cfm/section/news/ext/rosesellers001/category/ 1091

43 Cohen defends 'racist' Borat film, BBC News, November 16, 2006. Seen 2/27/2010 at http://news.bbc.co.uk/2/hi/entertainment/6153420.stm

44 Statement on the Comedy of Sacha Baron Cohen, A.K.A. "Borat", ADL, Seen 2/27/2010 at http://www.adl.org/PresRele/Mise_00/4898_00.htm

45 Ibid.

46 Borat — Throw the Jew Down the Well!!, YouTube video. Seen on 01/26/2010 at http://www.youtube.com/watch?v=Vb3IMTJjzfo

47 Hate Number Symbols: 14 (words) — From A Visual Database of Extremist Symbols, Logos and Tattoos, ADL, 2005. Seen on 2/27/2010 at http://www.adl.org/hate_symbols/numbers_14words.asp

48 Hate Number Symbols: 88 — From A Visual Database of Extremist Symbols, Logos and Tattoos, ADL, 2005. Seen on 2/27/2010 at http://www.adl.org/hate_symbols/numbers_88.asp

49 Steven Plaut, "The Khazar Myth and the New Anti-Semitism," *Jewish Press*, May 9, 2007.

50 How To Tell A Jew, the German Propaganda Archive, Calvin College. Seen on 2/27/2010 at http://www.calvin.edu/academic/cas/gpa/story3.htm

51 "Google executives convicted over posted video," *The Age*, February 25, 2010. Seen 2/27/2010 at http://www.theage.com.au/technology/technology-news/google-executives-convicted-over-posted-video-20100225-p414.html

52 Serious threat to the web in Italy, The Official Google Blog, February 24, 2010. Seen 2/27/2010 at http://googleblog.blogspot.com/2010/02/serious-threat-to-web-in-italy.html

53 Andre Oboler, "Under Attack in a Virtual World," *PresenTense Magazine*, February 2010. Seen 2/27/2010 at https://wave.google.com/wave/#restored:wave:googlewave. com!w%252BNksERr6Qc.6

54 Oboler, "Facebook, Holocaust Denial, and Anti-Semitism 2.0."

55 Oboler, "Online Antisemitism 2.0. Social Antisemitism on the Social Web."

56 UN General Assembly (March 2007), The Holocaust and the United Nations Outreach Programme, http://157.150.195.10/holocaustremembrance/docs/res61.shtml.

57 Steve Busfield, "Irving Loses Libel Case," *The Guardian*, April 11, 2000.

58 Deborah Butler, "Holocaust Denial in England," *Web Journal of Current Legal Issues* 4 (1997). Seen 2/24/2010 at http://webjcli.ncl.ac.uk/1997/issue4/butler4.html.

59 Frank Knopfelmacher, *The Age*, March 1979, cited in Jeremy Jones, "Holocaust Denial: 'Clear and Present' Racial Vilification," *Australian Journal of Human Rights* 1,1 (1994): 169-180.

60 Ibid.

61 "Mark Weber: The Professional Denier, Holocaust Denial: An Online Guide to Exposing and Combating Anti-Semitic Propaganda," 2001. Seen 2/28/2010 at http://www.adl.org/Holocaust/weber.asp

VI

COMBATING
ANTISEMITISM

HOSTILE ENVIRONMENT
Campus Antisemitism as a Civil Rights Violation

Kenneth L. Marcus

In 2004, the Zionist Organization of America (ZOA) filed a complaint with the U.S. Department of Education's Office for Civil Rights (OCR) describing an extraordinary pattern of antisemitic intimidation, harassment, threats, and vandalism at the University of California at Irvine (Irvine).[1] At that university, pro-Israel Jewish students have been subject to stalking, rock throwing, and various forms of intimidation, and a Holocaust memorial was damaged or destroyed.[2] Signs have been posted on campus showing a Star of David dripping with blood.[3] Speakers at campus events have chastised Jews for arrogance and have spoken of the distinction between the "good Jews" and the "bad Jews."[4]

Despite the severity of these incidents, OCR dismissed the complaint in November 2007.[5] Yet in early 2008, an independent task force investigating the Irvine allegations concluded that the "acts of anti-Semitism are real and well documented" and that "Jewish students have been harassed."[6] Most strikingly, the Task Force urged that "[s]tudents with a strong Jewish identity should consider enrolling elsewhere unless and until tangible changes are made."[7] What prevented OCR from grasping the civil-rights violations at Irvine was in part its failure to understand how certain forms of anti-Israelism could constitute discrimination against Jews.

The OCR resolution in *In re University of California at Irvine*[8] demonstrates not only government failure to grasp the essential features of the new antisemitism but also the stakes involved when it fails to do so. The *Irvine* case, now a source of considerable controversy,[9] was OCR's first major case under its 2004 antisemitism policy.[10] In this case, ZOA alleged a substantial pattern of antisemitic harassment at Irvine over a period of several years.[11]

After a lengthy investigation, OCR found insufficient evidence to proceed against Irvine.[12] OCR's decision has provoked strong congressional response from Senate Judiciary Committee members who are concerned that OCR's resolution "is inconsistent with its prior policy statements."[13] The Senators are right.[14] OCR's decision in this highly publicized case not only disregards OCR's formal policy, but bespeaks a fundamental inability to grasp the two issues on which this case turns: the nature of Jewish identity and the character (and wrongfulness) of the new antisemitism.

THE FACTS

The complaint alleges with unusual specificity that Irvine has fostered a hostile environment for Jewish students, in violation of the prohibition on racial and national-origin discrimination contained in Title VI of the Civil Rights Act of 1964. Specifically, the complaint alleges that Jewish students have been physically and verbally harassed, threatened, shoved, stalked, and targeted by rock throwing; Jewish property has been defaced with swastikas; and a Holocaust memorial was vandalized. Jewish students have been called "dirty Jew" and "fucking Jew," told to "go back to Russia" and "burn in hell," and subjected to comments such as "slaughter the Jews."[15] One Jewish student who wore a pin bearing the flags of the United States and Israel was told to "take off that pin...or we'll beat your ass."[16] Another reported receiving hate messages such as "Jewish students are the plague of mankind" and "Jews should be finished off in the ovens."[17]

In addition, as OCR's investigation has confirmed, numerous campus speakers have delivered lectures that some Jewish students have considered to be either anti-Israeli, anti-Jewish, or both.[18] Many of these speakers were "known for strong rhetoric and criticism of the foreign policies and in some cases the existence of the State of Israel."[19] In May 2004, one speaker argued: "This ideology of Zionism is so racist, so arrogant, based on so much ignorance."[20] On May 18, 2006, another expressed the so-called Holocaust inversion, announcing, "They are the new Nazis . . . they're saying when you see an Israeli flag next to an American flag, they're saying we're with imperialism. We are down with colonialism. We are down with white supremacy."[21] The same speaker warned that:

> [Y]ou settle on stolen land, you gotta deal with the consequences. So now its [sic] time for you to live in some fear now, because you were so good at dispensing fear. You were so good at making people think that y'all was all that and the Islamic tide started coming up.[22]

On that same day, another Irvine speaker, Amir Abdul Malik Ali, succinctly expressed the classic stereotypes of Jewish deceptiveness, conspiracy, and control: "Liars. Straight up liars, Rupert Murdock, Zionist Jews."[23] Next, he used the conspiracy stereotype to anticipate and defuse the inevitable antisemitism charge: "They say that it's anti-Semitic if you say that the Zionists control the media."[24] Malik Ali argued that this claim reflects Jewish arrogance and racism:

> They have taken the concept of chosen people and fused it with the concept of white supremacy. Once you take the concept of chosen people with white supremacy and fuse them together, you will get a people who are so arrogant that that will actually make a statement [that] implies that [they] are the only Semites. That's arrogance and that's the type of arrogance they display every day and that's the same type of arrogance that's getting them into trouble today.[25]

Finally, Malik Ali perpetuated the blood libel: "You all definitely don't love children and you know why? Because you all kill them."[26]

OCR POLICY

Until 2004, OCR's practice was to decline prosecution of cases alleging harassment of Jewish students.[27] The rationale for this surprising practice was that Title VI of the Civil Rights Act of 1964 only prohibits discrimination on the basis of "race, color, or national origin" in federally assisted programs or activities such as colleges and public schools.[28] It does not, however, prohibit discrimination on the basis of religion.[29] Although Congress has subsequently extended this prohibition to cover discrimination on the basis of sex, disability, age, and membership in certain patriotic youth organizations, it has never prohibited religious discrimination in this manner.[30]

The Supreme Court provided a legal response to that objection in 1987, but OCR did not embrace its teaching for seventeen years. In *Shaare Tefila Congregation v. Cobb*, the Supreme Court held that, for purposes of construing the scope of civil-rights protections, Jews may be considered to be a "race" within the meaning of the Civil Rights Act of 1866.[31] The Court reasoned that Jews, like other groups now considered to be "white," were considered to be members of a distinct racial group when the 1866 Act was passed.[32] The Court did not, however, address whether Jews may also be considered members of a distinct race within the meaning of the Civil Rights Act of 1964. Some have considered this to be problematic, because scientific and colloquial understandings of race[33] and Jewish identity changed considerably between 1866 and 1964.[34] However, the Court did observe in dicta that the Equal Protection Clause of the Fourteenth Amendment prohibits racial discrimination as sweepingly as does the 1866 Act.[35] This is important because the 1964 Act was designed to enforce the rights established under the Fourteenth Amendment.

In 2004, OCR issued a series of policy statements regarding "complaints of race or national origin harassment commingled with aspects of religious discrimination against Arab Muslim, Sikh, and Jewish students."[36] On September 13, 2004, OCR issued a widely disseminated formal "Dear Colleague" letter informing recipient institutions that it would exercise its Title VI jurisdiction to defend members of groups, such as Jews, which exhibit both ethnic and religious characteristics.[37] Thus, for example, it would "aggressively investigate alleged race or ethnic harassment against Arab Muslim, Sikh and Jewish students."[38] OCR reasoned that "[g]roups that face discrimination on the basis of shared ethnic characteristics may not be denied the protection of our civil rights laws on the ground that they also share a common faith."[39]

The following month, in another guidance letter, OCR emphasized that, for purposes of extending civil-rights protections under the Civil Rights Act of 1964, "'Jewish' may be interpreted as an ethnic [or]...racial category...even if the alleged victims are Caucasian and American-born."[40] This guidance letter emphasized that "anti-Semitic harassment may include adverse action taken against individuals based on a victim's ethnic background or ancestry, notwithstanding the prospect that such harassment may constitute religious discrimination as well."[41] OCR concluded: "In short, OCR recognizes that Title VI covers harassment of students of Jewish heritage regardless of whether the students may be Caucasian and American born. OCR cannot turn its back on victims of antisemitism on the grounds that Jewish heritage may include both religious and ethnic characteristics."[42]

These two guidance letters established that OCR would prosecute antisemitism cases, except for rare cases in which anti-Jewish discrimination is based solely on the tenets of Jewish religion. OCR based this guidance upon *St. Francis College v. Al-Khazraji*[43] and *Shaare Tefila Congregation*.[44] In *St. Francis College*, the Supreme Court held that Arabs are a "race" within the meaning of the Civil Rights Act of 1866.[45] In *Shaare Tefila Congregation*, the Court extended this holding to encompass Jews.[46] The Court's reasoning in both cases was that the term "race," within the meaning of the 1866 Act, is not limited by contemporary usage of the term. Rather, the Court construed "race" broadly to include groups of shared "ethnic or ancestral heritage," finding that Congress had used the term this broadly at the time.[47] OCR's rationale in extending *Shaare Tefila Congregation* was that the 1964 Act was intended to enforce the same rights established through nineteenth-century civil-rights legislation.[48]

During the second George W. Bush administration, however, Assistant Secretary of Education for Civil Rights Stephanie Monroe took a narrow view of Title VI's protections, which appears to exclude Jews.[49] She conveyed this position in somewhat coded bureaucratic language: "OCR has jurisdiction to investigate complaints raising allegations of religious discrimination or antisemitic harassment *if the allegations also include discrimination over which OCR has subject matter jurisdiction*, such as, race or national origin (including discrimination based on a person's ancestry or ethnic characteristics)."[50] In late 2009, Jewish Telegraphic Agency reporter Eric Fingerhut discovered (and shared with the author) a letter from Monroe's Obama administration successor, Russlyn Ali, which appears to indicate that she plans to continue Monroe's policy in antisemitism cases.

Under this guidance, OCR will only prosecute antisemitism charges "if the allegations also include" other matters "over which OCR has subject matter jurisdiction."[51] In other words, OCR will not address antisemitism per se. In order to understand the import of this statement, one need only observe that one can substitute virtually anything for the term "anti-Semitic harassment," as it appears in her letter, and the meaning of the statement is unchanged. Thus, OCR will also unquestionably investigate "complaints raising allegations of," for example, UFO sightings, lost kittens, or gubernatorial philandering "if the allegations also include discrimination over which OCR has subject matter jurisdiction."[52] This is because OCR is mandated to investigate all complaints that contain allegations of discrimination over which it has jurisdiction, even if the complaints also contain extrajurisdictional material.[53] Needless to say, OCR will ignore the portions of the complaint that address only UFOs, kittens, governors, or antisemitism; but it will focus diligently upon the other, jurisdiction-conferring matters within the complaint.

OCR RESOLUTION

Having interpreted its own antisemitism policy in this manner — rendering it meaningless or incoherent — OCR is now unable to address serious antisemitism allegations in a meaningful way. After investigating the Irvine case for over three years, OCR dismissed the ZOA complaint in a way that demonstrates its inability to grasp the issues at stake. ZOA alleged, inter alia, that anti-Jewish and anti-Zionist conduct at Irvine created a hostile environment for Jewish students on the basis of their ethnic and ancestral heritage.[54] OCR dismissed the complaint without even addressing ZOA's ancestry claims because it no longer adheres to its policy for doing so.[55]

In a thirteen-page closure letter, OCR rejected ZOA's claims on the grounds of timeliness, sufficiency of Irvine's response, and failure to provide sufficient factual information to proceed.[56] Astonishingly, OCR entirely ignored ZOA's claims that Irvine's Jewish students faced discrimination on the basis of their ethnic and ancestral heritage (i.e., their "race" in the *Shaare Tefila Congregation* sense). Moreover, OCR reviewed ZOA's national origin claims only to determine whether Jewish students of Israeli origin faced anti-Israeli national-origin discrimination.[57] OCR's opinion does not even consider whether anti-Jewish ethnic bias constitutes national-origin discrimination in any other respect. OCR provides no explanation of its failure to address ZOA's allegations of anti-Jewish ethnic and ancestral discrimination. It simply ignores the allegations as if they had not been made.[58]

In light of this ruling, Irvine and its defenders declared a total victory. Irvine's law school dean, Erwin Chemerinsky, announced: "The Office for Civil Rights of the United States Department of Education did a through investigation and concluded that there was no basis for finding that there was a hostile or intimidating environment for Jewish students on campus at the University of California, Irvine."[59] Chancellor Michael Drake issued a statement that he was "very gratified with the outcome and closure of this matter."[60] Indeed, the local press echoed Irvine's account of this disposition, trumpeting: "Civil Rights Investigation Clears UCI of Anti-Semitism Charges."[61] Even more emphatically, Irvine's Muslim Student Union announced that ZOA's "assertions were found false after a year-long investigation by the United States Department of Education's Office for Civil Rights."[62] In an article in the *Nation* on "Bogus Campus Anti-Semitism," Jon Wiener, professor of history at Irvine, insisted not only that "OCR exonerated the UCI administration," but also that this should "have been the end of it."[63]

In fact, OCR's disposition was hardly what Irvine's defenders claimed. By its own terms, it was not a full exoneration, since many of the claims were dismissed only on technicalities, such as determinations that the claims were not timely filed. Other claims were dismissed only on the the ground that they did not constitute "national origin" discrimination under OCR's controversial standard — which is hardly the same as finding that they were not antisemitic harassment. Moreover, this letter was only a nonfinal determination, for which an appeal still remains pending before OCR's headquarters more than two years later. Many of ZOA's allegations against Irvine were not even addressed, since they remain subject to a separate case on which OCR has not even ruled preliminarily. On its face then, OCR's closure letter clearly does not support the ubiquitious claims of full exoneration.

Irvine's claim to full exoneration is, however, even more preposterous than it appears to be. In the course of writing a book-length treatment of this subject, *Jewish Identity & Civil Rights*, the author discovered two critical facts about the Irvine case which had not previously been reported.[64] First, OCR's San Francisco office, which conducted the Irvine investigation, had actually concluded the *opposite* of what the closure letter provides. Instead of finding that ZOA had produced "insufficient evidence" to go forward, OCR's career investigators had determined that there was in fact a hostile environment for Jewish students at Irvine.[65] They did not say so only because OCR's senior political appointees directed them to suppress this finding.[66] Second, OCR's top three regional officials in California have all sworn under oath that they believe that OCR headquarters was motivated by antisemitic attitudes when it reversed the regional office's determination and punished (as they view it) the career officials who were responsible for that finding. This extraordinary testimony, reported in *Jewish Identity & Civil Rights*, was elicited in a pending case brought by OCR's top California official alleging that, as a Jew, he faced unlawful discrimination *by OCR* because of the manner in which he attempted to prosecute the case against Irvine.

The closure letter which OCR's regional officials were directed to issue, notwithstanding their opposite recommendations, has been highly controversial. In a statement that was truer than its speaker could have known, California Assemblyman Chuck DeVore panned OCR's ruling as "a classic case of distant bureaucracy in action."[67] The OCR letter evoked greater criticism from U.S. Senate Judiciary Committee members, who lamented that OCR's resolution "is inconsistent with its prior policy statements."[68] Several members of the U.S. House of Representatives also complained that OCR's closure letter "reversed OCR policy, as clarified in 2004, of protecting Jews against anti-Semitism."[69] The more important point, however, is not that OCR failed to follow current guidance but that the approach it did take was wrong as a matter of law, policy and basic fairness.

Beyond ignoring its own publicly stated policies and Supreme Court precedent, OCR's *Irvine* approach fails to understand Jewish identity. OCR's current assumption that Jews are only a religion fails to appreciate that Jews share not only religion but also bonds of ancestry and ethnicity. Indeed, the U.S. Department of State has adopted Merriam-Webster's long-standing definition of antisemitism as "hostility toward or discrimination against Jews as a religious, ethnic, or racial group."[70] The notion that Jews are only a religious group without ethnic or ancestral ancestry is a gaping error, although it is one that follows from OCR's understandable squeamishness about associating Judaism with either racial distinctness or national separateness.

The use of an antiracism provision to protect Jewish Americans from discrimination inevitably raises sensitivities about whether Jews can be considered a distinct "race." The very utterance of the words "Jews" and "race" in a single sentence evokes memories of Dr. Mengele and the pseudoscientific notion that Jews are members of a biologically inferior racial grouping.[71] On the other hand, it is little more credible to assert that "race" exists as a biologically or anthropologically meaningful category that simply does not include Jews. Most commentators agree that contemporary science rejects not only the notion that Jews are a racial group, but the entire racial concept, except as a means of describing social constructions.[72] Jews are, in this sense, neither more nor less racially distinct than other groups except to the extent that they have been perceived, portrayed, and constructed as such by racists. Using antiracism provisions to combat antisemitism both respects original statutory intent and also reflects that antiracism efforts by their nature target a prejudice that is founded upon irrational or inaccurate group identifications. Moreover, the modern, post–*Shaare Tefila Congregation* understanding of antidiscrimination provisions asks only whether Jews are an ethnic or ancestral group — which Jews clearly are — not whether they are a biologically distinct race.[73]

If OCR's current practices misunderstand both Jewish identity and OCR's own policies, they also misconstrue contemporary antisemitism. Commendably, OCR investigators took the unusual step of attending several Irvine programs featuring speakers whose presentations, it was anticipated, would include antisemitic content. Setting aside any First Amendment issues that might arise in this review, however, OCR's ultimate closure letter clearly misunderstood the import of the events that it observed. Based on direct observation, OCR determined that "during these events many speakers criticized Israel, its governmental policies, its treatment of the Palestinians, and Jews throughout the world who support Israel."[74] Moreover, OCR found that some speakers failed to distinguish between their opposition to Zionism and their opposition to Jews.[75] As if to mitigate this finding, however, OCR observed that "their criticism of Jews was focused on their perceived support of Israel."[76] OCR also found that some Irvine speakers during the course of the investigation "made broad generalizations *about Jews*, which were offensive to Jewish students."[77] Nevertheless, OCR determined that "although offensive to the Jewish students, the . . . events at issue were not based on the national origin of the Jewish students, but rather based on opposition to the policies of Israel."[78] For this reason, OCR concluded: "These incidents, therefore, were not within OCR's subject matter jurisdiction."[79]

This blithe dismissal misses the point of contemporary antisemitism; namely, that it frequently assumes the guise of anti-Zionism in order to evade social censure.[80] As the State Department observed in 2008, a distinguishing feature of the new antisemitism is "criticism of Zionism or Israeli policy that — whether intentionally or unintentionally — has the effect of promoting prejudice against all Jews by demonizing Israel and Israelis and attributing Israel's perceived faults to its Jewish character."[81] This fundamental tenet of contemporary antisemitism has been confirmed by many authorities, including the U.S. Commission on Civil Rights, the European Union Agency for Fundamental Rights, and the United Kingdom's All-Party Parliamentary Group Against Antisemitism.[82]

OCR's headquarters dismissed the evidence because it failed to grasp that the anti-Zionist rhetoric at Irvine was not just anti-Israeli but more broadly anti-Jewish. To assume, as these OCR officials did, that the anti-Zionist rhetoric does not relate to the Jewish-American students' "national origin" is to misunderstand that anti-Zionist rhetoric is used to demonize both Israel and the Jewish people in a way that creates a hostile environment for Jewish students. The hostility is not based on any narrowly conceived notion of Jewish nationality, of course, but rather on the mixed religious/ethnic/ ancestral characteristics of Jewish identity.

Kenneth L. Marcus, Lillie and Nathan Ackerman Chair in Equality and Justice in America, Bernard M. Baruch College School of Public Affairs, the City University of New York, and director, Initiative on Anti-Semitism and Anti-Israelism, the Institute for Jewish and Community Research.

This essay is an abbreviated and updated version of Kenneth L. Marcus, "Jurisprudence of the New Anti-Semitism," *Wake Forest Law Review* 44 (2009). It benefits from conversations with participants in Wake Forest University Law School's symposium on "Equality-based Perspectives on the Free Speech Norm: 21st Century Considerations," the 2008 summer research workshop of the Center for Advanced Holocaust Studies at the United States Holocaust Memorial

Museum, and the Baruch College School of Public Affairs Faculty Research Workshop Series; comments from Richard Delgado and Stephanie Marcus; editorial assistance from the staff of the Wake Forest University Law Review; and research assistance by Amita Dahiya and Avital Eliason.

ENDNOTES

1   Letter from Charles R. Love, Program Manager, U.S Dept. of Education, Office for Civil Rights, Region IX, to Dr. Michael V. Drake, Chancellor, University of California, Irvine 2, 4–5.

2   Ibid.

3   OC Independent Task Force on Anti-Semitism, report: "The University of California at Irvine" at 11–12 (2008), http://octaskforce.files.wordpress.com/2008/02/orange-county-task-force-report-on-anti-semitism-at-uci.pdf.

4   "Campus Anti-Semitism," US Commission on Civil Rights, Briefing Report (July 2006), http://www.usccr.gov/pubs/081506campusantibrief07.pdf.

5   Letter from Love to Drake, 11.

6   OC Independent Task Force, the University of California at Irvine, 26.

7   Ibid., 27.

8   Letter from Love to Drake.

9   For example, the Conference of Presidents of Major American Jewish Organizations (the Conference) announced that it was "troubled" by the decision of the OCR, which the Conference explained "will affect Jewish students not only at UCI [University of California, Irvine], but also at other colleges and universities across the United States." Letter from June Walker, Chairperson, Conference of Presidents of Major Am. Jewish Orgs., & Malcolm Hoenlein, Executive Vice Chairman, to Stephanie Monroe, Assistant Sec'y for Civil Rights, U.S. Dep't of Educ. (Feb. 8, 2008). Press Release, Zionist Org. of Am., "ZOA Applauds Presidents' Conference for Criticizing Office for Civil Rights' Troubling Decision on Campus Anti-Semitism" (March 20, 2008), http://www.zoa.org/sitedocuments/pressrelease_view.asp?pressreleaseID=354.

10   The author drafted this policy while serving as the head of OCR. The policy is commemorated in two primary legal guidance memoranda. See Memorandum from Kenneth L. Marcus, Deputy Assistant Sec'y for Enforcement, Office for Civil Rights, U.S. Dept. of Educ. (September 13, 2004), http://www.ed.gov/about/offices/list/ocr/religious-rights2004.html. Letter from Kenneth L. Marcus, Deputy Assistant Sec'y for Enforcement, Office for Civil Rights, U.S. Dept. of Educ., to Sidney Groeneman, Senior Research Assoc., Inst. for Jewish & Cmty. Research 1–2 (October 22, 2004), http://www.eusccr.com/letterforcampus.pdf.

11   Letter from Love to Drake, 1–5.

12   Ibid., 10–11.

13   Letter from Senators Arlen Specter, Jon Kyl & Sam Brownback, Comm. on the Judiciary, to Margaret Spellings, Sec'y, U.S. Dept. of Educ. 1 (February 27, 2008), http://www.zoa.org/media/user/documents/publ/SenJudicCom0208.pdf.

14   The author drafted the policies to which the senators refer.

15   Letter from Love to Drake, 2, 4–5. While this summary is primarily based on OCR's findings, it is conspicuous that the Task Force's contemporaneous investigative report on the same allegations is considerably more detailed, comprehensive, and graphic. For example, while OCR documents numerous swastikas drawn, etched, or carved on the Irvine campus, the Task Force provides this example of a swastika display that one student found particularly intimidating: an Irvine Jewish student was accosted by another student who "said 'Fuck Israel' and then lowered his trousers to show a swastika tattooed on his body." OC Independent Task Force, the University of California at Irvine, 10.

16   Letter from Love to Drake, 2.

17   Ibid., 8 n.11.

18   Ibid., 5–7.

19   Ibid., 6.

20   Ibid., 6 n. 7.

21   Ibid.

22   Ibid.

23   Ibid., 6 n. 8.

24   Ibid.

25   Ibid.

26   Ibid.

27   Kenneth L. Marcus, "Anti-Zionism as Racism: Campus Anti-Semitism and the Civil Rights Act of 1964," *William & Mary Bill of Rights Journal* 15, 3 (2007).

28   42 U.S.C. § 2000(d) (2000).

29   Kenneth L. Marcus, "The Most Important Right We Think We Have But Don't: Freedom from Religious Discrimination in Education," *Nevada Law Journal* 7 (2005), 172.

30   42 U.S.C., *e.g.*, Age Discrimination Act of 1975, §§ 6101–07 (2000) (age); Boy Scouts of America Equal Access Act, 20 U.S.C.A. § 7905 (West 2006); Education Amendments Act of 1972, tit. 9, 20 U.S.C. §§ 1681–88 (2000) (sex); Rehabilitation Act of 1973 § 504, 29 U.S.C. § 794(a) (2000) (disability).

31   Shaare Tefila Congregation v. Cobb, 481 U.S. 615, 617–18 (1987).

32   Ibid., Giving some spin to the decision, the American Jewish Congress's Marc D. Stern commented that "[t]he Court thus added an additional level of legal protection for Jews, although it did so by emphasizing the identity of Jews as an ethnic group, not a religious one." Marc D. Stern, "Antisemitism and the Law: Constitutional Issues and Antisemitism," in Jerome A. Chanes, ed., *Antisemitism in America Today: Outspoken Experts Explore the Myths* (Birch Lane Press, 1995), 385, 394. Having reinterpreted Shaare Tefila Congregation in this way (as an ethnicity case, rather than a "race" case), Stern comments that "[p]erhaps by the end of the twentieth century, that description of American Jews was, in any event, more apt."

33 "Race" has been usefully explained as "an unstable and 'decentered' complex of social meanings constantly being transformed by political struggle." Michael Omi & Howard Winant, *Racial Formation in the United States from the 1960s to the 1980s* (Routledge, 1986/1989), 68.

34 Marcus, "Anti-Zionism as Racism." The tendency among contemporary commentators to "dismiss the discrepancy as a shift in the meaning of the word 'race'" is a mistake; in fact, it reveals changes in racial thinking of "who is who, of who belongs and who does not, of who deserves what and who is capable of what." Matthew Frye Jacobson, *Whiteness of a Different Color: European Immigrants and the Alchemy of Race* (Harvard University Press, 1998), 5–6.

35 St. Francis Coll. v. Al-Khazraji, 481 U.S. 604, 613 n. 5 (1987).

36 Memorandum from Kenneth L. Marcus, Deputy Assistant Secretary for Enforcement, Office for Civil Rights, U.S. Department of Education (Sept. 13, 2004) http://www.ed.gov/about/offices/list/ocr/religious-rights2004.html.

37 Ibid.

38 Ibid.

39 Ibid.

40 Citing Shaare Tefila Congregation v. Cobb, 481 U.S. 615, 617–18 (1987), http://www.eusccr.com/letterforcampus.pdf, 1.

41 Ibid., 1–2.

42 Ibid., 2.

43 St. Francis Coll. v. Al-Khazraji, 481 U.S. 604 (1987).

44 St. Francis Coll. v. Al-Khazraji, 481 U.S. 615 (1987).

45 St. Francis Coll. v. Al-Khazraji, 481 U.S. at 613.

46 Shaare Tefila Congregation v. Cobb, 481 U.S. at 617–18.

47 St. Francis Coll. v. Al-Khazraji, 481 U.S. at 613.

48 Marcus, "Anti-Zionism as Racism," 865–72.

49 Monroe resigned from this position during the presidential transition.

50 Letter from Stephanie Monroe, Assistant Sec'y for Civil Rights, Dep't of Educ., to Kenneth L. Marcus, Staff Dir., U.S. Comm'n on Civil Rights 1 (emphasis added) (December 4, 2006), http://www.eusccr.com/lettermonroe.pdf.

51 Ibid.

52 Ibid.

53 Ibid.

54 Letter from Love to Drake, 1.

55 Ibid.

56 Letter from Charles R. Love, Program Manager, Office for Civil Rights, Region IX, U.S. Dep't of Educ., to Susan Tuchman, Zionist Org. of Am. 2, 13 (Nov. 30, 2007).

57 Ibid., 1–2.

58   Ibid., Letter from Love to Drake, cf. Complaint, 10–11.

59   Erwin Chemerinsky, "Unpleasant Speech on Campus, Even Hate Speech, is a First Amendment Issue," *William & Mary Bill of Rights Journal* 17 (March 2009), 765, 766.

60   Orange County *Register*, http://www.ocregister.com/news/students-190211-jewish-campus.html.

61   Ibid.

62   Letter from the Muslim Student Union to the UCI Administration, October 13, 2009, http://www.msu-uci.com/.

63   Jon Wiener, "Bogus Campus Anti-Semitism," *Nation*, June 19, 2008.

64   For a full account of the Irvine case, *see* Kenneth L. Marcus, *Jewish Identity & Civil Rights* (Cambridge University Press, 2010).

65   In addition, the regional office found that Irvine's administration had taken adequate measures to address this problem. For this reason, the regional office would have closed the case without finding a violation. However, based on conversations with a senior OCR official, it appears clear that, all else being equal, this finding would likely have been followed by a finding of violation a year or two later when subsequent events demonstrated that the administration's actions had not been adequate at all. *See* ibid.

66   Ibid.

67   Orange County *Register,* http://www.ocregister.com/news/students-190211-jewish-campus.html.

68   Letter of Senators Arlen Specter, Sam Brownback and Jon Kyl to Secretary of Education Margaret Spellings, Feb. 27, 2008.

69   Letter of Representatives Brad Sherman, Steven Rothman, Linda Sanchez, Allyson Schwartz, and Robert Wexler, Apr. 30, 2008, http://www.zoa.org/media/user/documents/publ/ushousetoedsecyretitlevi.pdf

70   Global Anti-Semitism Report, 6, http://www.state.gov/documents/organization/102301.pdf.

71   Bat-Ami Bar On and Lisa Tessman, "Race Studies and Jewish Studies: Toward a Critical Meeting Ground," in Lisa Tessman and Bat-Ami Bar On, eds., *Jewish Locations: Traversing Racialized Landscapes* (Rowman & Littlefield Publishers, Inc., 2001), 1, 7 (describing the impact of the Shoah upon the racial self-perception of American Jews).

72   The notion of biological racial distinctions was rejected, for example, in the United Nations Economic and Social Council's 1950 Statement of Race, drafted by Columbia University anthropologist Ashley Montagu, which announced that "scientists have reached general agreement that mankind is one: that all men belong to the same species, Homo sapiens." Jon Entine, *Abraham's Children: Race, Identity and the DNA of the Chosen People* (Grand Central Publishing, 2007), 250–51.

73   At the same time, however, it should be acknowledged that at least some contemporary population geneticists have identified genetic patterns that are significantly more common to Jews, or to some Jewish sub-groups, than to other populations. See Entine, *Abraham's Children*, 351 (acknowledging genetically "identifiable human races

and ethnic groups, including Jews," but rejecting "simplistic racial stereotyping"); David B. Goldstein, *Jacob's Legacy: A Genetic View of Jewish History* (Yale University Press, 2008), 117 (observing that it is now possible "to predict accurately those individuals claiming Jewish ancestry on the basis of their genetic composition alone"). Surveying the literature, Hillel Halkin comments that the burgeoning field of Jewish genetics has demonstrated that there is a "high degree of Y-chromosome similarity among Jewish males from all over the world, coupled with a much lower degree when the comparison is made between Jews and non-Jews from the same region." Hillel Halkin, "Jews and Their DNA," *Commentary* (September 2008).

[74] Letter from Love to Drake, 6.

[75] Ibid.

[76] Ibid.

[77] Ibid., (emphasis added). OCR acknowledged that some Irvine Jewish students felt deeply offended, intimidated, and harassed. Ibid., The Task Force's report went further, indicating that at least one Irvine gentile testified that, "I am not even Jewish and I feel scared for Jewish students on campus." OC Independent Task Force, the University of California at Irvine, 9.

[78] Letter from Love to Drake, 6.

[79] Ibid.

[80] See generally Gary A. Tobin, Aryeh K. Weinberg, Jenna Ferer, eds., *The Uncivil University (Politics & Propaganda in American Education)*, (Institute for Jewish & Community Research, 2005), 95.

[81] Global Anti-Semitism Report, 4.

[82] Marcus, "Anti-Zionism as Racism," 845–49 and sources cited therein.

STANDING UP FOR ACADEMIC INTEGRITY ON CAMPUS

Rachel Fish

Speaking in Memorial Church on September 17, 2002, Lawrence Summers, president of Harvard University, made it clear where he stood on the issue of the divestment campaign against Israel.[1] He stated explicitly, "Serious and thoughtful people are advocating and taking actions that are anti-Semitic in their effect if not their intent."[2] His words reverberated across the campus, where many students and some faculty had taken strong and unwavering positions on the current Arab-Israeli conflict. Formed in the spring of 2002, a time of intensified conflict between Israel and the Palestinian Authority, the divestment campaign had drawn up a petition that called on universities to dissociate themselves financially from Israeli businesses and any companies conducting business in Israel.[3] Although the divestment campaign ultimately failed, the Harvard community remained polarized in its wake.

In the fall of 2002, some members of the Harvard community came to recognize the lack on campus of serious scholarly discourse on the Israeli-Palestinian conflict. Hoping to replace the existing platitudes and talking points with a nuanced discussion, a few sought to organize a conference on the Middle East that would focus particularly on the global increase in antisemitism. As a graduate student at Harvard Divinity School at the time, I, along with a few classmates, thought that this conversation should take place at the Divinity School.[4] Late in the fall 2002 semester a one-day conference on global antisemitism was held.[5] Speakers included Harvard faculty members, a representative of the Anti-Defamation League (ADL), and Charles Jacobs, who had recently set up the David Project, a non-profit organization that would provide students with educational materials about the Arab-Israeli conflict.[6] Jacobs stated that the Divinity School should be concerned with anti-Americanism and antisemitism coming to campus due to an endowed professorship in the name of Sheikh Zayed bin Sultan Al Nahyan, who was associated with antisemitic publications, lectures, and even Holocaust denial. It became apparent that in order to understand Jacobs' claims, I would need additional information about Sheikh Zayed and his associations, and the endowment and conditions of Harvard's agreement with him.

Sheikh Zayed bin Sultan Al Nahyan was the dictatorial ruler of the United Arab Emirates (UAE). In 1966 he succeeded his brother as emir of Abu Dhabi and in 1971 he became president of the UAE. Several times human rights organizations, including Amnesty International, had accused Sheikh Zayed of such abuses as corporal punishment of prisoners, denial of the right to form political parties, prohibition of freedom of expression, censorship of the local media, and complicity of the government in the slave trade of Bangladeshi children.[7] These children were often kidnapped from their homes and brought to the UAE, where they were given little to eat in order to turn them into jockeys in the country's popular sport of camel racing.[8] Sheikh Zayed was one of the world's wealthiest men, controlling one tenth of the world's oil supply; his fortune was estimated at around $23 billion.[9]

In September 2000,[10] Harvard Divinity School announced the establishment of the Sheikh Zayed Al Nahyan Professorship in Islamic Religious Studies. Sheikh Zayed was the president of the United Arab Emirates from 1971 till his death in 2004. In 1999 he established the Zayed Centre for Coordination and Follow-Up (ZCCF) "to promote solidarity and cooperation among the Arab nations in the light of the principles and objectives of the League of Arab States."[11] The Zayed Centre had five objectives: 1) to enhance political, economic, social, and cultural solidarity among the Arab countries; 2) to formulate an "Arab Strategic Vision" to meet present and future challenges; 3) to defend an Arab national identity; 4) to promote communication with international and regional organizations; 5) to establish cultural inter-relationships among Arabs based on the ideal of diversity within unity.[12]

Considered the official think tank of the Arab League, the Zayed Centre held symposia and lectures and issued publications. The ZCCF was directed by the deputy prime minister of the UAE, Sheikh Zayed's son. According to its website, the ZCCF was "the fulfillment of the vision of the President of the UAE His Highness, Sheikh Zayed bin Sultan Al Nahyan." One symposium hosted by the Zayed Centre was on "Semitism." According to the ZCCF, this symposium was

> ...to counter the historical and political fallacies propagated by Israel that has used a variety of means during the past few decades

and in particular after World War II. Israel has indulged in spreading lies and exaggerations about holocaust in order to squeeze out huge sums of money from European countries through worst forms of blackmail and to create false legends in support of the concept of Semitism and establishing a national home for the Jewish people in Palestine.[13]

Among the Zayed Centre's publications was a range of works promoting anti-Jewish, anti-Israel, and anti-Zionist beliefs. One publication, "The Zionist Movement and its Animosity to Jews," addressed the "...activities of the Zionist Movement and its role during the Nazi regime in killing and terrorizing Jews in Europe to force them to immigrate to Israel:"[14]

> In the first chapter, the book enumerates the similarities between Nazism and Zionism. The second chapter discusses the cooperation between Nazism and Zionism which was crowned by the agreement under which the Nazis supplied arms to the Zionist army in Palestine and forced scores of Jews to immigrate to Palestine.[15]

Another of the Zayed Centre's publications, "Does Israel Rule the World?" addressed the tensions between the U.S. government and Israel, explaining that "...the Jewish lobby in USA is behind Israel's excellence, more so because this lobby controls the media, the Congress and monopolies."[16]

The ZCCF not only promoted anti-Israel and anti-Zionist tracts and beliefs, but provided a platform from which Holocaust deniers could publicize their views. "Those who Challenged Israel" was a collection of articles by Holocaust deniers, including David Irving and Roger Garaudy.[17] Not only did the Zayed Centre publish Garaudy, but the wife of Sheikh Zayed bin Sultan Al Nahyan contributed the equivalent of $50,000, in cash, to him. In 1998 Garaudy was tried for violating a 1990 French law that made it illegal to deny the events of the Holocaust and to incite racial hatred; the money was to cover the maximum fine he would be required to pay if found guilty.[18]

The Centre also hosted speakers and sponsored symposia that promoted intolerance toward Jews, Judaism, Israel, and Zionists. In a lecture, "The Making of the Holocaust between Nazism and Israeli Racism," delivered on September 11, 2001, Dr. Mohammed Ahmad Hussain explained:

> Zionists, with their media machinery, have been organizing a long-term orchestrated campaign aiming at the perpetuation of the [lie of the] 'persecution of Jews' or what they call the Holocaust, behind which stand extensive efforts, several establishments and huge funds.[19]

He added that the motivation behind the Holocaust was to "force the Jews to immigrate to Israel; to breed hatred towards non-Jews; [and] to form lobbies around the world that serve the interests of Israel."[20] Dr. Mohamed Saeed Al Bouti, an Islamic Studies Professor at Damascus University and a religious scholar, spoke at the Zayed Centre on March 2, 2002, about the "Situation in Palestine." He stressed that "all military operations done by Palestinian militants [should be] classified as martyr operations and not suicidal operations."[21]

On June 19, 2002, Archimandrite Father Atallah Hanna, spokesperson of the Orthodox Church of Jerusalem and the Holy Land, lectured at the Zayed Centre about how the "Orthodox Church supports Palestinian Resistance." He maintained, "... Palestinian martyrdom is part [of] the Intifada which has to remain kindled until a resolution is achieved for the Palestinian cause."[22] Hanna informed his audience that "the conduct of the Zionist movement is characterized by its racist nature, and that it is completely in contradiction with the Moslem and Christian values."[23]

The Zayed Centre also provided a forum for Lyndon LaRouche, the notorious American antisemite, to spout his hateful diatribes about Jews, Judaism, Israel, and Zionism. In his lecture at the ZCCF, "The Middle East as a Strategic Crossroad," he accused "Jewish gangsters" and "so-called Christian Zionists" of being the major forces behind President George W. Bush's support for Israel.[24]

Sheikh Zayed bin Sultan Al Nahyan extended his power beyond the Zayed Centre to the Zayed bin Sultan Nahyan mosque in Gaza. There, in a Friday sermon broadcast live on official Palestinian Authority television, Dr. Ahmad Abu Halabiya, a member of the Palestinian Authority-appointed "Fatwa Council," characterized the Jews as terrorists "who must be butchered and killed," enlisting the words of Allah in his support:

> O brother believers, the criminals, the terrorists — are the Jews, who have butchered our children, orphaned them, widowed our women and desecrated our holy places and sacred sites. They are the ones who must be butchered and killed, as Allah the Almighty said: 'Fight them: Allah will torture them at your hands, and will humiliate them and will help you to overcome them, and will relieve the minds of the believers ... [25]

Dr. Halabiya continued,

> Have no mercy on the Jews, no matter where they are, in any country. Fight them, wherever you are. Wherever you meet them, kill them.

Wherever you are, kill those Jews and those Americans who are like them — and those who stand by them — they are all in one trench, against the Arabs and the Muslims — because they established Israel here, in the beating heart of the Arab world, in Palestine.[26]

These examples[27] of ZCCF activities, lectures and publications are illustrative of a consistent pattern. The venomous hatred espoused by the ZCCF, as well as the individuals associated with it, could not be ignored.

After conducting research, December 2002-March 2003, two classmates and I met with William Graham, dean of Harvard Divinity School. We presented the dean with a seventy-page dossier outlining the relationship between Zayed and Harvard and the activities of the Zayed Centre, and requesting that the administration seek funding from a credible source for the chair in Islamic studies rather than from an individual associated with the promotion of hate. Dean Graham, who had stated in September 2000 that the endowment was "a most welcome gift,"[28] assured us that he would direct an independent investigation into the matter and respond to our concerns within four to six weeks. Notably, Dean Graham was comfortable with taking a stand on Middle East issues. His name had appeared on the original divestment petition against Israel, though it was later removed. Both Dean Graham and President Summers were given copies of our research on Zayed and I notified the dean that I expected to hear from him within the time he had allotted.

One of the most important elements in the research highlighted the problematic relationship between Harvard and Zayed, as detailed in the Terms of Agreement. Although several aspects of the Terms were disturbing, most unsettling was the clause designating a Harvard University official as a "liaison officer" with the president of the UAE. "This person will advise the UAE on procedures relating to application and admission to the University" and "will encourage relations in other areas of research and development."[29] The commitment to privileging applicants from the UAE and encouraging "relations in other areas of research," which foresaw academic exchanges between Harvard faculty and individuals associated with the Zayed Centre, was suspect. That Harvard faculty should be associated with the activities held at the ZCCF seemed inappropriate and could only benefit the ZCCF, not Harvard.

As I waited for Dean Graham's response, I discussed the funding issue with Jewish students throughout Harvard University, Muslim classmates at the Divinity School, faculty members, and the Boston Jewish community. The majority of the Jewish students supported my efforts but, with a few exceptions, they were reluctant to get directly involved. They indicated that they were busy preparing for final exams, applying to graduate programs, or searching for jobs. Hillel also hesitated to get involved, explaining, "We don't deal with confrontation, we are an apolitical organization." I responded that "I didn't realize that Holocaust denial was something that Hillel would not combat." Hillel would help bring a speaker to campus, but that was not the kind of support needed at the time. After the campaign became more public, some professionals at Hillel helped behind the scenes, but the unwillingness of Jews on campus to support the campaign actively and openly disheartened — and alarmed — me. If this was the response at Harvard, I feared that Jewish organizations at other colleges and universities also responded passively to similar threats against Israel and Jews.

When I met with the Muslim students (MSA) at the Divinity School I explained that as a student of Islam and Arabic, I recognized the need for a position in Islamic studies at the Divinity School; however, the funding should come from reputable sources. The Muslim students responded that "you can do good things with bad money, and even though we recognize that the money may be tainted it is more important to create the position." Some students even claimed that the antisemitic rants "were just words coming from the UAE and should be ignored." I rejoined that "I as a Jew know that words have consequences."

The majority of faculty responded to the issues I raised with silence. A few — less than a handful — were supportive behind the scenes.[30] Both tenured and untenured faculty refused to take a public stand. Many of the faculty with whom I spoke about the endowment ushered me into their offices, closed the door, and whispered, "This is very important. What are *you*, the student, going to do about it?" The reluctance of faculty to take a stand sent the message not to rock the boat. This was an unacceptable position for me. But they refused to make their concerns public.

In order to raise awareness beyond the gates of Harvard Yard I organized a group called Students for an Ethical Divinity School and set up a website "Morality not Money."[31] The site included a petition that called on Harvard to return the Zayed endowment and seek reputable funding for the chair in Islamic studies. The website informed the public about the endowment and the associations with the Zayed Centre, and provided contact information so people could express their concerns directly to university administrators.

After eight weeks passed without any response from Dean Graham to my list of concerns, I concluded that he was hoping time would run out, since graduation was approaching. Thus, when the *Boston Globe* contacted me, I decided to speak. I hoped that the publicity would pressure the university to respond. From March 2003 until the end of July 2004 I continued my efforts to raise awareness about the Zayed endowment — I gave numerous interviews to the media, wrote letters to newspapers, spoke to concerned Harvard alumni, and shared my research with the broader community. In the beginning of the campaign Graham emailed those who wrote to him expressing their disapproval of Harvard's acceptance of the endowment that "Zayed is the most liberal voice in the Arab world." (Liberal compared to whom? Qaddafi? Saddam Hussein?) Clearly, he was not engaging with the issues.

On graduation day, with the help of the David Project, I organized high school students to hand out flyers outside the gates of Harvard Yard outlining the relationship between Harvard, Zayed, and the ZCCF. When my name was called to receive my degree I approached Dean Graham and rather than shaking his hand presented him with 130 pages of evidence against Sheikh Zayed's Centre, an open letter calling on him to publicly denounce the antisemitism coming from the Arab world, and the petition with over 1,500 signatures expressing concern about the endowment. That afternoon the same materials were also delivered to President Summers' office.

Shortly after graduation in August 2003, the President of the UAE, Sheikh Zayed, announced his decision to close the Zayed Centre because the activities "starkly contradicted the principles of interfaith tolerance."[32] Within weeks of the ZCCF's closure, Harvard University announced that it would freeze the funds of the Zayed endowment during the current academic year and would assess whether the university should use the funds as originally planned. The Divinity School assured its constituents that it would appoint a professor of Islamic studies in order to promote understanding between the world's religions.[33] In July 2004, after the endowment had been suspended for about eleven months, Zayed withdrew his donation to the Divinity School. On July 26, 2004 the Divinity School issued the following statement:

> . . . representatives of the UAE informed Harvard of the donor's desire to withdraw the gift for the Zayed Professorship, in advance of the University's scheduled consideration of the matter later this summer. Harvard has agreed to honor this request and to return the funds. Harvard remains strongly committed to advancing the understanding of Islam, and the Divinity School is actively pursuing two faculty appointments — one senior, one junior — in this important field.[34]

This completed the campaign that had begun in December 2002. The immediate goals had been accomplished: disseminating information about the Zayed endowment and stopping Harvard from accepting the donation.

However, the larger issue remained unresolved because other universities, such as Columbia University and Georgetown University, had received donations from Zayed and the UAE and they showed no signs of relinquishing these funds. I soon recognized that similar problems existed on many other campuses. Thus in the summer of 2004 I opened the David Project's New York office and began working with students in the greater New York area to develop strategies to counter the anti-Israel and, in some cases, antisemitic propaganda on their campuses.

At Columbia University I met a with the pro-Israel political action student group, LionPAC,[35] who expressed a desire to confront the overt, and in some cases implicit, discrimination on campus against supporters of Israel and Zionism. These students believed that the situation in Columbia's Middle East and Asian Languages and Cultures department (MEALAC)[36] could be addressed by educating alumni about the problem. Alumni would then alert the university administration to the nature and dimensions of the problem, and it would respond accordingly. The students were concerned about a handful of MEALAC faculty who used the classroom to promote a particular, anti-Israel agenda, intimidating any students who supported Israel and Zionism. The university lacked a grievance procedure that would allow students to voice complaints in a manner that protected them. The students asked if the David Project could help them with this matter. It was also known that Zayed had given Columbia about $200,000 toward the creation of the Edward Said Chair of Middle East Studies. Despite Harvard's recent actions, Columbia was unwilling to return the funds.

The David Project agreed to support the students and asked them to provide corroborated examples of egregious behavior occurring in the MEALAC department. We requested that the students keep journals of classroom incidents in order to assess the dimensions of the problem. After exploring the situation for a number of months, it was decided that the students needed to communicate their situation and their distress to an audience beyond the confines of the campus. The students suggested making a film.[37] The David Project supported this effort and began working closely with students to make a film that would document some of the problems they had encountered.

In 2004 the David Project, in collaboration with the Columbia students, produced the film *Columbia Unbecoming*.[38] The film documented dozens of cases of intimidation of pro-Israeli students by MEALAC faculty. Not intended to be a full documentary account, *Columbia Unbecoming* was an effort to collect students' testimonies about classroom incidents and campus experiences. The testimonies revealed an alarming trend of bias, intimidation, hostility, and opposition to open discussion and debate. The purpose of the film was to provide a platform for the students to express their concerns and garner support for their efforts to change the environment within the MEALAC department. The goal was also to alert Columbia University to the problems in the hope that they could be resolved internally. In the film, American and Israeli Jews studying at Columbia recounted how professors and classmates silenced and intimidated them for holding views sympathetic to Israel or simply for being Jews. The students believed that academic integrity was being subordinated to a rigid political agenda. Columbia students contended that the administration had allowed professors in the Middle East studies department to create a hostile environment and to conduct classes lacking in rigorous scholarship or balanced academic inquiry.

Moreover, in violation of the university's code of ethics, professors had been allowed to intimidate students based on their ethnicity or national origin. In one episode, a tenured professor stated that a Jewish student could have "no voice" in discussing the Middle East conflict because her green eyes meant she was "not a Semite." Another professor, who taught a course on the Israeli-Palestinian conflict, challenged an Israeli student: "You served in the IDF — how many Palestinians have you killed?"

I also conducted over two dozen off-the-record interviews with tenured and non-tenured faculty at Columbia, who expressed their concerns about the MEALAC department and academic intimidation on campus. Although they reiterated many of the students' sentiments and experiences, they were unwilling to appear in the film for fear of reprisal. They saw participating in the video as "career suicide," and most indicated that expressing their views in the current intellectual environment would jeopardize their credibility as academics. Even some students felt the need to hide their identities in the film and asked that their voices be altered and their faces masked, to protect their future academic standing. The students struggled to understand why so many professors and administrators remained silent.

The film explored ways in which professors, administrators, and alumni could create a safe campus environment in which academic standards would be upheld. The film ended with students' pleas to Lee Bollinger, president of Columbia, to help the university live up to the ideals of the academy and create an intimidation-free environment for all students. The film was shown to members of the Columbia administration, alumni, donors, trustees, and faculty for six months before public debate began. Senior administrators, including the provost, Alan Brinkley, viewed the film and were informed of student concerns. Students, forming an independent group called Columbians for Academic Freedom, were deeply involved in the effort to change Columbia's classroom culture and to have their grievances recognized and addressed. When the administration did not issue a response to the students' concerns during those six months and the president of Barnard College, Columbia's sister school, publicly disclosed the existence of the video, the students, not the David Project, decided to publicize the issue.[39] Thus in October 2004 *Columbia Unbecoming* was publicly released.

As a result of the ensuant outside pressures, President Bollinger created an ad hoc faculty committee to address the students' charges. Composed of five professors from the School of Arts and Sciences, the committee was tasked with examining the "...set of issues and complaints that gave rise to the current controversy....Its focus will be the character of interactions between faculty and students occurring within the classroom and the broader pedagogical environment."[40] Of the five professors on the committee, two had signed the divestment petition against Israel; one was the dissertation advisor of Joseph Massad, the professor most often accused by students of intimidation and incitement towards racism; one wrote that America went to war in Iraq for Israel's benefit and that Israel is ultimately responsible for the increase in global antisemitism.[41] Lastly, one professor was a university administrator who had ignored multiple complaints by students regarding this situation. Moreover, the individual responsible for selecting the committee members was Nicholas Dirks, vice president for Arts and Sciences, who was married to Professor Janaki Bakhle, who co-taught a class with Massad. Both Dirks and Bakhle signed the original divestment petition although Dirks' name was later removed.

Clearly, this committee could not inspire any confidence in its objectivity. Thus students were not convinced that they could safely voice their complaints to this committee. In December 2004 students wrote to President Bollinger, stating that they "...fear[ed] speaking to the committee will have real repercussions on their academic and professional advancement..."[42] Still, some students who appeared in *Columbia Unbecoming* ended up speaking to the ad hoc committee and those who remained reluctant to do so were encouraged to submit the transcript of the film as evidence.

The ad hoc committee report,[43] issued March 28, 2005, recognized that one of the accused professors, Joseph Massad, had silenced student voices and had acted in a manner that could be perceived as intimidating, but overall—and not surprisingly—the report cleared faculty of statements "...that could reasonably be construed as anti-semitic."[44] Notably, the students had never accused the MEALAC faculty of antisemitism, but of intimidation — yet the committee did not seriously address this matter.

Since the campaign, Columbia has instituted no substantial changes. The MEALAC department remains largely unchanged and the tendency toward one-sided instruction persists. Columbia did introduce new grievance procedures, although their effectiveness remains unclear. And in July 2009 Joseph Massad was granted tenure after his earlier bid for tenure had been denied.[45] What then was accomplished by *Columbia Unbecoming*? Martin Kramer summarized it best: *Columbia Unbecoming* "... put a human face on the dysfunction of Middle Eastern studies;" it empowered students to speak out publicly; that this occurred in the academic home of Edward Said and his disciples made the story all the more powerful;[46] and the kind of student revolt that occurred at Columbia can spread to other campuses.[47]

Academic freedom is a cornerstone of democracy and should be upheld. In no way were the students or the David Project working to suppress this important freedom. Universities should be concerned with protecting free speech, including the right of professors to offer courses that take a view of the Middle East that differs from that of the pro-Israel community. However, universities also have a responsibility to ensure an environment in which all responsible views can be articulated and carefully assessed. An environment that is hostile to the presentation of alternative scholarly points of view is troubling precisely because it does not allow for the kind of free expression the public reasonably expects at a university. Thus the David Project and the students exposed a problem of rampant bias, hostility and vilification of pro-Israel students and viewpoints that precluded free intellectual discourse on the Arab-Israeli conflict at Columbia University.

This situation is not unique to Columbia; students at many other American universities routinely encounter highly politicized Middle East studies departments. The differences are only in the levels of professorial misconduct. The endowment situation at Harvard and the faculty abuse of the classroom at Columbia are merely those cases that received public attention and highlighted the anti-Israel bias and, in some cases, the antisemitism now appearing on numerous campuses. Perhaps the most insidious element of this campaign is professors' utilization of their classrooms and academic positions to mis-educate, and at times incite, students against Israel and, in some cases, even against Jews. To be sure, most students, including most Jewish students, are politically apathetic, and the problem is mainly confined to certain fields in the humanities and Middle Eastern studies departments. But the impact is significant.

"Palestinianism" has become the *cause celèbre* — and even the litmus test — for progressives on too many campuses.

Although criticism of Israeli and American policies is certainly legitimate, campus campaigns on the Middle East are often devoted to delegitimizing and demonizing the state of Israel, and sometimes the criticism morphs into antisemitism. The insensitivity or indifference of many university administrators to the problems on their campuses facilitates this extreme hostility toward Israel. Some university presidents struggle to distinguish between free speech and hate speech and academic instruction and propaganda. The issue is complicated, however, by the anti-Israel groups' abuse of the language of human rights in their framing of the conflict. Students, faculty, and alumni need to make university administrators aware of the problem on campus, and to pressure them to ensure academic integrity and an environment that always encourages open, scholarly and systematic discussion of the issues in the Middle East.

Rachel Fish is a doctoral candidate in Israel Studies in the department of Near Eastern and Judaic Studies at Brandeis University. Her dissertation examines the concept of bi-nationalism from pre-1948 Israel to the present.

ENDNOTES

[1] The divestment campaign at Harvard and MIT began in May 2002. By early September 2002 approximately 75 Harvard faculty members had signed the divestment petition. The campaign called on universities to divest from companies with holdings in Israel. Some faculty members merely signed the petition while others were actively engaged in the campaign. Depending on the version of the petition, some faculty encouraged the divestment of funds from businesses in Israel, others also encouraged removing funds from companies conducting business in Israel, and some faculty sought to divest from companies and governments that sell arms to Israel.

[2] http://www.thecrimson.com/article/2002/9/23/summers-stifles-israel-debate-university-president;http://www.thecrimson.com/article/2003/12/4/you-say-you-want-a-resolution.

[3] In March and April, after suicide bombers had killed many Israeli civilians, Israel launched Operation Defensive Shield. The operation increased the apprehension of many Palestinians associated with militant groups, who accused Israelis of massacring Palestinians, although the evidence belied the claim. Twenty-three Israeli soldiers and fifty-two Palestinians were killed in this campaign. At the time human rights organizations accused Israel of war crimes, although ultimately the United Nations found no evidence to support such claims.

4   The Divinity School is the oldest graduate institution at Harvard. It is where students study religion and the role of religion in societies. We felt it appropriate that the Divinity School should be engaged in discussing religious hatred and intolerance in the twenty-first century.

5   Approximately 40-50 people attended, including students, faculty, and administrators at the Divinity School. The conference was organized by Rachel Fish and Noah Bickart, both second-year graduate students at the Divinity School.

6   Jacobs was president of the David Project and co-founder of the American Anti-Slavery Group.

7   U. S. Department of State 2008 Human Rights Report: United Arab Emirates. http://www.state.gov/g/drl/rls/hrrpt/2008/nea/119129.htm

8   Ibid., and http://www.sightsofdubai.com/camel-racing-in-uae. In 2002 the UAE banned the use of children as camel jockeys, but it was not until 2005 that the government actively enforced the ban.

9   Forbes, July 3, 2000. http://www.forbes.com/forbes/2000/0703/6515256a.html.

10   Wendy McDowell, "Divinity School establishes new Islamic studies chair," *Harvard University Gazette*, September 28, 2000.

11   http://www.zccf.org.ae. The Zayed Centre website is no longer available. I have included the URL for the websites in which I found the original material, though much of this information has been removed from the internet. As I researched the Zayed Centre, I noticed that it was removing the controversial materials, so I made hard copies of the website pages. The Centre has been defunct since 2003. It was founded in the United Arab Emirates as the official think tank for the League of Arab States, an association of 22 Arab nations. The Centre was principally funded by UAE president Sheikh Zayed bin Sultan Al Nahyan. His son, His Highness Sheikh Sultan Bin Zayed Al Nahyan, was its founding chairman.

12   Ibid.

13   http://www.zccf.org.ae. According to the Los Angeles *Times*, August 31, 2002, Jews were labeled the "enemies of all nations." The ZCCF organized the conference "under the umbrella of the Arab League" to "expose the fallacious claims and concocted legends of the Zionists and to counter their nefarious propaganda against Arabs and Muslims after September 11."

14   http://www.zccf.org/ae/e_PubDesc.asp?Pubid=160.

15   Ibid.

16   http://www.zccf.org.ae/e_PubDesc.asp?Pubid=142.

17   Garaudy is a Frenchman who wrote *The Founding Myths of Modern Israel* (Les Mythes Fondateurs de la Politique Israélienne) (1996), in which he claimed that "...there was no Nazi program of genocide during World War II, and that Jews essentially fabricated the Holocaust for their financial and political gain." http://www.adl.org.holocaust.denial_me/western_deniers.asp.

18   Ibid.

19   http://www.zccf.org.ae/e_TitleDescription.asp?Tid=243.

20   Ibid.

21   http://www.zccf.org.ae/e_TitleDescription.asp?Tid=119.

22 http://www.zccf.org.ae/e_TitleDescription.asp?Tid=43.

23 Ibid.

24 http://www.zccf.org/ae/e_TitleDescription.asp?Tid=39 and http://www.zccf.ae/e_TitleDescription.asp?Tid=44.

25 Palestinian Authority Television broadcast calling for killing Jews and Americans, October 13, 2000. http://www.memri.org/bin/opener.cgi?Page=archives&ID=DP13800.

26 Ibid.

27 For a further sample of activities associated with the ZCCF, see the Middle East Media Research Institute (MEMRI): http://www.memri.org/bin/opener.cgi?Page=archives&ID=SR1803.

28 McDowell, "Divinity School establishes new Islamic studies chair."

29 The University Terms of Agreement for the Sheikh Zayed Al Nahyan Professorship in Islamic Religious Studies at Harvard Divinity School, Summer 2000. The document was signed by Mansour bin Zayed Al Nahyan on behalf of Sheikh Zayed, Harvey Fineberg, provost, for the President and Fellows of Harvard College, and Bryan Hehir, Chair of the Executive Committee of Harvard Divinity School.

30 Professor Jon Levenson of the Divinity School became very involved in the campaign, speaking publicly about the problems with the endowment. A few other faculty members also raised the issue with the university administration. I will always be indebted to these faculty members. See also Jonathan Jaffit, "Fighting Sheikh Zayed's Funding of Islamic Studies at Harvard Divinity School," in Manfred Gerstenfeld, ed., *Academics Against Israel and the Jews* (Jerusalem Center for Public Affairs, 2007), pp. 108–113.

31 The website was formed with the aid of the David Project, one of the few organizations willing to take an active role in the campaign. http://www.petitiononline.com/zayedno/petition.html

32 http://www.hds.harvard.edu/news/article_archive/zayed.html.

33 Ibid.

34 http://www.hds.harvard.edu/news/zayed_update.html.

35 Many of LionPAC students became intimately involved in the Columbia campaign.

36 MEALAC is an inter-disciplinary department offering courses in literature, culture, history, and the languages of the Middle East. See Noah Liben, "The Columbia University Report on Its Middle Eastern Department's Problems: A Paradigm for Obscuring Structural Flaws," pp. 95–102 and Martin Kramer, "Columbia University: The Future of Middle Eastern Studies at Stake," pp. 103–107, both in *Academics Against Israel and the Jews.*

37 The head of LionPAC, Daniella Kahane, recommended that students who had experienced anti-Israel bias recount their experiences on camera.

38 Avi Goldwasser was the Executive Producer.

39 Judith Shapiro, president of Barnard College, mentioned *Columbia Unbecoming* and the incidents of abuse in the classroom on October 18, 2004, when she spoke at the Lion of Judah Conference, a forum of over 500 people, including the press.

40 http://www.columbia.edu/cu/vpas/adhocgrievancecommittee/guidelines_to_procedure.html.

41 Lisa Hirschmann "Committee Draws Fire, Keeps Investigating MEALAC," *Columbia Daily Spectator*, January 27, 2005, http://www.campus-watch.org/article/id/1557. The individuals who comprised the committee were: Lisa Anderson, dean of the School of International and Public Affairs; Mark Mazower, history professor; Farah Griffin, professor of English literature and comparative literature; Jean Howard, professor of English and vice provost for Diversity Initiatives; and Ira Katznelson, professor of political science and history.

42 For a more detailed account, see Liben, "The Columbia University Report."

43 Ad Hoc Grievance Committee report. March 28, 2005. http://www.columbia.edu/cu/news/05/03/ad_hoc_grievance_committee_report.html

44 Ad Hoc Grievance Committee report.

45 Martin Kramer notes about Massad, "The member of MEALAC at the center of the controversy did his PhD at Columbia, had it published by Columbia University Press, and received his tenure-track teaching appointment at Columbia. He is the ultimate Columbia product; to deny him now would throw into question the entire quality control mechanism of the university." Address to a conference on "The Middle East and Academic Integrity on the American Campus," convened at Columbia University on March 6, 2005, reprinted as "Columbia University: The Future of Middle Eastern Studies at Stake," pp. 103–107 in *Academics Against Israel and the Jews*, p. 106.

46 Ibid, p. 105.

47 Ibid, p. 107.

MODERN LANGUAGE ASSOCIATION AND CAMPUS MADNESS

Evelyn Avery

In the late 1960s and early 1970s, the Modern Language Association (MLA), one of the largest academic organizations in the country, became highly politicized, positioning itself against the Vietnam War and condemning American imperialism. The door was open to subverting the original intellectual purpose of the group for political ends.

Increasingly engaged with social and political issues, in 1998 the MLA recognized the Radical Caucus (RC), which would take extreme positions on various issues. A tightly knit group of the disaffected, the RC gained notoriety by embracing the Palestinian cause and almost succeeded in persuading the MLA to censure and condemn Israel. Anti-Zionism intensified from 2007 through 2009 at three conventions in which anti-Israel resolutions were accepted by the Executive Council and transmitted to the Delegate Assembly. They were heatedly debated and rejected one year, approved, sent to the whole membership and adopted the next, and finally quashed by the Executive Council in 2009.

The first shot was fired at MLA on December 28, 2007, when an impassioned Zionist interrupted the panel "Never Again? Representations of Anti-Semitism in Jewish American Literature," warning of the RC proposal to censure Israeli scholars for their country's treatment of Palestinian educators. Out of an audience of twenty-five, four of us agreed to attend the Executive Council meeting and then the General Assembly. Little did we realize that the decision would become part of an all-consuming process for the next three years.

I expected the meetings to be civilized, the tone tempered, logic and evidence exhibited. Wrong on every count. Professor Ann Shapiro and I, assisted by MLA member and head of the American Association of University Professors (AAUP) Cary Nelson, challenged the depiction of Israel before the Council, where the Radical Caucus, led by Grover Furr, Margaret Foley and a room full of supporters, denigrated Israel as fascist, oppressive, undemocratic. Their proof was a swath of biased articles from the strongly pro-Palestinian Middle East Studies Association (MESA), the *New York Times*, and other sources. Outnumbered, we listened to the strident voices of our opponents, whose case depended upon depicting Israel as the monstrous Goliath and Palestinians as helpless victims.

The next day the attack continued — this time in a huge room with about 120 delegates who were to vote on several resolutions, the Israeli-Palestinian one emerging late in the afternoon. Though the five Israel supporters were seated in the observers' section, and only two of us spoke, Furr and friends had allies amongst the delegates, members of the RC, to support them from the floor. This was a year before the incursion into Gaza, so the radicals dwelled on the Lebanon War, blaming Israel for defending itself against Hezbollah. With protesters outside the meeting waving anti-Israel banners, the majority of delegates listened as the Zionists supported the only democracy in the Middle East. It seemed a hopeless cause — until far in the front of the delegate assembly a black man jumped up and, signaling frantically, motioned me outside to the lobby. It was Christopher Bell, a temporary lecturer and colleague at Towson University. "Do you want me, as a delegate, to speak for your side, for Israel?" he asked. Seeing my shocked look, he explained that he had toured concentration camps in Europe, had visited Auschwitz, and could never forget what Jews had suffered during the Holocaust. Furthermore, he related that as an instructor of African-American literature and disability studies, he had researched the long history of Jews and empathized with their suffering, but more importantly, admired their ability to overcome their painful past and build a new life in Israel. A realist, he was familiar with the Arab history of involvement in the African slave trade in the past and the present.

Astonished and relieved, I embraced Chris and instructed him to do "what he could" to defeat the anti-Israel resolution. Within minutes Chris had the floor and in a passionate voice identified himself as a black gay man who understood other people's suffering. He criticized the attempt to censure Israeli academics, the most open-minded in the region. The courageous support of Israel by a gay black man visibly moved the delegates and ultimately swayed the majority to vote against the resolution that "The MLA defend the Academic Freedom and the Freedom of Speech of faculty and speakers to criticize Zionism and Israel."[1] The resolution was, in effect, an attempt to sanction disruptions of pro-Israel speakers, without protecting Israel's advocates at anti-Zionist presentations. Without Bell, who died last spring, and the help of Cary Nelson, the outcome could easily have been different. However, as Nelson warned us, "they will be back next year with another resolution; be prepared."

I was not able to attend the MLA convention in 2008, and a Jewish literature session, involving some of my colleagues, was held at the same time as the Delegate Assembly debated the RC's latest, even more egregious, anti-Israel resolution. Nelson was right; they were back and this time they were armed with news of Israel's invasion of Gaza. The stage was set, I heard from colleagues. Outside the hall were demonstrators ranting about Gaza and the occupation. Inside the Delegate Assembly, Grover Furr and compatriots railed against imperialistic Israel with little opposition, except that Cary Nelson removed references in their resolution to "Zionist groups" and "Palestine" which would have delegitimized Israel. The modified 2008 Resolution passed the Assembly, and was transmitted to the whole MLA membership for an online vote by December.

We had nine months in which to organize and persuade colleagues to support Israel by commenting online and voting for our resolution instead of the RC's anti-Israel one. I contacted SPME (Scholars for Peace in the Middle East), an organization with thousands of American, Canadian, Israeli and European members, dedicated to fair treatment of Israel and a just settlement of Middle Eastern conflicts. My article, published in their online newsletter, alerted sympathetic MLA members to the dangers of the 2008 anti-Israel resolution, which exceeded the previous one by asserting that:

> Whereas those teaching and writing about the occupation and the Middle East culture have come under fire from anti-Palestinian groups on extra-academic grounds; Whereas education at all levels in the occupied territories is being stifled by the occupation; Be it resolved that the MLA endorses teaching and scholarship about Palestinian culture, supports members who come under attack for pursuing such work, and expresses solidarity with scholars of Palestinian culture.[2]

My note to the online Jewish Faculty Round Table elicited support from additional MLA members, who pledged to attend the convention and oppose the anti-Israel resolution. Professors Ann Shapiro, Carole Kessner and I collected signatures for the pro-Israel resolution, which we crafted through e-mails, phone calls, and a day-long New York meeting. During an intense seven months, we gathered articles from the *Wall Street Journal*, *Jerusalem Post*, *Washington Times*, *Washington Post*, and even the *New York Times*, illustrating Israel's vulnerability to terrorism, its repeated offers to negotiate, its reluctance to invade Gaza, and its efforts to avoid civilian targets. Equally important, we included proof of the harassment of pro-Israel speakers on American and Canadian campuses and of radical Islamists propagandizing at universities.

Our evidence indicated that it was Israel advocates who were under assault in U.S higher education, not Palestinian or Arab supporters. Instances of disruption and indoctrination have been legion at Columbia, University of California at Irvine, Georgetown, and even Brandeis, where former president Jimmy Carter refused to share a platform with Alan Dershowitz, professor of law at Harvard, who would directly challenge his contention that Israel was an "apartheid state." Lesser-known schools, such as Central Connecticut State University and Towson University, had also become the scenes of anti-Israel activity. Rather than just rejecting the pro-Palestinian resolution, we offered an alternative one supporting Israel:

> Whereas Israeli culture, literature and scholarship support open inquiry and debate;
> Whereas Israeli scholars and universities have been subjected on political grounds to boycotts and censorship at conferences, campuses and in print;
> Whereas the MLA is committed to academic freedom;
> Be it resolved that the MLA reject the radical attacks on Israel's democratic institutions and support Israeli professors and scholars, as well as others who pursue scholarship on Israeli and other Middle Eastern literature and culture.[3]

Our case for Israeli democracy was bolstered when Professor Neve Gordon of Ben Gurion University called for a boycott of "apartheid Israel" and was supported by colleagues defending his freedom of speech. Notably, there were no Palestinians who publicly condemned Fatah or Hamas or acknowledged that Israel was responding to sustained attacks on its people. Where were the Neve Gordons or groups like *Peace Now* among the Palestinians?

Despite the double standard, our 2009 resolution, unlike the RC one, affirmed the 2007 statement, which supported all Middle Eastern scholarship and refused to censure either side. Although we presented sufficient signatures and evidence to the MLA, our resolution was never forwarded to the general membership for a vote. Instead, the 2008 RC anti-Israel resolution was posted online for members' comments prior to a vote before the December 2009 convention.

We assumed that our resolution would appear the following year along with the even worse anti-Israel one. Meanwhile, we worked to defeat the 2008 anti-Israel resolution. With the assistance of SPME and the efforts of Yael Halevi Weiss (McGill), Edna Aizenberg (Latin American Jewish Studies Association), Irving Rothman (University of Houston), and others, we urged MLA members to support fairness through online comments and votes against the RC resolution. Although a number of comments were pro-Israel, with many scholars even questioning the wisdom of MLA politicizing the issue, the final tally, 863 to 540, supported the pro-Palestinian side.

Despite all our efforts, the Radical Caucus had succeeded in its assault on Israel. An informal survey determined that most of the 33,000 members had not voted and that many who had were ill-informed about the Middle East, swayed by propaganda depicting the Palestinians as helpless victims. However, all was not lost; we anticipated ushering our 2009 pro-Israel resolution to passage the next year, since we had met all the requirements and would be even more organized. We were therefore surprised when MLA Executive Council Director Rosemary Feal e-mailed me the following message on November 17, 2009:

> I am sorry that your resolution cannot go forward, especially after all the work you have put into it.... I should add that yours was not the only resolution that dealt with the Middle East; the committee came to the same conclusion on both resolutions.
>
> On a personal note, I must say that I would welcome a reduction in the number of resolutions that divide our membership.... It seems to me that the more energy we spend focusing on "research in...modern languages and their literatures," the better. If I could personally erase some resolutions ratified in the past, I'd do so in a flash. But the MLA is a democratic association in which a small minority of members vote. Perhaps this year with electronic balloting, things will be different.

The December electronic balloting passed the RC 2008-1 resolution. For the first time, MLA was on record as favoring one side in the Middle East, though it had passed an even-handed resolution in 2007. However, the RC 2009 resolution, more viciously condemning Israel for its Gaza incursion, was rejected, according to Ms. Feal, along with ours as too political and not in the interests of the MLA. Doubtless, our members' comments had an effect.

The Radical Caucus would no longer be the sole voice on Middle Eastern scholarship, or so we hoped.

Obvious lessons were gleaned from this experience, which paralleled those learned on our campuses. Persistence, patience and presence were essential in combating the enemies of Israel, who were always on the offensive. Experiences on my own campus, Towson University, illustrated the dangers of allowing ideological Islamists to insinuate themselves at a university. Until 2002 Towson had been a large but quiet campus in the University of Maryland system, situated in a middle-class suburb of Baltimore. About 30% of its 17,000 students came from nearby states such as New York, New Jersey, and Delaware. With a Jewish population of approximately 10%, it had a Hillel and a Jewish Studies program, which my now-deceased colleague Arnold Blumberg and I initiated in 1997, with the approval of the administration. For years we had offered courses in Jewish literature and Jewish history. We organized film festivals, lectures, celebrations of Yom Ha'atzmaut and commemorations of Yom HaShoa. Coordinated by myself and the History Department chair, the Jewish Studies program committee met once or twice a semester to plan activities — non-controversial, informational events about Jewish life and Israel, such as the showing of "Operation Moses and Solomon," on the immigration of Ethiopian Jews to Israel.

Until 2002, radical Islam and Israel-bashing did not exist on our campus. Then, during that year, the professor of Indian history retired and the search for a replacement was broadened to include hiring a historian who could teach about the Middle East. On a campus where there was no intellectual demand for Middle Eastern studies and few Muslim students, the position seemed extraneous. However, some at the university did not want to be left behind in the trend towards Middle Eastern studies. After all, it was reasoned, every self-respecting history department would soon have its Islamic expert.

Enter a professor with a PhD from a history department and Institute of Middle Eastern Studies. Although as Director of Jewish Studies, I had a vital interest in the Islamic history search, I was not asked to participate, but was assured by the history chair that the department would choose a real scholar, dedicated to fairness and balance, who would treat Israel as part of the Middle East. When the professor was selected, the chair (who was Jewish) shared his relief with me, convinced that the search committee had accomplished a real coup — hiring an impartial educator to teach Islamic history.

It didn't take long to discover how wrong they were. Six months after her arrival she, along with an Israeli co-host, organized the showing of a Palestinian film "Rana's Wedding," the story of a Palestinian love affair thwarted by Israeli barriers and occupation, by "the stress and despair that an occupied people must deal with." Although the history department chair refused to urge her to balance the event with another film or discussant with a pro-Israel perspective, he encouraged me to do so.

When I called her and requested that she consider offering a "fair, more balanced program," she rejected my recommendation on the basis that the film was fair; there was no other side, since there was no parity. Mighty Israel was heavily armed while the Palestinians had nothing. As a scholar fluent in Arabic and well-traveled in the Middle East, she considered herself different from American Jews who were single-mindedly pro-Israel, adding that there were Israelis who agreed with her. Asked if she had shared these views with the search committee during her interview, she replied that they hadn't asked for them.

Although she insisted that she presented a range of views in her classes, Jewish students had already begun to complain. When an elderly Holocaust survivor challenged some of her statements in class, he reported that he was ordered to take a seat in the back of the room, an episode confirmed by his outraged wife. Another student, a young Russian immigrant, described feeling suppressed, fearful that her grade would be lowered if she disagreed with the professor. Within a year the word spread around Hillel and Jewish students generally avoided the Palestinian-Israeli conflict course she had introduced, in addition to her Islamic history classes. Her open support for extracurricular Islamic activities also telegraphed her sympathies to faculty and students.

Although as the Jewish Studies advisor, I counseled students about courses and occasionally contributed to holiday and commemorative activities at Hillel, I had avoided attacking Arabs, Palestinians, or the Intifada. In my ethnic literature classes, I have taught Islamic novels, comparing the image and treatment of women in them with those in ultra-Orthodox Jewish fiction. In both my Jewish and ethnic literature courses I have had students of many ethnicities, including a few Muslims, who enriched class discussion and from whom I have learned.

This professor's approach was alien to me — *chutzpadic*, in your face, shameless. And as an assistant professor of one year, she was getting her way, having found allies among other leftist colleagues and having persuaded the dean that academic freedom protected her activities and approach. Jewish Studies was told it could offer its own programs but could not expect to be involved in direct rebuttal. Of course, this signal was interpreted as encouraging the anti-Zionists.

Within two years, this professor coordinated a major presentation, "Jerusalem Women Speak," described by *CAMERA* (Committee for Accuracy in Middle East Reporting in America) as three women speaking with a "unified voice against Israel, [designed] to spread vicious and false propaganda." And it was scheduled on Simchat Torah, when observant Jews could not attend. However, members of Tigers for Israel (the campus Zionist group) were there and took pictures and notes, despite being warned by campus police to stay away. Someone had (mis)informed the police that the group would cause trouble. According to reports, a good time was had by all, except for the minority of non-observant Jews who managed to attend. The room was packed with curious Muslim students, community members and sympathetic faculty, and was festooned with Palestinian flags and signs. The panel of three women, a 22-year-old Palestinian Muslim, a 48-year-old Israeli Jew, and a 61-year-old Palestinian Christian, competed in blaming Israel for Palestinians' woes. The few dissenters could barely be heard.

The next anti-Israel program (2007) featured the Syrian envoy to the United States. Alerted to the event, Shalom USA, the Jewish radio hour, advertised it, which resulted in a peaceful pro-Israel counter-demonstration outside the auditorium. Despite the envoy's silken tones and the distinction he made between Israelis — Zionists, on the one hand, and Jews (some of whom were his friends), on the other — his biases were transparent and critical questions were limited by the moderator.

The necessity of having a friendly, uncritical audience was again evident when the professor conducted a *New York Times*-sponsored discussion of the Gaza incursion. For the last few years, the *Times* has been distributed free on campus and has supported monthly, professor-led discussions of its articles. Having read the *Times'* pieces on Israel, the Hillel director, Jewish students and faculty gathered for this meeting to hear her perspective on Israel's retaliation against Gaza. Misinformation abounded, as the suffering of Gazan civilians and the numbers of disaffected Israeli soldiers were exaggerated. Hamas's provocation and Israel's painful 2005 withdrawal from Gaza were buried, while Israel was indicted and judged guilty of crimes against Palestinians.

However, we came prepared with facts, assembled from many sources, to challenge the professor. Although she refused to recognize my raised hand, she could not ignore my colleagues' rebuttal of her propaganda, which they exposed as baseless. However, dedicated anti-Zionists are never intimidated by occasional setbacks. Thus, after a quiet year (2009) without any anti-Israel activity, I learned a few days before Passover that a Palestinian professor, Salim Tamari, had been invited to speak about "Jerusalem, the Making of an Unholy City."[4] Because it was scheduled for 6 p.m. April 6, the last day of Passover, I and other observant colleagues could not be there, but we could protest to the administration about the event's timing and encourage others to attend. According to reports, Tamari apologized for the "mistaken title" of his address, which was supposed to be advertised as "Jerusalem, The Unmaking of a Holy City" — not quite as insulting as labeling Jerusalem an "unholy city." Although the subject was potentially inflammatory, the talk turned out to be technical and diffuse. Moreover, the scheduling conflict and exclusion of observant Jews backfired, since the new dean and new history chair apologized, instructing the event's coordinators to check the religious calendar before scheduling such activities again.

Since academia rightly supports freedom of ideas and speech, there cannot be censorship of Israel's non-violent critics. Israel's advocates should expect equal time and funding, open civilized forums for discussion of the Middle East, and scheduling which respects all religions.

Evelyn Avery is professor of English and director of Jewish Studies at Towson University, Maryland. Her books include *Rebels and Victims: The Fiction of Richard Wright and Bernard Malamud* (1979), *The Magic Worlds of Bernard Malamud* (2001), and *Modern Jewish Women Writers in America* (2007). She is founder and coordinator of the Bernard Malamud Society.

ENDNOTES

[1] Modern Language Association Delegate Assembly, discussion of 2007-1 resolution.

[2] Radical Caucus 2008-1, pro-Palestinian Resolution at Delegate Assembly, Modern Language Association, December 2008.

[3] Avery's proposed 2008-1 pro-Israel Resolution.

[4] Salim Tamari, sociologist at Birzeit University in the West Bank and visiting professor at the Center for Contemporary Arab Studies, Georgetown University. Prolific writer and speaker, critic of Israel, and advocate for Palestine.

THE ACADEMIC LEGITIMIZATION
OF ANTI-ZIONISM AND EFFORTS
TO COMBAT IT
A Case Study

Tammi Rossman-Benjamin

Under the mantle of academic freedom, falsehoods and distortions about Zionism and Israel — for example, that Zionism is racism, that Israel perpetrates genocide and ethnic cleansing, and therefore the Jewish state should be dismantled — are heard in classrooms and at departmentally-sponsored events on many university campuses. This essay will analyze the problematic nature of academic anti-Zionism,[1] the factors within the university that allow it to flourish, and the attempts of a small group of concerned faculty to address the problem within the university governance structure. It will focus on one campus — the University of California Santa Cruz — where the problem is particularly acute, and analyze an academic conference on Zionism that took place there in March 2007.

I. THE PROBLEM

Anti-Zionism at the University of California Santa Cruz

Over the last several years, faculty members at the University of California Santa Cruz (UCSC) have injected anti-Zionist rhetoric into their courses and departmentally-sponsored events.[2] For example, a Community Studies class designed to train social activists was taught by an instructor who described herself in her on-line syllabus as an activist with the "campaign against the Apartheid Wall being built in Palestine."[3] Her recommended readings included such unreferenced statements as: "Israeli massacres are often accompanied by sexual assault, particularly of pregnant women as a symbolic way of uprooting the children from the mother, or the Palestinian from the land."[4]

The previous summer, the same lecturer taught a Community Studies course on the Israeli-Palestinian conflict, in which she used the class email list to encourage students to participate in a demonstration outside the Israeli consulate in San Francisco protesting Israel's "destructive actions" in Lebanon and Gaza.[5] UCSC students also report that some professors insert into class lectures anti-Israel or anti-Zionist materials unrelated to the course, as when a full class period in a course on women's health activism was devoted to a lecture on the ruthless treatment of Palestinians at the hands of Israeli soldiers.[6]

Since 2001 a number of UCSC departments and research centers have sponsored more than a dozen events dealing with the Israeli-Palestinian conflict, all of which have been biased against Israel.[7]

"Alternative Histories Within and Beyond Zionism": An Academic Conference

A conference on "Alternative Histories Within and Beyond Zionism," which took place on March 15, 2007 with the sponsorship of eight university departments and research units, was perhaps the most egregious expression of academically-legitimized anti-Zionism at UCSC.[8] The primary goals of the papers presented by four professors and a graduate student were the deconstruction, delegitimization and elimination of Zionism and its realization in a Jewish state:

- David Theo Goldberg, Director of the University of California Humanities Research Institute and Professor of Comparative Literature and Criminology, Law and Society at UC Irvine, delivered a paper on "Racial Palestinianization," in which he claimed that from its inception Israel has been a racist entity, which has used its racist state policies to protect the purity of the Jewish "race" and exclude and oppress the Palestinians. He further suggested that such a state does not deserve to exist, and that, like in the case of the anti-apartheid resistance in South Africa, suicide bombings are a legitimate means for bringing about Israel's justly deserved downfall.

- Judith Butler, professor of rhetoric and comparative literature at UC Berkeley, presented a paper on "Hidden Histories of Post-Zionism," in which she revived the pre-state Zionist critiques of Jews such as Hannah Arendt and Martin Buber in order to argue that the Jewish state should be replaced by a bi-national secular state. She claimed that besides redressing the "longstanding issues of legal injustice and political violence" perpetrated by Israel, bi-nationalism had the added advantage of being able "to subject nationalism to a deconstruction," in this way defeating Zionism on the battlefield of ideas rather than through the violent destruction of Israel.

- Hilton Obenzinger, Associate Director for Honors and Advanced Writing at Stanford's Hume Writing Center, in a talk entitled "Jewish Opposition to the Occupation Since 1967, A Personal and Public Journey," recounted his experiences as a Jewish anti-Zionist activist. He portrayed Israel as an imperialist and colonial-settler state in partnership with the U.S., and encouraged members of the audience to take responsibility for "ending this empire."

- Terri Ginsberg, a scholar of cinema studies and adjunct professor at Purchase College, spoke on "Holocaust Film and Zionism: Exposing a Collaboration," arguing that Holocaust films have propagated and justified a racist Zionist ideology and facilitated its realization in a state that perpetrates ethnic cleansing and genocide against the Palestinians. She called on fellow Leftists to confront the Holocaust-Zionist conspiracy head-on, in order to "transform radically the ideologies and institutional structures of Zionism as we know it."

- Ryvka Bar Zohar, a graduate student at New York University, presented a paper on "A History of Zionism and the Politics of Divestment," in which she charged that Zionism grew out of Eastern European Jews' attempt to recover from the "shame of the diaspora" and the Holocaust by finding "pride in domination." She claimed that Zionism was a racist doctrine that led to the creation of an apartheid state, and argued that the movement to divest from Israel was a justified and effective strategy for mounting an opposition to the Jewish state.

Although advertised as an academic event, the conference violated well-accepted norms of scholarship and university protocol. Rather than providing a forum for the presentation of legitimate scholarly research in order to advance knowledge and educate participants and audience, the conference was an open exercise in political indoctrination, bent on promoting an anti-Zionist agenda and encouraging activism against the Jewish state. Moreover, the speakers left little room for doubt about their partisanship: most identified themselves in the course of their talks as anti-Zionists, and Obenzinger and Ginsberg openly expressed their solidarity with the Palestinian people. Most of the speakers were explicit about their political motivation and advocacy efforts: Obenzinger and Bar Zohar's talks were wholly devoted to justifying and promoting their anti-Israel political efforts; Butler began her talk by stating that she had committed herself "to speaking out, and to encouraging other Jews to speak out," and Ginsberg said that her goal was "to transform Zionism in the name of social justice." It is hard to imagine that the conference organizer, who had publicly acknowledged her own opposition to Zionism and Israel, was unaware of the fact that all the speakers she had selected had identified themselves as anti-Zionists and were actively engaged in efforts to undermine the Jewish state.[9]

Given the highly politicized nature of the conference, it is not surprising that much of the discourse was tendentious and unscholarly. For example, numerous unsubstantiated claims about Zionism and Israel were made:

- All the speakers charged that Zionism is racist in its formulation and realization in a Jewish state.
- Goldberg, Obenzinger, Ginsberg and Bar Zohar claimed that Zionism was a brand of European colonialism and imperialism.
- Bar Zohar labeled Israel "an apartheid regime," and Goldberg called Israel's actions "worse than apartheid."
- Butler, Obenzinger and Bar Zohar claimed that Zionism is discontinuous with Jewish historical experience and is therefore a historically and religiously illegitimate ideology.

In addition, some of the speakers made claims that were untrue or gross misrepresentations of the facts:

- Goldberg, Ginsberg and Bar Zohar accused Israel of ethnic cleansing.
- Goldberg and Ginsberg accused Israel of genocidal intentions and insinuated that Israel used Nazi-like practices to achieve this end.
- Butler, Obenzinger, Ginsberg and Bar Zohar stated or implied that Zionists have engaged in a vicious, immoral campaign to silence all criticism of Israel.
- Ginsberg claimed that literary scholar Alan Mintz "commits the *shanda* of dedicating his book, [*Popular Culture and the Shaping of Holocaust Memory in America*,] to Baruch Goldstein, the right-wing Orthodox Jewish settler who, in 1994, murdered 29 Palestinians in cold blood while they were praying in a Hebron mosque." In fact, the Baruch Goldstein to whom Mintz dedicated his book is *not* the same individual whom Ginsberg reviles in her comments.[10]

Finally, much of the discourse at the conference can be characterized as antisemitic, according to the broad working definition of the term adopted by the U.S. State Department, which focuses on the commonalities of its contemporary manifestations, including the specific targeting of the state of Israel. Numerous statements made by the speakers — which challenged the legitimacy of the Jewish state or called for its elimination; demonized Israel; compared Israel's treatment of the Palestinians to the Nazis' treatment of the Jews; and accused Israel of exaggerating the Holocaust for immoral purposes — correspond to the following examples given in the State Department's 2008 report on contemporary global antisemitism[11]:

- Denying the Jewish people their right to self-determination.
- Applying double standards by requiring of Israel a behavior not expected or demanded of any other democratic nation.
- Drawing comparisons of contemporary Israeli policy to that of the Nazis.
- Accusing the Jews as a people, or Israel as a state, of inventing or exaggerating the Holocaust.

II. FACTORS WHICH ALLOW THE PROBLEM TO FLOURISH

Academic Freedom and Its Abuses

> I want to welcome everyone to what I consider to be an historic event on our campus. This is a conference — the Alternative Histories Within and Beyond Zionism — that I think exemplifies the highest ideals of academic freedom: the ability to debate and discuss and have dialogue on controversial issues. That, I think, is the highest ideal of academic freedom. So I'm very happy to see all of you participating in this historic event. –Conference organizer Lisa Rofel, UCSC professor of anthropology.

In her brief introductory remarks, the conference organizer indicated that the presentations to follow were not only protected by academic freedom, but were exemplars of the highest ideals of that freedom. Given the scholarly questionable, politically-motivated and antisemitic quality of the five presentations, these remarks beg the question: do the conference presentations constitute bona fide expressions of academic freedom, or are they abuses of it? Answering this question requires a brief discussion of the nature of academic freedom.

Although often misconstrued as coterminus with the freedom of speech guaranteed by the First Amendment, academic freedom has never been legally understood in this way. According to legal scholar Robert Post, "The function of academic freedom is not to liberate individual professors from all forms of institutional regulation, but to ensure that faculty within the university are free to engage in the professionally competent forms of inquiry and teaching that are necessary for the realization of the social purposes of the university."[12]

Implicit in this understanding is the existence of three sets of evaluative processes for determining whether academic freedom is being exercised properly. The most important set consists of the professional standards for assessing "competent forms of inquiry and teaching." For Post, professional self-regulation — what he calls "the unimpeded application of professional norms of inquiry" — is the *sine qua non* of academic freedom, which is vital for the advancement of knowledge.[13] When research or teaching does not meet these standards of competence, it constitutes an abuse of academic freedom.

The other two sets of evaluative processes, while less central to the functioning of academic freedom, are still important in determining its limits. The first of these evaluates the extent to which teaching and research conform to "institutional regulation." Even if a faculty member's research and teaching are deemed scholarly competent after the application of "professional norms of inquiry," there may still be violations of the university's rules of faculty conduct, which render his teaching or scholarship an abuse of academic freedom. Finally, academic freedom is deemed necessary for "the realization of the social purposes of the university," above all "to promote inquiry and advance the sum of human knowledge."[14] Summarizing an argument in the "1915 Declaration of Principles on Academic Freedom and Academic Tenure" on why scholars should enjoy freedoms not afforded other members of society, Post writes: "Academic freedom is conceived of as the price the public must pay in return for the social good of advancing knowledge."[15] I.e., the very concept of academic freedom is seen as the consequence of the public's social contract with the university. Thus, as partners in such a pact, the public can play a role, albeit indirect, in limiting academic freedom when it suspects that the university is not upholding its part of the bargain, and knowledge is not being advanced.

The academic freedom rules that governed the University of California from 1934 to 2003 conceived of competent scholarship as a dispassionate duty, hostile to ideological conversion: "Where it becomes necessary...to consider political, social, or sectarian movements, they are dissected and examined — not taught, and the conclusion left, with no tipping of the scales, to the logic of the facts."[16] This older set of the rules included the policy that the University "assumes the right to prevent exploitation of its prestige by unqualified persons or by those who would use it as a platform for propaganda." Judged by the standards of competent scholarship and university policy set forth in this statement, the conference presentations analyzed above constitute clear abuses of academic freedom.

But things are far less clear when the conference is viewed through the lens of the current rules, which were revised by Robert Post in 2003 at the request of UC President Richard Atkinson, in order to allow the instructor of a controversial course at UC Berkeley, "The Politics and Poetics of Palestinian Resistance," to engage in unabashedly pro-Palestinian polemics.[17] As a result of these revisions, the references to standards of competent scholarship that existed in the previous document were removed, including the requirements of "dispassionate" scholarship, which eschews the goal of making ideological converts, and the concern with objectivity and "the logic of the facts." Similarly, all language proscribing the use of the University as "a platform for propaganda" was deleted.

Although the new statement acknowledges that academic freedom "requires that teaching and scholarship be assessed by reference to the professional standards that sustain the University's pursuit and achievement of knowledge," these standards are no longer spelled out in the rules. And while the new regulation mentions that "the exercise of academic freedom entails correlative duties of professional care when teaching, conducting research, or otherwise acting as a member of the faculty," the reader must consult another document, the Faculty Code of Conduct (APM-015),[18] in order to determine what these duties are, as well as to deduce how they may limit academic freedom.

By excising those sections whose purpose was to define the limits of academic freedom with respect to competent scholarship and university policy, Post was not denying that academic freedom had limits, but only shifting the responsibility for defining those limits from the academic freedom policy itself to faculty and administrative bodies. How, then, do these bodies monitor academic freedom and ensure that it is not abused?

The University's Two-headed Monster

Faculty and administration share the governance of each campus of the University of California. The faculty controls all academic matters through its representative body, the Academic Senate, whose responsibilities include the authorization, approval and supervision of all academic programming.[19] Often, as in the case of new course approvals, academic programming is first evaluated by faculty at the departmental level and then sent to an Academic Senate committee of faculty from across the university for final review and approval. Both reviewing bodies are charged with determining if a course or program meets a number of criteria, which, in theory, include "the norms and standards of the profession." In practice, however, these norms and standards have been selectively or wholly ignored by both reviewing bodies. For example, even before the UC Academic Freedom rules were emended in 2003, both the UC Berkeley English Department and the Academic Senate Committee on Courses of Instruction reviewed and approved the remedial writing course, "The Politics and Poetics of Palestinian Resistance." Yet the egregiously tendentious, unscholarly and anti-Israel course description included the contention that the "brutal Israeli military occupation of Palestine, an occupation that has been ongoing since 1948, has systematically displaced, killed, and maimed millions of Palestinian people," and it ended with the exhortation, "Conservative thinkers are encouraged to seek other sections."[20]

Notably, although statements about standards of scholarly competence were removed from the revised Academic Freedom rules, in a 2007 document entitled "Academic Freedom: Its Privilege and Responsibility Within the University of California" the UC-wide Committee on Academic Freedom warns: "Professors who fail to meet scholarly standards of competence or who abuse their position to indoctrinate students cannot claim the protection of academic freedom."[21] Nevertheless, as indicated above, courses in which faculty openly promote anti-Zionist perspectives, and even encourage students to engage in activism against the Jewish state, exist at UCSC and on other UC campuses.

Although the content of all academic programming falls within the purview of the Academic Senate, ensuring that its implementation meets the standards set by university policy is the responsibility of the Chancellor, chief administrative officer of a University of California campus, though it may be delegated to a divisional dean.[22] Based on a statute in the California State Constitution, which provides that the University of California "shall be entirely independent of all political and sectarian influence,"[23] there are several university regulations that effectively limit the freedom of faculty to promote a personal or political agenda while engaging in their academic duties. These include:

- Directive issued by Clark Kerr, President of the University of California, September, 1961[24]: "University facilities and the name of the University must not be used in ways which will involve the University as an institution in the political...and other controversial issues of the day."

- The Policy on Course Content of The Regents of the University of California, approved June 19, 1970 and amended September 22, 2005[25]: "[The Regents] are responsible to see that the University remain aloof from politics and never function as an instrument for the advance of partisan interest. Misuse of the classroom by, for example, allowing it to be used for political indoctrination...constitutes misuse of the University as an institution."

- Directive issued by Charles J. Hitch, President of the University of California, September 18, 1970, "Restrictions on the Use of University Resources and Facilities for Political Activities"[26]: "The name, insignia, seal, or address of the University or any of its offices or units...equipment, supplies, and services...shall not be used for or in connection with political purposes or activities."

- Academic Personnel Policy (APM) 015 - Faculty Code of Conduct[27]: Types of unacceptable conduct: "Unauthorized use of University resources or facilities on a significant scale for personal, commercial, political, or religious purposes."

Although the word "political," which occurs in each of the above policies and directives, can be narrowly construed as limited to supporting or opposing candidates or propositions in elections, a consideration of the wording of the regulations and the context in which they were written suggests that their authors intended a much broader interpretation. President Kerr's directive, for example, linked "political" with "other controversial issues of the day." And both the Regents' policy proscribing "political indoctrination" in the classroom and President Hitch's directive prohibiting the use of university resources and facilities for political activities were issued in the wake of campus protests against the Vietnam War that spilled into the classroom and university-sponsored events. In a letter written to all UC faculty just three weeks before the Regents issued their Policy on Course Content, President Hitch noted that faculty involvement with anti-war activism had led many California legislators to "believe that the basic academic purposes of our campuses are being distorted and subverted, that academic credit is being given for work that is not appropriate, and that the atmosphere of the campuses has become politicized, with freedom for some views and not for others."[28] According to such an interpretation of "political," courses, academic conferences and other departmentally-sponsored events that permit anti-Israel propagandizing are in clear violation of these regulations, and yet administrators routinely ignore these violations.

Raising the Ramparts of the Ivory Tower:
Keeping the Public Out

Although the public plays an important role in sustaining the university and ensuring that it does not deviate from its educational mission "to promote inquiry and advance the sum of human knowledge," faculty generally perceive any attempt by the public to hold the university accountable as an unwelcome interference. This is particularly evident in the report of the American Association of University Professors (AAUP) published in September 2007, "Freedom in the Classroom." It was drafted by the AAUP's Committee A on Academic Freedom and Tenure, as a response to perceived challenges from groups outside the university that "have sought to regulate classroom instruction."[29] The authors of the report acknowledge that professors have been accused of indoctrinating rather than educating students and of failing to provide balanced perspectives on controversial issues, but they belittle these accusations and instead call those outside groups who would raise them "a modern menace."

On the heels of the publication of the AAUP report, five prominent academics, calling themselves The Ad Hoc Committee to Defend the University, issued a public statement condemning outside groups that have "defamed scholars, pressured administrators, and tried to bypass or subvert established procedures of academic governance" in order to achieve their political ends.[30] The Ad Hoc Committee's harshest condemnation was directed at "groups portraying themselves as defenders of Israel...[that] have targeted scholars who have expressed perspectives on Israeli policies and the Israeli-Palestinian conflict with which they disagree." The statement charged that in order to silence "their political enemies," these outside groups have made unfounded accusations of antisemitism; expanded the definition of antisemitism to include scholarship critical of Israel; promoted the withholding of donations if certain faculty are hired or awarded tenure; and attempted to restrict federal funding for programs on political grounds. To date, over 600 academics, including almost 80 at the University of California, have joined the Ad Hoc Committee and signed the statement, pledging:

- to speak out against those who attack their colleagues "to achieve political goals"
- to urge university administrators and trustees to defend academic freedom
- to vigorously promote their views in the media
- to mobilize their students "to defend the values and integrity of their institutions"

Perhaps in compliance with their pledge, three of the statement's signatories from UCSC, including one of its originators, figure prominently in an article, published in the UCSC student newspaper in November 2007, which was very sympathetic to the Ad Hoc Committee.[31] The article quotes all three decrying that pro-Israel groups are silencing debate on the Middle East by harassing and threatening scholars. Two of the professors were involved in the March 2007 conference, one as conference organizer and the other as head of a sponsoring department. Both harshly criticized the "radical pro-Israeli groups" Stand With Us and Scholars for Peace in the Middle East (SPME) for publicly voicing their objections to the departmentally-sponsored conference.

In fall 2009, two University of California professors — David Theo Goldberg, a panelist in the 2007 UCSC conference, and Saree Makdisi — co-authored an article in *Tikkun* magazine entitled "The Trial of Israel's Campus Critics" that was a broadside against "outside pressure groups" such as "AIPAC, the Zionist Organization of America, the American Jewish Congress, and the Jewish National Fund." Goldberg and Makdisi asserted that these groups constituted an insidious Israel Campus Lobby, consisting of right-wing Zionists who will not countenance any scholarly criticism of Israel and egregiously violate the academic freedom of faculty. According to the authors, these Zionists engage in tactics that "plumb the depths of dishonor and indecency and include character assassination, selective misquotation, the willful distortion of the record, the fabrication of falsehoods, and an utter disregard for the truth."[32]

Confronted by censure, members of the public appear reticent to voice their concerns about political indoctrination and egregiously one-sided discourse on university campuses. This is especially true within the Jewish community, where many individuals and organizations are reluctant to criticize faculty-sponsored anti-Zionism for fear of being charged with McCarthyism or collusion with the Israel Lobby.

III. EFFORTS TO ADDRESS THE PROBLEM

In response to the rising incidence of anti-Zionism in classrooms and at departmentally-sponsored events at UCSC and on other UC campuses, in 2004 a few concerned faculty, including myself, established a local chapter of Scholars for Peace in the Middle East. Our group has sought to document the problem, to use our evidence to raise the awareness of the faculty, the administration and the public, and to encourage each of these stakeholders in the University to address the problem with the means available to them.

Inside the University:
Addressing Administration and Faculty

Our earlier efforts within the university focused on influencing the highest levels of UC governance, both administrative and faculty. In September 2006, we presented an open letter with more than 3,000 signatories to the UC Regents, asking them to address the growing problem of anti-Zionism and antisemitism on UC campuses.[33] Although the Regents did not respond, in November 2006 we received a letter from UC President Robert Dynes recommending that we discuss our concerns with the head of the UC Academic Senate, Professor John B. Oakley. In early 2007 we met with Professor Oakley to discuss the problem and how the UC Academic Senate could address it. We presented him with a report in which we documented numerous examples of faculty-sponsored anti-Zionism on several UC campuses. We argued that such actions violated UC policies, eroded the core academic values of the University and created a hostile environment for Jewish and pro-Israel students, and recommended that an independent Academic Senate task force be established to examine the problem.[34] Professor Oakley refused to allow the UC Academic Senate to consider our concerns, but suggested that we build our case on individual UC campuses.

We decided to focus our efforts on one campus, UCSC, where we had documented the problem most extensively. Given the unresponsiveness of both the UC system-wide administration and Academic Senate, we concluded that we would be most effective if we formulated our concerns more precisely, addressing academic matters to the UCSC Academic Senate and matters of University policy to the campus administration.

Our first opportunity to test the two-pronged strategy at UCSC came soon after, with the March 2007 anti-Zionist conference. A week before the conference, we began a correspondence with the UCSC Chancellor, in which we argued that the event, sponsored by eight departments and research units, was politically motivated and directed and therefore violated several UC policies proscribing university-sponsored political activities. We urged him to address these violations.[35] Although the Chancellor did not respond directly, in May we received a letter from the UCSC Counsel, who contended that the conference did not violate University policy, in part because it was not "political," according to her interpretation of that term as limited to supporting or opposing political candidates or ballot measures. She concluded that the conference was a legitimate exercise of academic freedom and should not be censured.[36] Despite subsequent letters and emails that we sent to the

Chancellor and Counsel demonstrating that the UC Presidents and Regents who authored the regulations prohibiting university-sponsored political activities intended the word "political" to be understood broadly,[37] and that even the California Supreme Court had determined that the term included the espousal of any cause,[38] neither office responded.

We had a similar experience with the Dean of Social Sciences after we informed him of our concerns regarding a Community Studies course, which we believed violated both state law and University policy in promoting an anti-Israel political agenda and encouraging students to engage in political activity. The goals of the course "Violence and non-Violence in Social Change," taught in summer 2007, included training students to be nonviolent activists in "a current social conflict." Included in the on-line syllabus were the instructor's biography, indicating that she was an activist "with the nonviolent joint Palestinian-Israeli campaign against the Apartheid Wall being built in Palestine," and a reading list weighted with books and articles on the Palestinian-Israeli conflict written from an unambiguously anti-Israel perspective.[39] A student who had previously taken a Community Studies class with her reported that she had used the classroom as a platform for politically biased and unscholarly instruction, sought to indoctrinate students in her anti-Israel perspective, stifle dissenting opinions, and had encouraged students to engage in anti-Israel activism.[40] Before and during the more recent class, we sent letters to the chair of the Community Studies Department explaining why we believed the instructor was likely using her classroom as a platform to indoctrinate, rather than educate, students, and requested that the chair look into our concerns.[41] When we received no response, we turned to the divisional dean, who, after consultation with the department chair and campus counsel, reported that no state laws or University policies had been violated.[42]

Addressing the faculty's responsibility for ensuring the integrity of all academic programming at the University, in May 2007 we submitted to the Senate Executive Committee (SEC) of the Academic Senate a letter documenting a pattern of political bias and advocacy (predominantly, though not exclusively, anti-Zionist) in classrooms and at departmentally-sponsored events since 2001. We argued that such bias and advocacy are antithetical to the academic mission of the university and urged the Academic Senate to investigate this problem.[43] The SEC agreed to look into our inquiry and sent it to the Committee on Academic Freedom (CAF) for consideration. One year later, in May 2008, we received the CAF report,[44] along with a letter indicating that the SEC fully endorsed it. The report not only ignored our primary concern, but converted the committee's charge into an investigation of members of our faculty group for alleged violations of academic freedom. This is made clear in a letter sent by the chair of the CAF to eight UCSC professors soliciting reports of their negative interactions with members of our group, included in an appendix to the CAF report:[45] "Our committee does not plan to investigate incidents of this alleged bias, but seeks rather to determine if, connected to the complaint in any way, including the activities of those making the complaint, there is anything that threatens academic freedom on our campus." Also included in the appendix are testimonies from four professors accusing members of our group of infringing on their academic freedom. Although the CAF report ultimately upholds "the right of SPME, on freedom of speech grounds, to make their opinions and viewpoints heard," it is apparent that the investigation of our group and its inclusion in the report were intended to discredit us and to stifle further inquiry into this matter by members of our group or by other faculty members.[46]

Outside the University: Addressing the Public

Our group has also endeavored to constrain the university-sponsored anti-Israel bias and advocacy through a campaign of public exposure and education: we have published articles in the local and state press and in on-line periodicals,[47] organized a speaker series about anti-Zionism and antisemitism,[48] offered public lectures, participated in radio and television interviews, created a website,[49] and participated in a documentary about the issue of campus antisemitism.[50]

These efforts to engage the public have had mixed results. Several individuals have responded by becoming pro-active: some have written letters to UCSC administrators, faculty and local newspapers critiquing faculty-sponsored anti-Israel classes and events or decrying the administration's unresponsiveness to antisemitic incidents on campus. Others have posted our materials on their blogs and initiated email campaigns targeting responsible administrators and faculty.[51] A few organizations, most notably the Zionist Organization of America and Stand With Us, have written formal letters to the UCSC Chancellor urging him to address these matters. However, administrators and faculty have largely ignored these expressions of public concern, and in some cases, as indicated above, they have even repudiated them.

IV. TAKING STOCK AND MOVING FORWARD

This analysis has demonstrated that anti-Zionist, anti-Israel and antisemitic discourse has found academic legitimacy on at least one major university campus. Intentional lies, half-truths and distortions about Zionism, Israel and the Jews — statements that Zionism is racist, imperialist and fascist; that Israel uses Nazi tactics to perpetrate genocide and ethnic cleansing; that Zionists have engaged in a vicious campaign to silence all criticism of Israel; and that Zionism should be eliminated and the Jewish state dismantled — would not have been heard in classrooms and at departmentally-sponsored events ten years ago. Today, however, they receive the imprimatur of the UCSC Academic Senate and the blessing of the campus administration.

The problem is not unique to UCSC. Indeed, faculty-generated anti-Zionism and anti-Israelism have been documented on at least five other UC campuses and at many other universities in the United States, Canada, Great Britain, Europe, Australia and Israel.[52] Moreover, the problem appears to be increasing in severity. Since the March 2007 conference at UCSC, when the expression of such sentiments at an academic conference were still rare, similar departmentally-sponsored panels, whose purpose is to demonize and delegitimize the Jewish State and even advocate its elimination, have been organized on many college campuses across the United States and around the world. For instance:

- In March 2008, seven departments at the University of Hawaii (UH) sponsored "Who are the Palestinians? Remembering the Nakba," a ten-day symposium consisting of anti-Israel lectures, films and other events, including a workshop on "Divestment and Boycott" presented by a UH professor of Ethnic Studies.[53]
- In June 2009, a conference entitled "Israel/Palestine: Mapping Models of Statehood and Paths to Peace"[54] took place at York University in Toronto, Canada, as part of York's 50th anniversary celebration. The conference was sponsored by 4 academic units and 6 administrative units from York University and Queen's University, as well as by the Social Sciences and Humanities Research Council of Canada.[55] It featured a number of speakers, well-known for their support of boycott, divestment and sanctions against Israel, who demonized and delegitimized the Jewish State and promoted its elimination.[56] Although several Jewish organizations raised concerns prior to the event, the York University president issued a statement defending the conference and portraying criticism of it as attacks on academic freedom.[57] An official York University

statement suggested that there was no reason that elimination of the Jewish State should not be discussed at a university in Canada.[58]

- In fall 2009, the Norwegian University of Science and Technology (NTNU) in Trondheim hosted an academic seminar series on the Palestinian-Israel conflict that featured speakers such as Ilan Pappe and Stephen Walt, whose animus towards the Jewish State and its supporters is well-known.[59] All three of the series organizers had called for an academic boycott of Israel and were part of a group of 32 professors who had petitioned the NTNU Board of Governors to adopt the boycott.[60] Nevertheless, the University Rector saluted the organizers on his official university blog, and characterized the seminar series as a "praiseworthy initiative."[61]

Clearly, university students are the greatest victims of such discourse, whose one-sided, tendentious nature not only limits their access to vital information and analyses of complex topics of global importance, but also violates their fundamental right to be educated and not indoctrinated. For many Jewish students, the academic legitimization of anti-Zionism, anti-Israelism and antisemitism has helped to foment an atmosphere on campus, both inside and outside the classroom, which is intellectually, emotionally, and at times even physically threatening.

On some campuses, the situation has become intolerable. For example, the Orange County Task Force, an independent body established to investigate antisemitism at UC Irvine (UCI), recently determined that "acts of anti-Semitism are real and well documented. Jewish students have been harassed. Hate speech has been unrelenting."[62] Although much of the problem at UCI is linked to the Muslim Student Union (MSU) and the administration's unwillingness to condemn that group's antisemitic hate speech, the task force also implicates faculty "who use their classrooms as a forum for their anti-Israel agenda" as contributing to the hostile campus environment: "The anti-Israel bias on the part of many in the faculty provides a fertile environment for the MSU and its anti-Israel and anti-Semitic rhetoric and actions."[63]

The situation on college campuses is unlikely to improve until faculty and administrators acknowledge the severity of the problem and commit themselves to solving it. Given their persistent intransigence, it is clear that new strategies are needed to achieve this goal.

One strategy has been to enlist the help of the federal government. In 2004, the U.S. Department of Education's Office for Civil Rights (OCR) announced its new policy of protecting Jewish students from antisemitic harassment under Title VI of the 1964 Civil Rights Act, which requires that federally-funded public and private universities ensure that their programs and activities are free from discrimination based on "race, color or national origin." The first test of the new policy came soon after it was announced: The Zionist Organization of America's Center for Law and Justice filed a complaint on behalf of Jewish students at the University of California, Irvine, which the OCR agreed to investigate. The complaint alleged that Jewish students had been subjected to a long-standing pattern of antisemitic harassment and hostility, most of it fueled by the anti-Israel programs and activism of members of the Muslim Student Union.[64] After a three-year investigation, the OCR decided that there was no Title VI violation. However, according to Susan Tuchman, Director of the ZOA's Center for Law and Justice, the decision did not mean that the OCR did not find antisemitic harassment and intimidation on the UC Irvine campus, but that it was based on a shift to a pre-2004 interpretation of Title VI policy, which did not include Jewish students as a protected group. In April 2008, the OCR opened a new investigation based on other incidents of antisemitic harassment, intimidation and discrimination that the ZOA had reported. This investigation is still open and on-going.[65]

Encouraged by the ZOA's example, in June 2009 I filed a Title VI complaint against UC Santa Cruz with the OCR. I alleged that anti-Israel discourse and behavior in classrooms and at university-sponsored events was tantamount to institutional discrimination against Jewish students, and had resulted in their intellectual and emotional harassment and intimidation. Besides providing extensive documentation of the longstanding and pervasive nature of the problem, I chronicled the failure of the numerous efforts that I and others had made to encourage UCSC faculty and administrators to acknowledge and address the problem.

The OCR has not yet announced a decision regarding my complaint. If the OCR decides to investigate it, whatever the outcome, this will be a landmark case, as it will represent the first time that the Department of Education has agreed to investigate a Title VI complaint alleging discrimination against Jewish students perpetrated by university faculty. The OCR's decision to open an investigation would also represent the recognition by the federal government that the anti-Israel rhetoric of faculty in classrooms and at departmentally sponsored events has the potential to create a hostile and intimidating environment for Jewish students, and that university administrators have not adequately protected them. Most importantly, such an investigation could provide the necessary impetus for faculty and administrators at UCSC to finally confront this longstanding and pervasive problem, and might encourage other universities to follow suit.

In the meantime, the Orange County Task Force has offered two other approaches. Among the recommendations in the task force's report are:[66]

- Students with a strong Jewish identity should consider enrolling elsewhere unless and until tangible changes are made.
- Jewish organizations and Jewish benefactors should be aware that their continued support of an antisemitic campus is, in the end, counter-productive and works against their own interests.

Fear of losing their student and donor base, along with the stigma of being labeled an antisemitic campus, may be sufficient impetus for faculty and administrators to finally address this alarming problem.

Tammi Rossman-Benjamin is a lecturer in Hebrew at the University of California Santa Cruz and cofounder of the UCSC chapter of Scholars for Peace in the Middle East.

ENDNOTES

[1] For the purposes of this paper, "anti-Zionism" refers to an opposition to Zionism, understood either in its classic sense as a belief in the centrality of the land of Israel to Jewish historical and religious experience, or in its modern manifestation as a movement to re-establish a Jewish homeland in the historic land of Israel. Anti-Zionist criticism denies the legitimacy of the Jewish state's founding ideology, and by extension, the legitimacy of the Jewish state itself.

[2] Leila Beckwith, Tammi Rossman-Benjamin and Ilan Benjamin, "Faculty Efforts to Combat Anti-Semitism and Anti-Israel Bias at the University of California-Santa Cruz," in *Academics Against Israel and the Jews*, edited by Manfred Gerstenfeld (Jerusalem: Jerusalem Center for Public Affairs, 2007), p. 122.

[3] Syllabus for Community Studies class "Violence and Non-Violence in Social Change" http://web.mac.com/spme_at_ucsc/iWeb/Site/Anti-Israel%20Course_files/CMMU%20124%20Syllabus.pdf.

[4] Nadine Naber, "A Call for Consistency: Palestinian Resistance and Radical US Women of Color," in *Color of Violence: the INCITE! Anthology*, edited by INCITE! Women of Color Against Violence (Cambridge, MA: South End Press, 2006), p. 75.

[5] See Appendix 1 in letter to UCSC Community Studies Department Chair, http://web.mac.com/spme_at_ucsc/iWeb/Site/Anti-Israel%20Course_files/Letter%20to%20Prof.%20Pudup%206-18-7.pdf, pp. 3-4.

[6] See Appendices 2 and 3 in letter to UCSC Senate Executive Committee, http://web.mac.com/spme_at_ucsc/iWeb/Site/UCSC%20Academic%20Senate_files/Report%20to%20SEC.pdf , pp. 6-8.

[7] See Appendix 4 in Ibid, pp. 9-10.

8 The following UCSC departments and research units sponsored the conference: Feminist Studies, Anthropology, Community Studies, Sociology, Politics, History, Institute for Humanities Research, and the Center for Global, International and Regional Studies.

9 For example, Goldberg, Butler, and conference organizer Lisa Rofel all signed a University of California petition for Divestment from Israel, and Obenzinger has been part of divestment campaigns at Stanford and with the Presbyterian Church; Butler, Obenzinger and Ginsberg all signed a petition for U.S. Jewish/Muslim Solidarity calling for cutting off all military and economic aid to Israel; Butler signed a petition boycotting Israeli academics and research; Ginsberg is a member of Jews Against the Occupation; and Bar Zohar helped to organize "Israeli Apartheid Week" in New York City.

10 In a personal communication, Mintz wrote: "The Baruch Goldstein to whom I dedicated my book was a rabbi and Hebrew school teacher who taught me in Worcester, MA, in the late fifties and early sixties; Rabbi Goldstein is now quite old. He is the first Holocaust survivor who told me his personal story."

11 Section on "Defining Anti-Semitism," from United States Department of State, "Contemporary Global Anti-Semitism: A Report Provided to the United States Congress," 2008: http://www.state.gov/g/drl/rls/102406.htm#defining.

12 Robert Post, "The Structure of Academic Freedom," in *Academic Freedom after September 11*, edited by Beshara Doumani (New York: Zone Books, 2006), p. 64.

13 Ibid, p. 70.

14 Ibid, p. 70. Post is quoting the "1915 Declaration of Principles on Academic Freedom and Academic Tenure," published by the American Association of University Professors.

15 Post, "The Structure of Academic Freedom," p. 73.

16 University of California Regulation Academic Personnel Manual APM-10 1934 – 2003. (See http://www.universityofcalifornia.edu/senate/assembly/jul2003/jul2003ii.pdf, Appendix A).

17 See Martin Trow, "Reflections on Proposed Changes in the University Regulations Bearing on Academic Freedom in the University of California," NoIndoctrination.org, 24 July 2003, http://www.noindoctrination.org/uc_cas.shtml.

18 See: http://www.universityofcalifornia.edu/senate/manual/apm015.pdf.

19 See: http://www.universityofcalifornia.edu/aboutuc/governance.html.

20 Robert C. Post, "Academic Freedom and the 'Intifada Curriculum'," *Academe Online*, Vol. 89, May-June 2003.

21 "Academic Freedom: Its Privilege and Responsibility within the University of California" was presented by the University Committee on Academic Freedom to the University of California Academic Council on February 16, 2007, and distributed to UC campus Academic Senate offices.

22 See: http://www.universityofcalifornia.edu/regents/bylaws/so1006.html.

23 Article IX, Section 9 of the California Constitution establishes the constitutional autonomy of the University of California.

24 See: http://content.cdlib.org/xtf/view?docId=kt900015wg&doc.view=frames&chunk.id=div00028&toc.id=0&brand=calisphere.

25 http://www.universityofcalifornia.edu/regents/policies/6065.html.

26 http://www.ucop.edu/ucophome/coordrev/policy/9-18-70.html.

27 http://www.ucop.edu/acadadv/acadpers/apm/apm-015.pdf.

28 Letter from Hitch to UC faculty, discussing the actions taken by the California legislature to deny salary increases for UC faculty, dated May 29, 1970.

29 "Freedom in the Classroom" (2007): http://www.aaup.org/AAUP/comm/rep/A/class.htm.

30 http://defend.university.googlepages.com/home.

31 Marc Abezeid, "Silencing Debate in the Middle East," *City on a Hill Press*, November 15, 2007. http://www.campus-watch.org/article/id/4467.

32 *Tikkun*, September/October 2009. http://www.tikkun.org/article.php/sept_oct_09_goldberg_makdisi.

33 SPME Open Letter to the Governor of California, University of California Board of Regents, Board of Trustees of the California State Universities, Chancellors of the University of California, and the Presidents of the California State Universities: http://web.mac.com/spme_at_ucsc/iWeb/Site/Home_files/Open%20Letter%20to%20the%20Govern.pdf

34 Executive Summary of Scholars for Peace in the Middle East Presentation to John B. Oakley, Chair, Academic Senate, University of California, January 29, 2007: http://web.mac.com/spme_at_ucsc/iWeb/Site/Home_files/Executive%20Summary.pdf.

35 Our first letter to the Chancellor, dated March 9, 2007, was sent prior to the conference: http://web.mac.com/spme_at_ucsc/iWeb/Site/Anti-Zionism%20Conference_files/Letter%20to%20chancellor%203-9-7.pdf. Our second letter, dated March 20, 2007, was sent the week after the conference, and included a report of the event: http://web.mac.com/spme_at_ucsc/iWeb/Site/Anti-Zionism%20Conference_files/letter%20to%20chancellor%203-20-7.pdf.

36 Letter from UCSC Counsel Carol Rossi, dated April 30, 2007: http://web.mac.com/spme_at_ucsc/iWeb/Site/Anti-Zionism%20Conference_files/From%20UCSC%20General%20Counsel.pdf.

37 Letter to the Chancellor: http://web.mac.com/spme_at_ucsc/iWeb/Site/Anti-Zionism%20Conference_files/letter%20to%20Chancellor%205-11-7.pdf.

38 *Gay Law Students Assn. v. Pacific Tel. & Tel. Co.*, 595 P.2d 592, 610 (Cal. 1979).

39 See endnote 2.

40 See endnote 4.

41 Our first letter to the chair was sent on June 18, 2007, approximately one week before the course began: http://web.mac.com/spme_at_ucsc/iWeb/Site/Anti-Israel%20Course_files/Letter%20to%20Prof.%20Pudup%206-18-7.pdf. Our second letter was sent on July 2, 2007, over a week into the course: http://web.mac.com/spme_at_ucsc/iWeb/Site/Anti-Israel%20Course_files/letter%20to%20Prof.%20Pudup%207-2-7.pdf.

42 Our letter, dated September 4, 2007: http://web.mac.com/spme_at_ucsc/iWeb/Site/Anti-Israel%20Course_files/Dean%20Kamieniecki%209-4-7.pdf; the dean's response: http://web.mac.com/spme_at_ucsc/iWeb/Site/Anti-Israel%20Course_files/from%20Dean%20K.%209-21-7.pdf.

43 http://web.mac.com/spme_at_ucsc/iWeb/Site/UCSC%20Academic%20Senate_files/Report%20to%20SEC.pdf.

44   http://web.mac.com/spme_at_ucsc/iWeb/Site/UCSC%20Academic%20Senate_files/CAF%20report.pdf.

45   Inquiry email from CAF chair and four faculty responses: http://web.mac.com/spme_at_ucsc/iWeb/Site/UCSC%20Academic%20Senate_files/emails%20to%20CAF%20re%20SPME.pdf.

46   In a letter dated May 29, 2008, we expressed several points of dissatisfaction with both the CAF's report and the SEC's endorsement of it: http://web.mac.com/spme_at_ucsc/iWeb/Site/UCSC%20Academic%20Senate_files/letQuentinSEC.pdf.

47   http://web.mac.com/spme_at_ucsc/iWeb/Site/Publications.html.

48   http://web.mac.com/spme_at_ucsc/iWeb/Site/Speaker%20Series.html.

49   http://web.mac.com/spme_at_ucsc/iWeb/Site/Home.html.

50   "Tolerating Intolerance: Hate Speech on Campus," a Stand With Us documentary.

51   For example, see: http://www.bluetruth.net/2007/03/pro-israel-voices-muzzled-at-ucsc.html.

52   Gerstenfeld, *Academics*.

53   See: http://www.kaleo.org/2.13219/free-hawai-i-free-palestine-1.1792655. See also: http://hawaiiandpalestine.googlepages.com/panels.

54   See: http://www.yorku.ca/ipconf/.

55   See: http://www.yorku.ca/ipconf/sponsors.html.

56   B'nai B'rith Canada report: "York University Conference Lives up to Anti-Israel Expections" http://www.bnaibrith.ca/files/260609.pdf.

57   See: http://www.yorku.ca/yfile/archive/index.asp?Article=12652.

58   See: http://www.yorku.ca/yfile/archive/index.asp?Article=12783.

59   "'All-star team of Israel-haters' at Norway school raises concern," *Ha'aretz*, October 18, 2009. http://www.haaretz.com/hasen/spages/1118684.html.

60   Ragnhild Sodahl, "Will the NTNU University of Trondheim Norway, Boycott Israel?" *Verdens Gang*, October, 26, 2009. Reprinted: http://spme.net/cgi-bin/articles.cgi?ID=6121.

61   See: http://commonweb.ntnu.no/rektors-side/2009/09/forskningsbasert-om-israel-palestina-konflikten/#comments

62   *Report of the Task Force on Anti-Semitism at the University of California, Irvine*, 2008, p. 26: http://octaskforce.files.wordpress.com/2008/02/orange-county-task-force-report-on-anti-semitism-at-uci.pdf.

63   Ibid, p. 26.

64   Leila Beckwith, "Anti-Zionism/Anti-Semitism at the University of California-Irvine," in *Academics*, p. 119.

65   See: http://www.jewishpolicycenter.org/comments/223

66   *Report of the Task Force on Anti-Semitism at the University of California, Irvine*, pp. 27–28.

RESPONDING TO CAMPUS-BASED
ANTI-ZIONISM
Two Models

Alvin H. Rosenfeld

In March 2007, a conference entitled "Alternative Histories within and beyond Zionism" took place on the campus of the University of California at Santa Cruz (UCSC). According to Tammi Rossman-Benjamin, a faculty member at the university who attended the conference, the following points were made: Zionism is a form of racism; Israel is an apartheid state; Israel commits heinous crimes against humanity, including genocide and ethnic cleansing; Israel's behavior is comparable to that of Nazi Germany; Jews exaggerate the Holocaust as a tool of Zionist propaganda; Israel should be dismantled as a Jewish state; morally responsible people should actively oppose the Jewish state by, for instance, supporting divestment campaigns.[1]

Given this bill of indictments, it is clear that the UCSC conference was designed as a propaganda exercise and not a scholarly forum. Protected by what the conveners take to be the rights granted them by academic freedom, they willfully abused such freedom and, in the process, recklessly subverted normative academic standards. Out went anything like reasoned discourse by well-informed scholars — according to Rossman-Benjamin, none of the 5 speakers was a scholar of Israel or Zionism — and in came slanderous accusations against the Jewish state and appeals for audience members to engage in anti-Israel political activism. Such abuses are all too common today, and similar gatherings rigged to score the same polemical points, as well as other blatant forms of Israel-bashing, have taken place recently at UCLA, UC Berkeley, UC Irvine, UC Santa Barbara, UC Davis, San Francisco State, San Jose State, Harvard, MIT, and Columbia. The aim of these efforts is to delegitimize Israel by presenting it as a brutal, criminalized state and, thereby, to argue, by whatever means necessary, that it is unworthy of moral, financial, diplomatic, and political support.

Seen in these terms, today's campus wars are recognizable as part of a broad-based ideological assault on the State of Israel. At universities in Great Britain and in parts of Europe, efforts to demonize Israel are already far along, with the result that Jewish students have found themselves embattled and sometimes under the threat of physical attack. Could the same happen at North American universities? On some campuses, it has already happened, and the potential for it to get worse is real. In order to develop effective strategies for combating such hostility, it is first necessary to recognize the nature of this assault and who is behind it.

Campus-based ideological battles are typically angry, bitter affairs, and they are unlikely to be won by mounting carefully composed counter-arguments based on verifiable facts. Such arguments are the stock-in-trade of academic scholarship, and they should not be set aside as if they are of no value. If they can be employed to good effect, of course they should be. But as campuses become a venue for more intense anti-Israel animosity, the careful marshalling and lucid presentation of empirical evidence may not be enough to carry the day. This is because the people responsible for most anti-Israel agitation on university campuses are simply not open to hearing rational arguments in support of Zionism and Israel. The grievances that drive them and the resentments they nurse are not amenable to being softened by those who speak from another point of view, least of all one that is contrary to the identity politics in which so much campus-based anti-Zionism is invested. For some, such politics serves as a quasi-religion and has its own rituals, moral hierarchies, leadership cadres, symbol systems, and the like. For those in need of a sense of community, it can provide the comforts of belonging, binding people to one another on the basis of shared affirmations — paeans to "peace" and "justice," simplistically understood, are part of the familiar political chants — and shared denigrations: one is expected to be "anti" a number of declared social and political evils, of which "Zionism" and the allegedly "exclusivist, oppressive, racist, apartheid" state it created are high up on the enemy list. In past decades, such a politics served to validate its loyal adherents as "revolutionaries" fighting for the "cause." That language has largely faded today, but the passions it once evoked can sometimes still be detected at so-called "progressive" anti-Israel gatherings on college campuses.

In its most acute form, the problem in the United States is to a large degree coastal, with much of it occurring on west coast (specifically California) campuses and, to a lesser degree, on the east coast (Columbia, Cornell, Harvard, MIT). Universities elsewhere are obviously not immune, but there is little evidence to date of chronically persistent anti-Israel manifestations on campuses between the two coasts. Norman Finkelstein and other extreme anti-Israeli polemicists like him may visit these campuses for a day or two to give inflammatory lectures lambasting Israel, but it is doubtful that they have much impact on anyone other than those who invite them in the first place. Ideologically committed to a range of extreme positions, these fervent people are typically unrepresentative of the political culture of most of America's academic institutions and generally lack significant influence in shaping campus opinion. They believe otherwise, of course, and no doubt will continue to press an impassioned anti-Israel agenda with the ardor of true believers. How their usually baseless and often hateful messages will be received, however, is another matter.

Much of today's campus-based anti-Israel activity is advanced by people in two discrete faculty and student groups. Each may have fellow travelers among other people, but much of the energy behind today's most strident anti-Zionism is generated in the main by politically active Muslims and so-called "progressive," anti-Zionist Jews (the latter are not to be confused with mainstream liberal Jews, the great majority of whom are not anti-Zionists). If, for argument's sake, we could temporarily bracket out the activists in these two groups, such phenomena as "Israel Apartheid Week," UC Irvine's recent hate-fest, "Israel: The Politics of Genocide," petitions for universities to end their study programs in Israel, and pressure to force universities to strip their endowments of funds in companies that deal with Israel would be greatly diminished, if not disappear altogether.

Given these geographic and demographic dimensions of our subject, strategies need to be developed that are specifically suited to combat anti-Israel hostility at those academic institutions where anti-Israel activists are most prominent. It is critical to recognize that most of these people are part of a social and political configuration that sees a Jewish state as aberrant and unacceptable. Such a state runs contrary to their sense of how political reality should be constructed and disrupts and threatens their worldview. In fundamental ways, Israel appears to them anachronistic and objectionable and needs to be opposed. Some would like to see it dissolved altogether. Inspired by a diverse range of intellectual and ideological currents — Islamism, Third-Worldism, Marxism, postmodernism, multiculturalism, post-colonialism, anti-Americanism, certain strains of feminism — these self-proclaimed "anti-Zionists" comprise a small but vocal minority of university faculty members and students. The various "isms" that shape their thinking are distinct, yet each may encourage a predisposition to regard Israel from an adversarial posture. In general, for instance, many postmodernists are unsympathetic to the idea of nation states and national identities and on these grounds may be biased against Israel as a Jewish state (even as they may readily support Palestinian nationalism and national identity). Post-colonialists stand strongly against imperialism and colonialism and will see Israel as heavily corrupted by both (they will be less inclined, however, to voice dissent against the imperialist schemes of radical Islamists to create a global caliphate). Multiculturalists typically look to redress what they perceive to be historic wrongs against marginalized, "oppressed" peoples; the Jews, however, are not recognized as such a people but are lumped together with "mainstream," "white," "majoritarian" culture. In America, multiculturalists in the main give little or no recognition to Jewish culture as a discrete entity worthy of inclusion in the rainbow of "reclaimed" or "newly enfranchised" cultures. Internationally, they treat Israel as an oppressor state, worthy of outlaw or pariah status.

This preliminary, still tentative account of the possible links between postmodernism, post-colonialism, multiculturalism, etc. and a predisposition to react negatively to Israel as a Jewish state needs to be far more deeply researched before any hard conclusions can be drawn. Nevertheless, it is already clear that the various intellectual and ideological trends alluded to above have helped to shape the political identities and thinking of two or more generations of American academics, especially those situated in humanities and social science departments. Almost by reflex, numbers of these people seem to be inclined to view Israel in a severely critical way, and, especially on the coastal campuses, some of them have organized to actively oppose the Jewish state and even call for its elimination. Most other faculty members and students at their colleges and universities are uninvolved in their causes and are likely to stay uninvolved unless certain hot-button issues draw them forth. The question then becomes one of limiting the negative influences that numerically small but strongly determined anti-Israel coalitions can have. What, in short, can one do to make sure their propaganda tactics do not succeed?

First, and this point cannot be stressed enough, it is necessary to expose their work as being propagandistic and thereby antithetical to the spirit of open inquiry and the balanced search for truth that universities exist to foster. Biased scholarship is a contradiction in terms and should have no place on college campuses. It undermines academic standards and procedures and turns the classroom and the conference hall into instruments of political advocacy, manipulation, and coercion. These are the inevitable consequences of anti-Israel activity, and when they occur, the main casualty is not so much Israel's image on campus but campus culture as such, which, in becoming heavily politicized, is seriously compromised and ultimately corrupted. Because those in the anti-Israel crowd will be immune to such arguments and are likely to counter them by decrying assaults on their rights of free speech by militant representatives of the "Zionist lobby," talking constructively with them about such matters becomes virtually impossible. What is needed, then, are appeals to those at the highest levels of university administration — department chairs, deans, chancellors, and presidents — to enforce their institution's own regulations safeguarding academic integrity. The argument, in other words, is not a Zionist one but one involving the proper understanding and application of established university policies. The University of California Regents Policy on Course Content, for instance, explicitly states that "misuse of the classroom by...allowing it to be used for political indoctrination... constitutes misuse of the University as an institution."[2] Documents endorsed by the same university's Academic Senate Committee on Academic Freedom affirm similar policies.[3]

If appeals to university administrators based on their institution's own stated policies on the abuse of academic freedom prove fruitless, then the argument can be taken higher still — to university trustees and, in the case of state-sponsored institutions, to state legislators and governors. It may also prove useful to enlist the support of community groups with a stake in university affairs as well as the parents of students, who want their children to be educated and not indoctrinated by their mentors. Such an effort takes an inordinate amount of time, energy, commitment, dedication, and hard work, but short of making such efforts, anti-Israel activity will go unchallenged and its proponents will reap some of the propaganda gains they seek to achieve. If they have not yet accomplished these to the extent they would like at the UCSC, it is because the reactivist model of opposing anti-Zionism that I have just described has been effectively developed and put into place by a few dedicated faculty members at that university. It is a demanding strategy but seems to be what's called for on the California campuses where anti-Israel agitation has been most intense. For present purposes, it seems appropriate to call it the "Santa Cruz model."

There is another model, which is proactive rather than reactive and aims less to defend Israel against its detractors than to discourage such hostility from arising in the first place. At its most effective, it succeeds by integrating coverage of Israel within a broad range of university activities. Because this model has long worked well on my own campus, I will refer to it as the "Indiana model."

I teach at an Israel-friendly, and not an Israel-hostile, university. Every spring when students elsewhere mount "Israel Apartheid Week," students on my campus put on "Israelpalooza," a celebratory event that annually draws hundreds of people to the campus green. The tone is upbeat and affirmative; and while there are occasional exceptions to it, such a tone tends to be typical of the reception that Israel has had at Indiana University (IU) over many years. In fact, during my long tenure as a faculty member in Bloomington, I cannot recall a single conference on the conflict in the Middle East that resembles the propaganda exercises that have recently taken place at UCSC, UCLA, UC Irvine, Harvard, and MIT. Israel is addressed from diverse points of view at IU and is not immune from proper critical scrutiny; nor should it be; but neither are the country and its people habitually discredited, maligned, and demonized. We must be doing something right. What is it?

In part, the explanation lies with a prevailing institutional ethos that directs the university's educational mission in a spirit of non-partisan, generally collegial cooperation. The old virtues of free inquiry, intellectual openness, scholarly balance, and social amicability are valued here and have kept IU from becoming as politicized as some of the coastal campuses are. As a consequence, it would not be easy for small groups of politically active faculty members and students to set an ideological agenda that would seriously change the tone and direction of campus thinking. Even during the tumultuous Sixties, when universities were heavily impacted by the pressure of radical politics, the Bloomington campus by and large kept its inner poise. There were frequent debates about the Vietnam War, but in the main the storms that blew through Berkeley, Wisconsin, and Columbia were not so violent and disruptive at IU. At least on the evidence to date, then, IU is not a campus that would be hospitable to the kinds of anti-Israel agitation that one finds at universities on the coasts. There are likely a number of factors at work here, but, simply put, one is this: the political culture that readily accommodates those hostile activities elsewhere lacks a strong presence on my campus. Neither the student body nor the great majority of faculty members and university administrators would be ready to pay the price in campus harmony and overall good-will that radical political propaganda exacts.

In addition, and in keeping with IU's encouragement of multi-disciplinary study, some 38 years ago, key administrators of the university approved a proposal to have study of Judaism and the Jews incorporated into the college curriculum. With the establishment and development of the Borns Jewish Studies Program, IU has encouraged scholarly engagement with all aspects of the Jewish experience. Attention to Israel has been part of this pursuit from the start and over the years has enabled us to introduce numerous courses on Israel, build a first-class Hebrew language instruction program, sponsor a multitude of lectures, conferences, and cultural events, conduct research and produce scholarly publications, develop links to Israeli universities, and more. In short, by integrating Israel Studies into Jewish Studies, which itself was long ago successfully integrated into campus academic and cultural life across the board, we have normalized Israel as a legitimate focus of scholarly and cultural endeavor. By "we," I refer not only to faculty members within the Jewish Studies Program but colleagues and administrators throughout the university.

In the summer of 2008, for instance, the President of IU visited Israel with his wife as part of Project Interchange. It was their first time in the country, and they returned enthusiastic about what they encountered there, so much so that President McRobbie has urged us to deepen our ties to Israeli universities and encourage more of our students to spend junior-year abroad studying in Jerusalem and Tel Aviv.

In June of 2009, the director of the India Studies Program visited Israel under the auspices of a high-level visiting scholars' program (The Israel Studies Institute, which is based at Touro College). It was, he reports, a positive, eye-opening experience. Prior to his visit, the director of Turkish Studies was a participant in a similar program and likewise returned feeling enlightened and rewarded by his time in the country. And the director of Iranian Studies has expressed a desire to make such a visit as well. Ties among Jewish Studies and these various area studies programs are strong at IU and allow them to do meaningful work together. For example, Jewish Studies has co-sponsored lectures and conferences with Turkish Studies on Sephardic Jewish culture and also on present-day antisemitism. With Jewish Studies as co-sponsor, India Studies brought Ambassador Jassal Singh to campus for a lecture on "India, Israel, and the Middle East." In April 2009, the Directors of India Studies and Turkish Studies joined me in sponsoring a symposium entitled "From Mumbai to Gaza: Indian, Israeli, and Turkish Responses to Global Terror." Further work among us will take place in the future, as will collaborative projects between Jewish

Studies and Iranian Studies on questions involving Iran and Israel. These are normal, mutually beneficial ties that are typical of IU's long-standing tradition of multidisciplinary cooperation. If such ties can be replicated on other campuses, the need to constantly "defend" Israel against campus assaults would likely diminish; should they not diminish, then colleagues elsewhere might do what we can readily do in Bloomington if faced with such problems, namely, look to our colleagues in India Studies, Iranian Studies, Turkish Studies, and in other departments and programs for support. I have no doubt it would be forthcoming, for all of us are allied against efforts to turn the university into an arena for the ugly battles brought on by partisan politics. Most importantly, IU's president, Michael McRobbie, is with us, as he demonstrated in August 2007, in signing a widely circulated protest against Britain's University and College Union's drive to boycott Israeli academic institutions. Shortly before then, he hosted a large dinner for Ehud Barak, who presented a public lecture at IU to an audience of 1,000 people. And at the time of our "Mumbai" symposium, President McRobbie hosted a similar dinner in honor of Professor Boaz Ganor, a specialist on terrorism and counter-terrorism at the International Institute for Counter Terrorism in Herzliyah, Israel, who spoke at the symposium.

Knowing that we have sympathetic colleagues like these and others, we have felt free to pursue scholarly work in Jewish Studies, including Israel Studies, with no fear of being isolated on campus and without any need to assume a defensive posture. We study the history and culture of the Jews, including Israeli history and culture, in as natural and unapologetic a way as our colleagues elsewhere on campus study the history and cultures of other peoples. That is the way universities are meant to function, and I am pleased that my own does so.

So what exactly have we done? A brief review of our activities includes the following: to help educate people on campus and in the broader community about Israel, we have sponsored more than 100 public programs over the past three decades. These have featured talks to large audiences by such prominent figures as Abba Eban, Yigael Yadin, Benjamin Netanyahu, Ehud Barak, and Natan Sharansky; literary events featuring such writers as Yehuda Amichai, Aharon Appelfeld, Amos Oz, and Etgar Keret; academic lectures by more than 85 scholars from every major university in Israel; a dozen or more additional lectures on Israel by American scholars; musical programs; film showings; poetry and fiction readings; art exhibitions, and more.

In addition to offering a broad array of courses on Israel taught by our own faculty as well as by visiting Israeli faculty members, we have sent hundreds of students to the Rothberg International School at the Hebrew University and to similar programs at Tel Aviv University and Ben Gurion University. In addition, our local Hillel House takes 25-40 students to Israel each year on the Birthright Israel program; and another 30-50 students annually participate in other Israel-related programs. Hoosiers for Israel is another active Hillel-sponsored group, as is IIPAC (Indiana/Israel Public Affairs Committee).

Through IU's Kelley School of Business, a group of about 30 MBA students devoted 8 weeks in the spring of 2010 to exploring the economy, politics, and culture of Israel, culminating their study with a 10-day trip to Israel, where they were exposed to diverse businesses, met with government representatives, and became personally acquainted with Israeli society and culture.

If our funding requests are successful, we will introduce a new course entitled "Three Thousand Years of Jerusalem: In Jerusalem," which will begin study of Israel's capital city on campus in Bloomington and cap off with students spending part of the summer in Jerusalem itself. This course will continue a tradition of focusing study of Israel on site. For more than a decade, for instance, we took students to an archaeological site not far from Jerusalem to participate in the excavation at Tel Bet Shemesh. One of our faculty members helped to initiate this historic dig, and many of our students spent parts of their summers there.

In addition, IU Press publishes the important journal *Israel Studies* as well as a large number of books on Israel.

The upshot of all of this activity is that, by providing extensive, variegated exposure to Israel — through courses, programs, cultural events, publications, and time spent in the country itself — and also by building constructive relations with sympathetic colleagues on campus, the "Indiana model" has proven effective and should be seriously considered as a strategy for engaging Israel at other colleges and universities. Obviously, it is a long-range strategy and is not designed to address immediate issues of the kind mentioned in the first half of this essay. For those, the "Santa Cruz model" of combating blatant manifestations of anti-Israel propaganda by exposing these as abuses of academic freedom will be more effective. But over the long term, it makes sense to proceed in the way we have at IU, by integrating Israel within the curricular and cultural offerings of the university. That has been done at other Midwestern universities as well, including the University of Michigan, in Ann Arbor, and the University of Wisconsin, in Madison, with similarly good results. A key factor in all of these cases is the pursuit of scholarly work on Israel in a normative fashion and on the highest of academic levels. Good scholarship earns respect and retains the power to drive out bad scholarship. In the end, it may be the most effective counterweight available to pseudo-academic assaults by anti-Israel polemicists. As political theater, anti-Zionism no doubt will continue to play a role on university campuses, but unless the campuses have already become hopelessly politicized, it will be a limited role, more a source of irritation than a prod to widespread, damaging change.

One of the aims of Zionism was to normalize the condition of the Jewish people. That is still a work-in-progress, but by normalizing Jewish Studies, including Israel Studies, in the ways described here, our chances for success go up considerably. There are no guarantees, for on any given campus a few determined individuals who know how to exercise leadership can make a difference, both for the good and the bad. The political predispositions of particular student and faculty bodies on different campuses are also factors in how Israel is likely to be viewed. Add as well the influential role of our government leaders who can use their bully pulpits to convey particular points of view on the Israeli-Arab conflict, and the picture becomes still more complicated.

Nevertheless, university professors have voices of their own and should not look on passively if campus assaults against Israel gather force at the places where they teach. To be successful, however, it is vital that we avoid copying the tactics of our foes and instead remain faithful to the highest values and principles of our profession. On the level of faculty involvement, what is needed over the long term to effectively combat or, better yet, preempt, anti-Israel political advocacy on campus is not more pro-Israel advocacy but the pursuit of balanced, honest scholarship. That plus a healthy measure of good will and fair-mindedness on the part of our students and colleagues should help to mitigate some of the more severe manifestations of campus-based hostility to Israel and its supporters.

———

Alvin H. Rosenfeld, professor of English and Jewish Studies at Indiana University, Bloomington, has taught at Indiana since 1968. He holds the Irving M. Glazer Chair in Jewish Studies and is director of the university's Institute for the Study of Contemporary Antisemitism. He is the author of numerous scholarly and critical studies on American poetry, Jewish writers, and the literature of the Holocaust. His publications include *Thinking about the Holocaust: After Half a Century* (1997) and *The Writer Uprooted: Contemporary Jewish Exile Literature* (2009). *The End of the Holocaust* is due to be published in 2011.

ENDNOTES

1 Tammi Rossman-Benjamin, "Anti-Zionism and the Abuse of Academic Freedom: A Case Study at the University of California, Santa Cruz," *Post-Holocaust and Anti-Semitism*, No. 77, 1 February 2009.

2 "The Policy on Course Content of The Regents of the University of California," approved June 19, 1970 and amended September 22, 2005. (http://www.universityofcalifornia.edu/regents/policies/6065.html)

3 "Academic Freedom: Its Privilege and Responsibility within the University of California" was presented by the University Committee on Academic Freedom to the UC Academic Council on February 16, 2007, and distributed to UC campus Academic Senate offices.

Index

Comintern, 175, 178, 181
Commager, Henry Steele, 86
Commentary, 47, 193, 236–37
Committee for Accuracy in Middle East Reporting in America (CAMERA), 391
Committee for Justice and Peace in the Holy Land, 190
Committee for Open Debate on the Holocaust, 304
Communist International.
See Comintern
Communist Party, Britain, 255, 260, 263
Communist Party, Czechoslovakia, 193–94
Communist Party, East Germany, 184
Communist Party, Hungary, 173, 193
Communist Party, Soviet Union (CPSU), 197–98
Communist Party (CP), United States, 176–77, 184, 200, 202–3, 293
　abandons assimilation, 184–85, 206
　accuses Arab armies of using Wehrmacht veterans, 166
　on Arab leadership, 185–86
　concerns about suppression of Soviet Jewish culture, xiii, 197–200
　defames Jewish Legion, 176
　denial of Soviet bloc antisemitism, 167, 192–93, 195–97, 199, 206
　and displaced persons, 182–83
　during Popular Front, 178
　during Third Period, 175–78, 182, 206
　during World War II, 179–81, 192, 206
　ignores Communist role in Hungarian pogroms, 173
　and Nazi war criminals, 182–83
　and 1936–39 Arab revolt against Jewish immigration, xiii, 178
　opposes boycott of German goods, 177
　opposes postwar British Palestine policy, 182–83, 185–86

　optimism about revitalization of Soviet Jewish culture, 199
　and Suez War (1956), 198–99
　support of Palestine partition, 181, 186–89, 191
　supports anti-Jewish Palestine pogroms (1929), xii, 174–77, 206–7
　switch to anti-Israel position, 192, 197, 206
　and War of Independence (1948), 166, 188–89, 191
　1966 Draft Resolution on the Jewish Question, 202
Community Security Trust (CST), 53, 70, 274
Conant, James, 130
Confederate States of America, 141, 156
Conference of Presidents of Major American Jewish Organizations, 364
Congress of South African Trade Unions (COSATU), 284–85
Conversion to Christianity, xiv, 106, 116, 245
Cooper, Rabbi Abraham, 322–24
Corbin, Arthur, 128, 130
Corbyn, Jeremy, 61
Cornell University, 83, 97
Corrie, Rachel, 60, 72, 287–88
Coser, Lewis, 82, 85
Coughlin, Charles, 144, 178
Council on American-Islamic Relations (CAIR), 3, 5
Court Jews, viii, 30
Cramer, Richard Ben, 252
Crossman, Richard, 55, 189
Crouch, Stanley, 225
Crown Heights riots (1991), 326
Czechoslovakia
　supplies arms to Haganah, 1948, 189–90, 203
　Slansky trial, 193–95

Dabashi, Hamid, 302
Dachau, 164
Dahl, Roald, 57
Daily Northwestern, 305

Duke University, 14
  lacrosse case, 7–8
Duke, David, 249
Durban Conference (2001), 34, 280
Dutt, R. Palme, 178
Dynes, Robert, 404

Eaks, Louis, 257–58, 262, 275
East European Jews, ix, 56, 77, 94–95, 97, 204, 395
East Timor, 303
Eban, Abba, 421
Eddy, David, 154
Egypt, 42, 166, 175, 202, 223–24, 235, 241, 288, 303
  anti-Jewish pogroms in, 170, 186
  occupation of Gaza by, 288, 311
  and Suez War, 198–99
  and Yom Kippur War, 258
Ehrenburg, Ilya, 192
Eichmann trial, 247
Eichmann, Adolf, 227
Einstein, Albert, 79–80
Eisenhower, Dwight, 143
Eisenhower, Mamie, 82
Elliott, William Yandell, 191
Ellis, Marc, 245
Emerson College, 100
Emerson, Ralph Waldo, 35
Empire State Black Arts and Cultural Festival, 298
Engels, Frederick, 241
English departments, 27, 50, 52, 231
  barring of Jews, 78, 85, 87, 96, 109, 114–15, 133, 138
  hostility to Jewish literature, 31
  Lionel Trilling, 78, 114–15
  "The Politics and Poetics of Palestinian Resistance" course at Berkeley, 50, 52, 400
Epstein, Hedy, 283
Epstein, Melech, 176–77
Equal Employment Opportunity Commission, 16
Erikson, Erik, 221
Esack, Farid, 277

Essex University, 263
Ethiopian Jews, 389
European Monitoring Center on Racism and Xenophobia, 281, 288
European Union Agency for Fundamental Rights, 363
Exeter University, 272
Exodus 1947, 187, 189

Facebook, xviii, 331–33, 336, 339–40, 344–48
Faculty searches and diversity requirements, 8–15, 18, 31, 36, 309
Fadiman, Clifton, 78
Fagin, 41
Fair Educational Practices law (Massachusetts), 26
Fairbanks, Jr., Douglas, 143
Fard, W. D., 218, 224–25
Farrakhan, Louis, 217–19, 224, 226, 229–30, 320
Fast, Howard, 199, 207
Fatwa Council, 372
Feal, Rosemary, 388
Featherstone, Ralph, 173
Fedayeen, 198
Federal Communications Commission (FCC), 149
Federal Reserve System, 141–42
Federation of Conservative Students, 263
Federgruen, Awi, 317
Feffer, Itzik, 186
Ferdinand, Archduke, 143
Fernberger, Samuel, 107
Feynman, Richard, 78
Fifteenth Amendment, 144, 151, 159
Final Call, 218, 231
Fingerhut, Eric, 359
Finkelstein, Norman, xv, 19, 43, 50, 245–47, 250, 252, 282–83, 416
Fire, 166–68
First Amendment, 4, 14, 17–19, 22, 297, 308, 312, 348, 362, 397
Flavor Flav (William J. Drayton, Jr.), 319, 327
Foley, Margaret, 385

Molotov-von Ribbentrop Non-Aggression Pact, 178–79, 192, 206
Mongrelization, Jews as agents of, 139, 144, 151, 155
Monroe, Stephanie, 359, 364, 366
Moonman, Eric, 267–68
Morgan Stanley & Company, 155
Morgen Freiheit, 175–77, 198
Morgenthau, Henry, 144, 194
Morocco, 42
Moscow, 184, 197, 256
Moseley, George Van Horn, 140, 144, 146–47, 150, 152–55, 157–58
Mosley, Oswald, 55
Mozambique, 256
MPACUK, 334, 336
MPLA, 256
Muhammad, Ashahed, 231
Muhammad, Elijah, 224–25
Muhammad, Khalid, 224, 228–29
Multicultural offices at universities, 8, 15, 18, 31, 34–36
Multiculturalism, 8, 54, 63, 330, 416–17
Munich Olympics (1972), murder of Israeli athletes, 168–69
Munich, Germany, 79
Münsterberg, Hugo, 96, 102, 106
Murphy, Stanley M., 145, 147–48, 150
Museum of Tolerance, Los Angeles, 324
Muslim antisemitism and anti-Zionism in Britain, ix, 53–54, 58, 61, 63–67, 312, 320
Muslim antisemitism and anti-Zionism in Europe, 241
Muslim antisemitism and anti-Zionism in the Middle East, xii–xiii, xviii, 54, 58, 61, 66, 167, 169–70, 178, 186, 240, 245, 248, 306, 370–75, 381
Muslim antisemitism and anti-Zionism at South African universities, iv, 277–89
Muslim antisemitism and anti-Zionism in the United States, xii–xiii, xviii, xxiii, 3–5, 19–20, 34–35, 167, 169–70, 186, 216, 241, 295, 302–3, 336, 391, 416

Muslim Brotherhood, 256
Muslim Council of Britain (MCB), 67
Muslim Public Affairs Committee (Britain), 61, 336
Muslim students at American universities, Muslim Student Union (MSU), Muslim Students Association (MSA), viii, xv, 3–5, 14, 17, 19–20, 34–35, 216, 360, 373–74, 389–91, 408–9
Mussolini, Benito, 180, 301
My Name is Rachel Corrie, 60, 72
Myerowitz, Molly, 26–27, 37

Nadel, Aaron, 103, 106
Namibia, 256
Nasrallah, Hassan, 306
Nasser, Gamal Abdel, 46, 169–70, 198, 200, 224–25, 238
Natchez, Mississippi, 138, 140–41, 148, 151, 155–56
Nation, 85, 87, 237, 239, 360
Nation of Islam (NOI), xvii, 32–33, 168, 208, 217–19, 221, 224–26, 228, 230–31, 319–20, 322, 326
National Association for the Advancement of Colored People (NAACP), 83, 217, 320
National Council of American-Soviet Friendship, 201
National Guardian, 170, 191–93, 196, 198, 202
National Liberation Front (NLF) (Vietnam), 256
National Organisation of International Socialist Students (NOISS), 255, 265, 269–70, 276
National Organisation of Labour Students (NOLS), 255, 263
National Public Radio (NPR), 44, 252
National Research Council, 99
National Research Fellow, 86
National Union of Israeli Students, 271
National Union of Students (NUS), xiv, 255–65, 268, 270–75, 336
Native American students, 31
Nazareth, 42

World War II, x, 26, 46, 55, 57, 77, 104, 106, 108, 121–22, 125, 128, 132–33, 139, 143, 154, 166, 173, 176, 180–81, 184–86, 190, 268, 293, 305, 345, 371, 381
Wright, Fielding, 148

X, Malcolm, xiii, xvii, 207, 217, 219, 224–29, 232, 319, 323

Yacub, 218
Yad Vashem, 234, 271
Yadin, Yigael, 421
Yale University, 6, 36–37, 85–86, 100, 221
    anti-Jewish quota, 23, 94, 121
    fear of being overrun by Jews, 24, 78
    Law School, x, 121–26, 128–30, 133
    Medical School, 121, 134
Yazdanpanah, Hadi, 296
Yerkes, Robert, 99
Yeshiva College, Yeshiva University, 80
Yevtushenko, Yevgeny, 214
Yiddish language, literature, culture, 27, 31, 46, 83–84, 111, 175, 185–86, 192, 198–200, 207, 247
Yiftachel, Oren, 243, 251
Yishuv, xii, 174, 176, 186–88, 190
Yockey, Francis Parker, 304
Yom Ha'atzmaut, 389
Yom Hashoah (Holocaust Remembrance Day), 305, 389
Yom Kippur, 35, 237, 240, 245
    scheduling exams on, 29, 34

Yom Kippur War, xiv, 165–67, 202–5, 224, 235, 247
York University (Britain), 263–65, 268–69, 275
York University (Canada), 310, 407
Young Communist League (South Africa), 278
Young Liberals (YL), xiv, 255, 257–58, 263, 275
Young Socialist Alliance (YSA), 202, 204–5
YouTube, xviii, 331–32, 340–47

Zaccari, Ronald, 19
Zapiro, 282, 288
Zayed Centre for Coordination and Follow-Up (ZCCF), xix, 370–75, 381
Zayed bin Sultan Al Nahyan, xix, 370–76, 381–82
Zener, Karl, 99
Zimbabwe, 42
Zionist Occupied Government (ZOG), xviii, 335, 345
Zionist Organization of America (ZOA), 80, 309, 314, 355, 359–61, 403, 406, 409
Zionists, vii, xii, xiv–xv, xviii, xxiii, 3–5, 20, 41, 43, 56–57, 61–70, 80, 83–84, 141, 143–44, 150, 153, 157, 164–68, 171, 175–76, 181, 185–86, 189–97, 202–6, 217–24, 227, 234, 241–42, 244, 247, 250, 255, 257, 259–73, 283–86, 288, 299, 303, 307, 325, 335–37, 345–46, 357, 371–72, 384–86, 391, 394–96, 403, 407, 414, 418
Zundel, Ernst, 345

CPSIA information can be obtained
at www.ICGtesting.com
Printed in the USA
LVHW012243211220
674801LV00004B/326